DYNAMICS AND SKILLS OF GROUP COUNSELING

LAWRENCE SHULMAN

University at Buffalo (SUNY)

BROOKS/COLE
CENGAGE Learning™

Australia • Brazil • Japan • Korea • Mexico • Singapore • Spain • United Kingdom • United States

Dynamics and Skills of Group Counseling
Lawrence Shulman

Acquisitions Editor: Seth Dobrin

Assistant Editor: Nicolas Albert

Editorial Assistant: Rachel McDonald

Technology Project Editor: Dennis Fitzgerald

Senior Marketing Manager: Trent Whatcott

Marketing Assistant: Darlene Macanan

Marketing Communications Manager:
   Tami Strang

Content Project Manager: Rita Jaramillo

Creative Director: Rob Hugel

Art Director: Caryl Gorska

Print Buyer: Paula Vang

Rights Acquisitions Account Manager, Text:
   Roberta Broyer

Rights Acquisitions Account Manager, Image:
   Leitha Ethridge-Sims

Production Service: MPS Limited,
   A Macmillan Company

Text Designer: Diane Beasley

Copy Editor: Laura Larson

Cover Designer: Diane Beasley

Compositor: MPS Limited,
   A Macmillan Company

For product information and technology assistance, contact us at **Cengage Learning Customer & Sales Support, 1-800-354-9706.**

For permission to use material from this text or product, submit all requests online at **www.cengage.com/permissions.** Further permissions questions can be e-mailed to **permissionrequest@cengage.com.**

Library of Congress Control Number: 2009940482

Student Edition:
ISBN-13: 978-0-495-50195-4
ISBN-10: 0-495-50195-6

Brooks/Cole
20 Davis Drive
Belmont, CA 94002-3098
USA

Cengage Learning is a leading provider of customized learning solutions with office locations around the globe, including Singapore, the United Kingdom, Australia, Mexico, Brazil, and Japan. Locate your local office at **www.cengage.com/global.**

Cengage Learning products are represented in Canada by Nelson Education, Ltd.

To learn more about Brooks/Cole, visit **www.cengage.com/brookscole.**

Purchase any of our products at your local college store or at our preferred online store **www.CengageBrain.com.**

Printed in the United States of America
1 2 3 4 5 6 7 13 12 11 10

For my sons David and Stuart, sources of great pride and joy.

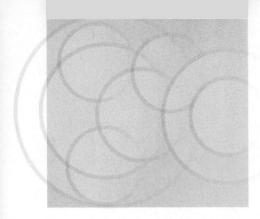

Brief Contents

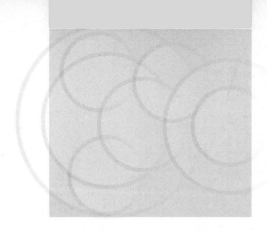

Contents

CHAPTER 2

Mutual Aid Processes in the Group 22

CHAPTER 3

Group Formation 39

The Beginning Phase with Groups 60

CHAPTER 5

The Middle Phase of Group Counseling 99

CHAPTER 6

The Middle Phase Skills 110

CHAPTER 16

Group Counseling in Marital and Family Settings 484

Association for Specialists in Group Work (ASGW) Best Practice Guidelines 612

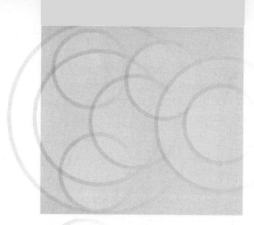

Preface

Overview

My purpose in writing this book is to present and illustrate an approach to group counseling that incorporates the powerful healing process of mutual aid in all types of groups (e.g., psychotherapy, psychoeducational, counseling, activity focused) and in the full range of settings in which group counseling is practiced (e.g., substance abuse rehab centers, schools, mental health clinics). I also wish to describe and illustrate how the use of mutual aid can enhance existing group practice models including those defined as evidence based.

The development of *Dynamics and Skills of Group Counseling* was guided by theory, empirical research, and the practice wisdom of colleagues, my own group practice, and my teaching efforts over the years with thousands of group leaders who were students in my classes or participants in training workshops. Above all, this book is practical in nature. Detailed illustrations including dialogue from actual groups are used to connect theory to practice and to address the day-to-day realities of leading counseling groups. I wrote the book as if I were responding to the most common, natural questions and concerns of the reader, and in a conversational tone that I hope the reader finds more engaging and lively than other textbooks.

Writing a book that would be beneficial to both beginning and experienced counselors who may one day apply their group counseling training into several different settings, I have divided the book into two major parts. Part 1 consists of 13 chapters in which the core group dynamics and leadership skills that make up what I call the "constant" elements of group practice are presented and illustrated with detailed examples from different settings, group types, memberships, and group leadership styles. A central theme is that while setting, group purpose and structure, and population and group member issues may make up the "variant" elements of group counseling, a common core exists to all group practice. Also included in Part 1 is a detailed discussion of the phases of work, a framework of time that can help students both understand how groups work and develop a model for intervention. Part 2 of the book contains six chapters that focus on the implementation of the key concepts presented in Part 1, organized according to counselor specialties, settings, populations, and problems. The central themes introduced in Part 1 are now adapted, each in their own chapter, to working in the following settings and problem areas:

- Substance abuse
- Schools
- Marital and family
- Community mental health
- Job and career
- Medical and rehabilitation

The six areas chosen for inclusion appear to be the ones most often involving group practice. Although the chapters focus on different forms of setting-specific group counseling, readers are encouraged to explore each of them for concepts and examples that may be relevant to their work in another setting.

Features

Throughout the development of this book, reviewers who provided their input made helpful requests for including examples to illustrate concepts presented in the text. The examples come from a number of sources and are presented in three basic formats. First, some of the examples are in straight dialogue format with the first names of the participants or "group leader" or "group counselor" indicating who was speaking. I have identified my comments as "Practice Points" in the text, and when appropriate, a "Practice Summary" may be provided at the end. In this way I have sought to provide not only clear examples but also additional information that students will find useful as they learn to think critically about their own methods and group counseling skills.

The second format is a simple process recording in which a description of the actual group conversation is provided in paragraph form, and it may include remarks by the group's leader as part of the record as well as my comments on content and relevance to the section.

The third format is a more formal structure entitled a *record of service (ROS)*. The structure of the report includes a description of the group, its membership, the particular issue the group was dealing with (formation, developing a culture for work, dealing with a "deviant member," scapegoating, etc.), and the time frame for the series of meetings. This record includes excerpts of the work selected by the group leader addressing the identified group problem over a number of sessions. The material often includes the retrospective analysis of the group leader and a description of the leader's thoughts and feelings over time. At the end of the ROS, the group leader may describe where the problem defined in the introduction stands at the end of the last reported meeting and in some cases what next steps need to be taken.

Another helpful feature is a glossary of key terms, which are italicized in the text, at the end of the book.

Ancillaries

A full suite of instructor's ancillaries is available for faculty teaching the course. A teaching guide and a test bank are available on the instructor's companion website, as well as a series of videos. The same resources are also available on a PowerLecture DVD that you can request from your local Cengage Learning representative.

Acknowledgments

I would like to acknowledge the many people who contributed to the development of this book.

William Schwartz, my good friend and mentor, developed the original model on which much of my work is based. Bill initiated a paradigm shift for the helping professions and was the first to introduce the ideas of mutual aid, contracting, the demand for work, and other concepts. He died in 1982 and is still missed; however, he remains very much alive in this text.

I would also like to thank my wife, Sheila, who has always been supportive of my work in more ways than I can say.

I am especially grateful to a number of faculty members who responded to a request from the publisher to review drafts and to submit suggestions while the book was under development. Many of their suggestions have been carried forward in this text and have significantly improved the organization and content.

I would also like to give special thanks to the editorial team at Cengage, headed by the sponsoring editor, Seth Dobrin. Seth worked closely with me over the 2 years of writing and revising, making many suggestions that significantly improved the structure, presentation, and content of the book. I particularly appreciated his patience and persistence as I, at times, appeared reluctant to accept what turned out to be important advice.

I want to also thank Laura Larson who served as the copy editor for the text. It became clear, chapter after chapter, that she was engaged with the material, not only as an editor but also as an interested reader. Her editing was excellent and her comments along the way very encouraging.

Production of the book was handled by Macmillan Publishing Solutions (MPS), a merger of ICC-India and Macmillan. The project manager was Gunjan Chandola who worked closely with myself and all of the others involved in production to produce the book on time and looking good. Rita Jaramillo provided oversight from Cengage.

Special thanks also to Trent Whatcott, senior marketing manager, for his enthusiasm about the book and his efforts, such as webinars, that allowed me to communicate my approach to group counseling to a larger audience.

Finally, and most important, I want to extend my appreciation to two additional groups. One group is the many clients who are cited in the numerous examples in the book. Their efforts to deal with and overcome many of the issues in their lives are evidence of their courage and an endorsement of the strengths perspective. Second, this book would not have been possible without the contributions of practice examples from hundreds of my students and professionals I have worked with through my workshops and consultations. Their willingness to risk themselves and their honesty in their sometimes overcritical analysis of their practice are tributes to their professional integrity and bode well for their development as competent group leaders. They are making what I like to call "beautiful mistakes" along the way and learning from them. This will definitely lead to more sophisticated mistakes in the future.

About the Author

Lawrence Shulman is a professor and dean emeritus at the School of Social Work at the University at Buffalo. He continues to hold a part-time appointment as a professor with the Research Foundation of the State University of New York and currently directs school violence prevention projects in the Buffalo Public School District. He also holds an appointment as a research associate with the University at Buffalo Research Institute on Addictions.

He obtained his master's in social work (MSW) from Columbia University in 1961 with a major in group work and his doctorate in educational psychology (EdD) from Temple University in 1974 with a major in group methods in classroom teaching.

He is a member of the National Association of Social Workers (NASW), the American Counseling Association (ACA), the American Psychological Association (APA), the Association for Specialists in Group Work (ASGW), and the Association for the Advancement of Social Work with Groups (AASWG). In 2007, he received the AASWG award for the Lifetime Outstanding Contribution to Group Work Practice and Research.

Dr. Shulman served for 5 years as the coeditor of the interdisciplinary journal *The Clinical Supervisor: The Journal of Supervision in Psychotherapy & Mental Health*. He co-founded and co-chaired the International and Interdisciplinary Conference on Clinical Supervision funded by the National Institutes of Health. He also serves on the editorial boards of five journals including *Social Work with Groups, Group Work* (England), and *The Journal of Human Behavior and the Social Environment*.

He has published 7 books and over 40 book chapters and articles dealing with the skills of helping, group counseling, professional impact, mutual aid, teaching, and supervision. His most recent books include *The Skills of Helping Individuals, Families, Groups and Communities*, sixth edition (Cengage Publishers, 2008); *Interactional Supervision*, third edition (NASW Press, 2010); *Mutual Aid Groups, Vulnerable and Resilient Populations and the Life Cycle*, third edition, co-edited with Alex Gitterman (Columbia University Press, 2005). A number of his books have been translated into Croatian, French, Swedish, Chinese, and Iranian and published in the respective countries.

Dr. Shulman's innovative empirical research formed the basis on which he has built his models of the helping process. During his academic career, he has received 13 research grants totaling $2,877,260 from federal (United States and Canada), state, and private foundations for research into individual and family practice, group counseling, classroom teaching, school violence prevention, child welfare, doctor-patient relationships, and other studies. His central research interest has been in method: What does the practitioner say and do, and how does that impact the working relationship (therapeutic alliance) with clients, group members, other professionals, and, eventually, the outcomes for clients?

Dr. Shulman has also used his own practice experience as well as the work of his students and other professionals in the field to develop practice models and to ensure they stay rooted in the realities of day-to-day practice. Over his academic career he has led at least one client group each year including support groups for married couples, single parents, students suspended from school for violence, persons with AIDS in early substance abuse recovery, foster parents, community center activity groups, and more. Many of these group sessions are described in this book.

While partially retired, he maintains an active consultation program providing workshops on group counseling, supervision, general practice, and teaching in the United States and other countries. Over the past number of years, he has provided training for thousands of practitioners in the United States and has presented in other countries including Cuba, Bermuda, France, Norway, Denmark, Hong Kong, and Australia, among others.

Finally, Dr. Shulman has produced a series of seven sets of video programs, containing multiple individual programs, that have been widely distributed on tape and DVDs. These include programs on group practice (e.g., the 1st and 19th sessions of his married couples group); classroom teaching, teaching about practice and diversity; the middle phase of practice; supervision for field practicum instructors; and research on individual, family, and group practice (e.g., a category observation system for analyzing group sessions).

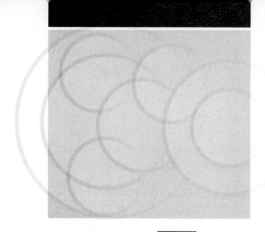

Introduction: What Is This Book About?

This is a book about method. The focus is on the group leader's understanding of the skills required to form and lead effective counseling groups. A simple definition of a *group* for our purposes is two or more people who meet, usually face-to-face, to pursue a commonly agreed-on purpose. *Group method* is defined here as more than a collection of "techniques." Rather, it is a collection of skills that are integrated into an overall understanding of how groups work and how counselors help group members do their work.

Group counseling is an important practice modality that includes a broad range of specific arenas, including career, educational, college, school, guidance, community, marital, family, health, mental health, substance abuse, behavioral disorders, and gerontological counseling. Graduates of accredited counseling programs pursue careers in community mental health and human services agencies, educational institutions, private practice, government, business, hospitals, and industrial settings. Group counselors also lead different types of groups, such as educational, psychoeducational, task, support, single session, open-ended, activity, substance abuse prevention, and recovery groups.

The Association for Specialists in Group Work (ASGW, 2000) defines group work as follows:

> A broad professional practice involving the application of knowledge and skill in group facilitation to assist an interdependent collection of people to reach their mutual goals, which may be intrapersonal, interpersonal, or work related. The goals of the group may include the accomplishment of tasks related to work, education, personal development, personal and interpersonal problem solving, or remediation of mental and emotional disorders. (p. 330)

Group leadership roles and personal styles also vary, and the setting of the group will have an impact. For this reason, this book is divided into two major parts. Part 1 consists of 13 chapters in which the core group dynamics and leadership skills that make up what I call the "constant" elements of group practice are presented and illustrated with detailed examples from different settings, group types, memberships, and group leadership styles. A central theme is that while setting, group purpose and structure, and population and group member issues may make up the "variant" elements of group counseling, a common core exists to all group practice. Another core concept is the idea of *mutual aid*, in which members of a group are helped to help each other. More detailed introductions to the core and variant elements are provided later in this introduction.

Core or Constant Elements in Group Counseling

Chapter 1 sets the stage for the rest of the book by exploring the underlying assumptions that guide this framework for practice. It begins with a brief description of what constitutes a practice theory and some comments on models, skills, and empirical testing. A view of our clients is presented that integrates an understanding of the impact of oppression (e.g., race, gender, sexual orientation, class, physical and mental ability) with an argument for resilience and a strengths perspective. A description of the elements of the *working relationship* or *therapeutic alliance* between the counselor and the group members and its crucial impact on the effectiveness of group leadership is presented and illustrated. In addition, more recent concepts and research around the impact of the group *members' alliance* with the group-as-a-whole are also shared. Finally, an argument is made for developing the ability to integrate our personal and professional selves in our practice so that group members perceive and relate to us as real people. I will be suggesting this is a life long development task that allows us to "use" ourselves rather than "lose" ourselves in our professional tasks as group leaders.

The Phases of Work

The framework of time can help us both understand how groups work and develop a model for intervention. Although the wording may differ, most group counseling authors also use time as an organizing principle (e.g., Corey, 2008; DeLucia-Waack, 2006; Gladding, 2003). The framework used in this book, made up of the following four phases, is effective not only for viewing the life of the group over time but for analyzing each individual session as well:

- The preliminary or preparatory phase
- The beginning or contracting phase
- The middle or work phase
- The ending and transition phase

The Preliminary or Preparatory Phase

This phase is addressed in Chapter 3 on group formation. With some exceptions, such as friendship groups in a high school, most counseling groups are formed by the leader. Chapter 3 explores group formation decisions such as membership, length and frequency of meetings, recruitment, whether a group is open-ended (new members can join) or has a closed membership policy, and so forth. The chapter also examines the skills involved in working with other professionals to encourage them to refer group members as well as the skills required for effective group member recruitment.

This preparatory phase is also a time for the group leader to develop a preliminary empathy about issues and concerns group members may bring to the first session. I refer to this process as "*tuning in.*" The concerns may relate to the group leader (*authority theme*), the group itself (*group themes*), or the content of the group (*work themes*). Because many of the most important issues brought by new members to a first session may be raised indirectly, the process of tuning in prepares the group leader to hear the indirect communications and to respond directly, when appropriate.

The Beginning or Contracting Phase

We know from our practice experience and research that two of the early questions on the minds of group members at a first session are "What is this group all about?" and "How does this group connect to my needs?" We also know that when group members are clear about the group's purpose in a first session(s) and can see a personal connection, they are more likely to make an effective start in their work. This maxim is true for all of the groups described (e.g., psychoeducational, therapy). Given the importance of structure in creating freedom, a core set of skills for all group leaders is described in Chapter 4 as the *contracting skills*. These include clarifying purpose (whatever it may be), clarifying the group leader's role, reaching for feedback from group members, and identifying the connections between the purposes of the group and the members' felt needs. As discussed in Chapter 4, other issues need to be addressed in a first session, such as those related to confidentiality, which form part of the common core of group counseling.

We also know that another important question usually on the minds of group members in the beginning phase is "Who is this group leader, and what kind of person is he or she going to be?" This suggests that some attention to the authority theme—the relationship between the leader and the members—would be wise in a first session. For example, group members in a parent education group, noting a young group leader without a wedding ring, may wonder, "Does this leader have children?" It may be an unstated question that is just beneath the surface, or it may be raised directly. This apparently simple question may actually be raising other reasonable questions, such as "Will this group leader understand what it's like for me as a parent?" or "Will this person be able to really help me, or just criticize and give me theoretical suggestions that are not practical?"

As discussed in Chapters 3 and 4, it is important for the group leader to be able to respond directly to the underlying issues, stated or implied, in a manner that is not defensive but instead opens up a discussion of the early concerns for all group members. A defensive response would cut off that conversation and indicate the group leader's own anxiety. One common example of a defensive response is "We are here to talk about you, not me." Another might be "I don't have any children, but in my counseling graduate program we take a number of courses on child development theory." Here is one alternative and less defensive response, though not the only one:

> No, I don't have any children. Why do you ask? Are you concerned that I might not be able to understand what it's like for you as parents? I'm concerned about that as well since if I'm going to be helpful to all of you, I'm going to have to understand, and you will have to tell me what it's like for you.

As discussed in later chapters, if this response is genuine and reflects an ability to empathize with the group members on issues related to the authority theme, my practice experience and research suggests that it will contribute positively to the development of the working relationship, also referred to in the literature as the *therapeutic alliance*. It is this relationship that creates the medium for the group leader to be influential.

I recognize that readers may have some questions about this issue: "Won't the group members have less respect for me if I admit I don't have any children?"; "I have been told never to share any personal information"; "I have kids, so does that mean I don't have this problem?" Some of these questions, and others, will be explored in detail later. For now, the main point is that the authority theme will be one of the constant elements in the beginning phase of work with all groups. The variant elements will be associated with how this theme is introduced. For example, substance abuse recovery group members may wonder if the group leaders have "walked the walk" (been in recovery) or "talked the talk" (been in AA); members of an activity group for the elderly in a community center may wonder if someone so young can really understand the meaning of loss; or African American teens in a school group for students suspended for violence may wonder what their white leaders from the suburbs could possible know about their lives of racism, poverty, and community violence. These issues, all explored in detail in subsequent chapters, are introduced here as illustrations of how the constant or core elements of practice are elaborated differently as we introduce the many variant elements that affect our work.

The Middle or Work Phase

The middle or work phase is often described as the most complicated in group counseling. As one student put it, "I'm terrific at beginnings, and I handle endings well; it's the part in the middle that gives me a hard time." Chapter 5 will present a model I developed for understanding the role of the group leader in the middle or work phase group counseling sessions. The chapter will describe how the group leader helps individuals reach out to the group for help and the interventions required to help the group respond. Examples from a range of populations and settings will illustrate how the group leader helps the group become an effective mutual aid system, with members helping each other, and how the group leader can avoid the trap of doing individual counseling in the group. It will be argued that these concepts and skills—in particular, the potential for mutual aid—are important in all types of group counseling. In those situations where a particular evidence-based practice is employed, such as a cognitive-behavioral approach, these skills and the development of mutual aid can enhance the effectiveness of the group. A number of these evidence-based as well as emerging models will be described later in Part 1 with illustrations of how mutual aid can be integrated. In addition, the mutual aid model can serve as a stand-alone form of practice while still integrating strategies and skills from other models of group counseling.

Chapter 6 continues the discussion of the middle phase, focusing this time on the communication, relationship, and problem-solving skills required in a single session. Once again, I adopt time as an organizing principle, suggesting we think of each group session as having a preliminary, beginning, middle, and ending stage. Specific group member behaviors and leader interventions will be identified for each of these stages. The interventions or skills are applicable to all types of groups. For example, "sessional tuning in" for each individual meeting, undertaken by the group leader prior to the session, might involve thinking about issues raised in the previous session, specific life events for individual members or the group-as-a-whole, events in the community such as the drive-by shooting of a school friend or the impact of a community-wide traumatic event such as the 9/11 attack on the World Trade Towers.

A less dramatic event might be to tune in to how students in a school counseling group may feel on the day they receive poor report cards. As described in more detail in Chapter 6, this preparatory work prior to the group meeting will be helpful to the group leader in hearing what might be indirect communications by members or understanding the impact of the event on their thoughts and feelings. As examples drawn from group sessions for persons with cancer will show, the group leader's anticipation of the impact on him- or herself and on the group participants of a member's death, symbolized by an empty chair, can help the group deal with the loss and its effect on concerns about their own illness.

The Ending and Transition Phase

The ending and transition phase is discussed in Chapter 9. The unique dynamics and group counseling skills required to help a group bring the experience to an end and make the transition to other experiences are explored. Common phenomena, such as "doorknob therapy" in which group members leave the most important issues to be raised during the last few sessions, are explained.

Another way I like to think about the phases of work is that in the beginning the group members have to make a "first decision" about whether they want to participate. Even in mandated groups where members are ordered to attend by a judge, they still need to make this decision rather than participating superficially—what I will be describing as the "*illusion of work*." That's why clear contracting in the first session is so important.

In groups where painful and difficult issues must be discussed—for example, moving past denial and accepting that one has a substance abuse problem in a court-mandated DWI (driving while intoxicated) group—members must make a "second decision," which is to address real issues in a nondefensive manner. In an example in Chapter 14, in Part 2, this involves an honest examination of the *triggers* that lead to drinking or drug use—those feelings that members have been able to avoid by using alcohol or drugs to dull the pain. In the ending and transition phase, group members must make the "third decision," which is to deal with the most difficult and painful issues before the group ends. In the DWI example in Chapter 14, Pete, who has been the "gatekeeper," preventing the group from dealing with painful discussion, and who also is the most resistant group member, finally faces and shares the fact that his trigger is when he thinks about the time he drove under the influence and crashed his car, killing his wife.

Thus, the first nine chapters will focus on the underlying assumptions, core dynamics, and skills that I believe apply to all group counseling efforts. Many of the ideas, concepts, models, and research are from my own practice, teaching, and research over the years. These are supplemented with material from other theorists and researchers dealing with group practice. These ideas will be central to each chapter.

Some variations will be introduced as the core concepts are illustrated in Chapters 10 and 11. Chapter 10 examines the impact of group structures including the dynamics and skills involved in leading a single-session group, or an open-ended group in which the membership may be constantly changing, as well as the use of activity in groups (e.g., art, games). The recent emergence of the use of the Internet and technology in group work is also examined. The discussion and illustrations in the first nine chapters introduce these unique elements, but they are brought to the forefront in Chapter 10.

It is not possible to consider group practice without understanding the impact of cultural and ethnic diversity. Gladding (2003) points out that "[b]ecause many different groups of people live in the United States and other pluralistic nations, *most group work is multi-cultural in nature*. Indeed, the term *multicultural*, which stresses this diversity among people, has become quite common in the professional helping literature as well as society at large" (p. 204).

DeLucia-Waack and Donigan (2004) emphasize the importance of attention to cultural diversity as both a potential problem for a group as well as a potential strength: "[W]e think it is essential for group leaders to recognize how the purposes of task groups, psychoeducational groups, and counseling and therapy groups may interact with different cultural values and expectations. Group leaders must learn how to effectively utilize the inherent power that rests within the collective diversity of the groups they lead" (p. xix).

Chapter 11 addresses crucial issues in recognizing and addressing diversity in group membership and leadership such as race, ethnicity, sexual orientation, age, and class. Illustrations allow the reader to see how respect for difference requires adaptation by the group leader but not abandonment of the core concepts described in Part 1.

The second half of Chapter 11 addresses what I refer to as intercultural and *intracultural,* issues that may be evident between the group leader and the members and between the members themselves. *Intercultural* refers to differences between people (e.g., a white leader with a group with clients of color; a female leader with a group of men); *intracultural*, to similarities (e.g., a Hispanic leader with a group of Hispanic members; a gay leader with group members who are gay).

Issues of race, ethnicity, gender, sexual orientation, and so forth can be both powerful and taboo in our society. When these concerns and stereotypes remain under the surface, they can impact the development of the working relationship. In one illustration in Chapter 11, two white female middle-class group leaders must address intercultural issues as they work with a group of inner-city African American girls in trouble with the juvenile justice system. In an example of an intracultural issue, an African American male group leader working with African American high school students in an inner-city school may face complicated and painful feelings the first time an angry group member calls the counselor an "Oreo"—black on the outside and white on the inside.

Both inter- and intracultural issues can also emerge as forces that affect the relationship among members, what I refer to as the *"intimacy theme."* The resulting dynamics need to be addressed. It is not enough to intellectually understand these powerful forces; specific interventions are needed to bring these issues to the surface, address them, and hopefully remove them as barriers to effective group practice.

In Chapter 12, the focus is on different models of practice, including some that have been designated as evidence based because of their consistent support in research (motivational interviewing, cognitive-behavioral, and solution focused) and others that have not yet been acknowledged as such but have been supported by practice experience and some research evidence (e.g., feminist, spiritual and religious, and crisis intervention).

The chapter starts by discussing the criteria for determining if a practice model could be considered evidence-based practice (EBP). Three examples of current EBP models are selected because of their wide use: motivational interviewing, and cognitive-behavioral practice. A number of other models of practice not yet formally designated as EBP, are briefly presented too, including feminist practice, religion and spirituality, and trauma and extreme events. Elements from all of these models have been introduced and integrated when appropriate into Part 1 of this text; however, the brief summaries in Chapter 12 bring them to the forefront of discussion.

A central theme of the chapter is the way in which mutual aid processes described in Chapter 2 can be integrated into group practice within any of these distinct models. In addition, techniques and strategies from different models can be combined into an integrated approach that is not limited to one framework. Over the years of my own practice, I have come to believe that group leaders need to be open to a range of interventions and models and not be too rigid in adopting only one.

Chapter 13, the last chapter of Part 1, returns to a number of issues introduced in earlier chapters that relate to values, ethics, and legislation. This chapter provides a more detailed discussion of ethics, ethical dilemmas created by conflicting values as well as social changes (e.g., managed care), and the impact of legislation and court decisions. For example, while Chapter 3 dealing with group formation and Chapter 4 dealing with first group sessions both explain the importance of confidentiality and informed consent, these concepts are presented in more detail and with background in Chapter 13. These 13 chapters in Part 1 can stand alone as a group practice textbook.

Part 2 of the book contains six chapters that focus on the implementation of the key concepts presented in Part 1, organized according to counselor specialties, settings, populations, and problems. The central themes introduced in Part 1 are now adapted, each in their own chapter, to working in the following settings and problem areas:

- Substance abuse
- Schools
- Marital and family
- Community mental health
- Job and career
- Medical and rehabilitation

These chapters are not designed to be in-depth discussions of practice in these different settings. That would be beyond the scope of this book. Each setting deserves a book of its own, and the reader can find books that focus on these unique aspects of practice. Each chapter does provide a brief introduction to the area and then a number of illustrations of how the core dynamics and skills of Part 1 are varied in group practice. The six areas chosen for inclusion appear to be the ones most often involving group practice.

While the chapters focus on different forms of setting-specific group counseling, readers are encouraged to explore each of them for concepts and examples that may be relevant to their work in another setting. For example, if you work with children, you can find illustrations of practice with children in chapters with schools and, substance abuse prevention and treatment settings, as well as in the other setting-specific chapters. The case example index at the end of this book will help you identify age and stage of the life cycle examples (e.g., children, adults, the elderly), problem-related examples (e.g., AIDS, substance abuse, school violence), and types of groups (e.g., short term, open-ended) throughout the book. Although group practice is influenced by the setting, the core of the practice presented in Part 1 remains the same.

Mutual Aid in Group Practice

Another central question explored in this book is "Why do we work with people in groups?" Yes, we can serve more people if we use a group modality rather than individual counseling, but I do not believe this is the most important reason. Instead, I argue that there is something very distinct, unusual, emotionally moving, and powerful about helping when it takes place in a group. This is *mutual aid*, defined as the process in which members are helpful to each other in a way that is different and supplemental to the help provided by the leader. Mutual aid involves giving and taking help in a reciprocal manner. In most cases, as group members provide help to an individual member, they also help themselves.

Most group counseling authors who address the question of why use groups cite the unique advantages of group practice. Jacobs, Masson, and Harvill (2006) point to efficiency, commonality, a greater variety of viewpoints, sense of belonging, an opportunity to practice skills and receive feedback, vicarious learning, real-life approximation, and commitment (pp. 2–5). These processes are central to mutual aid and are described using different terms in some detail in Chapter 2.

Corey (2008) points out that as

> a microcosm of society, the group provides a sample of reality—members' struggles and conflicts in the group are similar to those they experience outside of it—and the diversity that characterizes most groups also results in unusually rich feedback for and from the participants, who can see themselves through the eyes of a wide range of people.
>
> The group offers understanding and support, which foster the members' willingness to explore problems they have brought with them to the group. The participants achieve a sense of belonging, and through the cohesion that develops, group members learn ways of being intimate, of caring, and of challenging. In this supportive atmosphere, members can experiment with new behaviors. As they practice these behaviors in the group, members receive encouragement as well as learn how to bring their new insights into their life outside of the group. (p. 6)

Even in a single-session, education-focused group structured to provide a significant amount of information through a presentation format, mutual aid processes can be tapped to increase the possibility that what is said will be heard, understood, valued, and remembered. For example, anxious new students in a school or college, or in a professional counseling program, may find much of their concern diminished as they discover they are not alone and, in fact, are "all in the same boat" with shared feelings. The potential for mutual aid will be described as another constant element in all groups regardless of the specific group type, practice model, or setting. The different ways in which group members can help each other are described in Chapter 2 and then illustrated with detailed examples throughout the book. Mutual aid is not presented as a separate practice model but rather a powerful process that can be integrated to enhance all forms of group counseling.

This understanding of the mutual aid potential on the part of the group leader can help avoid the trap of doing *individual counseling in a group*, and it may increase the possibility of the group itself becoming a powerful force for learning and healing. Although the potential for a positive group counseling experience exists in all groups, there are many obstacles, including unhelpful past group experiences, that may impede the process. That is why the group leader needs to clearly understand his or her role, group development, and group processes. Central to this role are the skills required to help group members help each other.

Case Examples Used in This Book

The examples used in this book come from a number of sources and are presented in three basic formats. First, some of the examples are in straight dialogue format with the first names of the participants or "group leader" or "group counselor" indicating who was speaking. My commentary is identified as Practice Points in the text, and when appropriate, a Practice Summary may be provided at the end.

The second format is a simple process recording in which a description of the actual group conversation is provided in paragraph form, and it may include remarks by the group's leader as part of the record as well as my comments on content and relevance to the section.

The third format is a more formal structure entitled a *record of service (ROS)*. The structure of the report includes a description of the group, its membership, the particular issue the group was dealing with (formation, developing a culture for work, dealing with a "deviant member," scapegoating, etc.), and the time frame for the series of meetings. This record includes excerpts of the work selected by the group leader addressing the identified group problem over a number of sessions. The material often includes the retrospective analysis of the group leader and a description of the leader's thoughts and feelings over time. At the end of the ROS, the group leader may describe where the problem defined in the introduction stands at the end of the last reported meeting and in some cases what next steps need to be taken.

A major reason for including the ROS report is that it allows the reader to see the change in practice over time as the group leader gains insights and develops new strategies and interventions. These examples make a strong argument for reflective practice where beginning and experienced group leaders are continuing their learning process.

Examples also include some of my own work from early and more recent practice. I clearly distinguish when the illustration is from my own practice. Examples of my work with married couples, single parents, teenagers, and persons with AIDS and in recovery from substance abuse, among others, are used to illustrate key concepts such as the dynamics of first meetings. Other examples come from seasoned professionals as well as students illustrating a range of levels of practice skill. I believe the reader can learn as much from an analysis of mistakes as from a more sophisticated practice, so I have included illustrations of both. It is also encouraging for beginners to see how quickly a group leader can catch a mistake if willing to examine the work with a critical eye.

For all of these examples, normal Health Insurance Portability and Accountability Act (HIPAA) rules of confidentiality were followed so that clients could not be identified. In addition, I asked each person submitting an example for permission to include the record or a modified version of it in my future teaching and publications. In most cases, the writer was pleased to have the report selected and included in this text.

The illustrations are particularly helpful to students who may not have concurrent group counseling practicum experiences. They are also reassuring. A constant theme in this book stresses the importance of having the courage to be imperfect and to learn from mistakes. The process recordings can be used to help students understand the dynamics and skills required in classroom group leadership exercises. I believe the numerous illustrations are one of the strongest elements of the book, and each helps bring life to the theory and research. Each one has been purposely selected to illustrate major concepts associated with the chapter.

Appendix A includes a description of my research methods and findings and provides a framework for understanding and judging my studies shared in the book. Other appendices provide summaries of other research and of the best practices guidelines and professional standards from major group counseling associations together with accreditation standards. A glossary, index of topics and authors, and an index of case examples complete the book.

The "Fear of Groups Syndrome"

Finally, I want to address an issue that is often under the surface when beginning and even experienced counselors begin to consider working with groups. In my group leadership training workshops, a moment arises—usually early on the first morning—when I sense a general unease in the group. Sometimes the first clue of what I call the "*fear of groups syndrome*" emerges during their personal introductions, when some participants indicate they have never led a group. Their tone of voice suggests that if they could have their way, they never would. When I explore these clues, I often hear that some counselors were sent to the workshop by an administrator or supervisor who decided that group work would be a good idea. More recently, the pressures of managed care and requirements to meet performance goals have pushed settings to expand their group services, often for the wrong reasons.

Whether participants are in the workshop voluntarily or not, and whether they are experienced or new counselors, the underlying feelings are often the same: They are scared of leading a group if new to this modality of practice. As one experienced counselor said of group members, "There are so many of them and only one of me!" A commonly expressed concern relates to working with a group of people who are judging your work. The counselor is more exposed in group practice than in individual work. If an individual client does not return after a few interviews, the counselor can always chalk it up to the client's "lack of motivation." However, if five clients don't return to a group session, the counselor may feel that he or she was off track or failed in some way.

Another concern involves the potential for direct negative feedback from members. Anger from a single client is one thing, but an angry group is something else. Of even greater concern is the possibility of a boring group. Counselors tend to feel completely responsible for the success of a group and dread the possibility of long silences, rambling conversations, individuals who dominate the discussion, or the sight of 10 pairs of eyes glazing over.

Beginning group counselors often raise their fear about losing control. One workshop participant put it this way:

> When I'm conducting an individual interview, I know where it is going and can keep track of what is happening. In a group session, the members seem to take control of the session away from me. It feels like I am on my motorcycle, pumping the starter to get going, and the group members are already roaring down the road.

It takes some experience and time for a group counselor to realize that moments such as this may mean that the group is actually well on its way to success and that members have accepted the leader's invitation to "own" the group. One of the benefits for group counselors who also do individual work is that they realize they can relinquish some control in their one-to-one interviews by following the client rather than the other way around.

The complexity of group practice also intimidates less experienced counselors. In individual counseling, they needed to concentrate on the relationship between themselves and the client and the content of the conversation; with a group, they now have to concentrate on the relationships among group members as well. As they gain group counseling experience, they become more conscious of the entity called the *group-as-a-whole*, which is discussed in detail in Chapter 8. I describe the ways in which one can become more observant of this entity—the group—which is more than the sum of its parts—the members. In one-to-one interviews, counselors have to concentrate only on the individual; now they also must pay attention to the group and develop the ability to observe both the "one" and the "many" at the same time. The reader should not be discouraged. This is a skill that can be learned and learned quite quickly.

In Chapter 7, which focuses on the individual in the group, I suggest that the common concern that the leader must choose between the individual or the group—for instance, by paying attention to an individual's behavior and thus ignoring the needs of the group—can be resolved by examining the connections between the individual's behavior and the group-as-a-whole. A teenage girl in a group for survivors of sexual abuse, for example, may act out and disrupt the group when the discussion turns to a painful area such as the disclosure of the facts of one of the other member's abuse. She may actually be acting as a "gatekeeper" for all of the members who share these feelings. This can be a signal to the group leader of a need to open up a discussion of how hard it is to address such painful memories—not just for the individual but for the whole group. In an example in Chapter 7 drawn from just such a group, we find that the acting-out member turns out to be the one teenager who had suffered the worst abuse, in part explaining why she plays the gatekeeper role. This chapter looks at the most common individual roles in the group, such as scapegoat, deviant member, monopolizer, silent member, and others.

These concerns of new group leaders are understandable. On reflection, however, beginning and experienced counselors soon realize that their concerns are similar to those they felt when they first began as counselors. Skills in work with individuals, with which they now feel more comfortable, seemed beyond reach during their first interviews. Group leaders continually learn more about the dynamics of the relationships between themselves and clients, as well as the dynamics between group members. Confidence in the skills they have allows them to worry less about the skills they still need to learn and to better tolerate areas of ambiguity. They are better able to resist the understandable desire to come to closure quickly, sometimes adopting techniques and oversimplified or rigid and controlling models of group leadership, and instead remain open to the challenge of continued learning. I also believe that when using manualized approaches to group practice that have been developed through research, the group leader keeps in mind the need, at times, to innovate and depart from a prescriptive intervention. This is the element of the art of group leadership that should be strengthened by the science (the research) and not extinguished. In learning the skills to work with groups, counselors often start with no confidence at all; as happens in their individual practice, they build confidence through experience.

Furthermore, I try to reassure counselors that they already know more about group counseling than they realize. Much of what they have learned about helping can be applied to the group situation. The ability to listen, to hear and understand indirect communications (e.g., the teenage client who begins by saying, "I have a friend with a problem"), to empathize, and to communicate caring and concern are all important skills in the group counseling context. Areas of uncertainty represent exciting opportunities for new learning that can take place over the course of their professional lives. I have seen many students develop quickly while working in the group medium, particularly when they chose to see the group and its members as a source of their own learning.

With both new and experienced counselors, I try to point out that the root of their fear is a misconception about their complete responsibility for the group process. When they realize that they have responsibility only for their part, and that group members will do some of the most important work, counselors can view group practice from a proper perspective. Certainly, they will become more effective throughout their careers as they develop group skills and gain knowledge and confidence. They can, however, still give a great deal to their first early groups.

A key concept that often helps is that skillful group counseling involves shortening the time between when the group leader makes a mistake and when he or she catches it. In the earlier example of the counselor responding defensively to the question "Do you have any children?" the counselor might revisit this question in the next group session, this time addressing the underlying issues. An example of such skillful practice follows:

> Last week, when Mrs. Smith asked me if I had children, I was taken aback. I have thought about it, and I realize you were all probably wondering if I, without children of my own, could actually understand what you go through as parents and whether I could be helpful.

Catching the mistake in the same session would be very skillful indeed. I also suggest to new group leaders that they will make mistakes, learn from them, and then make more sophisticated mistakes. The important idea is to free group leaders from the misconception that they have to be perfect at all times. Group members can forgive mistakes and in fact are impressed by group leaders who can own up to them rather than be defensive. The first time I respond to a student who shares an example or does a class role play and say, "That was a beautiful mistake since you can learn from it," they have trouble with the concept. Once they understand it, they are free to risk more, make mistakes, learn from them, and not be so hard on themselves.

When new group leaders reflect on situations where they feel they could have handled things much better, and they no longer have the group to catch the mistake, I urge them to "sign the painting" and hang it up. The suggestion is that they should admire what they did well, recognize areas for improvement, and begin a new "canvas." They can't hold themselves responsible for making mistakes that at the time they did not understand or not using skills they had not yet developed. They are, however, responsible for continuing to grow in their knowledge and skills.

My research has indicated that new counselors tend to underestimate the amount of help they can give to their clients. Group leaders face this same problem. Continued group experiences help correct this misconception. The marvelous feeling a counselor experiences when he or she sees the power of mutual aid in a group helps make up for the group leader's anxiety along the way.

Finally, a counselor's fear of groups must not interfere with the clients' right to receive the modality of service that is most appropriate to their particular needs. Consider, for example, populations of oppressed and vulnerable clients such as battered women, for whom groups may well be the service modality of choice, providing a crucial complement to individual counseling. These clients should not be restricted to what may turn out to be less effective service simply because their counselor did not receive training in group counseling or feels more comfortable facing one client at a time. As the reader explores the many examples in this book, the obvious healing power of groups makes the case for overcoming the fear of groups syndrome.

Conclusion

The development of this book was guided by theory, empirical research, and the practice wisdom of colleagues, my own group practice, and my teaching efforts over the years with thousands of group leaders who were students in my classes or participants in training workshops. It provides a structure that allows the group leader to use a wide range of models and group types. It offers a clear format on how to run a group and is practical in nature. Detailed illustrations including dialogue from actual groups are used to connect theory to practice and to address the day-to-day realities of leading counseling groups. It is written in a form that can be helpful for the beginning group leader as well as for one with more experience. Both will take something out of the content based on their current levels of understanding and skill. The book is written in a conversational rather than a strictly textbook mode, as if I were responding to the natural questions and concerns of the reader. The conversation continues with a discussion of underlying assumptions in Chapter 1.

PART I

THE CORE DYNAMICS AND SKILLS OF GROUP COUNSELING

Part 1 entails Chapter 1 through 13. It includes nine chapters that introduce the core dynamics and skills of the mutual aid model of group practice. These are the "constant" elements seen in all counseling groups in which the goal is to create a culture in which group members can be helpful to each other. This framework can stand alone as a group practice model, and it is also compatible for use in a range of groups, including counseling, psychoeducational, educational, therapeutic, and more. It can also draw on elements or be integrated within and enhance other group counseling models such as motivational interviewing and solution-focused and cognitive-behavioral approaches.

Chapter 1 sets the stage for the book by examining underlying assumptions about people, groups, and group counseling. It illustrates what I term an "interactional perspective" toward group counseling. An oppression psychology perspective is presented, balanced with a resilience and strengths perspective in understanding the challenges faced by members and their potential sources of strength for change. Central to the framework is the importance of the working relationship (therapeutic alliance) between the group leader and the group members. A discussion of the importance of the group leader integrating personal and professional selves closes this chapter.

Chapter 2 describes the many ways in which mutual aid can operate in a group. Processes such as the "all in the same boat" phenomenon, mutual support, and mutual demand are discussed in some detail and illustrated with examples from actual group practice. The obstacles to effective work are also identified, as is the group leader's role in helping the group create an enterprise in mutual aid.

Chapters 3, 4, 5, 6, and 9 use the framework of time—preparatory, beginning, middle, and ending/transition stages—to examine the tasks of the group leader in forming a group, contracting in first sessions, working with the group in the middle (work) sessions, and bringing the group to a close and helping members make transitions to new experiences. Detailed examples from a range of group types, purposes, populations, problems, and settings illustrate the theory and connect it closely to the day-to-day realities of group leadership. The constant elements of practice, such as the importance of contracting in first sessions and recontracting in later sessions, are described. The chapters dealing with the middle or work phase of group sessions use the concept of stages of work—preparatory, beginning, middle, and ending/transitions—for understanding each individual group session.

Chapter 7 focuses on working with the individual in the group. It presents the model of a group as a dynamic system and tries to understand the behavior of each individual member as partially a result of the individual's "personality" but also affected by the group process. Examples include scapegoats, deviant members, internal leaders, gatekeepers, defensive members, quiet members, and monopolizers. By understanding individual behavior in a dynamic framework, the group leader can see members in new ways that suggest effective intervention strategies with both the member and the group. For example, in some cases the deviant member, often viewed as the "enemy" by the group leader, can be seen in a new way as a potential "internal leader" and the group leader's ally. Examples from a range of actual counseling groups help illustrate the concepts.

Chapter 8 introduces the concept of the group-as-a-whole, which is an entity that is more than the sum of its parts. Using three classic theories (Bennis and Shepard, Bion, and Homans), models for understanding the stages of group development, the impact of emotions on the group, and the group as part of a larger system of interactions are presented and illustrated with additional practice examples. A more recent group theory developed by the Stone Center researchers, described as an intimacy and relational model, examines unique aspects of group development and process in groups for women. These four general frameworks will help the reader "see" the entity called the group-as-a-whole while at the same time being able to see each individual member. The models are illustrated with examples of helping a group develop a "culture for work" and helping the group deal effectively with "its" environment. Chapter 9 deals with the special issues involved in bringing groups to a close and helping members make the transition to other experiences.

Chapter 10 introduces some variations in structural elements of practice. These include open-ended versus closed groups, single-session groups, activity groups, and groups using the

Internet. Chapter 11 discusses the impact of diversity (race, ethnicity, sexual orientation, age, etc.). In these first 11 chapters, a number of constructs and strategies drawn from a range of group counseling models are introduced in the context of discussion and examples. These include elements of motivational interviewing, solution-focused practice, cognitive-behavioral therapy, and feminist group practice. In Chapter 12, I will revisit these models, as well as others, bringing them to the foreground and providing a more detailed summary of their basic ideas and intervention strategies. A general discussion of evidence-based practice is also presented.

The final chapter in Part 1, Chapter 13 returns to a more detailed discussion of content related to professional values, ethics, and legislation. Many of the concepts were first introduced in the earlier chapters in the context of the discussion and illustrations. For example, the importance of informed consent and confidentiality was discussed in the context of first group sessions. In Chapter 13, I return to expand the discussion of values and ethics, ethical dilemmas, risk management strategies, guidelines for group practice, confidentiality, informed consent, the duty to warn, and the impact of social changes and court decisions, to provide some background for how these areas impact and guide our group practice.

CHAPTER 1

Underlying Assumptions About People, Groups, and Group Counseling

This chapter introduces a number of the central ideas underlying the approach to group counseling presented in this book. The framework builds on the core knowledge of the counseling process important for work with individuals and families, and with other professionals. These concepts are elaborated in the group counseling modality. A preliminary discussion of the process of theory building will place this effort in context.

A central notion is that all group members are viewed as part of a *dynamic interaction* with their many important social systems, such as the family, peer group, school, and, of course, the counseling group itself. Discussion of the assessment process focuses on a strengths perspective rather than on group member pathology. This is illustrated using as an example group work with inner-city, poor, and mostly African American or Hispanic students suspended from school for violence, weapons possession, and drug use. An oppression psychology model helps us reframe the behavior and suggest specific intervention strategies.

Counseling skill in the early sessions is the method by which the group leader strives to develop a positive working relationship with the individual group members and the *group-as-a-whole*, a relationship that allows the group leader to be helpful. The impact of the group leader's personal self—that is, the effect of his or her feelings, *ethics*, or *values*—on professional practice is also examined.

What Is a Group Counseling Practice Theory?

All practitioners eventually develop their own practice frameworks, some more and some less explicit, and judge these frameworks by how well they explain and improve counseling practice. The framework for group counseling described in this book has been most helpful to me in my group practice, theory building, and research; however, it is not engraved in stone. Although the theory has evolved over many years, it will continue to be used as a framework only as long as it appears to do the job. You should test its ideas, as with all approaches, against your own sense of reality and use those portions that seem helpful. I encourage my students to "write your own book." I do not mean that literally—although I hope and expect that some will—but rather to suggest that they need to create their own models of the helping process.

Many of the skills and models in this book are not bound by one approach and can easily fit into other theoretical frameworks. Ideas from other models, some of which are identified and discussed in more detail in Chapter 12, are integrated whenever they help enrich the core framework. For example, strategies and interventions that underlie the motivational interviewing, cognitive-behavioral, and solution-focused approaches also fit nicely within this framework.

Practice Theory

Because I refer to practice *theory*, *models*, and *skills* throughout the text, a brief explanation of how I use these terms may be helpful. Any practice theory requires three related sets of ideas:

- What do we know about people in general and about people in counseling groups in particular?
- Based on what we know about people, what would we like to see happen—our valued outcomes?
- What interventions (strategies and techniques) will we use to achieve these outcomes?

This approach to thinking about group practice is used throughout the text. For example, new group members may have some degree of general uncertainty about how any counseling relationship, individual or group, can be helpful to them. They may also wonder how they can get help from other group members who have the same problems as they do. They may be worried about whether the group leader will understand their concerns. We know this through experience and research. Based on this understanding, the group leader might set the following goals, among others, for the first session:

- Aiding group members to understand the kind of help that can be offered in the group
- Clarifying the group leader's role
- Helping group members understand the potential overlap—or common ground—between their felt needs and the group's stated purpose
- Helping the group members see the common ground among members

Based on this understanding and these immediate goals, the group leader will use skills of clarifying purpose, clarifying his or her role, and seeking group member feedback. (These specific skills are described in more detail in Chapter 3.) For my purposes at this point, they demonstrate how our knowledge about group members in new situations (knowledge) defines immediate goals (valued outcomes), which in turn inform the group leader of the skills and interventions (contracting) needed in the beginning phase of work. These are the crucial building blocks of any practice theory and will be identified for all phases of practice.

Models and Skills

The term *model* is used to describe a representation of reality. One would construct a model to help simplify the explanation or description of a complex process or object. In this text, models are used to describe helping processes (e.g., the dynamics and skills required in a beginning, middle, or ending phase of group counseling sessions), individual and social psychologies (e.g., resiliency and oppression theory), and group dynamics (e.g., the stages of group development).

The term *skill* refers to a specific behavior or technique that the group leader uses in the helping process. Many of the skills described in this text are core relationship skills, which are useful in the performance of professional as well as personal tasks. For example, empathic skills are needed by parents, spouses, and friends. I have come to believe that, for many helping professionals, the development of self-knowledge and the enhancement of personal skills are an important part of what originally inspired us to consider the helping professions. Helping others—which every candidate's application for admission to a professional school identifies as a core motivation—is also important. The focus here will be on the use of these skills as they relate to the counseling professional *function*.

Empirical Testing

Finally, although I have been conducting empirical testing of the hypotheses contained in the practice theory, this work should be seen as an ongoing process. The *grounded theory* approach to theory building, first described by Glaser and Strauss (1967) in sociology, guides my work. Formal and informal observations from practice are used to develop constructs of the theory. Formal research is conducted both to test propositions and to generate new ones. Some of the most interesting findings of my earlier studies did not support my initial hypotheses. This helped me expand the theoretical constructs and led to the development of the more general and holistic theory presented in the text that complements this book (Shulman, 1991). Appendix A summarizes my research methodology as cited in this book, and an expanded version of this appendix is available on the book's website at www.cengage.com/counseling/shulman.

Many of the core findings about skill from my earlier research have been supported by research in a number of related fields. Some propositions have begun to reach the replication stage at which they may be described, as in Rosenberg (1978), as *theoretical generalizations*. These propositions have received repeated support from many research efforts. As these ideas are presented throughout the book, I shall provide citations to the supportive literature. However, even these propositions must be open to modification as further empirical efforts direct. It is in this spirit of continuous evolution that the ideas in this book are shared.

Underlying Assumptions About Individual Psychology and Social Interaction

For many years now, systems theory has profoundly influenced the way that helping professionals view their group members. One central idea has been the emphasis on viewing a group member in interaction with others. Instead of seeing a group member as the object of analysis, group leaders began to focus on the way in which the group member and the group member's important systems were interacting. In fact, according to this *systems or ecological approach*, one can never understand the movements of the group member except as affected by the movements of others. Group members are viewed in interaction with their immediate and larger social surrounding, each affecting and being affected by the other in a reciprocal manner. Another crucial assumption of the interactional model is a belief in the essential symbiotic relationship between individuals and their social surroundings, with each needing the other for their own growth and success.

A group member may be considered resistant, for example, until one looks closely at the way the group leader is attempting to engage the group member. The resistance may in fact be a direct result of the group leader's efforts, or past experiences with other group leaders, and not inherent to the group member. Close examination may reveal that this member is, in fact, acting out the resistance of the whole group. An example of how an individual is always interacting with the environment is described in the following illustration of students suspended from school for violence.

An Interactional Perspective

A Counseling Group for Students Suspended from School for Violence

I want to illustrate this idea with an example from the work I directed during a project to address the problem of school violence. The setting was a midsize, inner-city school district in which a significant percentage of the students who had been suspended from school for violent acts against teachers or other students, drug possession, or weapon possession were students of color, economically disadvantaged, and at least 1 year behind in school. The center we established on the university campus—Vision-Integrity-Structure-Accountability, or VISA—provided a short-term, 2-week academic and behavioral intervention program, as well as services for the students' families.

From the perspective of the school system, the problem was with the student, and the diagnosis was often "learning disability," "oppositional behavior disorder," "borderline personality," or "emotionally disturbed." The usual response was either to formally suspend the student, sending him or her home for 2 weeks to receive home instruction from a teacher for 1 hour a day, or to enroll the student in anger management programs at the school or through local agencies. The school district recidivism rate was high; many of the students were resuspended soon after they returned to school, some up to seven separate times.

From our perspective, the students' behavior was most often interpreted as a call for help in dealing with some life situation that these students faced. We started with the assumption that the behavior was not the problem but the symptom of a maladaptive way of coping with struggles that existed for them with their families, their schools, the community, and—on a larger social level—our society.

Many of these students and their families had experienced the impact of long-term and persistent racism. In the next section, I will be describing an *oppression psychology*, proposed by Frantz Fanon (Fanon, 1968; Bulhan, 1985), that suggests a number of maladaptive ways people cope with oppression. When viewed from this perspective, student behavior involving the use of violence and substance abuse can be seen in a different light and may call for different interventions.

The VISA Center was a voluntary alternative offered to the students and their parents at the time of the formal suspension hearing. In addition to academic instruction, the behavioral modules were all designed to focus on the issues and concerns that students faced from their perspective. For example, modules on substance abuse were not used as lectures warning of the damage done by drugs, which these students had heard many times, but instead focused on the damage done to the students' lives. This included, for example, substance abuse issues in their families, the difficulty they faced from peer pressure to use drugs, relatives who were serving prison time for possession and/or sale of drugs, and friends who were heavy users and whom they worried about but did not know how to help.

Support groups focused on issues in the lives of the students that ranged from physical or sexual abuse to involvement in fights out of fear of "losing face" or the need to "front" (putting up a tough personality), pressure to join gang activity in the neighborhood (if only for protection), posttraumatic stress as a result of witnessing family violence or drive-by shootings, depression because of the loss of family members to violence and prison, anger about perceived racism within both the schools they attended and the larger community, and a sense of hopelessness about their futures. The latter issue was poignantly characterized by one 16-year-old who said in one of the groups I led, "Why do I need to finish school? I'm not going to live past 20 anyway!"

This *interactional model* led to interventions that were designed to work *with* the students rather than *on* the students. More detail on this program will be shared in Chapter 15, dealing with group work in schools. For now, the main point is that by avoiding seeing the student as the problem and instead focusing on the reciprocal interaction between the student and the immediate and larger environment, we were able to shift the conversation. By understanding that a student's behavior in the VISA Center was constantly affecting and being affected by the interaction with staff and other students (e.g., group dynamics), we were able to see the student in a more dynamic and individualized way. Figure 1.1 illustrates this interactional perspective.

FIGURE 1.1

Relationship of Group Member and Systems

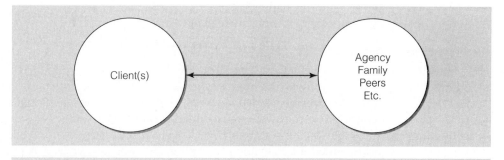

An Oppression Psychology Perspective

If a group member is a young female, a person of color, and economically disadvantaged, then she has the potential to experience triple oppressions related to gender, race, and class. Violent acting-out behavior, gang affiliation, or drug use may well represent a maladaptive but understandable defensive reaction to oppressive conditions. In Fanon's oppression psychology as described by Bulhan (1985), he suggested that prolonged exposure to oppression could lead group members to internalize the "oppressor without" and adopt negative self-attitudes and self-images. Internalized rage can lead group members to behavior that is maladaptive and destructive to themselves and others. "The oppressor without becomes an introppressor—an oppressor within" (p. 126). Such a person, according to Fanon, becomes an "autopressor" by participating in her or his own oppression. These ideas will be explored in more depth later in this book when we examine group practice examples with other "oppressed" groups, such as survivors of sexual or physical abuse, the mentally ill, people with physically challenges, or gay or lesbian group members.

Ironically, and conveniently, the maladaptive behavior that results from prolonged experience of oppression may then be used by the majority and more privileged group to justify continued stereotyping and oppression, maintaining a vicious cycle. We certainly observed this maladaptive pattern and the social response among the students we worked with at the VISA Center who had been suspended for violence. Many of their behaviors were self-destructive, and even their use of language and self-deprecating names and expressions often revealed a form of internalized negative image.

If the group member is also a vulnerable client—for example, he or she lacks a strong social support system of family or friends—then his or her essentially maladaptive responses become all the more understandable. In addition, given the group member's circumstances, one has to be impressed by the strength the group member has shown by simply surviving and continuing to struggle. By viewing the group member from a strengths and *resiliency* perspective while incorporating solution-focused strategies, discussed later in this book, the group leader can focus on the part of the group member that has demonstrated a capacity to deal effectively with life. Certainly, as we worked with over 350 suspended students during the duration of the VISA project, we were impressed with their survival skills and wondered whether we ourselves would have been able to cope, even maladaptively, if faced with their often overwhelming life situations.

A group leader starting from this *strengths perspective* will be more interested in identifying what is right than what is wrong with group members. For example, the group leader may want to help them identify times in their lives when they effectively coped and found the resources they needed rather than concentrating on when they were in trouble. This is a "solution-focused" technique that will be described in more detail in Chapter 12.

As another example, instead of focusing only on the causes (*triggers*) of *relapses* for members in a substance abuse recovery group, the group leader may want to help members focus on what seemed to help them maintain their recovery between relapses. As one member of a substance abuse recovery group I led said to me, "Relapse is part of recovery as long as you can learn from it and stay sober longer the next time." For our suspended students, their ability to survive longer periods of time in school before they were resuspended was viewed as a positive outcome in our discussions and in the research. If they were first suspended for a violent act and then resuspended for nonviolent behavior, this was also viewed as progress. These often subtle signs of life and strength are what the group leader will reach for in trying to help members overcome the effects of oppression.

At this point, you may have many questions and possibly some objections. What if the group member appears too weak to deal with the system, doesn't want help, or refuses to work on the interaction? Perhaps the problem is with the system—for example, the school. What about a situation where a group member's depression is related to biological factors for which pharmaceutical treatment is needed, perhaps in conjunction with counseling? These and other objections are pursued in some detail in the discussions that follow. For the moment, try to set them aside. At this point, it is important to grasp the fundamental concept that the group member—for example, the suspended middle or high school student—should be viewed as an interactive entity, often ambivalent, acting and reacting to the various demands of the systems he or she must negotiate. The systems will be viewed in this way as well.

Whatever the category of group members discussed in this book—the child in the residential center, the husband in marital counseling, the student who is failing, the group member with a terminal illness, the group member learning to live with AIDS, or the group member in the early stages of recovery from substance abuse—all will be viewed in the context of the interaction with their social surroundings and an understanding of their potential strengths.

A Resilience Model and the Strengths Perspective

Given our understanding of the life experiences of our group members, in particular the impact of oppression on their individual and social development, it might be easy to be discouraged about effecting change. That is why it is important to balance the preceding section with one that focuses on their sources of resilience and their potential strengths. Fortunately, a solid body of research informs this view. This literature will be briefly addressed in this chapter with a focus on children and parents, with a more detailed discussion later in the text when we look at resilience across the life span.

Resilience Theory and Research

During the 1970s and 1980s, developmental research focused on risk factors that appeared to be associated with negative outcomes for clients. A child growing up in an inner-city neighborhood besieged by drugs and violence faced a degree of risk in attempting to negotiate the passage to young adulthood and beyond. If the same child also experienced childhood trauma (physical or sexual abuse, abandonment, etc.) and had parents and family members who were active abusers of drugs and alcohol, research indicated that the degree of risk for the child's negative developmental outcome increased exponentially.

However, a recurring anomaly in our practice experience and literature indicated that not all children exposed to high degrees of risk and trauma had negative developmental outcomes. Examining the "anatomy of resilience," Butler (1997) pointed out that

> a growing number of clinicians and researchers were arguing that the risk factor model burdens at-risk children with the expectation that they will fail, and ignores those who beat the odds. Broad epidemiological studies, they say, don't explain why one girl, sexually abused by a relative, becomes an unwed mother or a prostitute while another becomes an Oprah Winfrey or a Maya Angelou. Retrospective studies can't explain why one man, raised in a harsh, crowded household in impoverished Richmond, California, becomes addicted

to crack cocaine and dies of AIDS, while his younger brother—Christopher Darden—graduates from law school, and goes on to prosecute O. J. Simpson. It's time, they say, to see what the Dardens and Winfreys of the world have to teach. (p. 25)

Given the widespread nature of substance abuse; the evidence of substantial emotional, physical, and sexual abuse; the increase in the nature and degree of violence in many communities; and the growing numbers of children living in poverty, it is little wonder that research shifted toward understanding why some children, families, and communities still thrive under these conditions. This focus lends itself to the development of both preventive and curative approaches to clients at risk.

Rak and Patterson (1996) identified four major groupings of *protective factors* associated with the "buffering hypothesis"—that is, variables that may provide a buffer of protection against life events that affect at-risk children (p. 369):

1. The personal characteristics of the children (e.g., an ability from infancy on to gain others' positive attention)

2. Family conditions (e.g., focused nurturing during the first year of life and little prolonged separation from the preliminary caretaker)

3. Supports in the environment (e.g., role models, such as teachers, school counselors, mental health counselors, neighbors, and clergy)

4. Self-concept factors (e.g., the capacity to understand self and self-boundaries in relation to long-term family stressors such as psychological illness)

Garmezy, Masten, and Tellegen (1984) suggested three models for understanding the relationship among risk, vulnerability, and resilience. These were the compensatory model, in which protective factors simply outweigh risk factors; a challenge model, which suggests that limited risk factors enhance competency; and the conditional model, which focuses on personal factors that increase or decrease the impact of the risk factors.

Masten (2001) reviewed the existing resilience models and research and identified two major streams of thought. One is the variable-focused study, which suggests that parenting qualities, intellectual functioning, socioeconomic class, and so forth, correlate with positive adaptive behavior. The second line of inquiry is the person-focused study, which tries to understand the whole individual rather than specific variables. Researchers who use the latter approach seek to identify groups of individuals with patterns of good-versus-poor adaptive functioning in life contexts of high-versus-low risks and then compare outcomes. After reviewing studies that use both approaches, Masten (2001) drew the following conclusions:

The accumulated data on resilience in development suggest that this class of phenomena is more ordinary than one was led to expect by extraordinary case histories that often inspired the study. Resilience appears to be a common phenomenon arising from ordinary human adaptive processes. The great threats to human development are those that jeopardize the systems underlying these adaptive processes, including brain development and cognition, caregiver-child relationships, regulation of emotion and behavior, and the motivation for learning and engaging the environment. (p. 238)

In reviewing more than 50 years of long-term studies of child development and resilience, the Harvard Mental Health Letter (December, 2006) pointed out that the first efforts to understand resilience tended to refer to "invulnerable" children suggesting innate characteristics that shielded them against any kind of stress at any time. Instead, researchers now refer to "resilience" meaning the capacity to endure stress and bounce back—a capacity that may be available to a given person at some times and not others, under some threats and not others. (p. 5)

As described earlier, researchers found that children's protection related to a number of factors that included finding relationships with competent and caring adults (family and community), the development of cognitive skills and positive self-image, and the motivation to be effective. The Harvard review points out that more recent research is focusing on "why and how resilient children develop these relationships, abilities, and attitudes describing it as an . . . . especially promising line of research involve the interaction between early experiences and genetically determined neurobiology" (p. 5).

Implications for Group Counseling

Whether one reviews the literature for young children or older adults (see Chapter 11), the findings consistently suggest the potential for strength and capacity for change. A key element throughout this line of research is the importance of social support. The counseling group is in many ways a microcosm of our larger society and can be the source of support that may be missing in family, friends, and community. A group approach that integrates the process of mutual aid—members helping each other—would be particularly useful in providing protective factors.

The research also supports the importance of the group leader bringing a strengths perspective to the group and always looking for and at times "demanding" that group members act in their own self-interest no matter how hard their lives and circumstances have been. The next section explores the assumption of strength for change.

Assumption of Strength for Change

Although it seems logical that past experiences affect the ways in which an individual attempts to negotiate new surroundings, the danger exists within this view of prejudging and underestimating a group member's (or the system's) resiliency, strength, and capacity for change. Within the framework presented here, the individual is best described by actions and is as strong or as weak as he or she acts in the present moment. The practice implication of this attitude is that the group leader must believe that the individual or the system has the capacity to move in its own self-interest, even if only by small steps, and that this movement will lead to increased strength and more change.

With this basic assumption in mind, the interactional perspective calls for the helping person always to place a "*demand for work*" before the individual and the group. The demand for work occurs when the group leader exhorts the individual group member and the group to work effectively on their tasks and to invest that work with energy and affect. The work itself—the goals of the process (even with mandated group members)—must be shared by the group member, not merely imposed by the group leader. In this way, the demand is to work on the very tasks that the group member has agreed need to be addressed. This demand also must be integrated with support in what could be called an *empathic* demand for work. When we press the individual or the group to take a difficult next step, to face painful feelings, to reach out to people who are important to him or her, or to take a risk, is exactly when the group members most need our support and empathy. A similar demand for work will be placed on the system (e.g., teachers), and I argue that our capacity for empathy with other professionals is just as important.

A familiar expression in this connection is "reach for the group member's strength," which suggests that the very act of reaching for strength—that is, believing in the potential of the work and refusing to accept even the group member's own self-description of weakness—is a central part of what helps a group member to act. Possibly the group member has reached the present impasse precisely because all the signals received from important others have reinforced belief in the group member's own impotence. The group leader, by contrast, operates on a basic principle: No matter how hopeless it seems, *there is always a next step.*

In an example from my own practice, described in detail in Chapter 14, I confront a group of people with AIDS in early substance abuse recovery who have apparently given up on their ability to have nonexploitive and drug- and alcohol-free intimate relationships with others. I tell them that they must set aside their own concerns and issues and become a *mutual support* group for one another. I suggest that they have the capacity to help one another and that, by giving help to others, they will be getting help themselves. This is a key concept in mutual aid support groups. My demand for work is rooted in the belief that even these group members, who have experienced years of polysubstance abuse, prison sentences, prostitution, and traumatic childhood experiences, still have the strength to reach out to one another within the group, which serves as a microcosm of larger society. The group members' response and their ability to care for one another are a tribute to themselves and an affirmation of the strengths perspective.

The assumptions just described will interact in important ways in the models and examples shared in this book. Group leaders will always search for subtle connections and demand that group members act on their potential for change. This view of practice is built on a deep investment in the concept of interdependence; a view of the group member as the source of energy for change, healing, and growth; a belief in group member strength; and a preoccupation with health rather than sickness.

This stance does not negate the fact that some group members, for many complex reasons, will not be able to use the group's help at a given moment. The helping process is interactional, with group leaders and other group members carrying out their parts as best they can. As such, group members have a part to play, and their strength helps determine the outcome. For example, no matter how skillful the group leader, he or she may not be able to reach a substance-abusing group member until the group member enters a detoxification center and stops using cocaine.

Using findings from my own research and that of others, we shall throughout this book explore the ways in which stress, acceptance of a problem, and motivation affect the group member's ability to receive and use help at any given moment. Another core concept, however, will be that a group member's inability to use help at a certain point in life does not mean that he or she cannot use it at a later time. In a child welfare project I recently directed, working with older foster children who were about to make the transition to independence (aging out of the foster care system), we found group member readiness to address problems at ages 17 and 18 that clearly was not there at ages 15 and 16. I believe that skillful work done by group leaders during the early years may have laid the groundwork for our progress once the group members were ready.

Socioeconomic factors, such as income, housing, and employment trends, also profoundly affect outcomes. Group leaders must therefore be concerned with social policies that affect the human situation. Becoming aware of and working for changes in social policies is part of the task of helping. Recognizing that a particular group member may be unable to use help at that time, the group leader will nevertheless always attempt to reach for the group member's strength because this is the way in which help is given.

Group Leader Skill and the Working Relationship

At the core of this interactional theory of counseling and group leadership is a model of the helping process in which the skill of the group leader helps create a positive working relationship, referred to elsewhere as the therapeutic alliance. In turn, this relationship is the medium through which the group leader influences the outcomes of practice. This simple model can be visualized as shown in Figure 1.2.

Although the model suggests that the applied skill leads to relationship, which then influences outcomes, the double-pointed arrows imply that the model is dynamic. For example, a change in the working relationship will affect the group leader's behavior as well. A group leader may be influenced in her or his interaction with a group member by the changing nature of the relationship (e.g., a positive relationship leads to more empathy on the group leader's part). Similarly, positive or negative outcomes for the group member may influence his or her sense of the relationship.

Another model incorporated into this theory involves the relationship between group members' ability to manage their feelings and their ability to manage their problems. These ideas were developed as part of the theory-building effort I have described in other publications (Shulman, 1978, 1981, 1991). The construct is based on the assumption that how we feel powerfully affects how we act. The relationship between feelings and action is reciprocal: How we act also influences how we feel.

To this feeling-behavioral connection we can add a third element: cognition. *Cognition* refers to the way that group members think about themselves and their environment. The contributions of *cognitive-behavioral psychology and theory* (Berlin, 1983; Watson & Tharp, 2007) have helped us broaden our understanding of how a group member's perception of reality can have a powerful impact on self-image, identification of the nature of a problem, and self-assessment of the ability to cope. Corey (2008) points out that

> [c]ognitive behavioral approaches are becoming increasingly popular in group work in part due to their emphasis on teaching clients self-management skills and how to restructure their thoughts. Clients can learn to use these techniques

FIGURE 1.2

Group Leader Skill and the Working Relationship

to control their lives, deal effectively with present and future problems, and function well without ongoing therapy. (p. 338)

I argue throughout this book that how group members think affects how they feel, which affects how they act, in a circular and reciprocal manner. The model presented could be termed a cognitive-affective-behavioral framework without confusing it with other models that incorporate cognitive-behavioral approaches.

For example, some female survivors of childhood sexual abuse describe themselves as "damaged goods" as they enter their teenage years. These group members may respond to the oppression they have experienced by internalizing a negative self-image and falsely assuming some form of responsibility for what was done to them. They could express feelings of guilt and concern that they may have been seductive toward the offending adult, thus shifting responsibility for the problem to themselves—a form of self-blame. This is an example of the internalized oppressor at work. Symptoms of depression and personal apathy often cover an underlying rage that the child learned to suppress in order to survive. The use of alcohol and drugs also provides an escape, a form of self-medication that is a flight from the pain associated with the abuse, and is an example of the self-destructive behavior described earlier, in which oppressed group members become autopressors.

The association between these perceptions of low self-image and the feelings (e.g., shame) that they can generate may lead these teenage survivors to enter into relationships and life patterns that perpetuate their exploitation. For example, a woman's low sense of self-esteem may lead her to relationships with exploitive men who use physical, emotional, and sexual violence to maintain control over the lives of women. The use of drugs and involvement in the street culture may lead to prostitution. These actions on the group member's part, related to the group member's feelings, may in turn deepen the sense of being "damaged." Thus, negative reciprocal relationships among how the group member feels, thinks, and acts result in a deepening of the problems in living. Of course, for many survivors, protective factors, such as the impact of a caring person in their lives (e.g., foster parent, teacher, group leader), may mitigate the impact of the abuse on their lives.

An intervention is needed to disrupt this vicious cycle. As the group leader helps the group members examine the underlying pain and rage, and face the oppressor within, the group members can begin to take control of their emotions and more effectively manage them rather than being managed by them. Effective practice can help the group member cognitively reframe the source of the problem and begin to perceive him- or herself as a survivor with strengths rather than a victim. Techniques associated with solution-focused practice or feminist group theory, also described later in this book, can help the group member see his or her strengths and begin the healing process. In the words of a poem written by a member of a support group for survivors, described in Chapter 9, group members can work through their pain and see themselves as "surviving and thriving."

The principle of dealing with feelings in pursuit of purpose will lead the group leader to help the group member connect her or his feelings and perceptions with her or his actions. Being aware of the connections among how we think, feel, and act is an early step in taking control over these thoughts and feelings and our resultant behaviors. As the group member better manages these feelings and develops a more accurate assessment of self and the situation, she or he can begin to manage life problems more effectively. Success with such problems, in turn, will influence her or his thoughts and feelings.

For example, a teenage survivor may begin to change her self-destructive behavior by taking a first step on her own behalf. Obtaining help with her addiction, leaving the streets for a shelter, or attempting to break off an abusive and exploitive relationship may be the first step toward breaking out of her trap. Each step that she takes in her own self-interest, however small, can contribute to a more positive feeling about herself and strengthen her to take the next step. Thus, managing her feelings helps her manage her problems, and managing her problems helps her manage her feelings.

As this model is explored, we shall see that if the group leader is to help group members manage their feelings, the group leader must be able to manage his or her own emotions. For example, as a result of feeling a group member's pain, a group leader who is helping a survivor of sexual abuse may prematurely attempt to reassure the group member that she is not damaged. Or the group leader may take on the woman's anger against the men who have exploited her, which may preempt the group member's essential work in facing her own anger. Both of these understandable emotional reactions by the group leader may block the group member's ability to manage her own feelings.

PRACTICE POINTS

The group leader instead needs to share his or her sense of the group member's pain without trying to relieve it. For example:

> As I listen to you, I'm feeling how much pain you are in, how damaged you must feel. A big part of me wants to say, "Don't feel that way! You are a person of value." But I know that no matter what I say, the pain is there, and I can't make it go away.

The anger against the exploitive men—for example, a sexually abusive father—can also be shared, but in a manner that helps the group member face her own anger rather than doing the work for her. For example:

> It makes me angry when I think of what was done to you by someone you expected to take care of you and to protect you. But from what you are saying to me, it seems that your feelings are mixed right now. It sounds like a big part of you wishes your family could be different, could change, and that you could still be like a real family.

The group leader's sharing of her or his feelings, in what I refer to as the integration of personal and professional selves, is a crucial and somewhat controversial element in this framework. Borrowing from the medical profession, a general injunction has been suggested by many in the field as well as in the literature, whereby the group leader does not share his or her feelings at any time. I will argue and illustrate throughout the book that this is a false dichotomy; in fact, based on some of my own research into the doctor-patient relationship (Shulman & Buchan, 1982), it does not even work for the medical profession from which it was borrowed. The issue is, instead, how do we "use ourselves" appropriately and professionally, within appropriate boundaries, rather than "losing ourselves" through the presentation of a supposed blank slate of emotions. I will say much more about this question throughout the book.

The eight skills examined in my study (Shulman, 1991) were drawn from those that proved to be most important in my prior research (1978, 1979b). Twenty-two specific skills were reviewed in the earlier research, with 10 of the 22 associating at a significant level with developing a positive relationship and counselor helpfulness. Although all of these skills (and others) are discussed in the chapters that follow, a particular emphasis is placed here on the eight skills studied in the more recent work. (For a clearer understanding of the methodology, findings, and limitations of this research, review a more detailed outline of this research in Appendix A and a further elaboration on the book's website at **www.cengage.com/counseling/shulman**.) These eight skills have been organized into two groupings, as follows:

Group leader's skills for helping group members manage their feelings

- Reaching inside of silences
- Putting the group member's feelings into words
- Displaying understanding of the group member's feelings
- Sharing the group leader's feelings

Group leader's skills for helping group members manage their problems

- Clarifying the group leader's purpose and role
- Reaching for group member feedback
- Partializing concerns
- Supporting group members in taboo areas

All of these skills are important in all phases of practice. However, each skill may have various meanings or impacts at different stages of the relationship. Because the helping process is so complex in individual and group practice, it is useful to analyze it against the backdrop of the different phases of work. The four phases of work described earlier are as follows:

Preliminary (or Preparatory) Phase

Beginning (or Contracting) Phase

Middle (or Work) Phase

Ending and Transition Phase

Each phase of work—preliminary, beginning, middle, and ending and transition—has unique dynamics and requires specific skills. Taft (1949), referring to the beginning, middle, and ending phases, was one of the first to draw attention to the impact of time on practice. Schwartz (1971) incorporated this dimension into his work, adding the preliminary phase and modifying the ending phase to the "ending and transition" phase. Most current models of group counseling also consider time as an organizing principle although they may not use the same wording when describing the phases (e.g., Corey, 2008; Gladding, 2003; Toseland & Rivas, 2005).

The Integration of Personal and Professional Selves

As suggested earlier, another carryover from the medical model was the importance placed on maintaining one's professional self. Most helping professions emphasized the professional role and the need to suppress personal feelings and reactions. For example, when working with stressful patients, one might have to keep one's real reactions in check to avoid appearing judgmental. A professional group leader has been described as one who maintained control of emotions and would not become angry or too emotionally involved, would not cry in the presence of a group member, and so forth. The injunction to the group leader appeared to be "Take your professional self to work, and leave your personal self at home." This image of professionalism was (and still is) widely held; many of my students started their careers wondering if they would have problems as a group leader because they "felt too much."

The practice framework presented in this text will suggest that we are faced with a false dichotomy when we believe we must choose between our personal self and our professional self. In fact, I argue that we are at our best in our work when we are able to synthesize the two by integrating our personal self into our professional role.

The conflict of views about what defines the professional self was brought home dramatically in a workshop I led on practice. One young counselor on a pediatric oncology service described an incident in which a mother appeared at her door after being referred by the attending physician. The mother had just been told that her 7-year-old daughter had a terminal illness. After explaining this to the group leader, the mother broke down and cried.

When I asked the counselor what she did, she described how overwhelmed she felt by the mother's grief. All that she could do was sit and hold the mother's hand, softly crying with her. I maintain that, although much work would need to be done in this case (e.g., helping the mother figure out how to get home, how to talk to her family, how to deal with her dying daughter and her family over the next few months), at this point what the mother needed most was not advice but someone to be with her. In fact, as the counselor partially experienced the mother's pain and shared it with her through her own emotions, she gave that client the important gift of her own feelings. The counselor was being professional in the best sense of the word. Other counselors, who might not cry with a client, may make the same gift in different ways—through facial expressions, a respectful silence, or a hand on the shoulder—each counselor responding in a way that is consistent with his or her own personality. The crucial factor is the group leader's willingness to be honest and to share his or her feelings.

In this example, the counselor continued her story by telling us that her supervisor passed the open door, called her outside, and berated her for unprofessional behavior. The supervisor said, "How could you let yourself break down that way? You can't help your clients if you become overwhelmed yourself." When I asked the counselor what she took from the experience, she replied, "I learned to keep my door closed!" Although many who hear this story are upset with the supervisor, I am not. I realize that she may have been trained as I was, during a time when personal expressions of emotion were considered unprofessional.

I encouraged this counselor to talk to her supervisor, because I felt that it was crucial for her to obtain support from her supervisor and colleagues if she were to continue to provide this kind of help to group members. My research (Shulman, 1979b) has emphasized the importance of formal and informal sources of social support for counselors. This counselor was making a gift to the client of her willingness to "be with" her at a terrible moment in her life. The counselor's capacity to continue to be there for clients depends somewhat on her having someone—supervisor, colleague, or both—be there for her. (This issue will be explored in more detail in Chapter 12 when I discuss groups for dealing with trauma and vicarious traumatization for group leaders.)

This often artificial split between personal and professional selves was created from the profession's understandable concerns with the inappropriate use of self by helping professionals. For example, concern arose about *countertransference*, a process in which group leaders may project onto group members their own unfinished family business (e.g., relating to a father in a group member's family as if he were one's own parent). The profession was troubled by group leaders who used the argument of spontaneity to justify acting out with group members, such as getting inappropriately angry or judgmental or sharing personal problems ("If you think you have troubles with your kids, let me tell you about my family").

Unethical behavior with group members, such as abusing the powerful forces of the helping bond to sexually exploit a vulnerable group member, provides another example. Each of these examples illustrates a lack of integration of personal and professional selves. The concerns about the use of the personal self were—and continue to be—well founded. Unfortunately, the solution of separating the personal from the professional led to more problems than it resolved.

The argument advanced throughout this text will be that each of us brings our own personal style, artistry, background, feelings, values, and beliefs to our professional practice. Rather than denying or suppressing these, we need to learn more about ourselves in the context of our practice, and find ways to use ourselves in pursuit of our professional functions. We will make many mistakes along the way—saying things we will later regret, apologizing to group members, learning from these mistakes, correcting them, and then making what I called earlier "more sophisticated" mistakes.

In other words, we will be real people carrying out difficult jobs as best we can, rather than paragons of virtue who present an image of perfection. As we demonstrate to our group members our humanness, vulnerability, willingness to risk, spontaneity, honesty, and lack of defensiveness (or defensiveness for which we later apologize), we model the very behaviors we hope to see in our group members. Thus, when group leaders or students ask me, "Should I be professional or should I be myself?" I reply that the dualism implied in the question does not exist. They must be themselves if they are going to be professional.

This position also puts to rest another artificial dichotomy between science and art. I believe each of us brings our unique artistry to our work; however, we have a professional responsibility to make sure it is guided by science. Fortunately, we have the whole of our professional lives to learn how to effect and refine this synthesis.

Chapter Summary

The chapter began with a brief description of what the elements of a practice theory are and descriptions of the terms *model* and *skill*. Underlying assumptions about individuals and their social interactions are discussed and illustrated. An oppression psychology perspective combined with a resilience model help readers both understand group members' sometimes maladaptive behaviors as well as identify their potential strengths for change.

The key skills for helping group members deal with their problems and deal with their feelings are described with supportive research findings. A cognitive-emotional-behavioral model is suggested as important to understand the nature of the change process. Group leader skills designed to develop the "working relationship" (therapeutic alliance) are also described.

Finally, central to the effectiveness of the group leader is her or his ability to integrate the personal self with the professional self.

Related Online Content and Activities

For learning tools such as glossary terms, InfoTrac® College Edition keywords, links to related websites, and chapter practice quizzes, visit this book's website at **www .cengage.com/counseling/shulman**.

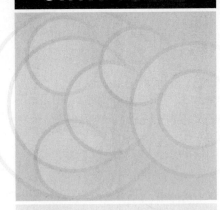

Mutual Aid Processes in the Group

I suggested in the introduction that although there are many different group purposes, models, and structures serving different populations in different settings, the potential for facilitating some form of mutual aid exists in all groups. The mutual aid process in which members are a source of help for one another is a central concept in this framework for group counseling. I believe mutual aid can be integrated as an element in group practice that uses other theoretical frameworks (e.g., psycho-dynamic, solution focused, cognitive-behavioral, motivational interview-ing). The resilience discussion in Chapter 1 underlined how important social support can be as a buffer and a protective factor. The mutual aid process in a group is a form of social support that can provide that help. Whether the group is a support group for the elderly, a substance abuse prevention or recovery group, or a counseling group for children who have lost a parent or someone else close to them, providing and receiving caring and help from other members is one of the major rea-sons we work with people in groups.

Because I will be discussing and illustrating how the mutual aid process works, and how the group leader helps make it happen, I will use this chapter to describe the dynamics of mutual aid that can occur when a group of people with a somewhat common agenda and similar concerns is brought together. The reader will find that many of the pro-cesses and skills discussed in this chapter are equally applicable when working with individuals and families; however, my focus is practice in the group context. I will also highlight the unique features involved in the use of group method, as well as specific obstacles that need to be overcome to create a mutual aid system. I will outline the mutual aid processes and examine the group leader's role in the group.

What Is Mutual Aid?

In a seminal article introducing the *mutual aid* concept, Schwartz (1961) defined the helping group as follows:

> The group is an enterprise in mutual aid, an alliance of individuals who need each other, in varying degrees, to work on certain common problems. The important fact is that this is a helping system in which the group members need each other as well as the leader. This need to use each other, to create not one but many helping relationships, is a vital ingredient of the group process and constitutes a common need over and above the specific tasks for which the group was formed. (p. 18)

The idea of the group as a "mutual aid system" in which the leader helps people help one another is an attractive one, yet it raises many questions in the minds of students and counselors whose experiences in groups, as members and leaders, have led them to question the potential of mutual aid. Exactly how can a group of people sharing the same set of concerns help one another? Isn't it a bit like the blind leading the blind? How will members be able to talk about their most intimate concerns before a group of strangers? What about the coercive power of the group? How can individuals stand up against the odds? What is the job of the group leader if the members are helping each other? These questions and others are legitimate. They sometimes reflect leaders' past group experiences, which may have been hurtful, nonproductive, or boring—far from being enterprises in mutual aid.

My response is that the potential for mutual aid exists in any group, but simply bringing persons together does not guarantee that it will emerge. Several obstacles can block the group members' ability to reach out to one another and offer help. Many of these hurdles are similar to those observed in individual counseling, but their effect can be magnified in the group context. Because all members will bring to the group their own concepts, based on past experiences with groups (e.g., school, camp, committees), and because many of these past experiences may have been poor ones, the group leader is needed to help the group members create the conditions in which mutual aid can take place. The tasks of the group leader in attempting to help group members develop the required skills are related to these obstacles.

Developing mutual aid in a group is a complex process, with members having to overcome many of their stereotypes about people in general, groups, and the helping process itself. They will need all the assistance they can get from the group leader. Because the leader has also been affected by past group experiences, one of the leader's early tasks requires facing her or his own feelings and examining stereotypes. Without this self-examination, the leader may be unable to convey to the members a belief in their potential for helping each other. Faith in the strength of the group will make an important contribution to the group members' success in their struggles.

In the balance of this chapter, I will begin to address the leader's hesitancy and questions by listing some of the ways in which group members can help another; these are the processes of mutual aid. The obstacles that can emerge to block this potential are briefly reviewed. An overview of the role of the group leader is then presented.

The Dynamics of Mutual Aid

In the chapters that follow, the mutual aid process will be described in detail and illustrated with examples from a range of groups. To help you conceptualize mutual aid in a general way, I present a number of illustrations here.

Sharing Data

One of the simplest yet most important ways in which group members can help one another is through the sharing of relevant data. Members of the group have had different life experiences, through which they have accumulated knowledge, views, values, and so forth, that can help others in the group. For example, in a married couples' group I led (described in Chapter 4), one of the couples is in their late 60s. They have experienced many of the normal life crises as well as those imposed by societal pressures (e.g., the Great Depression of the 1930s). As other group members who are in their 50s, 40s, 30s, and 20s describe their experiences and problems, this couple is often able to share an insight that comes from being able to view these crises from the perspective of time. As the group leader, I often found myself learning from this couple's experiences. We created in the group a form of the extended family in which one generation passed on its life experiences to the next. In turn, the older couple was able to use the group not only for their immediate problems but also as a place for reviewing their 50 years together. (This may be an important part of their work at this stage in their life cycle.)

In another group, working mothers were able to share ideas that have proven helpful in organizing their daily routines. The power of the Internet allowed many group members to have access to information about resources that would never have been available before. Members shared the names of community services that they had discovered, and each mother tapped the experiences and the ingenuity of the others. Whether the data consist of specific tips on concrete questions (jobs, available housing, money management, etc.), values, or ideas about relationships, each member can contribute to the common pool of knowledge. The leader will also contribute data that, when combined with that of the others, provide a rich resource for the members.

In a group of persons with AIDS who were in early recovery from substance abuse (referred to as an AIDS/recovery group and co-led by this author), specific information about the recovery process and coping with AIDS and its treatment was shared on a regular basis. For example, one group member told another, "This is the start of your second year in recovery—the feelings year—so don't be surprised about all of the pain you are feeling because you don't have the drinking and drugging to cover it up." At another meeting, group members shared their experiences with the, at that time, new triple-drug therapy and provided information for those who were not in the trial groups about how to get connected.

PRACTICE POINTS In this example, group members provided tips on how to increase one member's chances for acceptance into a special housing program for people with AIDS. My job as group leader was to help connect the group to the member to facilitate this form of mutual aid.

I pointed out that, earlier, Theresa had mentioned her interest in getting into this independent living facility. I wondered if we might help her just by addressing that issue as well. She told us she was concerned about putting an application in because she didn't think she had established enough credibility in her single-room occupancy housing. At this point, Jake and Tania started suggesting strategies and ideas about how to approach the living facility and what would maximize her ability to get in. They strongly encouraged her to make an application right now, since there were openings, and a few months down the road these openings might close, and there would be no place for her. They said they thought it would be wonderful if she could move into the building.

Tania (a transgendered member) pointed out that the building was supposed to be for people with AIDS, but, if you took a look at it, your guess would be that it was essentially for gay men. She said she was the only woman in the whole building—the only single woman in the whole building. She said to Theresa that if worse came to worst, you could always tell the staff it's discrimination and that'll get their attention. She said, "That's how I got in."

They continued to talk with Theresa about ways she could demonstrate her responsibility, things that she had done, her commitment to recovery, the fact that she wanted to leave the place where she currently lived. Even though it was supposed to be a safe building, everybody knew drug dealing was going on there all the time, and it was scary to be there. She took it all in, thanked them for their advice, and said she was going to apply.

The Dialectical Process

An important debate of ideas can take place as each member shares views on the question under discussion. Group members can risk their tentative ideas and use the group as a sounding board—a place for their views to be challenged and possibly changed. It is not always easy to challenge ideas in the group, and I will discuss later how such a "culture for work" can be developed. When this kind of group *"culture"* is present, the argument between two or more members takes on a dialectical nature. Group members can listen as one member presents the "thesis" and the other, the "antithesis." As each member listens, he or she can use the discussion to develop a personal "synthesis."

An illustration of this *dialectical process* in a couples' group I co-led occurred when one couple in their 50s discussed a problem they were experiencing with their grown, married children. They described their negative perception of the way in which their children were handling their marital difficulties and how this was affecting their own marriage. As they spoke, I could see anger in the eyes of a younger couple in their 20s. They were experiencing difficulty with the wife's parents, whom they viewed as "meddling" in their lives. When I reached for the verbal expression of the nonverbal cues, the battle was on. The older couple had to defend their perceptions against the arguments of the younger couple, who could see the problem through the eyes of the 50-somethings' children. In return, the younger couple had to look at their strained relationships with the wife's parents through the eyes of the older couple, who could understand her parents' perspective. For each couple, the debate, moderated by myself, led to some modification of their views and new insights into how the respective children and parents might be feeling. It was obvious from the discussion that other group members were making associations to their own experiences, using the dialogue taking place before them.

It is important to note that confrontation is a part of mutual aid. Instead of being suppressed, differences must be expressed in an arena where they can be used for learning. I believe that group members often present strongly held views on a subject precisely because they have doubts and desperately need a challenging perspective.

The skills involved in helping group members use these conflicts constructively in a mutually respectful and caring manner are explored later. This example also illustrates the fact that the group can be a laboratory for developing skills such as asserting oneself, so that the individual members can become more effective in their outside-the-group relationships. The conversation between the older and younger couples constituted a rehearsal for the important discussion that needed to take place with their respective children and parents. The group members were able to use the experience for this purpose when the leader made this point.

Discussing a Taboo Area

Each group member brings to the group the *norms of behavior* and the *societal taboos* that exist in our larger culture. Norms are the rules of behavior that are generally accepted by a dominant group in society. These norms can be re-created within a counseling group or other system. The existence of the norms is evident when the group members behave as if the norms exist. For example, one norm of group behavior may be to avoid discussion of a societal taboo.

In the beginning phase of work, the group re-creates in this *microsociety* the general community "culture," consisting of norms, taboos, and rules that the group members have experienced outside the group. Thus, direct talk about such subjects as authority, dependency (on people and/or drugs), death and dying, and sex is experienced as taboo. One of the group leader's tasks will be to help the group members develop new norms and feel free to challenge some taboos so that the group can be more effective. This is referred to as helping the group develop a *culture for work*.

Each group member will feel the urgency of discussing the subject somewhat differently from the others, and each group member will experience the power of the taboo differently. As the work proceeds and the level of comfort in the group increases (the skills for helping this happen are discussed in later chapters), one member may take the first risk, directly or indirectly, that leads the group into a difficult area of discussion. By being first, the member allows the more fearful and reluctant members to watch as the taboo is violated. As they experience positive work, they are given permission to enter the formerly taboo area. Thus, all the group members are able to benefit from the particular sense of urgency, the lower level of anxiety, or the greater willingness to risk of the member who leads the way.

In my AIDS/recovery group, one member spoke about her own abusive past history and how she had escaped her family and turned to the streets and "to every kind of drug and drink you could imagine." She went on to describe her experiences prostituting in order to raise money for drugs and how she was not proud of herself or what she did. She said, "While I was on the street, I was with many men, but I was really with no man." These revelations opened the door for other members to share their own sexual experiences, often degrading and exploitive, as they went on "coke dates" to raise money for their drugs. The ability to discuss their emotions in a supportive, nonjudgmental environment appeared to have a cathartic effect, creating a culture in which other taboo issues were discussed, such as their own illnesses, their rejection by friends and family, painful losses of people close to them, and their own fears of debilitation and death associated with AIDS.

In another example of a counseling group, for 8- to 10-year-old children, all of whom had lost a close relative (e.g., parent, grandparent), the session involved the use of drawing materials. The group leaders recognized that the taboo related to talking about painful issues such as death and loss was preventing a discussion of the members' feelings. Instead, the children were acting out their pain through maladaptive behavior. At the start of one meeting, one youngster drew a picture of his grandfather and then drew lines through it. The group leader pointed out the meaning of the drawing that his grandfather was dead, and the boy started running around the room saying he "doesn't want anyone to talk about his grandfather." A young girl in the group said he is running around because he doesn't want to talk about his grandfather's death. Another child said no one wants to talk about death because when you talk about it, you have bad dreams. The work begins as they started to verbalize their feelings having been led into the topic by the first boy's drawings.

The All-in-the-Same-Boat Phenomenon

After the group enters a formerly taboo area, the members listen to others' feelings and often discover emotions of their own that they were unaware of, feelings that may have been having a powerful effect on their lives. They also discover the reassuring fact that they are not alone in their feelings, that group members are *"all in the same boat."* Knowing that others share your concerns and feelings somehow makes them less frightening and easier to deal with. When, as a group member, one discovers that one is not alone in feeling overwhelmed by a problem, or worried about one's sexual adequacy, or wondering who one is and where one comes from (e.g., a foster teenager), or experiencing rejection because of "the virus" (AIDS), one is often better able to mobilize oneself to deal with the problem productively.

Discovering that feelings are shared by other members of the group can often help release a group member from their power. Guilt over "evil" thoughts and feelings can be lessened and self-destructive cycles broken when one discovers they are normal and shared by others. For example, a parent of a child with a physical or mental disability who hears that other parents may also feel that their child's condition represents "God's punishment" may be better able to cope with his guilt. This can be one of the most powerful forces for change resulting from the mutual aid process. There is not the same impact when a leader in individual work tries to reassure the group member that the same feelings are shared by others. Hearing them articulated by others in the group sessions makes a unique impression.

In another example from the AIDS/recovery group, one member talked of her fears of being rejected by her boyfriend because she had AIDS and he didn't. Even though the boyfriend knew about her AIDS and seemed to accept it, she was afraid to ask for a stronger commitment from him because she thought he would turn her down and she would lose him. Although she was an attractive young woman, she feared that no one else could ever love her because of the virus. A male member of the group responded, saying, "That's the thing you fear most—the rejection. I just disconnect my telephone and stay in my room because I know if I get close to someone, I'm just going to be rejected again."

Developing a Universal Perspective

Developing a universal perspective is a special case of the all-in-the-same-boat phenomenon just described. Many group members, particularly those belonging to oppressed and vulnerable populations, may internalize the negative definitions assigned to them by the larger society. Thus, battered women, survivors of sexual abuse, persons of color, the mentally ill, or people with AIDS may assume the blame for their troubles and see their difficulties as a product of their own personal shortcomings. This can be reinforced by mental health professionals who focus on personal pathology while ignoring the socioeconomic factors that created and constantly reinforce the negative self-image.

In groups where common experiences of oppression are shared, it becomes easier for group members to recognize that a source of their problems in living may be external to themselves. Early in the women's movement, this process was exemplified in the *consciousness-raising groups* designed to help women become more aware of gender stereotyping and oppression issues that affected their lives. With a more universal perspective on one's problems, the additional burden of taking all of the blame for one's troubles may be lifted. The anger against the oppression—anger that often lurks just beneath the outward signs of depression, submission, and apathy—can be released and converted into positive energy for dealing with personal as well as social issues.

In an example described in some detail in Chapter 9, a group of young female survivors of sexual abuse support each other in recognizing the social roots of the gender oppression and violence they have experienced. In a pivotal meeting, the leader announces that a "Take Back the Night" march against violence toward women will occur in their town the following week and wonders if group members might want to participate. An important discussion between the women, which highlights how these women have been taught to accept their "victim" status, leads to their decision to attend the march as a group. This group experience, resulting from their ability to universalize their perspective, may well have been one of the most therapeutic aspects of the group.

In an example from the AIDS/recovery group, one woman talked about the sexual exploitation she has experienced both from her "johns" while prostituting and from her boyfriends over the years. A transgendered female member of the group angrily declares that in her experience, sex is all most men are interested in, and they will use and exploit you and your feelings, if they can, in order to get it. To underscore her point, she declares, "And I know, because I have been both!" After the group members stopped their good-natured laughing at her comment, they discussed intimate relationships, how hard it is to find people who really care, and how painful it is when you lose someone who does.

In a vocational counseling group for unemployed men and women, the discussion led to the recognition that all of the members had lost their jobs just when they had reached senior status in the organization and had been replaced by younger, lower-salaried employees. It became clear to them that they were "let go" not because they were no longer productive but that they were experiencing a pattern of age discrimination. This realization led to a discussion of how to continue their job search but also what legal remedies might be open to them and how to access them.

Mutual Support

When the *group culture* supports the open expression of feelings, group members' capacity to empathize with each other is evident. With the group leader setting the tone through expression of personal feelings and understanding of others, each member is able to observe the powerful effect of *empathy*. Because group members share some common concerns, they are often able to understand each other's feelings in a deeper way than the leader. This expression of empathy is an important healing agent for both the group member who receives it and the one who offers it. As group members understand the others' feelings, without judging them harshly, they begin to accept their own feelings in new ways. For a member struggling with a specific concern, the group's acceptance and *caring* can be a source of support during a difficult time.

I have just used the expression "the group's acceptance and caring," which introduces a new concept to be explored in detail in Chapter 8. The important element here is the group, the entity that is created when people are brought together. This entity, which I will call the group-as-a-whole, involves more than just the simple sum of the parts (members). For example, support in the mutual aid group often has a quality that is different from support received in interaction with a single empathic person. It is more than just a quantitative difference of more people equaling more empathy. At crucial moments in a group, one can sense a general tone or atmosphere, displayed through words, expressions, or physical posture, that conveys the caring of the "group" for the individual. One can almost sense it "in the air." This seems to have a special meaning and importance to the individual group member. The properties of the group-as-a-whole are described in detail in Chapter 8, in which I will explore the idea of working with the group as the "second client."

In the following example of support, also from the AIDS/recovery group, the group member who is reluctant to confront her boyfriend for fear of losing him asks the transgender member how she looks.

PRACTICE POINTS — I sense the underlying question related to the impact of having AIDS and articulate Theresa's feelings:

> Once again, Theresa asked Tania how she looked. She said, "You're a woman. I know, as a woman, you will be honest with me and just tell me what you think. Do you think I look OK?" Tania seemed confused and said, "Well, sure, you look wonderful." I said, "I wonder if Theresa is really asking, 'Am I pretty enough? Am I attractive enough? If my boyfriend leaves me, can I find someone else who could love me even though I have AIDS?'" She said, "That's it," and came close to tears. She said, "I'm so afraid, if I lose him, I won't find anyone else." She said, "I know I could have guys, and I know I could have sex, and I like the sex. I sure missed it during the time I was in prison, but can another guy love me?"
>
> The group members tried to reassure her that she was a wonderful person, and Tania said, "It's not what you look like on the outside, it's what you're like on the inside." And she said, "And you, honey—you've really got it where it counts."

In another example, also described in detail in Chapter 14, one member in a DWI (driving while intoxicated) group finally reveals that the trigger for his drinking is the memory of having driven his car while drunk, crashing, and the resultant death of his wife. The worker describes how all of the men leaned forward toward him, physically and verbally supporting him as he struggled with his loss while also experiencing the feelings associated with their own losses due to their drinking.

Mutual Demand

Central to this practice framework is the concept of the helping relationship consisting of elements of both support and demand, synthesized in unique, personal ways. The same is true in the group counseling context. Mutual aid is provided through expectation as well as through caring. One illustration is the way group members confront each other. For example, in my couples' group, two male members were able to challenge a third who was maintaining that the source of the problem was his wife, that she was the identified "patient," and he was coming to group merely to "help her out." Both of the confronting group members had taken the same position at our first session and had slowly modified their views. They had lowered their defenses and accepted the idea that the problem was a "couple" problem. This *mutual demand* on the third member had a different quality coming from group members, rather than the group leader.

As the group culture develops, it can include expectations that members risk their real thoughts and ideas, listen to each other and set their own concerns aside at times to help another, and so on. These expectations help develop a productive culture for work. Another group expectation can be that the members will work on their concerns. At moments when group members feel overwhelmed and hopeless, this expectation may help them take a next step. The group cares enough about them not to let them give up. I have witnessed group members take some difficult action, such as confronting a boss or dealing more effectively with a close relative. When the action was discussed the following week, they indicated that one of the factors that had pushed them to make the move and take a risk was the thought of returning to the group and admitting that they hadn't acted. Mutual demand, integrated with mutual support, can be a powerful force for change.

In my AIDS/recovery group, members often used their insights and understanding about the recovery process, gained through participation in 12-step groups such as Alcoholics Anonymous (AA) and Narcotics Anonymous (NA), to confront each other when their behaviors threatened their recovery. In one example, a group member who had just spent 2 weeks in a detoxification program after relapsing into cocaine use described how hard it was for him not to "hang around" the pool hall where all of his friends were but also where drugs were sold. He described how he wavered each day, wondering if he could connect up with them and not relapse again. One of the other members, using an analogy obviously known by the others through their AA experiences, said, "You know, John, if you hang around a barbershop long enough" (pause) and the rest of the group, in a chorus, replied, "you are going get a haircut!" The group members all laughed, and John replied, "I know, I know, you're right—I would definitely be risking my recovery."

Individual Problem Solving

A mutual aid group can be a place where an individual can bring a problem and ask for assistance. For example, in one group a young woman discussed the strained relationship between herself and her mother. Her mother lived nearby and was constantly calling and asking to come over. The group member had been extremely depressed and was going through periods where she neglected her work at home (dishes piling up in the sink, etc.). Each time her mother came over, she felt, because of her mother's actions, that she was being reprimanded for being a poor housekeeper and a poor mother to her young children. The resulting tension produced many arguments, including some between the husband and wife. The group member felt her mother still treated her like a child even though she was 27.

The group member presented the issue, at first indirectly and later with much feeling and tears. The group members reached out to offer support and understanding. They were able to use their own experiences to share similar feelings. The older members of the group were able to provide a different perspective on the mother's actions. They could identify with her feelings, and they pointed out how uncertain she might feel about how to help her daughter. Conversations and incidents described by the group member were discussed, and new interpretations of the interactions were offered. It became clear that the group member's perceptions were often distorted by her own feelings of inadequacy and her harsh judgments of herself. The problem was described by the leader (this author) from a new perspective, that of a normative crisis in life as the young couple sought new ways to relate to her parents, and the parents, in turn, struggled to find ways of being close while still letting go. Other issues were involved as well, related to some of the reasons for the group member's depression, such as her feelings of being trapped at home and trapped as a woman. These emerged in later sessions.

It is important to note that as the group members offered help through *individual problem solving*, they were also helping themselves. Each group member could make associations to a similar concern. All of them could see how easily the communications between mother and daughter were going astray. As they tried to help the group member clarify her own feelings, understand her mother's reactions in new ways, and see how the mutual stereotypes were interfering with the ability to communicate real feelings, the other group members could relate these ideas to their own close relationships. This is one of the important ways in which giving help in a mutual aid group is a form of self-help. It is always easier to see the problem in someone else's relationships than in your own. The general learning of the group members can be enhanced through the specific problem-solving work done with each member. The group leader can help by pointing out the underlying common themes.

This mutual aid process offers another example that challenges the false dichotomy often posed between meeting the needs of the individual or the needs of the group—that is, group leaders' feeling that they must choose between the individual with a specific problem or attending to the group. This false dichotomy can lead to doing *individual counseling in the group* or ignoring individual issues for fear of losing the group. As I will illustrate later, if the group leader sees his or her job as helping individuals reach out to the group and helping the group respond, then there is no need to choose between the one or the many. The group leader can be with both at the same time.

Rehearsal

Another way in which a mutual aid group can help is by providing a forum in which members can try out ideas or skills. In a sense, the group becomes a safe place to risk new ways of communicating and to practice actions the group member feels may be hard to do.

 PRACTICE POINTS To continue with the previous example of the problem the younger member was experiencing in dealing with her mother, as that session neared the end, the group leader pointed out that the group member seemed hesitant about taking up the issue with her mother and suggested she practice the conversation in the group. The following excerpt from the process recording starts with the group member's response.

> **ROSE:** I'm not sure I can talk with my mother about this. What would I say?
>
> **LEADER:** That's a good question. How about trying it out right here? I'll pretend to be your mother calling to ask to see you. You can practice how you would respond, and the group can give some ideas about how it sounds. Does that sound all right?
>
> **ROSE:** (She stopped crying now and is sitting straight up in her chair with a slight smile on her face.) OK. You call me and tell me you want to have lunch with me and that I should keep the kids home from school so you can see them.

LEADER: (Role-playing) Hello, Rose, this is Mom.

ROSE: Hi, Mom. How are you and Dad feeling?

LEADER: Not so good. You know, Dad gets upset easily, and he has been feeling lousy. (The group member had indicated that her mother often used her father's health to try to make her feel guilty.)

ROSE: That's it! That's what she would say to make me feel guilty. (The group members are laughing at this point.)

The discussion picked up, with the group members agreeing about how easy it is for others to make them feel guilty. The leader inquired how Rose would feel at that point in the conversation. It became clear that the rest of the discussion would consist of her indirect responses to what she perceives as her mother's "laying on a guilt trip." After some discussion of what the mother might have been really feeling and having trouble in saying (e.g., how much she and her father really care about Rose and how much she needs to see her—an admission she might find hard to make), the group strategized with Rose about ways to break the usual cycle of indirect communications. The key moment in the informal role play came when the mother asked Rose to keep her children home for the mother's lunch visit. Rose had complained that the mother never wanted to see her alone—it was always with the children. She was always asking to have them at home when she visited. She thought her mother didn't trust her with the kids and was always checking up on her.

PRACTICE POINTS One of the advantages of this form of rehearsal is that the group member, by the way she handles the conversation, may reveal her underlying *ambivalence*. At one point the leader, sensing ambivalence on Rose's part, confronted her by asking if she really wanted to talk to her mother.

LEADER: (Speaking as the mother) I wonder, Rose, if part of the reason I always ask to have the kids there is that I'm uncomfortable when we get together. I'm not sure what I would say to you for a whole 2 hours. I want the kids around to help fill the conversation.

ROSE: You know, I'm not sure what I would say to my mother, either. I really don't know what to talk to her about.

FRAN: (Another group member) Can you try to tell your mother that you get upset when she asks to keep the kids home because you want to have some time alone with her? Maybe your mother could understand that. (Silence)

LEADER: Rose, do you really want to spend some time with your mother?

ROSE: I'm not so sure I do.

LEADER: Then that's the first step. When you're sure, I think the words will come more easily. If you tell your mother how you really feel, it could be the start of some honest talk between you. Perhaps she could share some of her real feelings in response, instead of always doing it indirectly and in ways which are open to misinterpretation. Maybe if you could do this, then your mother would see this as a sign of your maturity.

Rose tried to articulate her feelings more clearly but was obviously still having difficulty. She reported the following week that she had talked with her mother about how it made her feel when the mother tried to do things for her (e.g., wash the dishes when she came over), and the mother had responded by describing how she never really knew what to do when she came over—should she help out or not? Rose felt it cleared the air, even though other issues and feelings were not discussed.

PRACTICE SUMMARY

The interesting thing about the role-playing device as a form of rehearsal is that is often reveals the underlying ambivalence and resistance that the group member feels but has not expressed in the discussion. The rehearsal not only offers the group member a chance to practice but also reveals to the group, the leader, and the group member some of the feelings that need to be dealt with if the group member is to succeed in his or her efforts.

In my AIDS/recovery group, at one point the group member who had raised boyfriend problems used the group to consider how to approach him with her concerns. One member helped by role-playing how Theresa could handle the conversation:

We returned to Theresa, and I said, "Is the question really, Theresa, that you're afraid that he might not stay with you—that if you actually confront him on this issue of the other women, he might leave you?" She agreed that it was her concern. At this point, I wondered if it might help Theresa to figure out what she might say to her boyfriend. Theresa said that would be helpful because she didn't know when and how to say it. Then she laughed and said, "Maybe I should say it in bed." Tania said, "Oh, no. Don't say it before sex and don't say it after sex." And I added, "And don't say it during sex." Everyone laughed at this point, and Tania, a professional stand-up comedian, did an imitation of having a conversation with Theresa's boyfriend, while pumping up and down as if she were in bed having sex with him.

Tania then said, "You have to find a quiet time, not a time when you're in the middle of a fight, and you have to just put out your feelings." I asked Tania if she could show Theresa how she could do that. She started to speak as if she were talking to Theresa's boyfriend. I role-played the boyfriend and said, "Oh, but Theresa you're just insecure, aren't you?" Tania did a very good job of not letting me put her off and, instead, putting the issue right where it was: whether I (role-playing Theresa) was prepared to make a commitment or whether I was too insecure.

PRACTICE POINTS

Ambivalence and fear often underlie our clients' inability to take a difficult step. In the earlier example in the previous section, the young woman was not really sure if she wanted to speak with her mother, even though she expressed disappointment at her mother not wanting to spend time alone with her. In Theresa's situation, ambivalence about confronting her boyfriend is related to not being sure she wants to hear the answer. This, in turn, is connected to the purpose of the group: exploring the impact of having AIDS on their lives.

Theresa said, "I know I have to talk to him, but, you know, he's told me that he's not sure he wants to be tied down, that he likes to have his freedom." Jake nodded his head and said, "Yeah, that's the problem, they want their freedom and they don't want to make a commitment, and you're afraid, if you push him, he'll leave you because you got the virus." Theresa said she realized she had to sit down and talk to him because it couldn't keep up the same way. She would just get too angry and do something crazy and screw up her recovery. She said when she had a fight with him on Thanksgiving, he did call his sponsor and came back much more gently. She felt she had gotten through to him, but she had to find another way to get through to him and talk to him. Otherwise, this thing was just going to continue and it was going to tear her up inside.

The Strength-in-Numbers Phenomenon

Sometimes it is easier to do things as a group than it would be as an individual. In one example described earlier, a group of female survivors of sexual abuse attended a "Take Back the Night" march. The *strength-in-numbers phenomenon* worked to decrease their feelings of isolation and individual risk involved, which encouraged the group members to make demands for their rights to feel safe. An individual's fears and ambivalence can be overcome by participation in a group effort as his or her own courage is strengthened by the courage of others.

In a recent public television rerelease of the documentary *Eyes on the Prize*, which chronicles a period in the civil rights struggle in the Jim Crow (segregated) southern states, one could see the enormous impact of large groups of people marching and demonstrating for the rights guaranteed to them by the civil rights act that had been recently passed by Congress. The film documented in dramatic fashion the attacks on the marchers by the Mississippi state police trying to stop the demonstration. This particular march was undertaken to continue a march led by a civil rights leader who had been shot along the way. The strength-in-numbers phenomenon was evident as the marchers continued on their way in the face of racist verbal and physical threats and attacks by whites along the way. It was clear that even in the face of danger, the support of the group, marching and singing for their inherent rights, provided the fuel that helped to power their incredible courage.

In a less dramatic fashion, group members who have a difference with the group leader may be reluctant to raise it as individuals. However, with the support of other members, they have the strength to confront the leader.

Summary of the Dynamics of Mutual Aid

A number of examples have been shared to illustrate how the dynamics of the mutual aid process can work. Sharing data, the dialectical process, discussing taboo areas, the all-in-the-same-boat phenomenon, developing a universal perspective, mutual support, mutual demand, individual problem solving, rehearsal, and the strength-in-numbers phenomenon are some of the processes through which mutual aid is offered and taken. It is important to note that I am not suggesting that working in groups is a preferred method. The choice of individual or group counseling is influenced by many factors, particularly the comfort of the group members in dealing with their concerns on a one-to-one basis as opposed to within a group setting.

As I will explain in detail later, it is often helpful for a group member to have both individual and group counseling available so that both experiences can be used productively. Each would have a slightly different focus, and each could be expected to provide important stimulation for the other. For many group members, the group can offer (under certain circumstances) unique forms of help in dealing with their life problems. I have attempted to identify some of these mutual aid processes, but it is important to realize that groups will not provide this kind of help just because they have been brought together. In the next section, I will examine some of the obstacles that can make mutual aid a difficult process indeed. These obstacles, and others, will be explored in detail in later chapters.

Obstacles to Mutual Aid

In the early phases of a group's development, one potential obstacle to mutual aid is the apparent divergent interest each group member brings to the engagement. Even in a group with a narrow, clearly defined purpose, some group members may perceive their sense of urgency differently from the others. Even though the mutual threads of concern may exist, group members may not identify their common ground. Various group members may feel their concerns and feelings are unique and unrelated to those of other members. The attractions between members may be partial, subtle, and difficult to perceive. In many ways, the group is a microcosm of the larger society, and this diffusion of interest between "self" and "other" reflects the individual social encounter in society. Thus, as each member becomes oriented to the group engagement, that member will be asking, "How am I the same or different from the other members?"

Identifying the Common Ground

One of the early tasks of the group leader will be to help group members begin to identify their common ground. As the group develops a mature way of relating, individual members can begin to understand that they can learn and grow by giving help as well as receiving it. As each individual member develops the skills required to offer help and to take help, these same skills will be found to be related to their individual concerns outside the group. For example, group members who learn how to identify their feelings and to share them in the group may be able to apply these skills in other intimate relationships with family and friends. Nevertheless, at the beginning stage and periodically during the life of the group, members' inability to perceive their connections to the others will present an important obstacle.

The Complexity of the Group-as-a-Whole

A second set of obstacles will emerge from the fact that even a small group can be a complex system that must deal with a number of developmental tasks if it is to work productively. As soon as more than one group member is involved, a new organism is created: the group-as-a-whole. This group is more than the simple sum of its parts (i.e., the individual members). For example, this new organism needs to develop rules and procedures that will allow it to function effectively. Some will be openly discussed, whereas others may operate beneath the surface by mutual although unspoken consent of the members. Roles may be subtly distributed to group members, such as scapegoat, deviant member, internal leader, and so on. Some of these role assignments will represent ways by which the group-as-a-whole may avoid dealing directly with a problem. For example, the group *gatekeeper* may intervene to distract the group each time the discussion approaches a painful subject. Many of the unstated rules for relating will be counterproductive to the purpose of the group. These factors, and others to be discussed in Chapters 7 and 8, are properties of this complex organism called the group, and the leader must deal with them if the group is to function effectively.

Difficulty of Open Communications in Taboo Areas

A final major source of potential problems for the group is the difficulty of open communication. I have already discussed some of the barriers that make it difficult for group members to express their real feelings and concerns. These are related to a social culture that has implicitly and explicitly developed a number of norms of behavior and identified taboo areas in which honest communication is hard to achieve. Each group member brings a part of this culture into the group, and thus the group culture, in early phases of work, resembles the culture of the social surroundings.

This often makes it difficult for group members to talk with and listen to each other in areas of central concern. With the group leader's help, group members will need to develop a new culture—a culture for work—in which norms are modified and taboos lose their power, so that members may freely communicate with each other.

I have just outlined three major areas of potential obstacles to mutual aid: the difficulty individual members have in identifying their self-interest with that of the other group members, the complex tasks involved in creating a mutual aid system, and the difficulties in communicating honestly. The existence of these potential obstacles helps define the job of the group leader. These problems are not arguments against the use of groups as mutual aid systems; rather, they represent an agenda for the group leader. If groups were not faced with these problems, and if people could easily join together to offer aid and support, then there would be no need for a group leader.

The Role of the Group Leader

Although the role of the group leader may vary depending on the type of group, purpose, membership, and other factors, Schwartz (1961) suggests the general function of mediating the individual-group interaction. This leads Schwartz to argue one of his most central and useful ideas about group practice: that the group leader always has "two clients"—the individual and the group. The role of the group leader in this *two-group construct* is to mediate the engagement between these two entities. Figure 2.1 illustrates this role with the individual in the left circle, the group in the right circle, and the group leader below in a third circle.

As the group process unfolds, the leader is constantly concerned both with each individual member and with the group. For example, as an individual member raises a specific concern, the leader will help the member share that concern with the group. Because it can be difficult for group members to describe their concerns, a number of crucial skills will be needed to implement this role. Some have been men-

FIGURE 2.1

Relationship of Group Member, Systems, and Group Leader

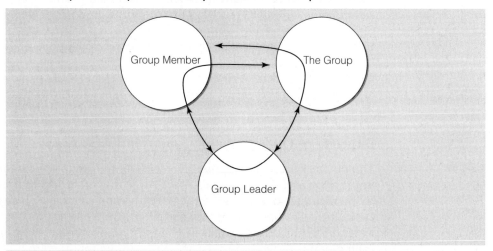

tioned already, and others will be discussed in more detail later. These skills include, for example, reading indirect communications and responding directly; articulating group members' concerns and feelings, when needed; reaching for feelings; and encouraging elaboration. The goal will be to help individual group members talk to the group and clarify their concerns. As the leader helps the one (the individual) talk to the many (the group), the interaction will also be monitored to see if the group members appear to be listening and relating to the individual. If they seem to be turned off, the leader will explore their feelings and reactions. Perhaps the individual's problem is painful to the group members, raising related feelings of their own and making it hard for them to listen. Whatever the realities may be, the group leader, with a clear sense of role, will pay attention to both the individual and the group at exactly the same time.

Attention to the group will require that the leader help group members deal with the obstacles described earlier. For example, if the group culture is making it difficult for members to discuss their real feelings about a specific issue, then the leader can call this to the attention of the group members. An effort to bring the obstacle out in the open is a first step in helping the group members become more conscious of their own processes. With the assistance of the group leader, group members can discuss how the blockage of open communication in a sensitive area frustrates their work. With understanding comes growth as the group becomes more sophisticated about its ways of working. A new agreement, including new norms that are more productive, can be openly reached. In many ways the group leader serves as a guide for the group members faced with the complex task of developing an effective mutual aid system. The important point is that this is the members' group, the work to strengthen it is theirs, and the group leader is there to help them to do it.

In a general way, these two areas of work characterize the group leader's responsibilities: helping the individual and the group relate effectively to each other, and helping the group become more sophisticated about its way of working, so that it releases the potential for mutual aid. Of course, this process is more complicated than this simple explanation implies. In the remaining chapters, I will explore the underlying assumptions about how mutual aid groups work and the tasks and skills required of the group leader.

Once again, the process will be analyzed step-by-step. For example, Chapter 3 on the preparatory phase will include a discussion on setting up a group, dealing with questions of group composition, recruitment of members, and the important work required with fellow staff members to gain their support and avoid possible "sabotage." The dynamics of initial group meetings will be discussed and illustrated in Chapter 4 using examples from a number of groups. The discussion in Chapters 5 and 6 of the middle or work phase will include a section on the individual-group interaction. In Chapter 7, I will explore the role of the individual in the group and the tasks of the group-as-a-whole, and describe how the leader can assist in the group's development.

Chapter Summary

In this chapter, I explored a number of ways in which group members can help one another through mutual aid, which is a process that can be employed in all types of groups. These included sharing data, the dialectical process, discussing taboo areas, the all-in-the-same-boat phenomenon, developing a universal perspective, mutual support, mutual demand, individual problem solving, rehearsal, and the strength-in-numbers phenomenon.

Three major areas of obstacles to the mutual aid process in groups were defined and illustrated. These included the difficulty members may have in identifying their common ground, the tasks that must be accomplished by a group in order to develop a positive culture for work, and the general difficulty of open communication. The role of the group leader was defined as an extension of the mediating function described earlier in the book into the group context. The group leader was seen as mediating between two group members: the individual and the group-as-a-whole.

Related Online Content and Activities

For learning tools such as glossary terms, InfoTrac® College Edition keywords, links to related websites, and chapter practice quizzes, visit this book's website at **www .cengage.com/counseling/shulman**.

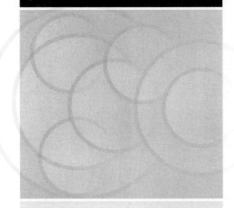

Group Formation

In this chapter, I will explore in detail the steps required to establish a group and to increase its chances for success. Work with the staff system (e.g., other counselors in an agency or teachers in a school) is dealt with first, since much that follows depends on these efforts. Next, issues related to group formation (timing, composition, etc.) are explored. The impact of ethnicity and culture in the group formation stage is discussed, as well as problems of recruitment. Finally, I return to the tuning-in skill, this time applying it to a first session of a group.

Preparing for Group Practice

The preparatory (group formation) phase can be one of the most complex in work with groups, as a number of crucial issues must be addressed before the first meeting takes place. The literature on group practice pays surprisingly little attention to the problems of this phase, beyond discussion of questions of group type (e.g., psycho-educational, educational, therapeutic, support), structure (e.g., frequency and number of sessions), group composition, and so on. For example, it is not unusual for a counselor to decide that a group would be helpful and to approach colleagues for appropriate referrals. General agreement may be reached at a staff meeting to support the group; however, the counselor waits 2 months without getting a single referral. In analyzing examples of this kind, I have consistently found that the counselor had left out the important step of involving the colleagues in a meaningful way. I could often determine the moment in the staff meeting when the groundwork was laid for the frustration that followed.

In like manner, a counselor may launch a group and prepare for a first meeting with 10 group members who have promised to attend. The evening of the meeting arrives, and after waiting 30 long and painful minutes for latecomers, the leader must face the reality that only two members have come. Once again, the source of the disappointment can often be traced to steps that were left out in the preparatory work with clients as the counselor or other counselors began the referral process. In analysis of interviews and telephone conversations, it is often possible to identify the moment the counselor sensed the ambivalence of the prospective group member but did not reach for it—a skill I call *"looking for trouble when everything seems to be going your way."*

These and other group formation issues will be discussed here, with an emphasis on illustrating strategies that may increase the possibility of launching effective mutual aid groups.

Engaging Other Professionals in Developing the Group

An important first principle is to recognize that a group in an agency, school, or another institution must be related to the service. If a counselor attempts to establish a group because of a desire to develop new skills or because he or she has decided (without involving the rest of the staff) that there is a need for such a group, the group may be doomed to failure. A common example is the student who is placed in an agency for practicum experience and is taking a course in group counseling. Although simulated class groups are often used to meet the requirement for the student to lead a group, most would agree that a real-life group leadership experience would be helpful, so the student endeavors to set one up in the field. Quite often the group never has its first meeting because the student's need for it is not a sound reason for developing a group. The idea for a group must begin by identifying an area of the potential unmet needs that the group method may be able to meet. The group must reflect the consensus of the department or team involved so that it is not seen as being personally "owned" by the group leader.

The difficulty or ease involved in establishing a group may depend on the group experience of the setting. In those settings where groups are a common form of service and where all staff members take their turn at leadership, many of the problems of formation may be minimized. In other settings, where groups are unusual as a form of service, these problems may be intensified. For example, a counselor who attempts to introduce group counseling into a setting that has never had groups must recognize that a threatening situation may be created for other staff. As discussed in the introduction, the "fear-of-groups syndrome" may be common.

Some counselors may be concerned by the idea of facing more than one client at a time or doubt their abilities to lead groups. If they do not have a fund of good group experiences to draw on or if they unsuccessfully attempted to establish a group when they were students, they may be hesitant about working with groups. The counselor attempting to initiate a group service must recognize that, on some level, colleagues may wonder whether, if the service is successful, they will be asked to carry a group next. This fear is often expressed indirectly with comments such as "Groups would be great but do we really have the time?" The development of group service can have an important impact on the staff system, and the counselor should make use of the tuning-in skill in preparing to negotiate the establishment of the group.

Staff resistance can also be noted when the administration of an agency or organization, because of the pressures of managed care or other cutbacks in resources, has decided to move into group counseling as a cost-cutting measure. In reality, group practice may actually increase costs, because it rarely serves as a substitute in those situations where individual counseling is required. In many cases, issues that emerge in the group for one member may generate the need for more intensive individual counseling, rather than less counseling, for other group members. Group counseling should be the practice modality of choice only if it is the best modality for the particular population and problem. When cost cutting is the only rationale offered, staff resistance due to fears about competency is often masked by staff anger at the "top-down" imposition of group practice. Whether the reasons for developing group counseling practice are sound or spurious, there is little question that there has been an explosive expansion of the use of group counseling in practice.

Achieving Consensus on the Service

The idea of a group may emerge in many ways: client feedback, a counselor discovering a common concern among a number of individual clients, or a staff team discovering an important gap in the service. However the idea of a group is initiated, it is important that all staff involved have the opportunity to comment honestly on the potential service. A common mistake is for a counselor to decide on the need for a group and then to set about "selling" colleagues on the idea. Rather than presenting their own views on the need for it and inviting feedback and discussion, counselors may try to unduly influence their colleagues, creating the illusion that they are involving others in the process. The counselor might find an artificial agreement expressed through apparently unqualified support. Once again, the skilled group leader would not leave the session without first reaching for the underlying reservations. For example, the counselor might say, "It's great to see such quick support for my idea, but, you know, it's going to cause some problems and inconveniences for the rest of you. Don't you think we should also talk about these?"

The counselor often senses the underlying resistance but fears to reach for it. The belief is that if one leaves the negatives unexpressed, they will perhaps go away. They never do. These reservations, negative reactions, fears, and the like, all come back to haunt the counselor in the form of conscious or unconscious sabotage of the counselor's plans. If the group is to become a reality, the counselor must insist that it be a service of the team and the organization, not just the counselor's personal group that happens to be taking place in this setting. Without real support from the rest of the staff, the counselor will be alone when problems emerge.

I have seen excellent work done with school principals, for example, when after the principal has given perfunctory agreement to allow a group to meet in the school, a community-based counselor has asked, "Would you be very upset if we couldn't offer this group to your kids?" After a moment's pause, the principal responded, "The only reason I OK these groups is that the people at the school board like to see them in the schools. Actually, staff and I often find they are more trouble than they are worth." Only at this point does the real discussion begin, and the counselor can start serious contracting with the agency or setting. If this stage is skipped over in the counselor's eagerness to gain a toehold, then the lack of real investment will hurt when the going gets rough in the group.

Fortunately, counselors usually have the opportunity to go back after making a mistake and to try again. This is important, since counselors who propose groups in a setting without connecting the purpose of the group to the general service of the setting are often seen as simply requesting space. When administrators and staff members perceive the connection between their service and the purpose of the group, they will be more likely to invest themselves in the group's development. A counselor offering to lead a group for children who have been identified by teachers as having trouble at school will be more easily accepted by the staff than one asking to lead groups for general discussion (e.g., "I would like to work with children who need a socialization experience").

It is also important to discuss the issue of confidentiality with other staff. From the point of view of the helping role that is being elaborated in this book, the mediating approach, acting as a communication bridge between group members and the system, is very much a part of the work. If the counselor begins work with staff by stating they will not be included in discussion of group content, their fears and anxieties may lead to direct or indirect efforts at sabotage. In one such case, a counselor in a group home for teens had completely ignored the residential counselor's concerns, particularly her fear of complaints, and had indicated that all discussions would be confidential. When the counselor arrived, the residential staff member rang a bell and shouted, to the counselor's consternation, "Group therapy time." In other examples, the counselor's colleagues have described the group to their individual clients in a way that served to heighten the clients' fears of involvement: "We are going to offer this group, but you don't have to go if you don't want to."

If the counselor's sense of function involves a commitment to helping in the process between client and system, including the agency, then this must be part of the contract. Child care counselors, teachers, and other counselors must be viewed as colleagues, with each having a part in the operation. Discussions should focus on how the group leader and the other staff members will handle feedback. The meaning of the feedback and the way in which clients might use either the individual counselor or the group counselor as a channel must be recognized. The agreement can include ways to achieve the optimum outcome, in which each will attempt to assist the group members' efforts to provide direct feedback to the other. I have found that this discussion often takes much of the threat out of the possibility of negative feedback and, instead, turns it into an important technical issue for both counselors. The details of how the fears of the group members can be handled and how a counselor can effectively share feedback with other staff will be dealt with in later chapters.

When I explore why counselors are reluctant to follow this course of action—that is, to treat other system people as colleagues and to work out agreements for mutual sharing of relevant information—they usually express concern about the member's acceptance of such a contract. Although there is some basis to this concern, I also often uncover their own fears about confronting a colleague with "bad news." How do you tell a fellow staff member, with whom you have coffee each day, that his client or student or patient doesn't feel he understands her? Confidentiality then really serves as a protection for the group leader not the client.

Often counselors reveal that they have developed stereotypes of their colleagues as "lousy" counselors (or poor teachers, insensitive doctors, etc.), so what good would sharing be? I can understand their reticence to take on this function, yet if the group counselor accepts that the colleague is actually closed to change, such acceptance means that an important part of the service to members will no longer be available. The counselor will inevitably be in a serious quandary when the strength-in-numbers phenomenon described in the previous chapter leads the group members to share their real feelings. A situation will have been set up that makes it impossible for the counselor to do anything about the problem except empathize, ignore it, or defend the system. This often leads to apathy and disengagement on the part of the group members.

The question of confidentiality has broadened during this discussion to encompass a much larger issue: the role of the helping person within his or her own helping system. This will be explored with a number of examples in other chapters. For now, I would summarize my view as being that this concern may be a central issue for other staff members when group formation is discussed. I would want it out in the open, and I would want to contract with both staff and group members for freedom of communication of group content in a responsible manner.

Identifying Group Type and Structure

Colleagues can also be helpful in considering the question of type of group and its structure. For example, will it be a group of fixed membership meeting over a period of time, or will it be an *open-ended group* in which different members arrive and leave each week? Special problems, dynamics, and strategies associated with open-ended groups will be discussed in Chapter 10; however, for some purposes and settings, they provide a better alternative than a fixed membership group. In contrast, a group for teenage survivors of sexual abuse will need some time to establish the levels of trust required to explore painful and formerly secret experiences. An open-ended group with a continually changing membership would not be appropriate for such a population. Some members might be added after the initial sessions, but at some point, such a group would need to be closed.

Groups are sometimes formed from ongoing natural groups, such as in a residential setting or a school. A group home is a good example, because it represents a living group, operating 7 days a week, 24 hours each day. For 2 hours twice each week, house meetings are held at special times within the ongoing group life to focus on issues of group living, such as problems among residents and between residents and staff. These meetings represent structured incidents in the life of the ongoing group designed to improve everyone's ability to live and work together.

Another issue is related to the content of the group meeting. People can provide mutual aid through means other than just talking—through other "mediums of exchange" between people (Shulman, 1971, 2009). For example, senior citizens in a residential center might use activities that they have developed to structure their time, provide enjoyment or education, give them the opportunity to develop new skills, or just to enjoy the company of others. In Chapter 10, I will discuss in more detail the place of program activities in the life of the group and the group leader's tasks. In the formation stage, it is important to consider whether interaction through activity represents an important part of the purpose of the group and fits within the general mission of the setting.

Community center–type activities offered during the school day to a group of children who are not doing well in their classes may be viewed by the school staff as a "reward" for acting badly, even if the group leader argues that the students are helped indirectly. When these activities are used in work with children as a substitute for discussions about class problems or because the counselor is concerned that the youngsters would not come to a "talking group," they may frustrate the essential work rather than assist it. This issue will be considered in some detail in the Chapter 15 discussion on group work in schools, but for now the important point is that a decision on group type (talk, activity, or both) needs to relate directly both to the mission of setting and to the needs of the group members.

Group Versus Individual Counseling

Another issue that can create problems for the group counselor is the compatibility of group and individual counseling. Some group counselors take the position that group members should not be seen individually because that will lessen the intensity of the group experience. Individual counselors also are often worried that clients will use their group session to discuss central issues. This can lead to a struggle over *"who owns the client,"* a misunderstanding of the interdependence of individual and group counseling, and an unacceptable attitude to client participation in decisions about service.

On the first issue, clients may use both individual and group help for different issues, as they see fit. For example, as the group works on a particular member's concern, the discussion may raise a similar concern for members who want a chance to discuss a special case of the general problem and may not have enough time in the group to do this. Individual sessions can provide this opportunity. Group discussion, rather than robbing the individual work of its vitality, will often enrich the content of the individual counseling sessions. As members address issues, as they understand how others are experiencing problems, they may be put in touch with feelings of their own that were not previously evident. Finding out that others have fears related to taboo areas, such as sex, may greatly speed up clients' willingness to discuss their own concerns in individual counseling.

In like manner, the work in the individual sessions can strengthen a client to raise a personal concern in the group. Some clients may find it too difficult to start to talk in a group context about some of their most private feelings and concerns. As they find they can share these with an individual counselor and not be harshly judged, they may be more willing to share these feelings in the group. Thus, the group and individual counseling can be parallel and interdependent, with the client free to choose where and when to use these resources for counseling. The question of client choice raises the second issue. In my view, these choices, at any particular moment, rest with the client. Feeling comfortable about dealing with issues in one context or the other, the client will make these decisions. I may share my opinions, offer support, and even provide concrete help (e.g., role-playing in an individual session to show how the client might raise an issue in the group).

With two and possibly more helping people working with the same client, good communication between the helpers becomes essential. Structures should be established that guarantee regular communication so that each understands how the client is choosing to deal with issues and so that the counselors can help each other in their related work. For example, in a couples' group that I have led, two co-leaders sat in on each session. They were seeing most of the couples on an individual counseling basis. In the "tuning-in" session we held prior to each group meeting, they summarized the specific concerns dealt with in the individual sessions. We used this preparatory work to anticipate potential group issues. I maintain a policy of not directly raising concerns in the group that were discussed in the individual counseling unless the couples wish them raised. The group member has to have control of what is raised in the group, how it is raised, and when it is raised.

Through the tuning-in process, I became more effective at picking up their indirect cues. Because co-leaders sat in on the sessions, they were able to incorporate content from the group experience into their individual counseling. If they were not able to sit in, I shared copies of my group process and couple summary reports so that they would be aware of the couples' progress. When sessions were videotaped, the tapes were also available for their use. Rather than competing for client ownership, we had three professionals, each providing a service through different modalities. As pointed out in the earlier discussion on confidentiality, without freedom to share information, this open communication would not have taken place.

This raises the issue of *informed consent*. Informed consent will be discussed in more detail in Chapter 13 dealing with values, ethics, and legislation that impact group practice. Informed consent is defined as follows:

> The client's granting of permission to the counselor and agency or other professional person to use specific intervention procedures, including diagnosis, treatment, follow up, and research. This permission must be based on full disclosure of the facts needed to make the decision intelligently. Informed consent must be based upon knowledge of the risks and alternatives. (Barker, 2003, p. 114)

In this instance, part of the informed consent process would be an explanation of how communications will take place between the individual counselor and the group leader. The client needs to grant permission for this cross-discussion and needs to know that he or she will be in control over what is shared. Other elements of informed consent will be discussed later in this chapter.

Agency or Setting Support for Groups

In addition to support from colleagues, help from the agency or setting administration may also be needed. For example, special expenses may be incurred in carrying out a group program. Mothers' groups held during the daytime may require babysitting services. Recruitment publicity, transportation expenses, coffee, and other items may be involved in some group programs. In addition, the counselor developing a group may need support in the form of a reduction in individual cases and consultation from an outside consultant if one is not available on staff. These issues should be discussed when the group is formed.

In some settings, where groups have not been an integral part of the service, the approach to group counseling programs may require that the counselor take personal responsibility for their implementation. For example, counselors are encouraged to develop groups if they can do so "on their own time." Many counselors, eager to see the service begin or to develop new skills in group practice, accept this responsibility and soon regret it. If a service is part of the agency function, it should not have to be carried as a personal "hobby" by the counselor. Groups take time, and if counselors do not see that the group is viewed as a part of their responsibilities, the additional demands on them and their feelings about these demands will often affect their work with the group.

Even when agencies support the development of group services, they sometimes do so for the wrong reasons. Administrators may believe that seeing clients in groups can save time and so encourage a swing to group programs as a way of providing more service to clients without increasing staff. With cost containment programs on the rise, there are some situations in which seeing clients in groups will save time. For example, orientation meetings for parents in a high school can be an effective way of starting communications with more than one person at a time. As pointed out earlier, however, more often than not the development of group services tends to increase the staff's workload, as new issues and concerns are discovered that require additional individual counseling. Groups should be viewed as an important service in their own right rather than as a service substitute. A counselor in a group will need time to follow up with individual members, to meet with other staff, to develop a system for recording the group work for agency accountability, and for personal learning.

To start a group service on a sound footing is better, even though the formation process may be slower and more frustrating. Time taken by the group counselor to interpret the group's purpose as well as to identify the special needs and potential problems related to instituting new group services will pay off in the long run. In those cases where doubts exist about the benefits of group practice, the counselor can propose the group as an experimental service to be closely monitored and evaluated. Records can be kept on the costs and benefits. The agency staff and administration can use the first groups as a way of developing experience with a new form of service. The important point is that the group service be owned by the setting, not the personal project of a concerned counselor. With the latter, it is not unusual to have a good first group only to discover that the service dies when the counselor is no longer able or willing to provide it personally.

Group Composition, Timing, and Structure

A conversation I had with a group of students who observed my weekly group sessions with a married couples group helps illustrate some of the myths and questions involved in planning a group. The group consisted of five couples in marital difficulty. The client group was videotaped and simultaneously observed by the students on a monitor in another room. After each meeting, I met with the observers and my co-leaders to discuss the session. At the end of a first session that was marked by excellent group member involvement (excerpts from transcripts of this group are shared in Chapter 4), I was peppered by questions on how the group had been formed. The first request was for my principles of group composition that had led to such a lively, interactive group. One couple was in their 20s, another in their 30s, a third in their 40s, a fourth in their 50s, and the oldest couple was in their late 60s and early 70s. I explained, much to the students' disappointment, that these were the only five couples referred for the group.

Another student asked how I had decided on five couples. I pointed out that we were using a studio, and with myself and my co-leaders, there was only enough room for five couples. Another effort to tease out principles followed as they inquired how we decided on the number of sessions. I pointed out that many long-standing issues were involved, and a short-term group did not seem to offer enough time. "How did you settle on exactly 23 sessions?" was the next question. Once again I disappointed the group by explaining that we decided we couldn't do the advance work needed to start the group before October 15. We simply counted the weeks until the end of the academic year. We then went on to discuss the differences between what I felt to be the myth of scientific group composition versus the reality of how decisions were made.

The students wanted prescriptions and rules, and I argued, perhaps more strongly than was needed, that the rules were not really that clear. In reality, we often "take what group members we can get." Our experiences, and some research findings, have provided us with some guidelines. For example, we know that extremes often lead to problems. Groups can clearly be too large to provide opportunity for everyone to participate or too small to provide a consistent core of members. Although groups can tolerate some degree of age range, as in my married couples' groups, extremes for some populations, such as teenagers, can create serious problems. For example, a 12-year-old child faces life tasks that differ significantly from the concerns of a 17-year-old. One person of color in an all-white group may experience a sense of isolation that the addition of another might well alleviate. A group of survivors of sexual abuse may have significant difficulty in achieving intimacy if it is structured as open-ended, with new members constantly joining the group and other members leaving it.

The literature provides hundreds of observations on questions of group composition and structure, but unfortunately it also provides conflicting opinions and evidence in support of rules. For example, there are conflicting reports on the optimum size for effective discussion groups, with support for different numbers argued persuasively. A balance has to be struck between ignoring these issues completely and depending too much on rigid rules and structures.

For example, Corey and Corey (2006) suggest the following:

> What is a desirable size for a group? The answer depends on several factors: age of clients, experience of the leader, type of group, and problems to be explored. For instance, a group composed of elementary school children might be kept to 3 or 4, whereas a group of adolescents might be made up of 6 to 8 people. There may be as many as 20 or 30 children in developmental group guidance classes. For a weekly ongoing group of adults, about 8 people with one leader may be ideal. A group of this size is big enough to give ample opportunity for interaction and small enough for everyone to be involved and to feel a sense of "group." (p. 117)

Jacobs et al. (2006) suggest a smaller group size would be appropriate for most groups.

> Group size can definitely affect group dynamics, so the leader should pay much attention to the decision of how many members to have in the group. The size of the group will depend in part on its purpose, the length of time of each session, the setting available, and the experience of the leader. We suggest 5 to 8 as the ideal number of members for most groups. For multicultural groups, the leader and the members may be more comfortable with groups of no more than 5. (p. 42)

The position argued here is that each setting must develop its own rules, based on its experiences as well as those of others. Given this reality, a group leader must address a number of questions, using the experiences of colleagues and of other settings to develop some tentative answers. Each group represents an experiment that can contribute to the fund of experience the counselor will draw on in starting new groups. Some of the questions requiring discussion are highlighted in the remainder of this section. I will not provide definitive answers to these questions but, rather, a way of exploring the issues.

Group Member Selection

The crucial factor in selection of members is that there is some *common ground* between their individual needs and the purpose of the group. Whether this purpose has been defined broadly or narrowly, each member must be able to find some connection between a personal sense of urgency and the work involved. Even if this common ground is not apparent to the prospective members at the start, the counselor should have some sense of its existence. In the example of the couples' group, each couple was having severe marital problems. Another point in common was that all five couples had some commitment at the start to trying to strengthen their marriages. Couples who had already decided to separate and who needed help in doing so without causing additional pain to each other or their families would not have belonged in this group.

In an AIDS/recovery group I co-led early in the emergence of the epidemic, the five members included one white, gay male, a transgender woman, a heterosexual woman, and two African American males. Although their life experiences differed significantly, all of the members shared in common the disease of AIDS, and all were in relatively early recovery (1 week to a little more than 1 year) from polysubstance abuse (alcohol, cocaine, heroin, etc.) and had experienced some form of early trauma. Group members differed in their status with respect to AIDS. Two members were on what was at that time an experimental treatment that had lowered their AIDS viral loads (counts) to almost zero and had raised their T-cell (protective) counts to near normal. One client was waiting for her viral load and T-cell count to reach the point at which she could enter the experimental clinical trials with the new drugs. Another client was eligible but refusing treatment. The health of the fifth had been damaged so badly by her use of hormones and illegal substances that she was too ill for the experimental treatment. For this client, her viral load was climbing each week, her T-cell count was nonexistent, and she was experiencing a range of opportunistic infections common to later-stage AIDS. In spite of these significant differences, each member was able to relate to the others on the basis of their shared struggle with AIDS, early substance abuse recovery, and the interaction between the two.

Group Composition and Age of the Members

As the group leader defines the purpose of the group and considers potential members, common sense can help identify potential differences that might create difficulty in reaching group consensus on the focus of the work. Group purpose will be important in thinking about age and group composition. For example, in the couples' group described earlier, the differences in the ages of the five couples provided unexpected dividends. Each couple was experiencing the crises associated with their particular phase of life and phase of their marriage; however, there were common themes cutting across all phases. In many ways, the older couples were able to share their experiences and perspectives with the younger ones, and the group often took on the appearance of an extended family. After one session in which some of the problems associated with the older couples' life phases were clearly delineated, the husband in the youngest couple said good-humoredly, "I'm beginning to wonder if this is what we have to look forward to going through!" The wife of the oldest couple, who had been married 49 years, responded, "Yes, but you will have the advantage of having had this group to help you face these problems."

Whether to include males, females, or both will similarly have to be determined according to the group's purpose. In those groups where gender issues are central, then gender may be a legitimate inclusion or exclusion criterion. For example, although there are male and female survivors of sexual abuse, the impact of the abuse and the issues that have emerged from it may have gender differences and require a homogeneous gender membership. Chapter 8 explores a number of theories that help us understand the entity I call the group-as-a-whole. One model described specifically refers to the dynamics in women's groups, and Chapter 12 explores feminist models of practice. Membership in these groups would be restricted to women.

I find some of the other factors often discussed when deciding on group membership, such as judgments about a member's "personality," somewhat questionable. For example, I have seen a group meticulously assembled with a proper number of relatively passive schoolchildren balanced by a manageable number of active ones. The theory was to guarantee interaction—the active members would stimulate the passive ones. In addition, some limit on active members was thought to help the leader with potential problems of control.

Unfortunately, nobody informed the group members about their expected roles. The leader was observed in the first session desperately trying to deal with the acting-out behaviors of the "passive" members, while the "active" members looked on in amusement. The fact is that clients do not act the same in every situation. A passive client in an individual interview or classroom may act differently when exposed to a new context. Clients will not remain in the "diagnosed" box long enough to be clearly identified. Their reactions will be somewhat dependent on the actions of those around them, particularly the group leader.

Race, Ethnicity, and Language

The impact of diversity on group practice will be discussed in detail in Chapter 11. For now, race, ethnicity, and language issues need to be considered when composing a group. The counseling literature addresses the importance of understanding the multicultural context in group practice. Corey (2008) suggests:

> In a pluralistic society, the reality of cultural diversity is recognized, respected, and encouraged. Within groups, the worldviews of both the group leader and the members also vary, and this is a natural place to acknowledge and promote pluralism. Multicultural group work involves strategies that cultivate understanding and appreciation of diversity in such areas as culture, ethnicity, race, gender, class, religion, and sexual identity. We each have a unique multicultural identify, but as members of a group, we share a common goal—the success of the group. To that end, we want to learn more about ourselves as individuals and as members of diverse cultural groups. (p. 11)

Some authors have focused on multicultural group work issues (e.g., DeLucia-Waack, 2006), and the Best Practice Guidelines adopted by the Association for Specialists in Group Work (Thomas & Pender, 2007) stress the importance of attention to this issue. However, there is a paucity of research on the impact of diversity on counseling group composition decisions.

Though not specifically addressing group composition, Rodriquez (1998) studied the impact of within-group value diversity on personal satisfaction, group creativity, and group effectiveness. He reported this finding: "After accounting for diversity in race/nationality, gender, and age, value diversity predicted greater personal satisfaction, and higher perceived group creativity and effectiveness" (p. 744).

Davis (1979, 1981, 1984, 1999) has addressed the impact of race on group composition and practice, basing his observations on anecdotal as well as empirical evidence. In reviewing the literature on the impact of racial composition, Davis (1981) identified a number of observed processes that emerge when a racial ratio changes and minority membership is increased. These included such processes as cleavage, tipping points, and white flight. In *cleavage*, the group splits into distinct racial subgroups. The *tipping point* is the number that creates in majority members' anxiety, resulting in aggression toward members of the "out" group. He suggested that white persons are so often in the majority that when they are placed in a group in which they are in a smaller-than-usual majority—for example, with more than 10% to 20% persons of color—they may experience a mental state of being in the "psychological minority," at times leading to a *white flight* reaction (Davis & Proctor, 1989, p. 103). Conversely, members of the minority group faced with this ratio may experience being in the "psychological majority" even though their absolute numbers are less than 50%.

As with many such observations, these concepts of psychological minority and majority may not significantly affect the decisions related to the composition of one's group. Rather, they serve to attune the group leader to potential group dynamics resulting from a composition that may affect the group's functioning. Awareness of the process by the group leader, as well as a willingness to address these issues when and if they emerge, may help the group cope more effectively.

In summarizing the literature on race and group in the late 1980s, Davis and Proctor (1989) suggest, "There is some evidence that whites and minorities may prefer different racial compositions: neither whites nor minorities appear to like being greatly outnumbered. The language spoken in the group may also be important. For example, if some members speak Spanish, while others do not, the nonbilingual speakers may become isolated" (p. 115).

Davis and Proctor (1989) also summarize the findings on group leadership: "Leaders who differ in race from their group members may receive less cooperation. Biracial co-leadership may enhance communication in racially heterogeneous groups. However, biracial co-leaders must remain alert to the possibility of one leader being perceived as the leader and the other as his helper" (p. 116).

Finally, in addressing the paucity of empirical research, they note:

> There is no evidence which suggests that group treatment is more or less suitable for any particular ethnic group. Furthermore, there is little evidence that either racially homogenous or racially heterogeneous groups are superior in their outcomes. Very few studies have attempted to assess the effects of the group leader's race on group member outcomes. Furthermore, reports from studies involving the race of the leader are mixed. However, these studies are consistent in that they have found that prior group leader experience in counseling with minorities appears to have beneficial effects for the group. (p. 117)

The impact of diversity in general on group practice as well as the issue of diversity between members and between members and the group leader will be explored in detail in Chapter 11. Specific strategies for addressing intercultural (the leader is different from the members) and intracultural (the leader is the same as the members) will be discussed and illustrated, as will inter- and intracultural issues between members.

Group Timing

There are a number of time-related factors to consider when setting up a group. How often will the group meet? How long will the meetings last? For how long will the group meet (e.g., six sessions, 4 months)? Once again, each of the answers must draw on common sense, the experience of the agency, and the literature, and all must be related to group purpose. In the married couples' group, we chose to meet once each week, for 2 hours each session, over a period of 23 weeks. Meetings had to be held in the evening so that both partners could attend. The group was designed to provide long-term support to the couples as they dealt with their marital problems. The alternate option of intensive weekends, for example, was not considered. For couples in crisis, it seemed that the intensive, short-term experience might open up more problems while leaving the couples unable to deal with them. Weekend workshops for marital enrichment groups, in which the relationships are strong to begin with, may be beneficial as educational and skill development experiences.

The decision to meet weekly was based on the recognition that longer breaks between meetings might diffuse the intensity of the experience, making each session seem like a new beginning. Two hours seemed to be enough time to allow for the development of central themes and issues in the beginning phase of each meeting, while leaving enough time to deal effectively with specific individual and group concerns. More than 2 hours might be wearying for both group members and group leaders.

Whatever decisions are reached for a particular group, discussing and clarifying the plan with group members is important. Group members have a sense of the group's time frame and will be affected by the particular phase of the meeting or the phase in the life of the group. As pointed out earlier, the "doorknob therapy" phenomenon can accelerate the presentation of important issues; however, the members need to know when the time to reach for the door is close at hand. It is possible for group members to work more effectively if they have less time to carry out their tasks.

Reid and Shyne (1969) have discussed the impact of time on both the counselor and the client in their work on short-term treatment. There is a limit, however, to how much can be dealt with, so judicious balance needs to be developed, allowing enough sessions to deal with the anticipated themes of concern. This limit will come from experience as an agency evaluates each group, using the group members as part of the evaluation process. Group members can be used quite effectively in setting up the initial parameters by exploring their reactions to time proposals before the group is established. Feedback on the day of the week or the specific time for starting may help a group counselor avoid unnecessary conflicts.

Form Follows Function in Group Formation

An expression borrowed from architecture, "Form follows function," is useful in thinking about time in the group formation stage. The form of the group in relation to time needs to be connected to group purpose. Agency conceptions about time can change as experiences with new group services are evaluated. In one example, I served as a consultant to an agency providing extensive group services to persons with AIDS (PWAs) as well as their friends, lovers, and family members. These groups were offered early in the AIDS epidemic and before the use of the triple-drug therapy treatments. Under the original plan developed by the agency prior to my work with them, a group would start with clients diagnosed as HIV-positive and continue as members progressed through the stages of the illness (AIDS-related complex, or ARC) and AIDS itself. The group would continue as a minicommunity as members became progressively more ill and most finally died. This structure seemed to make sense if the purpose of the group was to provide an alternative source of support for its members, many of whom felt cut off from other systems in their lives (e.g., family, work, and friends). In reality, the groups did not work this way. Most of the groups began to dissolve as members observed some members dying or becoming seriously ill.

The experience caused a rethinking of group purpose. Rather than the agency providing the substitute community, the groups were conceptualized as time limited, with a focus on helping the members deal with transitions to the various stages of the illness (e.g., one group for recently diagnosed HIV-positive clients; another group for clients facing the onset of serious medical problems). Another group focused on living with AIDS. This was not always easy to do, as the course of the illness was neither always smooth nor predictable. However, instead of the agency attempting to provide the substitute community—a task that would eventually become overwhelming, given the number of potential clients involved in the pandemic of AIDS—the focus changed to one of helping group members mobilize existing support in their own family, friendship, and community systems.

Analysis of process in the groups indicated that group leaders had been too quick to accept their group members' contention that such support was closed to them and that only the group could provide it. Work in the groups became more demanding, and members were asked to look closely at their own efforts to connect with their social support systems. The move to time-limited groups had an important and positive impact on the nature of the work. Once the "function" of the group had been clearly defined, the questions of "form" were easier to resolve.

In my more recent experience co-leading a group for PWAs in early recovery from substance abuse, new issues of timing presented themselves. For example, with a number of our group members on the then new triple-therapy drug regime, and with their resulting improvement in health, we were viewing the group as one of the ongoing support systems designed to help the members cope with (for most of them) living with AIDS rather than dying from AIDS. Also, the recovery issues required more long-term support than if the members were dealing with AIDS alone. This group began in October of one year, focusing on helping members get through the extremely stressful holiday season of Thanksgiving, Christmas, and New Year's Eve when attending parties with friends and families posed a serious threat to their substance abuse recovery efforts. The group reconvened in the new year and continued until a summer break, with the understanding that the members would assess the need to reconvene in the fall. Individual group members received ongoing support from my co-leader, who served as their substance abuse counselor.

In another example, in a consultation session with private practice mental health counselors, a group leader revealed he had been working with the same group meeting regularly for 6 years. This seemed excessive to me, so I asked why it had gone on so long. With some difficulty, the group leader finally shared that when he had ended a similar group earlier in his career, a member had committed suicide. It became clear that he had experienced a vicarious trauma himself and that his judgment on the continuation of the current group was affected by unresolved personal and professional issues. I suggested he consider ending this group, working on how to help the members make a safe transition to other sources of support, and then find a group for himself to deal with his grief and fears for his clients.

Group Structure, Setting, and Rules

A number of questions are related to group structure and setting in the formation stage. For example, the meeting place needs consideration. Ease of access by public and private transportation might be a factor. Holding a session on sensitive and potentially embarrassing issues (e.g., child abuse) in a public setting where members might fear being identified could be a mistake. The room itself should offer group members face-to-face seating (e.g., in a circle or around a table) and privacy. Comfortable chairs and surroundings often add to the group members' comfort during the first sessions. Even with larger information-focused groups, rather than setting chairs in straight lines, some sense of group involvement can be conveyed by simply curving the rows into semicircles amphitheater-style so that members can more easily see each other when asking questions or responding to the discussion.

Work with children, where activity is going to be part of the work, may require facilities that are relatively "activity-proof," so that members and the group counselor can relax without constant worries about order and decorum.

Finally, group "rules" need clarification prior to the first group meeting. For example, limits on physical activity may be set with children's groups. Even with some adult groups, it may be necessary to clarify the boundary on the use of physical force. In a group session for prison parolees, for example, one member pulled out a knife and began to clean his fingernails in a manner meant to be threatening to another member. The counselor recontracted with the members on the issue of bringing weapons to the session and made clear that threatening behaviors would not be tolerated.

Expectations about attendance are also important. The expectations the members have of the setting and the group and those the counselor has of the members should be discussed. In addition, what can each member expect from the others (e.g., confidentiality of material shared)? In my couples' group, for example, the three rules discussed in the first session are that each member is expected to come each week as long as he or she is not ill, that a couple wanting to quit the group will come back for one additional week to discuss it, and that confidentiality will be respected by group members. In the example of my AIDS/recovery group, meetings were held in a "clean and sober" residence (three members lived in this house). Members were not to bring substances to the group or be under the influence of substances when they attended.

There are many differences of opinion on the question of group rules. For example, some would argue that group members should not have contact with each other outside the meetings. The field of group counseling is far from the point where we can come to agreement on these questions. My general bias is that group members own their own lives and that my group is simply an incident in their week (albeit an important incident, I hope). I would, therefore, have difficulty insisting on a rule preventing them from having contacts outside the group. In fact, in many groups the bonds of mutual aid that have developed through telephone calls and informal contacts outside the group have been powerful supports for individual members.

Group leaders in some groups, who fear that group members may get involved in "acting out" outside the group (e.g., having sexual contact), appear to me to take more responsibility for the lives of the members than they should. In some groups, such as the AIDS/recovery group, such outside activity could be a distinct threat to the members' recovery at a particularly vulnerable time in their lives. These issues need to be discussed as part of the structure of the group.

In addition, group members should be free to bring their outside interactions into the group if they wish, because they can represent an important entry into the content of the group work. In general, the rules stated in the beginning of the group should be firmly rooted to the reality of the situation rather than the group leader's arbitrary authority or personal preferences. They should be seen by group members as emerging from the necessities of the work. A full discussion of these rules should be included as part of the informed consent procedure.

Returning to my married couples group, which met in a room in a health science center, after the fifth week I discovered that group members were having a second meeting over coffee in the cafeteria. I believe that their interaction as a social group was actually beneficial, allowing them to deal more effectively in the counseling group. Sometimes I was not even sure which meeting was helping more!

Section Summary

A number of issues related to group composition, timing, setting, rules, and structure have been raised in these sections for the purpose of alerting the reader to questions requiring consideration prior to the start of the group. My opinions on these questions have been shared not as the truth, but rather as an illustration of how one practitioner develops his own views from his experiences and those of others. As with all the ideas shared in this book, the reader will have to test them against her or his own sense of reality and ongoing group experiences.

Interviewing Prospective Members

After administration and staff support have been mobilized, potential obstacles to cooperation identified and discussed, and decisions made on the formation questions, then one more step remains: recruitment of group members. In contrast to individual and family work, very rarely does a group of clients arrive at the agency door and request services. It may happen with some naturally formed groups, as when a group of teens in a school approach the counselor for help. These are the exceptions rather than the rule. Most group counseling practice requires outreach, where the counseling service must be brought to the potential clients. Recruitment of group members is therefore a crucial element in the formation stage.

This process can also be complex, because clients feel a general ambivalence about taking help as well as unique concerns related to the group context. Some degree of ambivalence is usually present when people consider joining any group. I will focus this discussion on examples of mutual aid groups designed to deal with problems of living (e.g., marital difficulties, parenting skills, alcohol or drug addiction, school difficulties) in the belief that some of the principles can be applied to other types of groups as well.

Clients may become prospective group members by identifying themselves in response to posters, newspaper stories, letters from the agency, or other means of publicizing the existence of a group service. If handled well, the steps involved in making potential group members aware of the group can help turn the potential client toward the service. For example, posters or letters should be worded clearly, without jargon, so that the prospective member has a clear idea of the group's purpose. This would be a first step in the informed consent process. It may be helpful to identify some of the themes of concern that may be related to the client's sense of urgency. If the counselors' embarrassment results in the use of euphemisms, or if the counselors have the idea of changing the client "up their sleeves," a form of hidden agenda, and try to hide this by general and vague offers of service, prospective group members may be turned away. It can be helpful to test the letters or posters with colleagues and clients to get their sense of the meaning and suggestions as to how to make the wording direct but still nonthreatening. The group leader may be very surprised at a potential client's interpretation of the wording of the offer, particularly at the use of professional jargon unintelligible to the typical reader.

Other clients are referred by colleagues or other helping professionals or are selected by counselors from their caseloads. Whatever the case may be, even when the client has initiated the contact, the gap between thinking about joining a group and arriving at the first meeting can be a big one. Many of the skills already identified can be helpful in increasing the chances of a successful start. Two areas I will now examine are working with colleagues after they have agreed to recruit group members (a real agreement) and telephone or in-person contacts between the counselor and prospective members.

Strategizing for Effective Referrals

A counselor may have done an effective job with fellow staff members on the establishment of a group and even have their genuine support but still be disappointed by a relatively low number of referrals or clients showing up to a first meeting. An important question often overlooked is how the colleague will conduct a referral interview. It is a mistake to assume that even a motivated colleague will be able to make an effective referral without some joint work and strategizing as to how it might be done. For example, the colleague may have a general sense of the group purpose but be unable to articulate it clearly. One who has not worked with groups may not be sensitive to some of the underlying feelings and ambivalence that the client may share indirectly, thereby missing a chance to help overcome some of the obstacles blocking access to the group.

It is often helpful to suggest a "tuning-in" session, either one-on-one or with a staff group, in which counselors pool their efforts to sensitize themselves to the concerns clients may have about joining the group and the indirect ways these may emerge. Staff can then share strategies for discovering the underlying concerns through questioning or articulating them for the client. In addition, a brief role play of the referral interview may reveal to the group counselor that the colleagues are not able to articulate purpose, and work can then be done on this skill. For example, if a school counselor describes a group as a place for the student to deal with the stresses from teachers, school, parents, and friends in a way that does not get him or her into trouble, rather than suggesting that he attend an "anger management" group, the message might be heard differently. Such a process may also bring to the surface ambivalent feelings on the part of the counselor or unanswered questions that need to be dealt with prior to the actual referral interviews.

Recruiting Men Who Have Been Physically Abusive to Their Partners

An example of this process is a referral workshop that I conducted for social service professionals in connection with the establishment of a new and (at that time) experimental group service for men who had physically abused their wives or partners. Recognizing the importance of professional referrals to launch the program and knowing that the referral process might be extremely difficult in this situation, we provided an opportunity for tuning in and joint strategizing. To keep the discussion focused on skills, I asked for examples of difficult referrals of a similar nature.

One counselor described from memory a referral he had recently attempted with the common-law husband of a client. The client was a prostitute who had been beaten by the husband, who was also her pimp, but she had refused to report the incident or leave him (the existence of many situations like this had led to establishing groups for the men involved). As the counselor's interaction with the husband was analyzed, it became clear that he had never mentioned the physical abuse, attempting instead to lead the husband indirectly to agree to seek help.

When this point was mentioned during the analysis of the example, the counselor revealed that he had feared angering the husband and risking that the husband might then take the anger out on the wife. An important discussion followed in which others spoke of their fears of possible retribution on not only the partners but also themselves. Of course, this raised ethical issues in terms of informed consent. The workshop participants felt they faced an ethical dilemma because they wanted to protect the partner from further physical abuse yet knew they would be misleading the potential group members on the purpose of the group.

Their dilemma was discussed, and strategies were developed for broaching the subject directly in a manner that tried to avoid exacerbating the abusing partner's defensiveness. The first counselor tried to role-play how to recruit the member while being honest. Without this preparatory work, counselors would have been blocked, thus indirectly affecting this group because of their fears: Once the men arrived at the group, it would have become clear they had been misled.

Let us consider another illustration of the problem of stating group purpose. In a role play of how to describe the group purpose, it became clear that the counselors were describing the group in a way that would lead the prospective member to believe his worst fears: that the group was designed solely to chastise him for his behavior and to educate him to appreciate his impact on his partner. When I pointed out that the counselor seemed angry at the prospective group member, my comment released a flood of feelings, echoed by many in the room, of anger at the men. All of the professionals had agreed earlier that these groups could not be effective unless the men could both be held accountable for their violent actions toward women and also see the group as designed to help them as clients in their own right. This intellectual agreement evaporated in the role play. It was replaced with an essentially punitive and thereby ineffective offer of service.

The counselors' ability to discuss and be in touch with these natural yet often denied feelings might help ensure a presentation of the group that might turn prospective members toward the service rather than reinforce their resistance. For many of these men, even the most effective offer of service might not elicit a response. For some, it would take their partner leaving them or a court order to get them to come to the first meeting. Although this group example may be an extreme one, I believe that in most cases the counselor forming a group would be well advised to take some time with colleagues to discuss the technical aspects of making the referral.

Counselor Skills in the Initial Interviews

Group leaders often have initial contacts with individual members, in person or by phone, to discuss their participation in the group. These interviews can be seen as part of the exploratory process in which the counselor describes what the group has to offer and checks with the client to determine what may be needed. The skills described briefly earlier of clarifying purpose, clarifying role, and reaching for feedback are useful in this interview. Describing the structure of the group (how it will work) as well as timing provides information needed for the prospective member to make a decision about using the service. It also helps to fulfill another aspect of the requirement for informed consent.

In addition to the normal tuning in to the client's feelings about beginning a new relationship with a helping professional, it is also important to tune in to the specific concerns related to beginning in a group. The general population has been exposed to a number of reports on groups ranging from group psychotherapy to encounter groups. In addition, clients may bring stereotypes of groups based on their past experiences (e.g., class groups at school, camp experiences) that will have some effect on their feelings about attending. Questions about how people with the same problems can help each other will also be on their minds.

Recruiting a Member to a School-Based Parents' Group

Much of this hesitancy and fear may be just beneath the surface. It can be expressed in indirect ways, and the counselor must listen for it and reach directly for the indirect cues. In the following example, a school counselor has been describing a parents' group and has found the parent apparently receptive. The cues emerge when the counselor gets specific about the dates.

> **COUNSELOR:** We are going to have our first meeting in 2 weeks, on a Wednesday night. Can I expect you there?
>
> **PARENT:** (Long pause) Well, it sounds good. I'll try to make it if things aren't too hectic that week at work.

If the counselor quits right there and accepts the illusion of agreement, she may be guaranteeing that the parent will not show up. Even though counselors can sense the ambivalence in the client's voice, they often refrain from reaching for the negative attitude. When I have inquired why counselors refrain from exploring such cues of uncertainty, they tell me that they are afraid that if they bring the doubts out in the open, they will reinforce them—what I call the fear that if they reach for the problem, they will bring it about. They believe that the less said, the better. In reality, these doubts and questions are valid, and the counselor is missing an opportunity to help the client explore them.

Without this exploration, the client may simply not show up at the first meeting despite having promised to attend. When the counselor calls later, the client will express a lot of guilt and profuse explanations for his absence (e.g., "I really meant to come, only it got so hectic that day it just slipped my mind"; "Was it this week? I thought it was next week").

PRACTICE POINTS Returning to the interview with the parent, you should note the turn in the work when the counselor reaches for the cue.

> **COUNSELOR:** You sound a bit hesitant. Are you concerned about attending the group? It wouldn't be unusual; most people have a lot of questions about groups.
> **PARENT:** Well, you know I never do too well in groups. I find I have a lot of trouble talking in front of strangers.
> **COUNSELOR:** Are you worried that you would have to speak up and be put on the spot?
> **PARENT:** I don't mind talking about parenting; it's just that I get tongue-tied in a group.
> **COUNSELOR:** I can appreciate your concern. A lot of people feel that way. I can tell you right now that except for sharing your name, no one will put you on the spot to speak. Some people always talk a lot at the early meetings, while others prefer to listen. You can listen until you feel comfortable about speaking. If you want, I can help you begin to talk in the group, but only when you're ready. I do this all the time with people who feel this way.
> **PARENT:** You mean it's not just me who feels this way?
> **COUNSELOR:** Not at all. It's quite common and natural. By the way, are there any other concerns you might have about the group?
> **PARENT:** Not really. That was the biggest one. Actually, it doesn't sound like a bad idea at all.

PRACTICE SUMMARY Once again we see the importance of exploring the indirect cue so that the counselor has a clearer idea about the source of the ambivalence. Many group leaders would hesitate to explore the cue because they feel it was a sign of polite rejection of the group (and the counselor). When asked why they assume this unnecessarily, they often reply that they are unsure about their own competency and the quality of the group. They respond to the client's ambivalence with their own feelings. In the case just cited, the fear of speaking in the group needed to be discussed. Knowing that the counselor understands and that it is all right to feel this way can strengthen the client to overcome an obstacle to undertaking group experiences. In other cases, it may be memories of past group experience, or horror stories recounted by friends or relatives about harsh and confronting group encounters, or embarrassment about sharing personal details with strangers. The counselors need to clarify the reality when possible, empathize genuinely with the fears, and still attempt to help the client take the first difficult step. With this kind of help from the counselor, many prospective group members will be able to overcome their fears and doubts and give the group a try. A source of great support for the client is knowing that the counselor understands his or her feelings.

One other not uncommon type of resistance occurs when a group in a community mental health agency is offered to the caretaker, support person, or relative of a client. In one example, a counselor was recruiting a group for relatives of elderly Alzheimer's patients who were caring for their family members at home.

PRACTICE POINTS Note that in the face of the initial, hinted reluctance, the counselor reached for the concern:

> "You sound hesitant about coming to the group, Mrs. Smith. Can you tell me why?" The client responded, with some feeling, "Just one more thing on the list for me to do to take care of my

mother. I don't have time for myself!" The counselor replied, "Mrs. Smith, I think I can appreciate how demanding caring for your mother must be. But I don't think I made the purpose of this group clear when I described it. This group is not for your mother. This group is for you. Other group members will also be feeling overwhelmed by the demands made on them by their relatives with Alzheimer's, and part of what we can discuss is how you can get the support you need."

PRACTICE SUMMARY By reaching for the lurking negatives and the ambivalence, the counselor creates an opportunity to clarify group purpose to a potential member. A common trap that counselors fall into when they hear the indirect or direct cues of some reluctance is to try to "sell" the group even harder.

Chapter Summary

In this chapter, I explored three major areas of work involved in the formation stage of group counseling practice. The first focused on the skills required to work with one's setting and colleagues to engage them as active partners in developing the group service. Strategies were suggested for coping with underlying obstacles that can lead to sabotage of group counseling efforts. The second area involved issues of group composition, timing, and structure. A model was suggested for exploring issues in advance to maximize the possibility of success in forming the group. The final area of work examined the skills required to recruit members who may be ambivalent about attending a group session. In particular, the skill of looking for trouble when everything was going the counselor's way was identified as important for avoiding the illusion of agreement, in which the client promises to attend but doesn't show up.

Now that the counselor has completed the group formation tasks and the clients are ready to attend, the counselor needs to pay attention to the beginnings and the dynamics of first sessions. These topics are explored in the next chapter.

Related Online Content and Activities

For learning tools such as glossary terms, InfoTrac® College Edition keywords, links to related websites, and chapter practice quizzes, visit this book's website at **www.cengage.com/counseling/shulman.**

The Beginning Phase with Groups

Many of the issues related to beginning work with individuals are equally applicable to first sessions with groups, with an important addition: The individual client must also deal with a new system—the group. The first two central questions for the client in the individual context are "What are we doing here together?" and "What kind of person will this counselor be?" In the group context, a third question is added: "What kind of people will these other group members be?" Many of the uncertainties and fears associated with new beginnings will be present in a first group session, but they will be increased by the public nature of the engagement. For example, the member's fear of being manipulated by someone in authority may be heightened by the thought that any potential inadequacy displayed, and the resultant humiliation, may be witnessed by peers. For this reason, among others, special attention to first sessions is important, so that a proper stage can be set for the work that will follow. The task of the group leader in these first meetings will be described as *contracting*.

In this chapter, I provide an overview of the general structure of a first group meeting, reviewing some of the underlying assumptions outlined in Chapter 1 and considering some of the unique dynamics associated with group counseling. The tasks of both the group members and the group leader are outlined, and a number of specific skills are identified. With this overview as a backdrop, the dynamics of a first group session are illustrated using a detailed analysis of a first session of a married couples' group led by myself.

The issue of *recontracting* is also explored. This is the process in which the leader reopens the issues of contracting by providing a clearer statement of purpose or exploring the group members' resistance or lack of connection to the service. I will discuss the not-uncommon situation in which a leader joins an ongoing group in which a clear working contract has not been developed. The skills in working with the co-leaders and the group in initiating a recontracting process are illustrated with a detailed example. The chapter ends with a discussion of the potential problems involved in co-leadership and strategies for dealing with them.

The Dynamics of First Group Sessions

In exploring each of the phases of work—beginning, middle, and ending/transition—I will use the model of practice theory building described in Chapter 1. First, I will discuss what I know about people in general in relation to the phase described. In this case, it would be our general understanding about people attending a first group session. Then, based on this knowledge, I will explore what we would like to achieve based on these assumptions. Finally, I will identify and illustrate strategies and interventions designed to achieve the valued outcomes.

What Do We Know About First Group Sessions?

Most clients begin first group meetings, as they do all new encounters with people in authority, with a degree of tentativeness. Their normal concerns about adequacy and being up to the demands that will be made on them can be heightened by the fact that the encounter is taking place in public view. Most clients bring to first meetings an extensive fund of group experiences (e.g., classrooms, summer camp), many of which are associated with painful memories. We have all either witnessed or experienced the excruciatingly difficult moments in a classroom when an individual student has been singled out to answer a question, solve a math problem on the board, or give some indication of having completed the assignment. One could feel the embarrassment of a classmate when exposed to sarcasm as a punitive weapon in the hands of an insensitive teacher. In fact, whereas new encounters in a one-to-one counseling situation generate fears of the unknown, new group encounters tend to reawaken old fears based on past experiences.

Corey (2008) stresses the importance of the first meeting as follows:

The initial stage of a group is a time of orientation and exploration: determining the structure of the group, getting acquainted, and exploring the members' expectations. During this phase, members learn how the group functions, define their own goals, clarify their expectations, and look for their place in the group. At the initial sessions members tend to keep a "public image"; that is, they present the dimensions of themselves they consider socially acceptable. This phase is generally characterized by a certain degree of anxiety and insecurity about the structure of the group. Members are tentative because they are discovering and testing limits and are wondering whether they will be accepted. (p. 77)

The requirement of early clarification of purpose, required in individual counseling, is also central in the group context. It is only through presenting a clear structure that the leader can help lower the members' anxiety. The clients' first question will be "What are we here for?" Once you have clearly described the boundary of the group experience, members will find it easier to select appropriate responses. When the expectations of the group leader and the setting or agency within which the group takes place are clear, the group members' feelings of safety can increase. If purpose remains ambiguous, then all the fears of inadequacy will grow. In effect, I am arguing that the dichotomy often suggested between "structure" versus "freedom" is a false one and that, in fact, structure can create freedom. Of course, it has to be a structure that is designed to create freedom, not one that will take it away. This point will become clearer in the discussion to follow.

As the group starts, the group members will watch the group leader with keen interest. Having experienced the impact of powerful people in authority, they know it is important to "size up" this new authority figure as soon as possible. This leads to the clients' second central question: "What kind of person will the leader be?" Until the group members can understand clearly how this leader operates and the way in which they will be affected, they will need to test the leader directly or indirectly. Defenses will remain in position until members are certain that their individual safety is assured.

All these dynamics are similar to the ones experienced in the beginning of any new helping relationship. The major difference in the group setting involves the presence of other clients. As the group session proceeds, each group member will also be appraising the others. Many questions will arise: Who are these other people? Do they have the same problems as I do? Will I be embarrassed by finding myself less competent than they? Do they seem sympathetic and supportive, or are there people in this group who may attack and confront me? Although the client's primary concern in the first session is the group leader, questions about fellow members follow closely behind. Not only do members wonder what they can get out of the experience to meet their own needs, but they also wonder why it is necessary to get help in a group: "How can other people help me if they have the same problems as I have?"

DeLucia-Waack (2006) points out:

Providing specific information about what will happen in the group sessions and the role of the leader will help to reduce group members' anxiety. Their anxiety will also be reduced by participating in the screening interviews and the first session. Disclosing about their situation and finding that others have similar situations and/or reasons for being in the group is particularly helpful in alleviating initial anxiety related to group participation. Instillation of hope occurs through connections, identification of how groups work, and the discussion of specific activities to develop new skills. (pp. 95–97)

Although there is unanimous support in the literature for the importance of clarifying purpose in first sessions, Kurland and Salmon (2006) point out that group leaders commonly make six mistakes in the beginning phase of practice:

1. Practitioners promote a group Purpose without adequate consideration of client need.

2. Practitioners confuse group Purpose with group content.

3. Practitioners state group Purpose at such a high level of generality that it is vague and meaningless and therefore provides little direction for the group.

4. Practitioners are reluctant to share with the members *their* perceptions and ideas about the group's Purpose.

5. Practitioners function with a hidden Purpose in mind that they do not share with the group.

6. Practitioners do not understand Purpose as a dynamic, evolving concept that changes over the life of the group. Instead, they view Purpose as static and fixed. (p. 108)

With these cautions in mind, I now address what we want to achieve in first group sessions.

What Would We Like to Achieve—Our Valued Outcomes?

The leader should design the structure of first meetings to meet the following objectives:

- To introduce group members to each other
- To make a brief, simple, nonjargonized *opening statement* that tries to clarify the school's, agency's, or institution's stake in providing the group service as well as the potential issues and concerns about which group members may feel some urgency
- To obtain feedback from the group members on their sense of the fit (the contract) between their ideas of their needs and the setting's view of the service it provides
- To clarify the group leader's role and method of attempting to help the group do its work
- To deal directly with any specific obstacles that may obstruct this particular group's efforts to function effectively: stereotypes group members may hold concerning groups or people in authority, or group members' feelings of anger if attendance is involuntary
- To begin to encourage intermember interaction rather than discussion only between the group leader and the group members
- To begin to develop a supportive group culture in which members can feel safe
- To help group members develop a tentative agenda for future work
- To clarify the mutual expectations of the agency and the group members. For example, what can group members expect from the leader? In addition, what expectations does the leader have for the members (e.g., regular attendance, meetings starting on time)? Such rules and regulations concerning structure are part of the group contract.
- To gain some consensus on the part of group members as to the specific next steps. For example, are there central themes or issues with which they wish to begin the following week's or future week's discussions? How do the members' interests fit with the content outline if the group content is already structured?
- To encourage honest feedback and evaluation of the effectiveness of the group

At first glance, this list of objectives for a first meeting may appear overwhelming. A person new to leading groups might review this list and decide to stick to individual counseling. Actually, many of these objectives can be dealt with quickly, and most are interdependent in that work on one simultaneously affects the others. Obviously, however, these objectives cannot be achieved in the first session unless a clear *structure for work* is provided. The approach to creating such a structure, which is detailed in the remainder of the chapter, is offered as a general statement recognizing that the order of elements and the emphasis may vary depending on the leader, the group members, the nature of their work together, and the setting.

The Contracting Skills: Establishing a Structure for Work

The following is a list of skills and interventions designed to accomplish our *valued outcomes*, as listed in the prior section, in the first few sessions of a counseling group.

- *Clarifying the group's purpose*: a simple, "nonjargonized" statement made by the group leader (usually incorporated into the opening statement to the group) that describes the general purpose of the group in terms the members can connect with. For example, instead of telling fifth graders referred to a group because of their behavior in class that it is an "anger management" group, the leader might open by saying that each member was sent by their teachers because their behavior in class was getting them in trouble and probably making school not much fun for them. The leader could continue that the purpose of the group was for each of them to help each other find ways to deal with their feelings, such as anger and sadness, and figure out how to make school and their classes better for all of them.

- *Clarifying the role of the group leader(s)*: a statement of the role the group leader and co-leaders will play, offering some idea of how the group leader can help. In the school group, for example, it may be simply "My job is to help each of you talk to and listen to each other, to figure out what your problems in school are, and to help you help each other."

- *Reaching for the group members' feedback*: an effort made by the leader to determine the group members' perceptions of their needs and what they hope to get from the group. I call this work "problem swapping." For example, continuing in the school group, the leader might say, "How about it? Is school not much fun for you? Are your teachers and maybe your parents on your back? Are other kids giving you hard time? Are you worried about passing or even getting suspended from school?" This intervention provides "handles for work" for the members, which frees them to grab onto the one that hits home.

These statements need to be phrased from the group members' perspective and how they are likely experiencing their problems. It is important that they do not sound like blaming. Such an opening also states the contract from the children's perspective and the feelings and issues they struggle with that can lead to problematic behavior. This approach contrasts with an opening in which the behavior itself is the problem and the children feel blamed, as when the group's purpose is called "anger management." In addition to clarifying the kinds of things that can be discussed, the group leader is starting to demonstrate some empathy with the members, which is the beginning of developing the working relationship, a part of the group's beginning working "contract" that notes the overlap between the services offered and the felt needs of the group member as well as the common issues.

- *Identifying the common ground*: shared by group members. Continuing with this example, after some sharing by members, the group leader could say, "It seems like all of you are having the same problems in class and at home. Maybe if we talk about these things, you can all help each other. That's why the school asked me to set up this group: to help you find ways of dealing with these concerns and feelings that won't get you into so much trouble and maybe can get the teachers, your parents, and your friends off your back, so that maybe you even start to enjoy school."

- *Supporting members in taboo areas*: helping group members talk about issues and concerns that are normally treated as taboo (e.g., sex, death, authority, dependency). For example, in the school setting, it could be something like this:

    When I talk with kids like you, I sometimes find out that they have had very sad things happen in their lives and in their families. Some kids have seen drive-by shootings or have had friends or families hurt by others. Some worry about the family a lot and even friends who are doing too much dope. Some are being pushed to join gangs even though they don't want to but are afraid to say no.

- *Dealing with issues of authority*: the group leader's efforts to clarify mutual expectations, confidentiality issues, and the authority theme. The group leader has to make clear right from the start that what gets discussed in the group is confidential except if members reveal that they are thinking about hurting themselves, hurting others, or doing something else that is illegal. The leader also has to make clear that it's part of his or her job to make sure that everyone feels safe in the group so that fighting in the group or even outside the group cannot be allowed. This part of the work also addresses any questions they have about the leader as a symbol of authority, such as "Are you a teacher?"

The confidentiality issue must be addressed in the first session. In part, it relates to the earlier ethical discussion related to informed consent. In addition, the group leader is a *mandated reporter*, someone who is required by law to report when working with children and, in most states, the elderly if someone is at risk to themselves or to others. Chapter 13 discusses this and other ethical and legal issues governing a group leader in more detail.

Even as I describe these basic contracting skills, you may have many questions in your mind. For example, what if this doesn't go smoothly and the members start to act out? What if teenagers just sit there and stare at you? What if it is a mandatory group of DWI offenders sent by a judge or men who have battered their wives and partners but don't believe they have a problem with anger and violence? All of these issues represent variations on the central theme and will be explored in detail throughout the book. Let me just be clear here that these skills, designed to achieve that long list of valued outcomes, in one form or another, are central to making a start in the work no matter what the setting, group membership, issues to be dealt with, and other factors may be.

Illustration of a First Group Session: The Couples' Group

This section illustrates in some detail a first meeting using excerpts from a video-taped recording of the first session of a married couples' group I led a number of years ago. The group was conducted under the auspices of a university mental health setting's outpatient clinic.[1] Five couples were referred from a variety of sources. All had experienced problems in their marital relationships, and in each of the five couples, one partner was identified by the other as the "patient." The youngest couple was John and Louise, in their 20s, married for 6 years with two young children. Rick and Fran were in their 30s and had been married for 7 years with no children. Len and Sally were in their late 40s, had been married for 20 years, and had college-age children. Frank and Jane, in their 50s, were recently married after prior marriages and divorces. Jane's teenaged sons were living with them at this point. Finally, Lou and Rose were in their late 60s with a number of married children, who in turn, had children of their own. Louise and Rose had recently been inpatients at the hospital. Sally had been seen at the hospital and was considering entering as an inpatient. Frank, Jane, Rick, and Fran had been referred to the group for marital counseling. Each of the couples had been interviewed individually by one of my two co-leaders in the group; however, they were meeting me, the senior group leader, for the first time that evening. My two co-leaders, one male and one female, were also present.

The Initial Stage of the First Session

The group meeting room was carpeted and had comfortable chairs set in a circle. The session was recorded on video cameras placed in an adjoining studio. Cameras and the cameraman were on the other side of one-way glass partitions. In addition, a group of graduate students were observing the video in another room as part of their group counseling course. The couples knew of the observation and had consented with the understanding that they could request that the cameras be turned off if they felt uncomfortable discussing an issue. As the couples arrived, I met them at the door, introducing myself to each partner and encouraging them to take a seat. Len, Sally's husband, had to miss the first session, as he was out of town on business. Frank and Jane, who had expressed the most ambivalence and uncertainty about attending the group during the week, were not present at the beginning of the session. I began by suggesting that we go around the room so that the members could share their names, how long they had been married, and whether they had any children. I said this would be a way for us to get to know each other.

---

1. It has been my practice to lead different types of groups over the years, and this was one identified by the hospital as important for its mental health and family services. Two full-time employees at the hospital were co-leaders although I had primary responsibility for group leadership. One co-leader, a male counselor, had been a student of mine. The other, a psychiatric nurse, had offered to co-lead to expand her experience. The names of the members have been changed in this text. These sessions and other DVDs I have produced are available from Insight Media (www.insightmedia.com). Members of the group provided informed consent for the use of the group content for teaching and publication purposes, and they had an opportunity to view both video sessions before they gave their final consent. As one member put it when giving final consent: "This group has been so helpful to us I want it to be used to be helpful for others." The names in this text are not the real first names on the DVD. This change was implemented because of the wider distribution of the text version of the sessions.

PRACTICE POINTS
Note that I start to encourage the members to talk to each other and not only to me.

> **LOUISE:** I am Louise Lewis. We have been married 6 years, and we have two children.
> **LEADER:** Go ahead, John (speaking to Louise's husband sitting next to her), please share it with the group members. (I pointed to the rest of the group.)
> **JOHN:** My name is John. (Pause)
> **LEADER:** (Smiling) With the same kids!
> **JOHN:** (Laughing along with the rest of the group) Yes, I hope so.

The group members continued around the circle, giving their names and the data on their families. The advantage of introductions is that they help group members break the ice and begin to speak from the start. In addition, the leader conveys to them the sense that knowing each other will be important. Often during these introductions, someone will make a humorous comment followed by nervous laughter; however, even these first contributions can help the members settle down. It is important that a minimum of relevant information be requested at this point, since discussion of working contract—the group's purpose, the co-leaders' roles, and so forth—has not taken place. Group members will have the opportunity later to share the reasons why they have come. This will come after clarification of group purpose, which will provide the necessary structure. An alternative approach would be to make a brief statement of purpose before asking for introductions. This could be particularly important if group members had no idea of the group's purpose.

PRACTICE POINTS
Although the members had provided informed consent for the videotaping and observation, I believed they needed another opportunity to address their decision. Following the introductions, I brought up the videotaping issue since I knew it might be on their mind.

> **LEADER:** I realize you discussed the taping with my co-leaders, but I thought I would like to repeat the reasons for taping these sessions and also to give you another opportunity to share your reactions. As you know, this is a training institution, and we are involved in teaching other health professionals a number of skills, including how to work with groups. We find it helpful to use videotapes of groups such as these so that new group leaders can have examples to assist them in their learning. In addition, the co-leaders and I will use these tapes each week as a way of trying to figure out how to be more effective in helping this group work well.

I went on to explain that if segments of the tape were kept, they would have an opportunity to view them and could decide if they wanted them erased. I asked if there was any response, and after a few moments of silence and some verbal agreement that there was no problem, I proceeded. I believed the tapes were still on their minds and would come up again; however, they were not quite ready at this point to accept my invitation.

Clarifying Purpose and Role

With this acknowledgment of the taping issue, I moved to begin the contracting process. The first skills involved were similar to those described earlier in this chapter: clarifying purpose, clarifying role, and reaching for client feedback.

I had prepared an opening statement in which I attempted to explain the stake the clinic had in providing the group, to identify their potential interest in the counseling of the group and to state our roles as leaders. This statement had been reworded a number of times with the assistance of my co-leaders until we felt it was jargon-free, short, and direct.

> **LEADER:** I thought I would begin by explaining how we view the purpose of this group and the role that we would be playing, and to get some feedback from you on what you see the sessions to be all about. All of the couples in the group—and there may be one more here later this evening—are experiencing some difficulties in their marriages. This is a time of crisis and not an easy time. The way we see it, however, is that it is also an opportunity for change, for growth, and a chance to make a new marriage right within the one you presently have.
>
> Now we know that isn't easy; learning to live together can be tough. That is why we have organized this group. Essentially, the way we see it, it will be a chance for you to help each other—a sort of a mutual aid group. As you listen to each other, as you share some of the problems, some of the feelings, and some of the concerns, and as you try to help each other, we think you will learn a great deal that may be helpful in your own marriages. So that's pretty much the purpose of the group.
>
> Now, for our role as group leaders, we have a couple of jobs. The first is that we are going to try to help you talk to and listen to each other, since it's not always easy to do that, particularly with people you don't know. Second, we will be sharing our own ideas along the way about close relationships, some of which may be helpful to you. Does that make sense? Do any of you have any questions about that? Does that sound like what you thought you were coming to? (Most heads were nodding; there were murmurs of yes.)
>
> I thought to get us started, it would be worthwhile to take some time to do some problem swapping. What I would like you to do is to share with each other, for a little while, some of the problems and difficulties you have found between you as couples. I would like you also to share some of the things you would like to see different. How would you like the relationship to be? We can take some time to find out the kinds of issues that you're concerned about and then move from there. Would someone like to start?

Reaching for Feedback on the Purpose: The Problem-Swapping Exercise

The purpose of the problem swapping is twofold. First, it provides the feedback necessary to begin to develop the client's side of the working contract. These are the issues and concerns that will be the starting point for the work of the group. It is quite possible that in the initial stage, group members will share "near" problems that do not bear directly on some of the more difficult and hard-to-talk-about issues. This is their way of testing, of trying to determine how safe it is to use the group. The group leader has to respect and understand their defenses as an appropriate way to begin a new experience. In this particular group, each couple actually indirectly raised a core issue in their relationship in this first session that only emerged clearly during the last five sessions—the ending and transition phases. The work in the middle phase was solid and dealt with other important but not as potent issues. Watching the video of the first session after the last session of the group, I could see how they were indirectly sharing the problem and making what I have called the "first offering."

The second function of the problem-swapping exercise is to encourage inter-member interaction. For most of their lives, clients have participated in groups where the discussion has essentially been between the group member and the leader, the person in authority. This is a long-standing habit. They will need to learn new ways of relating in a group, and the problem-swapping exercise is a good way to start.

As each individual member shares a problem or a concern, the group leader pays attention to the two clients. The first client is the individual who is speaking at the moment. The second client is the group. Attention is paid by *monitoring the individual* and *monitoring the group*—their reactions as revealed by their eyes, their posture, and so on. The mediation function of the group leader can be seen in action during this exercise as he encourages individual members to speak to the group and share the concerns they are bringing to the forefront and at the same time helps group members respond to the individual. As group members hear others describing problems, they become better able to identify those issues for themselves. In addition, when they hear their own concerns echoed by other group members, there is some relief at finding out that they are "all in the same boat." The onus that each member may feel over having somehow failed as a human being and as a partner in a marital relationship can begin to lift as they discover that others share their feelings and their concerns.

Silence in the First Session

After the opening statement, silence is not unusual at this point. This silence can represent a number of communications, a different one for each group member. Some may be thinking of what they are willing to share with the group at that time. Others may be shy and afraid to be the first one to speak. Still others are expressing their wariness of being put on the spot if they raise a concern, because they do not know how other group members or the leader will react.

These are the moments that inexperienced group leaders dread. The silence, they feel, confirms a recurring nightmare they have had about their first group session. They are worried that after they have made their opening statement and invited feedback, nobody will speak. It is not unusual for group leaders to take over the group at this point and to offer subjects for discussion or, in some cases, to present prepared films or presentations.

Doing so, however, only leads to a self-fulfilling prophecy, where the message conveyed to the members is that although their participation is being asked for, there is no willingness to wait for it. An alternative, after a brief delay, is to explore the silence by acknowledging, for example, that it is hard to begin and that it is difficult to discuss such subjects with people one doesn't know. Often, this supportive comment frees a member to risk. If not, the group leader can ask if members might discuss what makes it hard to talk in a first group session as well as what would make it easier. This strategy is very effective because as the members discuss why it's hard to talk, they inevitably start the problem swapping as well. As they share what would make it easier, they are starting to develop a supportive culture for work.

A Member Begins: The Authority Theme Emerges

In the case of this couples' group, Lou, the member in his 60s, had a strong sense of urgency about beginning to work and was ready to jump right in. He was seated directly to my left. (As will be discussed in more detail in Chapter 8, this specific chair took on special significance with members, because the member who had chosen to there, sit next to me, often wound up revealing powerful emotions. One member thus called it the "crying chair.") As Lou spoke, he directed his conversation to the other members. He began by describing the problem as his wife's depression. The effect was flat in his voice, and his wife sat next to him stone-faced, without any change in expression. This is a position she held throughout the session, almost until the end, not saying a word, although she appeared to be hearing everything said by others. As Lou spoke, the rest of the group listened intently, obviously relieved that he had started. If he had not started, I would have acknowledged it was difficult to begin, which, as noted, often is enough to encourage a response.

PRACTICE POINTS

Note that as Lou keeps referring to his wife, I concentrate on expressing my empathy for him. When he says it has been tough on her, I acknowledge that and say that it was hard for him as well.

> **LOU:** To begin with, as you heard, we have been married for 45 years. Our relationship has been on a rocky road due in a great degree to tragedies that have happened to our family. While that was a real contributing factor, social conditions, economic conditions, and family relationships were also contributing factors. I'm making this very brief because most of this will come out later on. I think the outline on this will be enough for us to get our teeth into. As a result of the things I have mentioned, Rose, particularly, went into some real depressions. All the threads of her family seemed to go. As a result, it became difficult for her to operate. The problems were so strong, she decided she had to go to a psychiatrist. She went and I went with her for 2½ years. The psychiatrist opened up some doors for her but not enough to really make her free to operate. The unfortunate thing about her depression is that it developed into hostility toward me and the children. Now as soon as the depression lifted, as far as she was concerned, things straightened out. As soon as her depression lifted, we had no problems. (This is said emphatically, facing the group leader.) We had differences of opinion, but we had no problems.
>
> **LEADER:** It sounds like it has been tough for her and also tough for you.
>
> **LOU:** Oh, yes! The unfortunate thing as far as we were concerned is that we did not have a psychiatrist who understood what the relationship was. He took our problems as a family problem. His suggestion after a while was that if we weren't getting along together, we should separate. I felt I really didn't like that because I knew that wasn't the problem. The problem was getting Rose out of her depression.

PRACTICE POINTS

Lou had begun presenting the problem the way one partner often does in a couples' group. The problem was essentially the other partner who, in some way, needed to be "fixed." This is the way one partner often experiences things, and it is important that the group leader attempt to understand and express that understanding of the members' feelings as they are presented. When I show this session to students, one will often confront me for "allowing" Lou to talk about his wife as the "identified patient." Many students in the class identify with his wife and become angry with Lou for not taking responsibility for his part in the problem. Some suggest I should have asked Lou to use "I statements." (This was a popular artificial contrivance in group work that required members to talk only about themselves—the "I" rather than the other.)

I point out to my students that in the first few minutes of this session, this couple is acting out the very problem they have come to get help with. Lou is saying, "Do you want to see how I deny the problem and blame it all on Rose? Just watch me!" Rose is saying, "Yes, and watch how I sit here passively, letting Lou talk about me." I point out to the students that it doesn't make sense for me to get angry at these clients for having the very problems and maladaptive patterns of behavior the group was established to deal with. Also, before I confront Lou, I have to build up a fund of support. In this case I attempt to do that by commenting about this experience being tough on his wife and on him. He talks about his wife, while I come back to him. Later in the session, this same client drops some of his defenses.

Some observers wonder about my letting Lou continue to talk instead of immediately involving other members. It seemed obvious to me that the second client, the group, was listening to what Lou had to say and did not mind his going on at some length. Group members begin first sessions with various patterns of behavior. Those who are used to being quiet and withdrawn in new situations will begin that way. Those who are used to speaking and jumping in quickly, such as Lou, will begin that way. Each member is entitled to his or her own defenses in the beginning, and it is important that the group leader respect them. When a group member speaks for a period of time, keeping to the subject, usually only the leader feels nervous. The other group members are often relieved that someone else has begun the discussion.

PRACTICE POINTS

In this case, the tuning-in work from the individual session had alerted us to Lou's strong feelings toward helping professionals, which he raises at the end of the excerpt, who he felt had not been helpful. Understanding that the authority theme and the question "What kind of group leader will this be?" are always present in a first session, I had strategized to reach directly if I felt there were indirect cues related to us, the group leaders. I did so at this point in the following way:

LEADER: Are you worried that I and the other group leaders might take the same position with you and Rose?

LOU: Well, I don't know (voice slightly rising with annoyance). I'm not worried; I'm past that stage (accompanied with a harsh laugh). I'm just relating what happened, because I know where I'm at (said emphatically). To be very frank, my opinion of psychiatrists is very low, and I can cite 2 hours of experiences of what I have been through, my friends have been through, to show you exactly what I mean. This was a good case in point, his making a suggestion that we should separate because of the problem.

LEADER: After 45 years, I can imagine that must have hit you as a terrible blow.

LOU: Well, sure it did.

LEADER: Lou, do you think we could move around the circle a bit and also hear from the others as to what they see some of the problems to be?

In retrospect, I think Lou responded somewhat angrily partly because of the way I made my statement: "Are you worried that I and the other group leaders might take the same position with you and Rose?" I wanted to open up Lou's concerns about what kind of leaders we would be; however, my attempt was neither direct nor clear enough. Instead of asking for further *elaboration* from Lou or, perhaps, asking if others in the group had similar experiences or relations, I suggested we allow others to exchange problems by "moving around the circle." It is important to encourage such an exchange of problems; however, further exploration of the authority theme was also important. Fortunately, I had an opportunity to "catch my mistake" later in the session when I returned to the initial concerns raised by Lou. Lou responded to my suggestion that we "hear from the others" by turning to his wife.

LOU: Sure, you're on. Go ahead, dear. (He turns to his wife.)

ROSE: I think I'll pass right now (said in a slow, even way, with no evidence of affect).

LEADER: That's fine. How about some others? You don't have to go in order, and you know, you can also respond to what Lou just said if you like, as well as adding some of your own issues. We won't solve all of the problems tonight; I hope you realize that. (Some laughter by the group members) But what we would like to try and do is get a feel for how they seem to you right now. That can help us get a sense of what we need to talk about, and I think Lou has helped us get started. (At this point, John takes off his coat and seems to settle back in his chair.)

PRACTICE POINTS

Having witnessed how the leader responded to Lou, accepting and acknowledging his feelings, others in the group felt ready to share. Note that Louise reinforces Lou's issues with helping professionals as well as sharing her problem. Note also that I ask Louise to focus on how the feelings she raises affect her relationship to her husband since the marital relationship is what the group is about.

LOUISE: (John's wife, who is now speaking directly to Lou) I can understand what Lou means because depression has been our problem as well. I have gotten into such a state of depression that I can't function as a mother or a wife. I feel I have lost my identity. (This is all said with a very flat affect.) And I don't think that separation is the answer, either. And I have had some pretty bad psychiatrists as well, so I can really feel for you when you say that, Lou. I can understand that. But the problem is to be able to sort out and find out what feelings I really have and recognize them for what they are and try to get myself out of the hole that I fell into, and that's the tough part.

LEADER: How does it affect your relationship with John?

LOUISE: It's very strenuous. There is a lot of strain and tension when I'm sick and down and I put the responsibility for taking care of the household on John's shoulders. There is a breaking point for him somewhere there; I want to catch it before we get there. (Pause, leader is nodding and other members are listening intently.) That's about it. (Brief silence)

JOHN: Our biggest problem, or Louise's biggest problem, is due to her migraine headaches. She's had them ever since she was 5 years old. This is where the whole problem stemmed from, those migraine headaches and this new depression which she seems to have gotten in the last few months.

LEADER: Anything special happen within the last few months?

JOHN: No, it has been actually a very quiet time this summer.

LOUISE: I think it is things that have been festering for a long time.

LEADER: For example?

LOUISE: I don't know. I can't put my finger on what they are.

LEADER: (Speaking to John) This depression came as a surprise to you, did it?

JOHN: Yes, it did.

LEADER: How do you see the problem, John? What would you like to see different in the relationship?

PRACTICE POINTS

My effort to encourage John and Louise to become more specific about what has been going on recently is politely rejected. John goes on to describe how they don't do much together as a couple anymore and that he would like to see Louise get back on her feet so they can have some fun the way they used to. Discussion continued around the circle, with Fran and Rick looking at each other as if to ask who would go first. I verbalized this, and Fran begged off, saying that she didn't feel comfortable starting right away and that she would get in a bit later. Her husband, Rick, responded to my question by saying he was wondering why he was there because he knows that he has, or rather, they have, a problem, but what the problem is, is hard to define. Fran coached him at this point by whispering in his ear the word "communication." They seemed to agree that that's the problem, but when I asked for elaboration, Rick said, "That's not my problem—that's Fran's problem."

PRACTICE POINTS Rick then took a further step for the group by entering a taboo area and raising sexual intimacy.

RICK: I guess if you get right down to basics, it would have to be sexual intimacy. I have been going along for a little over 7 years, and now I find that I'm all alone. Fran's gone on a trip, and we're really in the very rocky stages of breaking up. (There is some emotion in his voice as he is speaking.) For the last 6 months, we have sort of been trying to recover, but it's still pretty shaky.

LEADER: It must feel pretty dicey for you right now.

RICK: Right. (With resignation in his voice)

LEADER: What would you like to be different? What would you like to see changed in your marriage?

RICK: (After a deep sigh to get his breath) There are times when everything is just fine, it seems to be going along smoothly, but just to say what I would like would be tough to put my finger on.

LEADER: How would you like the relationship to be with Fran?

RICK: I think I would like it to be peaceful at all times. We have been getting into a lot of fights, and just recently we have been getting into a lot of physical fights. A peaceful relationship, that's what I would really go for.

LEADER: How about you, Fran—do you have any ideas now?

FRAN: No, can we come back to me?

LEADER: Sure.

PRACTICE POINTS As stated earlier, each group member (and in this case, each couple) has to have control over how much they share. My approach is to ask for elaboration but also to be respectful of the member's defenses by not pushing too hard too early. The discussion continued with Sally talking about her marriage. This was difficult because her husband, Len, was not present. She described it from her perspective. Her description was filled with interpretations that had obviously been gleaned from years of involvement in various forms of analysis. The group listened intently to her stories. She also responded to Louise's comments about migraine headaches, mentioning that she had had them as well, and then she and Louise exchanged some mutual understanding. After Sally finished her description, there was a long silence as the group seemed unsure about where to go. Note that I had decided to get back to the authority theme and Lou, whom I felt I had cut off before.

LEADER: (Turning to Lou) I didn't mean to stop you before, Lou, if you want to get in again.

LOU: No, that's OK (laughing). I could go on for hours.

LEADER: Oh, they won't mind, you know (pointing to the group); they would be glad. (Most of the group members laugh at this.)

LOU: I want to give others the opportunity to speak because, after all, I have been married over 45 years, so I have an accumulation of incidents.

Returning to the Authority Theme

At this point, I picked up the theme that had been common to many of the presentations: "helping people" who had not really helped. I had reached for this theme earlier in the session in relation to the role played by me and my co-leaders, but Lou had not accepted my invitation. I believe the relationship between the group and the group leader is a central question at the beginning of each new group. Some discussion needs to take place on this issue so that the group can begin to work on what I have referred to as the "authority theme," the relationship between the person who offers help and the person who takes help. It is a powerful factor in the first group session; and for the group to develop properly, the group leader must begin to deal with it.

During the problem-swapping exercise, I had attempted to express my empathic responses to the concerns as they were raised, taking care not to express judgments on their feelings and actions. Even this brief period had let me build up a sufficient fund of positive relationships so that I could reach for some discussion on this difficult theme. If the group were to start to develop as a healthy organism, it would need to begin to sort out its relationship to me as the leader and my co-leaders as the persons in authority. Because this is a taboo subject, it would require considerable effort on my part to make it clear that the topic was open to discussion.

I decided to return to the theme of helpers who had not helped. It is important to note that I returned to this issue directly by pointing out to the group members that I thought such a discussion might be important, so that they could be involved with full knowledge of the process. The group discussion that followed, led by Lou who was an internal leader on this issue, was a critical factor contributing to a striking change in the group atmosphere and to its successful beginning.

LEADER: I have noticed a theme that has cut across a number of your presentations that I think is important for us to talk about. A number of you have commented on helping people who have not been very successful—psychiatrists you have had in the past, doctors, and so on. (Group members all nod, saying yes.) Can you stay on that for a minute in terms of the things in your experiences that you found difficult? The reason I think it is important is because it would be a way of your letting me and my co-leaders know what you would not find helpful from us.

This is the second time I reached for some comments about the group members' concern about us. This time, because a relationship was beginning, and because I reached in a way that was less threatening, they were ready to take me up. Lou volunteered to begin the discussion. He took us back to 1940 when he had his own business. He described some of the pressures on him concerning economic conditions and a rash he had developed on his leg. His doctor referred him to a psychiatrist who was brand new at the hospital. It was his first job. Lou's enthusiasm and feelings while describing this experience captured the attention of the group. They smiled and nodded agreement with his comments as he continued his story.

Integrating the Late Couple and Maintaining the Discussion

As he was about to describe his encounter with the psychiatrist, the door to the group room opened, and the fifth couple, Frank and Jane, arrived late. It is not unusual for group members to arrive late for a first session. It usually presents a dilemma for the group leader: What do I do? In this case, I had the new couple introduce themselves, and I asked the other couples to give their names as well. I then briefly summarized the contract, explaining that we had been hearing about some problems to help get a feel for the concerns that had brought the couples to this session, and pointed out that one theme that kept recurring had to do with helping people who had not been very helpful. I said that we were focusing on this right now and that just before they had entered, we had been with Lou in 1940. With that, I turned back to Lou to continue, and the group picked up where it had left off.

PRACTICE POINTS I think that it is important to recognize the entrance of the new group members and help them connect to the group; but, at the same time, I think it would be a mistake to take a great deal of time to start again. As will become clear later in this group session, these group members were late for a reason; their lateness was their way of handling a new and frightening experience.

Lou continued his story of his first encounter with the young psychiatrist, indicating that the psychiatrist had tried to lead him indirectly to recognizing that he had a marital problem. As Lou put it, "I was talking about the economic conditions and the problems of the time, and he kept coming back to the wife and the kids, and the wife and the kids, and the wife and the kids until I said to him, 'Are you trying to tell me my problem is with my wife and my kids?'" Lou went on to say that when the psychiatrist indicated it was, he stood up, called him a charlatan, and quickly got out of the office as he described the enraged psychiatrist coming out from behind the desk and shaking his fist at him.

> **LOU:** OK. I knew that my wife and my family were part of the problem, but I also knew that they were not at the core of the problem. They were a contributing factor because of the social and economic conditions. I went to this guy to get rid of this rash on my leg and not to have him tell me that my wife and my kids were giving me the problem. It took a while for the rash to go away, but eventually it did. That was item number one. I am going to skip a lot of the intervening incidents that had to do with families, and I will go to the one which we just experienced recently. We went to a psychiatrist in the community for 2½ years (and then with emphasis)—*2½ years!* I knew I had to go with her to give her some support, plus I wanted to find out what made her tick. I couldn't understand her depression. I had been down in the dumps and felt blue, but I had never felt as depressed as she seemed to feel. He asked her a lot of questions, asked me a lot of questions, tried to have us do some play acting, and had us try and discuss the problems. "You're not communicating" was his term. I didn't know what he was talking about when he said we didn't communicate, so we tried to communicate. But nothing really came of it because we saw we weren't communicating.

As Lou related his experiences, he was describing a number of techniques that apparently had been used to try to help him and his wife deal with their problems. The central theme appeared to be that of a helping person who had decided what the problem was and was now trying to educate them as to its nature.

Lou was resentful of this approach and resisted it in most of the sessions. Yet, part of him deep inside knew that there was a problem that he attempted to deal with in his own way. He described an incident when he had taken a tape recorder home and recorded a conversation with his wife, listening to it later. His description of the aftermath of this tape recording contained the first overt expression of the sadness and the pains the couple had felt but were not ready to share.

<table>
<tr><td>

PRACTICE POINTS

</td><td>

In this case, I believe it was necessary for Lou to share first the anger and the frustration at the helping people who had not understood him before he was willing to share his hurt and pain. My telling him to "take your time" and giving him some water was my natural response to his emotions. Lou was sitting in the chair next to me and was the first to cry in the group.

</td></tr>
</table>

LOU: We talked for about 15 minutes, and I realized when we played the tape back, that I was screaming at Rose. Now I never realized that I was screaming at her. But I heard my voice. (Lou clears his throat at this point and begins to choke up, obviously feeling emotions and trying to fight back his tears.) This is a little rough for me. Can I have some water?

LEADER: (Getting a glass of water from the decanter) Sure, you can, Lou, take your time.

LOU: It's kind of tough to get over the fact that I was screaming at her. Then I realized that when I was screaming at her, I was treating her like a kid. I took this tape to the psychiatrist, and he couldn't hear the screaming. He got nothing out of it.

LEADER: He didn't seem to understand how it felt to you to hear yourself screaming?

LOU: That's right. He didn't even hear me screaming. The other thing he tried to get us to do which I found really devastating is he tried to get us to reverse roles; she should be me and I should be her. OK, we tried it. But while we were doing it, I was thinking to myself, "Now, if that isn't stupid, I don't know what is." (Turning to me at this point) But you're a psychiatrist; you know what the score is. How can you reverse roles when I'm not feeling like she's feeling and she doesn't feel like I do? How can I communicate? Well, it was things like that that had been going on for 2½ years, and when we had finished, I was nowhere nearer being helped to be able to live with Rose than I was when we started. Now that's 2½ years! It isn't that we didn't try; both of us used to discuss this. Rose went back to the doctor, but I said I wouldn't go because I found I was just getting more frustrated.

At this point, some group members discussed the use of the tape recorder. Rick thought it was a good idea and wondered if Lou had tried it again. Lou said he hadn't. The conversation returned to his feelings of frustration and his sense of not having been helped.

<table>
<tr><td>

PRACTICE POINTS

</td><td>

My understanding of Lou's story was that he wanted to be sure that I and my co-leaders would listen and try to understand. This was my opportunity to clarify our roles as group leaders. Although I had indicated what our role would be in the opening statements, I'm not sure anyone really heard and understood the statement. Now was the time to address it again.

</td></tr>
</table>

LOU: I felt stupid. The psychiatrist kept telling me something, and no matter how hard I tried, I simply couldn't understand.

LEADER: You also seem to be saying, not only couldn't you understand him, but he didn't seem to understand you.

LOU: Well, yes. Peculiarly enough, that thought had not occurred to me. I felt, well, you are a professional (facing the leader at this point), so what you're doing, you're doing on purpose. You know what you're supposed to be doing. And whether you understand me or not is immaterial. That's not what the game is. It's my responsibility to understand what you, if you are the psychiatrist, are saying. (There was anger in his voice.)

LEADER: If you're asking us (referring to the other co-leaders) in this group, that's not the way I see it. I think that if we can be of any help to you or the other group members, the help will be in our listening and in our trying to understand exactly how you see it. The gimmicks and the things that seem to get tried on you is not my idea of how we can help. You'll have to wait to see if I mean that.

LOU: Yeah, we'll see.

LEADER: I think you folks have a powerful lot of help to give each other. And essentially, what I will try and do is to help you do that. And I'll share my own ideas along the way. But I have no answers or simple solutions.

LOU: Then, well, OK. (General silence in the group as the members appear to be taking in the meaning of the words)

CO-LEADER: I'd like to know, Lou, as we go along, how you see things. So, if you're feeling stupid or whatever, you'll let us know.

LEADER: It might be because we've said something dumb. (Some subdued laughter in the group)

PRACTICE SUMMARY

Although I had described the group as a mutual aid group in the opening statement, it was only at this point that the members really began to have a sense of how the group might work. Also, the clarification of the group leader's role contained in this exchange was actually "heard." Lou, playing the role of an internal group leader, was able to articulate the fears and concerns that group members felt about the potential power invested in the group leader's role. He provided the opportunity for an initial clarification of who we were as group leaders and what we did. Skills of accepting and understanding his feelings and his frustrations, and of helping connect his past experiences to the present moment, were crucial in this session. The feeling in the group was that we had moved past the first step in building our relationship. The authority theme was not finished as a topic of discussion; however, one could sense that an important start had been made. Following this exchange, the group members were able to move into work on their contract with more energy, involvement, and intermember interaction.

On another note, I had indicated that each of the couples had indirectly raised a central issue in the first session that I could not hear and understand until it was raised at a much later session. In Lou's case, he said he was going to skip some of the other experiences with psychiatrists. He was referring to a traumatic experience for him and his wife when speaking on the phone with their married son, living in another city, who was undergoing psychotherapy. The son had told his wife that his psychiatrist had said that all of his problems were her fault and that he never wanted to see her again. According to Rose, the son said, "Don't ever come to see me, or I will kill you!" As we discovered near the end of the group sessions, this was the precipitating event that led to Rose's severe depression over 2 years before and her recent hospitalization.

The Middle Stage of the First Session

With a 2-hour session, we could move past problem swapping and clarification of purpose and the group leader's role into beginning efforts to focus on an example of what happens in a group.

Frank and Jane and Issues of a Blended Family

Interestingly enough, Frank and Jane, the couple who had arrived late, provided an opportunity to do this. Frank began to share, with some elaborative assistance from me, a problem that they were experiencing in relation to his wife's teenage sons who were living with them. It was an interesting example of a group member raising a problem tentatively, moving quickly back and forth between the implications of the difficulty for the couple and his relationship to the children. He spoke of the sexual difficulty they had, while attributing most of it to his medical problem and also to the lack of privacy in their home. The bedroom door was not locked at any time, and the children would wander in without notice. As Frank was sharing this dilemma, he phrased it in terms of his problem with his stepsons, but one could hear throughout the discussion hints of the implications for his relationship to his wife. Each time I would acknowledge, even gently, the implication for the relationship, Frank would back off slightly, and both he and Jane would be quick to reassure the group of the positive nature of their communications.

It is not unusual for group members to use the early sessions to raise "near" problems in a way that presents them as issues and at the same time defends them from discussion. This is in part an expression of the member's ambivalence to deal with real concerns. It is also necessary for the group members to test the reaction of a group leader and the other members. Group members often feel it would be unwise to rush right in until they know how their feelings and thoughts are going to be treated, whether they will be met with support or confrontation, and whether it is OK to share their real feelings and concerns.

Not only are the group members worried about the leader and the other members, but they are also concerned about their partners. Each of the couples has developed a "culture" in their marriage that has included certain norms, behaviors, taboo areas, rules for interaction, and so on. The group will in many ways be a place for them to learn how to change that culture, or at least those parts of it that are not conducive to strengthening their marriage. With so many factors to consider, however, it is not unusual for group members to come close to a concern while watching to see how the partner, the other group members, and the group leaders will react. Timing is important in a first session, and it would therefore be a mistake for a group leader to confront and to attack defenses at a point when the group member needs them.

PRACTICE POINTS As Frank began to describe his efforts to deal with the children about this issue of privacy, I suggested that we might use this as an example of one of the ways in which the group members might help each other: (Speaking to the group) "Perhaps we can use this as an example of how we can be helpful. Frank can describe the conversation he had with his son, and the rest of the group members might respond by suggesting how they would have reacted if they had been the son. We could do some thinking with Frank about how he might handle this kind of an issue." The group members agreed, and Frank went into some details of a conversation in which he sarcastically implied to the son that they needed some privacy. After a number of group members supported his right to privacy, the co-leader pointed out that it would be difficult to take his comments seriously because he always seemed to be joking as he described things and never seemed as if he could really get angry. This triggered a response on the part of his wife, Jane.

> **JANE:** Aha! That's it exactly. Frank has trouble getting angry. Ever since he has been a kid, he has been afraid to be direct and angry with people. I keep telling him,

why don't you let yourself get angry and blow off steam? He says that he feels that it is just not the thing to do. You just don't do it. I do it all the time. I didn't use to, but now I do, and I get angry at least a couple of times a day.

FRANK: You know the kids are scared of you because you get angry so much.

LEADER: (Noticing that Sally appears to want to say something) Go ahead, Sally, get in.

SALLY: (Laughing as she speaks to Frank) You've got to meet my Len (the absent husband)! (The whole group, including Frank, erupted in laughter.) You sound like two of the same kind, and you're hard to live with.

LEADER: Frank, what made it hard for you to speak seriously to your son right then?

FRANK: I don't know. Well, you know the image of a stepfather like in the fairy-tale books, he is like a monster. I've got a nice thing starting to build with these boys, and I don't want to ruin it.

LEADER: You are afraid they would get angry if you were direct and honest.

JANE: (Laughing, but with a touch of anger) It's all up in your head.

LEADER: You know, Jane, I think Frank really is worried about that.

FRANK: I do worry about that. I really do.

In response to the leader's question, "What are you afraid might happen?" Frank goes on to describe the relationship the children had with Jane's former husband, of some of his fears of being unable to prevent the continuation of the same coldness and the problems that he envisioned in that relationship.

FRANK: It was because I didn't want to hurt that relationship that I more or less symbolized what I really meant.

LEADER: You kind of hinted at what you felt rather than saying it directly.

FRANK: Well, it's like you are in a washroom and you saw a fellow peeing on the floor. You would probably say, "Hey, you missed, fella." (Group members and leaders roar with laughter at his story.)

Frank went on to describe how he finally had to speak directly with the son. He described, much to his wife's surprise, a very direct conversation in which he explained the problem to the son. Frank's point was that since that time, the son had been much more understanding about not interrupting.

Lou the Internal Leader: How Do We Handle Anger in Our Relationships?

At this point in the group session, Lou, who had been listening intently, moved in and took responsibility for the group process. In a striking illustration of internal leadership at an early stage in the group development, Lou moved directly from the general discussion of anger and indirect communication to the implications for each couple. The leader had noticed during the discussion that on a number of occasions Lou had attempted to whisper to his wife, Rose, and to ask her a question, but she had refused to respond, instead remaining impassive and expressionless.

PRACTICE POINTS

Lou now used the group and this theme to deal with his concern—a concern that was common to all members. I believe that he was able to make this direct intervention and assume some leadership responsibility in the group because the way had been cleared through our earlier discussion of the leader's role. This was an example of Lou accepting my invitation for the group members to begin to own their own group.

LEADER: (Noting Lou's indirect communication of his desire to get into the discussion) Were you going to say something, Lou?

LOU: Something has come up here which I would like each couple in turn to answer if they can. (Turning to John, he asks his name, which John gives him.) I would like each couple to add to this in turn if they can. John, do you get really mad at Louise? I mean really mad, peed off? Do you yell at her—do you tell her off?

JOHN: Not really.

LOU: Why not?

JOHN: That's my style; that's the way I have been all my life.

LOU: Louise, how about you?

LOUISE: I'll probably hold back until as long as possible and then usually end up to where I'm in tears, or slam cupboards or dishes, or give John a cold shoulder rather than coming right out and saying that I'm angry. (As Louise is speaking, Lou is nodding and saying yes.)

LOU: Why? By the way, I am referring to Rose and myself right now when I'm asking this question, and I want to hear from everyone.

JOHN: It happens sometimes, but it is really rare that we actually yell at each other. (Louise nods her head, agreeing.)

LOU: Are you afraid to get angry, either one of you?

JOHN: I don't think I'm afraid. I don't have a problem yelling at other people. It's kinda strange. I don't know why.

LOU: How about you, Frank and Jane?

Jane and Frank both discussed her getting angry regularly, blowing her top all the time. She indicated that it worried her. Frank said he had trouble getting angry directly at Jane and gave an example of her not sharing her load of chores (they are both working); he had been getting angry at that because it was setting a bad example for the kids, but he had not told her. He paused when he said that, and then said, "I guess I hadn't said that to you until tonight."

As the conversation went on, I was monitoring the members, making sure they were involved and paying attention. Occasionally I would comment on some of the feelings associated with the comments.

LOU: (Directly to Jane) You have no aversions about getting mad, I mean spontaneously mad?

JANE: What other way is there to get mad?

LOU: You don't build anything up and then have it boil over?

JANE: Not anymore, not now.

PRACTICE POINTS

For a novice leader, the fact that Lou had actually taken an internal leadership role in the group and was providing direction for the discussion would have been disconcerting. From my perspective, it was a process that indicated to me that the group was off to a great, and unusually quick, start. After a pause, the leader turned to Lou and said, "Stay with it." Lou responded, "Fine, because something is happening here that happens to us [pointing to his silent wife, Rose], and I would like to hear from everyone in the group on this." At that point he asked Fran, who had declined to speak thus far, if she got mad.

FRAN: I hold it for a little while, and then I start and I pick, and I can't stop at the issue. Often I can't even determine what the issue is at the time. Since I can't figure out what it is, I go through the whole gamut to make sure I get to the right one. And—maybe I should let Rick speak for himself—my opinion is that he's quiet. He listens to all of this without a comment back. That really drives me out of my mind. I can't stand the silence. If only he would yell! Even if I'm wrong, then I know I'm wrong. But like I said, I go over the whole ballpark because I know I may hit the right one, since the right one is in there somewhere. There's not much of a reaction, because Rick is the quiet type. He doesn't like to argue or fight. And the quieter he seems to get, the angrier I get. I have to push even harder. It's just recently, the last couple of months, that we've started to fight physically. We've been married for 7 years, and this is just coming out now. Well, I didn't think that Rick had a breaking point and that he could get that mad. And I wasn't even aware that I could get that mad, but I can. I'm the pusher, I'm the one—the things that I could say could definitely curl your hair.

RICK: She basically said it all for me.

FRAN: And that's usual, too.

LOU: (Smiling in a supportive way) Your hair looks pretty straight to me, Rick.

RICK: (Sighing) It's been a long day. Yes, I am the quiet type, and I have a very long fuse, but once it gets to the end, look out. I've done some stupid things in my time, and they usually end up costing me. I guess I just reach my breaking point and take the frustration out somewhere. If it happens that Fran is taking hers out on me, I try and cool it as long as I can, but then I can only take so much of that, and we end up going at each other. That's about it.

LOU: Let me ask you a question, Rick. When Fran is at you like she does, is it that you don't want to or are you afraid of hurting her feelings so that she'll come back at you again and this thing will snowball, or is it that you have a reluctance and you feel you'll let her get it off her chest and then things will calm down again? Which of these is it?

RICK: I guess I'm just hoping that she'll get it off her chest and things will calm down again. But it doesn't work that way.

LEADER: (Turning to Lou) If I can just ask Rick this before you go on, Lou: What's going on inside of your guts when Fran is pushing that way? What do you feel?

RICK: (Takes a big sigh before he speaks) Well, I guess I'm trying to just block everything out of my mind. That's the reason I become quiet, even go to the point of reading the newspaper and just completely try to wipe it out.

LEADER: Because it hurts?

RICK: Right.

PRACTICE POINTS

This is a striking part of the session as Lou asks each couple in succession how they handle anger in their relationship. When I view the videotape of this session with students, they often ask me, "Why did you let Lou take over your group?" They particularly note that I turned to Lou to ask him if I can ask Rick a question before he goes on. I have to point out to them that it is not my group. The students perceive Lou as trying to usurp my role as leader. I believe this view comes from the students' insecurity. From my perspective, Lou is an "internal" leader; and when he starts the questioning, I watch the other members closely and would intervene if they were distressed, but in fact they were not distressed at all. They were responding to Lou, and I was feeling that the group had taken up my invitation to move past the authority theme and to begin to own the group. When students begin to realize what a contribution Lou is making to what turns out to be a dynamic first session, I jokingly suggest I should have set up a "rent-a-Lou" service for their own groups.

Lou continued, turning to Sally, who also described how she saw herself in Fran since her husband, Len, is like Rick, the quiet type. She described a number of similar examples, finally ending by saying, "I don't think I have ever found his boiling point. Heaven help me if I ever do."

LEADER: That must be as hard as having found it.
SALLY: Yes, I guess it is. The problem is that you hoard the hurts, and when you get a chance, zap, you give them right back. The sad part is that I really don't think Len has a mean bone in his body.

Rose Decides to Speak

There is a long silence after this as the group waits in anticipation. The next speaker should be Rose, Lou's wife, who has not said a word or changed her expression during the entire session. She has been watching and listening intently. Because of her silence, her comments at this point have a stunning impact on the group members as well as the group leaders.

ROSE: Well, I think there is a common thread running through with everyone, and part of it is anger, and there may be some recriminations amongst the couples here. Some people have learned to live with it, but obviously, those of us here have not. And no matter how long you're married, it's still something you don't know how to handle. I found that I got very angry here, and I wanted to tell Lou to stop talking about me that way.
LEADER: You mean here tonight?
ROSE: Yes, but I wasn't going to interrupt my husband to tell him that I didn't want him to say that or I didn't like what he was saying. So, I'm back to zero, not just one. I can pack my bags and go back to the hospital. (At this comment, her husband, Lou, flinches almost as if in pain and looked toward the leader.) And I don't feel comfortable talking about it.
LEADER: It's hard even now, isn't it?
ROSE: Yes, but I made up my mind I was at the point where I would pack my bags or talk.
LEADER: I'm glad you talked.
LOU: (His face brightening) Well, I have been thinking that that was about the only way I could get Rose to talk and to burst open.
ROSE: Sure, well, I knew that's what was going on.
LOU: She wasn't going to say anything to me. I asked her during the group if she was mad, and she said she was. I asked if she would say something, and she said no.
ROSE: Right, I said no.
LOU: Plus the fact that what goes on is that all our lives both of us have always been afraid of hurting each other.
ROSE: So, we kept quiet. Or else one spoke and said too much. I always felt that Lou had spoken lots more than I did. Now, I had an opportunity to do a lot of speaking at the hospital for 5 weeks, and certainly I found it helped me quite a bit. I told myself and the people there that I was going to try and remember to use everything they taught me. And there's really no way. Because different things come up and, say, they're not in the book that I went by.
LEADER: I guess you have to write your own book, then.
ROSE: That's right. I'm not very quick on my feet, and I don't think my mind operates very quickly, either. But how to deal with anger seems to be everyone's particular problem. (There is a pause in the group as Rose's words sink in.)

The Ending and Transition Stage of the First Session

The 2 hours have sped by quickly, and it is clear we must wind down the group and bring this first session to an end. My goal at this point is to summarize and credit their work as well as to make the transition to the next session. I also want to start the process of asking them to reflect on the session and provide some feedback to me and to each other.

> **LEADER:** It's close to the end of our session, and I wonder if what we haven't done is identify a common theme and issue that we might want to look at in more depth next week. Perhaps you could be prepared to share some of the incidents and difficulties, because I think if you can bring some of those arguments from the outside into here, where it is a little safer, and where there are people around to help, maybe it's possible to learn to do what Rose did just now without hurting. Perhaps it is possible to say what you are really thinking and what you're feeling without having to store up the hurts. My own feeling is that any real, intimate relationship has to have both some loving and some fighting. That comes with the territory. But it's a hard thing to do. We simply haven't learned how to do it. So maybe this could be a safe area to test it out. Does that make any sense to the rest of you? (Group members nod.) Maybe we could pick up on this next week as something that we're interested in. How do you find a way of saying what you're really thinking and feeling toward each other without wiping each other out?
>
> **JANE:** Is there a way to do that?
>
> **LEADER:** I think so, but why don't we test that out here in the group? If there isn't, though, then I think we're in trouble, because I don't think you could really care for each other if you can't also get angry at each other. Does that make some sense to the whole group? (Once again, there is some nodding in agreement.) What we could do is different couples could bring some examples. Maybe you'll have a hard time during the week that's tough to handle. Well, we could go over that with you here in the group and see if we can find a way of helping you identify what you were really feeling and also be able to say it directly and clearly in a way that keeps communication open. I think this is the way it would work. Even if one couple raises a specific example, the rest of us could learn in helping them with that example. So, you would get something out of each week's session even if you weren't talking about your own marriages.

With a clear contract and some work in the beginning of the session that helped create the safe conditions within the group, group members felt free to begin to risk themselves. With Lou's help in addressing the authority theme, the group members were able to get into the work with more comfort. This authority theme will continue throughout the life of the group, but at least we have made a start in dealing with it.

In addition, the group has moved directly to one of the core issues in marital relationships. What is striking is the way the group members themselves directed the emergence of this theme. Each group is different, because it reflects the strengths and experiences as well as the weaknesses of its members. Lou brought a sense of urgency and a willingness to risk himself to the group that helped it not only tackle the issue of authority directly and constructively but also move past its early defenses into the common concerns they had about their relationships with each other.

Although the particular way in which this group worked during its first session is unique, I do not believe the level of its work or the speed with which it began is at all unusual. I believe it reflected the sense of urgency of the group members, the clarity of group purpose, and leader role. The members were willing to attack the issue of authority directly, and the leader consistently tried to articulate the feelings expressed by the group members, even being slightly ahead of them. Given these core conditions, the impetus of the group members carried them toward productive work.

Wrap-up and Session Evaluation

Now that the session was nearly over and a consensus had been reached on a theme for additional work, the ending and transition phase of this session continued with an opportunity for evaluative comments. I wished in the first session to encourage members to talk about the way the group was working.

LEADER: We have 5 minutes left. This was our first session. I would like you to take a few minutes to share with each other and with us what your reactions are. What are your feelings and your thoughts? How has this session hit you? What will you say to each other on your way home in the car about this evening's session? It's important that you say it now.

ROSE: Well, I have the feeling that the first thing out the door, Lou is going to ask me what it is he said that made me angry. I can't define it right now. I'd have to pull it out of my head.

LOUISE: That's tough. That's really tough trying to figure out what it is that makes you angry. I feel that way, too. When I was an inpatient and someone showed me that I was angry at a resident and why I was angry, well, that was fine; I was able to do a little bit of yelling and get it off my chest. But it's not always easy to put my finger on what it is I'm feeling.

LEADER: Maybe that's what we can do here—help you figure out what those feelings are. (Turning to Lou) What's your reaction? I'm really interested in your reaction because I have a feeling that you came in here thinking about all of the people in the past who haven't been helpful. Where do we stand so far?

LOU: So far I feel that we're beginning to break a little new ground. Actually, the most important thing that happened to me tonight was Rose getting mad.

LEADER: Is it easier to handle it when you know where she stands?

LOU: No, not really, I don't know where she stands. I knew she was mad; I asked her to tell me what she's mad about, but she said no. The reason I am feeling good about this is that she has just gone through 5 weeks as an inpatient, and I can assure you (voice cracking) I've just gone through the same 5 weeks.

LEADER: I think these things change step by small step and perhaps tonight made a beginning. Perhaps if you aren't too harsh with yourself and demand too much, you have a chance of doing it. I am glad it hit you that way. How about the others—what will your reactions be tonight?

FRANK: Whew!

JANE: (Laughing) I think we were so apprehensive about what would happen here tonight it wasn't funny.

LEADER: What were you afraid of?

JANE: Well, I guess it was the fear of the unknown, and yet when we got here, we immediately started to sense that here are people who are concerned, who care, and this came right to the fore.

LOU: Larry, I'd like to make a comment here. Our youngest son is 36, and one of the things he complained about to us was that "You never taught me how to argue with my wife." I wondered where in the world he got the idea that it was necessary to argue with each other. As time went on, I realized that we used to argue and keep things on the inside. My son today is having problems, and he even called me last night on the very same subject. The important thing he said was, "You haven't taught us how to argue." Oh, yes, not only that but "You haven't taught us how to argue and to win the argument." (The group and leaders roared with laughter.)

Other members of the group were given a chance to comment. Frank pointed out that he and Jane were late partly because they were ambivalent about coming. He had been telling my co-leader all week that he wasn't sure whether he really belonged here. As he described his conversations, he laughed along with the other members of the group. They all acknowledged that coming to the first session had been frightening. Frank went on to say that what impressed him was the people in the group; they all seemed to be a really "super bunch," and that helped a lot. Lou commented that it was reassuring to find out that he wasn't alone and that others had the same feelings.

Reaching for the Negatives

After some additional positive comments, I pointed out that it would also be important to share their negative reactions or questions; these were tough to share but were also important. Sally indicated her concern about whether the group would really help, whether anything would really change. She was also worried about her husband Len having missed the first meeting. We talked about this, and I asked the group to strategize how we might bring Len into the second meeting quickly, because he would be feeling a bit like an outsider, having missed this first session. Once again, I was communicating a sense of their ownership of the group and their needed involvement in helping make it work. It was not just my responsibility to help Len join the group in the second session; they had some responsibility as well.

I then told Sally that there were no promises, no sure answers or easy solutions. Marriage is hard work, as she knew, but perhaps through the group we might be able to offer some support and help with their difficult tasks. She nodded in agreement. Fran and Rick responded that they had felt a bit shy and found it difficult to talk in the group. John and Louise jumped in and reassured them, saying that they thought they had participated quite a bit. I pointed out that they had risked some very difficult and hard-to-talk-about subjects in the discussion with the group, giving them credit for that. Rick said that after a week or two, he would probably find it easier getting in; I told him to take his time, that he would get in as he felt comfortable.

The Rules of the Group

As the evaluation seemed to be coming to an end, I pointed out that there were three rules we would follow in the group. I explained that members were expected to come each week and that it was OK to come even if your partner could not make it because of illness or some other reason. I said that material they shared with each other should be treated as confidential so that they could all feel that the other couples in the group would not be talking about them to outsiders. I also asked that if they wanted to drop out of the group at any time before the 23 sessions we had planned were over, they would agree to come back and discuss it with the group before quitting. All agreed that these seemed to be reasonable rules. I then complimented them on what I thought was an excellent start. I told them I could understand how nervous they must have felt at the beginning, since I felt a little of that nervousness, too, but that I thought they were off on some important work, which boded well for our future. The session ended at this point, but people did not leave immediately; instead they milled around talking to other members and the leaders. Then, slowly, the group members left the room.

Reflections on the First Session

This has been a detailed description of the first session of one kind of group. Perhaps the reader will immediately be thinking about some of the differences in the groups he or she has led. For example, these were generally articulate group members. They had volunteered to come to the group session and were not there under the duress of having been mandated to attend. Of course, there are differences between groups depending on the setting, the members, the purpose, and so forth. Some of these are illustrated later in this chapter with brief excerpts from first sessions of groups from different contexts. Nonetheless, the basic dynamics and skills involved in effective beginnings with groups cut across these differences. You will find in our examples that when these principles are respected, they more often than not lead to an effective start. When these principles are ignored, they haunt both the group leader and the group members. First sessions are important because they lay a foundation for the difficult tasks to follow. If handled well, they can provide a fund of positive feeling as well as a clear framework, both of which will influence the remaining sessions.

Returning to the comment made by more than one student after watching Lou taking the initiative in asking the couples about anger in their relationships: The video images reveal my facial expression, which clearly indicates my delight at his moving into a leadership role to the extent that I asked permission to interrupt. I pointed out that the fact that they accepted my invitation to take over in the first session was a very positive sign and an indication of the strength of the group members. This exchange often triggers an important discussion of the fear of an inexperienced group leader of "losing control of the group." It takes some experience and growing confidence for the group leader to realize that the process of "letting go" is central for leading effective groups.

Recontracting After a First Session

Another common student reaction to the videotape of the couples' group just described is to feel somewhat intimidated. As they often put it, "My first session didn't go that way!" I reassure them that neither did my early efforts. Even if the neophyte group leader has done excellent preparatory work, is clear about the contract, and has role-played an opening statement with a supervisor, unexpected events and problems may occur. Retrospective analysis often reveals that the leader has left something out or the words did not resemble the carefully constructed and rehearsed opening statement. New group leaders are understandably nervous leading their first groups and should not be too hard on themselves. They also need to realize that they usually have an opportunity to recontract with a group if they don't get it right the first time. Even if they are able to begin exactly as planned, group members may not hear or understand the opening statement. Contracting in an ongoing group always takes place over a number of sessions.

Another common problem may arise when leaders join an already functioning group and have to recontract around their role as leader and the purpose of the group. Joining an ongoing group as a co-leader and discovering that the contracting was never done or has been done badly can also be disconcerting. One student put it this way: "This sounds great in class, but I don't think the psychologist running our group has ever read your book!" In some circumstances, the ongoing group leaders have adopted a group practice model that operates under assumptions that differ from the interactional, strengths perspective, mutual aid model put forward here. The student needs to be reassured that many frameworks for helping are available, and this group provides them with an opportunity to see another model in action. Also, elements of the interactional model can often be integrated easily into other frameworks. In some examples, there simply is no model at all. Groups can be disorganized, unfocused, with members and the group leaders unclear about the purpose. Group sessions can resemble individual counseling in a group, with each member being "helped" by the group leader in turn. In the second set of circumstances, it becomes the group leader's job to try to influence the process with co-leaders and members to recontract for a more effective group.

Recontracting with Your Own Group

It is usually possible to come back at a later session and initiate the contracting discussion. In this section, we have two examples of recontracting.

An Open-Ended Group for Battered Women in a Shelter

In the example that follows, we see a counselor from a community mental health setting leading an open-ended group in a shelter for battered women. She begins a first session of a psychoeducational group with a mixed message about the group's purpose. In her opening statement, she briefly mentions a number of powerful themes related to the abuse and oppression that have brought these women to the shelter. In her structuring of the first session, however, she moves immediately to her agenda of providing information on "independent living skills." Rather than structuring time for problem swapping, which would have allowed the women some control over the agenda, the leader makes the decision for them. If one applies the oppression psychology outlined in Chapter 1, encouraging these women to take control of their own group could be seen as an important step toward independent living.

A number of group members signal that they are at a different place in their needs related to this group. Although independent living skills, job opportunities, and so on, are all important for these women, at this moment their sense of urgency may be more connected to their abuse and their living situations. The leader continues to control the first session, providing a sermon about the importance of "community support." As we will see, her understanding and skill evolve over the next few sessions as she recontracts with the women.

Session 1

I said, "The purpose of this group is to provide you with some helpful information that you can use once you leave the house. The group will also provide you with an opportunity to talk about your feelings, experiences, and concerns that you might have about the different topics we'll be discussing. Tonight's topic is independent living skills." I went on to say, "Some of you are here because of abuse by either a boyfriend or a husband. You may find tonight that you have some feelings in common with each other. Some of you may be here for reasons other than abuse, and you may have your own set of circumstances that you'll want to share. My role is to help you to talk and to listen to each other. So I hope that we can all learn tonight not only from the material I have brought but also from the comments that we share with one another."

PRACTICE POINTS While the leader has made a direct opening statement, she has not allowed for any feedback or identification of issues that the women have brought to the group. She has her agenda and moves directly into it with a presentation about job training programs. Some members respond, but others have a different sense of urgency and do not connect. The leader notes this but does not reach for the reason.

I began by giving the women information about two job training programs. One woman, Linda, talked about a job training program that she had attended and how she had landed a job afterwards. Two other women talked about the skills they had, one in accounting, the other in word processing and stenography. Four out of the seven women were interested. The other three women showed no interest at all. I didn't ask them why they seemed uninterested.

From there we moved on to the subject of community support. I stated that many people think asking for help is a sign of weakness. People, in many cases, think it's important to handle problems on their own. I said I disagreed with this type of thinking. I said people who think this way are oftentimes worse off because individuals aren't always equipped to handle situations that come up on their own. I said that people who look to their community for support could be better off in many ways. I then asked the women if they had any ideas or suggestions on where to find community support when they leave the house. No one had any suggestions off the bat, so I mentioned places such as churches, local community action programs, etc.

PRACTICE POINTS Although the leader wrote "we moved on to the subject," she should have written "I moved on"; clearly, the members did not move with her. The lack of response to her question is an indication they are not connecting with her information. In the next excerpt, an internal leader emerges to move the women to a discussion of the "here and now" of their experiences in the house and the pain of the abuse they carry with them. Although the information the group leader wants to share is helpful and important, it is not addressing where the group members are at the moment.

One woman said she was very glad to be at the house. She said she came into the shelter wondering what the other women would be like and found out that many of the women were just like her. She said, "It feels good to be with people who have the same problem." She said that when she lived with her husband, he would be on her mind all day long. She would worry about what he would be like when he came home. Before she came to the house, she would stay with her parents when her husband became abusive. Eventually, her parents would talk her into going back with her husband. She said, "Here at the house, you get support. You're told he has a problem, not you." She said she was very glad to hear that. I said, "So it sounds as if you're relieved to be here." She said, "Yes."

Another woman said she used to wonder what her husband would find wrong when he came home. She also said he wouldn't allow her to talk with friends. I said, "You probably feel good that you don't have that pressure over you now." She agreed. In addition, she said she planned to attend Al-Anon meetings for support once she left the house.

PRACTICE POINTS

In the next excerpt, one of the members sends a signal to the leader that the session is not meeting her needs. The leader's written comment about "reaction formation" indicates that she noted the negative feedback and reacted with internal anger and an external smile. The leader's early anxiety about doing a good job makes it hard for her to hear negative feedback. The group members' anxiety about their dependency on the shelter may make it hard for them to share it. The discussion finally turns to money and issues of economic oppression that are closely tied to a major source of anxiety experienced by these women—economic survival.

One woman who had left the group for 15 minutes came back and said, "What did I miss out on?" Angela, one of the uninterested women, said, "Oh, you only missed out on some boring information." I should have asked her why she found the information so boring. Instead, I just smiled at her (reaction formation?). Then Janice, a night staff person, joined the group. Everything was fine until she started talking with the woman next to her. They continued to talk between themselves for about 5 minutes. I didn't know how to handle this situation.

When we started to talk about the area of financial management and I mentioned budgeting, one woman said, "What do I want to know about budgeting? I don't have any money to budget." Then she said that actually she did want to know about budgeting. She felt that someone should have sat down with her at the welfare office and shown her how to get the most for her money. Angela said she was always worried about having enough money to make ends meet, and she didn't see what good a budget would do. Angela has four children, one of whom is handicapped. The group began to talk about how she could get help for the handicapped child with cerebral palsy. The women suggested that she or her social counselor call a cerebral palsy foundation. I turned to Angela and said, "You must get very discouraged at times." She agreed.

PRACTICE POINTS

Chapter 8 focuses in some detail on what I refer to as the *group-as-a-whole*, the entity that is formed when individuals are brought together. Bion (1961) describes an emotionality theory that suggests that in its early state, a group may have difficulty dealing with anxiety-producing emotions; and when faced with an issue such as economic security, one maladaptive response is for the group to go off into flight. This behavior in the group is a signal to the leader. The leader does not understand the meaning of the *flight-fight* behavior in the following excerpt and instead thinks that she will need to do a better job at setting out the rules—a step that would cut off the expression of feeling, rather than dealing with it.

As the discussion continued about financial management, the discussion became some what chaotic. People were talking at once, cutting each other off. The women were skipping from topic to topic. I finally asked them to please talk one at a time. For the most part three women were doing all the talking. I could see that the other women were not paying attention. Next week I'd like to lay down some ground rules for discussion and emphasize the fact that everyone has important comments to make and we should take the time to listen to one another.

With hindsight, the leader might have been able to address the second client, the group, by acknowledging that the discussion was hitting home for all of them. She could have identified the flight behavior—members talking all at once—as an understandable expression of the anxiety associated with the economic oppression and humiliation of being on welfare. These women had to demonstrate remarkable courage to overcome the economic restraints that our society places on them when they consider fleeing an abusive home. Inadequate financial supports function as a societal "shackle," helping keep women chained to oppressive family situations. The leader might have responded to the group with the same empathy she had demonstrated moments before when she said to Angela, "You must get discouraged at times." The leader is surprised when another staff person intervenes with the offer of going to church the next Sunday. There is the possibility that this staff member responded to the flight with what she felt might help.

Suddenly, Janice, a shelter staff person, asked if anyone wanted to go to church the following Sunday. This question was somewhat disruptive because we were talking about managing money at this point. She may have been responding to our discussion earlier about finding community support. It's difficult to say. The discussion became focused again when Linda asked for information about apartment hunting. One woman said that transportation was a big problem. Everyone chimed in on this. One woman said they should write a letter to the governor asking him to supply a car for the shelter. The women got excited at this point. I agreed that it sounded like a good idea, and I asked who would be in charge of writing the letter. Pam volunteered. Janice, the staff person, said they could talk about the letter the next day at the house meeting.

I told them that we had discussed a number of important issues. I said I hoped they would be thinking about questions and ideas for next week's session on single parenting, and said I would see them next Wednesday night.

A Chance for a New Beginning and a Different First Session

The next session described here is the 6th week following a number of sessions in which the leader allowed for more direction of the group to come from the group. As each session proceeds, the leader becomes more comfortable, still providing a structured agenda but letting the group members take more responsibility for the direction of the conversation. Even the members who seemed bored and disconnected become engaged and actually begin to exert internal leadership. Six new women attend this session, giving the leader an opportunity to start again.

I include this excerpt as a way of saying that one can learn from mistakes and grow rather quickly as a group leader if one is open to feedback and willing to be self-critical (although not too self-critical). The leader's continued growth is evident when this session is compared to her first session of only 3 weeks before.

Session 4

This week's group session consisted of six new women. Because of the new group composition, I told the women some information about myself and then asked them to tell me their names, how many children they have, and how long they've been at the shelter. Then, I stated the purpose of the group session. I said, "This group will give you an opportunity to talk and to listen to one another. This is what's called a mutual aid group. All of you here are experiencing some difficulty in your lives because of abusive relationships. This is not an easy time for you. In fact, it's a time of crisis. Because you've experienced similar difficulties, this group session will give you a chance to help each other. As you listen to each other, share some of your problems and feelings, I think you'll learn a great deal from each other."

PRACTICE POINTS Note the critical difference as the group leader moves from an opening statement to problem swapping instead of immediately presenting prepared material.

"In order to get the group discussion started, I'd like you to do some problem swapping—share with each other some problems and difficulties you've experienced in your abusive relationships. If you want to, you can share some of the things you'd like to see differently in your lives now. By problem swapping, we'll find out what your major concerns are, and then the discussion can focus on these issues. There's no sense in having a discussion if it's not about issues that you're concerned with." I said, "Who would like to start?" Joyce said, "My problem right now is that I don't have any money, and the last time I tried to apply for welfare, they told me I wasn't eligible." The women talked about this for a few minutes and tried to offer Joyce suggestions about receiving welfare. Next, Linda said that her life was very disorganized. At this point, she doesn't know where she's going.

PRACTICE SUMMARY The discussion continued going into some detail on their feelings of fear and oppression in the relationships they had just left. I will return to this group in a later chapter with a more detailed discussion of the way in which the women experienced the relationship to their male partners as a form of slavery. The key point here is that the *content* of the group emerges from the felt needs of the members. This does not mean the group leader never provides information, brings a film, or invites an outside speaker. This example illustrates how the contract with a group can evolve over time, and how the group process can educate a leader to deepen his or her understanding of group dynamics, group skills, and the themes of importance to the clients.

Co-leadership in Groups

Contracting issues are complex when starting a new group. They grow more complex when a leader joins an ongoing group that may have been operating for some time without a clear working agreement or with one that does not lead to effective work. In this situation, the new group leader has to deal not only with the members of the group but also with the ongoing leaders, who have an investment in the current status. Students often raise this as a perplexing problem when they report sitting in on group discussions as co-leaders and observing clearly the problems associated with poor contracting, co-leader conflict over the contract, or simply a lack of understanding of group process. Tensions develop as the students read about alternative models and listen in their classrooms to presentations that directly apply to their own groups. Yet, as a "mere student," they feel intimidated about intervening and effecting change. In a situation such as the one in the following example, their stress is increased when the team leader is also of another discipline, which introduces issues of status and power.

The discussion of joining an ongoing group brings us to the question of co-leadership. Whenever leaders raise the general subject of co-leadership, I inquire if they have had experience working with another staff member in a group. Almost invariably they have, and the experience was often a bad one. The list of problems includes disagreement on the basic approach to the group, subtle battles over control of group sessions, and disagreement during the group session over specific interventions—particularly those introduced by a co-leader that seem to cut off a line of discussion one leader feels is productive.

Underlying all of these problems is a lack of honest communication between co-leaders both within and outside the group sessions. Leaders often feel embarrassed to confront their co-leaders outside the session and believe it would be unprofessional to disagree during the session. This stance is similar to the "not arguing in front of the children" syndrome that many parents experience. There is an unreasonable expectation that they must appear to agree at all times. This lack of honesty usually reflects the insecurity of both leaders and often leads to defensiveness and the illusion of cooperative work. In addition, because of the importance of the authority theme in all groups, group members are very sensitive to signs of disagreement between co-leaders, whether they are openly expressed or lurk beneath the surface. My point is that you can't hide the differences anyway, so why not deal with them? Reflective practice, as described in the following section, offers one way to address the issues.

Reflective Practice in Group Co-Leadership

Atieno (2008) cites authors who have identified *reflective practice*, the ability of a counselor to reflect on their personal and clinical experiences, as critical to effective functioning of helping professionals. She cites Miller (2005) as identifying reflective practice in group work as "about helping people to reflect on their experiences of themselves and each other in the workplace in a way that builds insight and awareness so that people have increased choices about action" (Miller, p. 367).

Atieno argues that the lack of reflective practice in co-leadership can lead to many of the problems often experienced, such as "mistrust, competition, power struggles, personal or theoretical disagreements, intimacy overload, envy among co-leaders, and incompetence" (p. 237). The author suggests that reflective practice in co-leading groups involves a number of processes and that it evolves over time, requiring an investment of effort and commitment to the process on the part of the co-leaders. These processes include the following:

- An intrapersonal process: "An internal dialogue in which co-leaders critically and qualitatively contemplate their experiences in co-leader and group interactions" (pp. 239–240)

- An interpersonal process: "[R]eflective practice can be described as a verbal interaction characterized by systematic negotiations and self-disclosure influenced by insights gained from co-leaders' intrapersonal process" (p. 241).

- An evaluative process: "This evaluative function occurs at both the intrapersonal and interpersonal level. As co-leaders reflect on the interpersonal patterns in their relationships and on their interactions with group members, they engage in a process of evaluating the quality of relationships.

This process also involves co-leaders examining their individual performances as leaders, their co-leader performances, and the outcomes of their groups" (p. 242).

The ability to share this information between co-leaders both outside and, at times, in the group itself offers the possibility of an enhanced positive relationship between co-leaders and increased trust, cooperation, and effectiveness. Where it can get difficult, as described earlier, is when the thoughts and feelings are not always positive. If there also is a difference between the co-leaders in experience, training, theoretical framework, or a power differential (e.g., a supervisor and student co-leading a group), then honest sharing of the reflections on practice can be impeded. Many of the same skills required for effective practice may also be useful in implementing a reflective practice model in co-leadership, as will be illustrated in another example later in this chapter. First, however, I want to discuss the potential positives in co-leadership.

Positive Potential in Co-leadership

Co-leadership can be helpful in a group. A group is complex, and assistance by another leader in implementing the helping function can be a welcome aid. In my couples' group, one co-leader was female and a nurse. She was able to add perspectives to the work that were strikingly different from mine. For example, she reacted with a different mind-set to issues raised in the group related to women. Our ability to work well together was based on a number of factors. First, we had a basic agreement about an approach to the helping process. Although our theoretical frameworks differed and we used different conceptual models for understanding group member behavior and dynamics, we shared similar attitudes toward clients and a commitment to mutual aid and the importance of reaching for client strength. Within this common framework, our different conceptual models served, in fact, to enrich our work with the group.

Second, we structured time to discuss the group. We met before the start of the first group sessions to prepare strategy and also met before the start of each session to "tune in," using the previous session as well as any additional knowledge gained from individual contacts my co-leaders may have had with the couples. Time was set aside after each session to discuss the group. (In this case, the discussion took place with a group of students training at the school who, with the permission of the group members, viewed the group sessions on a video monitor.) Every effort was made to encourage honest communication about the sessions and our reactions to each other's input. This was not simple, since I was the senior group leader, and it was not easy for co-leaders to challenge me. As our relationship grew and trust developed, more direct communication was apparent. Finally, we had an understanding that we would feel free to disagree in the group. In many ways, the nurse co-leader and I were to be a model of a male-female relationship in action. It would be a mockery of our effort if we supported honesty and willingness to confront while maintaining professional "courtesy" toward each other in the group. Observing that co-leaders could disagree, even argue, in a group and still respect and care for each other can be a powerful object lesson for group members.

Group members are very observant, and they can pick up subtle cues of tension between leaders, no matter how hard leaders try to hide them. This was pointed out in the midyear evaluation session of this couples' group. A third co-leader in this group was a former student of mine, and although he participated in the sessions until that point, the presence of the other co-leader and his feelings about working with a former teacher inhibited him. We had discussed this concern in the sessions with the student observers, who had been quick to pick up his hesitancy. In the midyear evaluation session of the couples' group, I inquired how the members felt we could improve our group leadership during the second half of the year. Illustrating the perceptiveness of group members, Rose, our member in her late 60s (Lou's wife who had been silent during the first session), turned to my co-leader and said, "I hope you don't take what I'm going to say personally. I think you have a lot to give to this group, and I would like to hear more from you. I don't think you should let Larry [pointing to me—the senior leader] frighten you just because he is more experienced." He responded, "You know, Rose, I've been worried about my participation, too. It is hard for me to get in as often as I want to, and I'm going to work on it." In fact, this brief conversation was a turning point, with his participation in the group increasing substantially.

Skill in Dealing with Co-leader Conflicts in the Group

In this next example, I focus on the work done by a student in a mental health setting as she tries to influence the senior co-leader, a full-time employee from another discipline, into thinking about the group of psychiatric patients in a new and more strength-based manner. It becomes clear to her early in her work that the staff have a perception of psychiatric patients that underplays their ability to work effectively in a group.

PRACTICE POINTS At first, the student responds to her frustration with efforts that are not well received. After some reflection and the writing of an assignment analyzing her work, she develops a more professional sense of how to work effectively with her colleagues. She begins to internalize the idea that the environment itself and its staff are the "second client." Her report begins with her efforts to clarify group purpose with Dr. Brown, the senior staff member.

> When I continued to press at another time for group purpose, Dr. Brown finally asked what I would suggest:
>
> **LEADER:** Well, we could say something like, "This is a place where people can learn how to support each other and how to get along better."
> **DR. BROWN:** Hmm. I think that might be too frightening for them to hear. Schizophrenics have a hard time with relating to others, and they may just get scared if we try to tell them they have to talk to each other. I don't think we really need to tell them anything. We can just make it very general.
> **LEADER:** Like what?
> **DR. BROWN:** Well, we could say there's just so much to talk about, and we don't get enough chance to talk that much, so this is a chance for us to be with them.
>
> I did as he recommended at that point but continued to bring up the topic in future group supervision meetings.

By this point in the process the student was expressing, in class, increased feelings of frustration and anger. She decided to use a written assignment to focus on her work with the doctor, recognizing that influencing her co-leaders' and supervisors' perceptions about the group would require at least as much thought and skill as did her work in the group. This represented an important shift in her thinking from complaining about the existence of the problem to recognizing her responsibility to try to address it. At first, she still had difficulty tuning in to the concerns and feelings of her co-leaders.

The important change in her work, however, was her focus on taking some responsibility for her part in the interaction, which she can control. This is an example of good reflective practice.

I (the group leader) did eventually get some general answers about my co-leader's purpose, but I failed to tune in adequately to the team leader's place in the setting and its implications for what he could feel free to do. In the example above, Dr. Brown gave evidence of an important concern: the psychological feelings of safety of the clients. In the following excerpt, Dr. Brown notes other concerns.

DR. BROWN: I think you'll find that they don't react the way you're expecting them to. If we push them too far, I'm not sure what they'll do.

LEADER: Right. I wouldn't want to push them too far. But I think they may be able to handle some attention on relationships, and then we can see what happens and back off if someone is getting too upset.

The Leader's Reflections

By trying to convince him to do it my way, I failed to really give attention to his concerns or to explore what he thought might happen so that we might come up with some way to avoid it that really worked and that felt right to both of us. Since I wasn't really respecting his concern or trusting that it was a valid one, I was dismissing its importance and missing an opportunity to really tune in, to reach for the negatives, and to show empathy for the needs of the organization as well as of the clients. If I had this part to do over again, I would have asked for more information about his concerns, acknowledged them, and then tried to work with him to solve the anticipated problems. In fact, I did get to do it over again in a later session, and did better at tuning in at that time:

LEADER: I thought it was great how they were able to challenge each other and really interact with each other.

DR. BROWN: Yeah, but I was concerned. Fred seemed to be getting upset at what was going on.

LEADER: Does he have any history of having problems when he gets anxious like that?

DR. BROWN: Yeah, actually he was at XXX (a forensic psychiatric unit) a number of years ago for attacking somebody with a knife.

LEADER: Well, no wonder you're so concerned! I didn't know about that.

DR. BROWN: Yeah, it was a few years ago, but you never know with some of these people.

LEADER: We have never really talked about what we would do if someone became violent in the group. I've had some training in nonviolent self-defense, but what is the procedure on this unit?

Leader's Reflections

We were then able to talk about procedures and about other concerns about what could happen in the group. Again, I think I could have paid a little more attention to Dr. Brown's concerns by asking, "Do you think something like that might happen during group?" rather than by talking about procedures right away, but it did seem at least to acknowledge the importance of his concerns in a way I hadn't done before.

PRACTICE POINTS

It is important that the tuning-in and empathic responses to colleagues be genuine. When training has led professionals to respond with a pseudoempathy (speaking the words without feeling the feelings), an acute sensitivity to being "therapized" can be observed.

This will result in a negative response. In this example, as the student was better able to examine and manage her own feelings in the situation, her capacity for genuine empathy increased.

In the next excerpts, the student describes a strategy she has developed for influencing the team leader. Instead of confronting him with his "deficiencies," she invites him to join her in her own analysis of her work. She does this through the sharing of her process recordings, written for her supervision sessions, which include her own self-analysis of her practice.

> After the first session, I began to share my thoughts on what I would like to be doing in the group with my co-leader via process recordings. I began writing weekly a description of what happened in group, the main themes I saw, my overall impression, and my plans for follow-up, and I gave a copy of this to my co-leader each week. I hoped that if I shared my thoughts with him in a written format, he might be better able to take in my ideas without having to respond to them right away. I also felt that I could show in more depth in these recordings the scope of what I envisioned for the group, and that by giving me a chance to show him the things I would have liked to say, even when I wasn't yet able to say them, he might come to trust my judgment more.

Note in the group leader's comments that follow that she chose to share her concerns and issues about her practice and to invite her co-leader to discuss them with her. She was sharing her reflective practice and asking him to join her in the analysis. An example of what she shared with him follows, from the ninth group session:

Description

Helen started talking about her family and how her children and grandchildren kept her young. She also spoke about her job at the library and specific things she did there. I said it sounded like she really loved her job, and she agreed. She spoke more about this, addressing most of this to me, and I felt uncomfortable that the rest of the group was not being included, so I responded to her several times but then didn't pursue it further, hoping that others would be able to jump in then.

Reaction/Analysis

Not a great strategy, I see now! Perhaps I could have said how I felt and brought it to the group more, or said I thought it was interesting what Helen was talking about and wondered how other members were feeling as they heard Helen talk about her job, or asked her if she wanted anything from the group.

This strategy seemed to work well. When I saw Dr. Brown after he had read this, he said he had enjoyed reading it and looked forward to getting more. We then spoke more about the group and our plans for the next session. Although we rarely talked about the specific content of the recordings, it seemed that giving Dr. Brown the recordings did help him get to know me better and trust me more, and gradually we did come to working better together. I believe these recordings had a major impact on our relationship developing as well as it did.

Current Status of the Co-Leadership Relationship

Tremendous progress has been made in getting the team leader to accept some different possibilities for goals and formats for use with these patients. Through much discussion, he has been able to accept the possibility of their interacting with each other in a safe and empowering way, and, even more significantly, has begun to look at the system practices that work against the patients' being able to function independently in any areas. He has begun seeing possibilities for them to have more independence in the group that he didn't see before, and is showing interest in continuing to encourage that kind of independence. The structure of the group has been pretty well set by now, although the goals and purpose still need to be more clearly stated to group members and to the entire treatment team. There is a lot of work yet to be done, but a lot has been accomplished toward creating more empowering and effective goals and structure.

This example has not only illustrated a recontracting process over time but also the importance of the "two-client" idea, with the agency or setting as the second client. The attitude toward group practice in the setting was a reflection of the general attitude toward work with psychiatric patients. The student counselor was helpful to individual members of the group; however, her most important impact was on the system. Rather than just remaining distressed and angry about the deficiencies of the system, she began to see addressing these problems as central to her role. The effects of her impact on the system would be felt long after she had left her placement. She had also learned that in order to empower the client, staff must first deal with her or his own sense of disempowerment.

When I share this example or another like it, I often hear, "But I'm only a student! Wait until I am a professional—then I can deal with my colleagues, my supervisor, or the agency/setting." I understand the hesitancy, since the student will be graded, wants to pass the field practicum, and wants to eventually graduate. In some circumstances, perhaps unlike the one described here, the co-leader or the system may simply be too hard to influence. I tell my students that I believe it is important to take a next step and at least try. I think, as in this example, skill in having professional impact needs to be developed. The helping professions have become very good at recognizing the strengths in our client; however, we are not quite as good in seeing them in colleagues and the systems we work in. I point out to students that after they graduate, they will still have a supervisor, they will still be evaluated, and they could still lose their job, so that the magic of having the degree will not really protect them. So, I argue, they might as well as start implementing and learning about this aspect of their professional role while they are students.

A Final Comment on Co-leadership

In this example, I addressed the issue of co-leadership with a more senior co-leader. It is not uncommon for co-leaders to both be new to group practice. I believe it is difficult, but not impossible, for two beginning group leaders to work together. Their own anxieties are often so great that they often become more of a problem for each other than a help. Co-leading with a more experienced leader provides learners with an opportunity to test their wings without taking full responsibility for the outcome. When mutual trust and sharing develop between co-leaders, the leaders can be an important source of support for each other. The feelings of warmth and caring that develop between members and between the group leader and members must also exist between co-leaders as they tackle the complex task of working with groups. If a good working relationship exists between co-leaders, even two new ones, they can make the partnership work. Of course, the problems of co-leadership, only partially elaborated in this brief discussion, must be kept in mind.

Chapter Summary

The core skills of contracting in first sessions were examined in the group work context. Clarifying purpose, the group leader's role, reaching for client feedback, dealing with the authority theme, and so on, were all illustrated with a detailed analysis of the transcript of a first session of a married couples' group. Recognition that contracting does not always go well the first time, or that it may take a number of sessions for the group to deal with all the issues, was central to the discussion of recontracting—the process in which the leader raises contracting issues with an ongoing group.

In particular, strategies and skills for developing effective co-leadership relationships were discussed with the "reflective practice" model shared as one example. This was illustrated in an example where a student co-leader's ability to engage in a form of reflective practice with a senior staff member from another discipline had an important impact on group practice.

Related Online Content and Activities

For learning tools such as glossary terms, InfoTrac® College Edition keywords, links to related websites, and chapter practice quizzes, visit this book's website at **www .cengage.com/counseling/shulman.**

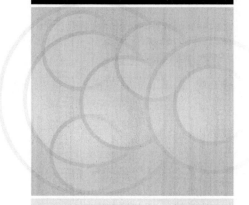

The Middle Phase of Group Counseling

The Middle or Work Phase in Group Counseling

In this chapter, I will return to the idea of the impact of time on our practice, applying the idea of the "stages" of work—preliminary, beginning, middle, and ending/transitions—to a single group counseling session. Just as looking at group counseling against the backdrop of time helps us understand the process over the life of the group, using the same backdrop for a single session is also revealing.

We begin in this chapter with a focus on the group leader's role. As pointed out in the previous chapter on beginnings and contracting, although strategies, interventions, and specific skills are important, they all need to be guided by the group leader's sense of role or function in the group. "What is my job in the group?" is the core question. There may be a range of views in response to this question, and some believe the "role" changes depending on the group's purpose, but I will argue that the core job does not change—it is only elaborated differently. I also believe that being clear about role and being able to implement it consistently helps a group leader deal with the unexpected events that always emerge in the life of the group.

In addition to the other responsibilities required in leading groups, a focus will be on how the leader helps individuals present their concerns and issues to the group and simultaneously assists the group members to respond. Once again I will be suggesting and illustrating the way in which indirect communications require the group leader to listen and understand what members of the group or the group-as-a-whole may be saying. In addition to helping individuals reach out to the group, I will focus on how the group leader helps the group respond and be helpful.

While the focus of this chapter is on the dynamic individual-group interaction, it is important to recognize that both the individual and the group require further detailed examination. In Chapter 7, I will analyze the individual's role in a group (e.g., scapegoat, monopolizer, gatekeeper), and in Chapter 8, I will concentrate on the group-as-a-whole.

Although most of the examples in this chapter address one form of counseling group or another, the model presented can just as easily be applied to any form of group work. In Part 2, when we will explore the variations on the theme introduced by setting and type of group (psychoeducational, substance abuse recovery, task focused, etc.), the same four-stage framework will help guide the group leader's interventions. All group sessions have beginnings, middles, and endings, and preparation for a group meeting by the group leader, before the actual meeting, is always important.

The Role of the Group Leader

What do we know about communications in a counseling group or, in fact, in any group? There are a number of barriers to open communication in the helping situation. These include ambivalence toward taking help because of the resultant feelings of dependency, societal taboos against discussion of certain topics (e.g., sex, substance abuse dependency), the member's painful feelings associated with particular issues, and the context of the helping setting (e.g., the impact of the helping person's authority). These blocks often cause a group member to use an indirect form of communication when sharing a problem or concern. This is similar to the use of indirect communications in individual or family work.

For example, members might hint at a concern (state a specific problem in a very general way), ask a general question in response to a presentation in a psychoeducational group that has a specific concern behind it, act it out (begin a session by being angry at the leader or other group members, using the anger to cover up the pain), employ metaphor or allegory as a means of presenting an issue (e.g., by telling a seemingly unrelated story), use art or other mediums (e.g., a child might draw a picture of an abusive parent), or send the message with *nonverbal forms of communication* (e.g., by sitting quietly with a pained expression or sitting apart from the group with an angry expression), or the classic "I have a friend with a problem."

In some cases, the group member may present the opposite of a concern or feeling. For example, a group leader may employ the *check-in* technique, to ask each member to report on any problems or how the week went. A member with a positive attitude and expression might respond, "The last few days have been great, not like the beginning of the week." When (and if) the leader inquires about what happened at the beginning of the week, the story, attitude, and affect change dramatically, revealing the real issue. The indirectness of these communications may cause the group members and the leader to miss important cues in the early part of the session. Alternatively, a member might raise a concern but do it in such a way as to hide the depth of feeling associated with it, thereby turning off the other group members. The leader's function is to assist the group in interpreting individual members' indirect communications.

Reaching for Individual Communication in the Group

Because of the problems involved in individual-group communication, in the early stages of each meeting, the leader should concentrate on helping individual members present their concerns to the group. The beginning of each group session should be seen as a tentative process of feeling out the group, endeavoring to determine which member or members are attempting to capture the group's attention for their own issues, and exploring how these issues may represent a theme of concern for the group. Even in a psychoeducational group that begins with a presentation, members may raise concerns indirectly through the questions they ask. For example, in a presentation to an adoptive parents' group on how children handle their concerns about their birth parents, one member might ask, "Do all adopted children want to know who their birth parents were?" The group leader who asks, "Has your child been raising this with you?" will find that the question was probably asked by the child during the previous week and the parent was unclear how to handle it. In a like manner, the group itself may be approaching a major theme of concern for that week, and the individual offerings may thus present specific examples of the central concern of the group.

Whether the concern originates with the single member or expresses the feelings of many, the leader's efforts in the early stages should be focused on answering the question "What are they (the group members) working on in this session?" As the information is shared, the leader must monitor the group members' reactions. It would be a mistake for leaders to rush in with their own agenda simply because the first productions (comments) of the group members are unclear. Likewise, it would be an error for the leader to believe that simply because the group had agreed to deal with a specific issue or an individual's concern at the end of the previous meeting, or even at the start of a meeting, this will be the issue for the current session. Even if the discussion picks up exactly where the members had agreed it would at the end of the previous meeting, the leader should monitor the conversation in the early part of the session with an ear either for confirmation of the theme or for hints that members are just going through the motions. In structured groups, such as a psychoeducational format, where an agenda for each session may be preplanned and a topic assigned for discussion, the group leader must still remain alert to the possibility that another or a related issue is emerging and must at least be recognized or that the topic presented has generated specific issues or strong emotions.

The important point is that the leader should be aware that even though the conversation may not seem directed toward the group's purpose, it is always purposeful. For clarity of exposition, I will focus here on examples where the early discussion is directed toward presenting a specific theme of concern. In Chapter 8, I will explore examples where the purpose of the early conversation is to raise an issue concerning the working of the group or the leader. In both cases, leaders should be asking themselves during the early discussion, "How does this conversation connect to our work?" or "What is troubling this particular member?" By doing so, there is a better chance of helping the individual relate a concern or raise an issue to the group.

A Group for Grieving Children

The following example involves a group for 10- and 11-year-old children who had lost a close family member. They were referred to the group because of behavior problems in school and elsewhere that signaled their difficulty coping with the death. The group members called themselves the "Lost and Found Group," because they had lost someone close but had found each other (Vastola, Nierenberg, & Graham, 1994). The authors describe how, at the start of a group session following one in which members had begun to open up and discuss their losses, Mark sends a mixed message using paper and pen. He repeatedly writes "Bob," the name of his grandfather who had recently died.

> **CARL:** Mark, your grandfather died?
> **MARK:** I don't want any damn body talking about my grandfather or I'll kick their butt.
> **LEADER:** You sound pretty angry.
> **MARK:** I'm not angry. I just don't want anybody talking about my grandfather.
> **LEADER:** It's very difficult.
> **MARK:** It's not difficult. I just don't want anybody saying that he died. (His anger is escalating.)
> **GLORIA:** Nobody wants to talk about nobody dying.
> **DICK:** Yes, we don't want to talk about that.
> **LEADER:** How come?
> **GLORIA:** That's why he (Mark) is running around. You can't force him if he doesn't want to.
> **LEADER:** Are you saying that perhaps that's what makes you run around—so you won't have to talk about something upsetting?
> **MARK:** Nope.
> **LEADER:** Maybe you feel it's too hard to talk about.
> **MARK:** No, it's not hard for me to talk about anything . . . but that reminds you, and you could be dreaming.
> **CARL:** Yup, you dream for about a week when you talk about your mother, then it takes about five days to try to get over it, but it comes back again and it stops and it comes back again. . . . Nightmares, I hate. I hate talking about my mother. (p. 87)

PRACTICE SUMMARY

Through his behavior, Mark has demonstrated his difficulty in dealing with the loss. The group members move to his defense, because this is their problem as well. The group leader's persistence sends a message to Mark (and the group) that she will not back off from this difficult issue. As she explores Mark's resistance by acknowledging the difficulty and asking what makes it hard to talk about his loss, the members begin to open up. It is interesting how often asking reluctant group members to discuss what makes it hard to address an issue actually leads to their addressing the issue. One can often interpret resistance as the group member or members saying to the group leader, "We need some help because this is a painful area."

In the preceding example, the leader was prepared to deal with the taboo subject of death and grieving—a very painful topic when children are involved. By responding to the behavior only, and attempting to set limits and stop Mark from running around the room, the leader would actually have been signaling her resistance to the discussion. The fight over the behavior would have been a means of avoiding the pain for both Mark and the leader. This is why it is so important for leaders to have access to supervision and support for themselves as they attempt to deal with these powerful issues (Shulman, 1991).

Grieving Adults: Loss of a Friend, Partner, or Relative to AIDS

Another example of behavior as communication comes from the beginning of a session of an ongoing, open-ended group for friends, lovers, and relatives who were grieving the loss of someone from AIDS. A woman who had just lost her son was attending her first meeting. The meeting started with a check-in ritual in which each member briefly shared what had happened to him or her during the preceding week. The new member began with an extremely rapid, nonstop monologue about how busy she had been keeping herself since her son died. She described a daily, hectic round of activity, showing very little emotion other than the hint of an underlying anxiety. She had clearly been in "flight" from her loss during the week and was indirectly communicating this flight by her opening conversation. It was as if she were saying, "Do you want to see how I am coping? Watch me!"

The leader responded by cutting her off after a while, pointing out that they needed to hear from all of the members as a part of the check-in. Later analysis by the leader revealed that he had sensed her anxiety and simply had not been able to deal with it. Had he been able to be honest about his feelings at the moment, he would have shared how he experienced her presentation—being uncertain about how to help, feeling her sense of overwhelming loss, and wondering about proceeding with the check-in. Any or all of these comments might have opened the door for further discussion and expression of the emotion that was under her expression of anxiety.

The group members joined in the collusion, in a flight process of their own. They were at a different stage in their grieving, and this new member's behavior may have reawakened feelings they would have preferred to have left behind. This example also reveals some of the problems associated with rituals such as check-in, which can take on a life of their own when adhered to dogmatically. Instead of providing an opportunity to deal with individual members' concerns, they can become a way to avoid deepening the work. In retrospect, the leader could have acknowledged the indirect communications of the member and raised, with the group, whether they wanted to respond right away or wanted to continue check-in. Either way, acknowledging the feelings underlying the individual's acting out of her pain would have laid the groundwork for dealing with her loss and the feelings evoked in the second client, the group.

A final example from the same group demonstrates how messages can be sent by more than just words. As the group started, the wife of a new couple attending their first meeting sat in the circle of group members, but the husband sat outside the circle by the door. When the leader invited him to join them, he responded, "I'm only here to drive my wife to the meeting." A powerful message was being sent about how the couple was handling the death of their son. The wife was facing the pain and doing the hard work on her own, while the husband was hiding behind his defenses sitting outside the group. This was a first session, and the leader did not directly confront the message or push the husband to join the group. In the meantime, the husband hears the other members dealing with their issues. Members are entitled to their defenses when they begin such a discussion. If the leader, when appropriate, again invites the husband to comment, these defenses against the deep pain of losing his son to AIDS may have been lowered by then.

The emphasis in this section has been on helping the individual reach out to the group. In many cases, particularly when the feelings expressed reflect those held by the group members, the leader's second client—the group—paradoxically appears to turn away from the individual. In the next section, I will discuss the meaning of this dynamic.

Reaching for the Group Response to the Individual

It is easy to see how a leader can become identified with a particular member's feelings as a theme of concern is raised. If strong emotions are expressed, the leader may feel supportive and protective. Not surprisingly, if the other group members do not appear to respond to the individual, a common reaction from leaders is to feel upset and angry. The leader is shocked and surprised to observe group members apparently not listening, to see their eyes glazing over as they appear to be lost in their own thoughts, to watch as two members start to carry on their own whispered conversation, or to witness a sudden change in subject or a direct rebuff to the group member who has bared some innermost feelings. At moments such as these, the leader's clarity of role and the notion of "two clients," the individual and the group, can be most critical. Instead of getting angry, the leader should view the group members' apparently disinterested response as a signal, not that they are uninterested in what is being said but that the theme may be having a powerful impact on them.

The mediating role calls for the leader to search for the common ground between the individual and the group at the point where they seem most cut off from each other. This clear sense of function directs the leader to empathize with the group members' feelings underlying their apparent resistance at precisely the same time as expressing empathy with the individual group member. The group leader must be with both "clients" at the same time.

A Psychiatric Day Patients' Group

The following example is from an outpatients' group for adults with a chronic mental illness. The focus is on family issues. In this fifth session, a member raises her depression on the fifth anniversary of the brutal death of her child.

The group members respond with silence, and the leader intervenes to support the second client—the group—and the individual member.

> At the beginning of our meeting, after group introductions and as people settled into their seats, Joan began speaking. She looked straight ahead of herself, eyes downcast most of the time, and occasionally made eye contact with me (one of the co-leaders) or looked furtively around the group as she spoke. Joan said, "Well, I just want to tell everybody that the fifth anniversary of my daughter's death (the daughter was raped and murdered) is coming up this week and it's bothering me a lot. It always has bothered me. I try to deal with it OK, but I just don't always know how. I get to thinking about it, and the more I think, the more I'm afraid that I'm going to lose it or do something against myself. I've tried to come to terms with it, but it's always hard when it comes around to when I lost her. So anyway, I've made arrangements to use the 24-hour bed (an emergency bed in the center) 'cause I'm too afraid when I get to feeling like this."

Note in the leader's next intervention how clarity of role and the two-client concept directs the leader to respond to the signal from the group—the silence—rather than rushing in to respond to Joan.

There was complete and utter silence in the group. I remained silent for a few moments as well. As I looked around the group, the members too were looking straight ahead, or down at their feet or acting uncomfortable and as if they didn't know what to say. I said, "Wow, that's some pretty heavy issue that you're bringing up. It seems like it is hitting people pretty hard." The group was still silent, and I paused, although, just as Elizabeth was about to say something, my co-leader said, "I'm wondering what people in the group are thinking or feeling about what Joan has just said, and if it's difficult to respond to it." There was a little more silence, and Joan went on, "Maybe I shouldn't have brought it up. Everybody here already knows that this is a problem for me. It's just that I felt so close to her. She was the one whose birth I remember. She was the one, instead of whisking her away and doing what they have to do right after they're born, they put her on me and I felt so much closer to her than the others. I remember it so much better. But maybe I just shouldn't bring it up here."

The group leader picks up the Joan's concern about the appropriateness of raising the issue and responds to her feelings by supporting her effort to use the group. She also helps identify the common ground between Joan and the group, which is the pain of losses of people you care about.

I waited a little and looked around the group once more and then said, "You're talking about a pretty big loss here, and especially with it being your daughter, it's very appropriate to bring it to this group. Everyone has had some losses with people close to them; maybe some of them don't seem as earth-shattering as others, but we all know the experience of loss in our families, one way or another."

Then Elizabeth, who had been about to speak earlier, said, "Whew. That's just it. Thinking about your daughter and the 24-hour bed; that's pretty serious." Wendy spoke up, saying, "Yeah, that's scary. I mean, I've been thinking about my accident (she had been in a car accident a few days before and has a long-standing fear that she may kill herself in a car) and thinking about losing my sons in the divorce like I did. It really troubles me." I said, "So, we're not only looking at family losses, but also at what we do to deal with them and look for ways to cope with them and feel safe."

With the leader's help, the group members revealed that their silence did not reflect lack of feeling or concern for Joan. In fact, it was the opposite, as Joan's feelings about her loss triggered many of their own. Joan was reassured that the group was the place to bring these issues, and she was helped by knowing she was not alone.

As I have described the role of the group leader, many of the dynamics and skills required in individual counseling can be recognized. These comprise the common core of practice skill, the generic element. The variant elements of the work derive from the presence of one of these important systems—the group—and the need for the leader to pay attention to its responses. The next section continues in describing the role of the group leader, this time focusing on other obstacles that may threaten the work.

Reaching for the Work When Obstacles Threaten

In this section, the connections between the process (the way of working) and the content (the purpose of the group) are explored. For example, the flow of affect between the leader and group members—the authority theme—was identified earlier as a potential obstacle to work as well as a source of energy for change. Attention needed to be paid to these feelings; they had to be acknowledged before the work could proceed. This same issue was highlighted in our analysis of first group sessions, when the importance of discussing the leader-group relationship was underlined. In the group context, one also has to deal with the interchange that takes place between the members—what Schwartz (1961) refers to as the "intimacy" theme. Both of these issues, authority and intimacy, are discussed more fully in the next two chapters, but they need to be mentioned now in the context of the middle phase of practice. For example, the process between members may help free individuals to *trust* the group enough to offer concerns in painful and sensitive areas.

Teenager in a Residential Center Raising a Difficult Subject

PRACTICE POINTS

In the next example, a youngster in a group for boys at a residential center wants to discuss a difficult issue but is hesitant about revealing himself to the group. By pausing and encouraging the group to discuss briefly the intimacy theme of trust, the leader frees the member to continue.

> I began the meeting by asking if there was anything that anybody wanted to ask or say before we got started. Mike said, "Well, I have some things, but I am not sure that I want to talk about all of it." I said that Mike wanted to get at what was bothering him, but he wasn't going to be able to do it right away. Perhaps he needed to test the group a bit to see if he could trust them? He said, "I don't know if I can always trust people." Terry came in here and said, "This is our group here, and we can say what we want to. What goes on in here does not go outside to others, isn't that right? If we have something that we want to talk about, something really personal, we won't let it out of our own group, right?" Terry got verbal approval from all the boys in the group. I also felt that Terry was demonstrating the basis of our contract. I said that I agreed with what Terry had said. To clarify the point further, I said that I saw our purpose as being able to talk about some of the feelings that we have around being here in the Boys' Center and that out of this might come family problems, work problems, and questions you may have, for example: What is going to become of me, or am I really worth anything? Steve elaborated this aspect by referring to his willingness to share his feelings with the group.

PRACTICE POINTS

The next intervention by the leader was important. After acknowledging the problem and restating the contract, the leader returned to Mike and his specific issue. This demonstrates the importance of not getting lost in a discussion of process. Sometimes it is necessary to discuss obstacles and to explore them in depth, as will be illustrated later; however, in most cases, the recognition of the obstacle is all that is needed.

Leaders can be "seduced" into expanding the discussion of the obstacle unnecessarily, thus subverting the contract of the group and substituting as a focus of discussion group members attempting to understand how they work as a group rather than exploring the issues and concerns that brought them together. In an extreme version, sometimes called a "process group," the purpose appears to be created just to talk about process with no external purpose. For example, members give feedback to each other about how they behave in the group. The fallacy here is that the members' behaviors are significantly affected by having no other purpose other than discussing process. This often leads to an artificial discussion. This admittedly controversial issue will be discussed in more detail in Chapter 8. In this group, the leader properly returned to the member, Mike.

> After this brief return to the contracting, I asked Mike if he thought he might feel like sharing some of the things he had said at the start of the meeting that were bothering him. He said that he thought that he could talk about part of it. John said that he thought that he knew what it was that was bothering him. I let this hang. I wanted to see if Mike would respond to John or if the others would respond to either John or Mike to help us work on what Mike had come up with. Terry reiterated what he had said earlier: "What is said in the group is for the group." John said, "I think that it is about your family, isn't it, Mike?" Mike: "Yes, that's part of it." I asked John what he meant by Mike's family. John: "Well, Mike doesn't have any parents, and we are all the time talking about troubles with our family, or we always have someplace to go if we make a weekend." Mike: "Yeah, that's part of it. Like I make a weekend and I stay here."

Mothers of Children with Hyperactive Diagnosis

Another way in which process and content are synthesized was described earlier in my discussion of the meaning of resistance. For example, the group member may appear to hold back from entering a difficult area of work, and the leader senses the member's reluctance to proceed. Such resistance was viewed as central to the work and a possible sign that the group member was verging on talking about an important area. The need to explore the resistance was suggested. In much the same way, a group may resist by launching a tacit conspiracy to avoid painful areas. This is often the reason the members of a group hold back in the early stages of a group meeting. Once again, the leader's task involves bringing the obstacle out in the open in order to free the group members from its power.

PRACTICE POINTS

In the following example of an educational counseling group with mothers of children who have been diagnosed as hyperactive, the early themes had centered on the parents' anger toward school officials, teachers, neighbors, and other children, all of whom did not understand. They also acknowledged their own anger at their children. The leader empathized but also pointed out a pattern of flight or avoidance of difficulty subjects, by saying:

> "It is terribly frustrating for you. You want to be able to let your anger out, but you feel that if you do so, it will make things worse." After a few comments, the conversation became general again. I told the group members that they seemed to be talking in generalities again. Martha said it seemed they didn't want to talk about painful things. I agreed that this appeared to be hard. Every time they got on a painful subject, they took off onto something safer. I wondered if the last session had been very painful for them. Martha said that it was a hard session, they had come very close, and she had a lot to think about over the weekend. Lilly said that she felt wound up over the last session, so much so that she had had trouble sleeping at night. I asked her to tell us what made it so upsetting for her. She said that she had felt so helpless when they had been talking about the school boards and the lack of help for children like her own. Doreen said it really wasn't so helpless. She had talked to a principal and had found out some new information.

It is interesting to note that when the leader asked, "What made it so upsetting?" the answer to the question designed to explore the resistance brought the group back to its work. This is a simple, effective, and usually underused intervention for exploring and moving past resistance. When a group member says, "I don't want to talk about that!" the leader's response "What would make it hard to talk about that?" is often all that is needed. As the group member talks about what makes it hard to talk about a topic, they usually find themselves actually talking about it. In this example, later in the same session, the leader picked up on the acknowledgment of the members' anger toward their children and the difficulty of talking about that anger with similar results.

It is easier for leaders to explore resistance if they do not view it as a commentary on their lack of skill. When sensing resistance, group leaders often ask themselves, "What have I done wrong?" This is ironic because in many cases, we sense resistance in the group because we have done something *right*. An important phrase that has helped me explore rather than run from signs of resistance is "resistance is part of the work." If the group is going well and has started to deal with tough issues, then we should expect resistance. If we never get it, the danger is that we are engaged in the illusion of work—superficial conversation without affect. Many phrases can help the group leader explore the resistance: "You are all quiet right now; is this hard to talk about?"; "The message I'm getting from you, all of you, is that you are not sure you want me to stay on this issue; are you finding it too hard to talk about?"; "Every time we get to this issue, you all seem to move away from it; any thoughts about why that is happening?" As pointed out earlier in this chapter, in many ways resistance is the group or group member's way of saying, "Help me out, leader—this is difficult for me."

Avoiding Individual Counseling in the Group

One consequence of failure to recognize the group leader's role as described here— that is, mediating between the individual and the group—is a problem raised frequently by beginning group leaders, particularly those who have done individual counseling. In an attempt to deal with a member's concern, they find themselves doing individual counseling in the group. This is a common pattern in which the group leader provides individual advice to a member within a group setting. Suppose, for example, a member raises an issue at the start of a session, and the leader responds with appropriate elaborative and empathic skills. The group member expands on the concern, and the leader tries to help deal with the problem while the other group members listen. When this problem has been explored, the leader then begins with another group member as the others patiently wait their turn. This contrasts with an effort to mobilize mutual aid for the group member by involving the other members.

After the meeting, the leader worries about having done individual counseling in front of an audience. In reaction to this feeling of uneasiness, the leader may strategize not to be trapped this way during the next session, thus making a different kind of mistake. Vowing to pay attention to the "group" aspect of group work, the leader attempts to do so by refusing to respond with elaborating skills when an individual opens the session with a direct or indirect offering of a concern. For example, one member of a parent group might say, "It's really hard to raise teenagers these days, what with all of the stuff they hear on the radio, that rap stuff, and what they see on YouTube." The leader quickly responds by inquiring if other members of the group find this to be true. One by one they comment on the general difficulty of raising teenagers. The discussion soon becomes overly general and superficial, and meanwhile the first group member is anxiously waiting with a specific concern about a fight with her daughter the evening before.

When trying to deal with individual concerns, leaders may find themselves doing individual counseling in the group; and when trying to pay attention to the group, leaders may find themselves leading an overgeneralized discussion. Both maladaptive patterns reflect the group leader's difficulty in conceptualizing the group as a system for mutual aid and in understanding the often subtle connections between individual concerns and the general work of the group. Schwartz's notion of the "two clients," discussed earlier, can help resolve the apparent dilemma. He suggests that the leader simultaneously must pay attention to two clients, the individual and the group, and the field of action is concerned with interaction between the two. Thus, instead of choosing between the one or the many, often a false dichotomy, the leader's function involves mediating the engagement between the two.

Chapter Summary

In this chapter, we have seen how individuals reach out, often indirectly, to raise their concerns with the group. I have also explored the group's ambivalent responses. The leader's function in mediating this engagement and the importance of paying attention to the process in the group have been analyzed, concentrating on problem areas such as members' reluctance to trust the group, the resistance that sets in when the work gets difficult, or the difficulties involved in helping in general terms, rather than specifically.

We also saw how the group leader needs to work with the individual and the group as they reach out to each other in the beginning stages of a session. We found that mutual aid deals with general themes of concern as well as specific problems of individuals. The examples in this chapter illustrated how groups can move from the general to the specific and from the specific to the general. The last excerpt illustrated the importance of striving for resolution and transition as meetings draw to an end. I have also addressed how to avoid the common problem of doing individual counseling in the group.

Related Online Content and Activities

For learning tools such as glossary terms, InfoTrac® College Edition keywords, links to related websites, and chapter practice quizzes, visit this book's website at **www.cengage.com/counseling/shulman**.

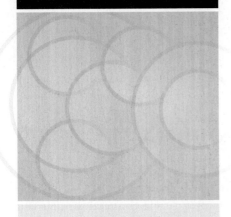

The Middle Phase Skills

During a training workshop, one participant expressed her feelings about the *middle or work* phase in a manner that sums up the experiences of many helping professionals: "I'm good at the beginning phase, and I can even deal with the endings, but I'm at a loss when it comes to what happens in the middle." Following a discussion session with group leaders about the problems of contracting clearly with children, one of the participants echoed this sentiment, saying, "I'm afraid that if I make a direct and clear offer to help the kids with their problems, they might take me up on it, and I would be in the middle phase. What do I do then?"

This chapter continues to explore the answer to the question "What do I do then?" That is, what is done after tentative clarity about the working contract has been achieved in the beginning phase? I have already established the importance of clarity of role in the previous chapter. I shall now examine the processes of the middle or work phase by once again using the time as a background—preliminary, beginning, middle, and ending. In this chapter, I will refer to "stage" of the meeting instead of "phase" to help distinguish between the phases of a group over time and the stages as applied to each group session. Each group meeting can also be analyzed using the model of the stages of work.

I will present an oversimplified model for understanding a single group session using time as the backdrop. I will first examine how the group leader prepares for each session using the tuning-in skill described earlier, but in this discussion it will be called "sessional tuning-in." The idea of contracting is also helpful in the beginning of a group session, but this time it will be referred to as "sessional contracting," with a slightly different meaning than in first sessions. A model for understanding the middle stage of a single session will be shared, as will another that addresses the ending and transition stage of each meeting. My discussion of the sessional ending and transition stage will stress the importance of resolution and transition to next steps or next meetings. Each of these stages and the requisite skills will be illustrated with process record material from a range of settings.

The concept of skill factors will also be shared in connection with each stage. A *skill factor* is a grouping of specific behaviors that have a common purpose—for example, expressing empathy or helping group members elaborate on their concerns. Although the groupings are somewhat artificial, as are their assignment to a specific stage of the session, they provide a structure to help in understanding how the group leader implements the role described in the last chapter. Each intervention is described, and most are illustrated with examples from group sessions. You should assume that the term *member* is used to describe an individual group member, the term *group members* or *the group-as-a-whole* would also be appropriate. (The concept of the group-as-a-whole will be discussed in some detail in Chapter 8.)

Skill Factors in the Middle Phase

The skills of the work phase have been organized into general categories called skill factors (see Table 6.1). A skill factor consists of a set of closely related subskills. The general intent of the leader using the skill is the element that is common to a given set of skills. The name of a skill factor reflects the common element among the subskills. For example, the skill factor called "empathic skills" in this work phase model includes all behaviors associated with the leader's efforts to deal with the group members' feelings.

TABLE 6.1

The Work Phase Model's Skill Factors

1. Preliminary Stage
   * Sessional Tuning-in Skills

2. Beginning Stage
   * Sessional Contracting Skills

3. Middle Stage
   * Elaborating Skills
   * Empathic Skills
   * Sharing Leader's Feelings
   * Exploring Taboo Subjects

   * Making a Demand for Work
   * Pointing Out Obstacles
   * Identifying Content and Process Connections
   * Sharing Data
   * Helping the Group Members See Life in New Ways

4. Ending and Transition Stage
   * Sessional Ending
   * Sessional Transition Skills

The Preliminary Stage

Sessional Tuning-in Skills

In the *preliminary or preparatory stage*, before each meeting, the leader attempts to anticipate themes that could emerge during the session using *sessional tuning-in skills*. A review of the previous session, information passed on by the group member or others, or the identification of subtle patterns emerging in the work can alert the leader to the member's potential current concerns. If a serious and possibly traumatic event has taken place—for example, the death of a member in a cancer survivors' group—one would tune in to the sense of loss but also the members' fear that they could be next.

Sometimes the leader's tuning-in takes place just before the start of the meeting. For example, at the first session of a three-session counseling group for single parents I led in a rural area, a member who arrived early spoke to another member of his difficulty in getting a babysitter in order to attend the meeting. I call this "pre-meeting chatter," which appears to be prior to the start of the meeting; however, if the group leader is listening, it is actually the start of the meeting, and the comments are meant for the leader to hear. The leader also develops some preliminary strategies for responding directly to indirect cues. This involves the use of the skill described earlier as putting the group member's feelings into words. In this example, I acknowledged in my opening statement that one of the difficulties when you are a single parent is just finding sitters so you could attend events like this one and be able to take care of yourself. I mentioned the comments of the early member, and as the session evolved, his very difficult and painful struggle became a major piece of work for him and the group.

The Beginning Stage

Sessional Contracting Skills

In the beginning stage of each session, the central task of the leader is to find out what the group member(s) or the group-as-a-whole is concerned about at the moment. *Sessional contracting skills* are used to clarify the immediate work at hand. As discussed in the previous section, sessional tuning-in may make a major difference in the group leader's ability to "hear" what the member or members are working on. In some cases, the leader may bring up issues that need to be addressed, and these will then be included in the contracting discussion. In a psychoeducational group or information session, an agenda may already be set for the meeting. Because group members often use indirect communication to indicate their concerns, leaders must take care to determine the member's current and perhaps more urgent agenda before moving quickly into the work. An illustration follows.

A Preadoption Parenting Group

In a preadoption information group, the leader might say, "I have scheduled a presentation on how and when to tell your child he or she is adopted. But before I begin, I wanted to check to see if there are also things on your mind you would like to discuss." In an actual example, they do not respond to the leader's invitation, but as the presentation goes on, the group leader picks up indirect cues that a major concern for them is how they will be judged as appropriate or not appropriate adoptive parents.

Until that discussion surfaces, one can see the group members saying what they think the group leader wants to hear, creating what I have called an "illusion of work," rather than saying what they really think and feel. When the group leader picks up the cues to this concern, and the members are reassured that if they made it this far, they are considered to be good candidates, they get to the hardest questions for the couples: "How do I know if the child will love me?" and "How do I know if I will be able to love this child?" Once sessional contracting is clear, the work is both moving and powerful as group members address their real issues related to their ambivalence about adoption. The group leader needs to reassure them that these feelings and concerns are normal and do not eliminate them as prospective adoptive parents.

The Middle Stage

When the sessional contract has been tentatively identified, the process shifts into the middle stage of the session. A priority in this stage is the leader's use of elaboration skills to help the group member or members tell their story. Empathy skills encourage the sharing of the affective part of the message. The leader must also be ready to share his or her feelings, in a professional manner and as spontaneously as possible. Because many concerns touch on taboo areas, the leader must be ready to help members overcome social norms that often block free discussion and to explore taboo feelings.

As the work progresses, it is not unusual to encounter some *resistance* from the group member or members, who are often of two minds about proceeding. One part of the person is always reaching out for growth and change, but another part is pulling back and holding on to what is comfortable and known. This ambivalence often emerges just as the work in the session starts to go well. It can be seen in evasive reactions (e.g., jumping from one concern to another), defensiveness, expressions of hopelessness, or other forms.

The leader needs to realize that resistance is a normal part of the work. Leaders often assume that group member resistance is a sign that the leaders have done something wrong. Ironically, just the opposite is often true. Lack of resistance may mean that the leader has not pushed hard enough; resistance is often a sign that the leader is doing something right. If you think of resistant behavior as the member's way of communicating that there is a difficult area to face, hard emotions to experience, a problem with taking responsibility for behavior, and so forth, you will welcome resistance rather than fearing it.

It's almost as if the group member or members are saying, "Look here, group leader. We are getting close to a tough area, and I need your help to explore what makes it tough." In the framework presented in this book, a premium is placed on *exploring resistance*, or the leader's ability to identify and discuss this resistance with the group member, which includes making a demand for work that can help the group member prepare to take the important next steps. Some other practice models suggest "rolling with," "circumventing," or simply "avoiding" areas that create resistance. In most cases, I disagree. Although I agree that timing is important—for example, respecting resistance in the early stage of work before a solid relationship is established—I believe it is a mistake to avoid it in the work or middle phase of practice. Such avoidance can lead to the *illusion of work*, in which the group member says what he or she thinks the leader or other members wants to hear. It also means that the issues, concerns, and feelings signaled by the resistance remain unexpressed, unexplored, and unresolved. A group leader's unwillingness to explore resistance may be a result of not understanding its importance in the process or the leader's own conscious or unconscious reluctance to deal with the difficult area.

Flow of Affect Between the Group Members and the Leader(s)

As the middle or work stage proceeds, obstacles may emerge that frustrate the member's efforts on his or her own behalf. For example, the flow of feeling between the group member and the leader may itself become an obstacle. As the leader makes demands for work, the group member may react to the leader, and this reaction in turn will affect the working relationship. Leaders and members must pay attention to such obstacles as they emerge. Because the leader–group member relationship resembles the member's other relationships, discussion of such obstacles can contribute to the member's understanding of his or her larger concerns. These obstacles are usually brought to light when the leader notices patterns in the work.

Another skill is called *identifying process and content connections*. The central idea underlying this category is that the *process*, or way of interacting between the leader and the group member, or between group members, often offers clues about the *content* of the work. In effect, the group member may (consciously or not) use the working relationship as a medium to raise and work on issues that are central to the substantive issues under discussion. For example, a group member working on developing independence of thought and action may demonstrate extreme dependence on the leader. It is as if the group member is saying, "Do you want to see what my problem around dependence and independence is all about? Watch me!"

In exploring the middle stage of a single session, let us return now to the skill factors introduced earlier and describe the specific interventions that are clustered under a factor, illustrating their use with examples from a range of settings, populations, and problems.

Elaborating Skills

The following skills are useful in helping group members tell their story and move from the initial offering to deepen our understanding of their issues:

- Containment
- Focused listening
- Questioning
- Reaching inside silences
- Moving from the general to the specific

Containment

As group member or members begin to tell their stories, group leaders too often attempt to "help" before the whole story is told. This is especially true for people who are new to helping; the desire to help is so strong that they will often rush in with unhelpful suggestions that are not directed at the group member's actual concerns. The elaborating skill of *containment* is an interesting one, because it suggests that not acting—that is, a group leader's ability to contain him- or herself—is an active intervention. As someone who grew up in New York City, I was used to a pattern of social communication in which one might begin to speak even before the other person had finished. Containment was thus an important skill to learn in my own professional development.

This skill should not be confused with remaining silent in the face of silence (discussed later). The group leader can be very active; however, the injunction is against jumping in with solutions or answers before the leader really knows the problem or questions.

Focused Listening

Listening is something we do all the time; however, *focused listening* involves attempting to concentrate on a specific part of the member's message. I discussed earlier how complex even the simplest interchange of *human communication* can be. In complex communications at the beginning of sessions, the group leader must focus on whatever the member or group is working on at that particular moment. By listening to the early communications with this purpose in mind, the group leader has a better chance of hearing the message.

A simple analogy is the difficulty of hearing two simultaneous conversations at a crowded social event. If one listens in a general way, all one hears is a loud buzz. If one attempts to focus on one particular conversation, however, it begins to stand out clearly, and the buzzing noise recedes. Similarly, when one is driving at night in a rural area, sometimes two radio stations are heard at once. The driver must tune in to one station and tune out the other in order to really hear anything. In the same way, the "noise" of the member's early communications may make it difficult for the group leader to understand the single strand that represents the basic concern. Focused listening—directed toward determining the concern—often makes the theme stand out clearly. More specifically, focused listening with the purpose of the group clearly in mind or the special purpose of the session will allow the leader to hear content that might otherwise be missed.

A common mistake a group leader makes is to take control of the session when he or she does not immediately understand the meaning of the communication. In effect, a group leader may answer a question before he or she actually knows what the question really is. Focused listening involves an attempt to hear the communication as the member's effort to work, and to search for the connections when they are not apparent. The group leader can ask for the member's help. For example, "Could you help me connect this discussion with the concern you raised about your daughter at the start of the meeting?" Group members will often be able to do so, either immediately or after some reflection. They do not get the opportunity if the group leader has already decided they are simply not working and more group leader activity is needed.

Group leaders often ask me how to handle a situation in which there is no real connection and the member evades work by changing the subject. Focused listening will clarify this as well. The member is actually working by avoiding the work; this may sound contradictory, but the member is signaling resistance to a particular topic—perhaps because it is too painful or embarrassing—and this resistance is what the group leader should hear and address. Once again, the *resistance is part of the work* if the group leader hears it for what it is: a call for help in facing difficult issues.

Questioning

Questioning in the elaboration process involves requests for more information about the nature of the problem. As a fledgling high school journalist, I was encouraged to answer the "five Ws" early in my articles: the who, what, when, where, and why of the story. These are useful areas for exploring the details of a member's concern. For example, in an earlier illustration with the mother and daughter, I left the process at the point where the member responded to the group leader's effort to move from the general to the specific by describing a fight with her daughter.

In the next part of the group session, we can see that the group leader's questions are designed to elicit more detail about what happened during the encounter.

> **MEMBER:** I had some row last night when Sue came home at 2:00 a.m.
> **GROUP LEADER:** What happened?
> **MEMBER:** She had told me she was going to a movie with a friend, but when she didn't get home by 11:00, I was really worried.
> **GROUP LEADER:** You were afraid something might have happened to her?
> **MEMBER:** Well, you know I have had some problems in the neighborhood with men.
> **GROUP LEADER:** What did you say to Sue when she came home?
> **MEMBER:** I let her have it good. I told her she was irresponsible and that I was going to keep her home for 2 weeks.
> **GROUP LEADER:** What did she say back to you?

As the conversation proceeded, the group leader helped the member elaborate on the details of the interaction and share these with the other group members. A term to describe this process between group leader and member is *memory work*, in which the member reaches back into her memory to recall the incident. In other situations, the group leader may aim her questions at getting a fuller picture of the member's concern.

Reaching Inside Silences

Silence during a group session may be an important form of communication, and thus *reaching inside silences* is a critical skill for the group leader. The difficulty with silences is that it is often hard to understand exactly what the member is "saying." In one situation, the member or all of the group members may be thinking and reflecting on the implications of the conversation. In another, a discussion may have released powerful emotions that are struggling to surface. The members may be at the critical point of experiencing suppressed and painful feelings. Silence can indicate a moment of ambivalence as the member pauses to decide whether to plunge headlong into a difficult area of work. This is not uncommon when the conversation deals with an area generally experienced as taboo. Silence may also signal that the group leader's preceding response was off base in relation to the member's expressed concern. The group leader has "missed" the member, and the silence is the member's polite way of saying so. Finally, the member may be angry with the group leader. Frequent silence in a group session may reflect a systematic attempt to express this anger passively by withholding involvement.

Because silences carry a variety of meanings, the group leader's response must vary accordingly. An important aid is the group leader's own set of feelings during the silence. For example, if the silence represents the emergence of difficult feelings, the group leader may have anticipated this reaction based on the content of the conversation or from the nonverbal communications the member sent. Posture, facial expressions, and bodily tension all speak loudly to the observing group leader and can trigger empathic responses. As such, the group leader may experience the same emergence of feeling as the member. At moments like this, the group leader can respond to silence with silence or with nonverbal expressions of support. All of these responses offer some support to the member while still allowing time to experience the feelings.

If the group leader senses that the member is thinking about an important point of the discussion or considering a related problem, responding with a brief silence allows the member room to think. Silence demonstrates respect for the member's work. However, a problem can arise if the group leader maintains the silence for too long. Silence can also be particularly troublesome if the group leader does not understand it or if it is used to communicate either a negative reaction or passive resistance. In such cases, the members may experience the silence as a "battle of wills." What started as one form of communication may quickly change to a situation in which the members are saying, "I won't speak unless you speak first." In this battle, both the group leader and members always lose. The skill of reaching inside the silence matters most during these kinds of silences.

This skill involves attempts to explore the meaning of the silence. For example, the group leader who responds to a silence by saying, "You've all grown quiet in the last few moments. What are you thinking about?" is encouraging the member or members to share their thoughts. In another case, the group leader could try to articulate what the silence may mean. For example, the member who hesitates as he describes a particularly difficult experience might be offered this response: "I can see this is hard for you to talk about." Once again, the group leader's own feelings guide her or his attempts to explore or acknowledge the silence. The group leader must be open to the fact that the guess may be wrong and must encourage the member to feel free to say so.

Group leaders often find silences in group sessions to be difficult moments. They have been affected by societal norms that create the feeling that a silence in conversation is embarrassing, and they may feel that the most helpful thing to do is fill the gap. When one works with group members from different cultures, one is struck by the differences in these social norms. For example, some American Indian group members describe how talking to non-Indian counselors is hard because they never keep quiet. As one Native group member said to me, "The problem with white counselors is that they never stop 'nattering.'" She pointed out that Indian culture respects silence as a time to reflect, but non-Indian counselors continue to talk because of their own anxiety, without giving the Native person a chance to think. In some cases, the Indian member might simply be trying to translate the non-Indian group leader's English into the Indian language and then a reply back to English.

Research Findings on Silence   A more detailed report on my research in this area can be found in Appendix A. I will summarize some of the related findings here. In my early research project on individual and family practice in a child welfare agency, the skill of reaching inside silences was one of the 5 skills used least often of the 27 skills studied (Shulman, 1978). However, another analysis showed it to be the one of the most significant. The 15 counselors (of 155 in the study) who had the most positive overall skill scores were compared with those counselors who had the most negative. The former were found to have more positive working relationships and were more helpful than were the latter. The practice skill profiles of the workers were compared according to their scores on 27 specific skills. The skill of reaching inside silences was one of the three most important skills in which the positive group of workers differed from the negative (p. 281).

Another finding from a separate design of the 1978 study yielded additional evidence that this important skill may often be lacking. In this part of the study, the individual interviews and group sessions of 11 volunteer counselors were videotaped and then analyzed by trained raters using a system I had developed. In an analysis of 32 individual interviews and 32 group sessions, raters scored the worker's or the client's behavior by entering a number that described the interaction every 3 seconds. A total of 103,248 individual observations of sessions were scored and then analyzed by computer. In one analysis, I was able to determine which behaviors most often followed silences of 3 seconds or longer, by pairing each number with the one immediately following to create pairs of numbers and then counting the pairs.

The findings were striking.

- Of all the entries scored, only 1,742 (4%) indicated that a silence of 3 seconds or more had taken place. Brief silences were rare in both the individual and group sessions.

- A 3-second silence was followed by another 3-second silence only 26% of the time. This meant that three out of four times when there was a brief silence, someone (worker or client) responded.

- Raters found that individual or group member comments followed 3-second silences only 38% of the time.

- The worker's active comments in response to silences occurred 36% of the time.

When these ratings were examined more closely, they revealed the following results:

- When counselors actively intervened after a silence, they attempted to encourage elaboration only 31% of the time.

- Their efforts to deal with the member's feelings or share their own feelings in response to silences were noted in only 4% of their responses.

- The most common active action in response to silence was to take the client or the group away from the member's presented theme of concern. This occurred 49% of the time.

Remember, however, that the subdesign involved only 11 workers in one agency, each of whom faced the unusual pressure of being videotaped as part of a research project. My attempt to generalize from these findings to other settings or counselors is tentative; even so, my observations as a training consultant and the findings of the more recent study support these conclusions (Shulman, 1991; see also Appendix A).

Why We Are Reluctant to Explore Silences?   I share these tentative findings with you because they reflect statistically my own observations that individual counselors and group leaders often seem reluctant to explore silences. In addition to the reasons already advanced, counselors have suggested that they often perceive silences to represent a problem in the interview or group session. If there is silence, the group leader must have done something wrong. The irony in the situation is that silence results more often from a group leader doing something right. The group leader often sees silence as negative feedback, even in those cases when it may mean other things.

A group leader's willingness to reach inside the silence when there is a possible negative response is directly related to feelings of comfort in the work and willingness to deal with negative feedback. Understandably, a group leader may be unsure about what to do with the feelings and concerns that might reside within the silence, and she or he may choose to change the subject rather than reach inside the silence. At this point, after the group leader has successfully helped the member elaborate concerns, the discussion needs to move to the question of feelings and how to deal with them.

When these findings are shared with group leaders in training sessions, their reactions provide further clues to the apparent low frequency of use of this important skill. Many indicate that their skill training specifically cautioned them not to put a member's thoughts or feelings into words. They report having been encouraged to only ask open-ended questions and to avoid "putting words into the member's mouth" or "doing the group members' work for them." One group leader reported being told by a supervisor that it was "like tying a member's shoelaces for him." Although these are legitimate concerns, and this is a controversial issue, these repeated findings and my own experience as a teacher and trainer suggest that group leaders make more errors of omission (failing to articulate the feelings) than errors of commission (articulating the wrong feelings).

Moving from the General to the Specific

Moving from the general to the specific has been mentioned in the sessional contracting stage, but it is important throughout the group sessions. Group members often raise a general concern that relates to a specific event. The general statement can be viewed as a first offering from the group member to the group leader. It may be presented in universal terms because the group member experiences it that way at the moment. The general nature of its expression may also reflect the ambivalence the group member feels about dealing with the concern in depth.

In one example, at the beginning of a single parents' group session, a mother stated, "It's hard to raise your kids these days when your mother is always criticizing you." Responding to the general theme, the leader and the group might have engaged in a discussion of changing mores, peer group pressure, drug availability, interfering in-laws, and so on. An example of moving from the general to the specific would be to ask, "Did you have a tough time with your daughter or your mother-in-law this week?" The group member's response in this case was to describe a fight she had with her 15-year-old daughter, who had returned home after 2:00 A.M. and refused to say where she had been. When she chastised her daughter, the girl had called her grandmother, who then called this client and accused her of being too hard on her daughter. This second offering of the concern was a more specific and manageable piece of work; in other words, the general problem of raising teenagers is pressing in our society, but this group member and this group leader could not do much about it. However, this mother's relationships with her daughter and mother-in-law were open to change.

Behind most early general statements is a specific problem or feeling. If the group leader does not encourage elaboration, the concern might emerge at the end of the session as a "doorknob" communication (offered as the group member is leaving the meeting). The teenager in a group who casually comments during a general discussion that "parents just don't understand" may be reacting to an incident that morning. The patient in a community health clinic who mentions to the nurse that "doctors must work hard because they always seem so busy" may still be reacting to terse comments from the doctor that the patient was too frightened or overwhelmed to inquire about. In each case, the leader's skill would involve reaching for more specific information.

Helping professionals have suggested to me two major reasons why they might refrain from reaching for the specifics behind general comments. First, they are not aware of how specific work must be; that is, they do not realize that they can only give help in terms of the details of a problem. One cannot help a parent deal with teenagers through general discussion alone. The learning will take place through the discussion of the specific interactions between parent and child. The group leader can help the parent and other group members develop general principles about her relationship with her children, but these principles must emerge from discussions of the specific events. Without the specific discussions, the group leader's attempts to generalize may be perceived by the mother as theoretical advice. Even in a parent education group with organized lectures that follow a prescribed outline, it is important to explore how the concepts actually apply in specific examples. Some may be given by the group leader and others by the group members.

For example, the parent in the earlier encounter might describe a conversation with her daughter in which she did not share her distress and hurt but instead gave way to the surface feelings of anger. After a while, the group leader may be able to help the group member see how, in incident after incident, she finds it hard to be open with her daughter about certain feelings. The group member may be able to understand this point because of the discussion of specific incidents. The discussion should develop an experiential base on which the group member can build new understanding, a reframing of her perceptions about the problem, and possible solutions. The group member may not be able to do much about changing mores in our society, but she can conduct her next conversation with her daughter in a different way. Lack of understanding of the power of specific discussion may lead the group leader to overlook the usefulness of this elaboration skill. A similar conversation could take place in relation to the mother-in-law.

The second reason why group leaders do not reach for the specifics—even when they sense the concrete problem connected to the group member's general offering—is that they are not sure they want to deal with it. Group leaders in a community health clinic, for example, suggest that they do not reach for a patient's comment about busy doctors because they are not sure what they can do about it. As one put it, "I find the doctors too busy to answer my questions, so how can I help the client?" The source of the group leader's ambivalence may vary, but feelings of ambivalence are common. I believe that, when group leaders feel more confident about offering help, they reach more easily for specifics. In the second part of this book, I will provide examples in which the group leader is attempting to have a positive professional impact on other staff members who have significant interactions with group members within the setting (e.g., teachers) and at other systems (e.g., a clinic).

A third, and less obvious, reason for failure to reach for elaboration has to do with the parallel process between group leaders and supervisors described earlier. Often, a group leader or student raises a question with a supervisor such as "Do you have any thoughts about techniques for handling angry group members?" Unless the supervisor inquires, "Did you have a tough group meeting?" the remainder of the conversation may stay at a general level. If the modeling is sound, the supervisor will always move from the general to the specific, thus teaching by modeling this skill. In turn, the supervisor is aided by having an administrator reach for her or his specific concerns behind the general offerings. My research on supervision of supervisors, however, has indicated that this is rarely done (Shulman, 1993). A supervisor may get general help in a case conference on how to deal with a difficult student or employee, but rarely is the process part of the conversation. It's no wonder, then, that the conversation in an individual or group supervision session often focuses on the case and not the process.

Empathic Skills

As group members tell their stories, group leaders may use a number of skills designed to keep the discussion meaningful by having group members invest it with feelings. Group members often share difficult experiences while seeming to deny the affect associated with them. For some, the experience may be so painful that they have suppressed the emotion to the point that their own feelings are not clear to themselves. For others, the emotions may seem strange or unacceptable, and they are fearful of discussing them with the group leader.

Whatever the reason, the affect is there, and it will exert a powerful force on the member until it can be acknowledged and dealt with. Group members can deal with affect in three different ways:

- Group members' sharing of feelings with the group leader can release an important source of energy.
- Group members can learn how emotions directly affect their thoughts and actions.
- Group members can develop skills that allow them to understand the sensations, accept them without harsh self-judgment, and disclose them to those who matter.

This can be described as the *feeling-thinking-doing connection*. How I feel affects how I think and act, and how I act affects how I think and feel. This interaction among feeling, thinking, and doing leads to the model described in this book, in which a group leader's skills for helping group members manage their feelings takes on such importance in helping group members address their problems.

Taft (1933) was one of the early practice theorists to discuss the power of feelings:

> There is no factor of personality which is so expressive of individuality as emotion. The personality is impoverished as feeling is denied, and the penalty for sitting on the lid of angry feelings or feelings of fear is the inevitable blunting of capacity to feel love and desire. For to feel is to live, but to reject feeling through fear is to reject the life process itself. (p. 10)

Rogers (1961), in writing about his "patient-centered" approach, stressed the importance of the helping person listening for the affective component of the communication:

> Real communication occurs when the evaluative tendency is avoided, when I listen with understanding. It means to see the expressed idea and attitude from the other person's point of view, to sense how it feels to him, to achieve his frame of reference in regard to the thing he is talking about. (pp. 331–332)

As group leaders allow themselves to get closer to group members—to experience group members realistically and not necessarily as group members present themselves—group leaders also give their group members permission to be natural. The acceptance and understanding of emotions, and the group leader's willingness to share them by experiencing them, free a member to drop some defenses and to allow the group leader and the member more access to the real person. The group leader also serves as a model of an adult with empathic ability. The member can learn to develop powers of empathy to be used, in turn, with those who need support.

Expressing empathy with the member or the group can prove difficult for the group leader in many ways. The capacity to be in touch with the member's feelings is related to the group leader's ability to acknowledge his or her own feelings. Before group leaders can understand the power of emotion in the lives of group members, they must discover its importance in their own experience. Group leaders often find it hard to express empathy in specific personal areas. Group leaders are human, and they face all of the stresses and difficulties associated with daily living, including crises. When group leaders hear their own difficult feelings expressed by group members, the capacity for empathy can be blunted.

The group leader's authority over the member may serve as another major block to empathy. For example, a group leader who is a mandated reporter and has had to report a possible child abuse situation revealed in a parenting group may find her or his empathic responses to the parent-member blocked at the time when they may be most needed.

Smalley (1967) described this process as follows:

> The self of another cannot be known through intellectual assessment alone. Within a human, compassionate, and caring relationship, selves "open up," dare to become what they may be, so that the self which is known by a group leader, a group leader at once human, caring, and skillful, is a different self from that diagnosed by one who removes himself in feeling from the relationship in an attempt to be a dispassionate observer and problem solver. As an adolescent girl once said to her new social worker, in referring to a former social worker, "She knew all about me, but she didn't know me." (p. 86)

Because of the difficulty of this skill area, group leaders must develop over time their ability to empathize. The capacity for empathy grows with experience. Group leaders who are open to this development can learn more about life from each group, which will help them better understand the next group. I believe every group leader should emerge from a group experience somewhat changed. Group leaders also learn more about their own feelings and true reactions to the plight of others. Awareness of the sensitive areas in one's own emotional armor will help one avoid the denial or intellectualization of difficult emotions when they are presented. The group leader will more readily allow a member to share more difficult emotions as the group leader becomes comfortable with their effects, particularly those of negative feelings—both the group leader's and the member's—which form a natural part of any helping relationship.

Supervision can play an important part in a group leader's emotional development. The concept of the *parallel process* suggests that the helping relationship between a supervisor and a group leader, or a practicum instructor and a student, parallels the relationship between the group leader (student) and the member. Thus, a supervisor must model effective empathic skills in the supervisory relationship. This is the meaning of the phrase "more is caught than taught"—supervisees watch their supervisors closely and learn a great deal from the nature of the interaction.

In one of my supervision studies, I found that the counselor's perception of the effectiveness of supervision was a powerful predictor of the counselor's morale (Shulman, 1993, 2010). Supervisory skill also contributed to the development of a positive working relationship with staff and to their sense of the supervisor's helpfulness. When I share these findings with supervisors, a short period of silence usually follows. When I reach inside the silence, one supervisor will often say, "But who listens to me?" The appropriateness of that question was suggested by other findings in the supervision study. The skill of articulating the supervisee's feelings—the skill parallel to articulating the member's feelings—was positively associated with relationship and helpfulness on every level of the study (supervisors–group leaders, managers–supervisors, executives–managers).

The three empathic skills described in the rest of this section are reaching for feelings, displaying understanding of the member's feelings, and putting the member's feelings into words.

Reaching for Feelings

Reaching for feelings is the skill of asking the member to share the affective portion of the message. Before proceeding, however, I should clarify one point raised briefly in a previous chapter. This process is sometimes handled superficially, in a ritualistic manner, thus negating its usefulness. The group leader who routinely asks a member, "How do you feel?" while not really being open to experiencing the feeling, may be perceived by the member as not really caring. Experienced group members have often reacted negatively to that repeated question. Of course, what they are reacting to is the group leader's intellectualizing, which is not effective practice. Genuine empathy involves stepping into the member's shoes and summoning an affective response that comes as close as possible to the experience of the other.

With the emergence of technique-centered training programs that focus on developing a patterned response from the group leader, the danger of expressing an artificial response increases. One group leader described how she had been taught by one program to reflect back the group members' feelings with the phrase, "I hear you saying . . . ." When she used this technique in one group session, the member looked surprised and replied, "You heard me saying that!" The reaching for feelings must be genuine, which means the group leader must be feeling something at the moment as close to the member's feelings as is possible. In most cases the group members will know when the leader's expression of affect is real or if it is just a technique. Although learning to use a technique without the associated emotions is faster and easier than learning to experience the affect, it is the latter that has real impact in practice and in life. I often point out to my students that if they feel more comfortable prefacing a statement with "What I hear you saying is . . . ," they should go ahead and do that, but they must actually try to feel the emotion. It's the client's sense of the leader's authenticity that really counts and not the words that are used.

Displaying Understanding of the Member's Feelings

The skill of *displaying understanding of the member's feelings* involves indicating through words, gestures, expression, physical posture, or touch (when appropriate) the group leader's comprehension of the expressed affect. The group leader attempts to understand how the member experiences the feelings even if the group leader believes that the reality of the situation does not warrant the reaction. The group leader may believe that the member is being too self-punishing or taking too much responsibility for a particular problem. Even so, the member may not agree at that moment, and the group leader must respond to the member's sense of reality.

Furthermore, the group leader needs to resist the natural urge to rush in with reassurances and attempts to help the member feel better. The reader should think back to moments when he or she had strong feelings of any kind and someone, a friend or relative, said, "You shouldn't feel that way." All that did was emphasize that the other person really did not understand the power and the reality of the emotion. Efforts at reassurance are often interpreted by the member as the group leader's failure to understand. As one member put it, "If you really understood how bad I felt, you wouldn't be trying to cheer me up."

Part of the healing process includes the members' sharing of feelings with a caring group leader as well as caring group members. Group leaders often express their fear of strong emotions. They are concerned that a member might become too depressed and that the group leader's effort to bring the emotions to the fore could result in more problems. Some group leaders worry that the members' feelings will overwhelm them to the point where they feel equally depressed and hopeless—they would then lose their ability to be effective. For many group leaders, the ultimate fear is triggering such deep feelings in the member that the member feels overwhelmed and commits suicide.

Note that the emotions themselves do not create the problems; rather, group members' inability to face their feelings or to share them with someone important does. The power that feelings can have over group members may be dissipated when these feelings are expressed and dealt with. The greater danger is not in the facing of feelings but in their denial. The only thing worse than living with strong emotions is the feeling that one is alone and that no one can understand.

The group leader's fear of being overwhelmed by emotions can be alleviated somewhat if the group leader is clear about the function and purpose of the engagement. The group leader's sense of function requires placing a demand for work on the member (as discussed in the next section). No matter how strong the member's feelings of hopelessness, some next step can always be taken. The group leader needs to experience the member's feelings of being overwhelmed (the empathy) while still indicating a clear expectation (the demand) that the member will do something about the situation, even in those cases in which doing something means coming to grips with the reality (e.g., the death of someone close) and picking up and beginning again (e.g., searching out new significant relationships). Belief in the strength and resilience of the member enables a group leader to make this demand.

With clarity of purpose in mind, the group leader can help the member find the connections between the emotions and the purpose of the discussion. Significant work with group members in painful areas can be done only after the expression and acknowledgment of feelings. The flow of affect and understanding between group leader and member, and between members, is a necessary precondition for further work. Group leaders who attempt to make demands on group members without first having experienced the affect with them will be perceived as "not understanding," and their demands will be experienced as harsh and uncaring. Empathic responses build a fund of positive affect that the group leader can draw on later. The word *fund* here suggests the metaphor of a bank account to describe this process: I put money in, and then I am able to draw it out when needed. This fund is a buffer that helps the members experience a group leader's later confrontation as a caring gesture.

Putting the Member's Feelings into Words

Thus far, I have described how a group leader might reach for feelings and acknowledge those that have already been stated. There are times, however, when a member comes close to expressing an emotion but stops just short. The member might not fully understand the feeling and thus be unable to articulate it. In other cases, the member might not be sure it is all right to have such a feeling or to share it with the group leader. *Putting the group member's feelings into words* is the skill of articulating the member's affect a half step ahead of the member. This occurs when the group leader's tuning-in and intense efforts to empathize during the session result in emotional associations as the member elaborates a concern.

In a common example when a participant in a mother's group asks the group leader if he has children, when he responds, "I don't have any children. Why do you ask? Are you concerned that I may not be able to understand what you go through as a parent?" the group leader has tuned in to that concern and expressed it for her. Instead of being "behind" the client by just asking how she felt, the group leader was half a step ahead of the client. I suggest a half step because I want to stay close to the expressed feelings and not get too far ahead of the client.

This is a controversial issue in the helping professions. Some advise never to put a client's feelings into words because one might be wrong. Others suggest it encourages dependency. My teaching, practice, and research have all suggested otherwise. I believe we make more mistakes of omission, the failure to risk our hunches, than mistakes of commission, suggesting feelings that are not there. In any case, as stated repeatedly, we can always go back and catch our mistakes.

Research on Empathy

Empathic skills have consistently been identified as important in helping relationships. One of the early pioneers in this area—working in the field of psychotherapy—Truax (1966) found a relationship between personality change and therapist empathy, warmth, and genuineness. Rogers (1969) points to several studies that found empathy to be central to the counselor's effectiveness. In the field of educational research, Flanders (1970) found empathy to be an important skill for teachers in improving student performance. A growing body of evidence following these early studies suggests that empathy is one of the core skills for all helping functions.

In a more recent qualitative study of empathy as an interpersonal phenomenon, Hakansson and Montgomery (2002, 2003) examined the experiences of 28 empathizers and 28 targets through analysis of their narrative accounts of situations in which they experienced empathy. Their subjects were 20 to 64 years old. The researchers focused on the constituents of both the empathizers' and the targets' experience of empathy. They examined four constituents: (1) The empathizer understands the target's situation and emotions, (2) the target experiences one or more emotions, (3) the empathizer perceives a similarity between what the target is experiencing and something the empathizer has experienced, and (4) the empathizer is concerned for the target's well-being. The data suggested that the actions associated with the fourth constituent concern make empathy an interpersonal phenomenon (2002, p. 267). The researchers' definition of the dimension of concern included such acts as "giving time, paying attention, giving the target advice, doing something for the target, being concerned for the target, being respectful towards the target, and performing coordinated acts demonstrating concern" (2002, p. 279).

This finding offers additional support for the construct that describes how skill—including empathy—develops a working relationship with the member. The expression of concern for the member corresponds to the term *caring* in my own research. All of the behaviors associated with concern could be perceived as contributing to the member's perception of the worker as "caring as much about me as my children" and "here to help me, not just investigate me" (Shulman, 1978, 1991).

My own research supports these findings. The skill of acknowledging the member's feelings appears to contribute substantially to the development of a good working relationship between counselor and client as well as to the counselor's ability to be helpful (Shulman, 1978). It was the second-most powerful skill in my research, ranking only behind the skill of sharing the counselor's feelings, which is discussed in a later section. This finding was replicated in both the study of supervision skill (Shulman, 1981, 1984) and the study of the practice of family physicians (Shulman & Buchan, 1982). Appendix A provides additional findings on this skill from my research as well as more recent research of others that generally supports the construct that acknowledging feelings is an important element in helping.

Although there is a consensus that the skills of empathy are important in the helping relationship or "therapeutic alliance," some researchers have suggested that some group members (e.g., unmotivated and volatile ones) would be better served by "therapeutic detachment" (Galloway & Brodsky, 2003). This view suggests the need for research that further defines and differentiates the mechanics of the process through which empathy affects a working relationship and outcomes. These researchers suggest addressing questions such as "Under what circumstances does empathy help?" "With which group members?" and "For what kind of problems?" Additionally, can the helper determine whether detachment would be more appropriate?

Sharing Leader's Feelings

An essential skill relates to the group leader's ability to present him- or herself to the member as a "real" human being. Theories of the helping process that follow the medical paradigm have presented the ideal group leader as an objective, clinical, detached, and knowledgeable professional. In these models, *sharing the group leader's feelings* is considered unprofessional. A concept of professionalism has resulted that asks the group leader to choose between the personal and the professional self. I believe this is another of the many false dichotomies that plague our practice; the real skill lies in integrating the personal and the professional.

Integrating the Personal and the Professional

One participant illustrated the effect of the personal/professional dichotomy in one of my training workshops. She described her counseling work with a woman who had just discovered that her child was dying of cancer. As the woman spoke, grief overcame her and she began to cry. The counselor felt compassion and found herself holding the woman's hand with tears in her eyes. Her supervisor, passing by the open door, criticized her for her "unprofessional" behavior. When I asked what she had learned from the experience, she replied, "I learned to keep my door closed." This comment led to a discussion in the workshop where I suggested the counselor needed to impact on her health care setting since it was clear that there was no built-in support for doctors, nurses, supervisors, and counselors that helped them deal with their own feelings when faced so often with death and dying issues related to children and parents.

My view is that the counselor was helping at that moment in one of the most important and meaningful ways I know. She was sharing the pain with the member, and, in expressing her own sorrow, she was making a gift of her feelings to the member. This counselor was responding in a deeply personal way, yet, at the same time, she was carrying out her helping function. The interactional practice theory suggests that the helping person is effective only when able to synthesize real feelings with professional function. Without such a synthesis of personal and professional, the group leader appears as an unspontaneous, guarded professional who is unwilling to allow group members access to the group leader's feelings.

The irony is apparent: The group leader asks group members to take risks and to be open, honest, and vulnerable in sharing feelings, while—in the name of professionalism—he or she is doing just the opposite. The result is often the "mechanical" group leader who always maintains self-control, who has everything worked out, and who is never at a loss for words or flustered—in short, a person who is difficult to relate to in any helpful way.

Group members do not need a perfect, unruffled group leader who has worked out all of life's problems. They require someone who cares deeply about the group members' success, expresses the group members' own sense of urgency, and openly acknowledges feelings. When group members experience the group leader as a real person rather than an automaton, they can use the group leader and the helping function more effectively. If the group leader shows no signs of humanity, the member will either constantly test to find the flaws in the facade or idealize the group leader as the answer to all problems. The member who does not know at all times where the group leader stands will have trouble trusting that group leader.

Remember the argument put forth earlier: A sound approach must be an integration of the personal and professional, and counselors need to guard against inappropriate expressions of emotions. Clarity of purpose of the group and the role of the group leader will be helpful in understanding these boundaries.

When the Group Leader Is Angry with the Member

If the group leader is angry with the member, it is much better to get the anger out in the open where it can be dealt with honestly. I realize this approach is controversial. Group leaders who fear the expression of angry feelings as signs of their own "aggressiveness" often suppress them, only to have them emerge indirectly through passive aggression in ways to which the group member finds it harder to respond. Professional expressions of anger—for example, through an unfeeling interpretation of a member's behavior—can be more hurtful than an honest statement of the feeling. A key factor is whether the anger is coming from caring or from the group leader's own frustrations. When it's the second, then an apology is in order.

Direct expression of feelings is as important for the group leader as it is for the member. A group leader who suppresses feelings must use emotional energy to do so. This energy can be an important source of help to the member if it is freed for empathic responses. The group leader cannot withhold his or her feelings and experience those of the member at the same time. The group leader may also become cut off from important forms of indirect communication in which the member uses the group leader's feelings to express his or her own. The concept of *projective identification* (Bion, 1961) will be discussed in more detail in Chapter 8 when we consider a number of group theories. For now, Bion suggests that a group or its members may project their own emotions onto the group leader. For example, if they feel defensive, they may make the leader feel the same way as a form of indirect communication. The members may not be aware of this process. If leaders are ignoring their own feelings, they may be missing an important message.

Consider the following example of this process, which comes from the 19th session of my married couples group described in earlier chapters (and in detail in Chapter 16). The couple had come close to breaking up the previous week, but because the group had agreed to deal with another couple's problem this session, the wife raised her concerns indirectly. At one point, she began to share in an intellectual manner that completely avoided the expression of any emotion and was a sign of resistance. After listening for a while, I finally confronted her, with mildly angry, perhaps better described as exasperated, affect in my voice that challenged this illusion of work as a way of continuing to avoid dealing with the painful feelings between them. It's important to note that this was in the 19th session and long after I and my co-leaders had built that fund of caring in our relationship mentioned earlier. (In addition to the frustration with the member, I had recently broken my thumb, and the painkiller was wearing off during the session.)

My expression of my feelings broke through her intellectualizing and freed my energy to respond to the member's feelings. She immediately moved to an affective level; and in what became an important turning point in the work of the couple, and the group, she responded to my pointing out that she had an angry expression on her face by agreeing she was angry. When I asked her exactly what she was feeling, she responded, "Screw the whole damn thing," referring to her marriage, and began to cry. When she stood up to leave the room, her husband followed her. When they returned a few minutes later, they finally addressed the core issues in their relationship. I believe it was my expression of frustration and exasperation that led to her ability to break through her veneer of intellectualizing.

Expressing a Group Leader's Investment in the Success of the Member

In the illustrations presented thus far, I have seen how the group leader's feelings of anger or frustration, when expressed openly in the context of a caring relationship, can help group members. This honest and spontaneous expression of feelings extends to a broad range of group leader responses. Another example is the feeling of investment a group leader can have in a member's progress. For some reason, the idea of self-determination has been interpreted to mean that the helping person cannot share a stake in the member's progress and growth. At points in the struggle toward change when group members feel most hopeless and ready to quit, group leaders sometimes suppress their own feelings of disappointment. In my view, this is a misguided attempt not to unduly influence the member's choices.

For example, consider a school counselor in a group for teenagers when one member states, "What's the use? I might as well just drop out of school." By the counselor indicating she believes in him and cares about his success and would be disappointed if he just quit, she may be sharing a feeling he very much needs to hear. Research on resilience cited earlier supports the idea that having even one person who believes in you and cares enough to set high expectations can be the crucial factor in coping with life and its stresses.

Sharing Feelings Associated with Life Experiences

Another way in which sharing the group leader's feelings can be helpful is when the affect is directly related to the content of the work, as when the group leader has had a life experience similar to that of the member. Self-disclosure of personal experiences and feelings, when shared in pursuit of purpose and integrated with the professional function, and within appropriate boundaries, can promote member growth.

In one dramatic example, a student group leader in my practice class was describing her work with a group of young men who were mildly mentally challenged. All of these group members had recently lost a significant family member. They had been brought together to discuss their losses because they had been exhibiting ongoing depression and denial. The group was started to help them face their feelings and to accept, or at least learn to live with, their sadness. Two weeks into the group, the group leader's father died, and she had to return home to take care of her own grieving. The group members were aware of her loss.

When she returned, she met with the group but did not mention the reason she had been away, even though she knew the members had been informed. One of the members said to her, "Jane, your father died, didn't he?" The group leader later described feeling overwhelmed by his comment and struggling to maintain her "professional composure." She reported that the group members must have sensed her emotions, because another member said, "It's OK to cry, Jane, God loves you, too!" In response to his comment, she began to cry and was joined by most of the group members. After a few moments, she commented to the members that she had been encouraging them to share the pain of their losses, but she had been trying to hide her own. The group members began their first serious and emotion-filled discussion of their own losses and reasons that they tried to hide their feelings, even from themselves. As the student described the incident in class, she cried again and was joined by many other students and me as well.

Even as I write about this incident, I can remember the many objections raised by group leaders when I advance the argument in favor of sharing the group leader's feelings. Let us take some time to examine these.

Boundary Issues in Sharing the Group Leader's Feelings

The first concern relates to the boundaries within which personal feelings can be shared. I believe that, if a group leader is clear about the contract (the purpose of the work with the member) and the leader's professional role, these will offer important direction and protection. For example, if a member begins an interview by describing a problem with his mother-in-law, the group leader should not respond by saying, "You think you have problems with your mother-in-law? Let me tell you about mine!" The member and group leader have not come together to discuss the group leader's problems, and an attempt by the group leader to introduce personal concerns, even those related to the contract area, is an outright subversion of the contract and a confusion of the group leader's role. If the student in the previous example had started to discuss the death of her father and her own loss, rather than using the moment to return to the group members' issues and to deepen their work on their losses, she would not have been synthesizing the personal and professional—she simply would have been unprofessional.

The member seeks help from the group leader, and the group leader's feelings about personal relationships can be shared only in ways that relate directly to the member's immediate concerns. For example, take a situation in which a group leader feels that the member is misinterpreting someone's response because of the member's feelings. The group leader who has experienced that kind of miscommunication might briefly describe his or her experience as a way of providing the member with a new way to understand an important interaction.

A second area of major concern for group leaders is that, in sharing their feelings spontaneously—that is, without first monitoring all of their reactions to see if they are "correct"—they risk making inappropriate responses. They worry that they will make a mistake, act out their own concerns, and perhaps hurt a member irretrievably. This fear has some basis because group leaders do, at times, respond to the member based on their own needs as well as countertransference. For example, a young group leader gets angry at an adolescent member's mother because this mother seems as overprotective as the leader's own. Another group leader experiences great frustration with a member who does not respond immediately to an offer of help but moves slowly through the process of change. Although the member makes progress at a reasonable pace, it still makes the group leader feel ineffective. Still another group leader misses several indirect cues from a group member in a residence about a serious problem with his family, whom he is about to visit during the holidays. The group leader responds to the resident's acting out of the feelings through behavior by imposing angry punishment instead of hearing the hidden message.

Spontaneous expression of feeling leads to all of these mistakes and others. In fact, a helping professional's entire working experience will inevitably consist of making such mistakes, catching them as soon as possible, and then rectifying them. In these cases, a good group leader will learn something about his or her personal feelings and reactions to people and situations. As this learning deepens, these early mistakes diminish. The group leader then becomes conscious of new, more sophisticated mistakes.

When teachers, supervisors, theorists, and colleagues convey the idea that the group leader should try during meetings to monitor her or his feelings continuously, to think clearly before acting, and to conduct the perfect group meeting, they are setting up blocks to the group leader's growth. Only through continuous analysis of some portion of their own work after the group meeting has taken place can group leaders develop the ability to learn from their mistakes. The more skillful group leaders, who are spontaneous, can catch their mistakes during the sessions—not by withdrawing and thinking, but by using their own feelings and by reaching for the cues in the member's responses.

What is often overlooked is that group members can forgive a mistake more easily than they can deal with the image of a perfect group leader. They are truly relieved when a group leader owns up to having "blown" a session, not having understood what the member was saying or feeling, or overreacting and being angry with a member. An admission of a mistake both humanizes the group leader and indirectly gives the members permission to do the same. Group leaders who feel group members will lose respect for their expertise if they reveal human flaws simply misunderstand the nature of helping. Group leaders are not "experts" with the "solutions" for group members' problems, as suggested by the medical paradigm often evident in the doctor-patient relationship. Instead, group leaders possess skills that can help group members develop their own solutions to their problems. One of the most important of these skills is the ability to be personally and professionally honest.

Sexual Transference and Countertransference Feelings

Finally, some group leader feelings are seen as too potentially harmful to be expressed. This is true; however, there are few such feelings. For example, many feelings of warmth and caring may flow between a group leader and a member or members. These positive feelings constitute a key dynamic that helps power the helping process. Under certain circumstances, feelings of intimacy are associated with strong sexual attraction. These mutual attractions are often understandable and normal. However, a member would find it difficult to deal with a group leader who honestly shared a sexual attraction.

Because of the authority of the group leader, as well as the process of transference, sharing feelings of sexual attraction—and, even worse, acting on them—constitutes a form of unethical sexual exploitation. Group members are vulnerable in the helping relationship and need to be protected. It is especially tragic and harmful when group members who are seeking help to heal their wounds from exploitive relationships find themselves in yet another one. Again, the problem is not that the group leader is sexually attracted to a member. This can be understandable, and the group leader should be able to discuss these emotions with a supervisor and/or colleagues. The unethical part is sharing or acting on feelings with the member.

Group leaders sometimes feel that they are in a bind if group members begin to act seductively toward them and even directly request some response from the group leader. For example, a young and attractive female worker described her reactions to the "come-on" of the paraplegic male client in a rehabilitation setting as "stimulating." She felt somewhat ashamed of her feelings, because she thought they revealed a lack of professionalism. Most group leaders in the consultation group in which this illustration was presented reported that they, too, had experienced these feelings at times. They had not discussed them with colleagues, supervisors, or teachers because they felt a professional taboo against doing so.

When the discussion returned to the interaction in the interview with the paraplegic, I asked the participants to tune in to the meaning of the sexual "come-on" in the context of the client's life situation and the contract—that is, the purpose of the work. They speculated that the young member feared he could not be sexually attractive as a paraplegic. With a new handle for approaching the issue, it was clear to the counselor that the client's feelings and fears about his sexual attractiveness might be a central issue for work that the counselor would miss if overwhelmed by her own feelings.

This example illustrates how the group leader can use the process (interaction with the member) as a tool to explore the content (the substantive content of the working contract). The counselor gently confronted the member directly about his comments to her, clarified her professional and ethical responsibilities and boundaries, and then reached directly for his issues with regard to relationships to the opposite sex. The work proceeded to explore this painful, yet crucial, area of content. (A later section in this chapter discusses process and content connections in greater detail.)

Research on Sharing Feelings   A number of helping professions have produced research on the impact of sharing a counselor's feelings. The findings indicate that this skill plays as important a part in the helping process as the empathic skills described earlier. The skill has been called "self-disclosure" or "genuineness," among other labels. In my 1978 study, the counselor's ability to "share personal thoughts and feelings" ranked first as a powerful correlate to developing working relationships and being helpful. Further analysis of the research data suggested that the use of this skill contributed equally to the work of developing the working relationship and the ability of the counselor to be helpful.

The importance of this skill was replicated in the more recent practice study (Shulman, 1991). It was one of the four skills in the grouping called skills to help clients manage their feelings. These skills had a strong impact on the development of the caring element of the working relationship and, through caring, a strong impact on the client's perception of the counselor's helpfulness as well. In addition, there was a low but significant influence on hard outcome measures.

What inferences can I take from these findings? It may be that, in sharing personal thoughts and feelings, the counselor breaks down the barriers that group members experience when they face the feelings of dependency evoked by taking help. As the counselor becomes more multidimensional—more than just a professional helping person—more "person" is available for a member to relate to. In addition, thoughts and feelings of a personal nature appear to provide substantive data for the member's tasks and therefore increase the counselor's helpfulness. Perhaps the personal nature of the data is what makes it appear more relevant to the member, easier to use and to incorporate into a sense of reality. This skill, like many others, may simultaneously serve two functions. By sharing feelings professionally and freely, a counselor effectively strengthens the working relationship or therapeutic alliance (the process) while contributing important ideas for the client's work (the content).

When I examined the workers' skill use profiles in the 1978 and 1991 studies, I found that clients perceived their workers as seldom sharing their personal thoughts and feelings. When these findings were later shared with counselors in various training groups, they always provoked important discussions in which the participants explored the reasons why they found it difficult to reveal themselves to group members. The group's first response was to cite a supervisor, book, or former teacher who had made it clear that sharing feelings was unprofessional. As one group leader put it, "I was told I had to be a stone-faced counselor."

After a discussion of these injunctions and their impact on the counselors, I would say, "Based on my research, my practice experience, my expertise, I am now telling you that it is no longer 'unprofessional' to be honest with group members and to make your feelings part of your work." I would then inquire how this new freedom would affect their work the next day. After a long silence, a typical response from a participant would be "You have just made things a lot tougher. Now I'm going to have to face the fact that it's my own feelings that make it hard for me to be honest. I'm not really sure how much of myself I want to share." At this point in the workshop discussion, the work would deepen.

I will also share the findings of my early doctor-patient interactional research related to the issue of sharing feelings (Shulman & Buchan, 1982). Although physicians believed that they were able to hide their feelings (especially negative ones) toward patients—part of what I have referred to as the "medical paradigm"—this study showed a high correlation between the doctor's expressed attitude toward the patient (positive, neutral, or negative) and the patient's perception of the doctor's attitude. In fact, the doctor's attitude was an important predictor of the outcomes. Thus, some members of the profession from which we borrowed the medical model may believe in a myth that they can maintain emotional neutrality.

Developing the ability to be honest in sharing feelings is difficult, but group leaders ask group members to do it all the time. It is an essential skill to provide effective helping. As one member said of her counselor, "I like Mrs. Tracy. She's not like a counselor. She's like a real person." This model suggests that Mrs. Tracy was both a real person and an effective counselor.

Making a Demand for Work

In constructing this model of the helping process, thus far I have presented the importance of five components: establishing a clear contract, identifying the member's agenda, helping the member elaborate concerns, making certain the member invests the work with feeling, and sharing the group leader's feelings. At this point, I should examine the question of ambivalence and resistance. Group members will be of two minds about proceeding with their work. A part of them, which represents their strength, will move toward understanding and growth. Another part, which represents their resistance, will pull back from what is perceived as a difficult process.

Work often requires lowering long-established defenses, discussing painful subjects, experiencing difficult feelings, recognizing one's own contribution to the problem, taking responsibility for one's actions, giving up long-held cognitive frameworks about life, and confronting significant people and systems. Whatever the difficulty involved, a member will show some degree of ambivalence.

Perlman (1957) describes member ambivalence as follows:

> To know one's feelings is to know that they are often many-sided and mixed and that they may pull in two directions at once. Everyone has experienced this duality of wanting something strongly yet drawing back from it, making up one's mind but somehow not carrying out the planned action. This is part of what is meant by ambivalence. A person may be subject to two opposing forces within himself at the same moment—one that says, "Yes, I will," and the other that says, "No, I won't"; one that says, "I want," and the other, "Not really"; one affirming and the other negating. (p. 121)

A crucial concept is that resistance is a part of the work. Less experienced group leaders who do not understand this may back off from an important area. Their own confidence in what they are doing is fragile, so when the member shows signs of defensiveness or unwillingness to deal with a tough problem, they allow themselves to be put off. This is especially true if group leaders experience their own ambivalence about the area. Communication of ambivalence in tough areas can be seen as the member's way of saying, "This is tough for me to talk about." It can also be a question to the group leader: "Are you really prepared to talk with me about this?" It is one of those life situations in which the other person says he or she is reluctant to enter the taboo area, hoping you will not really believe him. The surface message is "Leave me alone in this area," while the real message is "Don't let me put you off." These are the moments in interviews when the skills of making a demand for work are crucial.

The notion of a *demand for work* is one of Schwartz's (1961) most important contributions to our understanding of the helping process. He describes it as follows:

> The group leader also represents what might be called the demand for work, in which role he tries to enforce not only the substantive aspects of the contract—what we are here for—but the conditions of work as well. This demand is, in fact, the only one the group leader makes—not for certain perceived results, or approved attitudes, or learned behaviors, but for the work itself. That is, he is continually challenging the member to address himself resolutely and with energy to what he came to do. (p. 11)

The demand for work is not limited to a single action or even a single group of skills; rather, it pervades all the work. For example, the process of open and direct contracting in the beginning phase of work represents a form of demand for work. The group leader's attempt to bring the member's feelings into the process is another form of *empathic demand for work*. In a group for parents separated from their children, an angry father, commenting about the length of time he had not been able to see his kids because of a court order, said, "It's a long time for the kids." The group leader responded, "And for you, too." The father was talking about the children's feelings, while the leader consistently commented on his feelings. This is another illustration of the empathic demand for work.

Note that this demand can be gentle and coupled with support. It is not necessarily confrontational. I underline this point because of a tendency for people to see confrontation as negative and uncaring. Some models of practice, particularly in the substance abuse area, have been designed to use confrontation to break down defenses. Instead of allowing a group member to address the issues and to move past denial, it often hardens the resistance. It is quite possible for the group leader to make an empathic demand for work—and, as emphasized earlier, confrontation is experienced as caring if carried out in the context of a positive working relationship.

I have categorized several specific interventions as demand-for-work skills, each discussed in the following sections:

- Partializing member concerns
- Holding to focus
- Checking for underlying ambivalence
- Challenging the illusion of work
- Pointing out obstacles

Each is related to specific dynamics in group situations that could be interpreted as forms of resistance. Note that the consistent use of demand-for-work skills can only be effective when accompanied by the empathic skills described earlier. As the group leaders express their genuine caring for the group members through their ability to empathize, they build up a fund of positive affect that is part of the working relationship or therapeutic alliance. Only when group members perceive that their group leader understands, and is not judging them harshly, can they respond to the demands.

An integration of empathy and demand for work is needed. On one hand, group leaders who have the capacity to empathize with group members can develop a positive working relationship but not necessarily be helpful. On the other hand, group members will experience group leaders who only make demands on their group members, without the empathy and working relationship, as harsh, judgmental, and unhelpful. The most effective help will be offered by group leaders who can synthesize caring and demand in their own way.

This is not easy to do, either in the helping relationship or in life. There is a general tendency to dichotomize these two aspects of relationships, and group leaders might see themselves as going back and forth between the two. For example, caring about someone, expressing it through empathy, but getting nowhere leads to anger and demands, with an associated hardening of empathic response. However, it is precisely at this point, when crucial demands are made on the member, that the capacity for empathy is most important. With this stipulation clearly in mind, in the next section I explore four demand-for-work skills. A reminder to the reader: Although I will be referring to the individual group member, all of these dynamics and skills can apply to the group-as-a-whole.

Partializing Group Member Concerns

Group members often experience their concerns as overwhelming. A group leader may find that a member's comments, perhaps during a check-in, consist of the recitation of a flood of problems, each having some impact on the others. The feeling of helplessness experienced by the member and the other group members is as much related to the difficulty of tackling so many problems as it is to the nature of the problems themselves. The member feels immobilized and does not know how or where to begin. In addition, maintaining problems in this form can represent a form of resistance. If the problems are overwhelming, the member can justify the impossibility of doing anything about them.

Partializing the group member's skills is essentially a problem-managing skill. The only way to tackle complex problems is to break them down into their parts and address these parts one at a time. The way to move past perceptions of helplessness and feelings of being immobilized is to begin by taking one small step on one part of the problem. This is one way the group leader can make a demand for work.

When a group leader listens to the member's concerns and attempts to understand and acknowledge the member's feelings of being overwhelmed, the group leader simultaneously begins the task of helping the member reduce the problem to smaller, more manageable proportions. This skill is illustrated in the following excerpt from a parents' group.

> **GROUP LEADER:** You seem really upset by your son's fight yesterday. Can you tell us more about what's upsetting you?
>
> **MEMBER:** All hell broke loose after that fight [between her son and a neighbor's child]. Mrs. Lewis is furious because he gave her son a black eye, and she is threatening to call the police on me. She complained to the landlord, and he's threatening to throw me out if the kids don't straighten up. I tried to talk to Frankie about it, but I got nowhere. He just screamed at me and ran out of the house. I'm really afraid he has done it this time, and I'm feeling sick about the whole thing. Where will I go if they kick me out? I can't afford another place. And you know the cops gave Frankie a warning last time. I'm scared about what will happen if Mrs. Lewis does complain. I just don't know what to do.
>
> **GROUP LEADER:** It really does sound like quite a mess; no wonder you feel up against the wall. Look, maybe it would help if the group could look at one problem at a time. Mrs. Lewis is very angry, and you need to deal with her. Your landlord is important, too, and I should think about what you might be able to say to him to get him to back off while you try to deal with Frankie on this. And I guess that's the big question: What can you say to Frankie since this has made things rougher for the two of you? Mrs. Lewis, the landlord, and Frankie—where should I start?

The demand implied in the group leader's statement is gentle yet firm. The group leader can sense the member's feelings of being overwhelmed, but she will not allow the work to stop there. In this example, one can see clearly three sets of tasks: those of the group leader, those of the member with the problem, and those of the other group members who need to respond. The member raises the concerns, and the group leader helps her partialize her problems; the member must begin to work on them according to her sense of urgency; the other members need to focus on helping with one issue at a time. This is the sense in which work is interactional, with the group leader's tasks and those of the members interacting with each other.

When a group leader partializes an overwhelming problem and asks a member to begin to address the issues, she or he is also acting on a crucial principle of the helping process: *There is always a next step.* The next step is whatever the member can do to begin to cope with the problem. Even when a member of a hospice group is dealing with a terminal illness, the next steps may mean developing a way of coping with the illness, getting one's life in order, taking control of the quality of one's remaining time, addressing unfinished business with family members, and so on. When social supports, such as adequate housing, are not available for a member, the next steps may involve advocacy and confrontation of the system or, if all else fails, attempting to figure out how to minimize the impact of the poor housing. Although the group leader may not be able to offer hope of completely resolving the problem, the group leader needs to help the member and the other group members find the next step. When a member feels overwhelmed and hopeless, the last thing he or she needs is a group leader or a support group who feel exactly the same way.

In one of my practice studies, partializing was one of the four skills for helping clients manage their problems that contributed to the development of trust in the working relationship (Shulman, 1991). The other skills in the managing problems grouping included clarifying purpose and role, reaching for the group member's feedback, and supporting group members in taboo areas. The trust element of the relationship, in turn, contributed to the member's perception of the worker as being helpful. This is a logical finding, because counselors who help their group members deal with complex problems are going to be seen as more helpful.

Furthermore, when used in the beginning phase of practice, the partializing skill ranked fifth out of eight skills in the strength of its correlation with the caring element of the working relationship. It moved to second place in relation to the trust element of the relationship, and to first in importance in terms of its impact on helpfulness. This association between partializing and the working relationship replicated a finding in my earlier study, in which the skill appeared to contribute to the outcome of helpfulness through its impact on relationship (Shulman, 1978).

Why, then, does use of the partializing skill positively affect relationship building? One explanation may be that the group leader's use of the partializing skill conveys several important ideas to the member. First, the group leader believes the tasks facing the member are manageable. Second, the group leader conveys the belief that the member can take some next step—that is, that the member has the strength to deal with the problem when it is properly broken down into manageable pieces. Third, because partializing also serves to focus the work clearly, it may be another form of clarifying role and purpose. In any case, the findings on the partializing skill suggest that counselors might do well, especially early on, to help group members identify clearly the component parts of the concerns they bring to the group.

These ideas are consistent with the more recent evolution of the strengths perspective and solution-focused approaches (discussed in more detail in Chapter 12). Essentially, the group leader conveys to group members a belief in their ability to manage their problems if they can address them step-by-step. Asking group members to reflect on times in their lives when they were able to deal with issues more effectively—one of the basic solution-focused techniques—is an effort to help change group members' cognition about their life and their abilities.

Holding to Focus

As a member begins to deal with a specific concern, associations with other related issues often result in a form of rambling in which the member has great difficulty concentrating on one issue at a time. *Holding to focus*—asking the member to stay on one question—is a second problem-solving skill that incorporates a demand for work. Moving from concern to concern can be an evasion of work; if the member does not stay with one issue, he or she does not have to deal with the associated feelings.

PRACTICE POINTS

Holding to focus sends the message to the member and to the group that the leader intends to discuss the tougher feelings and concerns. This skill is illustrated in the earlier excerpt with the single parent. After the member decided to deal with Mrs. Lewis first (because of her fear of police involvement), the discussion continued:

MEMBER: When Mrs. Lewis came to the door, all she did was scream at me about how my Frankie was a criminal and that she would not let him beat up her son again.

GROUP LEADER: You must have been frightened and upset. What did you say to her?

MEMBER: I just screamed back at her and told her that her son was no bargain and that he probably asked for it. I was really upset because I could see the landlord's door opening, and I knew he must be listening. You know he warned me that he wouldn't stand for all of this commotion anymore. What can I do if he really kicks me out on the street?

GROUP LEADER: Can we stay with Mrs. Lewis for a minute and then get back to the landlord? I can see how angry and frightened you must have felt. Do you have any ideas about how Mrs. Lewis was feeling?

PRACTICE SUMMARY By acknowledging the distress (support) and then returning to the issue of dealing with Mrs. Lewis (demand), the group leader helped the member stay focused on this issue instead of allowing the member's anxiety to overwhelm her.

Checking for Underlying Ambivalence

One of the dangers in a helping situation is that a member may choose to go along with the group leader, expressing an artificial consensus or agreement, while really feeling ambivalent about a point of view or a decision to take a next step. *Checking for underlying ambivalence* is thus another important task of the group leader.

Group members may go along with the group leader in this way for several reasons. A member who feels that the group leader has an investment in the "solution" may not want to upset the group leader by voicing doubts. The member may also be unaware at this moment of his or her current doubts or the ones that might appear later, when implementation of the difficult action is attempted. Finally, the member may withhold concerns as a way to avoid dealing with the core of the issue. In this sense, the member shows another form of resistance that is subtle because it is expressed passively. In these circumstances, when words are being spoken but nothing real is happening, we have the illusion of work, which is the single most dangerous threat to effective practice. Having lived for 6 years in French Canadian Montreal, I learned to call this the "therapeutic pas des deux"—a form of a dance in which counselors and group members develop marvelous ways of maintaining the illusion that something real is happening, each for their own reasons.

Sometimes group leaders are aware of a group member's underlying doubts, fears, and concerns but simply pass over them. As one group leader put it, "I knew we were just spinning our wheels, but I was afraid to confront the member." Group leaders believe that raising these issues may cause the member to decide not to take the next step. They believe that positive thinking is required, and they do not wish to heighten the member's ambivalence by acknowledging and discussing it. However, the reverse is often true. It is exactly at moments such as these that the group leader should check for the underlying ambivalence. This is what I mean by the skill I called earlier as "looking for trouble when everything is going your way."

When a member has an opportunity to express ambivalence, the group leader and other members have access to the member's real feelings and can be of help. When discussed with the counselor and the group members, negative feelings usually lose much of their power. Perhaps the member is overestimating the difficulties involved, and the group can help clarify the reality of the situation. In other cases, the next step will indeed be difficult. The group's help consists of empathic understanding of the difficulty and expression of faith in the member's strength and resilience in the face of these feelings. Whatever the reasons for hesitation, they must be explored so that they do not block the member's work outside the session.

Group leaders need to struggle against a sense of elation when they hear group members agree to take an important next step. For example, in working with a group member with a substance abuse problem, an enthusiastic group leader might accept the member's agreement to enter a treatment program and then be disappointed when the member does not show up for the intake appointment. Careful examination of the session reveals that the member sent signals that he was still in the contemplative stage and not yet ready to move into the action stage of seeking help. Group leaders often admit to sensing a member's hesitancy but believing that it can be overcome through positive encouragement. This mistake comes back to haunt the group leader when the ambivalence and fears emerge after the session.

All is not lost if, in the next session, the group leader can admit to having moved too quickly and can encourage the member to explore the mixed feelings, which are normal at this stage of the process. This provides a good opportunity to elaborate on the earlier comment that resistance is part of the work. It would be a mistake simply to think of member resistance as an obstacle to progress; rather, there are important "handles for work" within the resistance itself. In the example of the member with a substance abuse problem, as the group leader explores the member's resistance, important work themes may emerge: concerns regarding acceptance of a problem with substances, how employers would view him, feelings of shame, and memories of traumatic events that serve as triggers, and so on. Other members of the group can be helpful if they share these concerns or have had them in the past and have been able to overcome them. This discussion does not take place unless the group leader encourages it.

In another example, a young university student who had been admitted to a psychiatric unit after a suicide attempt announced early in the first meeting that she would not discuss her boyfriend or her family because that would mean she blamed them. She simultaneously expressed resistance, and one of her central concerns related to guilt over her anger and resentment. Exploring why she did not want to discuss her boyfriend or her family could lead directly to her central theme of concern—the fact that she blamed her boyfriend and her family.

Challenging the Illusion of Work

As mentioned earlier, perhaps the greatest threat to effective helping is the illusion of work. Although helping can be achieved through nonverbal means such as touch or activity, much of the helping process takes place through an exchange of words. We have all engaged in conversations that are empty of real meaning. It is easy to see how this ability to talk a great deal without saying much can be integrated into the helping interaction. This represents a subtle form of resistance: By creating the illusion of work, the member can avoid the pain of struggle and growth while still appearing to work. For the illusion to take place, however, everyone must engage in the ritual. The group leader and the group members must be willing to allow the illusion to be created, thus participating actively in its maintenance. Group leaders have reported helping relationships with group members that have spanned months, even years, in which the group leader always knew, deep inside, that it was all illusion.

Schwartz (1971) describes the illusion of work in this passage about group practice:

> Not only must the group leader be able to help people talk but he must help them talk to each other; the talk must be purposeful, related to the contract that holds them together; it must have feeling in it, for without affect there is no investment; and it must be about real things, not a charade, or a false consensus, or a game designed to produce the illusion of work without raising anything in the process. (p. 11)

The skill involves detecting the pattern of illusion, perhaps over a period of time, and confronting the members with that pattern in a facilitative manner. An example from a marriage counseling group illustrates this process. A couple had requested help for problems in their marriage. As the sessions proceeded, the group leader noted that most of the conversation involved problems they were having at work, with their parents, and with their children. Some connection was made to the impact on their marriage; however, they seemed to have created an unspoken alliance not to deal with the details of their relationship. No matter how hard the group leader tried to find the connections from the topic they presented to how the couple got along, they always seemed to evade him. Finally, the group leader said:

> You know, when I started out, you both felt you wanted help with the problems in your marriage, how you got along with each other. It seems to me, however, that all we ever talk about is how you get along with other people. You seem to be avoiding the tough stuff. How come? Are you worried it might be too tough to handle?

The group leader's challenge to the illusion brought a quick response as the couple explored some of their fears about what could happen if they really began to work. This challenge to the illusion was needed to help the couple begin the difficult, risky process of change. In addition, their resistance itself revealed a great deal about their underlying problems. They were demonstrating to the group and the leader how they avoided talking to each other about their real problems. The other group members participated in creating and maintaining the illusion because of their own underlying hesitancy to address their own relationships.

Supporting Group Members in Taboo Areas

When moving into a helping relationship, the member brings along a sense of society's culture, which includes *societal taboos* against open discussion about certain sensitive areas. Taboos may be related to the general society or may be more specific to particular socioeconomic, ethnic, or community groups, or families. Whenever we bring a group of people together, one thing we can be sure of is that a culture is immediately established from the first meeting with a set of norms of behavior, roles (leader, member, etc.), rules both stated and unstated, and taboo subjects. (The concept of group culture will be addressed in detail in Chapter 8.)

For example, we are taught early in life that direct questions and discussions about sex are frowned on. Other areas in which we are subtly encouraged not to acknowledge our true feelings include, among others, dependency, authority, loss, and financial issues. The two examples in the next section illustrate the power of the taboo against discussing sex, incest, race, and authority.

Identifying Taboo Subjects

In one example of the impact of societal taboos, a counselor working with a teenager in a group for students exhibiting behavior problems in high school picks up hints that there may be a problem at home for one of the girls, including indirect suggestion of sexual abuse. The counselor, in an individual session, points out the obstacle by commenting to the girl after the session that a number of the girls she sees have experienced some form of abuse at home, and that this is always difficult for them to talk about for a number of reasons. The teenage girl does not respond in the moment; however, before the beginning of the next session, she discloses to the counselor that she has experienced incest with her father and has been too ashamed and afraid to tell anyone.

In another example of the impact of race and the authority theme, an African American high school student in a largely white school has difficulty discussing his experiences being bullied by white students with his white counselor. The counselor points out that it might be hard for the student to talk about what he is going through as a black student in a mostly white school when his counselor is also white. By pointing out this obstacle, the counselor opens the door for the discussion that followed.

Other taboo areas can be identified by the apparent efforts of group members to avoid discussing them even when they are relevant to the purpose of the group. For example, feeling dependent is often experienced as being weak. The unrealistic image of a "real man" or a "real woman" presents one who is independent, who can stand on his or her own feet, and who deals with life's problems without help. In the real world, however, life is so complex that we are always dependent on others in some way. Most people experience the bind of feeling one way, consciously or not, but thinking they should feel another way. The norms of our culture include clear taboos that make real talk about dependency difficult. These include dependency on people as well as substances such as alcohol or drugs and gambling.

Money is considered a taboo subject as well. Many families deeply resent questions related to their financial affairs. Having enough money is equated with competency in our society, and poverty is embarrassing. Reluctance to discuss fees with professionals is one example of the effect of the taboo in practice. Group members sometimes contract for services without asking about the fee, feeling that it would be embarrassing to inquire.

One of the most powerful taboos involves feelings toward authority. Parents, teachers, and other authority figures do not generally encourage feedback from children on the nature of the relationship. We learn early on that commenting on this relationship, especially negatively, is fraught with danger. People in authority have power to hurt us, so I can only, at best, hint at our feelings and reactions. In a group counseling situation, the fear is compounded by worrying about being embarrassed in front of peers. Revealing positive feelings to people in authority is almost as hard, because it is considered demeaning or in the vernacular—"sucking up." I already addressed the authority theme in the chapters on beginning group work as members wonder what kind of person the leader will be. Even if this is answered directly in the beginning (e.g., the illustrative responses to the question "Do you have children?"), issues of authority remain. The taboo against openly addressing authority theme issues can create an important problem in the working relationship between the group leader and the member throughout the life of the group.

Loss represents another taboo—one that takes many forms and affects various types of group members and areas of work. For example, the loss of a relationship because of death or separation may be considered too difficult to discuss directly.

A parent whose child has been born with a physical or mental problem may secretly mourn the loss of the perfect child he had wished to have. A survivor of childhood sexual, emotional, or physical abuse may mourn the loss of a normal childhood and her innocence. The adult child of an alcoholic may mourn the loss of the family once hoped for, but he may not feel free to discuss this because the family taught that the problem must be kept a family secret.

The elderly may grieve over the loss of family, friends, communities, and their good health and independence. In one example in a group meeting in a home for the elderly, members expressed dissatisfaction with the quality and variety of the food served in the dining room. The group leader helped them address this issue with staff but also opened up a discussion of the loss of their ability to cook their own favorite meals. Many of the messages of our society indicate that direct discussion of loss is not acceptable.

How does the group leader recognize a taboo exists? There is no sign on the wall or a written agreement not to discuss a specific taboo topic. The group leader recognizes the existence of the taboo in the culture of the group because the group acts as if it exists. The topic of understanding the culture of the group will be explored in more detail in Chapter 8, but for now, the concept is that we understand the culture of our group (norms of behavior, informal rules, roles taken on by members, taboos, etc.) because the group acts as if the culture exists. On recognizing the taboo, the group leader brings it out in the open and begins the negotiation of a new norm of behavior for the group session.

Changing the Culture of the Group

To support a member in *discussing a taboo area*, the group leader has to work with the group members to create a unique "culture" in the group. In this culture, it is acceptable to discuss feelings and concerns that the member may experience as taboo elsewhere. The taboo will not be removed for all situations, however. There are some good reasons for us not to talk freely and intimately on all occasions about our feelings in taboo areas, as the discussion on sharing group leader feelings showed (e.g., a group leader's sexual attraction to a member).

Discussing taboo subjects during the group session is meant not to change the member's attitudes forever and in all life situations but rather to allow work in the immediate situation. The group leader enables such discussion by monitoring the interaction of the work with the member and listening for clues that may reveal a taboo-related block in the process. Past experiences with group members and the tuning-in process may heighten the group leader's sensitivity to a taboo that lies just beneath the surface of the session.

The group leader needs to guard against a subtle subversion of the contract that can easily occur if the discussion of the obstacle becomes the focus of the work. The purpose of the helping encounter is neither to examine the reasons why the taboo exists nor to free the member from its power in all situations. Clarity of group purpose and the leader's role can assist the group leader to avoid the trap of becoming so engrossed in the analysis of the process that the original task becomes lost.

Dealing with the Authority and Intimacy Themes

Earlier I had suggested at any one time the group would be dealing with its work (contract) or its way of working (the authority theme and the intimacy theme). I need to examine this issue of authority and intimacy, also usually taboo subjects, to understand their impact on the group.

Schwartz (1971) describes the *authority theme* as a reference to "the familiar struggle to resolve the relationship with a nurturing and demanding figure who is both a personal symbol and a representative of a powerful institution" (p. 11). As the member uses the group leader's help to deal with this task, positive and negative feelings will arise. At times, the member will think fondly of this caring and supportive figure. At other times, the member will feel anger toward a group leader who demands that the members address painful feelings and take responsibility for the member's own part in the events of her or his life. Group leaders are not perfect individuals who never make mistakes. Even the most skilled group leader will sometimes miss a member's communications, lose track of the leader's role, and begin to sermonize or judge the member harshly without compassion for the real struggles involved in change. Reactions and feelings on the part of the member will result. As one enters a helping relationship, problems with the authority theme should be anticipated as a normal part of the work. In fact, the energy flow between group leader and member, both positive and negative, can provide the drive that powers the work.

Two processes central to the authority theme are transference and *countertransference*. Drawing on Freud's psychoanalytic theory, Strean (1978) describes their effects on the group leader–member relationship as follows:

> This relationship has many facets: subtle and overt, conscious and unconscious, progressive and regressive, positive and negative. Both client and counselor experience themselves and each other not only in terms of objective reality, but in terms of how each wishes the other to be and fears he might be. The phenomena of "transference" and "countertransference" exist in every relationship between two or more people, professional or nonprofessional, and must be taken into account in every counselor-client encounter. By "transference" is meant the feelings, wishes, fears, and defenses of the member deriving from reactions to significant persons in the past (parents, siblings, extended family, teachers), that influence his current perceptions of the counselor. "Countertransference" similarly refers to aspects of the counselor's history of feelings, wishes, fears, and so on, all of which influence his perceptions of the member. (p. 193)

Unfortunately, the authority theme is one of the most powerfully taboo areas in our society. Group members have as much difficulty talking about their reactions and feelings toward their group leaders as they do discussing subjects such as sex. When these feelings and reactions remain undiscussed, the helping relationship suffers. These strong feelings operate just below the surface and emerge in many indirect forms. The group member or the whole group becomes apathetic, is late for meetings, or does not follow up on commitments. The group leader searches for answers to the questions raised by the member's behavior. Group leaders may attempt to understand this behavior in terms of the member's "personality." However, the answers to the group leader's questions are often much closer to home and more accessible than the intangible notion of personality. The answers often may be found in the interactional process between the group leader and the members.

The skill of dealing with the authority theme involves continual monitoring of the relationship. A group leader who senses that the work is unreal or blocked can call attention to the obstacle and respond directly to it if she or he thinks it centers on the authority theme. Once again, as with other taboo subjects, the group leader is trying to create a culture in this situation in which the member perceives a new norm: "It is all right to treat the group leader like a real person and to say what you think about how the group leader deals with you." The group leader can begin this process in the contracting stages by responding directly to early cues that the member wants some discussion about what kind of group leader this will be (see Chapter 4). The new culture will develop slowly as the member tests this strange kind of authority who seems to invite direct feedback, even the negative kind. As the members learn that the group leader will not punish them, the feedback will arise more often and more quickly than before. Also of importance, the members get to see a nondefensive group leader demonstrate the capacity to examine his or her own behavior and to be open to change—exactly what the group leader will be asking the members to do. This is another example of integrating content and process.

Issues can also arise between members that remain under the surface and serve to create and support the illusion of work. As difficult as it may be to address issues with the leader, it can be equally difficult to deal with other members. Confrontation is hard when we have been generally taught to be polite and to avoid negative interactions. A member who is angry or hurt by another member's comment may hide these feelings while acting them out in withdrawal or indirect digs at the offending party.

Transference between members can also be an issue. Corey and Corey (2006) address the issue of transference and multiple transferences in the group context:

> Members may project not only onto the leaders but also onto other members in the group. Depending on the kind of group being conducted, members may identify people who elicit feelings in them that are reminiscent of feelings they have for significant people in their lives, past or present. Again, depending on the purpose of the group, these feelings can be productively explored so members become aware of how they are keeping these old patterns functional in present relationships. The group itself provides an ideal place to become aware of certain patterns of psychological vulnerability. Members can gain insight into the ways their unresolved conflicts create certain patterns of dysfunctional behavior. By focusing on what is going on within a group session, the group provides a dynamic understanding of how people function in out-of-group situations. (p. 211)

Research on Dealing with Taboo Subjects

In my early study, the skill of supporting clients in taboo areas was one of four skills that distinguished the most effective counselors from the least effective, from their client's perspective (Shulman, 1978). In the more recent study, this skill was only the sixth-most used out of the eight skills examined (Shulman, 1991). Clients reported that their counselors used this skill between "seldom" and "fairly often." This is not unexpected, because counselors face the same taboos that group members do. Group leaders need experience and supervision to find the courage to speak directly about many of these issues.

The introduction of time to the analysis of this skill yielded some interesting findings:

- Supporting clients in taboo areas, when used in the beginning phase of work (first sessions), was the third-strongest skill (out of eight) that correlated with the client's perception of the worker's caring ($r = .52$).
- The *correlation* for the use of the skill in the middle phase of work was slightly higher ($r = .58$).

These findings were expected, because support of any kind, particularly in sensitive and painful areas of work, could contribute to the client's perception that the worker was concerned about him or her. This provides some justification for the argument that it is better for the group leader to risk and be too far ahead of the member in addressing taboo subjects than to be overly cautious.

Identifying Content and Process Connections

Two group leader skills are associated with *identifying content and process connections*: (1) identifying these connections and (2) pointing them out to the group member. Members who are aware of the way in which they use process to deal with content may be able to learn from that awareness and take control of their interactions with others. For example, recognition of the meaning of the dependency on the leader may free group members to become more independent in the helping relationship by taking more responsibility for the work. In turn, this serves as a training medium for the group member to practice new skills of independence—skills that can later be transferred to other significant relationships.

In an example of helping group members see a connection between the group process and the content of the work, an African American high school student suspended from school for violence was confrontational with a white group leader during a group session at the Vision-Integrity-Structure-Accountability (VISA) Center I established at the State University of New York–Buffalo. When the leader skillfully addressed the just-below-the-surface and taboo intercultural issue that had emerged between the black teenager from the inner city and the white group leader from the suburbs, it was a major step in strengthening the working relationship. With an understanding of the connection between process and content, the discussion quickly moved to the conflicts between this student and his white teachers and administrators, who he experienced as racist. Thus, process (relationship to the group leader) and content (being black and dealing with white teachers and administrators) were integrated.

This discussion may help the student make a better assessment of when he actually experiences racism or when he, for many good reasons drawn from his life experience, may see it when it is not always there. It may also help him find more adaptive ways of coping with these highly charged interactions and create fewer problems for him. He may still have to confront racist professionals and students, but he may be able to develop more effective strategies and interventions in his response.

Another example was cited in the introduction, in which an angry mother in a mutual aid support group for mothers with chronically ill children in a hospital attacked a new leader during the first meeting. I suggested then that the mother was actually showing the leader how she used anger to avoid dealing with her painful feelings, and how she pushed helpful people away when she most needed them. This demonstrated how addressing the process (the authority theme) directly connected to the work of the group.

Process and Content That Relate to the Authority Theme

I suggested earlier that at any one time, the conversation during a group session is related to either process or content. However, because of the indirect nature of member communications, it is often hard to know which is really under discussion. For example, take a single parent in a group whose purpose is to work on issues related to dealing with children, employment, and relationships with friends and family. A member may begin a session apparently talking about content—how none of her friends or relatives understands her painful emotions. The issue is real to her, but she has also been angry with the group leader since the previous session, when the group leader missed or minimized her signals of distress.

This example emphasizes the importance of tuning in and group leader tentativeness in the sessional contracting stage of a group meeting, discussed earlier in this chapter. The group leader who is tuned in to the member's pattern of indirect communications around issues of authority may be better prepared to hear that the discussion is really about process (the group leader's ability to understand) rather than content (friends and relatives). If the group leader prematurely assumes that the discussion is only content related, the session may turn into the illusion of work, with the process issues buried under the surface.

Thus far, the terms *content* and *process* have been described and illustrated; however, the concept of the integration of the two requires further elaboration. One common mistake made by group leaders is to fail to see the possible connections between process and content that allow for synthesizing of the two. Group leaders often describe being torn between process and content. They describe trying to balance the two, spending some time on process (how the group is working) and some time on content. What they do not always realize is that they have fallen into the trap of accepting the false dichotomy of process versus content. When group leaders embrace this false dualism, they cannot avoid getting stuck. Instead, the group leader must search out the connections between process and content so that the discussion of process deepens the work on the content, and vice versa.

Returning to our single-parent example, the group leader who looks for this synthesis may recognize (usually between sessions, rarely during a session) that the way in which the member indirectly raised her anger and hurt feelings at the group leader's lack of compassion is a good example of the way this member deals with friends and other important people in her life. When her needs are not met, she gets angry because she expects other people to intuitively sense her feelings. She does not take responsibility for being direct about her pain and thereby helping others to understand. In this case, if the group leader opens up a discussion of the authority theme, the member can gain a deeper understanding of the skills she must develop to create and maintain a social support system. The member can be held accountable for her own responsibility in the relationship with the group leader as well as in relationships with other significant people in her life. Thus, I see in this example that the content of the work can be synthesized with process issues, and the process issues can be integrated into the content. After discussing the authority theme, the group leader can move from the specific issue of the member's way of dealing with the group leader or other members to the general issue of how the member seeks to have needs met by friends and family.

In another example, one group leader explored the difficulty a married member was having in allowing himself to feel dependent on the female group leader and the discomfort he felt at expressing his need for help. The difficulty seemed to relate to many of his notions of what a "real man" should feel. The work on the authority theme led directly to discussions of how hard it was for him to let his wife know how much he needed her.

In each of these examples, dealing with the authority theme served two distinct functions: It freed the working relationship from a potential obstacle and led directly to important substantive work on the contract. But this can only happen if the group leader rejects the process-content dichotomy and instead searches for the potential connections between the two.

The reader may have noted how often I challenge what I call false dichotomies and phony dualisms. This one is "Do I deal with group process or content?" Once one sees the connection between the two, the leader no longer needs to choose one versus the other.

Sharing Data

The group member must also be allowed access to the leader's own relevant data. Contrary to some views, which require a form of neutrality on the part of the leader, I argue that the leader's *sharing data* such as facts, opinions, and value judgments is an important part of the helping process. In some groups—educational and psycho-educational, for example—sharing data is the purpose of the group. Even in these groups, the leader needs to consider when sharing data is appropriate and how the data are shared. In order to be sure that the group leader is not acting on a "hidden agenda"—that is, attempting to manipulate group members—four conditions apply. The leader must take care to share only information that is

- otherwise unavailable to the group members,
- relevant to the members' work,
- shared openly, and
- shared in such a way that the group members are left free to accept or reject the leader's views.

I define group leader data as facts, ideas, values, and beliefs that group leaders have accumulated from their own experiences and can make available to group members. Furthermore, as Schwartz (1961) argues, "The group leader's grasp of social reality is one of the important attributes that fit him to his functions. While his life experiences cannot be transferred intact to other human beings, the products of these experiences can be immensely valuable to those who are moving through their own struggles and stages of mastery" (p. 23).

Sharing group leader data is important not only because of the potential usefulness to the member, but because the process of sharing the data also helps build a working relationship. The member looks to the group leader as a source of help in difficult areas. If the member senses that the group leader is withholding data, for whatever reason, this can be experienced as a form of rejection. As a member might put it, "If you really cared about me, you would tell me what you know."

During my professional training, a student who was majoring in group practice described his work with a group of teenage boys in a community setting. They were planning their first party with a group of girls and were obviously underestimating the quantities of food and drink required. When I asked if he had pointed this out to them, he replied that he had not interfered, feeling that they would learn something important about planning. I was shocked and felt that if they ever found out he knew their supplies would fall short and had not told them, their significant learning would be about him.

Although the skills of sharing data may sound simple, several misconceptions about how people learn—as well as a lack of clarity about the helping role—have served to make a simple act complex. The problems can be seen in the actions of group leaders who have important information for the member but withhold it, thinking that the member must "learn it for himself." These problems are also apparent in the actions of group leaders who claim to allow group members to learn for themselves while they indirectly "slip in" their ideas. This is most easily recognizable in group sessions wherein the group leader leads a member to the answer that the leader already has in mind. The belief is that learning takes place if the member speaks the words the group leader wants to hear. It is my observation, as both a group leader and a teacher, that students quickly sense this process and instead of working on an issue are hard at work trying to figure out what the group leader/instructor wants them to say. In the balance of this section, I shall identify some of the skills involved in sharing data and discuss some of the issues that often lead group leaders to be less than direct.

Providing Relevant Data

The skill of providing relevant data is the direct sharing of the group leader's facts, ideas, values, and beliefs that relate to the member's immediate task at hand. The two key requirements are that the data be related to the working contract and that they be necessary for the member's immediate work.

Regarding the first requirement, if the group leader is clear about the purpose of the encounter and that purpose has been openly negotiated with the member, then the group leader has a guideline as to what data to share. A problem is created when the group leader wants to teach something indirectly to the member and uses the interchange to subtly introduce personal ideas. This mistaken sense of function on the group leader's part is rooted in a model in which the group leader attempts to change the member by skillfully presenting "good" ideas. The problem is that the member soon senses that the group leader has a hidden agenda, and, instead of using the group leader as a resource for the member's own agenda, he or she must begin to weigh the group leader's words to see what is "up her sleeve."

This hidden purpose often creates a dilemma for the group leader in sharing data directly. On one hand, sharing may help the member. On the other hand, imposing an ideology on the member treats the member as an object to be molded. This group leader's ambivalence comes out in the indirectness with which the ideas are shared. If data are related to an openly agreed-on purpose, however, the group leader is free to share them directly.

The second requirement for directly sharing data is that the data be connected to the member's immediate sense of concern. Group members will not learn something simply because the group leader feels it may be of use to them at some future date, even if it relates to the working contract. The attraction people feel toward ideas, values, and so forth, is related to their sense of their usefulness at the time. One reason for the importance of sessional contracting is that the group leader needs to determine the member's current sense of urgency and must share data that the member perceives as helpful.

A Group for Preadoptive Couples

From my observations of educational groups for preadoptive couples, I can offer an example of sharing data that are not immediately relevant. Individual or group work is often employed for the dual purpose of evaluating the couples' suitability as adoptive parents and helping them to discuss the adoption. Group leaders will often prepare a well-developed agenda for group meetings that touches on all the issues that they feel the couples will need to face as adoptive parents. Unfortunately, such an agenda can miss the immediate concerns that preadoptive parents have about adoption and about agency procedures for accepting and rejecting potential parents. In the following illustration, preadoptive couples in a second group session respond to the group leader's query "Should one tell adopted children they were adopted, and when and how should we do this?"

The important point to remember is that these couples are still waiting to hear whether they are going to get children, and all are expecting infants. The issue of whether to tell the child will not present itself until a few years after the child has been adopted.

> **MR. FRANKS:** I think you have to tell the child, or you won't be honest.
>
> **MR. BECK:** But if you tell him, then he probably will always wonder about his real parents, and that may make him feel less like you are his parents.

(This comment starts a vigorous discussion between the men about how a child feels toward his adoptive parents. The group leader uses this opportunity to contribute her own views indirectly; she already has in mind an "acceptable" answer to her question.)

> **GROUP LEADER:** I wonder, Mr. Beck, how you think the child might feel if you didn't tell him and he found out later.

Recognizing that he may have given the wrong answer to the group leader, who will also judge his suitability to be an adoptive parent, Mr. Beck quickly changes his position.

> **MR. BECK:** I hadn't really looked at it that way. I guess you're right—it would be easier to tell right away.

When the group apparently reached the consensus that the group leader had intended from the start, she shifted the discussion to the question of when and how to tell. This is an example of what I have called the illusion of work. Unfortunately, the urgency of the issue of "telling" was not an immediate one. Preadoptive couples are more concerned with how they, their family, and friends will feel toward their adoptive child. This is a sensitive subject, particularly because preadoptive couples are not sure about the agency's criteria for acceptance. They often worry that they will be rejected if they don't express the "right" attitudes and feelings. This cuts them off from a supportive experience in which they might discover that most preadoptive parents face the same issues, that it is normal for them to have doubts, and that the agency will not hold this against them. In fact, parents who are in touch with their feelings, including such feelings as these, are often the ones who make excellent adoptive parents. Because the group leader was so occupied by "teaching" ideas for future use, she missed the most important issue.

Compare the previous example with the following excerpt. In this case, the parents raise the question of "Should one tell?" and the group leader listens for cues to the present concern.

> **MR. FRIEDMAN:** (Responding to a group member's argument that the kids would not feel that the adoptive parents are their real parents) I can't agree with that. I think the real parent is the one that raises you, and the kids will know that's you even if they are adopted.

Note how the group leader now opens the door for discussion of a taboo subject by raising their doubts about their feelings toward the child. In addition, she normalizes these feelings, thus giving permission for a real discussion of a tough issue.

> **GROUP LEADER:** You have all been working quite hard on this question of how your adopted child will feel toward you, but I wonder if you aren't also concerned about how you will feel toward the child? (Silence)

MR. FRIEDMAN: I don't understand what you mean.

GROUP LEADER: Each of you is getting ready to adopt a child who was born to another set of parents. In my experience, it is quite normal and usual for a couple at this stage to wonder sometimes about how they will feel toward the child. "Will I be able to love this child as if it were my own?" is not an uncommon question and a perfectly reasonable one, in my view.

MRS. REID: My husband and I have talked about that at home—and I feel I can love our child as if he were our own.

GROUP LEADER: You know, I would like the group to be a place where you can talk about your real concerns. Frankly, if you're wondering and have doubts and concerns such as this, that doesn't eliminate you from consideration as an adoptive parent. Being able to face your real concerns and feelings is very much in your favor. You folks wouldn't be in this group if I hadn't already felt you would make good adoptive parents. It would be the rare situation in which I would have to reconsider.

PRACTICE SUMMARY The group leader shared some important data with these group members that was relevant both to the general contract of the group and to their immediate sense of urgency. They learned that their feelings, doubts, and concerns were not unusual; that the agency did not reject prospective adoptive parents for being human and having normal worries; that the group was a place to discuss these feelings; and finally, that their presence in the group indicated that they were all considered good applicants.

This comment was followed by a deeper discussion of their feelings toward their prospective child and the adoption. These included their concerns over possibly getting a child from a "bad seed," their fears regarding the reactions of friends and family, and their anger about the delays and procedures involved in dealing with the agency. The data shared by the group leader in these areas were more meaningful to these parents than was information about future problems.

Providing Data in a Way That Is Open to Examination and Challenge

Group leaders are sometimes fearful of sharing their own fears, values, and other data because of a genuine concern with influencing group members who need to make a difficult decision. The unwed mother, for example, who is trying to decide whether to abort her child, to have it and keep it, or to have it and give it up for adoption faces some agonizing decisions—none of which will be easy. Each option holds important implications for her future. The skillful group leader will help such a member explore in detail these implications and her underlying feelings of ambivalence. During this work, the member may turn to the group leader at some point and say, "If you were me, what would you do?" Group leaders often have opinions about questions such as these but hold them back, usually responding to the question with a question of their own. I believe it is better for group leaders to share their feelings about revealing their opinions and then allow the member access to their views as representing one source of reality. For example,

When you ask me that question, you really put me on the spot. I'm not you, and no matter how hard I try, I can't be you, since I won't have to live with the consequences. For what it's worth, I think the way you have spelled it out, it's going to be an awfully tough go for you if you keep the baby. I probably would place the child for adoption. Now, having said that, you know it's still possible that you can pull it off, and only you know what you're ready for right now. So I guess my answer doesn't solve a thing for you, does it?

Group leaders who withhold their opinion do so because they fear that the member will adopt it as the only source of reality. Rather than holding back, however, a group leader can simultaneously allow the member access to his or her opinions while guarding against the member's tendency to use them to avoid difficult work. Schwartz (1961) describes this consideration that guides the group leader's movements as follows:

> The first consideration is his awareness that his offering represents only a fragment of available social experience. If he comes to be regarded as the foun-tainhead of social reality, he will then have fallen into the error of presenting himself as the object of learning rather than as an accessory to it. Thus, there is an important distinction to be made between lending his knowledge to those who can use it in the performance of their own tasks and projecting himself as a text to be learned. (p. 11)

Providing Data as a Personal View

Thus far, I have described how a group leader can provide data to group members in a way that is open to examination by making sure that the member uses the data as just one source of reality. An additional consideration is to make sure that what is shared is presented as the group leader's own opinion, belief, values, and so forth, rather than as fact. This is one of the most difficult ideas for many group leaders to comprehend, because it contradicts the normal societal pattern for exchanging ideas. Group leaders have an investment in their own views and will often attempt to con-vince the member of their validity. We are accustomed to arguing our viewpoint by using every means possible to substantiate it as fact. New group leaders in particular feel that they must present their credentials to group members to convince them that they know what they are talking about.

In reality, however, our ideas about life, our values, and even our "facts" are con-stantly changing and evolving. A cursory reading of child-rearing manuals would convince anyone that the hard-and-fast rules of yesterday are often reversed by the theories of today. I have found that inexperienced group leaders are often most dog-matic in areas where they feel most uncertain.

The skill of sharing data in a way that is open for examination means that the group leader must qualify statements to help group members sort out the difference between their reality and the group leader's sense of reality. Rather than being a salesperson for an idea, the group leader should present it with all of its limitations. A confident and honest use of expressions such as "This is the way I see it" or "This is what I believe, which doesn't mean it's true" or "Many people believe this, but others do not" will con-vey the tentativeness of the group leader's beliefs. The group leader must encourage the member to challenge these ideas when they do not ring true to the member.

Any nonverbal signals of disagreement mean that the group leader needs to reach for the underlying questions. For example, "You don't look like you agree with what I just said. How do you see it?" The member's different opinions need to be respected and valued. Even if all the experts support the idea, fact, or value at issue, it will only have meaning for the member if and when the member finds it useful. In many ways, the group leader is a model of someone who is still involved in a search for reality.

Every idea, no matter how strongly held, needs to be open to challenge by the evidence of the senses. The group leader is asking the member to do the same in relation to life, and the member should not expect any less of the group leader. Schwartz (1961) sums this up:

> As he [the group leader] helps them to evaluate the evidence they derive from other sources—their own experiences, the experiences of others, and their collaboration in ideas—so must he submit his own evidence to the process of critical examination. When the group leader understands that he is but a single element in the totality of the [group] member's experience, and when he is able to use this truth rather than attempt to conquer it, he has taken the first step toward helping the member to free himself from authority without rejecting it. (p. 25)

Ethical Dilemmas in Withholding Data

The question of providing data has taken on increased complexity as governments and other funding agencies have introduced economic and political issues into the equation. (Many of these and the ethical implications are discussed in more detail in Chapter 13.) For example, cost containment efforts in the health care system have led government and private third-party payers to develop a standard of care that dictates how many counseling sessions, on average, may be provided. Reimbursement to the agency may be a fixed amount, which means that patients who end treatment early earn money for the hospital, whereas those who continue may lose money for it. Counselors may feel pressured to close the case as quickly as possible.

The ethical dilemma emerges when a patient, family members, or even the group leader feels that a patient may not be ready to end counseling for any of various reasons, perhaps related to psychosocial issues or the availability of suitable community resources. The group leader has a responsibility to help the member negotiate the system, which includes working to advocate for the member's interest. The question here is whether the group leader should inform the patient of his or her right to appeal a decision to end counseling early, even if the patient does not ask. What if the administrative staff asks front-line staff not to share such information unless it is requested?

Another, even more striking example comes from the political controversy surrounding a decision by the U.S. Supreme Court in May 1991, which supported the right of the government to cut off funding for family planning centers that informed pregnant clients of the option of abortion—the so-called gag rule. Many of these clients were young, poor, and people of color. Even if clients requested information on this option for dealing with an unwanted pregnancy, or even if the member's health and safety might be in danger, any center that provided such information or referred a member to an alternative source of counseling where such information might be available would lose its funding. More recently, the executive orders of the George W. Bush administration continued this approach on an international and national level, although President Barack Obama reversed this policy in 2009. In another example, federal regulations have provided protection to health and human services counselors who claim a right of "conscience" not to be involved in such procedures that violate their beliefs. This issue is also being addressed under the Obama administration.

Many centers have indicated an unwillingness to accept restrictions on free speech and a client's right to be fully informed so that she can make a sound, personal decision on the issue. However, what if a center decided that continuing to provide family planning services to poor women was so important that they would accept this restriction rather than close down for lack of funding? For many counselors—regardless of their personal views on the issue of abortion—denying access to this information to women who are dependent on public social services is sexist, racist, and classist. Should a group leader try to subvert the policy? Should a counselor refuse to work in such a setting?

A number of professional associations' codes of ethics make clear the group leader's responsibility to the member in both of these examples. The ethical group leader would need to make available to the member all information required by the member to make a sound personal decision about her health care or her options in the face of unwanted pregnancy. Acting ethically, however, might require courage and might involve personal risk. This represents another example of how practice may be affected as much by ideological, financial, and political issues as by theories of human behavior. Ethical issues are explored in more detail in Chapter 13.

Helping the Group Members See Life in New Ways

A specific form of data is important enough to be included as a separate skill category. These are the skills with which the group leader is *helping group members see life in new ways*—that is, to reexamine perceptions (cognitions) about themselves, their life situations, or important people or systems in group members' lives (e.g., husband, parent, school). This skill can be central to a form of practice called cognitive-behavioral therapy (for a fuller discussion of this approach and others, see Chapter 12). To summarize briefly, group members have developed their views of life subjectively. Given the difficulties involved in communications, they quite possibly distort other people's actions or have internalized perceptions of themselves and their life experiences that lead to negative cognitions and feelings and self-defeating behaviors. By exploring alternative views in collaboration with the group members, the group leader attempts to help a member rethink his or her life situation and correct negative and inaccurate "automatic thoughts" and perceptions. This approach is also consistent with some of the solution-focused techniques and strategies also discussed in Chapter 12. The term *reframing* is also often used when thinking of this skill.

Redefining the Behavior of the Significant Other

One way the group leader can do this is by identifying the person or part of the system that may still be reaching out to the member. In a way, the group leader or another member plays the role of the missing person, articulating during the session the thoughts and feelings that might lie beneath the surface.

PRACTICE POINTS For example, following is an excerpt from a session with an adolescent who is having trouble in a class. He sees his teacher as pushing him because he hates him.

> **MEMBER:** Mr. Brown is always after me, always putting me down when I'm late with my work. I think he hates me.

> **GROUP LEADER:** You know, it could be that Mr. Brown knows that you're having trouble keeping up and is really worried about your failing. He may be keeping after you to try to get you going again.

MEMBER: Well, it doesn't help. All it makes me do is want to miss his class.

GROUP LEADER: He might not realize that what he says makes you feel so bad. Maybe it would help if I could let him know that you feel he is really mad at you.

The work continued with a discussion of the student's fears about what might happen if the counselor talked to the teacher and the counselor's reassurance about how he would handle it. Mr. Brown was surprised by the student's feelings. He had been frustrated because he felt the student did not care about school. A joint meeting was held to begin to discuss what each really felt in relation to the child's schoolwork. This started to open doors for collaboration.

After a period of bad experiences, the blocks in the reality of the relationship become the member's (and sometimes the system's) only view of reality itself. The group leader needs to help the member explore this maladaptive pattern and to break the cycle that prevents the member from connecting to people and systems that are important for success. At these moments, a group leader offers the possibility of hope and a next step by sharing a view of others in the system that allows the member to glimpse some possibility of mutual attraction. This is only possible when group leaders themselves see these possibilities, described earlier as the areas of common ground. For example, when a group leader helps a teenager see that his parents' setting of curfew limits may show that they care for him and recognize that he is growing up, the group leader has not solved the problem, but at least he has shed a new light on the interaction.

The Ending and Transition Stage

I now come to the skills factors involved in dealing with the *ending and transition stage* of any group session. Endings and transitions of group sessions present important dynamics and require the leader's attention. In addition, issues that have been raised indirectly throughout the session may emerge with some force when the group member is preparing to leave (the classic "doorknob therapy" phenomenon, discussed earlier). Finally, transitions need to be made to next sessions and future actions. The leader uses *sessional ending and transition skills* to bring a session to a close and to make the connections between a single session and future work or issues in the life of the group member.

As with beginnings and middles of any group meeting, endings contain unique dynamics and special requirements for leader skills. I call this stage the *resolution stage*. It is not unusual to find leaders carrying out their sessional contracting and demonstrating sensitive work with members in the group with regard to their concerns, but then ending a session without a resolution of the work. By "resolution of the work," I am not suggesting that each session end neatly, with all issues fully discussed, ambivalence gone, problems solved, and next steps carefully planned. A sign of advanced skill is a leader's tolerance for ambiguity and uncertainty, which may accompany the end of a session that has dealt with difficult work. If uncertainty is present for a member or members at the end of a session, the resolution stage might consist of identifying the status of the discussion. The five skills discussed in the balance of this section include summarizing, generalizing, identifying next steps, rehearsing, and identifying "doorknob" communications.

Before I examine these skills, a word on member activity between sessions is in order. Leaders sometimes act as if members have no life between sessions. They review a group meeting and then prepare to pick up the next session "where I left off." The leader needs to realize that the member has had life experiences, contacts with other helping systems, new problems that may have emerged during the week, and time to think about problems discussed in the previous session. After giving much consideration to how to help a member with a particular problem, a leader may be surprised to discover that the member has resolved the issue between sessions. It would be a mistake not to recognize and legitimate these between-session activities. Solution-focused practice, described in Chapter 12, incorporates inquiring about between-session activities as a major strategy. That is one reason why the sessional contracting skill, described at the beginning of this chapter, is so important.

Summarizing

Often, the group members are learning about life and trying to develop new skills to manage life in more satisfying ways. It can be important to use the last moments of a session to help the member or members identify what has been learned. How does the member add up the experiences? What new insights does the member have about understanding relationships to others? What has the member identified as the next, most urgent set of tasks? What areas does the member feel hopeless about and need more discussion on? I believe that the process of *summarizing* can help a member secure what he or she has learned. Sometimes the member summarizes the work, other times the leader does it, at other times the group members take on the task, and sometimes they do it together. Note that summarizing is not required in all sessions. This is not an automatic ritual but a skill to be employed at key moments.

Generalizing

Earlier discussion stressed the importance of the skills of "moving from the general to the specific." It can also be important to move in the opposite direction. For example, a parent raises a specific problem with her teenage son and after some work on the immediate problem, the leader may help the individual and the group identify the general principle involved. As the mother gives details, problem by problem and system by system, the leader helps her to generalize the experiences and to recognize how her learning applies to a whole category of experiences. *Generalizing* is a key skill of living, because it equips the member to continue without the leader or the group and to use the newfound skills to deal with novel and unexpected experiences.

Identifying the Next Steps

We have all experienced, at one time or another, frustration when we participate in some form of work that goes nowhere because of lack of follow-up. A good example is a committee or staff meeting in which decisions are made, but the *division of labor* for implementing the decisions is overlooked, and no action follows. The leader must make a conscious effort to help the member in *identifying the next steps* involved in the work. No matter what the situation is, and no matter how impossible it may seem, some next step is possible, and the leader will ask the member to discuss it. I call this the principle of "there is always a next step." The next step may be a small one or a hard one, but it will be available when all else fails.

Next steps must be specific; that is, the general goal the member wishes to achieve must be broken down into manageable parts. The next steps for an unemployed mother on welfare who presents the need to find a job in a work retraining group might include exploring day care centers for her child and meeting with an employment counselor. The next step for a couple in marital counseling who feel their relationship is worsening might be to identify specific areas of difficulty for discussion in the group the following week. In essence, the identification of next steps represents another demand on the member for work.

Lack of planning by the member does not always represent poor life management skills; it may be another form of resistance. Talking about a tough subject may be difficult, but doing something about it may be even harder. By demanding attention to future, specific actions, the leader may bring to the surface another level of fear, ambivalence, and resistance that needs to be dealt with.

Sometimes the expression of understanding, support, and expectation by the leader is all the member needs to mobilize resources. There may be no easy way for the member to undertake the task, no simple solution, and no easy resolution when two genuinely conflicting needs arise. For the member, verbalizing the dilemma to an understanding yet demanding leader and to the group may be the key to movement. At other times, the member needs help figuring out the specifics of how to carry out the act. For example, the member might need some information about community resources.

Rehearsing

Talking about confronting another person with regard to difficult, interpersonal material is one thing, but actually doing it is quite another. Agreeing to undertake a job interview may be quite a difficult next step. A member who protests with "I don't know what to say" may be identifying an important source of blockage. A leader can help by offering the safe confines of the group as a place for the member to engage in *rehearsal*. The leader or a group member takes on the role of the other person (boss, teacher, husband, mother, doctor, etc.) and feeds back to the member possible reactions to the member's efforts. All too often, the leader skips this simple yet powerful device for aiding a member by saying, "When the time comes, you will know what to say." Words do not come easily for most people, especially in relation to their most difficult feelings. With the help of the leader and group members, the individual may be able to say what must be said and, with some successful rehearsal under their belts, may feel a bit more confident about doing it. A leader who thinks she has done a marvelous job in helping a member learn to deal effectively with an important person may find that additional work needs to be done when the member formulates the words to be used.

Identifying "Doorknob" Communications

A *"doorknob" communication* is shared as the member leaves the group session, often with his or her hand on the doorknob, or during the last session or sessions. This commonly observed phenomenon, described in the literature of psychotherapy, refers to any comments of significance raised by the member toward the end of a session when there is too little time to deal with them. We have all experienced a session with a member, or a conversation with a friend, when—after a relatively innocuous discussion—he says, "There is just one thing that happened this week." Then we hear that he lost his job or found out that his girlfriend was pregnant or received an eviction notice or noticed a strange lump in his groin. Journalists refer to this as "burying the lead." Reflecting on the session, the leader may see that the first clues to the concern were presented indirectly during the beginning stage. Or, perhaps, there may have been no clues at all.

A doorknob comment signals to the leader the member's ambivalence about discussing an area of work. The concern is raised at a time when it cannot be fully discussed. It may be a taboo area or one experienced as too painful to talk about. Whatever the reason, the desire to deal with the concern finally overwhelms the forces of resistance. The urgency of the concern, coupled with the pressures created by the lack of time left in the interview, finally results in the expression of the issue. This kind of comment is actually a special case of obstacles that block the member's ability to work. As with all forms of resistance, it is a natural part of the process and provides the leader with an opportunity to educate the member about the member's way of working. An example from my married couples group follows.

Couples Group and Sexual Issues

The skill involves identifying the process for the member. For example, at the end of a second session of a couples group I led, a young woman concerned about her marriage directly revealed a difficult sexual problem between her husband and herself. I responded directly:

> LEADER: You know, you have just raised a really important issue, which we will not have time to talk about. You raised it at the end of a session. Were you feeling it was too tough to talk about, too uncomfortable?
>
> MEMBER: (Brief silence) It's embarrassing to talk like this to strangers.
>
> LEADER: I can understand how it would be hard to discuss sex; I mean, really talk about it, with anyone. You know, it's quite common for people to be reluctant to discuss this subject directly, and they often raise these kinds of difficult areas right at the end of the session, just like you did. (The member smiles at this, as do the other group members.) Would it help if I started the next session talking a bit about what makes it so hard for all of us to talk about sex? That might make it easier for us to discuss this important area. What do you think?
>
> MEMBER: That sounds OK to me. This is a hard one for me, and I would like to discuss it.
> LEADER: I think you are making a good start even by raising it at the end.

I did not blame the member for her difficulty but instead offered support for the strength she had shown in raising the issue. By identifying the lateness of the comment and the reason it came at the end of the session, I was educating the group on how easy it was to avoid difficult topics. In many ways, the difficulty in discussing this taboo subject in the group was a reflection of the difficulty in their marriages. After more incidents like this one, group members will begin to understand and control how they introduce material into the group session. In addition, the discussion of the source of the embarrassment in the session will open up related feelings about the difficulty of discussing sex in our society, as well as the couple's problems with open communication in this area. The discussion of the process in the group will lead directly to work on the content—another illustration of the process-content connection.

This discussion of sessional ending skills brings to a close our analysis of the work phase. The purpose of this analysis has been to identify some of the key dynamics in giving and taking help that follow the negotiation of a joint working contract. A final example of work with mothers of children diagnosed as hyperactive illustrates the importance of making the demand for work and transitioning to the ending stage.

Mothers with Children Diagnosed as Hyperactive

In this example, a leader with a group of mothers with children diagnosed as hyperactive helped the members move toward more realistic next steps in their work as a mutual aid group. In making this demand for work, the leader was endorsing the power of resilience, suggesting that no matter how hopeless the situation may seem, the group members could begin by taking steps on their own behalf.

> There was a lot of exchanging of problem situations, with everyone coming out with her problems for the week. There seemed to be some urgency to share their problems, to get some understanding and moral support from the other members. Through their stories, themes emerged: an inconsistency in handling their children's behavior (lack of working together with husband); the tendency to be overprotective; and their hesitancy at trusting their children. The issue of "nobody understanding" was again brought up, and I recognized their need to have someone understand just what it was that they were going through. Betty said that her son was never invited to play at the neighbors' houses, because he was a known disturber. Others had the same experiences with neighbors who didn't want their hyperactive son and daughter around. I expressed the hurt they are feeling over this, to which they agreed.

After acknowledging the importance of others' understanding, the group leader notes the members moving to the more difficult area of their own feelings toward their children.

> After further discussion about the impact of their children on others (teachers, neighbors, children), they moved to a discussion of how their children's behavior affected them. Rose said that she ends up constantly nagging; she hates herself for it, but she can't stop. Her son infuriates her so much. Others agreed that they are the biggest naggers in the world. I asked what brought the nagging on. The consensus was that the kids kept at them until they are constantly worn down and they gave in to them. Also if they wanted the children to do something, they had to nag, because the children wouldn't listen. I said that the children really knew them, how they reacted, and also exactly what to do in order to get their own way. They agreed, but said that they couldn't change they couldn't keep up with the badgering that these children could give out.

The group members have expressed two divergent ideas: on the one hand, they "couldn't change"; on the other, they could not "keep up with the badgering" from their children. They quickly moved to a discussion of medications as a source of hope for change. The leader pointed out that their hope in this solution was mixed with their recognition that the drugs were addictive and that they could not provide an answer in the long run. This is an example of another process in groups that Bion (1961) calls "pairing," in which the discussion of the group members appears to raise the hope that some event or person in the future will solve the problem.

For these group members, drugs provided this hope but also gave the group members an opportunity to avoid discussing what they could do to deal with the problem. In a way, it represented a "primitive" group response: attempting to deal with the pain of a problem by not facing it. As the session moved to a close, the leader sensed the heaviness and depression of the group members caused by their feelings of hopelessness. She had empathized with these feelings but now needed to make a demand for work on the members, asking them to explore what they could do about the problem.

PRACTICE POINTS When the members raised another hope for a solution in the form of an outside expert who would help, the leader pointed out their real feelings that no "outsider" could help and that they needed to find the help within themselves. In this way, the leader helped them resolve a difficult and painful discussion by conveying her belief in their strength and her sense of the concrete next steps open to them.

There was further discussion around the children's poor social behavior and the mothers' own worry about how these children will make out as adults. What will become of them? Will they fit in and find a place for themselves in society? I was feeling the heaviness of the group and pointed out what a tremendous burden it was for them. Our time was up, and I made an attempt to end the meeting, but they continued the discussion. I recognized their urgency to solve the problem and the need to talk with each other and get support from each other. Marilyn said that it was good; she came away feeling so much more relieved at being able to talk about how she felt, and she certainly was gaining some new insight into herself.

Discussion diverted to the problem with the children and how they were to deal with it. I asked what they wanted to do. Edna suggested they ask a behavior modification therapist to help them work out solutions. Others thought it was a good idea. I said that was a possibility, but I wondered if in wanting to get an "expert" involved, they were searching for someone to solve their problems for them. They agreed. I asked if they thought all these experts could do this. They said that it hadn't happened yet. I wondered if I could use the group for the purpose it was set up, to help each other problem-solve. I suggested that next week we concentrate on particular problems and work together to see what solutions we could come up with. They seemed delighted with this and decided that they should write down a problem that happened during the week and bring it in. Then we could look at a number of problems. Consensus was reached as to our next week's agenda, and the meeting ended.

This illustration of one form of sessional ending and transition work brings to a close our description of the work phase in a mutual aid group. Having looked at the general model of the individual-group interaction, we can now examine the elements in depth and explore some variations on the theme. In the next chapter, I will examine the individual's role in the group, concentrating on how members are informally assigned to play functional roles such as scapegoat, deviant, and internal leader. In Chapter 8, I will explore the needs of the group as a whole and the way in which the group leader can help the group work on its central tasks.

Chapter Summary

In an effort to describe this complex process in simple terms, I have had to oversimplify the central ideas. The work phase session does not proceed in four stages as neatly as I have outlined it here. Furthermore, the skill categories are not mutually exclusive. For example, as the sessional contracting proceeds, the leader will use elaborating, empathic, and demand-for-work skills. The advantage of describing this complex process in an oversimplified form is that it gives us a model with which to orient ourselves as I explore each stage and each skill factor in further detail.

I would like to reinforce an idea that will have already come to the reader's attention. This model of the middle phase of a group meeting could just as easily be written in the context of individual or family work, or other forms of counseling and task groups.

Related Online Content and Activities

For learning tools such as glossary terms, InfoTrac® College Edition keywords, links to related websites, and chapter practice quizzes, visit this book's website at **www.cengage.com/counseling/shulman.**

Working with the Individual in the Group

The model presented thus far suggests that the group leader always has two clients: the individual and the group. In this chapter and the next, an artificial separation of these two clients is employed to deepen your understanding of each in interaction with the other. First I will focus on the individual within the group, discussing how clients bring their personalities to bear in their group interactions. The concept of role is used to help describe how individual personality is translated into group interaction. Many common patterns of individual-group relationships are described and illustrated; for example, I look at scapegoats, deviant members, gatekeepers, and monopolizers. As these individuals are isolated for closer analysis, you will see that understanding individual clients without considering them in the context of their group interaction is often impossible.

In the next chapter, I will examine the concept of the group-as-a-whole. This is the entity that is created when more than one client is involved at a time. I will introduce an *organismic model* and illustrate some of the group leader's tasks when he or she must intervene to help in the growth of the second client, the group.

The Concept of Role in a Dynamic System

Two ideas central to the discussion of the individual in a group are role and dynamic system. Ackerman (1958) describes the ways in which the term *role* has been used and proposes his own definition:

> Sociology, social psychology, and anthropology approach the problems of role through the use of special concepts and techniques. They apply the term in two distinct ways, meaning either the "role" of the person in a specific, transient, social position or the characteristic "role" of the individual in society as determined by his social class status. Working in the psychodynamic frame of reference, I shall use the term to represent an adaptational unit of personality in action. "Social role" is here conceived as synonymous with the operations of the "social self" or social identity of the person in the context of a defined life situation. (p. 53)

Ackerman suggests that the individual has both a private "inner self" and a social "outer self" that emphasizes externally oriented aspects of his or her personality. I use this idea of social role in the following way: When clients begin a group, they present their outer selves as their way of adapting to the pressures and demands of the group context. Their pattern of action represents their social role. Ackerman argues that incongruity between the reality of the inner self and the outer self presented in a group can cause tension. In many ways, the task of the group leader involves helping individuals find the freedom to express their inner selves in the group. The central idea is that each member brings to the group an established pattern of translating a unique personality into social action.

The Impact of Oppression on Social Role

When we consider oppressed and vulnerable groups, we can integrate Ackerman's notions about role into the oppression psychology concepts described in Chapter 2. The outer self of survivors of oppression represents their adaptive behavior to the defined situation of oppression. We can understand the incongruity between the outer self, which they present in social situations, and the inner self as one of the defense mechanisms employed in an effort to cope. This resulting incongruity is a form of alienation from self-identity, as described by Fanon (Bulhan, 1985). The effort in the mutual aid group is to help members use the group to integrate their inner and outer selves and to find more adaptive mechanisms to cope with oppression, including personal and social action. The small group is a microcosm of the larger society. If we consider the impact of oppression, our understanding of the role played by a survivor of oppression within a group context deepens.

Keeping in mind the concept of individual roles, we can view the group as a dynamic system, in which the movements of each part (member) are partially affected by the movements of the other parts (the other members). This view is rooted in the work of Kurt Lewin (1935, 1951), who is often considered the founder of group dynamics. Thus, members bring their outer selves to this dynamic system and then adapt to the system through their social roles. All group members engage in this process of adaptation. The model presented thus far provides a general description of the individual-social interaction in a group. For our purposes, however, I shall concentrate on specific social roles that emerge over time and require special attention by the group leader.

More recently, the concept of *impression management (IM)* has emerged as a model for the way in which people present themselves to others to effect how they wish others to perceive them. This model is rooted in the early work of Erving Goffman (1959), whose book *The Presentation of Self in Everyday Life* explored the way we consciously or unconsciously shape the image projected to others. More recently, social psychologists have been exploring the topic of self-presentation, IM, and interpersonal behavior in a number of contexts (see, e.g., Learly, 1996; Schlenker, 2003).

Formal and Informal Roles in the Group

Patterned social roles are most easily illustrated using an example from a formal, organized task group, such as a students' association. To function effectively, the association usually identifies specific tasks that group members must assume and then assigns these jobs by some form of division of labor. For example, the association may need a chairperson, a secretary, a treasurer, and a program coordinator. The essential idea is that group roles are functionally necessary and required for productive work. In taking on any of these roles, specific members will bring their own sense of social role to bear. For example, depending on their experience, background, skills, and sense of social role, various members would implement the role of chairperson differently. Because the group is a dynamic system, the group and its individual members will also affect the chairperson's implementation of this role to a certain extent. The actions of the chairperson are best described as the product of the interaction among the individual's sense of social role, the role of chairperson as defined by the group, and the particular dynamics of the group and its members.

The roles just described are formal. Every group also creates less formal roles to help in its work, even though these might never be openly acknowledged. For example, in a group led by a professional group leader who guides the discussion as an external leader, one or more internal leaders may emerge as if they had been formally elected. The individuals who assume internal leadership in a group play a social role within the group that includes this function. By responding positively to them, group members encourage the internal leaders' assumption of this important role. The key and in fact crucial concept here is that the group itself has something to do with assigning and encouraging the playing of the individual role. Think back to groups you have participated in. Remember the class clown who you and your classmates encouraged by your laughter. Think back to your formal and informal social groups and how one or another member played a leadership role and by following that person, you recognized his or her leadership.

Other, less constructive functional roles can emerge in a group; these reflect maladaptation rather than healthy development. For example, *scapegoats* are often selected by the group because they possess the personal characteristic that members most dislike or fear in themselves. Thus, a group of young teenage boys who are worried about sexual identity may select as the group scapegoat the teen that seems least "macho" or least less sure of himself. The members, of course, do not hold an election for such roles. It is not as if the group members held an informal meeting, prior to the group session, and asked for volunteers to be the group scapegoats, internal leaders, deviant members, and so on. If the group has a need for these roles, however, they will go through a subtle, informal process to select members to fill them. The dysfunctional aspect of employing a scapegoat is that it often leads the group members to avoid facing their own concerns and feelings by projecting them onto the scapegoat.

Similarly, individuals do not raise their hands and volunteer to act as scapegoats, pointing out that they have successfully played the scapegoat role in their families and social groups for most of their lives. The scapegoat in the group usually subtly volunteers for this role, because it is consistent with that individual's concept of his or her social role. Adapting to groups by playing this social role is as dysfunctional for the individual scapegoat as it is for the group as a whole. Once again, the idea of the group as a dynamic system helps us understand the process of scapegoating in a dynamic way. (The next section explores the role of scapegoat in greater detail.)

In the sections that follow, I will look at informal roles that are developed in groups, such as scapegoats, deviant members, monopolizers, and gatekeepers. In each case, the discussion focuses on analyzing the dynamics as they reflect the individual's social role within the group. In addition, I will examine the skills of the group leader as he or she implements the individualizing part of the work while simultaneously addressing the second client, the group.

The Scapegoat

The discussion of individual roles in the group begins with the *scapegoat* because it is one of the most common—and one of the most distressing—problems in work with groups. The scapegoat is a group member who is attacked, verbally or physically, by other members. These members usually project onto the scapegoat their own negative feelings about themselves. The scapegoat role is often interactive in nature, with the scapegoat fulfilling a functional role in the group. Whether scapegoating is overt, as typically takes place in groups of children and adolescents, or more subtle, as in adult groups, the impact on the group and the group leader can be profound. As I explore this particular role in detail, I shall introduce several important concepts regarding social role in the group and the function of the group leader. These central ideas will reemerge as I examine other roles. This discussion can then serve as a general model to analyze individual roles in the group.

First, we must consider the history of the term *scapegoat*. Douglas (1995) attributes the term's origin to the 15th-century biblical scholar and translator Tyndale. Tyndale's translation of sections of Leviticus referred to an ancient ritual among the Hebrews that was practiced on the Day of Atonement. Two live goats were brought to the altar of the tabernacle. One was killed as a sacrifice and skinned with the separated skin of the goat called a "scape." After the high priest transferred his own sins and the sins of the people onto the scape of the first goat, it was placed on the second goat, which was taken to the wilderness and allowed to escape. Douglas suggests, "If Tyndale had read into the Hebrew idea that the goat was 'suffered to escape,' then his coining of the word 'scapegoat' becomes much clearer" (p. 8). Douglas describes the scapegoat ritual as essentially a process of purification, which means—in essence—that its practitioners felt that they were contaminated by the transgressions of their daily lives, and that the ritual of scapegoating would disperse that contamination and reinstate them as clean in their own eyes and, more important, in the eyes of their god (p. 14).

Whole populations, such as African Americans, Jews, people with mental illness and physical disabilities, immigrants, and gays and lesbians, have experienced extreme forms of scapegoating as part of the systematic oppression described in Chapter 2. These have included the projection of negative stereotypes as an underlying justification for slavery, as well as more current forms of economic and social oppression;

anti-Semitism and the Holocaust, in which millions of Jews (as well as many homosexuals, gypsies, and others) were systematically killed; and gay-bashing activities in which gays and lesbians are physically attacked on the street or serve as the butt of homophobic jokes. More recently, the immigrant population, both legal and illegal, has served as political scapegoats for politicians trying to use this group to tap into underlying stereotypes and biases held by a portion of the larger population. Shocking and random physical attacks on immigrants also have occurred in some communities.

Bell and Vogel (1960) have described the dynamics of this phenomenon in the family group, emphasizing the functional role played by the scapegoat in maintaining equilibrium in the family by drawing all of the problems onto him- or herself. Many scapegoats in groups have been socialized into this social role by their family experiences and are ready to assume it in each new group they enter.

Scapegoating is also discussed by Garland and Kolodny (1965), who provide an interesting analysis of the forms of scapegoating that are prevalent in practice:

> No single phenomenon occasions more distress to the outside observer than the act of scapegoating. Frequently violent in its undertones, if not in actual form, it violates every ethical tenet to which our society officially subscribes. As part of that society, the group worker confronted with scapegoating in the midst of interaction often finds himself caught up in a welter of primitive feelings, punitive and pitying, and assailed by morbid reflections on the unfairness of fate which leaves one weak and others strong. (p. 124)

In an early article of mine, I address the common mistake in practice I called the *preemptive intervention*, in which the group leader moves into the interaction between the scapegoat and group in a way that preempts the opportunity for either the group or the individual to deal with the problem (Shulman, 1967). Most often, when the group leader protects the scapegoat, the hostility of the other group members merely takes more covert forms. Appeals to fairness or requests to give the member a chance do not seem to help, and the group leader is usually left feeling frustrated, the scapegoat hurt, and the group members guilty.

As we think about scapegoating in the group, the concepts of social role and the group as a dynamic system provide us with clues to the meaning of this interaction. We cannot understand the behavior of the scapegoat simply as a manifestation of his or her "personality." Rather, it is a result of the interaction between the scapegoat's sense of social role and the group's functional needs. The relationship between the individual role and the group becomes clear if the group loses its scapegoat—if, for example, the member drops out of the group. As though operating on an unconscious command, the group immediately searches for a new candidate to take the scapegoat's place. One member is usually waiting to do so.

An example from work with a group of teenage girls in a school follows. The key concept for the reader to keep in mind is to avoid taking sides and to *be with the individual and the group at the same time.*

African American and Hispanic Teenage Girls in a School

This example illustrates the scapegoating process, some of the pitfalls the group leader faces, and effective strategies for intervention. We see a new group leader's interventions with a group of teenage girls over a 2-month period in a school setting. The group leader was white, and the girls were African American and Hispanic. The group leader started this work by developing insights into the scapegoating process and tuning in to her feelings.

Her protective responses toward the scapegoat were subtle; she tried to deal with the problem indirectly because of her concern with the possibility of hurting the member who was being scapegoated. Although she never directly confronted the scapegoating process, she did deal with the concerns of the second client, the group, which led the group to have less need for a scapegoat.

Client Description and Time Frame: This is a seventh-grade girls' peer support group of 12- and 13-year-olds (three African American and two Hispanic girls) from a racially mixed, low-income part of the city. The time frame is from December 5 through February 6.

Description of the Problem

This group is projecting its dependency needs onto one individual, causing the group to remain in the beginning stage of development. This individual, Rachel, acts out these dependency needs for the group. Rachel does her own thing, not involving herself in any group activities and keeping to herself. The group's investment in the role of the scapegoat both hinders and helps the development of the group as it pushes toward its next stage, intimacy.

How the Problem Came to the Attention of the Leader(s)

On January 23, I observed that Rachel sat away from the other members of the group and refused to join in the group activity (which was painting) and was unwilling to speak. This behavior brought a negative reaction from the group, and the other girls hypothesized about why she was acting like a loner. The group soon ignored this behavior when Lisa brought up a "hypothetical" situation in which she was involved. Lisa stated that she was tired of a girl she used to be friends with and now does not like anymore. Lisa asked the group for advice about what to do and how to tell this girl.

At this point, I realized that the girl she was discussing was Rachel. When questioned by the other girls as to who this girl was, Lisa would not say. At this moment, I was very unsure of my position as a group leader and what I should do about the situation. My first instinct was to see this as an issue that needed to be dealt with by Rachel and Lisa only, but, in thinking about it further, I decided it was indeed a group problem, especially considering our group goal of improving peer relations. It became clear to me that this need for the role of a scapegoat was an issue for the entire group.

The group leader's first tendency to see this as a problem between Rachel and Lisa is not unusual because she does not see the group-as-a-whole in a dynamic manner. She also is just beginning to understand the integration of process and content. That is, this apparent conflict between the two girls, handled in an indirect manner, is not at all uncommon for girls at this age and thus represents an opportunity to address the larger issue of peer relations.

Summary of the Work

December 5 (First Session)

We were discussing the purpose of the group, and I asked them what they thought some of the rules should be. Most of the members jumped in and offered suggestions, many of them expressing concern about confidentiality and "secrets." Rachel and Kim sat on either side of me, neither of them saying anything, but they nodded when Lisa and Amy asked them what they thought of a rule or an idea they suggested.

I attempted to engage Rachel and Kim in conversation, and I gave the group permission to make their own rules. I asked them both what they thought we should do as a group if someone broke our rule of confidentiality. They both replied by looking confused and shrugging their shoulders. Rachel said, "I don't know—what do you mean?" Lisa immediately jumped in, asked Rachel if she was "deaf or what?" and gave her idea of a "punishment," causing Rachel to sink in her chair and look down at the floor.

I could sense what was going on, but I did not know how to respond to it. Looking back, I can see that these were all issues related to the theme of authority. I did not want to discourage anyone from saying what she wanted, and I did not want to push anyone into talking if she did not want to. I was simply thrilled that anyone was saying anything, and that they were enthused about the group.

PRACTICE POINTS The group leader's honesty in this early session is refreshing. She is both pleased that any conversation is taking place but also unclear about how to implement the group's purpose and especially about her role. She is clearer in the next session as she tries to help Kim reach out for help from the group. However, as the group gets into the details and as the conversation flows, the leader is still unclear about how to respond.

December 12 (Second Session)

Kim had a problem, and I supported her in bringing it to the group. Kim told the group that she had a problem and that she wanted to ask everyone what she should do about it. She had been involved in a fight earlier that week, and now she had to go to court. She said she was afraid that she would be sent to a school where "they are real strict and don't let you do nothing you want to do." She asked me what she could do about this and asked if I could help her by talking to the principal for her. I told her I was glad that she brought this to the group. I asked the group what they thought about the situation. Lisa stated that, if the situation happened to her, she wouldn't worry about it because she knew her mother would not get mad at her and would not care. I completely missed the boat on this statement! Kim was discussing the entire incident with Mary, and the group became interested in the details of the fight. I became interested in who did what to whom and who was responsible for what, trying to determine if Kim was indeed going to be punished severely by the court system.

PRACTICE POINTS In hindsight, Lisa's comment about her mother not caring is also very potent. While it may not be appropriate for this moment at some time the group leader may want to get back to this issue. How about the other girls? Would their mother's care if they got into trouble?

Kim told the group that the reason she got into the fight was because someone in the school had spread the rumor that she was pregnant. She said that she had to let everyone know that she was not, and so she had no choice but to get into this fight with the person who started the rumor. The group agreed that she did have to fight this girl because, after all, she had no business saying such things, and she ruined Kim's reputation. (I missed an important issue the group was raising and asked the group to work on the more obvious issue.) I asked the group about other things they could do to avoid fighting in such a situation and did not focus in on the pregnancy issue, which, in retrospect, I think was the real problem.

With so many issues emerging at once, it would help if the group leader could partialize the problems raised by the girls and then help them address them one at a time: the fight, the court, parental reaction to the pregnancy, rumor spreaders, and, of course, the pregnancy itself. The group leader does note that Rachel, the group scapegoat, sits quietly during the discussion and picks a seat next to the leader. Taking this seat can be a communication of needing protection.

> Almost everyone in the group was actively involved in a discussion of who can and cannot be trusted in their class, and who the people are in the school that spread rumors. I missed the significance of Rachel not participating in the discussion. I realized toward the end of the group that Rachel did not participate actively in the conversation and, in fact, had sat next to me again. I also was able to recognize the fact that I was quite uncomfortable addressing the issue.

During a later session, the group leader realized that she had missed the central theme of concern for Kim. Although Kim raised her problem in terms of the fight and the resultant discipline, this was actually a first offering of her deeper concern—the fact that she was pregnant. The issue did not resurface until the fifth session. The next session followed the Christmas break for the group leader as well as a session before the break where the members expressed disappointment in not continuing to meet. Their competition for the attention of the leader emerges in some distress that one member, Rachel, is able to get out of class early to meet the leader. As the scapegoating of Rachel emerges indirectly, the leader senses it and feels a need to protect the scapegoat.

January 23 (Fourth Session)

Before group started, Rachel came in and told me that Lisa had been acting unfriendly toward her and that this upset her a great deal, because they were supposed to be best friends. We discussed some ways that she could confront Lisa on this and the friendship in general. Rachel told me that she wanted to meet two periods a week instead of one. I encouraged her to bring this up in group.

> When everyone arrived for the group, the girls all asked why Rachel got to get out of class early to come and talk to me. They appeared annoyed that Rachel may have received "special attention" but soon forgot this discussion when Lisa brought up a problem. I supported Lisa for coming to the group for advice, but I missed an underlying issue. Lisa told me that she had a problem and asked if we could please talk about her this week. She went on to say that this was a hypothetical situation and that it did not involve anyone they knew. Lisa said that she has a friend who is always doing everything she does, is always wearing the same clothes she wears, says the same things she says, and even likes the same boys she likes.

The specific conflict with Rachel emerges once again—what might be considered an escalation of the message to the group leader. The response to scapegoating described in the previous section—the preemptive intervention to protect the scapegoat—is evident in the following example. The leader thinks she is the only one who knows what's going on, but actually most, if not all, of the group members know. They are waiting for a signal from the group leader that they can address the issue.

I sensed that Lisa was talking about Rachel, and I felt a strong urge to protect the individual being scapegoated. The group members jumped in on this subject and stated how they all hate this behavior. Rachel sat in the corner of the room, watching the group and looking out of the window. I suggested that maybe this friend really likes Lisa a great deal and wants to be like her. Kim jumped in and agreed with me and told Lisa that she should feel complimented. I made a demand for work. I asked the group what they would do in this situation. I made the assumption that I was the only one who knew the entire picture and acted accordingly. Everyone was very involved in the pictures they were drawing and did not seem to feel like discussing the subject.

PRACTICE POINTS

It is at moments like these that the group leader identifies with Rachel, the scapegoat, which leads to the crucial question: If the leader is with Rachel, who is with the group? The obvious answer is no one. Once again, a false dichotomy traps the leader since her most helpful role is to be with the individual and the group at the same time. She is attuned to Rachel's discomfort but not connecting to the feelings of the group as expressed by Lisa.

In retrospect, I see that the group knew exactly what was going on and that it was my own feelings of discomfort that allowed me to avoid the issue. I avoided the main issues being raised in an attempt to protect the scapegoat. Lisa insisted on getting my opinion on the subject, even though I threw it out to the group for answers. I picked up on a conversation that Kim and Mary were having and began talking with Cindy about a teacher they disliked. Lisa put her problem back on the table for discussion. I was feeling very annoyed at her insistence, and I told her that we had answered her question and that she could come and discuss it with me later if she wanted to. As the members left that day, Lisa pulled me aside and told me that this person was Rachel and that she did not want Rachel to know. I was able to support her as an individual group member; I told her that I would be free to speak with her later that morning and gave her a pass to get out of class.

PRACTICE POINTS

The pattern of scapegoating is not directly addressed. Rachel, the other group members, and the group leader all know it is going on. The group leader's reluctance is rooted in not wanting to hurt Rachel, yet the persistent pattern of scapegoating is more painful than any direct discussion might be. Group leaders are often afraid to open up an issue such as this because they are not sure what will happen and where it will go. The group leader's indirect efforts to deal with the problem match the group members' own use of indirect communications, thus frustrating the growth of the group. As the group culture becomes more positive, the group members are able to deal with some of their issues and lessen their need for a scapegoat. Kim will introduce a major personal issue with the not uncommon "I have a friend . . ." opening.

January 30 (Fifth Session)

I supported Kim for bringing a problem to the group. Kim brought up a problem she was currently dealing with and asked the group for advice. She said that she has a friend who thought she was pregnant. Her friend's cousin told her to drink "this awful stuff" to get rid of the baby. She said her friend did not want the baby, but her friend's boyfriend wanted it very badly. Now her friend does not know what to tell her boyfriend. I reached for the group's feelings. The group immediately confronted Kim and wanted to know if she was speaking about herself. Kim said it was a friend. I said that this must be very difficult and was a scary situation to be in. I verbalized the group's nonverbal behaviors. I acknowledged that there seemed to be a great deal of tension around the subject of pregnancy and that it was a difficult topic of discussion. Cindy said that her mother would kill her if she ever came home pregnant and that she felt sorry for this girl. I pointed out to the group that the problem was not only an individual issue but also an issue for the group. The members appeared uneasy discussing the topic of pregnancy and were willing to change the subject and talk about something else.

PRACTICE POINTS

The group leader's growing sense of her role is evident as she immediately addresses the second client—the group. Their avoidance of a difficult and taboo subject is a signal that they need some indication from the leader that this topic is OK and that the leader is not afraid to discuss it. In the leader's comment about Kim's courage and the group's emotion, we see the group leader's integration of the job of being with the two clients at exactly the same time: Kim who is pregnant and the group members who are impacted by her comment.

The group tried to avoid the issue by concentrating on who among their classmates they thought could be pregnant. I made a demand for work. I stated to the group that a member had raised an important question and that it was an issue that demanded their attention. I asked the group what they would tell their boyfriends in a similar situation. Lisa stated that she would simply dump him and not tell him, since he must be crazy to think a 12-year-old should have a baby. Rachel stated that she did not have a boyfriend, and Mary said that she would tell him and hope he did not leave her. At this point, Kim broke in and told the group that it was herself that she was talking about. I said that everyone might be feeling a great deal of emotion, and that it must have taken a great deal of courage and trust to come to the group with this issue. The members focused in on the situation, giving Kim advice and reflecting the situation onto themselves, and they talked about what they would do in such a situation.

In this session, the group did not appear to need the scapegoat; the conversation was intense, and everyone worked together on the issue at hand. I began to feel that the group was progressing, and I felt much more in tune with my own feelings about things that happened in the group. I was able to catch myself more quickly and did not feel such a strong urge to protect everyone.

Where the Problem Stands Now

The group has entered the intimacy stage, and we are able to do "real work" and discuss issues that they want to talk about. Scapegoating still occurs at times, but I am able to recognize it and address it at some level. I have found that, when I call attention to the scapegoating, it is no longer an issue (at least at that time). Rachel has been integrated into the group more often and has not been in the role of the scapegoat in our last few sessions.

The group is able to discuss issues that are of concern to them, such as boys, friendship, and the violence that they frequently see in their neighborhoods. Other issues are still very difficult for them to talk about, such as racism, what it's like to be black or Hispanic in the city, and the fact that I am a middle-class, white group leader in a group for minority girls. The theme of authority remains an issue for the group—they have a difficult time understanding that they have control of this group. I need to work on letting them know this more often.

Note that this student group leader identifies race as an issue for the girls in their daily lives and also as an issue between the girls and her. She even includes it in her assessment of where the problem stands, although she identifies it as an issue that the members have difficulty discussing. Her struggle to deal with this crucial issue is not uncommon, and she will need support and supervision to recognize that her group members' difficulty in exploring the potentially explosive area of race reflects her own reluctance. When they are clear that she is ready, they will respond. This issue is discussed in more detail in Chapter 11 dealing with diversity under the heading "Intercultural Practice."

By understanding the dynamics of scapegoating, the group leader can more easily avoid the trap of siding with either the individual or the group. This natural response misses the essential message: that the group and the scapegoat are using the process as an attempt, albeit maladaptive, to offer a theme of concern. Because scapegoating may be the only way the group members know to deal with their thoughts and feelings, the group leader should not get too upset with either the group or the scapegoat. The group leader's task involves helping the group and the scapegoat recognize their patterns and find a new way to deal with concerns that are common to both. By viewing both the individual and the group as clients in need, the group leader can become better at understanding and empathizing with the feelings the two share.

Strategies for Addressing the Scapegoating Pattern

Work with the scapegoating pattern involves several steps.

- First, the group leader observes the pattern over time.
- Second, group leaders must understand their own feelings in the situation to avoid siding with or against the scapegoat.
- Third, by using the tuning-in skill, group leaders can attempt to search out the potential connections between the scapegoat and the group. What is it about themselves that they don't like and are projecting onto the scapegoat?
- If the group leaders are not clear about these connections, they can ask the group to reflect on the question.
- Finally, the next step involves pointing out the pattern to the group and the scapegoat. Thus, the group leader asks the group to look at its way of working and to begin the struggle to find a more positive adaptive process.

When group leaders challenge this scapegoating process, they must not criticize either the group or the scapegoat for having developed this way of dealing with their underlying feelings. In fact, the capacity for empathy and understanding of how hard it is to face these feelings is the very thing that allows the group leader to make this demand for work. This demand includes two tasks: (1) asking the group to consider why it is scapegoating and (2) asking the scapegoat to reflect on her or his reasons for volunteering for the role. Discussion of this process is designed to free the members to explore further their underlying feelings. It would be a mistake to support ongoing discussions of the individual's life pattern of being a scapegoat or the group's analysis of its process. When the discussion is honest, invested with feeling, and touches all of the members, the group will no longer need a scapegoat.

The discussion may help the members moderate their harsh judgments of themselves that lead to the need for a scapegoat. In turn, the scapegoat may discover that his or her feelings are not unique.

The Deviant Member

One of the most difficult clients for group leaders to deal with is the one they experience as the *deviant member*. In this discussion, the term *deviant* is used broadly to describe a member whose behavior deviates from the general norm of the group. This deviation can range from extremely inappropriate and disconnected behavior (e.g., a participant who refuses to stop talking at the first meeting or a member who manifests psychotic behavior) to one whose actions deviate only mildly or sporadically (e.g., a member who stares out the window while the rest of the group is deeply involved in a discussion).

In my practice, I have made two major assumptions about such behavior. First, deviant behavior is always a form of communication. The group leader's problem lies in figuring out what the member is saying. This difficulty is compounded by the fact that group leaders often experience the deviance as directed toward themselves, thus activating powerful emotions in the group leaders. For example, group leaders may see acting-out behavior in a children's group as a test of their authority, which at times it is.

Second, deviant behavior in a group may express a communication that has meaning for the group as a whole. That is, just as the group may use a scapegoat as a means to deal with difficult feelings, a deviant member may serve an important social role for other group members. This assumption is related to the view of the group as a dynamic system. In this section, I explore these two assumptions.

Extreme Versus Mild Deviance

Again, we can consider deviant behavior on a continuum that ranges from extreme to slight. On the extreme end would be a client or group member who evinces bizarre behavior that is totally inappropriate for the group. This can happen when meetings are open to the community or the screening of prospective members has not taken place. When this happens in a first session, the impact on the group leader and the group is profound. As the member speaks, one can sense the group shrinking in embarrassment and at times in fear. The leader needs to take responsibility for gently but firmly asking the member to withhold comment or, in extreme cases, to leave the session. Group members are not prepared, in an early session, to deal with extreme deviance and therefore depend on the group leader to clarify the boundaries and to enforce the limits if needed.

Parent Recruitment Group Example

In one such example, a woman attending a single-session, foster parent informational recruitment session responded to the group leader's opening contract statement and requests for group feedback by beginning a long, and essentially unrelated, tale of personal tragedy. When the group leader tried repeatedly to clarify the contract or to discover how the woman's concerns might relate to the discussion, she met with no success. The woman refused to allow others to speak and went on in detail about her personal problems and her fears that people were after her—even that the room was bugged.

The discomfort in the eyes of the group members was clear. The group leader, herself uncomfortable, finally moved to control the situation.

GROUP LEADER: Mrs. Pane, it is obvious that you're having a tough time right now, but I simply can't let you continue to use this group meeting to discuss it. I'll have to ask you to leave, but I would be glad to talk with you further about your concerns at another time.

MRS. PANE: You f- -ing workers are all alike. You don't give a s- -t about us; you're no different from the rest. You took my kids away, and I want them back.

GROUP LEADER: I'm sorry, Mrs. Pane, I can't talk with you now about that. You will have to leave, and I can discuss this with you tomorrow.

Mrs. Pane finally left, and the group leader turned to the group to acknowledge how upset she was feeling about what had just happened. The group members expressed their own feelings. After emotions had settled, the group leader picked up the group members' reactions to Mrs. Pane as a parent of children in the care of the agency. This led to a discussion of parents, their feelings about placements, and contacts between biological parents and foster parents. Once again, we see a skillful example of how to integrate process (the acting-out behavior of a disturbed biological parent) and content (possible contacts with biological parents).

The group leader followed up the next day with Mrs. Pane and did get to see her. There was a long, sometimes rambling and disjointed conversation during which the group leader consistently tried to reach Mrs. Pane and acknowledge her feelings. Mrs. Pane turned to the leader as she left and said, "I'm sorry for what I said last night. You know, it's just that I'm so angry—I miss my kids so much." Mrs. Pane's behavior at the meeting was an extreme example of the use of deviant behavior to express deeply held feelings. The group leader could not allow the session to be captured by Mrs. Pane, and, using all of her courage, she protected or, using another term, guarded the group's contract.

Reaching for the Underlying Message of Deviant Behavior

It is striking how often group leaders are surprised to find relatively normal reactions and feelings underlying initial deviant behavior that they have taken as personal attacks. For example, a group member whose first comment is to challenge the need for the group itself or who responds defensively about his own need for help may seem deviant at first but not after the source of the behavior comes to light. All that is needed, at times, is to confront the group member directly and to ask about the meaning of the behavior. Keep in mind the following three key concepts as you read the next example:

- The need to tolerate deviant behavior
- The importance of reaching for the underlying message
- Understanding the "deviant" as, at times, speaking for the group

A Group for Children Having Trouble in School

Consider the following example from a group for students having trouble in school. The meetings were held at the school in the afternoon, and John started acting up as he entered the meeting room. He picked a fight with Jim, knocked over the desk, and appeared ready to tackle the group leader next.

GROUP LEADER: John, what the hell is up? You have been roaring mad since you walked in here. (John remains silent, glaring, with his fists clenched.) Did you just come from a fight with someone? Or was it Mr. Smith [the teacher]? Did you have an argument with him?

JOHN: (Still angry, but slightly more relaxed) He's always picking on me, the bastard.

GROUP LEADER: OK, now slow down and tell me what happened. Maybe we can help you on this one. That's what the group is all about.

PRACTICE SUMMARY The group leader was able to reach for the meaning behind this behavior instead of getting caught up in a battle of wills with John, because he understood his own role, was clear about the purpose of the group, and understood that children often raise their problems indirectly by acting out. If the helping professional does not listen carefully and attempt to understand the feelings behind the behavior, it will only escalate. In this example, the group leader attempts to understand what happened just before this outburst, which leads to the feelings underneath and raises an agenda for work for the whole group.

The group member does not always immediately respond to the group leader's efforts to reach past the behavior; however, he or she often understands the group leader's meaning and will sometimes respond to the invitation later. Clarity of role is important, because if the group leader is concentrating solely on his or her limit-setting function (e.g., stopping the fight), he or she may miss the other part of the work. The skill often involves setting the limit and reaching for the meaning of the behavior at exactly the same time.

Deviant Behavior as a Functional Role

As mentioned earlier, deviant behavior may in some way reflect the feelings of the group as a whole. This notion stems from the idea of the group as a dynamic system, in that the movement of one member is somewhat affected by the movements of the others. The deviant member can be viewed simply as a member who, for various reasons, feels a particular concern or emotion more strongly than the others in the group do. This greater sense of urgency causes the deviant member to express the more widely held feeling, often in an indirect manner.

Schwartz (1961) refers to the function of the deviant member in the client group as follows:

> Such clients often play an important role in the group—expressing ideas that others may feel but be afraid to express, catalyzing issues more quickly, bringing out the negatives that need to be examined, etc. This helped us to see that such members should not immediately be thought of as "enemies" of the group, diverting it from its purposes, but as clients with needs of their own, and that these needs are often dramatic and exaggerated versions of those of the other group members. (p. 11)

It is critical, therefore, that group leaders not dismiss a deviant group member too quickly as simply acting out a personal problem. This would constitute the mistake of attempting to understand the behavior of one member of a dynamic system (the group) apart from the behavior of other members of the system. Although this member may bring this particular social role to all groups, one cannot understand him or her simply as a separate entity. The first hypothesis should always be that the member might speak for the group as a whole. In fact, this member who is often experienced by the leader as an "enemy" may in fact be an important "ally." In the first session of the couples' group described in earlier chapters, the older member (Lou) who attacked "professionals" was carrying out the important task of dealing with the authority theme, which was an issue for the whole group. His concerns and fears about how I and my co-leaders would run the group were clearly shared by other members.

Counseling Group at a Mental Health Center: What's the Purpose of This Group?

The following examples demonstrate two specific ways in which deviant behavior operates functionally: in opening up a discussion of group purpose and in deepening the work already in progress. In the following excerpt, a member attacks the purpose of the group in a session at a psychiatric center:

> **MR. WRIGHT:** (Who has been quiet for most of the first two sessions, although he seemed to have a critical look on his face) I think this is really all a bunch of crap! How in the hell is it going to do us any good sitting around and talking like this?
>
> **MRS. SAMUELS:** Well, you know, you really haven't had much to say. Maybe if you spoke up, it would be more worthwhile.

Most inexperienced group leaders would take the force of this attack personally because they would feel fully responsible for the group's success. It would not be unusual for the group leader to view Mr. Wright as negative, hostile, and resistant and to set out to challenge him or encourage the group members to "take him on." For example, the group leader might wrongly say, "Mr. Wright doesn't seem to think the group is too helpful. Do the others feel that way, or do they feel the way Mrs. Samuels does?"

Depending on how this question is asked, it could be heard by the group as an invitation to take on Mr. Wright. However, if Mr. Wright's behavior is viewed in the context of the dynamic interaction, and if the group leader sees him as a potential ally, he might instead help him elaborate.

> **GROUP LEADER:** I think it's important that we hear Mr. Wright out on this. If there are problems with the group, maybe we can work them out if we talk about them. What's bothering you about the group?
>
> **MR. WRIGHT:** Well, for one thing, I don't think we are leveling with one another. We're not really saying what's on our minds. Everybody is too busy trying to impress one another to be honest.

GROUP LEADER: You know, that often happens in the first few sessions of a new group. People are unsure of what to expect. How about it—have any of the others of you felt that way?

MR. PETERS: I didn't last week, but this week I thought the discussion was a bit superficial.

By treating the deviant member as an ally rather than as an enemy, the group leader gave permission for the group members to begin a frank discussion of how they were working. Others in the group felt the freedom to express their dissatisfaction, and, as a result, the members began to take responsibility for making their group more effective. This kind of discussion is essential for all groups, but it is often considered impolite to be direct in such settings. Members do not want to "hurt the group leader's feelings." As the group proceeded, the leader found that Mr. Wright—rather than not wanting to work—had several pressing issues he wished to deal with. His sense of urgency had forced him to speak out. Often, in a group, the member who seems most negative and angry is the one who wants to work the hardest. It is easy to understand, however, how the group leader's feelings might make it hard to see Mr. Wright in a more positive way.

Deepening Discussion in a Parenting Group

Expressions of deviant opinions in a group often serve as a lever for the group leader to deepen a discussion. For example, in one psychoeducational group on parenting skills, a major argument occurred when Mr. Thomas expressed the view that "all of this talk about worrying about the kids' feelings is nice for counselors but doesn't make sense for parents. Sometimes, the back of the hand is what they need." The other members pounced on Mr. Thomas, and a verbal battle ensued. Once again, for new group leaders who are not clear about their function, the expression of an idea that runs counter to their view of good parenting would arouse a strong reaction.

A new and inexperienced group leader might be particularly angered by the jibe about counselors and might set out to "educate" Mr. Thomas. Instead, this leader saw Mr. Thomas as expressing a feeling that was, in part, true for all of the parents but was not considered "proper" in this group. The principle articulated in the scapegoating section, being with the individual and the group at the same time, reemerges in this next excerpt. The leader reached to support Mr. Thomas:

GROUP LEADER: You are all attacking Mr. Thomas's position quite strongly; however, I have a hunch there must be many times when all of you feel the same way. Am I right? (Silence)

MR. FISK: There are times when the only feelings I'm interested in are the ones he has on his behind when I let him have it.

With the group leader's help, Mr. Thomas gave permission for the parents to begin to discuss the reality of parenting, which includes anger, loss of control over their temper, and frustration. The group leader continued by asking Mr. Thomas why he felt he had to express this position so strongly.

GROUP LEADER: You know, Mr. Thomas, you come on so strong with this position, and yet you don't strike me as someone who doesn't care about how his kids feel. How come?

MR. THOMAS: (Quietly, looking down as he spoke) Feelings can hurt too much.

GROUP LEADER: What do you mean?

MR. THOMAS: It wasn't easy to talk with my kids when their mother died.

GROUP LEADER: (After a silence) You really know what that is like, don't you? (Mr. Thomas just nodded.)

MR. SIMCOE: I've never had to handle something that tough, but I know what you mean about it being hard to listen when your kids are pouring out the hurt.

PRACTICE SUMMARY In summary, the deviant member who challenges the authority of the leader or provides negative feedback on the work of the group, raises a point of view contrary to the group's norm, or fights strongly and with emotion for a position may play an important functional role in the dynamic system of the group. The deviant member can be an ally for the group leader if the leader can deal with personal feelings and listen to the deviant member as a messenger for the group. This concept will be reinforced in many of the examples in this and later chapters. In the previous example, we can see how a deviant member may turn into an active participant over time.

The Internal Leader

Group leaders who are unsure of their role often experience *internal leaders* as a threat to their own authority, even viewing them as deviant members. However, if the mutual aid process is central to the work, leaders should understand that the work is going well when an internal leader emerges. The mistake of viewing the internal leader as a deviant member is most evident in work with teenagers and children, when the internal leader challenges the authority of the group leader.

Dealing with Acting-Out Adolescents: A Community Center Group

The following excerpt is from the first meeting of a group I led during my first year of professional training. As part of my field practicum, I wrote a *record of service (ROS)* of each group meeting for discussion with my supervisor. I share this example for several reasons. First, students need to realize that all group leaders start out with similar feelings and make most of the same mistakes. Many students who read examples or see videotapes of my work with married couples, single parents, or people with AIDS do not know about the many mistakes I made (and still make) during my professional development. Second, this particular group—acting-out adolescents—can be one of the most painful and stressful groups to lead. I still vividly remember dreading the early sessions, which seemed like a perpetual battle of wills—a battle both the group and I were destined to lose. Third, it provides a good illustration of how the group leader may at first see an internal leader as an enemy rather than an ally. Finally, it is an example of a community center group in which activities are a central part of the work. These kinds of groups often make up the bulk of group practice in some settings. (A more general discussion of the use of activity in groups appears in Chapter 10.)

The group consisted of acting-out adolescents (13 and 14 years old) who were members of a community center club. I had been warned that they were a difficult group and that they had given other group leaders a tough time in the past. Although the group was set up so that the club members planned their own activities, the agency had structured the first night by planning a mass sports program in the gym.

PRACTICE POINTS

The first issue on the group members' minds was "What sort of leader will this be?" but my supervisor had mistakenly led me to think that I must "demonstrate my authority in the first session and assert myself as leader," which in effect began the battle of wills.

Only five boys had shown up by 7:45 p.m., so we spent the first 10 minutes talking about the club last year. At this point, Al showed up and completely changed the tone of our meeting. It seemed as if the first five boys had been waiting for the catalyst that had finally arrived. Al was bubbling over about the school football game he had played in that afternoon. It was their first win in 3 years.

When I asked how it had gone, he described it abruptly. He then wanted to know what we were doing that night. When I explained the prearranged evening program, he became very negative about it. "Rope jumping [one of the competitive events] is for girls," he replied. I told him boxers use rope jumping for training, and he replied, "I'm not a boxer, and I'm not a girl." Although the other boys had not been overly enthusiastic about the evening program when I had described it earlier, their tone changed sharply as they agreed with Al.

Lack of clarity of role and initial nervousness led me to defend the program and to see Al as competition for leadership of the group. The group leadership model I had been trained under suggested that my skill in working with groups was in my knowledge of activities and programs and that I had to directly or indirectly influence members to go along. That framework was actually manipulative in nature, although I did not recognize it at that time. For example, if there were a scapegoated boy in the group, rather than dealing with it directly, as in the earlier example with the girls' school group, I should select an activity the scapegoat could do well. No one would know that I had this goal "hidden up my sleeve." By the term *manipulative*, I am describing group leader's secret use of power: I would be using my role as an adult and a leader to influence members without their knowing it. I later understood that this was problematic and would lead to distrust rather than trust.

PRACTICE POINTS

Getting back to my practice as a student, contracting was unclear, and an important discussion about the role of the group leader in relation to the group members was missed because of my own fears and misconceptions. As the meeting proceeded, I got myself deeper into trouble:

I tried to discuss next week's program with the guys. Girls from another club started pressing their faces against the window of the door, and, before I could stop him, Al was racing to the attack. The contagion was immediate, and what had been a quiet group of boys was now following its leader. I jumped up and asked them to ignore the girls. Instead, they chose to ignore me. I went over to the door, closed it, and politely guided them back to the desk.

This time, when they sat down, Al's feet were on the table (one of the wooden-finish types). Five more pairs immediately joined Al's (the testing was in full swing). All I could think of was my supervisor's advice, which amounted to "show them who's boss." I asked them to remove their feet, because they could damage the table. Joe and Ken responded, but the others didn't. I tried to maintain a light and firm stand. They slowly responded, stating that last year's leader let them keep their feet up that way. Another said there were a lot of things their leader let them do last year that I probably would not. I said that I would only allow them to do those things that were acceptable to the agency. One of the boys asked me what an agency was. I explained I meant the center (first week of fieldwork and I was already over-professional and using jargon). It was time to hit the gym for the games (much to my relief).

It is clear that my sense of role—that of "taming the group" and setting and enforcing limits—led me to miss important issues. Discussing the last leader's role would have been helpful. In addition, their relationships with girls were an emerging and uncomfortable theme for this group, given their age. The behavior was very appropriate for the members' age and stage of the life cycle, only I was missing its meaning. Al was the only club member to dance with girls later in the evening during the social part of the program. He asked about having a party with a girls' group, and I put off his request by saying, "We would need to plan this ahead of time." Al provided leadership in several areas, expressing the feelings and concerns of the group, but because I missed the importance of his role, a battle over "who owned the group" resulted, with me thinking that I did.

PRACTICE POINTS Because I missed the signals, the indirect testing continued. Al led the members in throwing paper around the club room and leaning out of the windows, spitting on other center members as they left. I kept trying to set limits while not allowing myself to get angry (which was considered unprofessional). Finally, my instincts got the better of me.

> I said that I would like to say a few words before we finished. I was attempting to reestablish the limits I had set earlier, but my own feelings got the best of me. I explained that this evening was really difficult for me and that probably it was for them, too. I said that if we couldn't relax enough to discuss further programs, there probably wouldn't be any. At this point, I said something that surprised me as I said it. I said their behavior better improve, or they could find themselves a new leader. They replied by saying that, compared with the group members who hadn't shown up this evening, they were well behaved. My reaction to this group was mild panic.

PRACTICE POINTS It is easy to understand my panic in this situation. My idea of being professional was to be able to "handle" the group without losing my temper. Actually, in these moments at the end of the meeting when I revealed my real feelings, I was starting to develop a working relationship with the group members. After a few more sessions of off-and-on-again testing, I moved to discuss the issue of the authority theme and to help the group members develop their own internal leadership and structure.

I told the boys that, because I had been with them for 5 weeks, they might be interested in hearing what I thought about the group. They perked up at this. Bert said, "You love us," and everyone laughed. I said that, during this time, I had been able to talk to each one of them individually and seemed to get along well. However, when we got together as a group, we couldn't seem to talk at all, right from the beginning. In spite of what they said, I thought that each one of them was concerned about stealing, acting wise all the time, and being disrespectful. Al said (very seriously this time) that it was different when they were in the group. I asked why that was so. Bert asked all the guys if they had stolen anything, and they all agreed that they had.

PRACTICE POINTS In the next excerpt, I confront the taboo I believed existed in speaking up and challenging the negative behaviors. This would be considered "sucking up," and peer group acceptance was crucial for this age and stage of the life cycle. My honesty opened the door for them to address the authority theme, which really amounted to the question: "Whose group is this?" My training had led me to believe it was mine, but my experience was rapidly telling me it had to be their group.

After some discussion, I told them I thought they were really afraid to say what they thought in the group. Bert said he wasn't afraid. I asked about the others. Al mockingly put up his fists and said, "I'm not afraid of anyone in the group." I laughed with the rest and said I thought it was easy to be brave with your fists but that it took a lot more courage to say something you thought the other guys would not like. I said it was their club, and, although it was important to me, it was really more important to them. Joel made a wisecrack, but he was silenced by Ken, who said, "That's just the kind of thing he [pointing to me] was talking about."

As the discussion continued, the boys explained that they often didn't like my suggestions for activities, and I encouraged them to say so in the future, because it was their club. A surprising amount of feeling emerged about the kidding around in the group, much of it directed at one boy who acted out a great deal but was not present that night. They talked about how they could plan their own programs. The group members suggested that I could bring in ideas from other clubs and that they would then decide what they wanted. At this point, Al suggested they have a president. After some discussion about the respective positions, a president (Al), vice president (Bert), and treasurer (Ken) were elected. A social committee was also formed to speak with the girls' club to discuss a party.

At this point in the meeting, I realized we were actively talking about something with no kidding around and no testing of me. I felt at ease for the first time. I commented to them about this. Al said, "We won't be able to do this all the time." I said I realized this and that there still would be a lot of kidding around. It would be all right as long as they could pull themselves together at times to get their work done. Al said that would be his job and that I could help by telling them when they got out of hand. I agreed.

At the end of the process recording, I commented that "all of the boys gave me a warm good-bye" as I left the building. From this point on, much of the work shifted to helping the group members develop their own structure. For example, I met with Al before sessions, at his request, to help him plan the agenda and to discuss his problems with chairing the sessions.

These group sessions were a painful initial lesson on the need to clarify my role and recognize the group's internal leadership. I had experienced Al as the group's deviant member, when, in reality, he was its internal leader. I had told them it was their group, but my early behavior had contradicted this; following a different paradigm of practice, I believed it was really my group for implementing my purposes. I encouraged them to plan activities when I already had the "appropriate" activities in mind. I experienced Al as my enemy, when he was actually my main ally. Chapter 8 includes further illustrations of my work with this group, in which I describe what the group taught me about helping group members negotiate the system—in this case, the school, their families, and the community center itself. I have always been grateful that they had not given up on me and began my group leadership education in a sometimes admittedly painful but very important way.

The Gatekeeper

Earlier we saw that the deviant member is often the one who feels the strongest sense of urgency about a particular issue. In a sense, the deviant behavior is an effort to move the group toward real work. The internal leader often serves this function in a healthier, more direct way. A group can be ambivalent about work in the same way an individual can be, and members can take on the function of expressing that ambivalence for the group. This is sometimes seen in the form of a *gatekeeper* role, in which a member guards the "gates" through which the group must pass for the work to deepen. When the group discussion gets close to a difficult subject, the gatekeeper intervenes to divert the discussion.

In one adult counseling group, every time the discussion appeared to approach the issue of the group leader's authority and behavior, one female member would light up a foul-smelling cigarillo or in some other way attract the group's ire. (This was prior to the emergence of the generally accepted "no smoking" policies.) The group would rise to the bait, and the more difficult authority theme would be dropped. After observing this pattern, at one meeting the group leader pointed it out, describing what he saw: "You know, it seems to me that every time you folks get close to taking me on, Pat lights up a cigar or says something that gets you onto her back. Am I right about this?" The group rejected the interpretation and turned on the leader with anger, thus beginning to deal with the authority theme. Later in the session, Pat commented that the group leader's observation might be accurate, because she had always been fearful of seeing her parents fight and probably had done the same thing in childhood. It was not appropriate in this group to discuss the reasons for the pattern—either Pat's or the group's—nor did the group members need to agree with the observation. The mere statement of the pattern offered the group an opportunity to face the leader directly, and Pat no longer needed to carry out this role.

People often use humor to protect the gates to difficult and painful areas. A group member, usually one who has learned to play this role in most areas of her or his life, will act out, crack a joke, make a face, and so forth in an effort to get the group members and the leader laughing and distracted. Note that humor can also be used to help advance the work of the group and does not always represent a means of gatekeeping. It helps, at times, to be able to laugh when facing painful work.

Professional staff groups, for example, at times use what I call *macabre humor* to deal with their tensions related to their work. For example, they may tell stories about clients, or others, that they would never share publicly. However, when this is the only means of releasing tension, and the underlying feelings that result from the stresses and traumas are not dealt with, such humor can lead to counselor *burnout* rather than preventing it. I have addressed this maladaptive reaction to secondary trauma, for example, in a book on supervision (Shulman, 1993). It is also explored in Chapter 16 in the section dealing with group work in response to traumatic events. With the client group, the group leader needs to observe the pattern over time and to note the results of the use of humor. If the humor consistently results in an illusion of work, the gatekeeper function is a likely explanation.

Teenage Survivors of Sexual Abuse

 PRACTICE POINTS In the example that follows of a group for teenage female survivors of sexual abuse, the reader should note the following:

- The gatekeeper's acting-out behavior always is associated with painful discussion.
- The role of blocking discussion of these painful areas is reinforced by the group.
- When the culture is changed and the taboo partially lifted, the gatekeeper is no longer needed.
- The gatekeeper turns out to be the member with the most reason for guarding the gate.

The group leader was careful to make sure that each girl had control over if and when she disclosed the circumstances of her own abuse. Whereas they had no control over their abuse as young children, it was important that they had control over disclosing it. One girl would act out when the discussion became serious and painful in response to a disclosure. She sang ribald songs, jumped on a table and danced provocatively, and otherwise exhibited sexualized behavior. The group eventually developed a more trusting culture through the disclosures of the details of abuse by a number of members. With the more positive, safer culture, the leader addressed the gatekeeper's behavior and reached for its meaning. The girl then revealed the extent of her abuse, in which her father had taken her to bars, had her literally dance on tables, and passed her around to patrons, trading sex for drinks. The gatekeeper is often the group member who has experienced the issue even more powerfully than the others and has the most to protect. In this case, the gatekeeper also had the greatest need for support, and her "deviant" behavior was a loud call for help.

The Defensive Member

Defensiveness represents its own social role, although other social roles may involve defensiveness as well. The *defensive member* refuses to admit there is a problem, to accept responsibility for his or her part in a problem, or to take suggestions or help from the group after a problem has been raised. The "yes, but . . ." syndrome is not uncommon as the defensive member has all of the reasons why he or she cannot deal with a problem and responds to every suggestion with a sentence that begins "Yes, but . . . ." Group members often respond to a defensive member by attacking the defense and eventually giving up and ignoring her or him.

Lewin (1951) described a model for change that can be applied to defensiveness on several levels—individual, group, family, and organizational. Stated simply, the individual personality in relation to its environment has developed a *quasi-stationary social equilibrium* in which some form of balance has been achieved. For the defensive member, denial has worked as a way to deal with painful problems. This would be roughly equivalent to the precontemplation stage of change (DiClemente, Prochaska, Fairhurst, & Velicer, 1991). The three steps for change involve "unfreezing" this equilibrium, moving into a phase of disequilibrium, and freezing at a new quasi-stationary equilibrium. The important point is that defenses have value to the individual, and to expect the unfreezing process to be easy misses the essence of the dynamics. The more serious the issue—the more deeply the individual feels a challenge to the sense of the core self—the more rigid the defense. Like resistance, a group member's defensiveness is a signal that the work is real. To begin the unfreezing process, the group leader or group must challenge the individual. However, the individual will need all the support, understanding, and help possible to translate unfreezing into movement and then into a new and healthier level of quasi-equilibrium.

Group leaders often underestimate the difficulty of what they and group members are asking people to do when calling them to move past defensiveness and denial. The difficulty of this process needs to be respected. Only a delicate integration of support and demand can create the conditions in which the group member may feel free enough to let down his or her barriers. The reader should note the following in this example:

- The group leader is with both the individual and the group.
- The group leader attempts to help the individual reach out to the group and to help the group to respond.
- The group leader recognizes that defensiveness and resistance are part of the work.

A Defensive Father in a Parents' Group

In the example that follows, a father describes a conflict with his 18-year-old son that has resulted in the son's leaving home and the family's being in turmoil. As the situation plays out in some detail, other parents point out that the father has been stubborn and failed to listen to what his son was saying. They try to pin him down to alternative ways of relating, but to each he responds in a typical "Yes, but . . ." pattern, not able to take in what they are saying.

PRACTICE POINTS

Finally, after a few minutes of this, the group grows silent. The group leader intervenes by pointing out the obstacle.

> GROUP LEADER: It seems to me that what has been going on here is that Ted has raised a problem, you have all been trying to offer some answers, but Ted has been saying "Yes, but . . ." to each of your suggestions. You look like you are about to give up on him. Are you?

ALICE: We don't seem to be getting anywhere. No matter what anyone says, he has an answer.

GROUP LEADER: Ted, I think you must feel a bit backed into a corner by the group. You do seem to have a hard time taking in their ideas. How come?

TED: I don't think they can appreciate my problem. It's not the same as theirs. They all seem to be blaming me for the fight, and that's because they don't understand what it really is like.

GROUP LEADER: Maybe it would help if you could tell them how this struggle with your son makes you feel.

TED: I gave this kid so much, raised him since he was a baby, and now he treats his mother and me like we don't matter at all. I did the best I could—doesn't he understand that?

GROUP LEADER: I think it's tough when you feel you love your child the way you do and you still see him as your kid, but he seems to want to pull away. You still feel responsible for him, but you also feel a bit impotent, can't seem to control him anymore. Can any of you appreciate what Ted is feeling right now?

The group members moved to support Ted in his feelings, with others recounting similar experiences and feelings. The focus had shifted for a moment to the common feelings among group members rather than the obstacle that seemed to frustrate them.

PRACTICE POINTS

The group leader sensed that Ted needed to feel understood and not be judged harshly by the other parents, precisely because he tended to judge himself more harshly than any of them. Having established this support, the group leader reached for the feelings underlying the resistance.

GROUP LEADER: Ted, if I were you, I think I would spend a lot of time wondering what went wrong in the relationship. I would be wondering how this could have happened when I had tried so hard—and if I could have done things differently. Is that true for you?

FRAN (TED'S WIFE): He stays up nights; he can't get to sleep because he is so upset.

TED: Sure, it's tough. You try your best, but you always wonder if you should have been around more, worked a little less, had some more time . . . you know?

GROUP LEADER: I guess that's what makes it hard for you to believe that anyone else can understand, and you feel so lousy about it yourself. Can the rest of you appreciate that it would be tough to listen if you were in Ted's shoes?

RAY: I think we are in Ted's shoes. When I see him getting stubborn in this group, I see myself and my own defensiveness.

PRACTICE SUMMARY

The group discussion focused on how hard it was to take advice in the group, especially when the members themselves felt uncertain. As the conversation shifted, the group leader could sense Ted physically relaxing and listening. After a while, Ted asked the group to take another crack at his problem. He said, "This is really tough, but I don't want to lose the kid completely."

Often, defensive members need more time than a single session to feel safe enough to "move." Group leaders will often find that the member has thought deeply, after the meeting, about the way he reacted, so that readiness to change and unfreezing appear in a later session. This is the client's part in the procedure; once again, the leader can only take responsibility for establishing the best possible conditions for change—the rest is up to the client and depends on many factors. One of my studies found that clients' acceptance of a problem contributed to their motivation to change as well as their ability to take and use help (Shulman, 1991).

In another example in the middle phase of work with a group of teenagers, a defensive member in the group was also responding with "Yes, but . . ." to every effort to help her. The group leader had a good relationship with her, having built up a fund of positive feelings in the relationship. At one point she gently confronted her by asking whether there was any way they could reach her on this issue, or whether she was so closed that they (the group) should just leave her alone and try another time. The member thought for a moment and then replied, "No, you can keep trying." At this point, in control of the process, she began to hear what they were saying.

For some clients, the stress of the issue is so great, or the issue so loaded, that they cannot accept any help at that particular point. Although such situations are frustrating and often sad, they exist. Accepting this is one of the most important things a new counselor can do. He or she must avoid taking responsibility for the client's part in the proceedings. Nonetheless, group leaders often feel guilty because of lack of clarity on this point and feelings of failure, and this guilt leads group leaders to feel angry with a defensive client for not cooperating. Note, in our example of the parents' group, that the anger from the other group members appeared to be a result of their seeing some of their own feelings and attitudes exaggerated in the defensiveness of the member. In fact, the more they pushed him, the more they heightened his defensiveness.

The Quiet Member

The *quiet member* is one who remains noticeably silent over an extended period of time. In small groups, the group leader and the other group members notice after only a few sessions that someone has said very little or nothing at all. A quiet member can create problems for the group, because the other members do not know what thinking and feeling goes on behind the facade. Group members will tend to believe that the quiet member is sitting in judgment of them, does not share their problems, or feels that others in the group talk too much. Group leaders, too, often grow uncomfortable, feeling that a member who is not speaking may not be involved.

The silence of a member in a group is similar to the silence in a one-on-one interview. It is a form of communication that, as we have seen, can be difficult to understand. For some group members, it simply means that they are uncomfortable speaking in the group. This is one of the most common explanations. Others may feel left out or uninvolved in the group because they feel that their problems are different. Some sit in judgment of the group's activity (as was the case in one of the deviant member illustrations dealing with the defensive parent). In my experience, sitting in judgment is the least stated reason for silence but, interestingly, is often the most frequent interpretation of silence by the active group members and the group leader; this probably reflects their own feelings. The two examples presented shortly will examine the quiet member who is afraid to speak and the quiet member who is left out. First, let us see how the group leader can help the group when they react to a quiet member.

Group Leader Strategies

Believing that all members need to speak an equal amount is a mistake. Social roles developed by individuals include patterns that involve active participation through speech as well as active participation through listening. On the one hand, a member may get a great deal out of a discussion without directly participating. On the other hand, small groups carry a sense of mutual obligation: Members who risk themselves feel that others should do the same. In fact, the silent member often feels uncomfortable about "taking" and not "giving." In addition, many silent members have been so used to being quiet in groups for so long that they have not developed skills required for intervention. Some quiet members say that they are always too slow with their thoughts. The group moves too fast for them, and, by the time they can get in, the idea has been stated and the group has moved on. Others say that, after they have been quiet in a group for several sessions, they are afraid the group members will "fall out of their chairs if I open my mouth." Whereas all members should be able to move into a group at their own pace, and although equal participation is not a goal, the quiet member often needs some assistance to participate in the group.

Group leaders sometimes try to deal with this problem either directly—through confrontation—or indirectly. Each tactic can backfire. For example, if a member has been quiet because of discomfort in speaking, a group leader who suddenly turns and says, "I notice you haven't spoken yet in the group and wonder what was on your mind?" may find the member even further immobilized by embarrassment. This direct confrontation may be exactly what quiet members feared would happen.

Indirect means can be just as devastating. The group leader has noticed a member not verbally participating in a discussion and turns and says, "What are your ideas about this question, Fran?" A member who is afraid of speaking often finds that any ideas she did have completely disappear in this moment of panic. The other indirect technique, of going around the room to get all group members' opinions when it really is only the quiet person's opinion the group leader seeks, may be experienced as manipulative and artificial by members. This is an example of what I described earlier as "acting on" the member rather than "acting with" the member.

PRACTICE POINTS The task, then, is to be direct and nonthreatening at the same time. My own strategy is based on the belief that people have a right to their defenses and their characteristic patterns of social interaction. As the group leader, my job is to mediate the engagement between each member and the group, so I feel a responsibility to check with a quiet member and see how that engagement is going. If there is an obstacle between the member and the group, I can offer to help.

The Member Who Is Afraid to Speak

As we have seen, members sometimes are merely afraid to speak. They have likely always held back in groups. The following conversation took place after the second meeting of a group. Richard had been particularly silent in both meetings, although his eyes seemed to indicate that he was involved.

> **GROUP LEADER:** Do you have a second to chat before you go?
>
> **RICHARD:** Sure, what's up?
>
> **GROUP LEADER:** I noticed you haven't spoken in the group these two sessions, and I thought I would check to see how it was going with you. I know some people take longer than others to get involved, and that's all right. I just wanted to be sure there were no problems.
>
> **RICHARD:** Well, you caught me.
>
> **GROUP LEADER:** What do you mean?
>
> **RICHARD:** I managed to get through all of my years in school without ever saying anything in class, and now it looks as if I've been caught.
>
> **GROUP LEADER:** Is it hard for you to speak in a group?
>
> **RICHARD:** I always feel unsure of what I'm going to say, and, by the time I've figured it out, the group has gone past me. Sometimes, it's just hard to get in with everyone speaking at once.
>
> **GROUP LEADER:** Look, I can tell from your eyes that you are actively involved in the discussion. However, after a while, you will probably feel uncomfortable not speaking, and then it will get harder and harder to talk.
>
> **RICHARD:** That's the way it usually is for me.
>
> **GROUP LEADER:** Not just you, you know. Lots of people feel that way. If you would like, I can help by watching for you; if I sense you want to get into the conversation by the look on your face, or your body, or if you give me a signal, I can reach for you and help you in. Would you like me to do that?
>
> **RICHARD:** That sounds all right. If I give you a signal, you'll call on me?
>
> **GROUP LEADER:** Exactly! I find that has helped people in the past.

PRACTICE SUMMARY The key here was turning control over the group leader's intervention to the member. At the next session, Richard avoided the group leader's eyes for the first 15 minutes; he was probably afraid of giving a false signal. He sat rigidly with his arms at his sides, also because he was afraid a sudden motion might be misinterpreted. The discussion was heated, and the group leader kept glancing at Richard. After a while, the group leader noticed Richard leaning forward a bit, with his eyebrows arched, looking at the group leader. The group leader simply said, "Come on in, Richard." The group paused, and Richard began to speak. Once again, it is important that the group leader always act *with* the member and avoid acting *on* the member.

The Member Who Feels Left Out

Another type of quiet member is one who feels that his or her particular concerns and issues may not be of interest to the group, or that his or her problems differ from the others'. Such members do not share problems with the group members; after a while, they feel left out, and the group members wonder what is happening. In the following example, Mrs. Trenke, who had shared some difficult experiences with the group, stated that she felt let down when the group did not respond to her feelings. Mrs. Davidson, who had been quiet in the group, supported Mrs. Trenke's comment.

The group leader encouraged Mrs. Trenke to elaborate:

> The group leader said, "Maybe we could hear how Mrs. Trenke felt let down by the group?" Mrs. Trenke continued, "I felt that I was not a part of the group and that I was not going to get anything out of it." Mrs. Davidson cut in, "Yeah! We didn't listen to other people's troubles because we had enough of our own!"
>
> The group leader turned to Mrs. Davidson and said, "Have you felt let down and left out of the group?" "No," said Mrs. Davidson, "I don't feel I have the same situation—they have husbands." (Mrs. Bennet reached out and touched Mrs. Davidson on the arm.) The group leader asked Mrs. Davidson how she felt about not having a partner. Mrs. Davidson replied, "Sad, depressed—I wonder if he could be as proud of the kids as I am?" She went on to say that maybe things would be different if her husband were still alive—maybe they could have made a go of it.

Now that the issue is on the table, the group leader suggested that it had been a problem for a while and that the members would like to know what it felt like to be alone. Mrs. Bennet, in the "gatekeeper" role, interrupts the work by challenging the importance of dealing with feelings.

The group leader points out the process, recognizing that all of the group members would have some difficulty with the pain raised by Mrs. Davidson. Most likely, that was the feeling and thoughts inside of the silence.

> The group leader said he felt that Mrs. Davidson had felt cut out of the group for some weeks. Mrs. Davidson agreed. Mrs. Bennet said that was probably due to the fact that she had not been able to share with the group the concerns she had. All agreed. The group leader responded after a silence and said, "I feel the group would like to know what it is like, what it feels like to be alone. What do you need help with?" Mrs. Bennet cut in, "There you go on that feeling theory again." The group leader asked if it worried Mrs. Bennet when we talked about feelings. "No," she said, "but is it important?" The leader said that it seemed important because everyone in this group was having trouble talking about and sharing feelings while at the same time they were interested in what others were feeling. "Do you see what we have done here? When we began to find out about Mrs. Davidson's feelings, someone suggested that we avoid it, and we all agreed. Let's go back to Mrs. Davidson's feelings!"
>
> Mrs. Davidson said, "I feel like s-h-i-t [spelled out] at home with the kids." The group leader cut in and said it was all right with him if she said shit—but why did she feel that way? "It rips me right across here [indicating midsection] when they are fighting. I've had nothing but fighting all my life—first in my own home, then with my husband, and now with my kids." "How do you see the fighting? What does it mean to you?" asked the group leader. "I feel on my own, all alone." Mrs. Trenke cut in, "I know that feeling. I had it with my husband—we used to argue. . . . What can I do? Why is it always me?" The group leader asked if Mrs. Davidson could share a specific problem with the group, and she did. It involved setting limits, then wavering on them and letting the kids have their own way.

Men's Group: A Member Reaches Out to the Quiet Member

As is often the case, simply acknowledging the lack of involvement by the member is enough to encourage the sharing of her concerns. Sometimes the initiative for reaching out to a quiet member starts with the group. It is not unusual, after a period of time, to have a group member turn to one who has been silent and ask, "What have you been thinking?"

Once again, the leader's concern for the two clients—the individual and the group—and clarity of role can help assist the group and the member in an important discussion.

RAY: I have been thinking about you, Fred. You have not said anything in the group so far. How come? (All eyes turned to Fred.)

FRED: (Looking very uncomfortable) Oh, I've been listening.

LEADER: (Addressing Ray) Does it concern you when Fred doesn't speak?

RAY: Yeah, I begin to wonder if I'm talking too much or he thinks I'm making a real ass out of myself.

LEADER: Have others in the group wondered about that as well? (Nodding of heads) I think it makes other people uncomfortable when you don't speak much, Fred, because they can't figure out what you're thinking. Could you react to that?

FRED: Actually, I've been sitting here thinking how much all of your problems are just like mine. I've wanted to share some, but I don't feel comfortable talking in a group.

LEADER: This wasn't easy for you right now, was it?

FRED: No, it wasn't easy at all, but I'm glad it came out.

RAY: Maybe if I shut up a bit, you would have more of a chance to talk.

LEADER: I don't think so, Ray. Some people speak more in a group, and others do a lot of work by listening. You also seem concerned about what others have to say, so I hope you wouldn't feel you needed to hold back. How about the rest of the group?

LOU: You raise interesting points, Ray, and it helps the group keep going. I would miss you if you just clammed up. (Ray smiles at this.)

LEADER: I can watch the talk in the group, and if I see someone trying to get in, I'll help make room for him. Is that all right? (Members of the group nodded in agreement.)

FRED: I'll get into the conversation. I just need some more time.

RAY: That's OK. Don't feel pressed. You can get in when you feel comfortable.

Once the communications had been clarified, the problem of the silent member receded. Fred did get into the discussion the following week, raising a concern to the group and meeting with a positive response.

The Monopolizer

The previous section on the quiet member brings up the opposite type of group member: the person who talks a great deal and is sometimes referred to as a *monopolizer.* My observation is that people who talk a lot are often more of a problem for the group leader than they are for the other members. In first sessions in particular, group members are pleased to see someone pick up the discussion. A problem arises, however, when the person who is talking does not also listen to others, cuts them off, and creates a negative reaction in the group. The group leader, who sees this happening as a pattern, rather than just the talkative response of a nervous group member at an early meeting, can raise the issue directly. One way would be to simply ask the member if she or he can hold off for a bit and give others a chance to get in. In most cases, just pointing this out directly and gently is enough to help the member become more conscious of the need for some restraint. It is also helpful to recognize that the member, like the rest of the group, must feel the issues and problems strongly and is anxious to get some help.

If the pattern persists and the group leader can sense through verbal or nonverbal signals that group members are unhappy with the repeated monopolizing of the conversation, a stronger intervention is needed. If the group leader directly points out what is happening and opens up a discussion of the process, usually this helps ease the problem. If the group leader inquires why the member acts this way in the group, the individual will often reveal that talking is a way of covering up feelings, avoiding a problem, or expressing concern about actions in the group. The overly verbal member's words are often a way of handling the same feelings that the quiet member handles, but in a quite different manner.

One pattern in groups is for the member to start to talk about an issue that seems unrelated to the theme of the discussion. Once again, understanding the meaning of this apparent changing of the subject is important. In some situations the discussion has hit a painful point, and the apparent monopolizer takes on a gatekeeper role as described earlier. A direct response would be for the group leader to point that out once the pattern is established and ask the member if it is hard to hear others talk about the issue and/or the feelings. In others, the member is so overwhelmed with his or her feelings and issues they appear not to have room for anyone else's issues. A direct response might be for the leader to say, "John, I think sometimes you, and maybe all of us, get so overwhelmed by our own pain it is hard to listen to someone else's."

PRACTICE POINTS Whereas some models of group practice prescribe indirect interventions such as "cutting off" the member, I believe a more direct approach that addresses the pattern is more helpful to the monopolizing member as well as the rest of the group. For example, as a member goes off on what appears to be a tangent, the leader could say, "John, I'm not clear about the connection between what you are raising right now and the theme of the discussion. Can you help us see the connection, or can anyone else in the group see the connection—or John, is this an issue you want us to get back to?" I don't believe it is enough to simply discipline or teach group behavior without understanding the underlying meaning.

A Psychoeducational Parents' Group for Children with Traumatic Brain Injury

The following brief excerpt illustrates how immobilized both the group leader and the other group members can feel when faced with a monopolizer. This member, Dawn, acted out her anxiety by responding to a doctor's presentation with an unstoppable stream of talk.

Agency Type: A rehabilitation center for children and adolescents

Group Purpose: A psychoeducational group to educate the group members about their children's medical and therapeutic conditions, as well as to inform them of safety precautions for children who have had a traumatic brain injury

Gender of Members: Three men and 11 women (including group leader)

Age Range: Mid-20s to early 40s

As soon as Dr. Thomas began to explain that children who have experienced traumatic brain injuries tend to be impulsive, Dawn started to describe what had happened with her child to demonstrate that she agreed with the doctor. She went on and on for almost 10 minutes, and nobody intervened. Then, she started to talk about her other child, Lisa, and what had happened at home during the past weekend. I turned to Dawn and said, "Dawn, I know you have many things to say, but why don't we go back to Eileen's behavior?" Dawn replied, "I know. I know. But let me finish. This is related to Eileen, too." People in the room rolled their eyes, but I did not object. She spoke for another 3 minutes or so and finished her story by saying, "So I told my children that school is always number one." I jumped in and said, "Good. Why don't we ask Melissa [the hospital tutor] about school?" People, including Dawn, laughed. When Melissa finished reporting on Eileen's school issue, I encouraged Dawn to ask Melissa questions. Then, I announced to the treatment team that we were running out of time so I would like to ask everyone to be short and precise. They nodded.

PRACTICE SUMMARY

In retrospect, this first meeting focused almost entirely on the concerns of one member. Although the other group members signaled their displeasure by rolling their eyes, the group leader, perhaps feeling unclear about how to intervene, let Dawn continue unchecked. Ironically, the doctor's presentation dealt with "impulsivity" of the children, and we have evidence of an impulsive parent. The leader would have been helpful to Dawn and the other members if she had intervened more directly and firmly. In a session such as this one, the monopolizer often feels embarrassed afterward for having dominated the conversation, and the other members wonder about the value of the group. In a first session, the group leader must take responsibility for providing structure. The leader is guided by the following strategies:

- Being direct but in a supportive manner
- Taking responsibility for maintaining structure
- Exploring the meaning of the monopolizing if it continues
- Attending to the thoughts and feelings of the second client – the group.
- Being aware of the integration of process and content

In doing so, perhaps the leader could say:

Hold on a second, Dawn. I know your child's injury and this discussion provoke a lot of feelings in you, and you probably feel you want as much help as you can get for your own child. But we need to allow room for everyone to ask their questions and make their comments, so I'll play traffic cop if it's OK with the rest of you.

If Dawn continued to test, such as by saying, as she did in the session, "Let me just finish," the group leader would need to say something like "Nice try, but we need to give someone else a chance." Continued persistence would require some discussion of the significance of being so full of one's own feelings that very little room remains for anyone else's. For example, "I know its hard to hold back when you feel so upset about your daughter." There is also a good chance that Dawn has just acted out the problem she has with friends and other family members—overwhelming them with her issues and not being able to respond to theirs. "I wonder if this is the way you ask for help from your friends and family members. I suspect at times it is hard for all of you to hold back when you feel so desperate about the situation. Am I right about that?" Once again, we see the integration of process and content.

If the group leader handles such interventions directly, openly, without anger, and—where possible—with nonhumiliating humor, he or she will reassure the group that the group leader will not let the monopolizing member subvert the purpose of the group or act out his or her anxiety. The problem is that such interventions go against societal norms, which encourage passively allowing the monopolizer to go on at length, intervening indirectly with little success, or intervening from anger as the group leader feels frustration at one member's domination of the group. In most cases, the monopolizer wants the group leader to set limits, because structure helps bind anxiety and helps the member feel more in control over what must be a devastating situation. Interestingly enough, there is a good chance that setting limits on the children's impulsive behavior is exactly what the parents need to do. The group leader needs to model it in the group since once again, "more is caught than taught."

Chapter Summary

This chapter examined common examples of individual roles in the group. The concept of social role helps explain patterned reactions by scapegoats, deviants, and gatekeepers, as well as by defensive, quiet, and monopolizing members. In each case, the group leader can best serve the group by understanding the individual member in terms of the dynamics of the group. For example, illustrations of how a perceived "deviant" member might actually be speaking for a larger number of group members suggested the importance of not trying to understand this behavior as just a product of "personality."

The scapegoating process in a group was defined in a similar manner, with the group projecting onto the scapegoat their own internalized negative feelings and the scapegoat, in some cases, volunteering for the role. The key element in the chapter was the concept of the group leader being with the "two clients"—the individual and the group—at the same time.

Related Online Content and Activities

For learning tools such as glossary terms, InfoTrac® College Edition keywords, links to related websites, and chapter practice quizzes, visit this book's website at **www.cengage.com/counseling/shulman**.

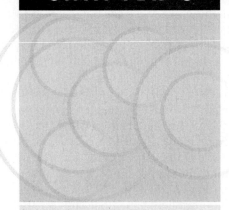

Working with the Group as the "Second Client"

In Chapter 7, I explored the various roles individuals play in a group setting—the interplay of one member within a dynamic system. In this chapter, I take a more detailed look at the group as an entity much like an organism, with its own properties and dynamics, and then I explore a strategy for the leader's intervention in relation to it. Next, I trace the tasks of the group as it attempts to deal with the relationships of members to the leader (the authority theme), relationships among members (the intimacy theme), the group's culture for work, and the group's internal structure (communication patterns, roles, etc.). A fifth task requires the group to relate to the environment—the setting that houses the group (the school, agency, institution). I address this task later in this chapter, when I examine the group leader's role in helping the client (the group, in this case) negotiate the environment.

A large body of group theory and research is available to the practitioner who wishes to better understand group dynamics. Our focus in this chapter is not on describing this body of literature, but rather on the practitioner's use of theoretical models and research results to develop his or her own integrated model of group practice. To illustrate this process, I have selected three classic theoretical models and one relatively new framework for discussion in relation to the group tasks: developmental (Bennis & Shepard, 1956), emotionality (Bion, 1961), environmental (Homans, 1950), and feminist self in relation (Fedele, 1994; Schiller, 1993). Although there are more recently published group theories, most in my view build their constructs on these earlier models. As will be seen in the discussion, each of these theories has ideas relevant to all of the group tasks.

The Group-as-a-Whole

It is not easy to describe this second client called the *group-as-a-whole*. In part, the difficulty comes from the fact that we cannot actually see the properties that describe a group. When we watch a group in action, we see a collection of individuals. Compare this to a solid object, such as a chair. When we are asked to describe its properties, visual references such as materials (plastic, wood, chrome), parts (back, seat, legs), shape, size, and so on, immediately come to mind.

Describing the properties of a group is more difficult. For example, *cohesion* in a group can be defined as a bond among members: a sense of identification with one another and with the group in its entirety. An observer cannot see a property of the group called "cohesion," but if we observe a group for a time, we can see all of the members acting as if the group were cohesive. Other properties of groups include shared norms of proper behavior and taboo subjects. We cannot see a group norm or a taboo, but we can see a pattern of behavior from which we can infer that a norm or taboo exists. For example, in our couples' group examples in previous chapters, I noted the members avoiding discussion of issues related to sex even though the members had indicated that there were problems in this area. From this pattern of behavior, we are able to infer that sex is a taboo area in our society, and as a result a norm has developed that it not be openly discussed. This norm was replicated in the couples' group and in fact also existed between the partners, which was one of the reasons it was difficult to deal with.

For beginning group leaders, when they look at the counseling group, what they see is a collection of individuals. As a leader begins to understand the properties of the group concept and to recognize collective behavior as an expression of the group's properties, the leader begins to "see" this group-as-a-whole. With practice, it is possible to see the collection of individuals and to see the group as well. With experience—and I am not suggesting a significant amount of time here—it becomes possible for the leader at one and the same time see each individual and the group-as-a-whole. This is a conceptual breakthrough that significantly enhances a group leader's ability to pay attention to the two clients: the individual and the group.

The Group as an Organism

We need to start by exploring the very idea of a group. When attempting to describe something as complex as a group, using a model is helpful. A *model*, as discussed in Chapter 1, is a concrete, symbolic representation of an abstract or real phenomenon. Most of us have been to a planetarium and sat in a room watching spheres in the ceiling circling a sun. Unless we were very young, we understood that this was not our solar system but a model that represented it. Having this model helped us understand the real thing.

To develop a model to describe a group, we must find an appropriate metaphor. Two common metaphors used in the literature are the machine and the organism. In the mechanistic model, the observer uses processes such as "input," "throughput," and "output" to describe the group. This was a popular model to describe organizations, work groups, and the like, in the mid-20th century. Alternately, many theorists interested in human social systems have adopted the organismic model as the most appropriate. The choice of an organism rather than a machine as a model reflects the organism's capacity for growth and emergent behavior. These terms describe a process in which a system transcends itself and creates something new that is more than just the simple sum of its parts.

To apply this idea to the group, we need to identify what is created when a group of people and a group leader are brought together that goes beyond the sum of each member's contribution. What properties exist that are unique descriptions of the group, rather than descriptions of the individual members? An example of such a property, described in Chapter 3, is the creation of a sense of common purpose shared by all the members of the group. This common purpose is a catalyst for the development of a tie that binds the members together. Group culture is a second example. As the group process begins, activities in the group are governed by a group culture made up of several factors including accepted norms of behavior. In a first session, the group culture generally reflects the culture of the larger society from which the members have been drawn. As sessions continue, this culture can change, allowing new norms to emerge and govern the activities of the members. Consider how important this can be, for example, in a group for adult children of alcoholics. The parent's problem with alcohol may have been the "family secret" that everyone knew but never discussed, certainly not outside the family. This taboo is re-created in the group in the first sessions, and changing this norm will be essential for effective work. Thus, common interests and group culture are two examples of properties of the group that transcend the simple sum of its parts, the individual members.

A third example is the group's relationship with its environment. As the group is influenced by its environment—for example, the agency, hospital, mental health setting, school or community—or the group leader as a representative of the agency, it (the group) must develop adaptive behaviors to maintain itself. This pattern of adaptive behavior is yet another example of a property of the group. I will be suggesting later in this chapter that one cannot think of the group without understanding that it is interacting with its environment all of the time. In fact, the immediate or larger environment may be having a more powerful impact on the group and member behavior than anything the group leader says or does. For example, in a psychoeducational group for children in a school, it may well be that the group members' behavior is in part in reaction to the way teachers and other staff relate to the students. Community violence, another example, may be directly contributing to the maladaptive way the group is coping. If school counselors ignore the impact of the environment, then they may be dealing with the symptoms and not the actual problem.

To summarize, we cannot actually see a group as an entity. That is why a model, such as the organism, is helpful. What we can see, however, are the activities of a group of people who appear to be influenced by this entity called the *group*. For example, when group purpose is clear, we can explain the members' actions as contributions in pursuit of that purpose. Again, group pressures, group expectations, and the members' sense of belonging all influence the members' behavior. The fact that a member's behavior changes as a result of believing in the existence of the group makes the group real. In the balance of this chapter, the key ideas to note are the following:

- I shall refer to the group as an entity,
- employ the organism as a metaphor, and
- focus on the group's developmental, internal, and external tasks.

Developmental Tasks for the Group

Two major group tasks have already been mentioned without each having been specifically described as such. These illustrate how a group can have tasks that differ from the specific tasks of each member. In Chapter 3 on group beginnings, I addressed what could be called the group's formation tasks. The group needed to develop a working contract that reflected the individual members' needs as well as the service stake of the sponsoring setting. In addition, a group consensus needed to be developed. This consensus reflected the common concerns shared by members as well as an agreement as to where the work might start. Reaching consensus on the work is a task that is unique to work with multiple clients (group, family, couples, etc.), because individual clients simply begin where they wish—there is no need to reach a consensus with other clients. The group's formation tasks also include initial clarification of mutual obligations and expectations. The group's effectiveness depends on how well it accomplishes these formation tasks. The skills of the leader in helping the group work on these formation tasks were described in Chapter 3 as contracting skills and illustrated with a range of first meetings.

A second critical group task involves meeting individual members' needs. For the group to survive and flourish, it must have individual members. Members feel a sense of belonging and develop a stake in the work of the group when they can perceive that their own related needs are being met. If these needs cease to be met, members will simply drop out of the group, either by not attending or not participating. In Chapter 5 on the work phase in the group, we saw how easily the group can miss a member's offered concerns or turn away from these concerns when they hit the group members too hard. In still other examples, individual members did not immediately see the relation between the work of the group and their own sense of urgency. In the previous chapter, we saw how members can play functional roles in the group, some of which cut them off from being able to use the group to meet their own needs. In each of these cases, leaders attempted to help members use the group more effectively, reach out and offer mutual aid more effectively or both simultaneously. All of these efforts were directed toward helping the group with its task of meeting individual members' needs.

Thus, in order to grow and survive, a group must address the tasks of formation and meeting individual members' needs. Other sets of tasks linked to the developmental work of the group are those in which the group works on its relationship to the leader (the authority theme) and the relationships among members (the intimacy theme). Schwartz (1971) describes these two critical tasks as follows:

> In the culture of the group two main themes come to characterize the members' ways of working together: one, quite familiar to the caseworker, is the theme of authority in which the members are occupied with their relationship to the helping person and the ways in which this relationship is instrumental to their purpose; the other, more strange and threatening to the caseworker, is the theme of intimacy, in which the members are concerned with their internal relationships and the problems of mutual aid. It is the interplay of these factors—external authority and mutual interdependence—that provides much of the driving force of the group experience. (p. 9)

The group's ability to deal with concerns related to authority and intimacy is closely connected to the development of a working culture, established through common interests and group norms of behavior. Finally, the group needs to develop a structure for work that will enable it to carry out its tasks effectively. For example, responsibilities may have to be shared through a division of labor, and roles may need to be assigned formally or informally.

The following five major task areas will be introduced in the balance of this chapter:

- The relationship to the leader (the authority theme)
- The relationship among members (the intimacy theme)
- The development of a working culture
- The development of a structure for work
- The relationship to the environment

Obviously, these tasks overlap a great deal: Work on one area often includes work on the others. Although somewhat artificial, the division is still helpful. Recall that discussion of these tasks will draw on elements of group theory from three foundations and one relatively newer model and will focus on constructs that seem relevant, applying them to practice examples.

The Relationship to the Leader: The Authority Theme

In Chapters 3 and 4, I discussed the authority theme, the relationship between the leader and the group members, as an important issue to address early in the life of the group. I suggested that the question "Who is this leader, and what kind of person will he or she be?" is on the minds of all group members as they begin in the group. Even if the issue is addressed directly in the first sessions, the authority theme does not simply go away. It remains as an important theme to be explored at different points in the life of the group. This next section explores this theme using a classic theoretical framework that still guides group practice today. The reader familiar with more recent group developmental models will recognize their debt to Bennis and Shepard (1956).

The Bennis and Shepard Model: The Issue of Authority

Bennis and Shepard (1956) address the themes of authority and intimacy in their model of group development, and several of their key concepts are useful in explaining group process. Their observations, however, are based on their work with laboratory training groups (T-groups), in which graduate students studied group dynamics using their own experiences as a group. As a result, some ideas in their theory may be group-specific and therefore might not apply to groups of the type discussed in this book. Our analysis will illustrate how a practitioner can use what he or she likes from a good theory without adopting it whole.

The examples that follow illustrate the two sides to the members' feelings: On one hand, they were afraid of the leader and the leader's authority; on the other hand, they wanted the leader to take responsibility for the group. Bennis and Shepard (1956) attribute these two sets of feelings to two types of personalities in the group: the *dependent member* and the *counterdependent member*. They believe that the dependency invokes great uncertainty for members, and that the first major phase of group development, the *dependence phase*, involves work on this question. They describe three subphases within this first phase.

- In the first subphase, *dependence-flight*, the group is led by the dependent leaders, who seek to involve the leader more actively in control of the group.

- In the second subphase, *counterdependence-flight*, the counterdependent leaders move in and attempt to take over the group. The group often shows anger toward the leader in this phase. Two subgroups develop—one that argues for structure and another that argues against it.

- In the third subphase, *resolution-catharsis*, members who are *unconflicted*—independent and relatively untroubled by authority issues—assume group leadership.

According to Bennis and Shepard (1956), this "overthrow" of the leader leads to each member taking responsibility for the group: The leader is no longer seen as "magical," and the power struggles are replaced by work on shared goals. In considering this model, it is important to understand that the groups studied by the authors were marked by group leaders who were extremely and purposively passive in the beginning, which, in my view, increased the members' anxiety about the authority theme. The theory was that if the leader were passive—and I mean remaining silent and unresponsive to group member appeals for some form of intervention—the group would eventually have to take responsibility and develop its own internal leadership. The authors described this as a *barometric event* that impacts the group and marks the shift from one phase to the next—for example, when the leader is "overthrown."

My observation of groups such as these during and since my own graduate training in educational psychology was that the first and most powerful barometric event was actually the passivity of the leader. The second was the lack of a clear external purpose other than that of examining the group's process. Thus, many of the interactions that followed were directly a result of the leader's early passivity and a lack of clear external purpose. At the same time, the idea that groups had to first address the authority theme and "overthrow" the leader and then take responsibility for the group and deal with the intimacy theme are useful constructs. This is a good example of how one can take part of a theory without adopting it whole. Although many of the specifics of the Bennis and Shepard model are restricted to the particular groups observed, we can apply to all groups the general outline of this struggle over dependency.

The following discussion explores these five issues of the authority theme:

- Who owns the group?
- The group leader as the outsider
- The group leader's demand for work
- The group leader's limitations
- The group leader as a caring and giving person

In the next example, we can see the early emergence of the authority theme over the question of "Who owns the group?"

Who Owns the Group? The Couples' Group and the Authority Theme

In the second session of the couples' group, following the session described in Chapter 4, the members were watching to see if I would carry out the role I had described in the first session. However, my intervention was actually an example of acting on instead of acting with a member. Once again, Lou, the 69-year-old member, signaled the members' concern about this issue.

Note that I catch my mistake and use this as an opportunity to further clarify the authority theme, with my encouraging members to catch me when I make a mistake.

One couple was presenting a problem that they were having that involved the husband's grown children from another marriage. I noticed each spouse was telling the group things about the other, rather than speaking directly to each other. I interrupted Frank, the member in his 50s who had remarried to Jane, and suggested he speak directly to his wife. After a noticeable hesitation, he began to speak to her, but he soon returned to speaking to me. I interrupted him again. Once again, he seemed slightly thrown by my action.

As this was going on, I noticed that Lou was looking distressed, staring at the floor, and covering his mouth with his hand. After watching this for a time, I reached for the message. "Lou, you look like you have something to say." He responded, "No, that's all right. I can wait 'til later." I said, "I have the feeling it's important, and I think it has something to do with me." I had been feeling uncomfortable but was unaware why. Lou said, "Well, if you want to hear it now, OK. Every time you interrupt Frank that way, I think he loses his train of thought. And this business of telling him to speak to Jane is just like the stuff with the other psychiatrists I described last week." I was surprised by what he said, and I remained quiet while I took it in.

Frank said, "You know, he's right. You do throw my line of thought every time you interrupt that way." I said, "I guess I ended up doing exactly the kind of thing I said last week I would try not to do. I have not explained to you, Frank, why I think it might help to talk directly with your wife rather than to me. I guess you must feel my comments, because you don't really understand why I'm suggesting this, as sort of pushing you around." Frank said, "Well, a bit." Lou said, "That's exactly what I mean." I responded, "I won't be perfect, Lou. I will also make mistakes. That's why it's so important that you call me on it, the way you just did. Only why wait until I ask?" Lou said, "It's not easy to call you; you're the leader." I said, "I think I can appreciate that, only you can see how it would speed things up if you did."

This second week's discussion was even more important than the first, because the members had a chance to see me being confronted with a mistake and not only acknowledging it but also encouraging Lou to be even more direct. The point made was that they did have rights and that they should not let my authority get in the way. At this point, you may be thinking that to reach for or encourage such negative feedback would be difficult for a beginning group leader. Ironically, the leader needs this kind of honesty from group members most when she or he is least confident and least prepared to hear it. Beginning group leaders should expect to miss these signals in sessions, but as their confidence grows, they should start to reach for the negatives later in the same session or in the session that follows.

The authority theme appeared many other times in similar discussions, for example, about the agenda for our work. When I appeared to return to an area of work without checking on the group's interest, members would participate in an obvious illusion of work. When I challenged the illusion, we could discuss why it was harder for them simply to let me know when they thought I was leading them away from their concerns. Another way to put this important point is that group leaders need to train the members to treat them as real people and not just as symbols of authority. I realize that for some this may be a different view of group leadership.

Issues of control also emerged in connection with responsibility for the effectiveness of the work. In the next example, one couple had spent an unusually long time discussing an issue without getting to the point. I could see the reactions in the group and inquired about what was going on.

Fran, the member in her 30s, responded by saying it was getting boring, and she was waiting for me to do something. Because this was a middle phase session, I found myself annoyed that everyone was waiting for me. I said, with some feeling, "How come you are waiting for me to do something? This is your group, you know, and I think you could take this responsibility, too."

The resulting discussion revealed that members felt it was risky to take one another on, so they left it to me. We were able to sort out that members, too, needed to take responsibility for the group's effectiveness. We discussed what the members were worried about if they were more direct with each other. In another example of how process and content can be integrated, I asked them if that was the same reason they had trouble confronting each other as couples. A major theme throughout the group sessions was how hard and risky it felt to be direct with each other particularly in uncomfortable areas of their relationships.

The Group Leader as the Outsider

Issues of control are just one aspect of the general theme of relationship to the leader. A second area concerns the leader's place as an outsider to the group. This arises particularly in groups in which the leader has not had life experiences that are central to the group members' themes of concern.

For instance, in a group for mother of children who have been diagnosed as hyperactive, the question arises of whether the leader who has no children can understand them and their problems. This is a variation on the similar question raised in the discussion of the beginning phase when parents inquired if the leader had children. The following excerpt illustrates this aspect of the authority theme struggle in the group context.

Note the importance of the group leader not becoming defensive and acknowledging that she was an outsider and had much to learn from the parents. This is most often seen by the group members as a sign of strength, not, as inexperienced group leaders believe, a sign of weakness.

Mother of Hyperactive Children: The Leader as the Outsider

Discussion got back again to causes of hyperactivity. Ann, who had thought it was hereditary, explained that her husband thought that he had been hyperactive as a child, except that nobody gave him the title. Marilyn said that her husband had also said that he had been like her son and had felt that her son would grow out of it. The group picked up on this idea and seemed to like the possibility. I was asked by Betty what I thought. I said I didn't know the answer but that, from what I did know, not enough research had been done. The group began throwing questions at me, related to general conditions and medications, and I couldn't answer them. I admitted that I knew very little about hyperactivity. I was certainly nowhere near being the experts that they were.

Someone asked if I had children. I said that I didn't. Beatrice wondered what work I had done with hyperactive children and extended this to children with other problems. I answered as honestly as I could. She wondered whether I was overwhelmed by their feelings. I replied that she and others present were really concerned about how I felt toward them, and whether I really understood what it felt like to be the mother of a hyperactive child. She agreed. I added that last week, when I had said I was feeling overwhelmed, I was really getting into what it felt like to have such a child. It was pointed out to me that I was the only one in the group who didn't have a hyperactive child—that I was really the outsider. Beatrice offered to lend me her son for a weekend, so that I could really see what it was like. Everyone laughed. (I think they were delighted at this.) I said that they were telling me that it was important that I understand what it's like, and I wondered whether I was coming across as not understanding. They didn't think so. I said that the more they talked, the better feeling I got about what they were going through. Toward the end of this, there was a lot of subgroup talking going on, and I waited (thankful for the break).

The Group Leader's Demand for Work

The third area of the authority theme relates to the group's reaction to the leader as a person who makes demands. For the group to be effective, the leader must do more than contract clearly and be empathic. The group will often come up against obstacles, many of which relate to the group members' ambivalence about discussion of painful areas. As the leader makes demands, group members will inevitably generate negative feelings. If the leader is doing a good job, group members will sometimes become angry with the leader for refusing to let them off the hook. If group members are *never* angry at their group leaders, they are probably not doing their job. Conversely, if group members are *always* angry at their leaders, that's a problem as well.

Of course, clients also have positive feelings associated with the fact that the leader is empathetic and cares enough about the group to make these demands. The negative feelings, however, need to be expressed; otherwise, they can move beneath the surface and emerge in unconscious expressions, such as general apathy. As we have seen, the leader must feel comfortable in her or his role to be willing to deal with this negative feedback.

In the example that follows, many years after the end of the Vietnam War, we see the delicate process of developing a good working relationship between a current group of still-traumatized, male Vietnam veterans in an outpatient clinic of a VA hospital and a young female graduate student who takes on the role of new co-leader, along with her supervisor. In a bold and creative manner, she challenges the men to address their internalized negative feelings that result from the way they were treated when they returned home from the war. Although the responses to today's soldiers returning from Iraq and Afghanistan are strikingly different—because most of the antagonism of antiwar protesters has been directed toward the administration, not the soldiers—there are still lessons to be learned from this example.

Note the following in these excerpts:

- The group leader's courage in addressing the issue of her gender
- Her capacity for empathy with their struggles on the issue of pride
- Her tenacious reaching for the group members' strength and finding it
- How the earlier described connections between how we feel, think, and act interact with each other

Posttraumatic Stress Disorder Vietnam Veterans' Group

Type of Group: Posttraumatic stress disorder Vietnam veterans' group

Age Range of Members: Early 50s through early 60s

Gender, Ethnic, Sexual Orientation, and Racial Information: On average, this biweekly group comprises 10 male individuals. Each member has been diagnosed with posttraumatic stress disorder (PTSD), and some receive a service-connected disability for this diagnosis. At the present time, the group is closed, and all members have been involved for a minimum of 2 years.

Dates Covered in Record Form: September 14 to November 9

Group Task: Relationship to the environment

Problem Statement: Beginning in mid-September 2006, this group was presented with a co-facilitator for the first time after a number of years. As a new authority figure in the group, my role as a young, female intern and group co-facilitator needed to be clarified. After the completion of this process, my goal was to confront the shame, hurt, and guilt when these veterans returned home to the United States after serving in Vietnam and receiving a very negative public response.

How the Problem Came to My Attention: After attending my first brief group session for approximately 20 minutes, in a nervous state of mind, there were mixed statements and body language presented that signified a welcoming to their group but also a level of uneasiness by some of the group members. I realized that I would need to promptly address these issues.

The first sessions described next deal with the issue of a new co-leader who is young and female. I believe these sessions lay the groundwork for her to make a later demand for work on the members, so they are described in some detail.

Summary of the Work

I entered the group room midsession because I was in between mandatory hospital trainings. My supervisor greeted me and introduced me as the visitor they were expecting. I addressed this comment by saying, "Hello, my name is Nicole. It is very nice to finally meet all of you." The male veterans all responded with a friendly hello and welcome, and one man, George, directed me to have a seat wherever I liked. After allowing the man who was speaking to finish the rest of his story, I further introduced myself. I spoke to the group by telling them that I am a graduate student and explained that my role at the VA hospital was as an intern. I explained I would be attending their group through next May, when I graduate. I explained that Barbara, their group leader, is my supervisor and mentioned that I had hoped to be employed at the VA in the future, after I graduate.

There was silence after I stated my role. This was followed by my supervisor requesting that each member tell me a little about himself and his background. To my surprise, the veterans were not shy about offering information until it came to George, the third group member to speak. He began to introduce himself by saying, "You know, I feel like there is tension going on in the room because you are very pretty. I don't know if the others are feeling this way, but I just wanted to get this off of my chest." Completely caught off guard—feeling my face become flushed out of embarrassment and noticing that no one was responding to George's statement—I responded by saying, "Well, thank you." I immediately felt that my appearance was a hindrance to the group members. As a young, inexperienced leader, I also feared that I would not be able to be looked upon as a leadership figure, but only as a sexual object.

PRACTICE POINTS The student's reaction was understandable, and it would have been hard to respond any differently. However, in reflection, one of the issues these men faced was their response to women, and George may have signaled their somewhat inappropriate way of handling such encounters. It was almost as if George were saying, "Do you want to see how inappropriate we can be dealing with women?" This issue would have to wait for another session, but one can see how process, once again, can connect to content. It's also apparent that one can be insightful after the fact but not so easy when the group leader is experiencing the moment. One man raises the issue of the intern as an outsider, and she responds directly without defensiveness.

The second-to-last man to introduce himself then asked me two questions in a forceful tone of voice regarding my comprehension of the subject he was discussing. He said, "Do you understand?" I responded with, "I think so," even though I felt somewhat confused. I stated, "I realize that I am new here and still have a lot to learn. I recognize that I am young and I may have some questions, so I hope that everyone will teach me even if some of my questions appear to be silly." The group members were very understanding as they responded with "Sure" and "No problem." I still wondered if they questioned how someone could help them if she or he didn't understand their experiences.

The last man to speak, named Dennis, was very friendly and reassured me that none of the group members would ever hurt me. I responded to Dennis by letting him know that was greatly appreciated, but I was not under that assumption. The group members spoke over one another with muffled responses of "Don't worry" and "Yeah." This comment made me feel as though the group members thought I viewed them in a frightening and negative manner.

PRACTICE POINTS Once again, with hindsight, we can see that the comment about not hurting the leader was also an indirect communication about the group members' concern as to how people reacted to them as Vietnam veterans. After presenting this excerpt in class, the student addressed this issue, at least in part. Note that she has tuned in to possible concerns on the part of the group members and shares her hunches directly.

During the third session, I initiated the group conversation by speaking to Dennis, who had previously stated that none of the group members would ever harm me. I presented to him that I was not clear as to what he meant by this and expressed that I felt that it was necessary that we speak about this because I did not want the group members to feel that I had any negative impressions of them. I explained that I had three different interpretations of the statement. Due to my age and my not fully understanding all war terms and experiences, I wondered if they either felt their discussions would be too traumatizing for me or that I feared them because I knew that they had killed people. I wondered if they thought I had negative images of them based on the nonsupportive media their war received and movies produced later that did not present the total reality of the war and their experiences.

Dennis disagreed with my perceptions and revealed to me that he did not want me to believe that the group members were nasty and miserable men who disapproved of my presence in their group. He stated, "In reality, we are all big teddy bears." I expressed to the group that I was not intimidated by them, that I trusted that no one would hurt me, and that I greatly appreciated everyone treating me nicely.

I brought up the statement I had made in the first session that I hoped the group members would teach me if I had questions that appeared to be silly because I was still learning. I specified to them that I recognized that this was their time to share their feelings with one another, explained that I was aware that their group session was time limited, and stated that I wanted them all to get the most beneficial experience out of their session without me interrupting to ask irrelevant questions. The men responded with comments including, "It is OK to ask questions," "Feel free to ask questions because you young people can help educate others about our experiences and real feelings," and "It is not a burden to our time limit."

PRACTICE POINTS Once again, with courage, she returns to the comments about her attractiveness in the first session by directly raising them with George.

I directed my attention to George, who had mentioned that he felt tension in the room because of my appearance. I instantly noticed that George appeared a little nervous when I brought this subject up, because he sat up and looked pink in the face. I described to him that I was not trying to make him feel uncomfortable or put him on the spot, but I wanted to know if my presence in the group initiated the same feeling of tension in anyone else. The group remained silent. I stated that I personally felt a little uncomfortable when that statement was made and wanted to know if my presence as a young female was going to impact the group in a way that would not allow them to disclose information as easily as they were able to before my entrance into the group. The group members replied that they did not feel this way and that they were used to working with an attractive female leader before my entry into the group.

PRACTICE POINTS This student's directness and willingness to reach for the meaning behind the previous comments demonstrated her strength and willingness to risk. Her honesty about her discomfort, a form of sharing her feelings, also contributed to the beginning of the working relationship and their respect for her in response to her respect for them. She still misses the implications of the comment in respect to their relationships to women and others outside the group; however, she is making sound progress in developing the working relationship. In the excerpt that follows, she begins the process of exploring their internalized negative feelings.

Based on group conversation concerning the humiliation and dishonor Vietnam veterans received when they returned home, it was evident that the members lacked feelings of pride for their military service and were embarrassed to admit that they served in Vietnam. I opened the fourth session with the topic of Veterans Day approaching in the next couple of weeks. I asked the men if they could describe whether they observed the holiday in a positive or negative manner. I specifically asked whether they could reflect on feelings of pride and/or shame on this special day. I received a number of negative responses. These included remarks such as, "It is a holiday that observes veterans from all wars except the Vietnam War," "If it was a real holiday, then only veterans would receive special sale prices on this day," "How could I observe this holiday and feel pride if I was afraid to even admit that I served in Vietnam?" "It is just another day to me," and "The only place I would feel safe celebrating this holiday is with other Vietnam vets who understand one another's experiences." The men came to a general consensus that they did not feel pride or increased levels of self-esteem on Veterans Day.

I asked the veterans if they could discuss specific events that influenced them to feel shameful on this holiday and in general. The veterans discussed their disappointment at how they were treated by their families and their employers when they returned home, the names they were called, the lack of interest people had in trying to understand their war experience, no one seeming to recognize that they had to do what they were commanded to do while in the military, and how difficult it was to adjust to civilian life because the average citizen did not seem to understand the reality of the Vietnam War. I stated to the group that I had great respect for them serving in Vietnam and that it angered me to know how badly they were treated when they returned home. I indicated that I was beginning to understand the severity of the traumas witnessed and experienced while in the war and commented that I gave them all a lot of credit for staying strong inside and seeking help through this group and individual counseling.

Because the Vietnam War is now more than 40 years' past, it may be hard for young group leaders to understand the turmoil in the country and the size and intensity of the antiwar movement and its impact on already traumatized veterans. This student would have experienced the wars in Iraq and Afghanistan. Although many in the United States objected to the original Iraq war and its continuation, these feelings do not generally carry over to the returning troops. This is in sharp contrast to the typical response to Vietnam veterans.

PRACTICE POINTS

This conversation provides an important education for the student and allows her to demonstrate her empathy and respect for the group members. This expression is important because it lays the foundation for her to make a demand for work—the group members will know it comes from caring and with an understanding of how hard the steps she asks them to take will be. In her most impressive moments, she refuses to accept the word *no* and insists that they take the steps needed to face their demons. Using humor and persistence, she even confronts them when they try to avoid public exposure by hiding and smoking. I commented to her on her assignment paper when she handed it in, "You are very strict." The key here is that—by making a demand that they be strong—she sends the message that she believes they are strong.

It was at this point that I asked the veterans to please bring in their medals from the war and wear an item of clothing such as a hat that identified that they served in the war to the next session, because it was 2 days before Veterans Day. I described to them that I wanted them to be proud of their duty in the military and that I hoped that they would be able to acknowledge that they could be recognized as Vietnam veterans without being retaliated against by the public. The veterans agreed to this after complaining that they really didn't want to do it and that they did not know where they had put their medals. I explained to them that we needed to work together to overcome these feelings and thoughts that have burdened their lives for many years.

The fifth session began with the veterans passing around their medals and certificates. To my surprise, six out of eight people who attended brought in their medals, seven men were wearing Vietnam hats, and one man brought in a catalog from which those who had misplaced their medals could order replacements. One veteran brought in red poppy pins, which represent veteran appreciation, and a roll of brand-new Canadian quarters, because every year a new word is printed on the back of the coin to represent veterans.

The exercise suggested by the group leader helped the men begin to address their lost pride in their efforts that had been overcome by the response on their return home. Her next step is to ask them to take their veteran selves outside the group room and face the public.

After the sharing process, I told the group that I wanted them to go down to the cafeteria or to the main waiting room near the outpatient entrance as a group for 20 minutes with their Vietnam apparel on. I disclosed to the group that I had chosen these specific places because they were areas in which there would be veterans from different wars, employees, and friends and family members who were not veterans. Their immediate response was a rejection of this suggestion. The group made comments such as "People in the halls are going to hide or put on protective gear if they see a group of Vietnam vets, because we are a bunch of crazies." I told them I knew that they could do it because they have one another for support. I persuaded them to hold their heads up high and be confident regardless of whether they were questioned about traveling through the hospital as a group. I made the group aware that I would be coming down to check on them in about 5 minutes to make sure that they really did go to one of the locations.

When I went down, I found the group outside smoking, and they had not gone to either location. They responded, "How did you know we were out here?" I joked with them and said, "If I can't have a cigarette, you can't either!" They commented, "Wow, I'm surprised you were able to walk out here and confront a whole group of males alone!" I laughed and said, "Just because you may feel that others are scared around you as a group, I'm not!" I then told them that we should go down to the cafeteria and get some coffee as a group.

We did this together and the veterans ended up staying longer than planned and talked to me and others eating in the cafeteria. The veterans showed an interest in speaking to me on a personal level without the presence of my supervisor. They questioned what I thought of working with their war population and what other things I was doing in the mental health clinic. I felt that this helped increase our comfort level and establish a stronger rapport.

The growth in the therapeutic alliance is evident as the men begin to see this counselor as someone they can use for individual concerns as well. After pushing hard for the men to take the difficult public step, the group returns to the group room, and the leader begins to explore their reactions to the experience.

When we returned to the group room, I raised the question, "In recognizing that you all were avoiding this experience by going out to smoke in an area where no others were present, was it as difficult of an experience as you originally perceived it to be?" The veterans stated that they were shocked to not receive any negative comments and to be as comfortable as they were together in an identified group of Vietnam veterans. The men responded positively to my asking whether or not this was a beneficial experience for them. One individual responded by recognizing that being in their group allowed them to normalize their feelings, but up until now, they had never left the safe space of their group room to perform an outside activity as a group. I asked if they would feel comfortable in the future doing a new activity outside their group room again. They responded in agreement to this.

Where the Problem Stands Now

I feel that I have successfully addressed and clarified my role as a new helping figure. I have shown that I am confident in attending to taboo subjects and interested in reaching for further clarification with the group members regarding my role and subjects discussed. I became self-assured that the rapport between me and the group had strengthened to a deeper level when the men felt comfortable enough to ask me self-disclosing questions and speak to me in the cafeteria from an educational perspective. It communicated to me that they were interested in getting to know me as a person and were willing to devote part of their limited group time to assist me in further understanding their feelings and experiences while in Vietnam and after returning home. I feel that positive change has occurred in the group and will continue to be reinforced when new interventions are presented and activities outside of the safety of the group room are conducted.

PRACTICE SUMMARY The student group leader has developed a positive working relationship with the men, working across gender, age and experience; she has also demonstrated her faith and belief in their ability to change. The excerpt of her practice over time has demonstrated her courage in addressing the issue of her gender; her capacity for empathy with their struggles on the issue of pride; her tenacious reaching for the group members' strength and finding it; and how the connections between how we feel, think, and act interact with each other.

The Group Leader's Limitations

A fourth issue is the need for the group to come to grips with the reality of the leader's limitations. Members hope that the leader, or some other expert, will be able to solve their problems. This is, in part, a result of the emerging dependency of the group. Once the group members realize that the leader has no solutions, their own work really begins. However, this realization is painful for the members and often for the leaders as well.

PRACTICE POINTS At the end of one particularly painful and depressing discussion in the parents' group dealing with their children's hyperactivity, when the members recognized that the drugs and the professionals were not going to "make the problem go away," a member appealed to the leader to cheer them up:

Mothers of Hyperactive Children: Can Someone Cheer Me Up?

We were way over our time. I started to sum up some of the feelings that came out today. I said that they had really been saying all along how helpless they felt that they couldn't do anything to help the children, and how hopeless they were feeling that there wasn't a solution for them. Marilyn said to me that that's how they felt, depressed and helpless. She said that I always came up with something at the end to make them feel better. I had better come up with something really good today, because they needed it. I said that I was feeling the same way, thinking to myself, "What can I say that's going to take the depression and hurt away?" I told her that I didn't have a magic formula, that I wished that I could suggest something. I knew how much she and all of them wished that I could help them with a solution. Rose said that they were feeling depressed, but they shouldn't blame themselves. I said that perhaps part of the depression was related to the fact that they themselves hadn't been able to help their children more, and they felt terrible about it. She seemed to be so terribly depressed, more than ever before. I know because that's exactly how I felt.

There was not too much discussion on the way out, as I didn't to know what to say to them (usually we joke around a bit). Marilyn said to me that I let her down—I didn't come up with my little blurb to pep them up. I said that she was feeling very depressed and looked to me to say something to make things easier. I said that she wanted a solution, and I didn't have one. She said to me that perhaps I did, and I was holding back. I said to her that she was very disappointed in me that I hadn't been able to make things easier. I wished that I did have the magic solution that they all wanted so desperately, but I didn't have one. After this, the members left.

The Group Leader as a Caring and Giving Person

A final aspect of the authority theme requires the group to deal with their reactions to the leader as a caring and giving person. The group members watch as the leader relates to them and to the others in the group. They can see the pain in the leader's face if he or she feels the hurt deeply; after a while, they can sense the genuineness of the empathy. This side of the leader provokes powerful responses in the group, and a mutual flow of positive affect results. An interesting discussion in my couples' group illustrates the importance of this aspect of the authority theme, as well as the group's awareness of this issue.

The Couples' Group and the "Crying Chair"

In the session before the Christmas break (the eighth session overall), one member arrived late and distraught. She sat down in the empty chair to my left, and, for the first time in the group, she shared a frightening medical problem her husband was facing. Until then, this member had appeared to be "without problems," because her husband was, in her mind, the identified patient. I comforted her while she told her story, and I tried to help her verbally and nonverbally—touching the back of her hand, communicating my empathic responses to her feelings. The group also reached out with support. In the second part of the session, after the immediate issue had been somewhat resolved and the member was in better shape, we carried out a planned midpoint evaluation of the group.

PRACTICE POINTS In discussing the way we worked as a group, one of the members raised the authority theme.

> Fran said, "I knew that this was Jane's night to get help the minute she walked in the door." (Jane was the member who had been crying.) When I inquired how she knew, she said, "Because she sat in the crying chair." She went on to point out that all of the people who had cried in sessions—4 of the 10 group members—had sat down in that chair at the beginning of the session. In fact, some had sat apart from their spouses for the first time in the group. Other members nodded in recognition of the accuracy of Fran's observation. I inquired whether they had any thoughts about why that was so. Rose said, "Because that's the chair next to you, and we sit there to get some support when the going gets rough." I responded, "Could you talk a bit about what it is about me that causes you to sit there or feel I can support you? This is important as part of our evaluation, but it can also tell us something about what it is you might want from one another."

The request for specifics was designed to encourage discussion of the members' feelings about the leader reaching out to them with caring. In addition, as is often the case, the process in the group can serve to assist group members in understanding their own relationships more clearly. The record continues:

> Louise said, "It's because we can feel free to say anything to you, and you won't judge us. We can tell you our feelings." Rose continued, "And we know you really feel our hurt. It's not phony—you really care." Lou, the 69-year-old member who had been most critical of helping professionals in the first session, and who had cried himself sitting in that chair, said, "It's safe next to you. We can share our innermost feelings and know that you won't let us get hurt." As I listened to the members, I felt myself deeply moved by the affect in their voices, and I shared that with them. "You know, it means a great deal to me to have you feel that way— that you can sense my feelings for you. I have grown to care about you quite a bit. It's surprising to me, sometimes, just how hard things in this group hit me—just how important you really have become."

The authority theme is a two-way street, and the leader will have as much feeling toward the members as the members have toward the leader. The countertransference dynamics need to be made a part of the discussion. The leader's honest feelings, freely expressed, are often the key to aiding the group as it comes to grips with its relationship to the leader.

In summary, some aspects of the authority theme to be dealt with during the life of the group include the leader's control, responsibility, and status as an outsider, and the group's reactions to the leader's demands, limitations, and caring. Although the phases in which a group deals with issues are never neat and orderly, a pattern emerges: as the issues of authority are dealt with, the group becomes more ready to turn to its second major developmental task—the relationships among members (the intimacy theme).

Group Member Relationships: The Intimacy Theme

A second major theme and driving force for a group is the *intimacy theme*. This refers to the way in which the members relate to each other. Recent research has highlighted that in addition to the therapeutic alliance to the leader, a therapeutic alliance has to develop to this entity called the group-as-a-whole.

Cohesion and Therapeutic Alliance to the Group-as-a-Whole

Recent research, for example, in the group psychotherapy field, has been paying increased attention to the concept of the group-as-a-whole, exploring both group development issues and their impact on outcomes. For example, while the concept of the "therapeutic alliance" between a therapist and patient has been examined, and its positive impact on outcomes has been evident in the literature, it has not been as widely examined in terms of alliance to the group-as-a-whole. Lindgren, Barber, and Sandahl (2008) have argued, "In treatment formats in which the group process is predicted to be a curative factor, it is counterintuitive to emphasize only the relationship between an individual patient and therapists" (p. 164).

In their own pilot study of patients diagnosed with burnout-related depression who received short-term psychodynamic group psychotherapy, these authors found an association between patient report of group alliance (using the group version of the California Psychotherapy Alliance Scales) and two of their three outcome measures.

> After controlling for initial level of outcome measures and group membership, mean alliance was significantly predictive of decreases in anxiety and global symptoms, but not in depression. Alliance to the group-as-a-whole explained 50% to 55% of variance in change of global symptoms and anxiety after control of initial symptom level and group membership, and 22% of the variance in change of depression. (p. 173)

Another interesting finding relates to the model presented in this chapter: that groups first develop the working relationship with the leader (the authority theme) and then with other members (the intimacy theme). The researchers found that alliance to the group-as-a-whole was lower in the early sessions of the research groups but became stronger in the middle or work phase of the group. In addition, the association of middle phase group alliance with the outcome measures was significantly stronger than the alliance at the beginning phase. Although this pilot study had a number of limitations, including the number of patients in the final analysis (19), the authors suggest that an increase in process research of the group-as-a-whole would be helpful.

In another study of group therapeutic alliance and cohesion, Joyce et al. (2007) examined the impact of each on outcomes in short-term group therapy.

> In the group context, then, treatment benefit may be facilitated by the patient's relationship with the therapist (alliance), the patient's signs of cohesion with the other patients, the patients' experience of cohesion to the group as a whole, or some combination of these relationships. In this study, our aims were to explore, first, how global measures of the alliance and cohesion may overlap and, second how they may jointly influence group therapy outcome. (p. 270)

In order to pursue these aims, the researchers used measures of cohesion that assessed the quality of the patient's relationship to the group as a whole (commitment) and the quality of the relationships with the therapist and other members (compatibility), from the perspective of each group member and the group leader (p. 273). Patients were matched on two personality variables and then randomly assigned to either an interpretative or a supportive group therapy, and each group was assigned a therapist. Of the 107 patients who completed the 12 sessions (32 attended less than 8 and were considered dropouts), a relatively equal number were in each group. The two groups were equally successful in achieving a number of positive outcomes including, for example, grief symptoms.

The authors reported, among others, the following significant outcomes:

- The patient-related and therapist-related alliance variables had a modest degree of overlap. Patients and therapists had similar views of the level of alliance.
- The therapist's view of the alliance was moderately associated with the patient's rating of commitment to the group and to the other members' rating of the patient's compatibility.

- The patient-rated alliance was directly associated with improvement on all three outcome factors: general symptoms, grief symptoms, and target objectives/life satisfaction.
- The group alliance variables were more consistently associated with outcomes than cohesion variables.

Although both studies report important limitations, nevertheless they mark an interesting venture into operationalizing key concepts such as group alliance, compatibility, commitment, and cohesions and their impact on each other and on outcomes. As this research continues, it will add to our understanding of this entity called the group-as-a-whole. It should also offer insights into the mechanisms of change in group practice. In the next section, I return to the Bennis and Shepard model but this time in relation to the intimacy theme.

The Bennis and Shepard Model

In addition to concerns about dependency, a second major area of internal uncertainty for group members relates to *interdependence*. This has to do with questions of intimacy—that is, the group members' concerns about how close they wish to get to one another.

In Bennis and Shepard's model, the group moves from the first phase, concerned with dependence and marked by a preoccupation with authority relations, to the interdependence phase, characterized by issues of peer group relationships. The two sets of member personalities that emerge in relation to this issue are the overpersonal and counterpersonal group members; these parallel the dependent and the counterdependent personalities of the first phase. Once again, three subphases are identified:

- the *enchantment-flight* subphase, in which good feelings abound and efforts are directed toward healing wounds;
- the *disenchantment-flight* subphase, in which the counterpersonals take over from the overpersonals in reaction to the growing intimacy;
- the *consensual validation* subphase, in which the unconflicted members once again provide the leadership the group needs to move to a new level of work characterized by honest communication among members.

As pointed out earlier, the specifics of the Bennis and Shepard model relate most directly to the dynamics of training groups (T-groups). However, ambivalence toward honest communications among members can be observed in most groups. After dealing with the authority theme, the group often moves through a phase marked by positive feelings among members, as the enchantment-flight subphase suggests. As the work deepens and members move beyond simply supporting one another and begin to confront one another, more negative feelings and reactions arise. As members begin to rub up against one another in their work, these feelings are quite natural and should be an expected part of the process. However, group members have learned from their experiences in other situations (e.g., family, groups, classes they attended as students) that talking directly about negative reactions to the behavior of others is not polite. This conditioning is part of the leader's experience as well. Often, then, the leader and the group become angry with members but nonetheless withhold their reactions.

Without direct feedback from the group, individual members find it difficult to understand their impact on the group, to learn from that understanding, and to develop new ways of coping. The leader's task is to draw these interpersonal obstacles to the attention of the members and to help the group develop the ability to discuss them. Leaders often fear opening up discussion of the angry feelings they sense in the group, because they are concerned that things will "get out of hand," they will be overwhelmed, individuals will be hurt, and the life of the group will be threatened. Actually, the greatest threat to the life of the group is overpoliteness and the resulting illusion of work. Expression of anger can free the caring and other positive feelings that are also part of the group's intimacy.

Of course, the leader needs to take care that the contract of the group does not get subverted. Sometimes, the discussion centers on intermember relationships, thereby losing sight of the original reason the group was formed. This is one of my major criticisms of the type of groups (T-groups) studied by Bennis and Shepard: They have no external group purpose other than to analyze the interactions among members. They are usually described as educational groups, wherein members can learn about group dynamics and their own interpersonal behaviors. A second possibility to which the leader must be alert is that the member involved may attempt to use the group to deal with a personal pattern of behavior in groups, another attempt at subversion of group purpose.

College Student Counseling Group and the Intimacy Theme

In the following illustration from a counseling group for college students experiencing difficulty in adjusting to their first year on campus, one member developed a pattern of relating in which she consistently cut off other members, did not really listen to them, and attempted to raise her own questions and concerns directly with the leader.

PRACTICE POINTS The leader sensed that she was relating only to him. The other group members showed elevating nonverbal signals of anger at her behavior, which she did not perceive. The record starts after a particularly striking example of this behavior.

> I noticed the group members had physically turned away as Louise was talking. Their faces spoke loudly of their negative reaction. I decided to raise the issue: "There is something happening right now that seems to happen a lot in this group. Louise is asking a lot of questions, cutting some people off as she does, and I sense that the rest of you aren't too happy about that. Am I right?" There was silence for a moment, and Louise, for the first time, was looking directly at the other group members. I said, "I know this isn't easy to talk about, but I feel if we can't be honest with one another about how we are working together, we don't stand a chance of being an effective group. And I think Louise would want to know if this was true. Am I right about that, Louise?" She answered, "I didn't realize I was doing this. Is it true?" Francine responded, "Frankly, Louise, I have been sitting here getting angrier and angrier at you by the minute. You really don't seem to listen to anyone else in the group."

PRACTICE POINTS The leader opened the door by pointing out the pattern in the group and breaking the taboo against direct acknowledgment of an interpersonal problem. This freed members to explore this sensitive area. The reader should remember that this was not a first session. This kind of confrontation before the leader had started to develop a working relationship and before the group members had experienced some positive work might have shut everyone down rather than opening the discussion up. A point to remember is that timing is crucial.

After Francine's words, there was a moment of silence, and then Louise began to cry, saying, "You know, I seem to be doing this in all areas of my life. All of my friends are angry at me, my boyfriend won't speak to me, and now I've done it again. What's wrong with me?" The group seemed stunned by her expression of feeling.

Because this was the first real discussion of an interpersonal issue in the group, the leader needed to clarify the boundary of the discussion, using the contract as his guide. I call this intervention *"guarding the contract,"* designed to prevent a member from subverting the working agreement by raising other issues. The group felt guilty, and Louise felt overwhelmed. The leader acknowledged both of these feelings:

> "I guess you all must feel quite concerned over how strongly this is hitting Louise?" Members nodded their heads, but no one spoke. I continued, "Louise, I'm afraid this has hit you really hard. I should make it clear that we won't be able to talk about the other areas in your life that you are finding tough right now—that wouldn't be appropriate in this group. I'd be glad to talk to you after the group, however, and maybe, if you want, we could explore other avenues of help. For right now, could you stick to what is happening in this group? How come you seem to be so eager to ask all the questions, and why do you seem so cut off from the group?" Louise was thoughtful for a moment and then said to the group, "I guess it's just that I'm feeling really concerned about what's going on here at school, and I'm trying to get some help as quickly as possible. I want to make sure I get as much from Sid [the leader] as I can." I paused and looked to the group. Francine responded, "You know, that's probably why I got so mad at you, because I'm the same way, and I'm sitting here feeling the same feelings—I want to get as much help as I can as well." Louise: "Well, at least you were straight with me, and I appreciate that. It's much worse when you can sense something is wrong, but people won't level with you."

After the exchange between Louise and Francine, the group seemed to relax. Louise's readiness to accept negative feedback without defensiveness had an impact on the group. In other circumstances, members may feel more vulnerable and would need all the help the leader could give in terms of support. When Louise was able to express the underlying feelings she experienced, other group members were able to identify with her, and this freed their affect and concern. Louise could sense their concern for her, making it easier for her to feel more a part of the group rather than relating only to the leader.

The leader proceeded to underscore the importance of honest communication among members and then guarded against preoccupation with process by reaching for the implicit work hinted at in the exchange.

> "I think it was really tough just now, for Louise and the rest of you. However, if the group is going to be helpful, I think we are going to have to learn how to be honest with one another. As Louise pointed out, it can be tougher not to hear sometimes. I think it is also important that we not lose the threads of our work as we go along. I noticed that both Louise and Francine mentioned their urgency about getting help with their problems right now. Could we pick up by being a bit more specific about what those problems are?"

Francine accepted the invitation by expressing a concern she was having about a specific course. From that point on, Louise was more attentive to the group and appeared a good deal more relaxed. The few times she interrupted, she good-naturedly caught herself and apologized. The leader spoke to her after the session and arranged an appointment for personal counseling. Members from that point on also appeared more involved and energetic in the discussion.

A group needs to develop a climate of trust that will allow the members to lower their defenses. On the one hand, a powerful barrier to trust can be raised and maintained by what members leave unsaid. Group members can sense both positive and negative reactions by other members. The effect of these reactions increases when they remain beneath the surface. On the other hand, open expression of these feelings can free members, who feel more confident when they know where they stand with the group.

Leaders usually experience intermember issues as particularly difficult. As they develop group experience, they become proficient at reaching for issues related to the authority theme; however, they take longer to risk dealing with the intimacy theme. So powerful are the taboos and so strong is their fear of hurting, and being hurt in return, that they will try many indirect routes before they finally risk honesty. The reluctance may be partly rooted in leaders' feelings that they are responsible for "handling" anything that comes from reaching for intermember negatives. As this excerpt illustrates, a group that has developed even a small fund of positive feelings is better equipped to handle its own problems. The group needs the leader's intervention to act as a catalyst, giving the members permission and supporting them as they enter the formerly taboo area.

The Stone Center: Intimacy and the Relational Model

Another theoretical model that helps us understand the intimacy theme is the relational model. This model has emerged from the work done at the Stone Center in Wellesley, Massachusetts, which is dedicated to studying the unique issues in the development of women and methods for working effectively with them. The center has built on the early work of Jean Baker Miller, whose publication entitled *Toward a New Psychology of Women* (Miller 1987; Miller & Stiver, 1991) laid the groundwork for the relational model.

Much of the evolving work in this area can be found in publications and a series of working papers from the Stone Center. This framework is often classified under the general rubric of self-in-relation theory. In one example of a group work elaboration of this model, Fedele (1994) draws on three central constructs repeatedly found in relational theory:

- Paradox (an apparent contradiction that contains a truth)
- Connection ("a joining in relationship between people who experience each other's presence in a full way and who accommodate both the correspondence and contrasts between them")
- Resonance ("a resounding; an echoing; the capacity to respond that, in its most sophisticated form, is empathy") (p. 7)

Paradox

Referring to therapy, Fedele (1994) identifies several paradoxes: "Vulnerability leads to growth; pain can be experienced in safety; talking about disconnection leads to connection; and conflict between people can be best tolerated in their connection" (p. 8). She also identifies the paradox between "transferential" and "real" relationships in therapy as well as the "importance of establishing a mutual, empathic relationship within the context of the unequal therapist-client relationship" as additional primary paradoxes in therapy (p. 8).

> These dilemmas are dramatically apparent in group psychotherapy. The therapists and group members collaborate to create an emotional relational space which allows the members to recapture more and more of their experience in their own awareness and in the group. The feelings of the past can be tolerated in this new relational space. It allows us to reframe the experience of pain within the context of safety. The difficulty of creating an environment that allows vulnerability in a group format involves the complexity of creating safety for all participants. (p. 8)

In applying this theory to group therapy, she identifies the "basic paradox" of a simultaneous yearning for connection accompanied by efforts to maintain disconnection as a form of protection from being hurt—a need generated from earlier painful experiences. The paradox of "similarity and diversity" describes a tension between connection to *universal perspectives* and fears of isolation because of difference. Fedele points out that "[t]he mutuality of empathy allows all participants to feel understood and accepted. The leader, creating a safe relational context, fosters connectedness within that safety by working to enlarge the empathy for difference" (p. 9).

Another related paradox is the fact that the very process of sharing disconnection can lead to new connection. For example, "When members phone the leader to report anger or dissatisfaction with the group, the leader can encourage them to share this experience in the group. Often, if one feels the disconnection, it is very likely that one or more of the other members experience similar feelings and resonate with the feelings of dissatisfaction" (p. 10). Thus, when members share the sense of disconnection, these feelings can lead to connection. Finally, the paradox of "conflict in connection" describes the importance of managing conflict and keeping anger within the context of safety and acceptance of divergent realities. As Fedele points out: "One way to view anger is to see it as a reaction to the experience of disconnection in the face of intense yearning for connection" (p. 11).

Connection

In describing the second major construct of relational theory, the idea of "connection," Fedele (1994) says:

> The primary task of the leader and the group members is to facilitate a feeling of connection. In a relational model of group work, the leader is careful to understand each interaction, each dynamic in the group as a means for maintaining connection or as a strategy to remain out of connection. As in interpersonal therapy groups, the leader encourages the members to be aware of their availability in the here-and-now relationship of the group by understanding and empathizing with their experiences of the past. But it is the yearning for connection, rather than an innate need for separation or individuation, that fuels their development both in the here-and-now and in the past. (p. 11)

Resonance

The third major concept, resonance, asserts that the "power of experiencing pain within a healing connection stems from the ability of an individual to resonate with another" (Fedele, 1994, p. 14). She suggests that resonance manifests itself in group work in two ways:

> The first is the ability of one member to simply resonate with another's experience in the group and experience some vicarious relief because of that resonance. The member need not discuss the issue in the group, but the experience moves her that much closer to knowing and sharing her own truth without necessarily responding or articulating it. Another way resonance manifests itself in a group involves the ability of members to resonate with each other's issues and thereby recall or reconnect with their own issues. This is an important element of group process in all groups but is dramatically obvious in groups with women who have trauma histories. Often, when one woman talks about painful material, other women dissociate. It is a very powerful aspect of group work that, if acknowledged, can help women move into connection. It can also cause problems if women become overwhelmed or flooded. The leader needs to modulate this resonance by helping each member develop skills to manage and contain intense feelings. (p. 14)

Many of the constructs of this theory, particularly its group work implications, fit well with the mutual aid framework presented in this book. The description of the process of resonance closely resembles the dynamic described as the "all-in-the-same-boat" phenomenon. As another example, Linda Schiller (1993) was able to use the self-in-relation framework to rethink a classic theory of group development known as the Boston model (Garland, Jones, & Kolodny, 1965), adapting it to a feminist perspective. We will return to a discussion of gender-related models when we discuss feminist group practice in Chapter 13. More recent insights from the Stone Center publications will be shared that raise questions about the appropriateness of this model for all groups for women since the initial observations were made with a largely white and middle-class population.

A Support Group for Women with Cancer

In the example that follows, from a community-based support group for women with cancer, we can use the relational model to explain the patterns of interaction over time. We see examples of paradoxes, connections, and resonance in each session of the work.

Members: Four 45- to 58-year-old white women from different ethnic and socioeconomic backgrounds. All have been diagnosed with breast cancer and are either in the midst of treatment or have just finished.

Dates Covered in Record: November 14 to December 5

Group Task: Individual need satisfaction

Description of the Problem

The task of this group is for members to reach out to one another to find support for painful issues related to their cancer diagnoses. One member in particular seems to be expressing the pain and anger for the group. The problem that I began to recognize was that this member was carrying a great deal of emotion about her cancer diagnosis. She demonstrated her emotion through anger and distrust projected onto group members and the medical staff in general. I suspect that all members shared similar feelings to some extent but were unable to recognize them as related to their illness. My co-leader and I found ourselves faced with two problems:

(1) We needed to find appropriate ways to address the emotions expressed by the angry member, or what appeared to be the deviant member, to get at the underlying message, and (2) we needed to help the group as a whole find the freedom to express and address their painful feelings rather than allow this individual member to bear the responsibility.

How the Problem Came to the Attention of the Leader(s)

Through conversation and the telling of individual stories, it seemed apparent from the beginning of the group that this woman was distrustful of people in general. I had originally suspected that she was someone who generally had not found people trustworthy throughout her life. After the second session, I began to wonder if this quality was not somehow related to her recent cancer diagnosis as well. She called my co-leader and expressed a desire to quit the group because her "ways of dealing with [her] illness [were] diametrically opposed to the other members' ways."

At this time, she also mentioned the name of one member specifically. Although she continued to attend, it was apparent that she was carrying anger with her, especially toward the member she had named. She would roll her eyes or mutter something under her breath whenever this woman spoke. The other members did not acknowledge this, nor did the woman to whom the behavior was addressed.

Summary of the Work

Session 1

After introductions, I went over confidentiality issues as well as the rules and the purpose of the group: "This is a support group for women with breast cancer. It was created because of their requests in the oncology clinic, and I hope that it will become a safe place for all of you to share your experiences and feelings about your illness as well as a place in which you can learn from one another." My co-leader then stated that she, too, hoped to make this a safe place for the women to share their stories, and then she invited each one to talk about her experiences.

Each member told her story, offering an account of what she had been through. I noticed that none of the women expressed their stories with much emotion, only offering descriptive accounts of their experiences. However, one woman, Joan, did stand out in her account. She expressed distrust of the medical system and said that, so far, she had not found any of the doctors or nurses helpful. "I do my own research and reading. I can't count on them to give me the answers. They're in and out in a flash." Another woman, Judy, added that she had a similar experience in the past and ended up switching doctors. Joan snapped at Judy, making an excuse for not being able to switch doctors, and said, "I just deal with it."

PRACTICE POINTS

If we consider our discussion of the group as a dynamic system and each member playing a role, then Joan's behavior can be understood as her potentially raising the feelings associated with the diagnosis they all experience and the underlying concern about whether they can trust their doctors. This is a difficult issue for the co-leaders because they must relate to the medical staff and must feel somewhat uncomfortable about the negative comments about doctors. This reaction is evident as they do not pick up on this issue.

Once each woman had shared with the group, my co-leader asked if any of them had been in groups in the past. Only one woman had been in a prior group, and she talked about how each member in that group had died. The room was silent. Instead of letting the silence stay and then addressing its meaning, I asked the woman what it felt like to be starting another group. She commented that it was a little scary and added, "But we have to keep going on. We have no other choice." I then asked the other members what it felt like to hear her talk about the other group.

They all commented about how it must have been an awful experience for her. My co-leader pushed, "Does it make you start to think about your own mortality?" A couple of members said that they had not really given it much thought, and Joan said that it did make her think about it, but that was all. Instead of pursuing this, both my co-leader and I let the conversation drift back to the members' telling Barbara how it must have been hard to be part of that group. Again, Joan had given us an opportunity to recognize her as really wanting to do the work in the group. First, she brought up the anger, and then she acknowledged thinking about death. Both are very real issues for all the members in this group. We failed to pick up on her desire to work.

We ended the meeting with my co-leader offering a summary of what she felt she had heard as being common among the women's experiences. Death and anger were not mentioned. We both thanked them for coming to the group.

In Joan's reaching out and at the same time seeming to use her anger to push people away—for example, by snapping an angry response to Judy—she demonstrates the basic paradox in the relational model of the simultaneous yearning for connection accompanied by efforts to maintain disconnection as a form of protection from being hurt. The co-leader reinforces the taboo in the group in relation to death and anger by not mentioning it in her summary.

PRACTICE POINTS In the next session, we see the leaders' attempt to encourage connection and resonance as Joan brings up how overwhelming dealing with her own cancer and taking care of others can be. This time it is Judy who demonstrates disconnection as she responds to Joan's emotional presentation by moving to an intellectual discussion.

Session 2
We asked each member to give a brief check-in so that everyone could get an idea of how the others were doing. Joan was the last one to check in, and she brought up the fact that her daughter was going through chemotherapy at the time and that she herself was presently taking care of a depressed friend. This opened up a discussion for all the women to find something in common. It turned out that each of them was caring for elderly parents; thus, all these women were acting as caretakers while dealing with their illnesses. I asked, "What's it like to not only have to worry about your own health and ability to live from day to day, but to have to worry about taking care of someone else as well?" Barbara said, "You gotta do what you gotta do." Everyone agreed.

Judy then began to change the subject to talk about how, when she was not caring for her mother, she was working on a proposal that addressed research on tobacco and cancer-related issues. She wanted to know if any of the other women would be interested in helping her out. Barbara and Gayle inquired about it, while Joan sat quietly, appearing to be somewhat annoyed. Neither my co-leader nor I said anything. I did not realize at the time that this was Judy's way of avoiding the work of addressing painful feelings, the group's way of going along with it, and Joan's silent plea to do the work.

As is usually the case, the group members will offer the leaders another chance at addressing the real issues. In thinking about the group as a dynamic system with members playing various roles, we can then see that Joan is actually trying to move the group deeper into the work through the expression of emotions, although the anger covers her pain. Judy is the member who reminds everyone, including the leaders, that this is hard to talk about by moving away from painful subjects. This time the leaders address the process but fail to name the members and to identify the roles that they play.

The women continued to talk about their own efforts in keeping busy, and then Joan chimed in, "I haven't been able to go back to work because of the amount of chemotherapy I receive. I have enough trouble trying to take care of everyone else and myself." Judy responded by stating that she knew how she felt because she wished she had more time to work on her proposal. She then went into how long a proposal takes to draft. Joan rolled her eyes. The other members seemed to fall into Judy's trap again. My co-leader said, "I've noticed that the group sort of shifts a focus off of issues that seem to bring up some painful emotions for each of you. Have you noticed that, Sandra? Has anyone else noticed that?" Gayle asked what she meant. She explained, without using names, that whenever the group got close to having to share how experiences or "realities" were affecting them, they seemed to shift to talking about less emotional topics. She then said, "I wonder why this happens."

Here we began to point out the pattern that the group was establishing in addressing painful issues. What we failed to do was to recognize and use Joan's experience in the group as a way to name the painful feelings that the members avoided discussing. Gayle stated that she hadn't noticed this. Judy and Barbara stated that they had not noticed either. Each of them was sort of smiling an embarrassed smile. Joan would not look at the group members; she just let out a very heavy sigh that caused everyone to look at her. No one said anything.

Proponents of the relational theory framework describe the importance of monitoring connection and resonance, keeping in mind that members can get "flooded" by emotions. Judy and Joan may be expressing the flooding in different ways, and the model would urge the leaders to help each member develop the skills to "manage and contain" intense feelings. Although the leaders press Joan to respond, they still avoid the expression of anger that remains a taboo in the group.

Barbara commented on how quiet it had gotten. This broke the silence, and the other members began to admit that they "might" have been avoiding painful issues. Joan still sat quietly. I remarked that she had been very quiet for a while and that our time was running out. I wondered if she wanted to share anything with the group. She said no. My co-leader said that she imagined her silence meant something. She said, very angrily, that it was sometimes easier to "just not talk." The group then began to inquire and stated that the reason they were together was to help one another and that, if they could help Joan, they wanted to. Joan just shook her head and said that she was fine. We, again, avoided bringing up the anger that was present. Maybe we (my co-leader and I) did not want to deal with it?

The group then began to talk about some side effects of chemotherapy. Judy was the only one in the group without hair. She expressed feeling fine about not having it: "It will grow back." Others talked about hair thinning and other side effects that they had read about. Joan joined in the conversation minimally. We still ignored the possible significance of her deviation from the group norm.

The call from Joan about wanting to quit the group easily fits another paradox in the relational model, in which the very process of sharing disconnection can lead to new connection. The leaders encourage Joan to bring her concerns to the group as a means to create the connection she both yearns for and resists.

In retrospect, what I think we were missing was that Joan represented the ambivalence of the group to face painful issues. In addition, we failed to really note what Judy represented to her, and possibly to other members. Judy is the only one who has completed chemotherapy and/or radiation, she is the intellectualizer (or initiator of flight), her baldness is a reminder of what might happen to others in the group, and she is getting back into her work and other parts of her life that she has put on hold, unlike the other members who are still faced with much uncertainty. The leaders make an empathic demand for work by asking directly who provides emotional support after members describe other forms of help.

Session 3

The group opened again by checking in with each of the members. Joan appeared somewhat more cheerful than I had expected. Barbara brought up feeling worn out about caring for her mother and herself. This opened up a discussion about how they each were giving support to other people. Directing the question to any member, I asked, "Who gives you support?" Judy began to talk about how her friends used to provide her with transportation and/or come over with meals when she was sick from treatment. Each of the other women shared her "support" stories as well. I finally stated that the kind of support that they had all just talked about was support around concrete needs: food, rides, and so on. I then asked who gave them emotional support. The room got silent. Judy began to intellectualize. Joan rolled her eyes and shook her head. I pointed out that they were "doing it again," referring to their established pattern of avoiding painful issues.

Everyone but Joan smiled embarrassedly. I said to them that everyone was smiling but Joan, and I wondered what they were really feeling. They were silent. I said that I imagined it was hard for all of them to be here and to talk about their illness, especially when they are still in treatment.

My co-leader took this opportunity to ask the group what it was like for them to still be in treatment and to have a member present who was through with it. Joan remained quiet. Gayle got tearful and began to pour out that she was "scared shitless" of what might happen to her hair, of how sick she might become, and of how there's no real guarantee the chemo would work. I stated that I had just seen more emotion pour out of her than I had seen before. I named what I saw: "You seem like you're feeling sad and scared and angry all at once." She had tears rolling down her cheeks.

PRACTICE POINTS In the next excerpt the group leaders finally confront Joan and do not let her off the hook when she expresses her anger directly.

I looked at Joan, who was tearful. My co-leader asked the group, "What do you do with all of these feelings every day?" Joan made a sound of irritation. My co-leader asked her what that sound meant. Joan just shook her head. My co-leader stated that Gayle's outpouring of emotion was understandable and that she thought it must be hard for her to carry those feelings around. I then took the opportunity to narrow the focus to the anger, because it seemed to be an emotion shared at that moment by more than one member (both Gayle and Joan).

At this time, I ended up taking advantage of an opportune moment to address Joan's anger without making her feel alone with it. When I mentioned that it must be hard to deal with the anger and asked how they managed it, Joan started right in about how angry she was at the hospital and about her depressed friend. The discussion continued until Gayle said that she just wished that she could get back to where she was before she got sick. Through this discussion, the group was able to talk about its anger, an emotion that all of them admitted to feeling. They acknowledged that it "might" be about their "unlucky" confrontation with cancer, but no one would give a definitive "yes" on that.

As the group ended that day, there was a sense of peace in the room. On reviewing my notes from this session, it appeared that much work was done to break through the obstacles that the literature speaks to. By reaching for the underlying feelings and the meanings of the nonverbal messages, we were able to open up some painful areas that the group obviously felt ambivalent about sharing. We were also able to take the individual's issue (the anger) and bring it out as a common feeling among all the group members, rather than leaving it in one person's possession. One thing that was not addressed, though, was Joan's anger directed at Judy. I think we were too afraid to touch this.

Session 4

The group started as usual with check-ins. The members shared some events that had taken place that week regarding new drugs that two of them were put on. A discussion opened up around side effects again, and this led Joan to discuss her anger about her visit with her doctor that week, as he had been "in and out in a matter of minutes." At this point, Barbara said to Joan, "You seem so angry at the doctors. I wish that your experience with them wasn't so dreadful. It makes it much easier if you feel like you are in good hands." The group began to discuss this thought, and Joan sat back and listened. She did not appear angry, just deep in thought. My co-leader asked her what was going through her mind. Joan said, "I just feel like my life is in their hands. They have all the power; the cancer has the power, the drugs have the power, I have none."

For the first time, the group members started to really talk about feeling helpless to their cancer diagnoses. After we had recognized and called attention to Joan's nonverbal messages, the group was able to benefit once again from Joan's ability to bring a common issue to the forefront. In addition, the members were beginning to feel comfortable bringing up the issues themselves.

The leaders have recognized that Joan plays an important role in the group, but they fail to see that Judy does as well. If they acknowledge this interaction—the direct and indirect expressions of anger from Joan toward Judy—they will probably discover that the part of Judy that Joan is angry at is the part of her own feelings that would also like to live in some form of denial. Connection and resonance emerging from disconnection as the relational model would describe it. They do open the door to the powerful feelings of helplessness dealing with a possibly life-threatening disease that underlies Joan's surface anger and is shared by the other members.

This example illustrates how difficult it is for group members and, at times, group leaders to deal with anger between members directly. In the misconception about relationships in general and groups in particular, the myth exists that anger is negative and is to be avoided. Anger is an emotion just like any other, and it needs to be faced and addressed if we are to get to the underlying feelings. Avoided, anger stays beneath the surface and blocks the opportunity for connection and resonance.

Anger in a Graduate Class on Practice: Impact of Trauma on the Practitioner

I would like to share one more example that comes from my graduate school teaching experience. While a class is an educational group, not a therapeutic encounter, mutual aid processes can nevertheless be powerful sources to enhance student learning. In a class I taught in Canada on group practice for second-year graduate students, most of whom had come from a practice background prior to attending school, I noticed a pattern in which one student, a Native Canadian in his 30s, continually took discussion about group examples presented by class members to a theoretical level, avoiding any emotional expression.

After the third class and having noticed other students beginning to roll their eyes in response, I pointed out what I saw happening in the class. When I opened the door for comments, a few students expressed anger toward this one student for his continuous intellectualizing. When I asked the class members why they seemed so angry at this pattern, the response was a brief silence. I waited and then one student said, "Because when I listen to him, I think that's what I have become here at graduate school. I'm full of theories and have forgotten why I got into school in the first place." Others joined in and continued a discussion of how they thought their first year of graduate school had focused on theories and research and was changing them in ways they were not sure they liked.

After a discussion with most of the students participating, except for the student who had been intellectualizing at the start of class, I asked him if he had any thoughts about why he kept talking about theories and seemed to avoid the emotions. After a brief pause he said, "I used to deal with feelings when I worked with homeless Native kids on the street. I got really close to one 16-year-old boy and began to feel like the father he never had and he like the son I would have wanted." After a long pause while he appeared to be struggling with his feelings he said, "And then one night he shot himself in the head." At this point he began to cry softly, as did others in the class. I found my own eyes tearing as I felt the profound impact of his emotions.

The remainder of the class was spent with other students discussing their experiences with suicides and attempted suicides, and the death of clients on their caseloads. They simultaneously provided support to the first student while pointing out that no matter what they did, they would never be able to prevent this from happening. They also suggested that as much as they intellectually understood this tragedy, when it actually happens they never quite get over it. They also pointed out how little help they and their colleagues received from instructors, supervisors, and agency administrators.

By my addressing the anger and trusting the process, I helped the class group achieve resonance and connection in the face of disconnection. Moreover, I learned another important lesson about my teaching: In addition to trusting the class group, I needed to trust myself. This was perhaps easier to do since I was a full professor with tenure at the time—not as easy for new faculty, PhD students, and new group leaders.

Kendler (2002) pointed out how difficult it is for group leaders, particularly new ones, to openly address anger and conflict in a group and calls for a process of personal introspection that allows group leaders to understand their fears.

No amount of professional experience will every fully banish the group leader's fear of addressing conflict in groups. Nevertheless, the distinctive potential and power of a group to foster personal growth and to allow mutual aid to thrive among its members absolutely relies on the leader's comfort and skill in doing precisely that.

Leaders with groups need to make conscious efforts to come to grips with their own fears and struggle to do so even after years of group work experience. Time and experience in leading groups surely and gradually help leaders to overcome their aversion to conflict so as to be able to hone their skills and interventions. But time and experience alone are not enough to bring leaders to a level of personal awareness and professional appreciation of conflict as a positive force in the life of a group. (pp. 25–26)

In developing their readiness and skills to address conflict in the group, I have observed that leaders often first achieve some measure of comfort in dealing with conflict related to the authority theme and anger toward themselves in their role as group leaders. It is then that they are more able to address conflict and anger between members, or what I refer to as the intimacy theme. Kendler makes five recommendations for addressing conflict in groups:

(1) do not cut off confrontation too early, before members have arrived at the heart of the conflict; (2) do not allow confrontation to continue for too long, to a point at which members denigrate each other or to a point at which the nonparticipating members who silently observe the conflict are no longer able to tolerate its presence; (3) empathize with and validate the feelings of each member; (4) point out the commonalities in the group; (5) refer to the overarching purpose of the group. (p. 26)

Of course this still leaves questions for group leaders of when, whether, and how to confront or manage it. I will return in Chapter 12 to Kendler's ideas on dealing with posttraumatic stress groups and her illustration of how she answered these questions in a group she led for New Yorkers coping with the September 11, 2001, terrorist attacks on the World Trade Center.

The descriptions of the difficulties that group members face in dealing with two major developmental tasks—the relationship with the leader and the relationship among members—refer to an even more general task: the development of a culture for work. In the following section, I explore the question of group culture in more detail.

Developing a Culture for Work

The term *group culture* has been used thus far in its anthropological/sociological sense, with a particular emphasis on group norms, taboos, and roles. In Chapter 7, I addressed the concept of role in some detail, so I will focus here on norms and taboos.

Norms and Taboos

Hare (1962, p. 24) has defined *group norms* as rules of behavior, or proper ways of acting, that have been accepted as legitimate by members of a group. Norms specify the kinds of behavior that are expected of group members. These rules or standards of behavior to which members are expected to conform are for the most part derived from the goals a group has set for itself. Given a set of goals, norms define the kind of behavior that is necessary for or consistent with the realization of those goals.

Taboos are commonly associated with primitive tribes who developed sacred prohibitions that made certain people or acts untouchable or unmentionable. As I have discussed, the term *taboo* in modern cultures refers to social prohibitions related to conventions or traditions. Norms and taboos are closely related; for example, one group norm may be the tradition of making a particular subject taboo. As groups are formed, each member brings to the microsociety of the group a strongly developed set of norms of behavior and shared identification of taboo areas. The early culture of the group therefore reflects the members' outside culture. As Hare points out, the norms of a group should be consistent with those necessary for realization of its goals. The problem, however, is that the norms of our society and the taboos commonly observed often create obstacles to productive work in the group. A major group task then involves developing a new set of norms, thereby freeing group members to deal with formerly taboo subjects.

We have already addressed the problem of helping group members develop their culture for work. For example, authority and dependency are generally taboo subjects in our culture; we do not talk freely about our feelings regarding either. Group experiences in classrooms over many years have taught us not to challenge authority and have alerted us to the dangers involved if we admit feelings of dependency on a person in authority in front of a peer group. The discussions of the authority and intimacy themes in the first part of this chapter described the group leader's efforts to help the group discuss these taboo areas and to develop a new set of more productive norms. The effort is directed neither at changing societal norms nor at exorcising taboos. There are sound reasons for norms of behavior, and many taboos have appropriate places in our lives. The work focuses instead on building a new culture within the group, but only insofar as it is needed for effective group functioning. Transfers of this experience beyond the group may or may not be relevant or appropriate.

For example, members in a couples' group had to deal with taboos against open discussion of sex, an area critical to the group's work. The frankness of the group discussion freed the couples to develop more open communication with each other outside the sessions. This change in the culture of their marriages was important for them to develop and was therefore an appropriate transfer of learning. However, if the couples used their newfound freedom to discuss issues of sexual functioning at neighborhood cocktail parties, they might quickly discover the power of peer group pressure (or perhaps be invited to more parties).

To illustrate the leader's function of helping the group work on its important tasks, I shall examine a number of efforts of leaders to develop a group culture. Then I examine the impact of ethnicity on group culture. This section uses the group theory outlined by Bion (1961) to illustrate again the way in which practitioners can draw on the literature to build their own models of group functioning. The reader familiar with more recent formulations about emotions and groups will recognize, once again, that they had roots in the early and innovative work of Bion.

Bion's Emotionality Theory

Bion (1961) can help explain difficulties with addressing emotions, a characteristic common to groups. His work was based on observations of psychotherapy groups, led by himself, in which he played the relatively passive role of interpreting the members' behaviors. Once again, as with the earlier theory, some elements of his model are specific to this type of group, whereas other aspects lend themselves nicely to generalizing. A central idea in Bion's theory is the *work group*, which consists of the mental activity related to a group's task. When the work group is operating, one can see group members translating their thoughts and feelings into actions that are adaptive to reality. For example, in the illustration from a parents' group for hyperactive children described earlier in this chapter, the work group was operating when the members spoke honestly about the deep and painful emotions they often experienced. As Bion describes it, the work group represents a "sophisticated" level of group operation. In the living-with-cancer group from another example, the honest discussion of the members' fears about the treatments, their anger, and their feelings of helpfulness all would represent what Bion would call the work group in action.

It is important to note that when Bion describes the work group, he is not speaking of a subgroup within the group or even of a separate group. This is a common misunderstanding of his theory. What he means by the work group, and other "basic assumption groups" described in the following paragraphs, is that the group members are acting as if they had come together under the basic assumption to do their work—or to avoid work—whatever it may be. So later, when I describe Bion's "basic assumption dependent group," it is still the same group of people, but their behavior now looks as if they came together not to work but to act on the basic assumption to be dependent on the leader. It is possible for a group session to start off as a work group, as we have seen in previous examples; however, when a difficult emotion is raised, the group may in an instant turn into the dependent group looking for the leader to help them resolve their pain.

Bion believes most groups begin with a more "primitive" culture, in which they resist dealing with painful emotions. Group development is therefore the struggle between the group's primitive instincts to avoid the pain of growth and its need to become more sophisticated and deal with feelings. The primitive culture of the group's early stages mirrors the primitive culture in our larger society, in which the direct and open expression of feelings is avoided.

In the following example of a parents' group, the leader described how the problem came to her attention, pointing out how the more painful subjects were dropped as the group took flight into a discussion of more superficial issues. This conforms to one of Bion's key ideas. He believes that the work group can be obstructed, diverted, and sometimes assisted by group members who experience powerful emotional drives. His term *basic assumption group* refers to the idea that group members appear to act as if their behavior were motivated by a shared basic assumption about the purpose of the group—an assumption other than the expressed group goal.

One of the three basic assumption groups he identifies is the *flight-fight group*. In a primitive group, when the work group gets close to painful feelings, the members will unite in an instantaneous, unconscious process to form the flight-fight group, acting from the basic assumption that the group goal is to avoid the pain associated with the work group processes through flight (i.e., an immediate change of subject away from the painful area; using humor to blunt an issue) or fight (i.e., an argument developing in the group that moves from the emotional level to an intellectual one). Bion is taking a concept from individual psychology and biology, the inherent *fight-flight* reaction to danger and applying it to this organism called the group. It may well be an unconscious reaction with group members not aware of how they are avoiding difficult work. For example, we saw in the previous chapter how the "clown" in a group used humor as a distraction just when difficult material was about to emerge.

This process in the group context parallels the ambivalence noted in work with individuals when resistance is expressed through an abrupt change of subjects. Bion's strategy for dealing with this problem is to call the group's attention to the behavior in an effort to educate the group so that it can function on a more sophisticated level. This process is illustrated in the next example. In reading this example, you should focus on the following:

- The way in which the group goes into Bion's fight-flight mode whenever the discussion gets to painful issues
- The importance of the leader pointing this out

- The leader's expressions of empathy that build the foundation for making the demand for work
- The leader's efforts to make a demand for work that gets to the underlying issues

Mothers of Hyperactive Children: Accepting Difficult Feelings

The first illustration is of a leader's efforts to help a group of mothers of hyperactive children share their painful, angry feelings about their children's problems. This is the same group cited earlier to illustrate the need for group members to deal with feelings that result from demands for work.

Description of the Problem

The members found it very difficult to talk about their own feelings about their hyperactive children. Instead, they continually focused on what other people—such as teachers, neighbors, husbands, and relatives—felt about the children. Despite their reluctance to focus on their feelings, they occasionally gave me clues that this was their underlying concern, and, as this was also part of the contract, I felt we had to explore their feelings and work on them.

How the Problem Came to the Attention of the Leader(s)

During the first few meetings, the members continued talk about how important this group was for them, as it gave them a chance to get together to discuss their problems related to their hyperactive children and get support from one another. The feeling was that no one, not even their husbands, understood what they were going through and how they felt. Any time they would begin to talk about their own feelings, they resorted back to discussing medications, school, and so on—in other words, safe topics. Yet the need to talk about how they felt was always raised by members in different ways. This pattern began in session two, when one member raised the question of hyperactivity due to emotional deprivation at an early age. The group superficially touched on it but dropped the subject, resorting back to something safe. As the members' pattern of flight became more obvious to me, I could help them understand what they were doing, and thus help them deal with their feelings.

PRACTICE POINTS

As I return to the leader's record of service on this problem, we will see that her early efforts were directed at systematically encouraging the expression of feelings and acknowledging these with her own feelings in an attempt to build a working relationship. As the pattern of using flight or, in Bion's terms, the emergence of the fight-flight group developed, the leader drew on this working relationship to point out the pattern of avoidance and to make a demand for work.

Summary of the Work

Session 3

I listened to what the members were saying, and I encouraged them to talk about their feelings toward their hyperactive children. Marilyn told us that, since she had begun coming to the sessions, she noticed that she had changed her attitude in relation to her hyperactive son, and now he was responding more positively toward her. She had always thought of him in terms of being a normal child, and it had frustrated her that he was unable to react as normal children do. In fact, she had set up expectations for him that he couldn't meet. I encouraged her to continue talking about her feelings toward him. She said that she supposed she really couldn't accept the fact that he was hyperactive, and then, after coming to the meeting, she began to accept this. I asked how she felt now. She felt better, but the hurt was there.

By the fifth session, the group had come close to discussing some of the more difficult underlying feelings; however, each time they had come up, they had used the flight mechanism to avoid the pain. Some of the feelings experienced by these parents ran so counter to what they expected themselves to feel that they had great difficulty in admitting the feelings to others and at times even to themselves. The leader had developed a fund of trust during the first sessions through her efforts to understand the meaning of the experience for the members.

PRACTICE POINTS In the following excerpt, the leader draws on that fund and makes a demand for work by pointing out the members' pattern of flight. Even as she does this, she tries to express her empathy with the difficulty the group experiences in meeting this demand.

Session 5
The group sometimes picked up on their feelings, and I tried to put a demand for work on them—that is, to stick with the subject and to really talk about their feelings. I pointed out their underlying anger and did not allow them to take flight. Betty started talking about George and the school again, and the others became very supportive, offering concrete help. She expressed anger at the school but also talked about George and how he didn't fit in—he couldn't read and cope with the courses, and he didn't care. I detected that some of her anger was directed toward him, and I asked how she felt toward him at this point. She said that she pitied him. I wondered if she wasn't also feeling somewhat angry at him for causing her so many problems and irritating her so much. I said that there were times when George made her very angry. Mildred agreed that she has reacted negatively, too.

PRACTICE POINTS The leader's synthesis of empathy and demand helped the group modify its culture and create a new norm in which the members would not be judged harshly for their feelings—even those they felt were unreasonable. As they expressed feelings of anger toward their children, the group members moved to a new level of trust and openness. With the leader's help, they described moments when they felt like "killing" their child, and, under her gentle prodding, they explored how they experienced having an "imperfect child" as a reflection of themselves as bad parents. This attitude, in turn, affected the children's sense of acceptance by their parents, which sometimes led to further *acting out*. Understanding and accepting these feelings was a first step toward breaking this vicious cycle. The leader's comments at the end of the session acknowledged the important change in the discussion:

I recognized how hard it was to talk about their feelings, and how much pain they felt. I credited them for their work and tried to create feelings among them that I understood. Denise had been talking about her own feelings about her son, and she seemingly had her feelings well under control. She had said that she was very sensitive and had trouble talking about it. I said that perhaps she was saying that she, too, had feelings that the others had mentioned, but she found them very hard to discuss. The others said that it was hard to talk about their concerns, to admit that these children weren't the same as the others, that you wanted to be proud of them but couldn't.

I agreed that it was hard—they were living the situation 24 hours a day, and they had feelings about these children. The members discussed how much they were criticized by their relatives and were very upset. I said that people just did not know what it was like to be a mother of a child like this, and also they did not feel the pain and frustration that the parents felt. I waited, and there was silence. I noticed that our time was up long ago, and I said that they had done some very hard work. It was not easy to talk as they had today, to share the feelings of depression and hostility toward their children, and to admit that they had wanted to kill them at times. I wondered how they felt now. Marilyn said that she couldn't understand everything I tried to get them to do, but I made her think and try new things, and also I made her look at things differently. I said that it wasn't easy for them to do this, I knew that, and I often felt their pain.

PRACTICE SUMMARY

We have already seen, in an earlier excerpt, how the leader needed to help this group articulate its anger in response to her demands for work. Bion might describe those exchanges as examples of the flight pattern of reaction in the flight-fight group. Another basic assumption group, as described by Bion, is the *dependent group*, in which the group appears to be meeting to be sustained by the leader. This is another form of avoidance of the work group and was illustrated in the earlier excerpt in which the group wanted the leader to "cheer them up." The third and final basic assumption group in Bion's theory is the *pairing group*. Here, the group, often through a conversation between two members (the "pair"), avoids the pain of the work by discussing some future great event. The event can be the discovery of a new drug or procedure that will cure the person who is ill. Another example would be the arrival of some person or organization that will solve the problem. The discussion in this group of "new drugs" or "outside experts" who might provide a solution to their problems is an example of the pairing group in action.

Bion's emotionality theory, his concept of the work group, and the three basic assumption groups (dependent; fight-flight; pairing) are rooted in the idea of a group unconsciously capable of acting without even the group members' awareness. One doesn't have to accept the model's strongly psychoanalytical core concepts to be able to observe the processes Bion describes. We have seen examples in this book where arguments between members (fight) or inability to stay focused (flight) emerged when painful issues were being discussed. We have seen numerous examples where group members hoped that the leader (dependent) could help them solve or resolve the problem so they would not have to deal with the associated feelings. We have also seen in the previous example how much easier it was for the group when two members (pairing) talked about a new miracle drug that might change their children so they could be "normal." Bion's writings are often dense, complex, and at times mystical, but these basic concepts I have described ring true and have helped me "see" and understand this organism called the group.

Helping Members Develop a Structure for Work

As a group develops, it needs to work on the task of building a structure for work: the formal and informal rules, roles, communication patterns, rituals, and procedures developed by the group members to facilitate the work of the group. Some rules are established by the agency or host setting and are not within the group members' control. At times, the group leader may try to help a group change a rule when conflict with the setting persists. In other cases, the rules emerge from the members themselves. The following example illustrates this process.

An Outpatient Group for Young Recovering Addicts

In the following example, one member of an outpatient group for recovering addicts raises the issue of bringing her baby to the group sessions. Underlying the issue of structure are several other concerns for this client, as well as questions for the leaders about the need for additional agency support for the group.

The setting is an outpatient alcohol and drug clinic in a hospital. This is a group for young recovering addicts. The purpose of the group is for the members to learn from and support one another as they cope with a sober lifestyle. Two men and two women are at the first meeting, and up to four more members could be added. The members range in age from 19 to 27 years old. The two women are black; one of the men is black, and the other is white. The co-leaders are white, and one is a counselor at the clinic.

PRACTICE POINTS While the agency rules were explained to the client, she decided to raise the issue in a meeting hoping to achieve support for her position. Note how the leader explains the agency position and then turns to the group members for their views on the matter.

We had just finished going over the group rules, and the group members were quiet. Beth (my co-leader) asked the group members if they wanted to add any more rules. There was a brief silence, and then Amanda said (to Beth), "You know what I would like to have for a rule?" Beth nodded and said that maybe Amanda could explain what she meant to the group. Amanda turned back to the group and said that she had a 3-month-old baby. The social service department had the baby now, but she hoped to get the baby back soon. She was not sure that she could find someone she trusted to watch the baby while she came to group. This was her first child, and she had been separated from her for so long that she didn't want to leave her. She said that when she was in group, she would worry about the baby, and that she had asked Beth in the pregroup interview if it might be all right for her to bring the baby along, but that we (Beth and I) had told her that she couldn't bring the baby. Amanda looked at Beth.

Beth said that, traditionally, the clinic hasn't had very many female clients, and that this issue hadn't come up before at the clinic, so she hadn't given Amanda an answer right away but had talked to me and to the other staff members; she said that she and I had thought that it could be disruptive and distracting to have a baby in the group. Amanda, still speaking to Beth, said that probably the baby would just sleep most of the time. Beth said that the problem was that the baby wouldn't be 3 months old for very long. Beth said that maybe Jen (another member) had some thoughts about the issue. Amanda turned to Jen. Jen smiled and said that she could remember when her daughter and her son were babies and that she had never wanted to leave them. She said that it's hard to leave your baby, but if there's a baby in the room, it's hard to ignore it even if it is asleep, because babies are so cute you always want to pick them up or play with them or touch them, so having a baby in the group could be disruptive.

Note how the supportive comments of the other members and their focus on Amanda's need are easier for her to hear. She is also raising through this request for a rule change a number of other potential issues:

- I'm really a good mother and am concerned about the baby.
- It's going to be hard for me to address my own needs and those of the baby at the same time.

Amanda appeared to take this comment in thoughtfully, and then she turned to Leo and Herb and said, "What do you think?" There was a brief silence, and then Leo said that he didn't personally have children but that he had a real soft spot for children and old people. He said that, from what he could tell, it was going to be hard for Amanda to leave her baby, and he could see why. He said it seemed like Amanda was between a rock and a hard place, because if she brought the baby, it might distract her and the rest of the group; and if she didn't bring the baby, it might also distract her because she would be thinking about her baby and worrying about her. He said that it was important for Amanda to take time to focus on her own recovery, and bringing the baby to the group could get in the way of that as well as be distracting.

Amanda seemed satisfied with this and turned to Herb, who said that he basically agreed with Leo. Herb said that he liked kids a lot but that he thought that a baby probably would be distracting and that it would be good for Amanda to take the group time to focus on herself. Amanda said that she could understand where everyone was coming from, and she still felt like she didn't want to leave her baby, but she'd do the best she could to get a babysitter. Leo suggested that maybe Amanda shouldn't get too worked up just yet, because it would be a few more weeks before she got the baby back and maybe a solution would turn up between now and then. He finished off by saying, "Easy does it," prompting Herb and Jen to follow quickly with two more Alcoholics Anonymous slogans. Everyone, including Amanda, wound up laughing. Then there was a brief silence.

The next intervention by the leader recognizes that she has two clients: the group members and the agency. Amanda's conflict raises a question about agency support for clients with similar issues. The leader's clear sense of her role leads her to suggest she will follow up with the agency on the need to consider additional supports.

I agreed with Leo and said that it was good that this issue had come up because it might be the first time it had come up in the clinic, but it almost certainly wouldn't be the last time. I said that I thought it showed a gap in the clinic's services, and it was something Beth and I could explore a little more and see if we could find a solution for. The members nodded, and Beth mentioned that there was a babysitting service in the hospital during the day, but that there clearly was a gap in the availability of services at night. Amanda said that she had not known about the daytime service, and it made her mad to know it wasn't offered at night. She said she thought that probably a lot more women would come to the clinic if there were someone here to watch their kids. The other group members agreed. Beth said that maybe something could be worked out, such as cooperative babysitting, and she asked me if I would bring that up at the staff meeting on Monday morning, because she isn't there on Mondays. I said I would be sure to, and I'd let them know what happened.

The discussion of the rule often raises many issues for the client—in this case, Amanda's concern about caring for her baby and not losing it to the child welfare agency again. The leader remains responsible for enforcing the agency policy on the issue of Amanda bringing her baby to the group. In this example, the leader involves other group members in addressing the rule and its impact on Amanda and the group. Most important, the leader's sense of the mediating role between client and system leads her to begin immediately to identify potential systems work on the issue of providing child care resources so that members can attend the group without being concerned about neglecting their children. In exploring the other issue that may be being raised indirectly by the member—that is, her concerns about the demands on her life that emerge from her parenting responsibility—the leader provides an example of how process and content can be integrated. By bringing the baby to the group, the client may be indirectly saying, "Look how hard it is for me to take care of my own life and the baby at the same time." The leader might also want to explore this as a theme of concern for Amanda and for other members as well.

Helping Group Members Negotiate the Environment

The discussion thus far has focused on the internal tasks of the group. However, a group does not exist in a vacuum but is located in an institution, a school, an agency, or a community-based service. In the description of the group as an "open social system," presented at the beginning of this chapter, the term *open* was used to imply that the boundary between the group and its environment is not closed. Even a group that is part of a private practice still exists and is affected by the larger environment. In fact, the activities of the group will have some effect on the relationship between the group and the environment. In turn, the interaction with the environment will have an impact on the internal operations of the group. In this section, I will explore an additional group task: negotiating the environment.

With the exception of Chapter 4 on contracting, I have been discussing the group almost as if it is cut off from the external world. In that chapter, I focused on finding the common ground between the service of the setting and the needs of the group members. Contact between the group and its external system continues after the beginning phase and is one of the ongoing realities to which the group must pay some attention. Two aspects of this group and environment interaction are considered in this section, the first being the group-environment relationship in terms of mutual obligations and expectations. The example is from a community center setting in which an acting-out group of young teens, an *activity group* I led in my first field practicum, finds itself in trouble with the agency because of its aggressive behavior.

Adolescents: Acting-Out Behavior in the Community Center

The example involves the young teenage club described earlier in my discussion of internal leadership in the group. The setting was a middle-class community center, and the group had a long history of acting-out behavior at the center. This group was one of my first as a student. I was in the building working on recording one evening when I was told by a staff supervisor to "get the kids in my group in line, since they were acting out in the game room." He was obviously angry at them. My first reaction was panic; I had been working hard to overcome our rocky start together, trying to undo my earlier mistakes of attempting to impose limits and establish my authority. I had just been getting somewhere in this effort and saw this confrontation as a potential step backward. When I explained this to the supervisor, his reaction was "What's wrong? Do you have trouble setting limits and using your authority?" As any student in training knows, a supervisor questioning your "problem" evokes a powerful response. I decided to face my responsibility, as defined by the supervisor, and went off to do combat in what I knew would be a battle of wills. Feeling upset about what I was doing only made me come on stronger.

I found the boys running and screaming in the halls, and I yelled at them to "cut it out." They slowed down for a minute, and I said to them, "Look, if you guys don't cut it out, I'm going to throw you out of the building." I continued, "What kind of way is that to behave, anyway? You guys know better than that. I thought I was getting somewhere with you, but I guess I was all wrong." My words seemed to be an additional catalyst, and I found myself chasing them through the building, catching them one at a time, and escorting them outside.

My mistake was a natural one. I was not clear about the concept of deviant behavior as communication at that time, so I did not attempt to find out what was wrong—why they were so agitated. Even if I had been clear about that, my functional confusion would have prevented me from dealing with them effectively. In the same situation today, I would be able to explain my functional role more clearly to my supervisor, suggesting that I speak to the boys to see what was going on and to try to cool them down long enough to talk to the supervisor about what was happening in the building and why. If I were unsuccessful, then the supervisor could throw the group outside, and I would go with them. I would have explained to the supervisor that at the point the boys were thrown outside, I would be available to them to figure out what had happened and to find a way to deal more effectively with the community center, since they would want to be accepted back. The center was concerned about this group's behavior, and this would be an opportunity to do some work on the relationship between the group and the center.

I am not suggesting there would never be a time when I felt bound to set limits on the boys and act on behalf of the agency or society. In the course of our time together, there would be many such occasions. For example, if physical violence were threatened, it would be my job to set limits and try to stop it so that we could develop safety for all members in the group. However, at this moment, when they were thrown out, they needed their leader the most. As I found out later, that day had been report card day at school, and most of the boys in the group were afraid to go home that evening and face their parents because of bad grades and reports of similar behavior problems in school. The acting-out behavior was an indirect call for help. A marvelous opportunity for work had been missed.

The Homans Social Systems Model: Relating to the Environment

A group theorist who could have helped me conceptualize the problem differently is Homans (1950). In his classic book *The Human Group*, Homans presents a general theory of human interaction using five well-known field studies of social interaction to illustrate his ideas. He describes three major elements of behavior, which he terms interaction, sentiment, and activity. Interaction refers to any contact between people, sentiment to feelings or drives, and activity to any action. Thus, Homans could take a descriptive social study and break it down into these three components: interactions, sentiments, and activities. His interest centers on the interdependence of these elements of social behavior—for example, how sentiment in a group can affect interaction and, in turn, how interactions can affect sentiment.

In the group example just described, the boys' feelings (sentiments) about their poor grades affected the way they related (interactions) to each other, which in turn generated behavior (activity) of the acting-out type. Homans's second major theoretical contribution is important here. He viewed activities, interactions, and sentiments within two interdependent systems—the "internal" system and the "external" system. The internal system consists of the interactions, sentiments, and activities within the group and their mutual interdependence. The external system consists of the same three basic elements (interaction, sentiment, and activity) between the group and its environment—in this case, the Y. It is important to note that Homans does not use the term *external system* to refer to the system itself—in this case, the community center. This is a common use of the concept system and a common misunderstanding in respect to Homans. The external system, to Homans, would be the three elements of interaction, sentiment, and activity between the group and the center.

The boys had developed a pattern of acting out within the center that generated negative sentiment on the part of staff, which in turn affected the interactions between staff and the group, which in turn generated more negative sentiment, and so on. Any effort to deal with the group members' behavior within the group must take into account the impact of the "external systems" of the school and the agency. I have oversimplified Homans's theory, but I think the central elements demonstrate once again how a theoretical construct can help a leader conceptualize a problem in a new way.

The issue of helping the group negotiate the environment will come back to the forefront in later chapters. I will argue that the counselor who believes he or she can take the group into a room and work with it with no regard to environmental issues will be missing an important aspect of the helping role and an opportunity to have a powerful impact.

Chapter Summary

The leader's second client, the organism called the group, must go through a developmental process. Early tasks include problems of formation and the satisfaction of individual members' needs. The concept of what I call the group-as-a-whole is receiving increasing research attention, with some focus on the impact of the development of group cohesion and what is called the therapeutic alliance to the group. Problems of dealing with the leader as a symbol of authority (authority theme) must be faced, as well as the difficulties involved in peer group relationships (the intimacy theme). Attention needs to be paid to the culture of the group so that norms can be developed that are consistent with the achievement of the group's goals. Taboos that block the group's progress must be challenged and mastered if the discussion is to be meaningful. A formal or informal structure must be developed. This structure will include assigned roles, assigned status, communication patterns, and a decision-making process.

Three classic group theories and one more recent theory were presented as models to help the group leader understand the group, its developmental needs, as well as its relationship to the environment. Effective work in the group will develop a sense of cohesion, which in turn will strengthen future work. Finally, the group exists within a dynamic system—the environment—and one of the leader's tasks is to assist with the interaction between the group and its social surroundings.

Related Online Content and Activities

For learning tools such as glossary terms, InfoTrac® College Edition keywords, links to related websites, and chapter practice quizzes, visit this book's website at **www.cengage.com/counseling/shulman.**

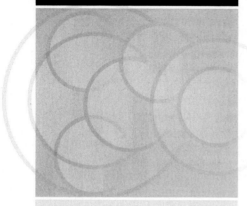

CHAPTER 9

Endings and Transitions with Groups

By examining the ending and transition phase of practice, this chapter completes the discussion of the phases of work. The chapter explores the unique dynamics and skills associated with bringing the helping process to a close and helping the group members make appropriate transitions. Practice examples will illustrate how this can be the most powerful and meaningful phase of work, as group members make the *third decision*—to deal with core issues that may have only been hinted at in the earlier phases. This chapter also examines the danger of this phase becoming a moratorium on work, in which both the group members and the group leader participate in an illusion of work. Specific skills to increase the possibility of positive endings and transitions will be described and illustrated.

The Ending Phase of Group Practice

Recall that, in the beginning phase, group members face a first decision. They must decide whether they are prepared to engage with the group leader and each other and to lower defenses if needed and to begin to work. In the second decision, the transition to the work phase, group members agree to take some responsibility for their part in problems and to face the emotional pain involved in work. In the third decision, group members must decide whether to deal with the most difficult issues as they approach the end of the working relationship.

The ending phase offers the greatest potential for powerful and important work. Group members feel a sense of urgency as they realize there is little time left, which can lead to the introduction of some of the most difficult and important themes of concern. The emotional dynamics between group leader and member are also heightened in this phase as they prepare to move away from the other. Termination of the relationship can evoke powerful feelings in both members and the group leader, and the group leader can often connect discussion of these to the members' general concerns and tasks. The ending phase holds tremendous potential for work, yet ironically this phase is often the least effective and can be characterized by missed meetings, lateness, apathy, acting out, and regressions to earlier, less mature patterns of behavior. Moreover, the group leader—as well as the members—shows these behaviors at times.

In many ways, the ending sessions are the most difficult ones for both the group leader and the members. The source of the strain stems from the general difficulty we have in dealing with the end of important relationships. Our society has done little to train us how to handle a separation; in fact, the general norm is to deny feelings associated with it. For example, when a valued colleague leaves an agency, the farewell party is often an attempt, usually unsuccessful, to cover the sadness with fun. The laughter at such parties is often a bit forced.

Delucia-Waack (2006) suggests the importance of addressing endings even in psychoeducational groups and addresses factors that may cause leaders to ignore the importance of this phase.

> Group leaders often underestimate the importance of the termination session and the consolidation of learning for a variety of different reasons. One is that psychoeducational groups tend to be so brief that it is difficult to consider giving a whole session to a topic that is not teaching a new skill or strategy. . . . [T]ermination brings up grief and loss issues, and sometimes group leaders may not want to experience emotions that go along with this stage, so they avoid it if at all possible. (p. 129)

Chen and Rybak (2004) also address the issues of loss in what they refer to as the "termination stage":

> The characteristics of the termination stage in a group are similar to those of the golden age in a person's life. Ridden throughout is a theme of loss and grief. A lot of feelings are triggered by the ending of the therapeutic relationship. Ending can be filled with sadness. Although the entire group experience may feel like a small life lived with others who have become significant in one's life, its ending may feel like a big loss. When sensing the ending approaching, some members start to feel a sense of separation anxiety. (p. 318)

The group leader–group members association is a specific example of this larger phenomenon. It can be painful to terminate a close relationship; when you have invested yourself meaningfully in a relationship, have shared some of your most important feelings, and have given and taken help from another human being, the bond that develops is strong. Strean (1979) has described the difficulties involved in terminating a close working relationship:

> Whether a leader-member relationship consists of five interviews or a hundred, if the leader has truly related to the member's expectations, perceptions of himself and transactions with his social orbit, the member will experience the encounter as meaningful and the leader as someone significant; therefore, separation from this "significant other" will inevitably arouse complex and ambivalent feelings. Still, a long-term relationship with a leader will probably include more intense emotions at termination than a short-term one.
>
> A prolonged relationship has usually stimulated dependency needs and wishes, transference reactions, revelation of secrets, embarrassing moments, exhilaration, sadness, and gladness. The encounter has become part of the member's weekly life, so that ending it can seem like saying good-bye to a valued family member or friend. (pp. 227–228)

Corey and Corey (2006) also emphasize the importance of the work to be done in this stage of the group.

> The final phase in the life of the group is the time for members to consolidate their learning and develop strategies for transferring what they learned in the group to daily life. At this time members need to be able to express what the group experience has meant to them and to state where they intend to go from here. For many group members endings are difficult because they realize that time is limited in their group. Members need to face the reality of termination and learn how to say good-bye. If the group has been truly therapeutic, members will be able to extend their learning outside, even though they may well experience a sense of sadness and loss. (p. 269)

Ethical Issues Related to Endings

Mangione, Forti, and Iacuzzi (2007) echo the importance of addressing endings, suggesting there are ethical issues to be considered.

> Loss and endings are potent factors in our client's lives, and potentially in their healing and growth. Therefore, we have the intersect of a cultural ethos that is not mindful of endings, clients with histories of complicated and conflictual endings, and at least some schools of psychotherapy postulating that well-worked endings are critical to client welfare. . . . Given the inherent difficulty and emotional upheaval that endings evoke, group psychotherapists need to be in possession of ethical tools for addressing the emotional tensions and conflicts that can arise in their clients and themselves and that can affect clinical decision making. (p. 27)

The authors also point to the importance of respecting racially, ethnically, and culturally diverse differential understandings and reactions to endings.

> In a culture that emphasizes continuity of relationships, an ending may be viewed as an interruption, not a permanent alteration. In another cultural group an ending may be seen as a permanent severing. Ethical difficulties can arise when these divergent views arise in the context of ending a therapy group. (p. 28)

In a survey of members of the American Group Psychotherapy Association on ethical issues related to endings, conducted by Mangione et al. (2007, pp. 28–34), 275 therapists (11% of the membership) responded. Half of these were in private practice and half in settings such as hospitals, schools, clinics or university settings. These are their findings on key issues:

- Virtually all of the seasoned therapists felt that endings were important and spent a good deal of time both preparing for and processing them.
- Fifty-nine percent endorsed discussing ending expectations in pregroup screening, and 13% said they did not talk about termination at all.
- Just over 36% said that ending should be jointly decided by therapist, client and the group.
- Over a quarter of the respondents had experienced verbal or acting-out appeals from members to extend the group and felt the need to extend the group in response to members getting more symptomatic even though they understood the ethical issues involved in changing the agreed-on framework.
- Twenty percent of the sample had extended a short-term group at the request of the clients despite ethical concerns. Fourteen percent expressed ethical concerns about not extending a group when some clients were in distress and follow-up was not available.
- In response to an offered scenario of a member leaving unexpectedly, three-quarters would want to discuss their perspective on the departure with the group members; however, the same number were aware of the obligation to protect client privacy if they did so.
- A small percentage of respondents had experienced a group member committing suicide, and they expressed the need for support for themselves as well as an opportunity to discuss the event with group members and to share in the grieving.
- Over half of the respondents had asked a member to leave the group primarily on the basis of disruptive behavior or a poor fit between the individual and the group.
- Over half of the respondents had experienced having to leave a group often because of life situations (e.g., pregnancy) and at times because of more complicated issues such as experiencing a physical threat from a group member.

This survey, as well as my own practice experience, suggests that endings can indeed be complicated, and they can raise ethical challenges for the group leader. An opportunity to explore these ethical issues and, as will be suggested in Chapter 13, the advantage of a collegial ethical review committee as well as a risk management model in place can be extremely helpful.

The Group Leader Takes a Leave of Absence: Transitioning to an Interim Leader

One more model of endings can take place when the primary leader needs to take a leave of absence and intends to return with the group led by an interim leader. While there is an expansive literature on endings with leaders or members leaving, the temporary leave of absence is not as well addressed. With roles in settings and in personal lives becoming increasing complex and demanding, this need for a leave can occur more often. Pudil (2007) uses her own experience on a leave from an adolescent HIV-positive group to develop and illustrate the model. She suggests five steps that need to be planned and implemented when a leave is known in advance:

1. Providing ample time for the announcement of the primary worker's (hereinafter referred to as the "PW") leaving.
2. Developing a system of transfer through meetings between the interim worker (hereinafter referred to as "IW") and primary leaders.
3. Introducing the group members to the IW.
4. Processing group member's feelings and reactions about the transfer.
5. Reintroducing the group members to the PW when the leave of absence ends and the IW departs. (pp. 218–219)

The author provides illustrations of the five steps drawn from the adolescent group with step 3, introducing the group members to the IW, being one of the most complicated. The PW and IW agreed to keep the first meeting brief to allow time for the group members to voice their concerns and feelings after the IW left the room. The IW introduced herself, and each member did the same in turn. Some of the introductions came closer to expressing the feelings of the members. For example, Akira said, "I'm Akira. I have one daughter and I'm currently pregnant. I live in Manhattan. I've been in the program for a long time and I don't like new people" (p. 224). It's not too hard to understand which "new people" she is referring to. Another member expresses the feelings of loss: "Hi, I'm Kim. I've been with Dr. C for a long time" (p. 225).

The PW invites the members to ask the IW any questions and is greeted by silence. After the IW left, the responses flowed, as described by the leader:

> They stated their dislike for her and her laid back, quiet personality. The members decided that she was too different and would not be able to meet their needs, alarming the PW, but it is important to remember they were still reacting to the idea that the PW was taking a leave of absence. Also, because a large number of members kept their HIV status a secret, they had historically tried to keep new people at a distance, automatically assuming that new people would be judgmental and reject them; in fact they had been in situations that regularly exposed them to rejection. (p. 225)

The strategy adopted for the transition involved having the IW attend a number of sessions with the PW and co-lead. Eventually, the IW began to take an increasingly active role in leading the group. In addition, the group members were provided with a chance to indicate the direction they wished the group to go during the interim period. The most important process in effecting a positive transfer was their ability to openly express their emotions, particularly their concern about investing themselves in yet another leader when the PW was returning and then the deeper connection to losses experienced in the past. A gradual reintroduction of the PW co-leading a number of sessions after months of absence allowed the group to successfully make the transition back.

Individualizing the Ending and Transition to Meet Individual Needs

Each individual member may experience the ending of the group differently depending upon their particular circumstances and life experiences. Gladding (2003) points out that regardless of how careful and thorough the leader is during the termination stage, a few group members may occasionally need more help. For these people he suggests three options:

1. Individual counseling, in which unique concerns can be given greater attention;

2. referral to another group or organization, in which more specific or specialized assistance can be rendered; or

3. recycling, in which the individual can go through a similar group experience again and learn lessons missed the first time. (p. 182)

Most authors, including those cited earlier, agree that the ending process in a helping relationship can trigger the deepest feelings in both the group leader and members. As such, both can do powerful work during this phase, as well as ineffective work if the feelings are not dealt with. This chapter explores the dynamics of the ending phase, identifies some of the central skills required to make effective endings, and discusses how group leaders can help group members make transitions to new experiences.

The Dynamics and Skills of Endings

Schwartz (1971) described the ending phase in the group context:

In the final phase of work—that which I have called "transitions and endings"—the group leader's skills are needed to help the members use him and each other to deal with the problem of moving from one experience to another. For the group leader it means moving off the track of the members' experience and life process, as he has, in the beginning, moved onto it. The point is that beginnings and endings are hard for people to manage; they often call out deep feeling in both group leader and members; and much skill is needed to help people to help each other through these times. (pp. 17–18)

Flow of Affect in the Ending Phase

One of the dynamics that makes endings hard has already been mentioned: the pain associated with ending a relationship in which one has invested a great deal. In addition to the pain, a form of guilt might surface. Group members may feel that if they had worked harder in the relationship, played their part more effectively, and risked more, perhaps they could have done a better job. This guilt sometimes emerges indirectly, with members saying, "Can't we have more time?"

As with many of the feelings in the ending phase, this sense of guilt is often shared by the group leader, who may feel that he or she should have been more helpful to the group. Perhaps, if the group leader had been more experienced or more capable, he or she could have been more helpful with regard to some of the unresolved issues. Instead of understanding that members will need to work continually on life's problems, the group leader feels guilty for not having "solved" them all. Counseling students often articulate this feeling as follows: "If only the group had a real group leader!" Usually, they underestimate the help that they have given.

Because of the general difficulty of talking about negative and positive feedback, both group leader and members may have many unstated feelings that need to be dealt with in the final phase. Things may have been left unsaid because of taboos against honest talk about the role of authority. This theme needs to be discussed before the relationship can properly end. For example, the group leader may have said and done things that made a member angry. The reverse might also be true, with the group leader somewhat frustrated about the member's inability to take risks and to open up to the group leader.

The group leader providing this feedback, if it is related to the group leader's real caring for a member, can serve to clear the air. Even if the leader and the group members have not been able to get along together, and they face the impending separation with a sense of relief, the discussion that takes place at the end should be real. What was it about the group leader that the group members could not relate to? In turn, the members should know what made it difficult for the group leader to connect with them. There may have been misconceptions on the part of either or both parties, and discussing these can help clear them up. The importance of feedback to the group leader is obvious, but this discussion also could be quite helpful to members who may choose to enter another helping relationship in the future. If the negative feelings are not dealt with, group members might transfer them to their next group leader.

Even more difficult for group leaders and members to handle than the negative feelings may be the positive ones. It is not easy for any of us to tell those close to us, particularly people in authority, that they have meant a great deal to us. Moreover, many group leaders find accepting positive feelings with grace extremely hard to do. I have repeatedly observed group leaders respond to a member's genuine expression of thanks for all that the group leader has done by protesting, "It wasn't really me; I didn't do that much—it was really all your work." One student asked during a class if it was all right for her to accept a fruitcake offered to her by an elderly group member at the end of their work together. This was not a case in which a member was trying to pay a group leader for her services, which were normally free. It was simply this woman's way of saying thank you to a group leader who cared. I asked the student if the fruitcake looked good and suggested that, if it did, the student ought to take it.

When I press group leaders about the cause of their embarrassment in such cases, they usually point to the general cultural barriers against appearing immodest, as well as their belief that they could not have really given that much help. The latter response reflects an underestimation of the effect of the help given. Group members respond with great feeling to a caring, honest group leader; they are not usually as critical as the group leader is about what the group leader might have done. Cultural barriers notwithstanding, mutual sharing of positive feelings at the end of a relationship matters a great deal because it enables both members and the group leader to value what has taken place between them and to bring it properly to an end. Both the members and the group leader can carry feelings of regret for unspoken words long after they have stopped seeing each other, thus making the actual ending process protracted and more difficult. The problem with delayed endings is that they tie up energy that both parties need to invest in new relationships.

Timing and the Ending Phase

The timing of this phase depends on the length of the relationship. For example, for weekly group sessions that last a year, the final 8 weeks or so usually constitute the ending process. In short-term work—for example, six sessions—evidence of feelings about endings may emerge in the fourth or fifth session as the group leader receives subtle cues to the members' reactions. Although these cues mark the beginning of the ending phase, thoughts about the end are present even in the beginning. Often, a member will inquire early in the process, even after a first session that was helpful, how long the sessions will continue. Time is an important factor, and group members will orient themselves accordingly. A long break in the work phase, whether caused by the group leader's illness, a vacation, or perhaps a holiday season, can provoke ending feelings as the member associates the break with the ending to come. It is not uncommon to observe apathy, withdrawal, and other premature ending symptoms immediately after such a break.

It is important for the group leader to draw the members' attention to these signals and initiate a discussion of whether they have begun to think about the ending. Then the group leader and the members can strategize about how to make sure they don't end prematurely and that they make good use of what might be the most important period of work rather than experience a moratorium on work.

Stages of the Ending Process

Schwartz (1961) has outlined the stages of the ending process in group work as follows:

- Denial
- Indirect and direct expressions of anger
- Mourning
- Trying it on for size
- The farewell-party syndrome

The reader who is familiar with the classic work by Kübler-Ross (1969) on the stages of death and dying will note similarities. Even though there is some question about the Kübler-Ross model itself and the discrete stages as described here, and the fact that they rarely proceed in such a linear manner, practice experience nevertheless tells us the model is useful for understanding group dynamics in this phase of work. Every ending represents a loss, not as powerful as death, but still evoking strong emotions.

Denial

First is the *denial of the ending*, in which group members appear to ignore the imminent end of the group. This is related to the general difficulty of facing feelings in all areas of our lives associated with the ending of important relationships. If the reader considers endings of personal relationships, it is possible to recall how hard it was to face them.

In the group context, the members are ending with the leaders—whom hopefully they have experienced as caring and supportive professionals—as well as ending with the other members. Recall the married couples' group that was illustrated in previous chapters: A number of excerpts revealed how close members were able to become to one another as they shared their life experiences. About halfway through this group, held in a room in the Health Science Center at the university, I discovered that the group members were getting together for coffee in the cafeteria after the regular session ended. The mutual aid process had created a bond between these five couples—so different in their ages, life experiences, and social situations—that was also coming to an end. The group had become a safe place where they could get help with their difficult family struggles. They would be losing the group leaders, but they would also be losing one another.

Following my own advice, given later in this chapter, I pointed out at the 20th session that we only had four sessions left before the group would come to an end. I indicated that if they had something to say in the group, the next four sessions would be the time to do it. One member of the group disagreed with me and indicated that I had said in the first session that the group would continue until the end of May, not the end of April. He said, "We actual have eight sessions left." The other group members agreed with him. Since all of the sessions had been videotaped, I decided to play the next week the section of the first meeting where I indicated we would end the last week in April. After the tape stopped, the same member said, "See, you said the end of May." Denial was in full force, and even the video evidence would not budge the members. My statement did, however, set the process in motion as we moved to the next stage the following week.

Anger

Denial is often followed by *anger about the ending*, which emerges in direct and indirect forms and is often focused on the group leader, who group members feel is abandoning them. At times, conflict between members of a group during this phase of work is actually an indirect way of expressing anger toward the group leader. In an example from a children's group in a school setting, one group leader describes the session that follows the one in which he told the group he must leave in a few weeks, not by his choice. There is no response in that session; the members continue with their activities as if they had not heard. The group had been established for boys who were in trouble for fighting and other forms of acting-out behavior.

Over the course of the school year, they had moved into being able to talk about their issues, such as their anger at teachers and parents, rather than acting them out through negative behaviors. At the start of the session the week after the announcement of the group leader's departure, the boys appeared to regress and began acting out, fighting, and not responding to the group leader's efforts to set limits. At one point, in a symbolic action, the internal leader of the group put masking tape over his mouth, an action that was quickly followed by the other members. The boys turned and shook their fists at the group leader. Finally, the group leader, who had also been in a stage of denial, said, "I know you are all angry at me for leaving, and that, underneath that anger, you are sad. I have to let you know I am sad as well. We have gotten very close to one another over the year. But we have been a talking group most of the year, and I hope you can take the tape off and we can talk about my leaving."

Adults can express their anger by missing group sessions or through dismissive comments about the value of the group. Regression may begin as group members report being unable to deal with problems in their lives that they had been able to address earlier in the life of the group. This regression may be an indirect call for help: "Don't leave us yet—we are not ready."

Mourning

The *mourning period* is usually characterized by apathy and a general tone of sadness in the group. This can be seen as a grieving period, as the reality of the ending begins to hit home. In the couples' group, in the second session that followed my reminder to group members that we only had four sessions left, and now only two, I entered the usually brightly lit group room to find that no one had turned on the overhead lights. In addition, each of the members sat silently, looking mostly at the floor, and did not participate in catch-up conversation with one another as usual. I articulated my first reaction by saying, "What's going on? This feels like a wake." One of the members—Lou, our 69-year-old member who had been angry at professionals during the first session reported in Chapter 4—said, "This is a wake. In a few weeks, the group will be over." This was followed by a discussion of the implications of the group ending for the members and the beginning of the transition phase work in terms of how they would get help in the future and on whom they could depend for support.

What I found most interesting with regard to this ending was the fact that my co-leaders and I would meet before and after the session with a group of students who observed the group on a monitor as part of their group course (with the group members' permission). When I entered the observation room to meet with the students after this particular group session, I suddenly realized that I was going to have to deal with two group endings on the same evening. When I mentioned the wake-like feeling in the observation room—which mirrored the feeling in the group meeting room I had just left—one of the students said, "I have felt so close to these people and their lives that it's tough to think about this ending." A second student commented that she had seen one group member in a supermarket checkout line and almost went over to say hello before she remembered that the group member had never actually seen her. Another student asked, "What am I going to do on Thursday evenings"?

Trying It On for Size

In the "*trying the ending on for size*" stage, the group members operate independently of the group leader or spend a great deal of time talking about new groups or new group leaders. I noticed this in my teaching (an educational group) when a second-year, last-semester seminar class was coming to a close. A student was making a presentation on the concept of continuing their learning when I made a comment. The class members turned toward me, looked for a moment, and then went right back to their discussion as if they had not heard me. When this happened a third time, I realized they were getting ready to graduate and would no longer have a professor to help them out. They would need to depend more heavily on their colleagues, and I could see that they were trying this on for size. I commented on this by pointing out what I thought was happening. They turned, looked at me, and then went right back to their conversation. I realized I needed to just sit back and watch and to be pleased with how they had learned to depend on and use one another.

Farewell-Party Syndrome

Finally, in the *farewell-party syndrome*, group members appear to protect the group by avoiding discussing its negative aspects. The group leader may ask for feedback on how the group has functioned: What were the positives, and what were the negatives? How had the group leader done, and how well had the members accomplished their goals? When the feedback is almost all positive, this is a sign of the farewell party—no group is *always* great. The group leader needs to reach for the negatives so that the group members do not "pad" the experience by only reflecting on the positives.

It is also not unusual for group members to suggest throwing an actual farewell party in an attempt to avoid the pain of the ending. What is often left out is a discussion of the loss that accompanies the ending of the group. I am not arguing against a good old-fashioned farewell party; however, it should not be a substitute for saying good-bye.

In another illustration of avoidance, consider a staff member leaving a residential institution. Staff members may have real farewell party while avoiding dealing with the affect associated with the staff member leaving. Consider that loss is central to the issues faced by the children in a residence. They may have already lost their parents, siblings, home, and so on. Losing a residential counselor is another loss for some of these children and needs to be openly discussed. Moreover, if staff members have not addressed their own feelings about the loss of their colleague, they may not be able to address those of the children.

Group Leader Strategies with Regard to Ending

Group leader strategies for dealing with endings in group work are similar to those in work with individuals and families. They are as follows:

- The group leader should bring the ending to the group members' attention early, thereby allowing the ending process to be established.
- The stages should be pointed out as the group experiences them, with the group leader reaching for the indirect cues and articulating the processes taking place: denial, anger, mourning, and so on.
- Because the group ending has meaning for the group leader as well, he or she can bring personal feelings and recollections to the group.
- Discussion of the ending feelings should be encouraged, with the group leader participating fully in the exchange of both positive and negative reactions.
- The group leader should also help the group members be specific as they evaluate their work together. For example, when a member says, "It was a great group!" the group leader should ask, "What was it about the group that made it great?"
- Finally, the group leader should reach past the farewell-party syndrome to encourage members to share negative feedback. For example, "I'm glad you all feel the group sessions were great, but they can't always have been great. Weren't there some that were not so great?"

Because members have different reactions to endings, the group leader should encourage the expression and acceptance of differing views. Not everyone in the group will experience it in the same way, and as pointed out earlier in this chapter, the ending may have more impact on some than others.

Group Leader Strategies with Regard to Transition

The group leader must also pay attention to the transitional aspect of the ending phase. For example:

- If members are continuing with other group leaders, how can they begin the relationship in a positive manner?
- If members have finished their work, what have they learned, and how can they use their learning in their new experiences?
- If members have found the group helpful, how can they find similar sources of support in their life situations?

In this way, the group leader can ensure that the ending discussion deals with substantive matters as well as the process of ending. In some situations, help can also take the form of a physical transition. In an example to be shared in Chapter 15, a group for sixth graders who were about to transition to middle school, the group leader arranged for the group to visit the school and meet with the principal and seventh-grade teacher. This also serves as an example of helping the group deal with its environment.

Finally, the group leader should search for the subtle connections between the process of the ending and the substantive work of the group. For example, endings for a group of young mothers about to give birth may coincide with separation from their children if they have opted to place them for adoption. In another example, teenage girls in a group for survivors of incest expressed strong feelings of anger toward their two female group leaders as the group was coming to an end after a year of hard and powerful work. The group members expressed feeling abandoned by the leaders. With the help of the leaders, the group members connected to this anger with their anger toward their mothers who had failed to protect them from the abuse. This had been a taboo subject and only emerged in the last sessions—an example of "doorknob therapy." These and other connections can help enrich the ending discussion. They represent the group members making the third decision referred to earlier. The next section illustrates these dynamics and skills.

Additional Group Illustrations

The ending phase of work offers a powerful opportunity to deepen the work by integrating process and content. The losses involved in ending a group often provoke issues of intimacy and loss in other areas of the members' lives. By constantly searching for the connections, however faint, between the dynamics of the ending process and the substantive work of the particular group, the group leader can help the members use the ending as an important learning experience.

In the first example that follows, a group leader opens up the discussion of her leaving with a group of people who have multiple sclerosis, or MS (the group will be continuing). The announcement of the impending ending initiates a powerful conversation about intimacy and loss related to the illness.

A Support Group for Patients with Multiple Sclerosis

Note that the group leader brings the group members back to their own endings in the here-and-now of the group experience. This example illustrates the following points:

- Endings provoke a range of feelings that can be connected to the work of the group.
- The members in this group talk about loss of a sense of self as well as loss of loved ones.
- The group leader needs to bring the members back to the imminent loss of the group.

> **GROUP LEADER:** As you know, I only meet with you one more time after today. You all will continue to meet until June. What are your thoughts about the group ending in a couple of months?
>
> **BOB:** I am not looking forward to the summer because of the hot weather . . . it makes my MS flare up.

ALBERT: I know . . . I always feel tired and run down when it gets too hot. And then the group breaks up, and I don't have anyone to really talk to about my MS. I used to look forward to the summer, but now I almost dread it.

BOB: I'm going to miss everyone, too. I don't have anyone to talk to, either. My wife is great, but she doesn't really understand what I am feeling.

GROUP LEADER: Do you guys keep in touch even when the group is not meeting during the summer months?

ALBERT: Not really . . . .

FRED: I talk to Rob from the other group pretty regularly.

BOB: Albert, you live not too far from me. We should get together once in a while this summer. Or at least talk on the phone.

ALBERT: I like that idea . . . I do want to stay in touch.

PRACTICE POINTS As the group approaches the end with only one more meeting with this leader, we see the "door knob therapy" phenomenon described earlier emerge as one member raises the powerful issue of physical appearance and how others appear to regard him. Another member points out the lack of visible symptoms also causes problems as others do not understand the pain of the disease. The leader encourages elaboration of both themes.

JAMES: (Who has been quiet up to this point) I used to dance and run track . . . and now I can't anymore. People look at me like I'm weird.

BOB: I always liked to dance, too.

GROUP LEADER: James, you said people look at you weird. What do you mean by that? How does that make you feel?

JAMES: I get mad because I am not weird. I am just in a wheelchair. They don't know what I used to be able to do. All they see is what I look like on the outside.

GROUP LEADER: You're right. Strangers do not know who you are or what you are like, as we do. They don't know you as a person, and it isn't fair that they should judge you by your appearance or being in a wheelchair.

FRED: That's the trouble—no one can see the MS. They can't see the pain we feel in our legs or the burning we have in our joints.

ALBERT: (Who is one of the members whose MS is not as extreme—he still walks) People don't even know anything is wrong with me because I am not in a wheelchair. But I still experience the MS symptoms. When they flare up, I get tired and sometimes walk off-balance, like I am drunk or something.

PRACTICE POINTS As the ending approaches, this conversation indicates that the members have made what I called earlier the "third decision." They are going to discuss some of the most painful and difficult issues, and the leader will try, as best as possible, to empathize with them.

GROUP LEADER: It must be hard for you, Albert, because people cannot see your illness, and they may not understand when you try to explain your physical symptoms.

ALBERT: Yeah, that happens a lot. When people find out I have MS, they don't believe me, because I am not in a wheelchair, and they automatically associate MS with being in a wheelchair.

FRED: I went through that a lot when I was first diagnosed. I fought going into this wheelchair for as long as I could. I was lucky to be able to work until I was 60. But a short time after I retired, I had to get the chair.

JAMES: Yeah . . . when I first got those symptoms, the military police on base used to stop me to ask if I was drunk because I staggered so much. That's when I first realized something was wrong. And then it just kept getting worse until I wound up in this wheelchair.

PRACTICE POINTS The group leader takes the discussion to another level by opening up an area that has been most painful for the members: the loss of loved ones. As this discussion evolves, note how the leader, also being affected by the strength of the feelings, picks up on their concern about symptoms, moving them off this painful theme.

> **GROUP LEADER:** You guys have lost important things associated with your identity because of this disease. Many of you had to quit working before you wanted . . . some of you lost important relationships.
> **JAMES:** That's what I miss . . . having a girlfriend. (He pauses.)
> **GROUP LEADER:** (After it looks like James won't continue on his own) Tell us more, James.
> **JAMES:** I just miss the company. I don't care about the sex. I just wish I had the companionship. I need someone to talk to, who will do things with me. I love my son and my parents, but I wish I had someone more my age to be with.

> (Group leader's note: James is a young guy—in his early 30s—and, in addition to being confined to a wheelchair, he has speech difficulties and shaking in his arms and neck. In retrospect, I wish I had explored more about how the change in his appearance and increasing disability affect his romantic possibilities. He has an 8-year-old son, but I don't know what his relationship with the mother was or if she left him when he became disabled. I'm sure this is something all the men have had to face—changes in their manhood, and how society views a disabled man.)

> **FRED:** I know, James. Companionship is important.
> **BOB:** There are a lot of symptoms of MS that people don't see and we don't talk about. Like our bladder and bowel problems. It's very degrading and embarrassing not to be able to control them all the time. (The others all voice their agreement.)
> **GROUP LEADER:** I know you were interested a few weeks ago in having Dr. C. (urologist) come to speak to you about these problems. Did she ever come?
> **ALBERT:** Not yet.
> **GROUP LEADER:** I will talk to the nurse again and try to schedule her as a speaker in the future. (I bowed out of a sensitive and embarrassing subject here as well. I probably should have explored their feelings more with regard to this subject.)

PRACTICE POINTS Although the discussion is important and raises powerful issues, it skirts around the group's ending and the losses involved in the group. It is as if the members of the group are waiting to see if the group leader will come back to the issue she raised at the beginning of the meeting. She does.

> **GROUP LEADER:** I want to talk some more about our ending. I know I've been mentioning it the last couple of times we've met. It's really hard when people come and go from your life.
> **ALBERT:** Yeah, it is. It seems like we just started with you and now you are leaving already.

GROUP LEADER: I want you to know that it is hard for me, too. I am in a field where I will have to say good-bye many times to people whom I have grown to care about. But I believe that, when I leave here, I will take a part of you all and internalize it, especially your courage. I have learned a lot from all of you about what it is like to live with MS, and how hard it is to deal with all the symptoms. But mostly I have seen how courageous and positive you are in light of all you have been through, and that encourages me. I believe I will be able to help other people in your position because of what you have taught me about dealing with a chronic disease like multiple sclerosis, and I thank you for this group and this experience.

BOB: I know you are going to do well. You are a kind person, and genuine and caring. I think I speak for everyone when I say we've enjoyed having you here. (The others nod and voice their agreement.)

GROUP LEADER: Thank you. That's nice to hear. I've really enjoyed being a part of this group and getting to know all of you. (The time was up, and we finished by saying good-bye and their talking about meeting again in 2 weeks.)

PRACTICE SUMMARY

As the ending approaches, there is always unfinished business between the group and the group leader that needs to be explored. Given the theme of internalized stigma, it was important for the leader to share her perspective of them as people of real courage. In the next example, we see an example of ending with a group over time.

Adult Female Survivors of Childhood Sexual Abuse: Ending over Time

As the previous examples illustrated, the ending and transition phase of a group takes place over time. The stages are noticeable during the last three or four sessions for an ongoing group, beginning with the group leader's reminder that the group is coming to an end. The next example provides excerpts from the last six sessions of a group for adult survivors of childhood sexual abuse.

The members of this group all experienced oppression on many levels. They were all sexually exploited as children, most often by people whom they knew and should have been able to trust. As women, they continued to experience oppression in relation to their gender. Some of the members were Hispanic and faced racism, which, when combined with sexism, strongly affected their lives. Finally, some were lesbians or bisexual, which also placed them in a group that commonly experiences prejudice and oppression. Thus, all of the group members carried a great deal of pain and internalization of their oppression.

As the group members moved into their ending and transition phase, and as they reviewed and evaluated their work together, note their courage, their love for one another, and their group leader's conviction about their inherent strength not only to survive oppression but to overcome it and fight it. In many ways, the work of the group followed the three developmental stages described in Chapters 1 and 2, in which oppressed people attempt to free themselves from the oppressor within and the oppressor without.

In addition, the discussion of a new psychology of women (Miller, 1987; Miller and Stiver, 1991), which laid the foundation for the self in relation model of group process drawn from the work of the Stone Center (see Chapters 8 and 12), helps explain some of the paradoxes evident in the work.

In particular, notice the notion that vulnerability can lead to growth, talking about disconnection leads to connection, and pain can be experienced in safety and the importance of resonance or empathy between members (Fedele, 1994). The group leaders are both experienced in group work in general and specifically in work with survivors, which is evident in their practice.

Member Description and Time Frame: This 24-week group for adult female survivors of childhood sexual victimization is offered by a community rape crisis center and is led by two co-leaders. The time frame of the meetings is August 28 to October 16. The seven members range in age from 22 to 28. All members are women from working-class or middle-class backgrounds. Two members are Hispanic, and the rest are Caucasian or are from various other ethnic groups. Two women are lesbians, one is bisexual, and four are heterosexual.

Description of the Problem

As the group begins its ending stage, members are reluctant to face the pain and loss of the impending termination and the potential effect of this transition on their lives. As survivors of sexual abuse, many of the women feel acute fear and discomfort when confronted with strong feelings. They have described families of origin in which the development and ending of relationships have been poorly modeled, and they have learned to keep silent about their feelings and fears. The tasks of the group leaders will be to help build a group culture in which the taboo subjects of endings and losses can be explored, freeing the members to grapple with the tasks of termination. We must help the group establish a norm that supports intimacy and risk but also profoundly respects each member's need for safety and self-protection.

How the Problem Came to the Attention of the Group Leader(s)

As my co-leader Jane and I prepared for termination, we tuned in to the potential problems of this stage, using both general knowledge of survivors' issues and our knowledge of the work and struggles of this particular group as a guide. Since the first sessions, safety had been vital to meaningful and productive work in the group. Members had worked hard to recognize when they felt unsafe or at risk and had learned to take steps to protect themselves. Because bonding and connection had been central to the group's creation of a safe and trusting culture, we hypothesized that the group might feel unsafe as members began to separate.

Note that even a group that had created a safe culture may need to work on that group issue again as the endings approach. The leaders are aware that this is still a vulnerable group of young women and that safety needs to be addressed regularly throughout the development of the group.

We believed that the group might need to create a different "safe culture" that could tolerate the coming ending. On August 28, we learned about the group's norms for saying good-bye and about subjects and feelings related to endings that were forbidden. Members responded with silence when asked direct questions about what the group's end meant to them, and they informed us that they usually run away from and ignore endings.

Summary of the Work

August 28

Linda was describing how she felt compelled to binge on salty and high-cholesterol foods lately and how it was very dangerous for her high blood pressure. I observed that, in the past, she had done this when she was having really strong feelings, and I asked how she was feeling these days when she seemed compelled to binge. She began to cry and said, "There's just so much pain, so much loss." She described her fear of losing her whole family if she confronted her mother (the perpetrator of her sexual abuse), the death of a cousin who had been missing and whose body had been found, the anniversary of a rape in which she had nearly been killed at age 18, her loss of me as her individual therapist, and the impending loss of the group, the first people who had ever believed in and supported her. In the face of this, she said that she was really isolating herself and wanted to eat.

PRACTICE POINTS

This powerful list of events, some earlier and some more recent, has emotional impact on the group members and the leaders. Given the ending stage, the group leader's focus on the support within the group and how to continue to get it even after the group has ended.

I tried to enlist the support of the group to combat her isolation. I said, "Linda, it sounds like you're feeling overwhelmed by all this pain, and at the very time you could use some support, you're all alone. Is there any way the group can help you right now?" She responded that she isolates most when she's most in pain but that the group could help by reaching out to her, that she needs to be with people when she feels this way. Some group members responded with expressions of support and offers to talk on the phone or be with her. People shared how hard it was to see her pain but how important it was that she share it.

PRACTICE POINTS

The group leader uses the opportunity of Linda's sharing about the simultaneous need for connection coupled with an effort to disconnect to address the rapidly approaching ending of the group.

I said that Linda had shared feeling really sad about the group, and I wondered how others in the group were feeling about the end approaching. There was silence. I waited, thinking they might need time to respond. Jane, the co-leader, asked group members how they usually say good-bye. Group members responded: "I just take off, usually." "Hey, I don't say 'good-bye,' I say 'see you later.'" "I never say good-bye, I just disappear." "I try to pretend nothing's changed." Jane said that she felt it was important for members to understand how they usually cope with good-byes so that they could make choices this time about how they want to handle this ending. Issues of trust, intimacy, and loss had been important in the group's work, and we could do vital work in these areas during our final weeks. Time was up, and I said that we would be spending more time next week talking about the approaching end of the group and how people wanted to work on it.

PRACTICE POINTS

The group leaders recognize that this stage in a group such as this one can be a time of the most important and powerful work or a moratorium on work as members and leaders avoid facing the painful feelings associated with separation. While wanting the group members to make the best use of the last sessions, at the same time the group leaders display their understanding of the importance of allowing these young women to have control over the issue of disclosing the details of their abuse. It is common that, as the end approaches, in what is I call doorknob therapy, group members will disclose their most difficult issues and "secrets." Not having had control over what was done to them in the past, often by family members, it is crucial that the group members have control over their disclosure.

September 11

A major goal for Martha had been to spend time in the group telling the story of her abuse, but each time she had planned to do it, she had felt unable to go through with it. She had felt flooded with fear and pain. The group had processed why it was so difficult and suggested different ways she could prepare and cope with this "disclosure," but to no avail.

This time, what came up was that she felt unable to risk and be vulnerable in the group when it was so close to ending and she could be rejected and abandoned by the group members. She said that it no longer felt safe in the group. I said that perhaps what she was telling us was that this goal was not right for her right now, that keeping herself safe was most important, and that she was making choices about how she needed to protect herself.

PRACTICE POINTS

Because child victims often learn to feel that they are not worth protecting and can never feel truly safe, safety and self-protection had been important in the group's work. The group leaders recognize that this is not only Martha's issue but one for the whole group. They use this as an opportunity to address group norms as they approach the last sessions.

I said that we needed to strike a careful balance as we approached the ending, trying to work as hard as we could and risk as much as we could but also respecting each person's needs for safety. I told Martha that if she wanted to do her disclosure, we would help her, but that no one would force her to do it. Martha and the group discussed this for a while, and then Jane talked about Martha's goal and goals in general and how it was important for us to review them and take stock of the work we needed to address in the next 4 weeks.

PRACTICE POINTS

In the next excerpt, the group members move past denial and begin to express the anger associated with the ending phase. The group leaders' efforts to evaluate the group and the progress achieved by members may have been an unconscious way of avoiding this painful part of the process. Once the anger is expressed, the leader's response connects it directly to the ending.

I asked if we could spend some time right now hearing from everyone about what they had accomplished so far, what they still needed to work on, and how they were feeling about the group ending. (I immediately sensed my error but didn't know how to correct it.) The group was silent. Jane then said that she understood how hard it was for the group but that it was important for us to take stock of where we were. We could still accomplish a lot but we needed to know. . . . Jodi burst in and said, "I just feel like telling you to shut up. You both keep talking and talking about this, and I'm feeling really angry. I wish you would let us move on to what we want to talk about and stop wasting time."

I said that she was clearly feeling really angry and that it felt to her like we were pressuring the group. I waited and then said that people often feel very angry when they face losing something that has been really important to them. I wondered if some of her anger was related to the ending itself. Rita said, "But we're not losing the group. We'll still see each other." Others agreed. I confronted the group's denial. "That's true," I said, "you can choose to continue your friendships as individuals and as a group, but this Monday night group is special, the way we work together here. It's like it has its own identity. That's what's going to end." Michelle said that she wouldn't know what to do with herself on Mondays anymore. Others joined in, saying how they would miss the group. Both group leaders reflected these feelings and shared their own feelings about the group ending.

PRACTICE POINTS

The group leader recognizes that she has pressed too much in asking about goals and is somewhat ahead of where the members are at the moment. She catches her mistake.

I said that I had asked for a lot at once during my earlier question about goals. This was really hard to talk about and might require some reflection. Perhaps group members could review their progress and future needs during the week, and we could set aside time to discuss them next week. We would also need to talk in more depth about the final session. For now, I wondered if we could just spend some time talking about how it felt this moment to be dealing with this. We discussed this for the last few minutes of the session.

PRACTICE POINTS

By addressing the process of ending and the associated affect, the leaders create the conditions where members can make the third decision—the addressing of the hardest and most painful part of the work. In this case, Martha, who has been the one member unable to disclose up to now, finally shares her painful childhood experiences.

September 18

I reminded the group that we had planned to spend some time this week taking stock of what the group has meant to people and where we needed to put our energy during these final four sessions. People had put quite a bit of thought into this, and the group spent some time evaluating and prioritizing. Martha had clarified the issue of disclosure for herself. She had discovered that, in trying to force herself to discuss the abuse before the group "audience" while feeling unsafe, she had been re-creating the dynamics of her abuse as a child in which her father had taken her to bars where she had been sexually abused by various strangers while others observed. With the support and understanding of the group, she was able to carry out a disclosure related to this specific abuse, checking with the group whenever she began to feel unsafe. We credited her growing ability to protect herself while achieving her goals. Both Jane and I offered positive feedback about Martha's growth and her ability to both keep herself safe and move forward with her goals.

PRACTICE POINTS

The leaders next address the structure of the final session. Although they share an example of how it has been handled in previous groups, they continue to make clear that the group is owned by the members and that they will have the last say in how the final session will be structured.

Later, Jane raised the issue of the final session, explaining to the group members that it is generally structured around feedback, both negative and positive. She asked the group to consider a structure that has worked well for other groups, in which each group member in turn gives feedback to each of the other members and the group leaders. Past groups have chosen to write a special message to each individual so that the feedback would be kept and remembered. Some members were eager to do this, whereas others expressed considerable anxiety about evaluating themselves and others. I said that some people seemed eager to do this, but others seemed really uncomfortable with it. Ultimately, the decision of how to handle the last session lay with the group, but I wondered if we could explore how people felt about it right now. What made it seem scary, and what seemed positive about it? This was explored for a while.

Then group members asked me to review information about the local "Take Back the Night" march with them. We had told them about the march against sexual violence against women a few weeks before, and, after some exploration of their fears about participating in a public demonstration, they decided to march as a group. I supported the group's readiness to act independently and support one another in new experiences. I shared with them how good I felt that they wanted to march together, and I gave them the information they needed.

PRACTICE POINTS A discussion of a feminist orientation to group practice will be included in Chapter 11 dealing with issues of diversity as well as in Chapter 12. One of the major themes will be the importance of empowerment of, in this case, young women who have experienced sexual and physical abuse. The march is an activity that allows the women, as a group, to assert their rights by overcoming their fears. This is an example of the "strength-in-numbers" phenomenon as described in the earlier discussion of mutual aid.

September 25

As the group processed how the march had felt for them, Jane and I shared how powerful it had felt for us to see them there, marching, chanting, and singing. We also shared that it was hard for us to see them and know that the group was ending. The group was special for us, and it would be hard to let it go.

(I fell for the illusion of work and let the group get off track.) Rita had been talking for some time about her problems and conflicts with her parents. At first, both group leaders and the group were active in discussing her problem, but I gradually began to feel that we weren't going anywhere and my attempts to involve the group proved fruitless. They seemed to have checked out. I now think that some of the anger Rita was expressing was indirectly aimed at the leaders and/or the group, but I missed this at the time because she had ample reason to be angry with her parents.

PRACTICE POINTS In the next intervention, this experienced group leader demonstrates her ability to be with each individual in the group and the group-as-a-whole simultaneously—what I have described as the "two clients." Her observation that the group appears to have "checked out" is recognition of their nonverbal cues. As she reaches for the underlying feelings associated with the nonverbal cues of one member, Linda, she opens up the powerful feelings of loss as well as the emerging feelings of hope and strength for all group members.

I had noticed for some time that Linda seemed very agitated and seemed to be struggling to contain herself. Rita had come to a long pause, and I asked, "What's going on with you, Linda?" Linda seemed startled: "Who, me? Why? What's the problem?" I answered, "Well, Rita's been talking for a while now about her family, and I know your family has been a source of a lot of your pain. You seem really upset right now, and I wonder what's happening." Linda began to talk of having a great deal of pain all the time. She said that her losses had totally overwhelmed her lately, and she just didn't know how she was going to make it. I immediately felt the group come back to life.

Linda and various group members talked for some time about how hopeless she felt. I reached for her ability to cope with her pain. "I'm just hearing that you have so much pain and sadness right now, Linda, and I wonder, what are you doing with all this hurt?" She said that she was crying a lot, just letting herself feel the sadness, and that she was also writing in her journal and writing poems. She mentioned that she had just written a poem today about her pain and where it was taking her.

Several people asked her if she would read it, and she did. It was called "Children of the Rainbow," and it described how beams of light are shattered and broken as they pass through a drop of water and how they emerge to form the vibrant colors of the rainbow. The poem said that she and all survivors in recovery are like beams of light; if they can make it through their pain, they will become vibrant, beautiful, and whole. Several of us had tears in our eyes (me included), and there was a powerful silence when she finished.

I remained silent to let the group control this moment. People thanked her for sharing such a personal, painful, and hopeful part of herself. I had been Linda's individual counselor for some time, and I was finding it very hard to leave her and the agency. I acknowledged her feelings, shared my own, and credited her ability to cope. I shared that I found the poem very moving, that I could feel that she had incredible pain, but that her art and ability to create were powerful vehicles for carrying her forward and transforming her pain. The group ended soon after.

PRACTICE POINTS In the next session, we can see the impact of Martha's finally being able to disclose her abuse in the group as well as her empowerment by participating in the Take Back the Night march. This process helps her now assert herself by confronting her father, who was her abuser.

October 2

Martha told the group that she had confronted her father with the abuse since the last group. We were all amazed, because this had been a goal that Martha had not hoped to attain for several months, if not years, in the future. Her abuse had been very sadistic, and her father had continued to hold incredible power over her when he was able to have contact with her. She had been with Linda before he called and described "just feeling very powerful and safe. I was able to see Linda and my roommate right there, and I could hold the whole group right in my mind and feel you supporting me and helping me to be safe. I've never felt anything like that before. And he was weak! He was the one who seemed powerless."

Martha had burned a picture of her father after the call as a way of exorcizing his control over her, and she had brought the ashes to group. Later, the group gathered and flushed the ashes down the toilet. Both leaders credited Martha's incredible and rapid growth and related it to the ending and how she had taken control of how she wanted to accomplish her goals and approach the end of group. The group gave Martha feedback and discussed how it felt to be part of her sense of safety.

PRACTICE POINTS In the next brief excerpt, the group leader, after the fact, makes an important connection between a member's anger at her psychiatrist and the anger toward the group leaders. This is an important point of growth for the group leader.

Next, Donna raised the issue of her psychiatrist and how he had told her to get on with her life and stop indulging herself with her depression and dwelling on her abuse. The group responded with explosive anger. I allowed my own anger and the real differences between my approach and the approach of the psychiatrist to blind me to the part of the group's anger that might have been directed at me, had I invited it. We did good work in helping Donna evaluate her therapy, but we missed another chance to explore the group's anger about the ending and our role as group leaders. I think that this group felt so special to me, and I was finding termination from individuals, the group, and the agency so hard, that I kept myself unaware of their anger.

October 16: Final Session

Each member and group leader had prepared written feedback for the other members and group leaders, and members took turns reading their messages to one another. (Group leaders passed out written individual feedback and gave verbal feedback to the group as a whole.) The material was very personal and moving and related the work of the group to strong feelings about ending. Group leaders assisted members in preparing to read and helped the group to respond. Some members cried and expressed deep feelings of pain and loss. Group leaders also responded directly to their own feedback.

A few of the women chose to hand out the personal feedback and speak to the group generally, while members read the personal material. Although I believe that the material was genuine, it focused on positives only, and both group leaders missed the opportunity to reach for negative feedback, falling for the farewell-party syndrome.

PRACTICE POINTS

Although this important task was not accomplished, the group leaders did accomplish their goal of creating a safe culture in which members could risk being intimate and trusting as the group ended. Once again resonance and connection through disconnection is apparent.

Martha had read each note and closed with "Love, Martha." At one point, Rita said, "This is really hard, but I have to ask. You said 'Love' to everybody, but you didn't say it to me. I'm sure you just forgot, but I have to say, it hurts. Don't you love me, too?" She began to cry with these last words. Martha had clearly just forgotten and turned to Rita, saying, "I'm so glad you told me. I was just finding this all so hard that I didn't even realize . . . I do love you. I'm sorry it hurt that I forgot you. Here, let me write it on yours."

I asked Rita how it had felt to risk this question, and I said that I remembered that she had entered the group 6 months ago saying she never let herself be vulnerable with others. Rita responded that this was a safer place than she had ever been in before. She had shared her story, her shame, and had been vulnerable with people here. She knew she could trust us. "It's true," added Martha, "I've never been anywhere that was safe the way this is, even more than individual therapy." Michelle added, "This place is like the safe home we never had. You guys were almost like parents for us. You were honest with us, and we learned to be honest with each other. And it never mattered, we could feel good, feel bad, disagree with each other and be mad, but it was OK. We could learn to be ourselves. You were there for us the way our parents should have been." Soon after, we ended the group. There was a long "group hug" at the suggestion of the members, and we ate some cake a member had ordered. The message on the cake said, "Survivors — Striving and Thriving!"

PRACTICE SUMMARY

The metaphor of Linda's poem, in which survivors in recovery are viewed as "beams of light; if they can make it through their pain, they will become vibrant, beautiful, and whole," is extremely powerful and moving. It captures beautifully the struggle of these young, oppressed, and vulnerable women to free themselves from the self-image of being "damaged goods" that had been imposed on them by those who should have been nurturing them. Their courage in joining a Take Back the Night march, when they felt so personally uncomfortable doing so, was an affirmation of their willingness to fight and overthrow their oppressors. It was a social parallel of their individual revolutions against oppression described in one member's efforts to confront her offending parent. The unique power of mutual aid groups is amply demonstrated in the content of their work together and in the "Survivors—Striving and Thriving" lettering on the cake at their final session.

This last example completes the illustrations of the ending and transition stage. This chapter also brings to a close the focus on the four phases of work. In the next chapters in Part 1, I will discuss additional elements which help us to understand the common core of group counseling in respect to different group structures and the major issue of diversity.

Chapter Summary

The ending phase of group work can be a powerful one as members bring to the forefront some of the most important and difficult issues in a process sometimes described as "doorknob therapy." However, because of the powerful issues involved in bringing a group to a close, both intimacy and authority themes need to be addressed to avoid the endings becoming a moratorium on work.

Group leaders need to help group members identify and move through several common but not universal ending stages: denial of the ending, anger over the ending, mourning, trying the ending on for size, and the farewell-party syndrome. Group leader interventions in this stage include *pointing out the endings early*, reaching for feelings, *identifying the stage of the ending process*, sharing the leader's feelings, making a demand for work to prevent avoidance of facing the ending, and, when appropriate, connecting the ending process with the purpose of the group.

The group members also need to consider transitions to new experiences and individual member "next steps" as the group is brought to a close. Special dynamics arise when the group leader leaves and the group continues.

Related Online Content and Activities

For learning tools such as glossary terms, InfoTrac® College Edition keywords, links to related websites, and chapter practice quizzes, visit this book's website at **www.cengage.com/counseling/shulman.**

CHAPTER 10

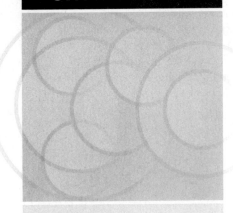

Open-Ended, Single-Session, Activity, and Online Chat Room Groups

This chapter first focuses on three common types of groups used with all populations and in many settings: open-ended, single-session, and activity groups. *Open-ended groups* do not have a fixed membership throughout the life of the group. At any one meeting some members may be beginning and others ending the group experience. This type of group is sometimes referred to as a "soft" open-ended group as compared to a "hard" open-ended group where new members are only added when a member leaves and, in some cases, only after the first few sessions. *Single-session groups*, most often educational or psychoeducational group types, contain all work in one session. For example, an information meeting for parents at a school might be held to update them on school activities, expectations, and other pertinent information. *Activity groups* use a wide range of modalities usually in addition to talking. For example, young children may be involved in a play group; older children or adults may use art or writing to address the group's purpose.

More recently, interest in using the Internet for online groups for basic group services, follow-up to face-to-face treatment groups, or psychoeducational groups has grown. This chapter discusses and illustrates these types of groups as well. While the types of groups are different, they all have in common the uniqueness of their structure. I believed that each deserved some individual attention prior to examining issues of diversity (Chapter 11) and models of group counseling (Chapter 12) and then moving to Part 2, which explores the impact of population, problem, and setting.

The Open-Ended Group

An open-ended group is one in which the membership is continuously changing. New members arrive and old members leave throughout the life of the group. This is in contrast to a *closed group* (or fixed-membership group), where the same people meet for a defined period of time. Members may drop out and new members may be added in the early sessions, but in general, the membership of a closed group remains constant.

Corey (2008) points out that

> [a]s a result of managed care, many groups tend to be short term, solution oriented, and characterized by changing membership. Whether the group will be open or closed may be determined, in part, by the population and the setting. But the issue needs to be discussed and decided before the group meets, or at the initial session. (p. 70)

The decision to run a group as open-ended or closed depends on several factors, including the nature of the contract, the characteristics of the clients served, and the structure of the setting. For example, in a couples' group dealing with marital problems, the difficulty of discussing personal issues such as sexual incompatibility would increase if membership in the group were constantly changing. The same would be true in a group for survivors of sexual abuse, such as the one described in the previous chapter, where disclosure of traumatic experiences is difficult in a group context. A stable membership is essential for such groups to develop the necessary mutual trust and culture for work.

Conversely, an open-ended group is more appropriate for teenagers in a group home, where residents are entering and leaving at different times. The problems associated with shifting membership in this type of group are outweighed by the advantages of having all the residents present. Thus, the decision to operate open-ended or closed groups must be made with the unique characteristics of members, the group's purpose, and the setting in mind.

An open-ended group provides certain advantages. For example, a group that has developed a sound culture for work can bring in a new member quickly. As the new members listen to the discussion, their own willingness to risk may be accelerated by the level of openness of the others. In addition, those who have been in the group for a while can assist new members with issues they themselves have already dealt with. A technical problem associated with open-ended groups is that each session may be a new beginning for some members, an ending for other members, or both.

Corey (2008) notes that

> [a] disadvantage of the open group is that new members may have a difficult time becoming part of the group because they are not aware of what has been discussed before they joined. Another disadvantage is that changing group membership can

have adverse effects on the cohesion of the group. Therefore, if the flow of the group is to be maintained, the leader needs to devote time and attention to preparing new members and helping them become integrated. (p. 70)

Toseland and Rivas (2005) address the question of the timing of adding new members.

If a counselor can control when members begin and leave a group, the counselor should consider during the planning process when it is optimal to add new members. For example, the counselor may decide it is best to add new members during the first few sessions and then close group membership. Alternatively, the counselor might plan to add no more than one or two new members in any given meeting. (p. 172)

In short-term groups, where members do not remain for a long time, the leader can take responsibility for bringing in new members and acknowledging the departure of the old ones. In groups with longer-lasting membership, the group members themselves can discuss this process and develop a system for dealing with the changing group composition. This will be illustrated in the example later in this section of bringing a new member into a group for persons with AIDS. Either way, the skills involved require that the leader be able to state the purpose clearly and briefly to a new member so that the group's ongoing work can proceed in spite of the changes in membership.

Open-ended groups, particularly short-term groups, are characterized by the need for more leader guidance. Because the group has little continuity, the leader needs to actively provide the structural supports. This does not mean, however, that the group members are excluded from taking some responsibility for dealing with structural issues. One common example is when a new member joins a relatively stable open-ended group. Often, the new member initially feels like an outsider. In turn, the ongoing group members may resent a new member and be concerned about the possible impact on the group dynamics.

Ongoing members may not be direct about their feelings, because they sense it is not OK to feel that way. Their heads may say, "Because I am receiving help, shouldn't it be available to others?" At the same time, their hearts may say, "I like the group just the way it is, and I'm afraid a new member will screw it up!" Unless this issue is openly explored, their real feelings may be acted out in the way they relate to the new member. The leader may have some ambivalence as well, accepting the agency policy of keeping the group open, yet feeling concerned that a "good group" might change with the addition of an unknown new member. The result may well be an illusion of work, in which the leader announces a new member is coming the next week and the group quickly moves on to a different topic. Or, if the group raises objections, the leader may side with the new member and completely miss the concerns of the second client, the group.

The alternative is for the leader to tune in to his or her own feelings, as well as the feelings of the group members, and to use the skill (described in Chapter 4) of looking for trouble when everything is going the leader's way. This scenario is illustrated in the next example.

Bringing a New Member into a Group for Persons with AIDS

The following example from a group for people with AIDS illustrates how the leader asks the group members to take real responsibility for bringing in a new member.

The leader must first challenge the illusion of work as group members appear to have no problem with a new member joining. Rather than accepting the first positive responses, the group leader uses the skill described earlier as "looking for trouble when everything is going your way"; that is, he reaches for the potential lurking negative.

> **LEADER:** I wanted you to know that we have a new member joining the group next week. As you know, agency policy is that we stay open to new members if we have room. I'm not asking for a vote here, but since we have been maintaining a regular membership recently, I wondered how you all felt about adding someone new.
>
> **JOHN:** It's not a problem. After all, we were all new at one point or another.
>
> **LEADER:** I appreciate that thought, John, but in my experience, even though it isn't completely rational, ongoing members sometimes resent and even fear adding someone new to a group that's working well. I wonder if anyone feels that way.
>
> **TED:** Does it mean we are going to go back to square one—I mean, starting all over? I've gotten to trust these guys, and I'm not so sure a new member is a great idea.
>
> **LEADER:** That's exactly what I meant, Ted. How about the rest of you? You have worked hard to build a good group here, and it wouldn't surprise me if the new member might make a problem for you.
>
> **RICK:** I'm not sure I want to see someone going through what we all went through when we first had that diagnosis. I mean, I'm past all of that now, and I want to work on other issues.

The leader's skill and understanding of his role and the role Ted may be playing as an internal leader allows him to credit Ted and reach for similar feelings on the part of other group members. Doing so opens up important concerns under the surface of the apparent acceptance of a new member. The leader then partializes by listing these concerns.

> **LEADER:** I think it's also a little scary to have someone come in who may reawaken all of the fear and anxiety. I hear three issues: Is the new member going to set us back to going over old issues? Are we going to lose our sense of trust in the group? And, How are we going to feel facing all of our initial feelings again? Let's discuss these and see if we can come up with a way to bring this new member in and cope with it effectively. I am willing to work with him in advance to help in the entry to the group, but I think you are all going to need to help as well. The faster we integrate him, the better chance we will not lose what we have.

At the leader's suggestion, the group members used the rest of the time to tune in to some of their own feelings when they first joined the group and what it was that either helped them connect or put them off. As the members put themselves in the new member's shoes, they developed strategies that both the leader and they could adopt in greeting the new member. These included acknowledging that he was coming into an ongoing group and that it might take some time for him to feel connected; making some room for him in the first session to handle the initial shock issues, while still making sure that they picked up on their own ongoing issues; letting him know he could get involved as he felt comfortable; and offering to provide a "buddy" from the group whom he could contact by phone if he wished.

After some further discussion, the leader raised another potential underlying issue associated with the entry of the new member. This was the fact that the space had opened up because of the sudden and unexpected death of one of the ongoing members. Even though it had been discussed when it happened, he explored with the group how their ongoing feeling of loss might affect their ability to attach to each other and to the new member.

The leader did not need to have this conversation for every new member who joined. Rather, the leader monitored the changing composition of the group and periodically raised the issue when circumstances required it. This concept is clearer if we conceive of the group as an organism, which is more than the sum of its parts. If we think of the group as an entity independent of its members, existing with a continuously changing membership, then the need to address its tasks in relation to new members is clear.

The Single-Session Group

Some groups are short-term or single-session groups. Examples include informational meetings or educational sessions (e.g., a session at a school designed to help parents assist their children with homework problems). These groups will often be larger than the small, face-to-face groups I have been describing thus far.

Jacobs et al. (2006) points out that clarity of purpose is particularly essential in a single-session group.

> The leader needs to be very clear about why the group is meeting and then plan a group that will accomplish the desired objective in the time allotted. The group's purpose may be to discuss and determine a treatment plan for a patient, to resolve a conflict, or to plan an event. Being clear will help the leader use the time effectively and accomplish the desire outcomes. Often at single-session group meetings, little is accomplished because the members keep switching topics and the leader fails to keep the discussion within the boundaries of the purpose. (p. 62)

Leaders of such groups often feel that the time limitations and size of the group will eliminate the possibility of group interaction or involvement, so they substitute direct presentation of the information to be shared, followed by a question period. Sessions structured in this way can be quite effective, but one drawback of straight didactic presentation is that people do not always hear, understand, or remember the material presented. If they are concerned about a specific issue or have feelings about attending the group, these may block their ability to hear. A second problem is when too much information is shared, causing group members to actually tune out of the presentation as they suffer from information overload. Questions raised at follow-up sessions too often suggest that, although the leader has shared the data, the group members have not taken it in. I am sure every reader can remember a speech, a workshop presentation, or a didactic lecture in a class that they experienced as overloaded (e.g., too many PowerPoint slides with small print) or just boring. You can remember the event but not the actually content. The challenge for the leader is to structure a session in a way that allows participants to interact with the information given and make it more meaningful.

Size of group and restricted time do not automatically rule out active participant involvement, and many of the principles discussed thus far can be adapted to such situations. The leader should begin by thinking about each group if it were a "small group" and by attempting to adapt the basic model to the group's limitations. For example, the idea of phases of work is still helpful, but the beginning, work, and ending/transition phases all must be encompassed in one session.

I have found it often helpful in an information meeting to reverse the usual order of talking first and listening later—that is, making a presentation and then asking for questions. Even a very brief, structured start to the meeting in which the leader asks the group members what they would like to get out of the session can make a major difference in their ability to connect to the presentation. Sharing some brief examples, what I have called "handles for work," will help the group members think of their concerns in the area and also reassure them that they are not alone. Contracting in the opening phase of a session is critical, as the following example from a foster parent recruitment meeting demonstrates.

Information Group: Foster Parent Recruitment

A major problem in child welfare is finding appropriate foster homes for children. The subsidies are usually too low, requiring the foster parents to cover some expenses from their own funds. In addition, many of the children referred to foster care have been seriously neglected and/or abused, and the result may be acting-out behavior. If the biological parent(s) are still involved, they may have supervised or unsupervised visiting rights. Reports of parents missing visitations or showing up under the influence of drugs or alcohol, with a resulting acting out by the children, are not uncommon. Foster parents report children returning from visits with the biological parent exhibiting strong emotional reactions (i.e., bed wetting). Given some of the negatives, there are still many families who feel a deeply held obligation to help these children. The first information meeting is designed to encourage group members to consider becoming foster parents and to address concerns real or imagined, or concerns heard in the neighborhood.

Note the following elements of the structure:

- A clear statement of purpose and role
- Reaching for feedback and concerns
- Articulating a number of concerns as "handles for work"
- Recognition of the time available

    I explained that the agency was holding these meetings to encourage families to consider providing a foster home for our children in care. The purpose of this first session was for us to share some information about fostering with the group, to try to answer their questions and to discuss the concerns they may have on their minds that might help them to determine if further exploration were feasible. I pointed out the group was large (over 40), and I realized that might make it hard for them to talk, but I hoped we could treat this evening as a conversation rather than a lecture. I would be interested as much in hearing from them as in sharing my own information.

    I then asked if this is what they had understood to be the purpose of the meeting. There was a general nodding of heads, so I continued. I said I thought it might be helpful if I could begin by asking them what some of their questions were about fostering—some of the things that were on their minds. I would keep a list of these and try to make sure we covered them in our discussion. There was silence for a moment, and then a hand was raised.

In this example, the leader chose to obtain feedback from the group before beginning her presentation. If the hand had not been immediately raised, this would be a good moment for the leader, after a short pause, to provide some "handles for work." For example: "Some folks who are new to fostering wonder about how much responsibility they will be taking on. It's not uncommon to wonder about the support they will receive from the agency—financial, emotional, and assistance dealing with the children. They wonder about contact with the biological parents as well as how having a foster child might impact their own children."

This is the listen first–talk later approach mentioned earlier to leading an informational group session. One advantage to this approach is that it helps the leader identify and address members' needs. If people have an urgent concern about the subject, listening to any other conversation can be hard for them until that concern has been dealt with or at least acknowledged. Once they know they are "on the agenda," their energy is freed to invest in absorbing other data. Just throwing out these examples will often stimulate a response from group members who are reassured they are not alone in their concerns, that it's OK to have these questions, and that the group leader appears to understand and want to address the real issues.

The amount of time taken to raise questions, or swap problems, is determined by the overall time available. For example, in a 2-hour meeting, one would not want to spend more than 15 minutes contracting and problem swapping, whereas in a 3-hour session, more time might be used to explore issues and develop a group consensus on the agenda. Timing is always important in group sessions, but it naturally takes on a special urgency in a single-session group. The leader needs to keep track of time and point out continually to the group the relationship between time and their work. For example, the leader might say, "You are raising so many good issues that I think we could probably meet for a week. However, we only have 2 hours. I wonder if it is possible for us to focus on one or two central concerns and dig into them." Or the leader could explain, "I would like some time at the end to discuss this evening's program, to evaluate the session, and to see what you feel you have gotten out of it. Can we be sure to leave the last 15 minutes to do this?"

Group leaders often suggest many reasons for not involving clients in single-session or large groups more actively in the work. First, they are concerned that they have so much to cover they do not have time for group process. However, as pointed out earlier, most of us have noticed in our own educational experience that a teacher who is busy covering the agenda does not necessarily teach anything. We are often better off narrowing the field of work and limiting our goals. Effective work with a manageable agenda is preferable to going through the motions of trying to cover a wide area. The first skill in handling such meetings, then, is to narrow down the potential area of work to suit the time available. I will tell my own short-term groups that "I would prefer to cover everything well than to try to cover everything."

A second area of concern is that the group may raise questions that the leaders are not prepared to answer. This is a particular concern for new leaders, who are nervous enough as it is. They may have little experience in the field and have prepared extensively to deal with the specific areas they have predetermined as important. Their notes are written out in detail, or they may have prepared a PowerPoint presentation, and the last thing they want is someone asking a question for which they are unprepared. This is understandable, because it takes confidence to allow the group to shape the direction of the work. When leaders realize they are being judged by group members not on whether they have all the answers but rather on how well they involve the group in the process, they are often more willing to risk opening up the session in novel and unexpected directions. When they do so, they find they learn as much from such sessions as do the group members. Each session helps the leader tune in and prepare for the next one, so that the ability to deal with the group's real concerns grows with experience. Also, it is always possible to admit not knowing a specific piece of information and offer to find out the answer and contact the participant later.

A third area of concern, particularly with large groups, is that a single member may take over the group for individual or personal issues unrelated to the contract. Our discussion of deviant members illustrated how the leader may need to be assertive in such a situation and guard the contract vigorously. This ability also comes with experience. Once again, the leader has to be willing to risk the hazards of such an approach if the benefits of more member involvement are to be gained.

Informal Event Group: Remembering the Holocaust

A short-term, informal, spontaneous group can be brought together to deal with an event or immediate circumstances. In Chapter 12, for example, we will discuss community crisis-related groups used for debriefing traumatized participants such as parents and children after the 9/11 attacks or students at a school after a shooting by an intruder. As another example, counselors have reached out to relatives and friends in the waiting room of an emergency ward to form an informal group to help them cope with their immediate stress. School counselors have organized groups for students following a classmate's suicide. Groups have been held in residential settings or schools following a catastrophe (hurricane, earthquake, flood, September 11) or the assassination of a political or movement leader. In each case, the work is short-term and focuses on the impact of the event and ways in which group members can more effectively cope with it.

In the following example, a counselor works with a group of elderly members of a Jewish community center day program. As part of a program designed to focus on the World War II Holocaust, when millions of Jews and others were killed, the center staff had mounted a photo exhibit during Yom Hashoah—the day set aside for remembrance. An informal group had spontaneously begun a discussion in the hallway, and the student was present. She noticed Sara, who often played the role of group scapegoat, expressing angry feelings.

PRACTICE POINTS

This excerpt also provides another example of Bion's fight-flight concept, discussed in Chapter 8, as the powerful feelings associated with the Holocaust evoke angry exchanges among the members.

> **SARA:** Why are we talking about this nonsense? Photo whatnots. Didn't used to be what we did for Yom Hashoah. We didn't used to have a bunch of foolishness pictures—it was taken more serious.
> **VICTOR:** (Referring to Sara) She doesn't know how to talk. There were community gatherings to remind us about what happened. Yom Hashoah isn't taken seriously now.
> **LEADER:** Somehow I get the feeling that we're not just talking about this particular day being taken seriously.

> **SARA:** No, we're talking about death gonna happen again if we don't do something about it.
>
> **ROBERT:** (To Sara, laughing mockingly) Well, what could you possibly do about it anyway?

PRACTICE POINTS In the next excerpt, the leader demonstrates the two-client idea by identifying with the individual (Sara) but also asking the group what may be going on for them. She does this by articulating what she thinks the group members may be feeling under the anger.

> **LEADER:** I wonder what's going on that people are talking to Sara this way.
>
> **VICTOR:** Because she is so strange!
>
> **LEADER:** I wonder why people are talking this way to Sara right now. To be honest, people seem angry.
>
> **ROBERT:** (To leader) Yeah, sure we're angry. You want us to dance? I would never dance with Sara!
>
> **LEADER:** I wonder if people are actually angry about the Holocaust not being taken seriously. (Silence.) Or maybe people are angry that nothing stopped it from happening in the first place.
>
> **SARA:** (To leader) *Gei kaken* (Yiddish for "Go shit"). You're a nice girl, but . . . (To Robert, loudly) Did you live in the war?
>
> **ROBERT:** (Stands up, loudly, to Sara) I'll tell you something! I saw my father shot, my mother was gassed, and my sister (makes gesture of hanging by a rope). You never had such a life! (Puts hands in pockets, jingles change, and begins to sob quietly, turns back to group. Silence follows.)
>
> **SARA:** (To Robert) That's a terrible thing. I wish I could say something to make you feel better.

PRACTICE SUMMARY Remembering an event as powerful and awful as the Holocaust is bound to generate many reactions to the associated pain. The flight-fight reaction in the group was maladaptive in that it turned survivors of oppression into antagonists, just when they needed each other the most. The leader's brief intervention illustrates the beginning of helping them rediscover their connections and to express their caring.

In summary, clients in a single-session group, even a large one, can be involved actively in a group process with beneficial results. I have asked groups with as many as 900 people to attempt a discussion, with some degree of success. There are many situations where direct didactic presentation at the beginning of a session can be extremely helpful. However, the leader must keep the presentation of material to a reasonable time (more than 40 minutes may be too much) and should monitor the group's reactions as the presentation progresses. The ability of group members to work effectively and with feeling in a single-session group, when the proper conditions are set by the leader, has never ceased to amaze me.

Activity in Groups

Activity group is a term usually applied to groups involved in a range of activities other than just conversation. *Program* is another term used to describe the activities implemented in such groups, such as the expressive arts (poetry writing, painting, dancing), games, folk singing, social parties, cooking—in fact, almost any recreational or social activity used by people in groups. In one of my earlier articles, I examined the ways in which people relate to each other, suggesting that to dichotomize talking and doing is a mistake (Shulman, 1971). Relationships between people were best described by a *mixed transactional model*. Let me explain.

In the complex process of human interaction, people express feelings, ideas, support, interest, and concern—an entire range of human reactions—through a variety of mediums. A mixed transactional model presents the idea that all of these mediums—words, facial and bodily expressions, touch, shared experiences of various kinds, and other forms of communication (often used simultaneously)—should be included when one considers the means by which transactions are negotiated and consummated. Leaders should not fragment human interactions by forcing them into categories such as "talking" and "doing" but should focus instead on the common denominators among transactions, defined here as exchanges in which people give to and take from each other. Group leaders are concerned with helping people who are pursuing common purposes carry out mutually productive transactions.

In my analysis of the ways in which group members might use shared activity for mutual aid, I reject grandiose claims that suggest specific activities might lead to creating "spontaneous or creative individuals" or "strengthened egos." Instead, I suggest the need to describe the specific and immediate functions that the activity in question may play in the mutual aid process.

Functions of Activity in a Group

Here are five of these identified functions:

- *Human contact*—activities that focus on meeting a basic human need for social interaction (e.g., Golden Age clubs for isolated senior citizens)
- *Data gathering*—activities designed to help members obtain more information central to their tasks (e.g., raising teenagers, preparing for employment, arranging a series of trips to business or industrial complexes)
- *Rehearsal*—a means of developing skills for specific life tasks (e.g., a teenage party creating an opportunity for members to practice the social skills necessary for the courtship phase of life)
- *Deviational allowance*—activities creating a flow of affect among members that builds up a positive relationship, allowing members to deviate from the accepted norms and raise concerns and issues that might otherwise be taboo (e.g., young teenage boys who have gotten to know each other and the leader through many shared activities being more willing to accept a leader's invitation to discuss their real fears about sex)
- *Entry*—specific activities planned by a group as a way to enter an area of difficult discussion (e.g., the play acting of young children as they create roles and situations that reveal their concerns of the moment, or artwork expressing issues for people in recovery from addiction)

Two Categories of Activity Groups

Besides these functions, we can see activity groups in terms of two general categories of groups in which activities are used as a medium of exchange. In the first, the activities themselves constitute the purpose of the group. Examples include a teenage club in a school or community center or an activity group in a day treatment center for the mentally ill. The group exists for the purpose of implementing the activity. A second category includes groups established for curative or educational purposes, in which an activity is employed as a medium of exchange with specific healing or educational goals in mind. A group for children who are dealing with grief through the use of drawing or art therapy is an example. Another would be a group for persons in substance abuse recovery who are asked to draw illustrations, for example, of how they see their addiction or how they envision their recovery would look. These two categories will be covered separately, because each raises special issues.

In the first type of group, the most typical problem is that the leader or the setting ascribes therapeutic purposes to the group that constitute a hidden agenda. The group members may think they are attending a school club, but the leaders view the group as a medium through which they can change the members. This view reflects an early and still dominant view of program activity as a "tool of the leader," which grew out of early efforts to distinguish the group leader from the recreational leader. The professional, so the thinking goes, would bring to bear special skills in selecting programs that would result in the desired behavioral changes. Take, for instance, the problem of the child who was scapegoated in a group. In this early model, the leader might ascertain what area of skill this child had and then select or influence the group to choose an activity at which the scapegoated child would shine. All of this was done without the knowledge of the group members or the scapegoat, and the meaning of the scapegoat phenomenon was ignored.

My own training was rooted in this view of practice. In one setting, my agenda involved attempting to influence group members (teenagers) toward their religious association. The agency was sponsored by the Jewish community, which was concerned that second-generation teenagers might be "drifting away" from their religious heritage. The program was the tool through which I was to influence the members by involving them in agency-wide activities—for example, in connection with religious holidays and celebrations. When such activities were conducted with the members' direct involvement and planning, they offered powerful opportunities for deepening a sense of cultural connection and community.

Unfortunately, at times I was so busy attempting to covertly "influence" the membership that I ended up missing the indirect cues group that members offered about their real concerns related to their identity as a minority group in a Christianity-dominated culture. There were important moments when the concerns of the community and the felt needs of the group members were identical; the common ground was missed because of the misguided view that I could influence the process covertly.

If the agency or setting has other agendas it feels are important for groups, then these must be openly presented in the contracting phase, and the group leader must attempt to find whatever common ground may exist. However, just as the leader will guard the group's contract from subversion by members, he or she must also guard it from subversion by the setting or agency. Members will learn a great deal about relationships, problem solving, and other areas as they work to create and run their groups; however, the leader must see the group as an end in itself, not a tool to be used for hidden professional purposes.

The second category of activity in groups where the activity has a direct therapeutic or educational purpose often includes expressive arts. Corey (2008) addresses one form of this use of activity called "expressive arts therapy." This specific approach is based on the work of Natalie Rogers (1993) who expanded on the person-centered approach of her father, Carl Rogers (1961), by addressing the use of expressive arts to enhance personal growth for individuals and groups.[1] "Group facilitators, counselors, and psychotherapists trained in person-centered expressive arts offer their clients or groups the opportunity to create movement, visual art, journal writing, and sound and music to express their feelings and gain insight from these activities" (N. Rogers, 1993, cited by Corey, p. 260).

Corey cites Rogers's principles underlying the expressive arts therapy, which include, among others, the following:

- All people have an innate ability to be creative.
- The creative process is healing. The expressive product supplies important messages to the individual. However, it is the process of creation that is profoundly transformative.
- Self-awareness, understanding, and insight are achieved by delving into our emotions. The feelings of grief, anger, pain, fear, joy, and ecstasy are the tunnel through which we must pass to get to self-awareness, understanding, and wholeness.
- Our feelings and emotions are an energy source. That energy can be channeled into the expressive arts to be released and transformed. (N. Rogers, 1993, p. 7).

While expressive art therapy as developed by Natalie Rogers is a broad personal growth model, I want to emphasize for my purposes here how the creative arts can be linked to emotional expression and discovery as part of what I termed earlier a mixed transactional model.

Another example of the use of expressive arts, described by Malekoff (2007), was the development of a classroom-based poetry club in an alternative school for young children (5-, 6-, and 7-year-olds) identified as having serious emotional disturbances. Malekoff emphasizes working closely with teachers and attempting to integrate group purpose and academic goals. For example, in kindergarten (p. 126):

- Grammatically correct language in complete sentences
- Participates in discussion, listens, takes turns
- Expressess originality and inventiveness
- Comprehends a story (poetry)
- Recalls a story (poetry)
- Identifies feelings and how to express them

One age-appropriate example described by Malekoff was beginning each session with a ritual: a "guess what" poem that described something for the members to discover together.

Key words were left out of the poems to create mystery. The group's assignment was to guess what the poem described. After the poem was read, the group was instructed to huddle up, like a football team might, and discuss what they thought the poem was about. Finally, when

---

1. Corey acknowledges writing this section on creativity and creative expression in collaboration with Natalie Rogers.

they thought they had arrived at the correct answer they would say so. The first poem was about a giraffe. (p. 127)

The children had to guess it was a giraffe after listening to poetic lines such as these:

- Because they hold their heads up high.
- Because their necks stretch to the sky.
- Because they're quiet, calm, and shy.

PRACTICE SUMMARY Malekoff describes the children enjoying the huddling, arms around their shoulders, the discussion, the decision, and then the "high fives" when they succeeded in guessing a giraffe. After that, the assignment was for each to create their own "guess what" poem and share it with the others. Longer term projects involved the members completing open-ended sentences about themselves described as "poem-under-construction." Members refined their work and then included them in a Poetry Club Journal as part of an ending project. The group members shared gift-wrapped copies of their journal with teachers, the principal, and other staff in the school.

This second category of activity group in which specific purposes other than the activity are the major focus and the activity is used to help achieve these ends is illustrated in the following example. In this group, the leaders help 8- and 9-year-old children deal with the trauma of separation and divorce through activities using drawing, puppets, and discussion of scenarios as mediums of expression.

Children Dealing with Their Parents' Separation and Divorce

I am sharing this example in some detail for a number of reasons. First, it is a good illustration of how relatively new group leaders analyze their work over time and develop increasing skill in exploring painful feelings with children. The first step for them, and most new group leaders, is recognizing their own resistance to this difficult work. Also, it reveals the use of a wide variety of activities including drawing, puppets, completing real and imagined scenarios provided by the group leaders, and doing simple completion exercises in response to drawings (e.g., a sad or a happy face) or questions: "What are the good things about separations, and what are the bad things?" Finally, it is an example of the strength and courage of young children dealing with a shattering experience in their families once they understand that the caring adults and the other children are willing to listen and help.

PRACTICE POINTS As you read these excerpts, note the following:

- The leaders become more courageous in reaching for painful feelings as they recognize their own resistance.
- The leaders use a wide range of activities, including drawing, puppets, responses to prepared scenarios, and scenarios created by the children.
- The leaders listen carefully to the cues, both direct through conversation and indirect through activities, and reach for their underlying meaning.
- The members become more comfortable with the leaders and each other and progressively deal with a range of emotions, including sadness and anger.

- The members are in control of the pace of disclosure, with the leaders gently prodding them as they come close to the most serious and painful areas of discussion.

> **TYPE OF GROUP:** This is an ongoing group to give children the opportunity to discuss their fears, to face change, and to find solutions to the painful crisis of their family disruption.
>
> **MEMBERS:** 8- and 9-year-olds; white; lower and middle-income; two girls and one boy
>
> **DATES:** October 31 to November 28

Summary of the Work

First Session

I was anxious about starting a group whose members were so young. My co-leader, Joanne, had a lot of experience working with children and did not share my anxiety, and this offered me some relief. She had some written activities for children from a former group she had run, and she and I together modified the activities to meet the needs of this group, knowing that it was important to allow for input from the members as well. Two of the members showed up early. For the first session we had expected three members and had been told one member would arrive late. We had a snack prepared and tried to make the two members comfortable, explaining that we would wait for the third member to arrive before actually starting group.

I felt a need to reach out to these two members. I introduced myself, asked their names and ages and where they went to school, and encouraged them to help themselves to the snack. Henry (age 9) and Stacy (age 8) were initially shy but with this invitation helped themselves to juice and crackers. Stacy began talking about her family. Time passed; the third member never arrived. Joanne and I decided to formally start the "group," recognizing that, with only two members, we might need to alter some of our planned activities to decrease the intensity for these two children. I asked if they knew why they were here. I wanted to get a feel for what they had been told about the group and note any reactions. Both were able to share that it was because their parents were "going through a separation."

PRACTICE POINTS

Once again we observe the problem of the group leaders not making some form of opening statement that will let the members understand what the group is all about—rather than just indicating why they were sent to the group. For example: "When parents go through a separation or a divorce, it can be very difficult for the children involved. They can feel sad and sometimes angry as well. Sometimes they feel they have to take sides with their mother or their father, which is hard when they love both. We have this group as a place where you can help each other and we can help you get through this difficult time by talking about what its like for you or having activities, like drawing, that will help you let us and the other group members know how you are feeling. We are going to start by doing some things that will help us to get to know each other." Although the children may not take all of this in and recontracting will most likely be necessary, at least the purpose of the group and the purpose of the activity are explained.

We began our first activity, which involved having the members draw or write their responses to benign questions: something they like, something they don't like, an animal each would like to be and one they wish they had, and then share their work as an effort to increase their comfort level with sharing. Henry drew a picture of not liking when kids fight, which he said was happening at school. I wondered, given this was a group dealing with separation and divorce issues, if he also had not liked when his parents fought—how that felt, the position it put him in. Stacy said she does not have to worry about this because "everyone in my class likes me."

PRACTICE POINTS

The group leader begins to make an effort to connect the child's comment about fighting to the fighting experienced in the family. Another possible connection is that when children are sad and upset about fighting and separations, sometimes they get angry, and that can lead to fighting in the school. Putting out both interpretations will help the child elaborate on this "offering" about fighting.

> I wanted to set a precedent in this first group that there would be an expectation that members would speak with one another and that by doing so members might find new ways of problem solving. I asked Stacy if she could give Henry some advice about how to avoid getting into situations where fighting might occur. Her response to Henry was to fight back if you had to. She said that is what her father had taught her to do.
>
> A wish that both Henry and Stacy drew was illustrated by a great amount of money (green rectangles). I missed the significance of this wish until a review of the literature helped me to understand how money, in the children's minds, could fill the void that each of them feels.

PRACTICE POINTS

Another interpretation of drawing money could be that since the separation and before, having enough money might have been a powerful issue between husband and wife. By asking why they were drawing money, the leaders may have been able to help them express the feelings behind the drawing. Both leaders are new to this work, so it will take some time to develop the appropriate interventions.

> The next activity involved each member drawing a picture of his or her family. Henry had great difficulty here. He drew a door, then a window, then asked to go to the bathroom. Stacy drew her entire family: all five members were smiling, Mom and Dad were next to each other, and a big heart encircled all of them. Henry's inability to draw his family members and Stacy's wishful illustration seemed to reflect some avoidance and some denial, respectively. (Henry did complete his drawing on his return and drew a smiling child with his mother's arm around him.)
>
> Because of their ages and the fact that this was the first group session, as with issues mentioned earlier, I chose not to explore the significance of how this activity was played out. I knew these would be ongoing and necessary themes to explore, as the artwork demonstrated, and that my co-leader and I would need to help these children name their feelings if the group was to be effective. I knew, too, I would need to pay attention to my own resistance or hesitation to explore these emotional, painful issues.

PRACTICE POINTS

Because the children know in a general way what the group is all about, we can assume the drawings relate to the family distress. The group leader may be on target when she identifies her own resistance to acknowledging the reason she refrained from commenting on the connection. Just identifying the expressed feelings can be helpful—for example, "It can be hard to draw your family when they don't feel like a happy family any more" or "I guess you may be drawing a happy family because that is what you would like your family to be." Both comments simply acknowledge the message and do not require "probing" in a first session. It is often the case that the group members are ready to begin, but when the content is painful, it is the leaders who are hesitant.

The group leader's recognition of her own resistance to explore painful issues is an important step in helping her reach for the members' underlying feelings of hurt, anger, and tremendous loss. At times such as these, leaders need supervision or consultation to help them explore their own resistance. These children are astute observers of adults around them and have already received the message that the feelings are taboo and not to be discussed. When they perceive that these adults are ready to hear them, the chances of their responding greatly increase.

Second Session

PRACTICE POINTS Although the intent of involving group members in explaining the group's purpose is understandable, given the early stage of the group and the lack of clarity in contracting with the continuing members, it would be better to make a clear statement to the new member first and then involve the others. Note that Tara knows why they are there but is unable to really describe the purpose of the group or how their being in it will help.

> Henry, Stacy, and Tara (age 9) participated in group today. Because Tara had missed our first group, I asked Henry and Stacy if they could share with her what took place in the first session. Both Henry and Stacy were able to tell Tara the activities we had done, and Henry even recalled the details of each of the drawing activities. Joanne and I asked the members if they could recall why each of them was here. Tara was able to say, as Henry and Stacy had the week before, that she knew it was because her parents had separated.

PRACTICE POINTS The leaders now move into an activity that is more focused on the purpose of the group. Again, in hindsight, it would not be hard to explain to even these young children why they were being asked to focus on the word *divorce* and that by hearing each other, they could help each other.

> For this session, the plan was to focus on the word *divorce*. The children were asked to brainstorm words that come to mind when they hear this word and determine whether the words have positive ("good") or negative ("bad") meanings to them. The members eagerly responded to this activity. Each took turns writing a word or phrase on the blackboard, and after they finished, we discussed what they had written. Their list was quite comprehensive: the "good" list included "no more fighting" and "parents still love us," and the "bad" list included "separation," "lots of crying," "children feel sad," and "some people think it's their fault." Because "children" was a big word and Stacy had trouble writing it, Henry suggested that she simply write, "We feel sad." I heard this as his ability to identify with her statement and bring its context closer to home.
>
> When Henry wrote, "Some people think it's their fault," I asked him, "Which people?" I wanted to reach into his words and bring what he was saying closer to the group. He responded by mentioning "the children," which led us into a discussion as to whether each of the members had ever felt it was their fault that their parents had separated/divorced. None of them believed that it was; each sounded as if she or he was repeating messages heard from their parents about not feeling responsible.

The work is starting to deepen, but the group leader holds back on a gut feeling that could be very helpful. For example, she could have said, "I wonder if you hear from your parents that it wasn't your fault, but even so, it still feels like it was your fault. It would be hard not to feel that way."

Following this discussion, the members drew pictures illustrating aspects of what had just been discussed. Henry's picture was incredible; the top of the page said, "Separation" and under this heading, he drew a crying child, alone, in the middle of the page with Mom walking off the right-hand side of the page and Dad walking off the left side. All you could see was one leg and one hand of each parent. It was a powerfully vivid and moving depiction of Henry's understanding of "separation."

The last part of the session involved reading a series of statements and the members deciding if these statements were true or false. Somehow, animal puppets had gotten passed around, to the leaders as well, and we all agreed to respond through the puppets. I did not know if it was due to difficult subject matter or the lateness of the hour, or perhaps a combination of both, but the group all seemed to be responding at once. I asked that one puppet speak at a time, while recognizing that this exercise was the most sensitive one in which the group had participated so far.

The children's strong need to deal with these feelings, at least with understanding adults such as the leader, leads them to use the activity as a powerful form of communication. The group leader's intervention to set the rules may actually be emerging more from her discomfort than theirs. As an alternative to repeating the rule, she could point out what is going on in the group: "You know, when we talk about these sad things, it can be hard to talk one at a time. You get so full of feelings you can't really hold them in. Maybe I can help by calling on you one at a time. Would that help?"

Again I noticed, however, that discussion seemed to travel between each member and my co-leader or the members and me. I once more tried to encourage discussion among the members. Each time someone responded to a statement, I would say, "Stacy and Henry, Tara thinks this statement is true because . . . . What do each of you think?" My effort at this time only resulted in their responding to me.

Sometimes the right intervention can seem so simple in retrospect. For example, if the leader trusted her gut, she could observe to the children that each time they speak or respond to a question, they speak to the leaders and not each other. She could ask them why they thought that was so. A discussion of the process would most likely reveal that they don't understand how talking to other kids with the same problem could be helpful. This could lead to the contracting piece left out at the start: What is mutual aid all about? How can kids who have the same problems and feelings help each other?

I wished that this last exercise could have been given more time. The statements had evoked a lot of feeling and a lot of sharing, but the session was over. In comparison with the previous week's session, I did feel discussion of feelings associated with separation and divorce had taken place and that through their words, pictures, and puppets, much had been shared. It was only the second group and the first group for the three members together. I am actually struck, as I write this, at the courage and vulnerability the members displayed. I hoped that next week's session would provide another opportunity for the members to share their feelings and recognize their capacity for mutual aid.

Third Session

Joanne asked the group what changes when parents separate or divorce. I overheard Stacy and Henry both say the word *disappear*. I commented that they had both used this word and asked each of them to share what they meant by this word. I was trying to create a bridge by showing the members there was similarity in their response.

PRACTICE POINTS By astutely listening and asking the children to elaborate on the use of the word *disappear*, they open up a new, powerful, and poignant theme in the group. It's not only physical items that disappear but important people as well. The leader is also respectful of the differences between the children; and, rather than putting Henry on the spot, she acknowledges how different separation can be for different families.

Stacy said that things disappear, like the couch or the television—one parent gets the couch, one the television. I looked to Henry for his response, and he immediately offered that a parent can disappear. Because I had learned through Joanne that Henry's father had left 4 years earlier, I knew there was a lot of feeling behind what Henry had shared. The two other members in the group had both parents very much in their lives, as well as brothers and sisters and new partners for their parents; Henry had only his mother. I do not believe the other members were aware of the significance of Henry's remark and therefore were not sensitive to what he had shared. I struggled with how to proceed. I chose to mention how divorce can be different in different people's homes. I discussed that for some people divorce may mean new people in their lives if mom or dad gets a new boyfriend or girlfriend and that this can be positive or negative; I also said that it can mean being single for a parent, which can be lonely for the parent and maybe for the child; and I added that it can mean leaving a place one has lived; leaving school, friends, grandparents, other family members; or perhaps moving to a place where one is closer to relatives or family friends. This created discussion among the children as they began to relate stories about their parents' partners, their grandparents, and their friends who were also experiencing parental separation/divorce.

PRACTICE POINTS Once again we see the group leaders using a creative idea to help the group members connect their feelings with issues related to the divorce. By writing them down and then sharing them, a structure is provided to discuss and share these feelings. It is sad that their view of the "best" thing about divorce is that family fighting has stopped.

Our activity for this session involved giving each member a sheet of paper with three faces on it, one face reflecting happiness, one reflecting sadness, and one reflecting fear. Each child was to write underneath each face the best, worst, and scariest thing about divorce, respectively. The children immediately responded to this task; all were clearly concentrating on what they were writing. When they were finished writing, they shared what they had written. All of them agreed that "no more fighting" was the best thing about divorce, a theme they had perhaps recalled from the previous week.

A variety of answers were written, and both Joanne and I encouraged each of the members to think about whether what the others had written applied to them. Not surprisingly, the children could identify with several of the examples. They all agreed with Tara's comment that another "best" thing about divorce is that "your parents still love you" and with Henry's comment that a "worst" thing about divorce is that "some kids think it's their fault." While many of these themes had been discussed the previous week, I saw that the members were incorporating some of what was being shared in our group. In addition, this week it seemed there was more feeling behind the words. I wondered if Joanne and I were functioning well as leaders and creating a safe environment in which the children's feelings could emerge, as the group seemed to be feeling more comfortable with one another, and in turn, more comfortable sharing.

In addition to tuning in to the general themes raised each week and to the developing group process themes, the leaders are tuned in to the impact of the calendar. Family separation and family functioning are affected by the holidays. The holidays may have been the times when the fighting was more pronounced, and the losses of family members and family structure will be more potent as Thanksgiving approaches. In the time before the conflict, holidays may have been important and positive family experiences that have been lost and may be missed.

Fourth Session

With the Thanksgiving holiday occurring this week, I thought it would be appropriate to focus our fourth session on how the members were feeling about the upcoming holiday and what it represented to them in terms of how and with whom they had spent it in the past, what has changed for each of them, and what they anticipated for this holiday. I spoke with my co-leader about this idea, and she agreed that it would be useful and that we could modify any activity to include this event. As has been described, each week so far had revisited discussion about expressing feelings of sadness, anger, and happiness in response to divorce. While in some ways it seemed redundant, my co-leader and I recognized that the purpose of this group was to get the members to feel increasingly comfortable acknowledging and voicing their feelings. The Thanksgiving holiday seemed a perfect vehicle to elicit current struggles each member might be experiencing.

When this session started, I noticed that all three members immediately began chatting, eating their snack, and asking about today's plans in a more animated display than I had seen in previous weeks. I used this opportunity to get right down to work, and I asked what was happening this week that made this week special. Each child mentioned that it was Thanksgiving. I asked if they could tell the group how each one would be spending the time. All three members began speaking at once. I asked the group if we could review the group contract. Tara and Henry raised their hands. I explained that raising hands was not necessary but that it seemed that they had the right idea. Tara said that only one person should speak at a time. I commented that it seemed all three of them had something interesting to say and that I did not want to miss anyone's contribution. Stacy asked if she could go first, because she was the youngest. The children described how they would be spending the holiday and then drew pictures of how they envisioned feeling on that day.

All three members reported that the previous Thanksgiving had been their favorite Thanksgiving; Joanne and I looked at each other skeptically, because we knew that for Stacy in particular, her parents' marriage had already been in serious trouble. Each child commented that they were with family and had good food. Stacy talked in great detail about her grandmother's soup. I recalled Stacy's difficulty in focusing on her personal situation in our first group session.

I mentioned that holidays can be very special because for many people they are spent with loved ones, but that they can also be difficult when families change or when someone wants to be in two places at once. The members continued to draw. Tara commented that she has an aunt who draws well, but not as well as Henry.

Despite the members' inability to tolerate what I was attempting to raise, this was the first time I had heard an unsolicited comment from one group member to another. While this may have demonstrated a member's aligning with another member rather than dealing with the issue at hand (flight), other examples of this interaction occurred in the session that supported my initial sense that the members seemed more connected and willing to speak to one another. Nevertheless, Joanne and I looked at each other and agreed we needed to move on to another activity; the members had become absorbed in their artwork and needed a push.

PRACTICE POINTS

As the group develops, the leaders introduce other creative activity forms that can facilitate the work. The sharing of vignettes can provide some structure for exploring difficult feelings. Once again, it would not be difficult to explain to the children, in simple terms, how the vignettes work and why it might be helpful.

Joanne and I took turns creating vignettes, and the members had to decide whether someone described in the vignette would feel happy, sad, angry, or disappointed. We spontaneously created scenarios that seemed relevant to what the children might be facing this week. I went first and offered, "Mary's father is supposed to pick her up at 10 a.m. on Thanksgiving. He calls her at 11 a.m. to say he can't make it because he's decided to go to his girlfriend's house. Mary feels . . . ."

The scenarios became more complicated as Joanne and I introduced stepparent and stepsibling issues and other conflicting themes that might involve the members. Each child responded quite positively to this activity. They were spirited and engaged, and each contributed sound reasons for feeling as the character might have felt. Often the members personalized the scenarios by saying how he or she would feel. After Joanne and I had each done two scenarios, Tara asked if she could make one up. Stacy followed. She described a situation where a mother's boyfriend was angry at a child and threw the child down the stairs. She wanted to know how the mother should feel.

Henry and Tara responded together that the mother would be sad the child was hurt. I felt an urgent need to make a stronger statement, as well as model for the members the acceptability of their own strong feelings. I added, in a very firm voice, that if I were the mother, I would be furious that my boyfriend had hurt my child and that no matter how my child behaved, no child deserved to be hurt, and that my boyfriend's behavior was absolutely unacceptable. Recalling the activity we had played in a previous session, Stacy acted like the judge and said I had given the best response for that scenario. It was a scenario Joanne and I would need to be alerted to.

PRACTICE POINTS

The scenario made up by Stacy raised a warning flag for the leaders that they need to address in an individual session. The group leaders are mandated reporters, and even an indirect communication of possible abuse must be explored, and if confirmed, shared with the appropriate child welfare agency. Even if the individual conversation does not provide confirmation, the leaders should alert the child protection office so that a more thorough investigation can take place. In retrospect, the discussion about confidentiality, so crucial in any beginning session, was not reported in this record of group meetings. If not explicitly expressed before, it should be addressed after this comment. A more complete discussion of confidentiality and mandated reporting issues can be found in Chapter 13.

The children's vignettes were complicated and revealing. Each member seemed to be an internal leader—creating a vignette and listening to each person's discussion as to why someone might feel as he or she did. This activity seemed to reduce the amount of denial and avoidance I had sensed earlier; by removing the focus from the three members, which in a group of three may have simply been too intense, the members could be more spontaneous in exposing their feelings. Time had run out, and the members did not want to leave. I told the group that everyone had made wonderful, creative, and sensitive contributions and that we would talk more next week. I wanted to praise and reinforce their willingness to take risks and to take ownership of their group by conceiving their own stories.

Fifth Session

My co-leader and I decided to focus this week's session on anger. Prior to group, she and I had agreed that we would use vignettes again because they seemed to be an effective way of getting each of the members to reveal their own feelings, sometimes in the guise of sharing through what the characters might feel and sometimes through making identifications with the characters as to how they, the members, would feel.

The group opened as it did last week; the members were snacking and chatting with each other and seeming comfortable as they discussed how they had spent their Thanksgiving holiday. The members asked what we were going to do today, and Joanne responded that we would be talking about anger. I felt a need to review why we were all together and to remind the group that there was a shared purpose to our meeting. I asked the group what we had been discussing in our previous weeks together and what it was that brought us all together. Tara immediately responded, "Divorce." I nodded and then asked if anyone could be more specific. Stacy said we talked about "happy, sad, and mad." I asked the group if this is different from what they do in school and, if it is, in what way. Everyone said it was different and that in school people do not discuss their feelings. I asked the group why they thought this was so. A silence followed.

I thought that the members might be feeling uncomfortable and that their silence reflected their own discomfort and sense of isolation regarding their ability to discuss their family situations freely at school and perhaps even in the group. I missed an opportunity to acknowledge their discomfort and instead tried to educate them and normalize their experience about the common occurrence of divorce. I asked the members if they knew other children at school whose parents were separated and divorced. My co-leader pointed out that almost half of all marriages end in divorce. Not surprisingly, the intellectualized response by my co-leader, and perhaps by me, generated little response, and my co-leader and I moved on to our planned activity.

PRACTICE POINTS The leaders here took the children to the edge of an important discussion. The question about what makes it hard to talk about these subjects was on target; however, the children's silence in response moved the leaders away from this conversation. This was the moment when reaching into the silence, perhaps by offering some specific possible reasons why it is hard, could help the children deepen the conversation. The group leader showed important insight in her learning process as she recognized her own intellectualizing response. Perhaps the silence and intellectualizing arose because talking about anger—the focus of the session—was particularly difficult for both the leaders and the children.

We asked the children what makes them angry about divorce. They came up with several responses. I tried to draw them out to have them reveal the depth that they had in previous sessions, and I pointed out connections to other responses when similarities were evident to me. Joanne and I then took turns creating vignettes that we knew would resonate for the members in our group. What followed was a lengthy discussion about absent parents, new partners in their parents' lives, and contending with the children of these partners.

Tara and Henry both described wanting to kill a new baby who was born to "Walter's mother and her boyfriend," characters in a scenario. I thought it was important to acknowledge the expression of their feelings and again tried to elicit from them why they might want to kill this baby, whom else might they be angry at, what would happen if they really did kill the baby, and what their loved ones might feel about them. Following this opportunity for them to play out this scenario, I asked if it was really OK to kill a baby. The members all said no. I then asked if anyone could think of other solutions to this dilemma, because killing a baby is really not OK. I hoped that this would instill confidence in the members' own capacity to problem-solve. Henry and Stacy smiled. Tara, who had a newborn in her home, did not. Henry, an only child, said maybe "Walter" could play with the baby; I asked Henry what that would do. He replied, "Walter might like it." I acknowledged that Walter might enjoy having a younger sibling after all, even though his feelings might remain mixed. This seemed to give Tara permission to discuss that it is hard having only younger siblings and that she wished she were not the oldest in her family.

One of the vignettes created a scenario of a friend wanting to talk to someone about his parents' divorce. I asked the group whom this friend could speak with. Henry said that he would tell this person to speak to a counselor or teacher. I said that this was a very good suggestion. I then highlighted for the group that each of them could be very supportive to a friend because they have gone through a similar situation and that it might help the friend to feel less alone. We again began discussing why talking about these feelings is difficult. I noticed that all three children had moved into the corner and were focused on a dollhouse, standing with their backs turned toward Joanne and me. This time I was not going to miss the opportunity to acknowledge their discomfort. I said to the group, "I have asked all of you a question. Is it hard for you to talk about this stuff right now?" I was stunned by the honesty of their reactions. Henry immediately nodded, and Stacy and Tara said, "Yes." I chose to reach further to have them identify their discomfort. "How come?" I asked. There was no answer, and this session was over. I again wanted to praise their willingness and bravery to take risks and share their feelings. I commented, "That's OK. You've all been doing a great job today talking about issues that are hard for everyone. It's not easy, and you've all been very brave."

PRACTICE SUMMARY As the group sessions approach an ending, preparing for termination sessions with a group of children for whom the loss of adults has been central will be important. A good start will be for the leaders to tune in to their own feelings given that the record reveals they have become close to these children and the children to them.

Internet Online Groups

Technology is having a growing influence on the way counseling is done, particularly the use of the Internet for individual, family, and group practice. Kennedy (2008), in a lead article in *Counseling Today*, points out:

More and more counselors have come to accept, even if sometimes begrudgingly, that their profession is not immune to technology's impact. Instead, they are actively looking for ways that technology can be of "help" to the helping professions. As such, new technologies are influencing how counseling is being accessed, delivered and taught. (p. 34)

Computer-mediated counseling is defined by Kennedy as "any type of counseling that uses a computer for delivery of services whether via e-mail, chat rooms, online support-groups or video conferencing" (p. 34). One concern raised by members of the American Counseling Association (ACA) in an association survey was the "possibility of inadvertent violations of licensing laws if the client being treated online resides in a state different from that of the counselor" (p. 34). Kennedy cites Goodrich, who advises some precautionary measures when considering computer-mediated counseling, including the following, among others:

- Encrypting conversations to ensure confidentiality
- Performing risk assessments—know the contact information and locations of clients so these clients can be referred to local resources in cases of suicidal ideation or instances of other severe mental health risks
- Being aware of client's access and basic computer knowledge
- Being cognizant of legal issues
- Knowing ethical codes for being a distance counselor[2]
- Acquiring proper licensure and credentials for distance counseling[3]

Although still a relatively new approach to group practice, the use of the Internet for online groups, including chat groups, has been growing. Haug (2008) points out:

Over the past few years, computer-mediated interpersonal communication via the Internet has expanded rapidly. Online therapeutic approaches like Internet chat groups create new opportunities for the prevention and treatment of mental health problems. . . . Such groups offer the possibility of serving people with limited mobility, time restrictions and limited access to mental health services, including individuals living in remote areas, those lacking access to appropriate therapists, or those lacking access to other patients with similar problems to form a therapy group. The only requirement for a patient or therapist to participate in the group is access to an Internet-connected computer and the ability to use this technology. (p. 36)

In this section, I will present three types of communications currently used in online groups: (1) text-only groups, (2) video groups, and (3) sound-only groups.

Internet Chat Text Group Providing Follow-up Mental Health Care

Essential elements to qualify as an Internet chat treatment group are that communications are synchronistic (there is the ability to have a direct response) and a therapist is present to guide the interaction. Haug (2008) states:

The model for therapeutic chat groups is the traditional face-to-face group therapy setting in which group members (normally between 3 and 15) meet at prearranged appointment times with a therapist or other mental health professional. The online chat group interaction takes place in a "chat-room" where

---

2. Goodrich suggests a source for more information is the 2005 ACA Code of Ethics, Standard A.12., "Technology Applications," and the National Board for Certified Counselors webpage at nbcc.org/webethics2.
3. For more information on credentialing and training, Goodrich suggests contacting NBCC at nbcc.org.

participants can simultaneously log on to a particular Web site to interact and communicate with each other. Compared to asynchronous forms of communication like e-mail or message boards, Internet-chats are more interactive as every sentence typed is immediately displayed on the screen for all the participants. (p. 37)

Haug adds that there are both advantages and disadvantages to the use of Internet chat groups. On the downside, there is a lack of facial expression and even emotional tone because communications are text based. Some ways of dealing with this include the use of emoticons (e.g., ☺) or sound words (e.g., hmmm). A number of authors have documented the difficulty of replicating face-to-face group process due to the lack of visual cues (e.g., Schopler, Galinsky, & Abell, 1997).

On the advantageous side, Haug (2008) points out that "[t]he anonymity of the Internet may make it easier for individuals to disclose information about themselves since barriers such as age, gender, social status, and appearance are less present" (p. 27).

An Online Web-Based Video Support Group for Caretakers

In another example of the use of technology in providing group services, Damianakis, Climans, and Marziali (2008) reported the results of an online survey of eight counselors and one nurse exploring their experience in making the transition from face-to-face to web-based video support groups for caregivers of family members with Alzheimer's, Parkinson's, stroke, frontotemporal dementia, and traumatic brain injury. Groups were offered using a 10-session, 1-hour-per-week. "The aim of these closed groups was to provide psychosocial support and to enhance caregiver's problem-solving and coping capacities while caring for their family members in their homes" (p. 103).

The researchers provided computer and webcam equipment for group leaders and participants. The group leaders were trained in the use of the equipment and received a manual on Internet delivery of group treatment focusing on the particular illnesses of those they cared for (e.g., Alzheimer's). The leaders' theoretical orientations included cognitive-behavioral, narrative, psychodynamic, and solution focused. All of the therapists were experienced in working with geriatric populations. The online survey was composed of six open-ended questions dealing with their experiences in six key areas:

(1) the experience of working online as compared to face-to-face, (2) the experience of transitioning from facilitative face-to-face groups to video Internet groups, (3) assessing the quality of relationships amongst group members and client outcomes, (4) advantages and disadvantages of working via Internet video conferencing, and (5) recommendations for other clinicians beginning to work online. (p. 104)

The researchers reported a generally positive experience as perceived by the therapists in spite of some technological challenges that impacted group processes. Online group interaction and therapeutic effectiveness were perceived as comparable to face-to-face support groups. The therapists reported that making the transition involved "(1) additional engagement of group members' in the pre-group phase, (2) attending to the group members' frustrations with glitches in the technology but also recognizing the potential advantages toward group bonding, and (3) adapting to change in group communication patterns as a result of structured technological sequencing" (p. 105).

An Online Audio and Text Educational Group for Graduate Students

These findings conform to my own experience as an instructor of an online graduate practice course. This was a model that provided more contact than a text-based group but less than one that also provided video. I made use of the university-based technology Blackboard®, using a version that allowed for online verbal communication but did not provide video of the participants or myself. All participants were graduate students who lived in different parts of the state. After they signed in, they could hear live my comments as well as the contributions of other group members. As the educational "group leader," I was able to electronically recognize participants who signaled they wanted to speak by clicking on their virtual hand on my screen. This capability maintained order and prevented voices from overriding each other. Finally, students could also type a response in a chat box that could remain confidential unless they wanted the text to be shared. Group members could also access online videos, Power-Points, or other visuals I had made available from a home page but not while the online group was operating.

Although evaluation of the web-based approach was not part of a formal research study, students' midsemester and final evaluations of the course were universally positive, with the ability to take an otherwise unavailable course from their home or offices far outweighing any technical issues or other negatives. My experience did, however, highlight the need for a technical support person who could directly respond to any technical difficulties experienced by participants. In addition, because many students were accessing the course through their county office computers, setup technical work was required before the course that allowed the students to connect to the university. This entailed developing a "tunnel" that allowed them to bypass their system's firewall to access the Internet.

My personal experience was that the lack of visual cues from individual students and my inability to see the group required extra efforts on my part to encourage verbalization of emotional reactions to the work for individuals and the group. For example, in a face-to-face group, when the group members remain silent, I can at least see their faces, which might help me understand or guess at the message in the quiet. In this model of educational group leadership, silences became very "loud" indeed. In another web-enhanced experience, most of the course was offered online, but the group members also attended three weekend full-day classes, one at the beginning, one during the middle, and a final class at the end. This mixed model was perceived positively by the student participants.

Finally, in another group consulting situation I conducted where videoconferencing was involved, the technological difficulties of connecting and working simultaneously with small groups in different locations were both expensive and loaded with technical problems. This type of videoconferencing requires "bridging" technologies and a host to control the sound and video feeds from the different sources; this necessity adds to the complexity and the cost of Internet groups. However, given the growth in this area of practice and the movement toward the use of technology for provision of health and social services, I suspect our knowledge of how to use this medium and the technology will increase significantly—and sooner rather than later.

Chapter Summary

Some differences in the core elements in group practice include, among others, the unique processes and skills required in working with (1) an open-ended group, in which members join and leave the group continuously; (2) a single-session group, often large, which meets for informational proposes or in response to a particular event or trauma; (3) activity groups, in which activities are used as "mediums of exchange" among members, for various purposes such as sharing information or working through problems; and (4) the emerging use of the Internet for groups for initial and follow-up counseling.

The three basic types of Internet groups described in this chapter involve text only, text and verbal connection, and text-verbal-video models. Leaders can apply to the four groups all of the core dynamics and skills discussed in the first nine chapters.

Related Online Content and Activities

For learning tools such as glossary terms, InfoTrac® College Edition keywords, links to related websites, and chapter practice quizzes, visit this book's website at **www.cengage.com/counseling/shulman.**

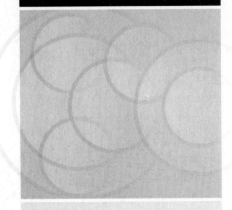

The Impact of Diversity on Group Practice

T his chapter is divided into two parts. The first deals with the impact of diversity on groups and group practice from a number of perspectives: race, ethnicity, age and stage of the life cycle, physical ability, and sexual orientation. Gender could also have been included; however, I chose to include the discussion of the impact of gender earlier, in Chapter 8, when I presented a gender-based theory of group development. I will address gender again in Chapter 12, which summarizes other models of practice, including some identified as feminist.

The second part of this chapter focuses more on the impact of differences and similarities between the group leader and members and among the members themselves. The term *intercultural* is used broadly to refer to differences in any of the categories just listed. For example, a white counselor who leads a school group for African American youth or an African American counselor leading a group with white members could be described as being involved with intercultural practice. By this expanded definition, a female leading a group of males would also be intercultural. A group with a diverse membership, such as gay and straight, could also be considered intercultural as defined here.

The term *intracultural* refers to practice in which the group leader and members share characteristics that are more similar than different. For example, the work of a Hispanic leader of a school group consisting of Hispanic students is considered to be intracultural practice. Interaction between the members of the same group can also have intracultural elements and issues as well. If not recognized and dealt with, inter- and intracultural issues can create problems in a group; however, if understood and addressed, they also can provide important energy that may deepen and enhance the work.

Common Definitions

Before proceeding to discuss and illustrate the impact of diversity, I want to provide some basic definitions. Devore and Schlesinger (1996) provide some term definitions used in this chapter, including *culture*:

> *Culture* is a commonly used concept that is difficult to define. It revolves around the fact that human groups differ in the way they structure their behavior, in their world view, in their perspectives on the rhythms and patterns of life and in their concept of the essential nature of the human condition. (p. 43)

They suggest there are a number of definitions of *ethnic group:* "Most definitions converge around the view that ethnic groups share important elements of religion, culture, physical appearance, or history, or some combination of these. These commonalities make for distinct differences among the various groups" (p. 45). They also suggest that the development and maintenance of ethnic identity is influenced by the following cultural factors (pp. 55–56):

- Language
- Rituals and celebrations
- Ethnic schools and parochial schools
- Primary groups

Lum (1996) introduces the impact of oppression and defines *culturally diverse practice* as a form that

> recognizes and respects the importance of difference and variety in people and the crucial role of culture in the helping relationship. Its primary group focus is on people of color—particularly African Americans, Latino Americans, Asian Americans, and Native Americans—who have suffered historical oppression and continue to endure subtle forms of racism, prejudice, and discrimination. In working with an individual, family, group, and or community, the practitioner draws on the positive strengths of diverse cultural beliefs and practices and is concerned about discriminatory experiences that require approaches sensitive to ethnic and cultural environments. (p. 12)

While this introduction has focused on culturally diverse practice mostly in terms of race and ethnicity, it could just as easily address similar concepts and models with other diverse groups. For example, as illustrations in the balance of this chapter indicate, the notion of culture could just as easily be applied to other subpopulations such as gays and lesbians; the differently abled; immigrants of first, second, or even third generations; and those of different ages and stages of the life cycle. Although Lum understandably emphasizes a primary focus on groups that have endured historical oppression, much of his concern about the need to be sensitive to the impact of oppression and about the importance of working with positive strengths can apply to these other groups as well.

Before exploring diversity issues and practices, it's important to understand the guidelines in this area provided by our professional associations.

Guidelines for Diversity Best Practices

The Association for Specialists in Group Work (ASGW) addresses diversity in its best practices guidelines published in 1998 and revised in 2007 (Rapin & Keel, 1998; Thomas & Pender, 2007). The guidelines state the following:

> Group Counselors practice with broad sensitivity to client differences including but not limited to ethnic, gender, religious, sexual, psychological maturity, and geographic location. Group Counselors continuously seek information regarding the cultural issues of the diverse populations with whom they are working both by interaction with participants and from using outside resources. (p. 8, Section B.8)

DeLucia-Waack (2004) believes the process starts when the group leader begins by examining his or her own cultural and ethnic values and racial identity.

> Group leaders must learn to recognize and separate their own cultural assumptions from the assumptions of their chosen theoretical orientation and those basic to group dynamics. Once the influence of culture and theoretical beliefs on their approach to group counseling is recognized, group leaders are more aware and communicate more directly how they approach counseling, and specifically group counseling, is from their own, rather than a universal, perspective—and thus, such leaders are more sensitive to differing perspectives. (p. 7)

Corey (2008) suggests that in order to practice in a culturally competent manner, you as a professional should first take an inventory of

> your current level of awareness, knowledge, and skills that have a bearing on your ability to function effectively in multicultural situations by reflecting on these questions:

- Are you aware of how your own culture influences the way you think, feel and act?
- What could you do to broaden your understanding of both your own culture and other cultures?
- Are you able to identify your basic assumptions, especially as they apply to diversity in culture, ethnicity, race, gender, class, religion, language and sexual identify?
- How are your assumptions likely to affect the manner in which you function as a group counselor?
- Can you be flexible in applying the techniques you use in your groups, depending on the specific makeup of the membership?
- How prepared are you to understand and work with individuals from different cultural backgrounds in a group?
- Is your academic program preparing you to work with diverse client populations in different kinds of groups?
- What life experiences have you had that will help you to understand and make contact with group members who have a different worldview from yours?

- Can you identify any areas of cultural bias that could inhibit your ability to work effectively with people who are different from you? If so, what steps might you take to challenge your biases? (pp. 34–35)

The requirement to develop cultural competence is often, but not always, put in the context of a member of a majority culture needing to understand a culture different than their own. However, the same set of issues can be raised when the group leaders come from a minority culture and attempt to work with group members who are different from them. Diaz (2002) describes her personal experiences as an Asian Pacific Islander who felt a level of conflict between her own cultural values and certain demands of what she perceived as group work values. She points out that the majority of literature published in this area focuses on Asian Pacific Island membership in groups but less on the issues involved in group leadership. She identifies some of her potential conflicts while appropriately pointing out, as I would put it, that there is diversity within diversity, with differences between specific populations (e.g., Chinese and Filipino) and even differences for individuals within a particular population.

> There are three demands of group work practice that I have found to be dissonant with Asian Pacific Islander cultural value: (1) the assumption of a role of authority that is non-hierarchical, (2) the exploration of conflict, and (3) the exploration of feelings within a group. While these aspects of group work are a challenge to all group counselors, especially for those beginning group work practice, the challenge is more poignant for group counselors who are Asian Pacific Islanders because of the contradiction with their values and beliefs. (p. 47)

Diaz provides examples such as working with students in an elementary school who did not accord her, on the first meeting, the respect for the authority due an older person. This practice had been very much a part of her own upbringing, and even in graduate school, it had made it difficult for her to address a professor by a first name, even if invited to do so. She describes a cultural norm that avoids direct conflict. The importance of "saving face" and not bringing "shame" to a family or others is a central construct. (This will be explored further in later sections of this chapter, including this author's own experiences teaching in Hong Kong.)

> As a group counselor who is an Asian Pacific Islander, I can attest to the feeling that direct confrontation is an affront to my sensibilities. In groups that I lead, I strive to explore conflict because that is what I have been taught to be good group work. My first reaction to conflict, however, is to squelch it as quickly as possible to avoid feelings of discomfort for myself and to prevent discomfort among members of the group. It is not easy to unlearn this reflex. (p. 53)

Diaz describes having difficulty with the third identified area in expressing her own feelings and exploring those of group members. Citing this author (Shulman, 1999) as an authority for the importance of the group leader to set a "tone" by expressing his or her own feelings that encourages members to empathize with each other, she points out:

> Asian Pacific Islanders who are group counselors may have difficulty setting this tone due to their unfamiliarity with experiencing other's expression of emotions in a group. . . . As a group counselor I am not obligated to express my emotions or self-disclose. But I have found that I often struggle with the facilitation of exploring feelings in a group because I myself would hesitate to expose my feelings in a group. (p. 54)

Diaz's personal disclosure of her own struggles in this article is, in itself, an effort that may run counter to her background. However, it is a sign—along with her efforts described in her group work practice—that she is making progress in responding to many of the questions raised earlier in Corey's (2008) list of steps toward cultural competence. I believe this article also speaks to those of us who teach group work practice about the importance of understanding the culture of our students who may not always feel free to share their dilemmas caused by the conflict between what they perceive to be group work values and those of their own culture.

Before presenting illustrative examples related to a number of populations and groups, it is important first to explore issues associated with addressing taboo subjects in our society. Each one of the diversity elements in this chapter has associated with it, some more and some less, taboos that make discussion sensitive.

Discussing Taboo Subjects

The key to effective cultural practice is first to recognize that discussion of these subjects, which tend to be taboo in our society, presents a challenge for a group leader; however, as long as they remain unacknowledged and unspoken, these factors can grow in power to have a negative impact on the group. Addressing them openly, rather than allowing them to remain below the surface, often diminishes the negative impact and strengthens the group. Nonetheless, for a number of reasons it is difficult for group leaders and members to address diversity issues. For new group leaders, it can be particularly stressful.

In my classes and workshops, I have tried to address this difficulty when an example or issue arises that has the potential for being problematic. One way I approach this is to point out that it's sometimes difficult to find a safe and supportive atmosphere in an educational group, and acknowledge that the participants may not always have had positive experiences. I then ask the group members to take a few moments to discuss what makes it difficult to have these discussions and what would also make it easier. What is interesting is that as participants share what would make it harder and easier to discuss these taboo subjects, they are actually discussing them.

For example, white participants when discussing race, male students dealing with issues of gender, or straight students addressing gay and lesbian issues describe how they have personally been, or witnessed someone else, verbally attacked for "using the wrong term" or asking a question that is negatively received. In their own words, they feel they have to either "walk on eggshells" for fear of making a mistake or say nothing at all. They also describe taking oppression or diversity courses in their professional training that they actually experienced as "oppressive." When asked what would make it easier to have these discussions, the most common response often describes a group atmosphere where no one "jumped" on them if they made a mistake, and where their questions and concerns were respected by the other students. These factors would contribute to the creation of a safe environment.

Participants who are members of a minority or other oppressed populations have described their need to be sensitive to the many direct and indirect slights they receive in daily life. The African American participants who describe no one taking an empty seat next to them on a crowded bus, women who are exposed to sexist comments by strangers on the street, or gay and lesbian participants who are not "out" but regularly hear homophobic comments and jokes from family or colleagues, all describe the need to keep their "antennae" up as a form of self-protection. When asked what would make it easier for them to participate in such discussions, they also often say they would be prepared to share information if they felt the person asking "really wanted to know" and was trying to be respectful. Also, they indicate it is important that others take the time and effort to inform themselves about diversity and do not depend on members of the minority groups to do it for them.

Another key factor, as noted, is that there is a great deal of diversity within diversity. For example, when discussing the Latino population, it would be important to appreciate differences between New York Puerto Rican Americans and California Chicano Americans or immigrants from Central America. All may share a language, but they have widely different experiences and cultures. The same may be true for southern rural blacks and northern urban blacks or blacks who have emigrated from Africa or the Caribbean. A common student complaint is being the "only one" of color in a class or group and having a white student ask, "And what do your people think?" as if they were representative of a whole population.

It is interesting to note that simply asking what would either facilitate or create barriers to a meaningful discussion can result in a change in atmosphere and a greater willingness to examine formally taboo subjects. This holds true in client groups as well as professional classes or workshops. The important point is that taboos exist in our culture for a reason, especially when deeply painful feelings are involved. It is important that group leaders understand how this pain may be expressed through anger, which may effectively close off discussion. The result is often that majority participants then say what they think others want to hear rather than what they themselves actually think and feel. This has been referred to earlier as one example of the "illusion of work."

With this preface addressing the taboo nature of this area of conversation, I will start with race and ethnicity and then explore other areas of cultural sensitivity. This chapter is not meant to address all types of diversity or even explore specific population cultures in depth, but rather to provide a way of thinking about the topic and illustrations of how it affects groups and group practice.

Race and Ethnicity

One of my important learning experiences occurred when I served as a consultant for one month with the Hong Kong Government Department of Social Services. I provided training workshops for a number of groups of social service professionals on how to organize and lead mutual aid groups for clients. Although I had tried to prepare by reading about Asian ethnic-sensitive practice, consulting with Asian friends and colleagues, and tuning in, nothing quite prepared me for the emotional impact and challenge to my adaptive skills as I led a number of short-term training groups for Chinese group leaders. I quickly understood that the process in the training groups would parallel what these counselors would face as they attempted to lead their client groups. In other words, the training group was an example of group work with a Chinese population, at least in the culture of Hong Kong. The members of the group would watch me closely and would learn about my views at least as much by how I led the groups as what I presented. This conformed to my observation that most often more is "caught" than "taught."

Also, I realized that although the month would be a difficult one, I would learn at least as much as I would be able to teach. I was aided in my education by the staff of the Hong Kong Social Service Department. I will use this personal experience to begin the discussion of and to illustrate key concepts in the remainder of the chapter.

Leading an Educational Group for Hong Kong Asian Counselors

My first important insight was that fundamentals of human and group behavior are universals across cultures; however, the roots of these norms, taboos, rules of behavior, and so on, can be traced to very difficult sources, and the intensity of their impact and the way they emerge will vary with different cultures. For example, I had prepared for the fact that the authority theme would be central in this group, as it is in all groups, in the beginning phase of work. With the Hong Kong groups, however, I was the "professor," to be accorded status and deference in a manner that persisted for the life of the group. Participants would not openly disagree with me, not so much because they feared my authority (as a Western group member might), but because, as a symbol of authority, I deserved respect and they would not want me to "lose face" in the group. In addition, as the "expert," I was expected to provide information, in a formal manner, which they were expected to learn. In an unpublished paper on group work, one of the participants, Mary Wong, points out that

> Chinese tradition allows great prestige and authority to the group leader. This echoes exactly the same position of the father in the Chinese family. As a person of knowledge, the group leader is entitled to respect and obedience from the group members who come to learn from him/her. Respect involves more than just ordinary politeness; it also involves agreement with the leader's view or at least abstention from open expression of disagreement. To disagree with a leader is to challenge his/her social role and hence harm his/her prestige.

My second insight was that principles of good practice also applied across cultures, but I needed to make serious efforts at adaptation in order to respect and work with ethnic and cultural differences. For example, rather than opening each group session with my usual problem swapping designed to engage participants, I prepared a brief and expected presentation. However, I did not abandon my requests for active discussion and involvement; I just delayed the demand and responded to their expectations of me. I also respected their early resistance to disagree with me; however, I pointed out my awareness of their reluctance and my hope that during our work together, we might find a way for them to provide feedback.

I was making a conscious effort to encourage them to share cultural differences without feeling they were offending me or that I would lose face. Here is an excerpt from my notes from one of the early groups.

> I am very pleased that I will have an opportunity to share my ideas about leading mutual aid support groups with you. However, I have a problem with which I will need your assistance. These ideas were developed in my work with groups in a Western culture. I believe many will be useful for your groups as well. Some will need to be adapted to respect your Chinese culture, and others may not fit at all. I understand and appreciate that your respect for me as a professor and your thoughtfulness will make you hesitant to disagree or suggest different ideas. It is my hope, however, that as we get to know each other, you

will see that I very much value your ideas and will find your opinions to be helpful to me. I am prepared to teach what I know about group leadership, but I am also hoping to be a student as well.

There was no response to this offer, but I believe it was heard and understood. After the session, one group member, who had been educated at Berkeley University, where the cultural expectations governing the interchange between faculty and students was somewhat different at that time, approached me privately to reassure me that it would take some time before I could expect a response and that I should not be discouraged.

I continued to try to find ways to encourage the group members to participate and provide feedback within their own cultural tradition. For example, when the group members reached the point where they felt safe enough to share some of their difficult experiences leading groups, and we had reached a point in the analysis of an example in which the skill of reaching for feelings or making a demand for work was appropriate, I would comment as follows:

If I were faced with this problem in a group I was leading back home, I would probably say the following at this point: (I would then share my specific intervention). Can you help me to see how we could modify this so that we can accomplish the same end but do it in a way that would be comfortable within your culture and your groups?

This often generated an excellent discussion in which the workshop members artfully found their own ways of making the same intervention. Because my request was presented in a cooperative, rather than confrontational, manner, workshop members appeared to feel free to respond without fearing they would be offending their group leader. An important additional benefit here was that I was modeling the same respect for culture in the workshop group that they would need to demonstrate in their own client groups.

Language was another area where it was important to understand the impact of culture. Hong Kong is bilingual, with all students learning English as well as Chinese. However, after working for years in Chinese only, many participants could understand English well but were embarrassed to risk speaking. I encouraged them to feel free to speak in either language, since I had translation assistance from the training staff. When no one spoke in Chinese after two sessions, I acknowledged the discomfort they may have felt at using their own language. So strong was the sense of embarrassment about not being able to speak English well, it was not until the fourth session that some participants felt free enough in the group to accept my invitation to use Chinese. After a few had broken the barrier, others were quick to join in, and I found myself often, and with good humor, having to slow them down so my translator could keep me involved.

Respect for authority was also evident in the pattern of participation within groups that included supervisors or administrators as well as front-line counselors. It quickly became apparent that most front-line counselors would refer questions and discussions to senior (and older) group members. Only after this pattern had been respectfully pointed out in the group did supervisory staff begin to play a less active role, which then encouraged front-line counselors to become more involved.

The desire to create a harmonious atmosphere was also evident in the group members' reluctance to criticize in any way the comments or presentations of their peers. Once again, by pointing out the process and relating it to similar dynamics that would be occurring in their client groups, I provided the avenue for a discussion of the importance of honesty and for the development of group guidelines for providing feedback in a respectful manner designed to allow a participant to maintain "face."

Issues of racism were never discussed in the workshops, even though early on I pointed out that I was a white, Western professor and that this might cause a problem. Sexism was also a generally taboo subject even though institutionalized sexist attitudes, stereotypes, and practices existed. There was a strong denial of problems such as sexual violence or incest, even though these issues were documented. It was clear that feelings of shame associated with revealing some "family problems" to an outsider were very difficult to overcome. Devore and Schlesinger (1996) describe this phenomenon with Asian clients as follows:

> Many people don't perceive problems as being lodged in or "belonging" to individuals, as is characteristic of mainstream culture. Problems may be seen as "belonging" to the family or the community. If something is wrong, the family is shamed. This is the case with many Asians. (p. 204)

PRACTICE SUMMARY

These personal experiences have been provided to introduce the idea of respect for ethnic and racial variations in understanding and supporting the development of an effective group culture. In addition, I hope I have illustrated how important it is for group leaders to also be active learners and to engage group members in the leader's education.

The immediate example that follows is of work with a group of Hispanic parents of children with cancer. It will illustrate some of the cultural issues raised in this section. The additional element of having to come to the United States to receive temporary treatment for their children with cancer introduces other complex issues to the analysis.

Hispanic Parents of Children with Cancer

Gladding (2003) argues the need to understand cultural differences and stresses the importance of understanding that there is diversity within diversity. He argues for understanding both the similarities and differences:

> Like other ethnic and cultural groups, there is considerable variety in populations that are characterized as Hispanic/Latino. Similarities and differences exist, for instance, among the three major Hispanic/Latino subgroups—Cuban Americans, Mexican Americans, and Puerto Ricans. (p. 212)

Schaefer and Pozzaglia (1994) provide an example of the impact of ethnic culture in their work with a group of Hispanic parents whose children have cancer. Many of the members of this group have come to the setting, a cancer treatment center in the United States, on a temporary basis so that their child can receive treatment. The group also includes different subgroups of Hispanics. Their challenges include special issues of dealing with their child's disease as well as living for a period of time in a foreign country. Many are also facing a transition from a rural area to a big city. According to Schaefer and Pozzaglia:

> The parent of a child who has a life-threatening disease such as cancer undergoes a uniquely devastating experience. A large body of literature addresses the multiple stresses in coping with child hood cancer and the need for

psychosocial intervention. A Spanish-speaking, nonnative Hispanic parent is separated from extended family, friends, and home. (p. 335)

These authors also point out that the term *Hispanic* includes many subdivisions of nationality, class, color, beliefs, customs, and race, and they all may experience linguistic and cultural isolation.

> However, important cultural commonalities do exist. While all families experience a sense of social isolation due to their child's disease and treatment, Hispanics additionally suffer from linguistic and cultural isolation. Hispanic families respond by grouping together informally for translating and support. (p. 335)

The observation of the natural tendency to group together for support caused the hospital setting to establish Spanish-speaking mutual aid support groups for this population led by Spanish-speaking group leaders. The authors point out there is a cultural norm for Hispanic families of providing support from both the nuclear and extended family members as well as friends when a stressful event is experienced. However, for many of these group members, their temporary condition of living in a foreign country cuts them off from this traditional support network.

The group leaders describe their observations in the hospital of the way Hispanic family members cope in ways that are different from the Anglo community and it was in part these observations that led them to offer a separate group:

> Our experience suggests that Hispanics tend to be more emotive of their feelings. When the child is hospitalized and is critically ill, family members congregate in the child's room crying and praying together. Under these stressful situations many Hispanics react with somatic complaints and *ataques de nervios* (nervous attacks). . . . This intense expression of feelings is sometimes misinterpreted by non-Hispanics as hysterical. Unlike this uninhibited expression of grief and sadness, Hispanics try to control their anger. This, however, is not necessarily the case with white, middle-class families who are more comfortable in openly expressing their anger at the disease and their frustration with the hospital system. The Hispanic family's strong belief in God and His will is used to explain why the child is ill and minimizes their anger. (pp. 336–337)

While the content of these group meetings varies depending on the group composition and member needs, the authors describe four general themes: "(1) environmental concerns, (2) family issues, (3) illness and treatment concerns, and (4) death and dying" (p. 339).

PRACTICE POINTS In the following excerpts from one meeting, we see how religion and faith guide the member's feelings and beliefs about the illness, treatment and death and dying. What also emerges is their personalized relationship to God:

> **MRS. MUNOZ:** (Said tearfully) And I was against the idea [of the catheter] from the moment Dr. S. explained it. How can I allow my son to go through more pain when I know he's going to die anyway?
>
> **MRS. LOPOZ:** You know something? I felt the same way when Dr. A. wanted to put a broviac [catheter] in Maria. I thought, "What's the use if she's just going to die? Better to leave her alone." But I finally agreed, and she had her chemo without having to get stuck much, and I've had her well for six months. Now she's not doing as well, but it's given her some time with me.

MRS. RAMIREZ: I look at it this way: why would God give man medicine if it wasn't for us to use and improve our lives? Whatever is going to happen to Joanne is in God's hands, but I believe He shows the doctors the way.

MRS. LOPEZ: Maria really prefers the catheter and she knows which is best because she's been sick one and half years. Why don't you come to my room after we're finished and I'll show you Maria's broviac.

GROUP LEADER: (To Mrs. L.) That's a wonderful idea. What do you think, Mrs. Munoz?

MRS. MUNOZ: Yes, I'd like to see what it looks like. At least then I'll understand what they're talking about. Thank you.

The excerpt also reveals the lack of immediate trust in the advice of the doctors. The authors point out that this trust, or *confianza*, is difficult to achieve in a large, somewhat impersonal health care facility. Most Hispanic patients prefer personalized health care from professionals who demonstrate *personalismo* that develops *confianza* over time.

PRACTICE POINTS

The group leader is careful not to identify with the doctors to try to convince Mrs. Munoz to accept the advice and instead supports the offer of mutual aid offered by another member. Finally, in the same session as the preceding excerpt, Mrs. Martinez states her strong religious affiliation and her belief in spirits:

MRS. MARTINEZ: When I heard Jose had leukemia, I prayed to God and called to Jesus over and over again until I felt relieved. I fasted for 5 days to prove that I really wanted my son to live and meant it.

MRS. LOPEZ: But didn't you get sick? I could never do that. I tried once.

MRS. MARTINEZ: Yes, they had to start an IV on me because I fainted, but that was a sign that my son would be saved. (p. 345)

PRACTICE SUMMARY

The authors point out that although to non-Hispanics this belief and behavior may seem extreme, it was accepted by other members of the group as a way of being active in a situation where Mrs. Martinez felt helpless and overwhelmed. They suggest that health professionals need to be respectful of these beliefs and traditions if they are to develop a positive relationship with this population.

Age and Stage of the Life Cycle: The Geriatric Population

Each stage of the life cycle introduces age-related dynamics to group practice. Because children through middle-aged adults are covered extensively in other chapters, I have chosen to focus on the geriatric population as the illustrative group here. What are some of the differences involved in working with older clients? What do we know about people in this age range in general and in groups in particular? How do our own attitudes toward older clients affect our group leadership practice? These questions are introduced in the sections that follow and then illustrated with excerpts from a geriatric reminiscence group.

Some Differences in Working with Older People in Groups

Toseland and Rizzo (2004) focus on some of the unique issues involved in working with older group members. They begin by discussing the impact of the lack of personal experience in aging for most group leaders.

> Most group counselors lack personal experience with the developmental issues faced by older adults. When working with younger people, group work practitioners can draw from their own life experiences. But, when working with older persons, most group counselors can only draw upon vicarious experiences with grandparents and other elders. . . . [I]t is often necessary for group work practitioners to sensitize themselves to the positive and negative aspects of aging, and to the developmental issues typically faced by older adults. To begin this process, it is helpful for counselors to identify their own attitudes and feelings about aging . . . group counselors' images of aging may be distorted by negative stereotypes. (p. 7)

While countertransference issues can emerge in working with any population, most group leaders have had some close and personal experience with older adults, including parents, grandparents, and other relatives. I remember showing a videotape in a group practice class a number of years ago illustrating the then-emerging group practices with Alzheimer's patients in a residential facility. Most of the group members could participate on some level in a very structured group, but all had significant recent memory loss. When I turned the tape off, I was greeted with what appeared to be a stunned silence. I had anticipated discussing the group practice, but it became apparent, when I explored the silence, that almost every student was associating to some current or past older family member in their lives. I had to begin by addressing their reactions and feelings to start the discussion, and as Toseland and Rizzo point out, that was the place to start.

Group leaders need to be attuned to age-related changes that can affect individual and group interactions. For example, Toseland and Rizzo note that in addition to a possible slowing of reaction time,

> [w]orking memory also . . . declines, but older people compensate with a storehouse of experience about how things work. Thus, these decrements in physical functioning often do not become severe enough to affect the day-to-day functioning of older adults until they reach advanced old age. Still, they can affect the pace of group meetings. (p. 8)

The authors quote Toseland (1995), who points out that while experiences may differ, common themes come up when older adults meet together:

> These themes include: (1) continuity with the past, (2) understanding the modern world, (3) independence, (4) physical and cognitive impairments, (5) loss of family members and friends, (6) spouses and other family of origin relationships, (7) children and grandchildren, (8) resources, (9) environmental vulnerability and adjustment, (10) religious conviction and ethnic pride, (11) leisure pursuits.

Most of these issues emerge in the geriatric reminiscence group illustration described later in this chapter. But first, I will present some data on resilience and life span theory as it applies to this population.

Resilience and Life Span Theory

Resilience theory, as discussed in Chapter 2, does not apply only to children and families. The life span theory and research described here focus on an individual's adaptive capacity to deal with life stresses.

Staudinger, Marsiske, and Baltes (1993), working in the area of aging, have attempted to integrate the notion of resilience with their work concerning developmental reserve capacity emerging from the field of life span psychology. *Life span theory* suggests that development throughout life is characterized by the joint occurrence of increases (gains), decreases (losses), and maintenance (stability) in adaptive capacity (p. 542).

Staudinger et al. (1993) suggest that this theory challenges a one-dimensional model in which aging, for example, might be seen as simply the loss of capacity. Plasticity, which can be positive or negative, is another central notion of life span theory. *Plasticity* can be defined as the individual's ability to be flexible in response to stress. This idea suggests that variable components of change can be attributed to the reserve capacity of individuals or populations and may be associated with cross-cultural or historical differences. The degree of an individual's plasticity may depend on the individual's reserve capacity, which is constituted by the internal and external resources available to the individual at a given point in time. Cognitive capacity and physical health are examples of internal resources; one's social network and financial status are external ones. Note that an individual's resources need not be fixed but may change over time (p. 542).

The authors describe two types of reserve capacity. *Baseline reserve capacity* is the individual's current "maximum performance potential" with existing internal and external resources. *Developmental reserve capacity* refers to resources that can be activated or increased. Life span theory argues that, as reserve capacity increases, so does the potential for positive plasticity.

Group intervention activities may be seen as focusing on helping older clients, for example, to use their baseline reserves while intervening to activate the clients' developmental reserves. For example, increasing the client's social network (external reserves) through involvement in an older citizens' program could directly improve the internal reserve capacity (health, emotional state, cognitive capacity), which in turn strengthens the client's capacity for developing stronger social networks. This client would have demonstrated positive plasticity in the area of social relationships.

Geriatric Reminiscence Group

In the example that follows, a geriatric reminiscence group is organized at a day center to help older members make social connections and strengthen external and internal reserves. The example also illustrates the scapegoating process, described in Chapter 7, and the "flight" and "fight" group responses, described in Chapter 8.

Scapegoating is most often associated with groups for children and teens because it is most obvious in those age groups. But it can also take place with adults, as is illustrated in this example of work with a geriatric reminiscence group. We also see the impact of age and stage of the life cycle as members of this group, who have experienced many losses in their lives, start to face some of the painful as well as positive feelings associated with their reminiscences about their lives.

The reader should note the following key points in the example:

- The importance of providing examples when making an opening statement of purpose
- The need to reach for the underlying message when an angry comment is made
- The importance of always searching for the connection between the conversation and the purpose of the group
- The need to be aware of how group members play various roles such as gatekeeper and scapegoat in this illustration and the reason they do so.

Type of Group: Geriatric reminiscence group

Age Range of Members: 68 to 101 years old

Gender, Ethnic, Sexual Orientation, and Racial Information: Male and female, primarily working-class. Most have only an eighth-grade education. The members are predominantly Italian, some Irish and Latino. All have physical problems. Some have slight mental retardation, chronic schizophrenia, dementia, and Alzheimer's.

Dates covered in record: January 21 to March 31

Description of the Problem

The task this group faces is to reminisce about the past, which can bring forth both good and bad memories. The group has not yet developed a culture to be able to talk, not only about the good times but the losses, such as death, functioning and mental capacities, as well. The group-as-a-whole goes into flight instead of talking about difficult or painful issues. The behavior itself is not the problem. The problem seems to be the communication within the group. Deviant behavior is a signal of this problem. The problem I face is helping the group find a way to talk about painful issues without scapegoating occurring.

How the Problem Came to the Attention of the Group Leader(s)

The problem of using a scapegoat to avoid talking about feelings came to my attention early in the life of the group. Throughout each group session, everyone was easily engaged and ready to share. Once a topic or an issue was touched upon that seemed sensitive or emotional, immediately "the fun would begin." Different members at certain points in the conversation would start making fun and picking on other members. When I addressed the jokes and the fun poking, the acting-out members often started talking in Italian. I realized that these issues needed to be addressed if the group was going to be effective.

Note in the first session that the group leader states the purpose of the group but does not share any examples or illustrations that would help the members to understand it more clearly. The leader acknowledges her discomfort at the silence and her reaction to fill the void by talking. It is at this moment she could provide what I have called in a previous chapter handles for work.

Summary of the Work

January 21

This was the first group session. My co-leader and I named 7 clients that we wanted in our group, and, when we arrived at the center, there were 17 members waiting for us. My co-leader and I worked at the center since last semester, so most of the members knew us quite well. I told the group that this was a reminiscence group, in order to clarify the purpose. I explained what reminiscing meant and told the group that, although we would be talking about the past, it could be any topic that they wanted to discuss.

Most group members stared at me without comment. I became anxious with the silence, so I continued to talk. One group member started to discuss the news from that morning. Instead of clarifying the purpose again, I allowed the conversation to continue. At the time, I did not think about bringing the topic of the conversation to the past. In retrospect, I realize that I should have mentioned that the past does not include 2 hours ago. Because I did not do this, it became a common theme in the group. I left the group feeling that not much work was accomplished.

When a group member starts to discuss the morning news, the leader feels they have not understood or responded to her opening statement on the purpose of the group. This may not be true since current events often can be connected to earlier life experiences if the leader helps. For example, as the United States faces a difficult current economic situation, members who raise the extreme loss of jobs reported in the morning paper can be helped to connect that news to past experiences in their lives—such as the Great Depression—and how it felt to them and how the country was able to emerge stronger. The key skill for the group leader is to find the connection between the conversation and the purpose of the group.

PRACTICE POINTS

Note in the next excerpt how Mary plays a gatekeeper role and how the group leader misses her message. Instead of asking, "Is it hard to talk about painful memories, Mary? How about the rest of you?" she encourages sharing of memories. In response, Mary leads the group in a form of flight by using Joe's entrance as a humorous distraction. Mary, whose feelings have not been addressed, responds to the next leader's intervention with anger. Mary's pain, still not addressed by the leader, is under this anger.

January 28

When my co-leader and I arrived, the conversation of the group already had begun. After being filled in by the group members that the conversation was about the North End in the "good old days," I helped facilitate conversation. I asked the group if their parents were born in the North End. Florence stated that her parents were from Canada. Another group member started talking about Italy and how her parents came to America. Mary stated that she lost her mother many years ago, so why bother talking about her? I replied by saying that one of the ways memories can be kept alive is by sharing them with others. Right after I made my comment, Joe walked in. Mary looked at Joe and started singing, "Joe, Joe from Buffalo. He kisses girls, then says hello."

The group started laughing, and another member started singing a different rhyme. I had to get in touch with my own feelings because, on one hand, I wanted to laugh with the group, and avoid the work as well. On the other hand, I realized that I was there with a purpose. I tried to bring the focus back to the group. I told Joe that we were discussing the North End and where our families of origin came from. I then asked him if he would like to share with the group when his family came to America. Mary looked at me and stated with anger, "Isn't the group over?" It was.

In the next excerpt, the group leader must deal with her frustration at her co-leader who joins in the separate conversation. Starting to demonstrate greater confidence in her role, the group leader pulls the co-leader in and responds to the apparently random conversation about food by skillfully connecting it to the purpose of the group. This is a good example of sessional contracting discussed in the chapters dealing with the middle phase of group practice.

February 4

When my co-leader and I arrived, there were 19 members waiting for us. Vinny started talking about a show that was on television last night. I asked the group what they wanted to talk about. Someone mentioned food, and eventually the group was out of control. Everyone was yelling out their favorite foods without listening to one another. I had to control my own feelings because my co-leader was having a private conversation. After pulling my co-leader into the conversation, the discussion of food continued. I reached for feelings and asked if everyone was hungry.

After laughter and agreement, I hoped to bring the topic back to the group purpose and examine what members had and lost. I stated that sometimes food and smells provoke a lot of memories. The group remained silent for a while, and then members started sharing their memories. After 2 minutes, the group was chaotic again. Members started talking about Paul Revere and Bingo. I became frustrated and copped out. I did not raise the real issue of reminiscing until the end of the group, and by then I was so frustrated with the group and my co-leader that I honestly just wanted to leave.

A major theme for a group at this stage of the life cycle is the many losses they have experienced. In addition to friends, relatives, and their work as homemakers or in other capacities, they also experience the loss of being able to prepare foods that had important meaning to them. The joking, which may be a form of flight, may be the way they signal the leader that this is a difficult area for discussion. In addition, the size of the group may add to the difficulty since it would be hard for them to find "space" in the middle of the conversation with so many present. It's also possible that they may not all be able to hear that well, which would be another impediment to a more orderly group discussion.

PRACTICE POINTS

The leaders would have to understand that in a group this size with this population, more structure may be needed—for example, agendas from the leaders reflecting the topics of interest raised by the members.

February 18

Before the group meeting, my co-leader and I realized that, although the conversations were funny and people were socializing, we were not accomplishing the group's purpose, which was to reminisce about the past. After getting seated, I stated, "Is everyone ready to work today?" Florence replied by saying, "What's the job?" The group started laughing.

I stated again that the purpose of the group was to reminisce. Grace began by talking about birth order. The group talked about family, siblings, and children. The topic then turned to the discussion of medical care and how much things have changed with technology. I was actually amazed. The group was communicating, listening to one another, and sharing opinions. I encouraged the communication to continue. Everyone was listening and respecting one another. When the group was over and I was getting my coat on, Lena grabbed my arm and stated, "Oh, yeah, Joan, what does reminiscing mean?"

PRACTICE POINTS Unfinished business from the first (contracting) session reemerges since the group leader had used a term, *reminiscing*, without illustrations or further explanation. Lena gives her an opportunity to recontract. Once again the group members, through Rose, use a member (Paul) to both avoid a discussion and at the same time raise an issue: lost love relationships.

February 25

I started the group by asking if anyone knew what *reminiscing* means. My purpose for doing this was because that is where the group left off last week. A group member volunteered with an answer by saying, "Thinking and talking about stuff from long ago." Other members chimed in to give their definition. I asked the group if they knew why we reflect on memories from the past. Rose stated, "More importantly, do you all know that Paul has a girlfriend?" Everyone started laughing. I asked Rose how that was relevant to the conversation. Rose stated that the present was better than the past. I asked if the past was too painful to talk about. Rose told me that the past was dead. Another member asked Paul if he was in love. I ignored the comment and asked the group if they thought that Paul wanted his love life told to everyone. I now realize that I was adding to the "flight" behavior. Fran looked at me and then said something to Rose in Italian.

PRACTICE POINTS When the group starts to talk about Paul's "love," they are actually working on an important issue—their own lost loves. The counselor's first response is to experience only the flight; however, she quickly catches this mistake and finds the connection between the joking and the theme for the day. Her acknowledgment of an intercultural issue, her being Jewish and most of the members Catholic, helps the group members discuss the sensitive area of intercultural romantic relationships. Note how Fran actually introduces a response about first loves by asking the group leader if she is Jewish.

I tried to turn an awkward moment into work and asked the group if anyone would like to talk about their first love. Fran turned to me and stated, "You're Jewish, aren't you?" After I answered yes, Fran turned to Rose and continued having a conversation in Italian. I avoided questioning Fran's comment because I knew they were angry and looked at my co-leader for help. My co-leader asked the group to share one trait that makes them different. Everyone started saying what makes them different from others. After the conversation ended, I took a chance and stated, "Everyone has different abilities and traits. One thing that makes me different is that I am Jewish while most of you are Catholic, but we are all the same inside." Fran seemed to get a kick out of my statement. She came over to me, gave me a hug, and then stated, "My first love was Jewish, but I was not allowed to date him." From there, the work began.

PRACTICE POINTS By now the leader has learned to understand the group's pattern of raising issues indirectly and using humor to do so. Each group develops their own culture and the method of discussing difficult topics. The group leader needs to learn the "language" of the group that helps her to "hear" the underlying issues.

March 4

Everyone seemed uninterested and was quiet when my co-leader and I arrived. We started by discussing the upcoming Academy Awards and movies from the past. No one seemed to want to participate. I asked everyone why they seemed down. No one responded. The group remained silent. One member reached into her pocketbook and took out her wedding picture. She told the group that she had been 20 years old at the time. Maria looked at the picture and stated, "You should have stayed 20. You seem happy there. Now you're a miserable old lady." In shock, I asked Maria why she said this. Shirley (the woman in the picture) said, "Forget about it. Let's talk about something else."

I would have liked to explore Maria's comment, but Shirley seemed uncomfortable. My co-leader asked the group what they wanted to talk about. Frank stated, "We talk about the same things over and over. Let's play cards." I asked if the past was too painful to talk about. Mary commented, "Why talk about the past? Who cares about the past? I agree with Frank. Let's play cards." Before I could respond, Rose states, "I live in the future, not the past." I tried to get Rose to elaborate. I asked her to describe her future, but she could not. I tried to keep a focus on the group and stated that, if we played cards today, then tomorrow that, too, would be in the past. I asked if that would be difficult to talk about. The group said no.

PRACTICE POINTS The underlying issue of the pain that can be associated with reminiscing for this population has finally emerged directly. Ethel, who questions the value of talking about the past, is actually the leaders' ally by raising an issue felt by others in the group. The group leader credits her since it has been raised so indirectly before and needs to be discussed.

Ethel said in a strong voice that so many people have so little time left that it is better to plan tomorrow than think about yesterday. I thanked the group member who stated this comment and acknowledged the fact that it took a lot of courage to make that statement. I then commented that it must be tough having so many losses. Lena said, "Enjoy it while you're young because it goes by too fast." With that comment, I truly empathized with what the members were feeling. I realized that they did not want to discuss the pain because they could almost count the time they had left. They would rather enjoy the time that they had left. I voiced my thoughts to the group. The response I received was, "Exactly. Now let's play cards."

PRACTICE POINTS As described in Chapter 9, the group leaders use the skill of introducing the impending ending of the group a few sessions in advance. They share their own feelings of loss, and this evokes an expression of feelings by the members. In another example of the integration of process and content, discussion of the ending of the group brings forth the issue of loss in the members' lives.

March 18

My co-leader and I mentioned that there would only be four more group meetings and that then the group would end. My co-leader explained that school would be over and so would our internships, which would be another loss in their lives. Mary said, "Four weeks is far away. Why are you bringing this up now?" I explained that termination is a process and that, although I would be leaving, I would miss all the members and wanted to start preparing myself to leave. I explained that it would be a loss for me as well. The group expressed sadness. Joe said, "Oh, well, just another person leaving my life." I validated that loss is difficult and facilitated a conversation on loss and sadness. Group members openly shared their sadness and grief with the group.

Mary shared with the group, "I may give these girls a hard time, but it is only because I know I can, because I know they care." The group turned its focus to friends that have left through the years. Frank seemed to get uncomfortable and started singing. I confronted Frank about his feelings and universalized to the group. As my co-leader and I left the group for the day, the group continued to share feelings with one another.

PRACTICE POINTS The leaders were alert to the connections between the ending of the group, their leaving, and the issues of loss. The stage of denial is evident in the next session as the group members decline the leaders' invitation to discuss the fact that there are only two sessions left.

March 30

The group started talking about Easter Sunday. The conversation was very general. We mentioned that there would only be two sessions left. The group did not seem to want to continue with this topic. I asked the group what they would like to do for our last session and where they pictured themselves in the future. The group mentioned that they enjoyed reminiscing (I found this to be quite funny, since that is the one thing they mostly wanted to avoid) and asked if the activities director would continue the group.

I was interested in what the group felt that they got out of the group. The group shared with my co-leader and I that "sometimes the old days are fun to remember." The group mutually decided that, for our last session on April 16th, they were all going to bring in pictures from different stages in their lives. I thanked the group for sharing their memories with me and encouraged the group process and the friendships to continue.

Where the Problem Stands Now

The group seemed to have developed some sort of group culture along the way, only I am not sure when it happened. The communication in the group has gotten better and the scapegoating has lessened, although it still occurs. The group has mutually decided that they can discuss the good memories, but not the painful ones, although they are now able to acknowledge that sadness and losses do exist.

I was very happy to hear that the group members wanted the group to continue, which only proves that sometimes you do not realize the impact that you make. Instead of going into flight and completely avoiding the painful topics or denying that they are sad, the group now communicates by saying, "Oh, let's not talk about that. That makes me think about too much heartache." The group has connected to one another, and friendships have emerged as well.

These two leaders demonstrated real caring for the group members, who responded with caring in return. As one member pointed out, she gave them a hard time because she knew they cared. It was important to be able to balance the group with both the positive and negative aspects of reminiscence. Another specific next step would be to help the group members connect their feelings, both current and past, with their behaviors. For example, not uncommon is a theme in groups such as these to avoid new close relationships because of the pain associated with past losses. The discussion of resilience research earlier in this chapter underlined the importance of having close relationships at this stage of life. In addition, in a group such as this one, the leaders need to be alert to the impact of loss of a member or someone close to a member due to death. Finally, a theme that emerged from time to time was the importance of finding new joys in their lives as the faced the ultimate reality of their own deaths.

Physical Ability and Group Culture

Clients who are differently abled also bring a sense of identification and a population-related culture to group sessions that require the group leader to be sensitive to important differences as they emerge. After receiving my degree, I worked at an agency with a year-round focus on helping children with disabilities integrate into community center agencies. We were just beginning to understand the concept of streaming these youngsters into regular programs when possible. This concept was beginning to emerge in public schools as well. It would be years later that the American with Disabilities Act of 1990 (ADA) would be passed to try to address some of the inequities in the way people with disabilities were treated.

A Summer Camp Group for Physically Challenged Adults

In both the winter program and the summer camp program, 6 weeks for children and 2 weeks for adults, I began to understand the level of stigmatization clients with disabilities face in attempting to negotiate the larger environment. For example, when we went into town and unloaded a van full of children or adults with polio braces, cerebral palsy spasticity, and other highly visible physical problems, they could see eyes averted or experience patronizing, even hostile, comments that had to be painful for them. What emerged in groups we led for this population was how important it was for them to be seen by others, including the group leaders, as more than their particular disability. Spastic adults who had great difficulty speaking did not want the listener giving up on them or thinking they were not capable of thoughtful conversation. Part of the training of new camp staff was helping them begin to understand that for this population, staff members were mostly outsiders who would need to work to understand their world. Physical ability differences were yet another example of an intercultural issue.

Even with this perspective, I look back now and see how in some subtle ways our own internalized biases and lack of understanding still emerged to be discovered. For example, in an adult group I led in this camp whose purpose was to discuss current events, there was a powerful session in response to the newspaper reports of the discovery of how the use of a widely prescribed drug, Thalidomide, had resulted in birth defects when used by pregnant women. Until this session, I had been unaware of the culture that separated the birth defect population, such as those with cerebral palsy or muscular dystrophy, from the disabled population of young (mostly) men who had lost limbs in accidents or who were disabled by polio as children.

As the conversation developed, the more recently and less visibly disabled members spoke about how abortion was the answer to Thalidomide babies. I had not recognized a caste system in the group in which birth defect members were scapegoated by the others, mostly, as it later became apparent, because of their own internalized feelings about their own disabilities. It was a maladaptive way to point out "At least I'm not as bad as them." This issue came forcefully to the surface when one extremely spastic, cerebrally palsied member said with great difficulty and anger, "Are you saying I should not be alive today, that I'm not a person because of my disability?" This became an opening for a discussion of the painful issues they all experienced as adults with disabilities, which helped them understand each subgroup with greater empathy and the common ground they shared. It also was an opportunity for me, the outsider and relatively new group leader, to deepen my understanding of the powerful social impact of disability.

Ending with Hearing-Impaired Teenagers' Group

In this illustration, a leader helps a group come to grips with her leaving and prepare for the arrival of a new leader. The group consists of teenagers who are hearing impaired. The beginning phase of work had been difficult, because the counselor had needed to develop a way to communicate with the members and to help them communicate with each other.

Their concern about the new leader was heightened by their fears that an "outsider" might not accept them because of their "handicap." The group had operated using a combination of discussion and activities. The planned activity for that evening was tobogganing:

> When I arrived, the members were already there. The usual greetings were exchanged, and we sat down to wait to see if more members would come. Billy said, "I think we should wait 10 minutes and then go." Kathy said she had spoken to several members, and they had indicated they wouldn't be coming, as it was such an awful night. I remarked that it was pretty cold for tobogganing. It was too bad we didn't know what the weather would be like. Billy said he had brought his toque, which would keep him warm. He proceeded to model it, which caused all of the members to laugh.
>
> At this point, Billy asked when the new leader was coming. I said that Barbara would be coming next meeting. Stephen said, "Is she like you?" I replied that she was a student like me; she was young and very happy to be coming to the group. I turned to Kathy and said, "We are talking about the new leader who will be coming to our meeting next week." Kathy turned to Amelia and Anna and indicated by sign language that the new leader would be coming next week. Amelia mocked a crying gesture, which bought a chorus of smiles from the other members.
>
> Stephen said, "Has she ever worked in a group like ours, like with deaf people?" Billy turned to Stephen and said, "Well, Lucille never worked with deaf people before us." Kathy replied, "That's right."

Just as group leaders need to develop the ability to monitor the group-as-a-whole, the content and process of the discussion, and the clock, they must also monitor each individual. In this group, because of the hearing disability of the members and their difficulty in seeing and reading others' lips, the leader must actively monitor signs of lack of involvement.

<table>
<tr><td>**PRACTICE POINTS**</td><td>In the next excerpt, the leader reminds the group to include everyone and also reaches directly for their concerns about losing her and about the possible attitude of the new leader.</td></tr>
</table>

> Amelia, Jo-Ann, and Anna were craning their necks to find out what was going on. I pointed out that some members were being left out of our conversation, and we had to try to remember to include everyone. Billy made a mock gesture to the effect of "here we go again," and he motioned the three members to move in closer. I said, "It's tough work letting everybody know what's going on," to which Billy replied, "Yeah!"
>
> I remarked that Billy and Stephen seemed sort of worried about the new leader coming in. Kathy smiled the sort of smile that says, "You hit the nail on the head." Stephen said, "We just want to know what she's like." I said that I think Kathy was thinking that, too. I said, "Was I right, Kathy?" to which she nodded her head.
>
> Amelia mumbled something that I didn't understand. Billy turned to her and then translated to me. Amelia had said it was like starting our group all over again. Jo-Ann asked what was starting over. Kathy explained to Jo-Ann what was going on. Jo-Ann shook her head. Anna, who is totally mute, was looking as if she were in another world; I was aware that she did not understand our conversation. I smiled at her, and she grinned back. Billy looked at me and said, "I'll explain to Anna."

The group counselor recognizes that for any group there would be interest in what the new leader will be like during the ending and transition period. In the case of these hearing impaired young people, a new hearing person raises concerns about how they will be viewed—as individuals or as their disability.

<table>
<tr><td>**PRACTICE POINTS**</td><td>While reaching for the feelings of concern, the leader does not directly raise the issue of having a hearing person lead the group.</td></tr>
</table>

> I then turned to Amelia and said, "You're nervous, like maybe it was like when you came to the meeting with me for the first time." Amelia mumbled, "Nervous? Nervous?" and turned to Stephen with a puzzled expression. Stephen very slowly said, "Remember what it was like the first time we came here?" Amelia gave him a look that said "I sure do." I said I guessed it was like that again, knowing a new leader is coming. Stephen nodded and said, "How come you're going?" then in a joking way added, "I guess you don't like us anymore." I said, "Of course I still like you." Stephen then patted Billy on the back. Billy said, "A good group, aren't we?" I smiled and said we'd been through an awful lot together. Kathy nodded her head, and this was a message that quickly got translated to all the members.
>
> Kathy said, "Gee, I wish we could have a leader that would stay in our group." Stephen said, "Yeah." I said I guessed that maybe people were also angry because I was going. Stephen said, "No, no, that's not right." Billy said, "We've had a good time in this group." I said, "Just the same, I understand it's a hard thing to have to face going through getting to know a new leader again." Kathy said, "Yeah, we just got to know you." Amelia made another mock gesture of crying. In the meantime, Jo-Ann and Anna were talking in sign language and I think were quite out of the conversation.

The leader's direct reaching for the anger at her leaving was too difficult a demand for the members at this moment. In flight from the painful feelings, they played a trick on her instead of responding directly:

Jo-Ann then said to Billy (in sign language), "When are we going to go tobogganing?" He translated for me. I said we had somehow passed the 10 minutes Billy had suggested we wait, and I asked her, "Are you ready to go?" Jo-Ann shook her head. I said, "You had a tough time knowing what was going on," and repeated this several times until she understood. She smiled and nodded and then smiled at Anna. Billy and Stephen then said they were ready to go. Billy poked Kathy and said, "Ready?" Kathy nodded. I said I thought Anna was being left out. Billy translated it to her, and she nodded.

I said I would go and get the two office toboggans and I'd be back in a minute. When I came back, to my dismay the group had all disappeared. I looked in several rooms and then decided to sit down and wait. In several seconds, Billy came whistling in. I jumped to my feet and said, "Gee, what happened to our group?" Billy, in a mischievous way, said, "Gee, I don't know. I just went for a walk." He said, "Why don't we look in the hall?" I said I guessed the members would come back, at which point he, in an insistent way, said, "No, let's look in the hall," which we did. Five beaming faces appeared with Kathy saying, "Surprise!" Everyone laughed, as did I; however, I said, "How come the group wanted to leave?"

Stephen said, "We wanted you to look for us." Amelia grinned and said, "Were you worried?" I said, "Did you want me to be worried?" to which there were several nervous titters. I then said, "I think this group wants to leave me before I leave them," to which there were vehement no's. Billy said, "We were just joking." I said, "Still, I wasn't sure that everyone knew why I was leaving." Stephen said, "You're going back to Saskatchewan—isn't that where you were from?" I said I would be working on my research 'til June. Kathy said, "We'll still have a good group." Stephen poked Kathy and said, "You'll still be here." Kathy said, "All of us members will be here." I said that I thought they could continue to have a good group, but that would depend a lot on them. Billy nodded his head as if he understood. Kathy said, "Like you always say, we got to work at it." The group members laughed and shared this last piece of information, and then we got ready to leave.

Another area that the group leader could have explored is the indirectly expressed concern by the members about how the new leader will view them. At a number of moments in these excerpts, the leader could have reached for these issues as the group prepares to make a transition.

This example brought back to me my own early reluctance to directly address the disabilities of my group members in my early camp experience. Even after one becomes so used to the physical aspects of, for example, entering a camper cabin with braces, crutches, artificial legs, and other such devices hanging from the rafters and folded wheelchairs, a person who is not disabled may feel reluctant to discuss the disability. On reflection, I think my own hesitancy was (and perhaps still is) related to my understanding of the anger often below the surface of those who have experienced yet another form of stigmatization and oppression and my own biases and prejudices that are deeply and socially ingrained. This can also be true in working with people who are differently sexually oriented, as described in the following section.

Sexual Orientation: Lesbians, Gays, Bisexuals, and Transgender Clients (LGBT)

In recent years, practice with lesbians, gays, bisexuals, and transgender (LGBT) clients has received greater attention both by the professions and within professional education. Writing in 2000, van Wormer, Wells, and Boes refer to social work but could also be speaking of other disciplines including counseling. The authors make the following point:

> Until recently the training of social work, like that of other mental health professions, included virtually no consideration of the knowledge and skills needed to work with gays and lesbians. To the extent that the needs of this highly invisible population were recognized at all, the focus was on causation and pathology. The change effort was directed to "the sexual deviant"; various forms of cures were tried. In recent years, as we have seen, social work has moved with psychiatry away from a view of homosexuality as an illness to be cured to a view of homosexuality as a viable alternative orientation. (p. 23)

Even today, the influence of politics and religion significantly impacts how this issue is handled by schools and professional associations. Van Wormer et al. (2000) assert that the helping professions had not yet developed an integrated approach to practice with this population.

> Indeed, there are a great many books on lesbian, gay, and bisexual existence, enough to fill whole libraries. At the level of the popular press, issues relating to sexual orientation—for example, same-sex marriage, gays and lesbians in the military—have become more and more prominent in public discourse. Social scientific research on homosexuality has been prolific as well. But, apart from anthologies, no contemporary volume offering an integrated, social work approach had appeared. (p. xiii)

These authors suggest that the understanding of and practice with this population is affected by popular attitudes, religious views, and politics. They note that attitudes toward homosexual conduct have evolved from viewing it as "sinful," "criminal," and "sick," to being "a normal variation," and back to "sinful" again (p. 7).

Definitions

Van Wormer et al. (2000) offer the following definitions of general terminology:

- *Sexual orientation* refers to the inclination of an individual toward sexual or affectional partners of the same sex, opposite sex, or both sexes.
- *Heterocentrism* is the term, parallel to ethnocentrism (as applied to ethnicity), to express this phenomenon of viewing the world through the eyes of the dominant group.
- *Heterosexual privilege* refers to the rights and advantages that heterosexuals have and take for granted every day: the right to marry a single person of the opposite sex, for example, or the informal privilege of holding hands in public.
- *Homosexuality* refers to sexual attraction between members of the same gender, often but not always accompanied by sexual behavior.

- *Gay* and *Lesbian* are used in this book as parallel and equal terms to refer to male and female homosexuality, respectively.

- *Queer* is an insider term that is being reclaimed—as in, for example, queer art and queer theory. The advantage of this term is that it can encompass all sexual minorities. The disadvantage is obvious.

- *LGBT* stands for lesbian, gay, bisexual, and transgender people.

- *Bisexuality* refers to those individuals who can be attracted to either men or women or, as they say, to a person, not a gender.

- *Transgender* is a term that has come to be used to encompass several different types of sexual identities and sets of behaviors that involve taking on the attributes of the opposite sex. (pp. 18–19)

The Oppression Perspective

The oppression perspective on human behavior and the social environment was introduced in Chapter 2. Many if not all of the concepts can be applied to this population as well. In a culture in which being openly lesbian, gay, or bisexual is risky, in terms of social status, employment, and physical safety, it is not surprising that passing for straight—otherwise described as being "closeted"—is not uncommon. Fear of being "outed," or having one's real sexual orientation revealed, is also common. Recent examples exist in which politicians and others, who outwardly led what were considered normal heterosexual lives (e.g., married with children), have either denied their true sexual orientation or accepted it as a reason to resign from their positions when revealed.

Although activist gay groups have worked hard to confront this oppressive culture through such activities as "gay pride" days and parades, legal challenges, and legislative initiatives, with some success, for many closeted and openly gay clients, Fanon's oppressor within, discussed in Chapter 2, is very much alive (Bulhan, 1985). The onslaught of negativity and homophobia can be unrelenting. The impact of listening to friends and colleagues, who may be unaware of one's sexual orientation, openly tell "fag" jokes takes its toll. For other oppressed populations, a greater awareness of the nature of sexism, racism, anti-Semitism, and so on, has tended to drive some of this behavior underground. This is not yet true for antigay behavior, which is too often tolerated. When antigay statements and stereotypical attitudes are held by the family members of gay individuals, it can be extremely painful.

Of course, many young men and women who come out to family and friends find acceptance, love, and support, which helps buffer the negative societal attitudes. For others, the response of family and friends can be both traumatic and lasting.

Petros Levounis (2003) describes his work as a gay psychotherapist with a gay patient named Stephen. He reports Stephen's description of coming out to his family:

He came out to his mother when he was eighteen years old and expected a sympathetic response. Instead, she experienced a "nervous breakdown," locked herself in her room for days, and eventually sought professional help from a "psychologist who worked with hypnosis." She asked Stephen to simultaneously see the same therapist for individual psychotherapy in an attempt for them to address together the fallout of his coming out. Stephen complied only to find out, two months later, that his mother had quit therapy shortly after the initial visit: now, the only patient was Stephen, and, in his mother's words, he was "the one with the problem." "The whole thing felt like a setup," he recalls: he felt "bamboozled" by his mother and left the weekly treatment after two and a half months. This was Stephen's only prior experience with psychotherapy. (p. 18)

In a support group I led for persons with AIDS in early substance abuse recovery, Tania, who was a transgender client, described her traumatic experiences growing up in a small, rural, midwestern town:

> I realized I was different and finally came to the conclusion that I was not just an effeminate boy but was really a woman in a man's body. I started to act more like the girl I felt I was which exposed me to ridicule at school, especially when I started to dress like a girl. When I told my family, they were shocked and angry at me and embarrassed. They tried to "straighten me out" but it didn't work. Finally, when I turned 16, my older brother grabbed me outside of the house and held a pistol to my head. He told me I had to leave town or he was going to shoot me. I knew he meant it. My being a girl scared them all. I decided to leave town, and I have never had contact with any of my family since that day. It was more than I could take.

At this point, Tania began to cry. A gay member of the group offered support and described how his family had rejected him and his homosexuality when he came out. Only his grandmother accepted him for who he was. Both members described a development of self-hatred for being who they were. This sense of self-doubt had begun to moderate only as they saw they were not alone, and they began to regain pride in themselves and how they had survived.

van Wormer, et. al (2000) discuss their interpretation of parental responses:

> A primary fear of parents regarding their gay or lesbian children concerns their happiness in a society that stigmatizes homosexuality. Is there anyone who has not heard derogatory "fag" remarks and jokes? Gays, lesbians, and their loved ones endure cruel, hurtful words on a frequent basis from thoughtless and ignorant people. Homophobia is fostered by our religious, educational, and legal institutions. Gays and lesbians have lost jobs, been refused housing, denied hospital visitation to their informed partners, been beaten, raped, and killed by homophobic heterosexuals or "wanna-be heterosexuals." Families have disowned their lesbian and gay children or siblings. Gays and lesbians have been devalued, been told they will burn in hell, and have been victims of aversion therapy. The roots of unhappiness are not due to sexual orientation but to hatred directed toward those who identify as or are perceived to be gay or lesbian. In spite of overwhelming homophobia, most lesbians and gays eventually state that they are happy. Indeed, research shows gays and lesbians to be as happy as are heterosexuals in the partner relationships. (p. 115)

For all clients, a strengths perspective may be important in helping change their cognition and feelings about themselves. For clients who have experienced brutal oppression, it is essential.

The Strengths Perspective for LGBT Clients

Van Wormer et al. (2000) provide guidelines for how to apply a strengths perspective to gay/lesbian sensitive practice:

- *How about Seed the positive in terms of people's coping skills and you will find it;* look beyond presenting symptoms and setbacks, and encourage clients to identify their talents, dreams, insights, and courage.

- *Listen to the personal narrative*, the telling of one's own story in one's own voice, a story that ultimately may be reframed in light of new awareness of unrealized personal strength.
- *Validate the pain* where pain exists; reinforce persistent efforts to alleviate the pain (of themselves and others) and help people recover from the specific injuries of oppression, neglect, and domination.
- *Don't dictate: collaborate* through an agreed-upon, mutual discovery of solutions among helpers, families, and support networks. Validation and collaboration are integral steps in the consciousness-raising process that can lead to healing and empowerment.
- *Move from self-actualization to transformation* of oppressive structure, from individual strength to a higher connectedness. (pp. 20–21)

Strategies for GLBT Sensitive Practice: The School Counselor

Elze (2006) focuses on work with youth in the school context. Her suggestions are useful in considering how one works with group members at this stage of their life cycle development both in recruitment to support groups and in the groups themselves. She describes how a school counselor can be GLBT sensitive in practice. This is a crucial stage of development for intervention, during which students attempt to come to grips with their sexual orientation, and the larger heterosexual population begins to develop its attitudes toward difference.

Elze suggests that the counselor needs to demonstrate that he or she is an "askable" person in response to all students:

The strategies that signal to GLBT youths that you are a supportive person may precipitate questions from heterosexual youths and colleagues, providing opportunities for consciousness-raising. Always correct myths, stereotypes and other misinformation that students and colleagues articulate about GLBT people. Normalize sexual orientation diversity and gender variant behavior, and educate others to affirm diversity in gender expressions. When explaining to students what you do in your job, include sexual orientation, gender identity, and sexuality concerns as examples of the issues that students come and talk with you about. (p. 861)

Elze describes a number of best practice principles when working with GLBT youth, which are summarized as follows:

- When providing services to GLBT youths, respect the students' confidentiality.
- Follow your professional code of ethics.
- Do not assume that GLBT youths' problems are related to their sexual orientation or gender identity, and do not assume that they are not.
- Remember that these young people are, first and foremost, adolescents, and may bring to you such issues as clinical depression and other mental disorders, parental substance abuse or mental illness, parental unemployment and financial stress, and domestic violence.
- Affirm, validate, and accept youths' expressions of same-gender attractions, desires, and behaviors, of any self-identification, and any confusion the youth may be experiencing.

- With transgender youths, respect their wishes by using their preferred names and pronouns, and do not demand or enforce gender stereotypical behavior.

- Avoid labeling young people, but instead help them safely explore and understand their feelings, thoughts, and behaviors related to sexuality or gender identity.

- Follow the youth's lead in using terminology. However, be able to say the words "gay," "lesbian," "bisexual," and "transgender" with comfort and without hesitation.

- For a highly distressed youth who cries, "I don't want to be gay," encourage further expression of feelings and explore his or her underlying beliefs and attitudes. The distress is often grounded in myths, stereotypes, and fears of rejection and stigmatization.

- Help young people build self-esteem by correcting their internalized myths and stereotypes.

- Believe students when they share their experiences with discrimination and prejudice.

- Be aware that the risks of "coming out" vary from person to person. Do not assume that "coming out" is the best choice for everyone. Immigrant youths, youths with disabilities, and youths of color, for example, may have more to lose by self-disclosure, especially if they are already marginalized within their schools. (p. 865)

Homosexual Veterans with AIDS: Dealing with the Effects of Oppression

In the next example, we see many of the oppression concepts as well as the strengths perspective in group work with homosexual veterans with AIDS. This example focuses on the impact of societal oppression on the development of a group culture. In this case, the group members are gay veterans who are HIV-positive or have been diagnosed with AIDS. Once their sexual orientation is established, these clients find themselves treated as outsiders by the larger, heterosexual population. They experience prejudice, discrimination, and assaults on their minds, hearts, spirits, and bodies. They can be the target of nasty private and public humor (e.g., television and movie stereotypes), which if expressed about other oppressed groups—for example, persons of color—would be considered racist and unacceptable.

Only more recently, as a result of growing militancy, organizational skills, and self-assertion by organized gay and lesbian groups, have laws been passed in some states to ban discrimination on the basis of sexual orientation. Although the taboo against recognizing homosexuality has been modified, as evidenced by the number of successful television shows with openly gay characters and actors, strong homophobic emotions are still easily aroused. More recently, the powerful, emotion-laden negative reaction to proposals for gay unions and gay marriage serves to support the idea that homophobia is still a strong current in our culture. The tendency to internalize the negative self-image of the oppressor society and to adopt defensive strategies, some of which are maladaptive, can be seen among some members of these populations as well.

Passing for heterosexual by staying "in the closet" about one's sexual orientation has been one means of surviving in an oppressive and often threatening society. While major strides have been made in establishing a general culture that supports open declaration and presentation of a gay or lesbian sexual orientation, leading many individuals to come out and declare themselves, many still keep their orientation hidden from friends, family, co-counselors, and the community. Such denial leads to Fanon's sense of alienation, as described by Bulhan (1985), from self, culture, and community, which can cause emotional pain and damage. When AIDS strikes, the negative connotation attached to the illness by our society increases the experience of oppression. The long period of time in which this disease was ignored by local and federal governments, a situation that changed only with the spread of AIDS to the majority, white, heterosexual community, is a powerful sign of the depth of oppressive attitudes. Against this backdrop of oppression have emerged encouraging signs of organized resistance by the gay and lesbian community, conforming to the third and healthiest stage of reaction to oppression, as described in Chapter 2.

A stark reminder of this discrimination was faced by every member of the group discussed in the following record of service. They had all served in the armed forces of the United States, where public acknowledgment of their sexual orientation would have led to dismissal. This policy, while modified slightly by the "don't ask, don't tell" position, introduced by the Clinton administration as a compromise, was in force in principle at the time of this writing, although it is not always enforced in practice. For most of the men in this group, their homosexual orientation was kept secret from the units in which they served, from friends, and from their families. Now that they are HIV-positive or diagnosed with AIDS, they face many difficult struggles that have been put off in the face of an oppressive homophobia.

PRACTICE POINTS The reader should note the following key points in these excerpts:

- In an ongoing health-related group in which members have advancing symptoms, open discussion can be difficult as they begin to worry about their own futures.
- Clear examples of flight (humor and distractions from important discussions about the advance of their illness) and fight (anger at the medical establishment) emerge at key moments.
- Intracultural issues emerge for the leader, who is also gay, which leads to his own fight-flight reactions.

Client Description and Time Frame: Support and stabilization group for men, 28–65 years old. All the members have HIV infection and consider themselves to be gay in some capacity. All the members are United States veterans.

Dates Covered in Record: October 16–November 20

Description of the Problem

The group members resist openly addressing issues around HIV/AIDS infection. Although the members identify with being gay, discussions of homosexual lifestyle issues are purposely avoided. Most importantly, the painful feelings associated with watching a fellow group member's health decline are suppressed by the group and not discussed.

The group described here preceded the success of the "triple-therapy" drug treatment and the associated diminishing of symptoms of AIDS and increased hope for at least a greater ability to live with AIDS if not an eventual cure.

October 16

I wanted the group to address their feelings on seeing one of the group members with an advanced stage of AIDS. I knew that Mr. Rooney was having a hard time coming to group due to the fact that some of the members had the physical signs of advanced AIDS. Roughly half the group members were fairly new to this ongoing group of 2 years. I hypothesized that they, too, were struggling with their own acceptance of their diagnosis and were very disturbed at the sight of Mr. Jergen, the member with advanced symptoms, who was hacking, wheezing, and struggling for air when he spoke.

Mr. Rooney, one of the new members, was so uncomfortable with this that he had skipped the meeting prior to this one. When I confronted him about this outside the group, he confirmed my suspicions and only reluctantly agreed to attend the session today. Having just been released from the hospital with a bout of shingles, Mr. Rooney discussed this experience with the group. In being careful not to single out Mr. Rooney, I asked the group how it feels to see each other becoming sick and being forced to spend time in the hospital. There was silence. Mr. Bane asked how bad Mr. Rooney's outbreak of shingles was. Just then, Mr. Downey arrived 20 minutes late, weighted down with lots of packages.

I copped out and allowed the "flight" reaction and the distraction of the late arrival to gloss over my demand for work. Jerry (co-leader) allowed this to take place also in asking what Mr. Downey had brought in all of his packages.

The group leader in this example is also gay and has experienced many personal losses to AIDS. This would be an example of intracultural practice described earlier in this chapter. Examination of the working circumstances in this hospital revealed a lack of social support for staff that contributed to their participation in the same flight-fight behavioral reactions as many of their clients. The counselor's retrospective analysis helps him understand his own participation in the illusion of work.

In the next excerpt, the fight reaction, also designed to avoid pain, emerges as the members attack the poor quality of medical care they feel they are receiving. Because institutional oppression in relation to medical care is a reality for this population, some of what Fanon referred to as "adaptive paranoia" is understandable and necessary. Persistence of this angry reaction on the part of the group members, in the face of evidence to the contrary, can be understood as the fight reaction. While the group members are furious at what they consider poor treatment because they have AIDS, at this stage in the epidemic with the close association between AIDS and homosexuality, believing they are being discriminated against because of their sexual orientation may also be present but has not surfaced directly.

PRACTICE POINTS The leader misses the underlying meaning of the struggle and instead confronts the group members trying to help them see the facts in the case. It is only in retrospective analysis that the counselor recognizes the pain and fear that lay just below the anger. In effect, his effort to convince the group members represented his own version of fight-flight.

November 6

I was forced to confront behavior that allowed a misunderstanding to continue. Mr. Williams needs an operation on his hernia and financially cannot afford to seek alternative medical services outside this agency. After several weeks of scheduled pre-op, appointments, and what was perceived by Mr. Williams as bureaucratic red tape, his operation was canceled. During this period, Mr. Williams took every opportunity in group to discuss the delays he was experiencing, his blame on the system, and the inconvenience of having to live with the hernia. For a while the group began to become incensed with what this implied (i.e., discrimination around not treating someone with HIV infection).

At this juncture, Jerry (co-leader) and I became involved in attempting to come up with a rationale for the indefinite postponement of Mr. Williams's surgery. It was the opinion of the chief of infectious diseases that Mr. Williams's overall health, even without regard to the HIV, was so poor that his risk was greater to have the surgery than to live with the hernia. This was then explained to Mr. Williams's satisfaction by the chief of infectious diseases (Dr. Smith). During the very next group session, Mr. Williams, when asked by Jerry as to his health, began again with blaming the system for his inability to get his surgery. It was at this point that I reminded Mr. Williams of his discussion with Dr. Smith and assured the group that no discrimination had occurred around his HIV infection.

It was during this session that Mr. Tippet had returned to group from a 3-week vacation. He asked Mr. Williams whether or not he had received his operation. Mr. Williams shook his head in disgust and said that the "bureaucrats still haven't gotten it together." Mr. Tippet was enraged at the seemingly bad treatment Mr. Williams had received from the hospital. I waited for a group member to confront Mr. Williams. Mr. Tippet went on about the injustice of it all and looked at me. I said, "It was my understanding that Dr. Smith spoke to Mr. Williams and explained that there were other serious medical considerations apart from HIV that put Mr. Williams more at risk by having the surgery." I asked Mr. Williams for validation. He nodded in agreement. Mr. Tippet thanked me for the clarification and said he felt better about the hospital.

PRACTICE POINTS

The group leader is surprised that the facts of the situation seem to be ignored in the expression of anger toward the "system." He feels it is necessary to represent the hospital and the medical staff rather than explore the apparent disparity between their anger in this specific case and the medical reality.

I felt that Mr. Tippet could not be allowed to continue to think it was the fault of the system for the indefinite delay in Mr. Williams's surgery, especially when the rest of the members were made known of the truth during Mr. Tippet's absence. I was shocked and upset to think that Mr. Williams would choose to continue in this behavior. I could not allow this misconception to continue. It would have created collusion between Mr. Williams and the rest of the group, with the exclusion of Mr. Tippet. If I had this to do over again, I would have put aside my own feelings, considered the second client, and said something like, "It must be very difficult to be forced to manage several different ailments at the same time." Nearly all of these gentlemen could relate to that scenario.

PRACTICE POINTS

The group leader was surprised when the other group members did not confront the member who was angry at the system. This is not surprising at all, if in the terms of Bion's theory, we consider Mr. Williams the group's fight-flight leader. Rather than confronting this member, the group will generally encourage his angry reactions. In the next excerpt, the group leader does address the stigma around homosexuality, and we see the impact of the oppression on the group members' ability to openly deal with their disease and their sexual orientation.

November 13

I wanted to allow the group to explore the feelings attached to the stigma around the HIV infection and the homosexual orientation. Mr. Tippet revealed that only one member of his family knew of his disease. Several other members expressed the same personal situation. Mr. Tippet said that he could only see himself telling one of his sisters about his HIV infection. I said, "Should you decide to tell her, what will you say if she asks how you think you got it?" Mr. Tippet replied, "Well, I'll tell you, Dan; once a man reaches the age of 62 and never marries, then I think it's pretty easy to figure it out." I smiled and asked how he thought his sister would react to the news. Mr. Tippet said he thinks she would be "OK" with it. I asked what the others thought. Mr. Bane began with his own situation regarding disclosure to his brother in a letter he had sent to the Midwest. I allowed him to go on, and Jerry subsequently questioned him further regarding the particulars around the disclosure.

I should have encouraged the group at that moment to look at the feelings associated with the taboo of homosexuality and the attached stigma of an AIDS diagnosis. Something like, "How hard is it for us to talk about this now? Maybe if we can talk about where these bad feelings about being gay come from, then discussing HIV infection with loved ones may not seem like such an impossible task."

PRACTICE POINTS

As the leader becomes more comfortable with opening up discussion in the up-to-now taboo area around their homosexuality and family acceptance, he also decides to address openly the group members' feelings when faced with the deteriorating health of other members. The leader encourages a member who can no longer attend because of his health to come one last time to say good-bye.

November 20

I wanted to attempt to reexplore the feelings behind seeing a few of the members develop full-blown AIDS. Two of the veteran group members had been unable to attend the last few sessions as it became just too much for them logistically to come in. My supervisor and I paid one of these gentlemen a home visit. Mr. Jergen agreed on the next Tuesday to attend the group in conjunction with his scheduled appointments with the HIV clinic. With the aid of a wheelchair, he came in early to attend group with the intent to say good-bye to the other members.

During the session, Mr. Jergen explained that he was taking his leave of the group as it had become too much for him physically to attend. He went on to say that his absence recently illustrated this but that he agreed with my supervisor and me, and he wanted to come in one last time to terminate with the group.

I asked the older members of the group how it feels to see the other original members getting sick and dropping out. Mr. Meany, who rarely speaks up, said that he has been in group for over a year and a half now and that, "At first you tend to feel bad for those who become sick and scared for yourself. You don't want to face it." He went on to say that, after one becomes sick a couple of times and gets well again, you begin to see others getting sick in a different way. Mr. Meany said, "You still feel for those that are too sick to come to group, but you begin to count your blessings that you feel good today." There was silence. I thanked Mr. Meany for his input.

Mr. Victor (who is asymptomatic) said he was also taking his leave of the group because he wants to be around other HIV-infected people that aren't sick. He wants the more upbeat experience from "The Center" downtown. He went on to say that he still feels he needs the support but that he has been with this group for almost 2 years and believes it is time to move on. Jerry (co-leader) said we are sorry to see you go and hope that you decide sometime in the future to come back. Mr. Victor said that he may do that. Much to my surprise, the remaining time in the session was spent vividly discussing the gay affairs each member had while they were in the service.

Where the Problem Stands Now

The group has managed to get at some of those feelings associated with witnessing the decline of a fellow member's health. Mr. Meany's comments were a beginning for the group to attempt to break through that negative group norm. In their defense, there exists no similar example in modern history of how to act when faced with a disease that has the stigma AIDS carries and offers, in most cases, only a slow and, in many instances, painful progression toward death.

If this record were written today, there would be more discussion of living with AIDS and less of the inevitability of an early death, although I doubt that the stigma issue would be very different. The group leader continues his analysis:

Society tells us at best to pity those afflicted with this disease and, at worst, to blame the victim. These men take with them into group the views of our society and an internalized guilt (stigma) for being "deviant" in their homosexual behavior. I believe, based on the last process excerpt (November 20), that ground has been broken in beginning to discuss openly issues around homosexuality and the inevitable progression of the disease which afflicts all the members in some capacity.

PRACTICE SUMMARY Although the group has been able to make some breakthroughs, there is evidence of the impact of the losses faced by the leaders having an impact on their own denial. Working in situations such as this one, with advanced illness, death and dying, and other challenging topics, it is important to develop a support group to assist the co-leaders, and other staff in the system to deal with all of the losses they were experiencing. Increasing attention to the issue of "secondary trauma" experienced by many helping professionals, discussed in Chapter 12, supports this argument. The need for such help became obvious to the counselor after a subsequent meeting, when the very ill member, who was attending a session in conjunction with a clinic visit, deteriorated so quickly that he had to request admission to the hospital. This had a powerful impact on the group and the counselor. In fact, he reported that shortly afterward he had an argument with the patient's admitting nurse, which he later recognized was caused by his struggle to deal with his own pain. This led to first steps to begin his work with the system.

Intercultural Issues: Group Leader–Member Differences

The authority theme needs to be addressed in all groups, but it can take on special significance when the group leader differs in some way from the group members. One example would be when a leader of a substance abuse recovery group has not "walked the walk and talked the talk"—been addicted and participated in some self-help group such as Alcoholics Anonymous. Examples of this difference are discussed in Chapter 14 focusing on substance abuse treatment. In a similar manner, a heterosexual male counselor with a group of gay men, a young counselor with a geriatric group, and a counselor of color leading a group with white members would all be examples of intercultural dimensions to the relationship. Open discussion of issues such as these in the context of the authority theme may be experienced as taboo by both members and the group leader. This can lead to an under-the-surface issue that can grow in power to obstruct the development of the working relationship (or therapeutic alliance) and thus block the full development of the group.

In such cases, it becomes the job of the group leader to challenge the taboo and confront the issue head-on whether never raised, raised indirectly or even raised directly. In the two examples that follow, the first illustrates the importance of addressing the intercultural dimension as a male counselor joins an ongoing group for women who have been abused. In the second, two white female counselors address differences in a group for inner-city African American high school girls.

A Male Counselor Co-leading a Group for Women Who Have Been Abused

This example describes the first session in which a male co-leader joins a female co-leader in an ongoing group for women who are mothers and have been affected by substance abuse of others (e.g., family, spouses). The purpose of the group is to explore their experiences in a supportive atmosphere. Meeting for a year, this group is part of a program that offers concurrent groups for their children and adolescents. All of the members range in age from 29 to 63. Their ethnicity is of Northern European descent, and they are from working-class backgrounds. Attending his first meeting, the new male leader decides to raise the issue of gender after waiting for a period of time.

The group has been working for 20 minutes discussing what they hope to gain from this year's group. None of the members has addressed the fact that I am male and what, if anything, that means to them as individuals and as a group. I asked the group if it was hard to have a male co-leader this year. I noted we had been talking for some time and no one has mentioned this issue.There was a tense silence, and I decided to remain silent. Mickey then states directly that this is the women's group, and she did not want to deal with a "strange man" as this is where she comes to "feel safe with other women" like herself. Patty then states that she is in the process of divorcing her substance-abusing husband and that she has too much to talk about to figure out if "you're OK or not." The other members nod their heads in what I perceive as agreement.

PRACTICE POINTS

The reaction to his comment indicates that there were feelings about his presence that were under the surface and were actually being expressed indirectly by ignoring him. His comment acknowledging the issue opens the door for them to respond. His experience in leading groups and his tuning in help him respond to the comments and the affect in a nondefensive manner.

I ask the group if they are afraid that as a man I won't be able to understand their experiences or feelings of how men may have let them down. The group was silent. I stated that it's a big risk to have a male in the group, and I wouldn't be surprised if you all had questions about trust. Wilma stated that she has no plans to remain silent in the room because a man is in the group. She continues: "I don't know if I want to trust you." The other members of the group vocalize their agreement with Wilma's comments. I respond to the group by stating that they are correct in not trusting me, as trust is something that is earned over time and not given away easily, particularly for women who have had their trust challenged by so many men in their lives. The group members agree some by nodding their heads and others by saying out loud, "That's right!"

It's important to note that this is the second year the group had been meeting. Attempting to introduce a male into the group might have been a greater problem in the first year before trust with the female leader and with each other had been developed. Also, one could argue that the women had to decide for themselves whether having a male co-leader would be helpful or would inhibit the work of the group. In this case, because of the male counselor's directness in addressing the issue and his nondefensiveness, they decided he could stay, and they would put him on "probation" to see how he worked out.

White Female Counselors with African American Inner-City High School Girls

In thinking about the example that follows, of group work with young African American inner-city girls, it is important to put their lives in the context of risk factors, vulnerability, and strengths as presented earlier in this chapter. An early landmark study in developmental psychology involved 698 infants on the Hawaiian island of Kauai who, in 1955, became participants in a 30-year longitudinal study of "how some individuals triumph over physical disadvantages and deprived childhoods" (Werner, 1989, p. 106). Werner stated that the goals that she and her collaborators shared were "to assess the long-term consequences of prenatal and perinatal stress and to document the effects of adverse early rearing conditions on children's physical, cognitive, and psychosocial development" (p. 106). She described their growing interest in resilience as follows:

> But as our study progressed we began to take a special interest in certain "high risk" children who, in spite of exposure to reproductive stress, discordant and impoverished home lives and uneducated, alcoholic, or mentally disturbed parents, went on to develop healthy personalities, stable careers, and strong interpersonal relations. We decided to try to identify the protective factors that contributed to the resilience of these children. (p. 106)

One of the findings indicated that a strong protective factor was having the opportunity to establish a close bond with at least one caretaker who provided positive attending during the first years. These resilient children were found to be "particularly adept at recruiting such surrogate parents when a biological parent was unavailable or incapacitated" (Werner, 1989, p. 108). These children were also able to use their network of neighbors, school friends and teachers, church groups, and so forth to provide emotional support in order to succeed "against the odds" (p. 110).

Werner pointed out that

> [a]s long as the balance between stressful life events and protective factors is favorable, successful adaptation is possible. When stressful events outweigh the protective factors, however, even the most resilient child can have problems. It may be possible to shift the balance from vulnerability to resilience through intervention, either by decreasing exposure to risk factors or stressful events or by increasing the number of protective factors and sources of support that are available. (p. 111)

Researchers and theorists have built on this basic set of ideas: life stressors can lead to negative outcomes for people at high risk; however, personal and environmental factors can buffer the individual, thereby providing the resilience to overcome adversity. Other researchers have applied the basic model to specific populations (as defined by race, ethnicity, etc.), economic status (poverty), or community variables (inner city, level of violence). For example, Daly, Jennings, Beckett, and Leashore (1995) make use of an "Africentric paradigm" to describe an emphasis on collectivity that is expressed as shared concern and responsibility for others: "Scholarship using this perspective identifies positive aspects of African American life richly embedded in spirituality and a world-view that incorporates African traits and commitment to common causes" (p. 241).

In a study of the risk and protective factors associated with gang involvement among urban African American adolescents, researchers found that youths with current or past gang membership documented higher levels of risk involvement, lower levels of resilience, higher exposure to violence, and higher distress symptoms than did youths with no gang affiliations (Li et al., 2002). The findings persisted when controlled for age, gender, and risk involvement. The authors suggest that gang membership itself is associated with increased risk and ill effects on psychological well-being. They also found that strong family involvement and resiliency protects against gang involvement.

Garmezy (1991) focused on the resilience and vulnerability of children in relation to the impact of poverty. He states, "The evidence is sturdy that many children and adults do overcome life's difficulties. Since good outcomes are frequently present in a large number of life histories, it is critical to identify those 'protective' factors that seemingly enable individuals to circumvent life stressors" (p. 421). The author points to a core of variables that serve as resilience factors. These include "warmth, cohesion, and the presence of some caring adults (such as a grandparent) in the absence of responsive parents or in the presence of marked marital discord" (p. 421). Similar findings in studies that examine the resiliency of children who are exposed to poverty and other traumas have identified emotional responsivity in the parent-child relationship as a buffering factor (Egeland, Carlson, & Sroufe, 1993).

In the powerful example that follows, it becomes clear that the young women who are having trouble "managing their anger" have understandable reasons for their rage. They have many of the risk factors—including a history of physical abuse, incest by a parent or sibling, poverty, and gang involvement—and few of the protective factors. It will important for the group leaders to develop a sense of trust and for them to become, at least for a time, that "one adult" who cares who can make a major difference in the lives of these children. While the group leaders' roles and the group itself are only incidents in the lives of these young women, they can be powerful incidents that can help them adopt less understandable and less self-destructive adaptations to the stressors in their lives. These maladaptive behaviors have gotten them in trouble with the legal system.

As is often the case, teens in this situation (on probation for their behavior) are mandated to attend a group with the title of "anger management." They bring with them traumatic experiences in their lives that need to be addressed. The very title of the group implies that they are the problem and they are going to be changed. It is clear from their early reactions that they experience being mandated to the group as a form of punishment.

The two white female counselors must address the authority theme issues, including race and class, if they are to get to the point of developing a culture for work that allows the girls to use the group for mutual aid and the beginning of a healing process. As is also often the case, in reading the group leader's report, we can see that the writer is much too critical of her work in progress and in fact demonstrates important growth in her understanding and skill. Once again, the trick is to reflect on one's practice, learn from mistakes, and then make more sophisticated mistakes.

The reader should note the following:

- The unclear opening statement that leads to "blank faces"
- The purpose originally described as the members' anger problem and terms such as *trigger* and *mandated* used without clear descriptions
- The emergence early of an internal leader challenging the leaders and the group
- The leaders using an "ice breaker" because they are unclear about how to proceed
- The change in the group when the leaders address their differences from the girls and the issue of developing trust with them and with each other

Type of Group: Anger management, psychoeducational, support group

Ages of Members: 15–16 years old

Gender, Ethnic, and Racial Information: All clients are female and African American. These girls were mandated to attend the group either through the courts or probation.

Dates Covered: August 31–October 6

Description of the Problem

The group has had difficulty since the first meeting discussing taboo topics. They are able to perform the educational tasks of the group but are unable to deal with the deeper issues that they are all facing, specifically, the trauma (incest) that they endured in their early childhoods. When the girls do discuss serious topics, they sometimes seem detached. This is an educational group; however, one of the group purposes is to acknowledge trauma and its relation to the anger that the girls experience.

How the Problem Came to the Attention of the Group Leader(s)

From the first meeting, it was clear that girls were uncomfortable discussing anything of a personal nature, which was understandable because it was the first time that we had all met. The only topics that the girls were really willing to discuss were issues such as the movies that they liked or where they went to school. When we tried to approach the subject of why the girls were there, they would only say that they had to be. We were hoping that they would explain what offense they had committed, if any, so that they could see that they were not alone. This pattern generally continued throughout the next three sessions. Anytime a personal subject was approached, the girls would "attack" or question my co-facilitator and myself. This pattern continued until about the fifth session, when we really got to the heart of the issues. The only hope that I did have for the girls was because they would—once in a while—share a small amount of personal information but then clam up.

Note that the leaders are unclear in their opening statement in the first meeting and that they avoid two powerful issues: the group members are mandated, and the group leaders are white. Although acknowledging the mandated nature of the attendance, they try to move past it too quickly. The term *mandated* may also need to be explained. The blank faces are a result of the use of jargon to explain the group's purpose and the lack of reaching for the group members' possible connections to the work.

Summary of the Work

First Session: Attempting to Establish Role and Purpose

I was nervous because this was my first time co-facilitating a group of this type and with this age group. As the group members began to trickle in, I immediately realized that they were all female and they were all African American. I was surprised at this mostly because there were 15 people scheduled to attend, and only 5 females had shown up. After the group members sat down and seemed ready to start (they were staring at me and co-facilitator Kim), I stated the basic purpose of the group:

"As you all know, this group is called Anger Management, but what I want to clarify is that we are not here to teach you how not to be angry. We are here for the next 6 weeks to discuss why we as humans get angry, and how we can better prepare ourselves to handle the situations that make us angry. Basically, what we are going to try to do is give you some tools to help manage those triggers or things that make you angry in different ways."

After I finished talking, I looked around the room at a bunch of blank faces. The girls seemed to be confused by what I had said, so I asked the group if they had any questions or if they wanted to comment on anything. Again, the girls' faces were blank, and no one said anything. I was beginning to get nervous because of the silence, but I let it go on for about another minute and then stated, "I realize that most of you are mandated to be here either by the courts or probation, so basically you have to be here. As much as most of you don't want to be here, I think that most of us could benefit from learning new ways to deal with our anger even if we don't think we have a problem." Almost before I finished talking, one of the girls—Monica—spoke up: "You're right, I don't want to be here, and I don't need to be here." This sentence was accompanied by nods of agreement from the other girls. At this point, I looked to my co-facilitator for some assistance. Kim promptly stated that the girls should give the group a chance and at least try to make it through the first meeting to see what they think.

This statement prompted another response from Monica: "What is it gonna matter if we decide we want to stay or not? We have to be here. I really just think it's stupid that I have to sit here with people I don't know and learn from two old women how I'm supposed to act." At this point, I was feeling defensive and somewhat out of ideas, so I suggested that we go around the room and discuss what had brought the girls to the group. The girls did complete this exercise, but they would only say that they had to be there because a particular judge or probation officer "said I had to." After that, we proceeded to complete an icebreaker. The rest of the session went relatively well once the girls began discussing things other than the group, such as movies, music, and so forth. We finished the group by establishing group rules (which were determined by the girls, except for the rule of confidentiality, which was established by Kim and me).

PRACTICE POINTS Both leaders are in the mid-20s, so the comment by Monica about "two old women" may really stand for two white women. The leader uses after-session reflection to tune in to the meaning of the exchange.

When Monica spoke, I hadn't realized what she was trying to tell me, or to ask me, which was basically, Who are you, and what are you doing here? When she said "two old women," I should have realized that she was taking on the authority theme, which is basically "issues related to the relationship between the client, the group, and the counselor." Not only was she questioning our ages, she was also questioning the color of our skin. Kim and I are both white women who are at least 10 years older than the group members. Had I realized this, or picked up on the underlying theme or statement, the session probably would have gone a little better. Looking back on the situation, I realize that I was "ducking" her question. Had I picked up on what she was saying, I would have been able to recognize her feelings and possibly the feelings of the rest of the group members. In the next session, Monica brought this up again, and luckily I was able to "get" the issue.

PRACTICE POINTS

In a striking example of how a group leader can honestly examine her work, rather than blame the group members, this leader identifies a number of crucial issues that need to be addressed. Race, age, and the mandated nature of the group are all issues that unless discussed can block the ability of the group to move past the formation stage and the authority theme. Note also the use of the word *mandated*, which, as already mentioned, the members may not understand because it is a technical term and part of our jargon. A slight change to "forced by a judge or probation officer to be here" would be clearer to the members.

Also, it helps in situations such as this one to point out although they were ordered to attend, no one can make them really participate. That is up to them. With courage, the leaders catch their mistake and jump in feet-first, in particular, addressing intercultural issues as white, older (comparatively), and middle-class group leaders.

Second Session

After the first session, I was feeling even more nervous because of the feelings the girls had about being in the group. I wanted them to realize that they all had similar issues and could discuss them with one another. I was aware that they had all been sexually abused in their early childhood. I was also aware that this type of trauma could lead to the types of acting-out behaviors that landed them in the group. I wanted the girls to be able to see this without having to discuss the issue—first, because I didn't want them to be embarrassed about the topic, but also because I didn't want any of the girls to think that I was breaching confidentiality.

I opened the session by asking the girls to go around the room and say one thing about their week. The girls did this with no problems until it came to Monica, who stated, "Why do you care about my week? None of you would understand what I'm going through anyway." I responded by asking Monica if she was concerned that Kim and I wouldn't understand because we are white and much older than her. Monica said that was part of it and that we both come from places that are different than where she lives. At this point, we were right in the thick of the authority theme (once again).

I said, "Monica, I realize that Kim and I may look different than you, and we are. And, to be completely honest with you, we probably won't understand all of the time what you or any of the other members are experiencing. The only thing that I can tell you is that we want to try and understand, but that we can only do that if you'll give us the chance." Monica seemed happy with this statement and one of the girls—April—raised her hand. Kim told her that she didn't have to raise her hand if she wanted to talk and reminded her that we had established that last week. April then said, "I get what you are saying, but how do we know that any of the rest of us have anything in common?" The other three girls nodded their heads in agreement with this. I asked the girls if they all felt that way, and, if so, what could we do to make it more comfortable for them to share?

By articulating the underlying issues of age, race, and background in a nondefensive manner, the group leaders grant permission for the issue to emerge. Monica, who takes on the authority theme directly, might be experienced by some group leaders as the "deviant member." But as pointed out in Chapter 7, this difficult member may be the group leader's ally and be serving as an internal leader. In addition to directly raising trust with the leaders, she also raises the second major issue in the group: trust with each other.

> The girls all started talking at once. Kim then asked if they could talk one at a time. Once again, Monica spoke up: "Really, does it matter if we have anything in common? I'm not going to be sharing anything in here anyway." At this point, Kim again explained the rules and limits of confidentiality, and that we all had to feel safe if any of us were going to share. Kim also explained that no one had to share until she felt comfortable doing so. The girls agreed, and Kim asked them if it was OK to move on. Once again, they agreed.
>
> The issues of intimacy and trust were very strong during this session, and I wasn't tuned in to them. If I could go back, I would have discussed these issues with the girls in the first session and been better prepared to address it in the second session. I should mention here that one of the girls—Lisa—was not at this session. We found out later that she was sent to detention and would not be back for the rest of the group meetings.

As is often the case, new group leaders are oversensitive to what they feel they have done wrong and are not comfortable crediting what they have done right. This second session represented a crucial breakthrough for the leaders and members, as they started to develop the working relationship they would need to create the trust and the culture for the more difficult sharing. They had the courage to put the taboo yet crucial issues of racial and social class differences on the table, which began to lessen their negative impact. They use the next session to return to issues of purpose and their role. The loss of members, one having been returned to the detention center for violating probation, impacts the remaining members with force.

Third Session: Establishing Rapport and Trust; Trying to Reclarify Purpose and Role

At the start of the group, I opened by explaining to the girls that we had lost two members and that they would be the only three left for the rest of the group. This statement prompted a tirade of questions about what happened to the girls. I explained to them that Lisa was in detention, and I did not know when she would be out (I had previously received permission from Lisa to explain to the girls why she was not there). As I looked around the room, the girls were all looking down at their feet and not saying a word.

I asked, "Is everything all right? I'm wondering if you all are sad or scared for Lisa. Have any of you ever been in detention?" Monica (who seems to have become my internal leader) said very quietly, "Yes." Once she stated this, the other two girls nodded their heads in agreement. I said, "It seems that all of you have been in detention—do you think that we could talk about why you were in detention?" The girls jumped at this; all at once, they tried to tell their stories. All three of their stories were very similar: the girls had gotten into fights at school, and the judge sent them to detention (it was not the first time any of them had been arrested for assault). The girls used the remainder of the group to discuss their time spent in detention and how they never wanted to go back.

Toward the end of the group, once the girls had settled down, I noticed that Monica was very quiet; she had been quite talkative in the previous sessions. Monica explained to the other two girls, April and Samantha, that she had spent 5 days in an adult county jail. As she went through the experience of being there with the girls, I realized that she was beginning to build trust with all of us. While she talked, the other two girls sat mesmerized by her words—they looked frightened and intrigued at the same time.

PRACTICE POINTS

The discussion is both powerful and frightening. As Monica describes women in the jail performing sexual favors for guards, it provokes a flight reaction from April, who begins to laugh. For young women who have experienced incest, in which a parent they were supposed to be able to trust took advantage of them, this discussion of women in prison being sexually abused by guards who are also in a position of authority had to evoke powerful emotions.

I began to notice that April was laughing and finally asked her why. April said that it was just funny the way that Monica was explaining how the women in the jail would perform sexual favors for the guards. Kim and I let her continue to laugh. For the rest of the group, Monica finished her story, and we all thanked her for sharing.

Once again, I had missed an opportunity to address the feelings that not only April may have been feeling, but Samantha and Monica as well. When April was laughing at what Monica was saying, I realized (looking back) that she was avoiding the importance and significance of what Monica was telling her—that it is scary being in an adult jail. I think that the feelings were becoming too real. These girls were getting older and approaching an age at which they would no longer be sent to detention or juvenile hall. I felt, at the time, that she was avoiding doing the work, but really she was expressing to me that she couldn't deal with the reality of the situation: that it was scary for her.

PRACTICE POINTS

Since this group is semistructured with agenda items set for discussion, the leaders decide to move ahead and raise the question of "forgiveness." With some level of trust between the group members and the leaders, and between each of the members resulting from the serious conversation the previous week, the topic evokes a powerful and negative response.

Fourth Session

Once Monica had broken the ice and started discussing some deeper issues, Kim and I realized that we should try to tackle the topic of forgiveness. Because the groups are set up to follow a certain structure with specific topics for each week, Kim and I decided to jump ahead and try to tackle the idea of forgiveness ahead of schedule. We chose to do this because forgiveness is such a strong topic that we wanted to be able to devote as many of the last sessions to it as we needed to.

Forgiveness in this context is an attempt at helping clients to move past the trauma or any bad experiences in their lives. After the 5 minutes of usual chitchat, the girls took their seats and Kim stated that we were going to discuss forgiveness. The girls looked very perplexed, so I decided I would try to explain to them what that meant: "You are probably wondering why the heck we are going to talk about forgiveness in an anger management class. Well, the reason we discuss it is because sometimes things happen to us in our lives that are bad, and sometimes we can't move past those experiences. Forgiveness to me means that we try to move past those experiences and not let the experience or person keep us down. I also want you girls to know that I am not saying that you need to walk up to whoever and say, 'I forgive you,' but to be able to say to yourself that the person or experience or situation isn't going to hurt you anymore." I then asked the girls if any of them had an experience that they could think of that they would like to talk about.

Monica started talking right away. It was at this point that Monica said, "I hope you don't think I'm ever going to forgive my f—in' father—when he's dead, I'll forgive him." I asked Monica if she was saying that because she was still angry with him for some of the things that he had done to her. Monica agreed. I then asked her if she would mind sharing a little bit about what happened. She began explaining a situation with her father. When she was very little, he had broken her arm in five different places because he was trying to keep his beer from rolling down the hill, and he slammed her arm in the car door. She went on to explain that, when she was 10 years old, her stepbrother had molested her; her father knew about it and didn't do anything.

The discussion has taken a powerful turn as Monica, again an internal leader, begins to describe her physical and sexual abuse. It is important that the leaders monitor the impact this disclosure has on the other members since they also have experienced trauma. The leader picks up April's nonverbal cues and reaches for her feelings.

While Monica was telling these stories, April was looking at the floor. She also looked very upset, and I was pretty sure that she had tears in her eyes. Monica was still talking, so I said, "I'm sorry to interrupt you, Monica, but I wanted to ask April a question. April, are you OK? You seem to be very upset right now, and I'm wondering if it's because you can relate to what Monica is saying." April looked at Monica and said, "I'm never going to forgive my father, either, or my mother." April looked back at me and said, "Why should I do that? You don't understand, and neither does she." I sat there for a minute, not really knowing what to say. Before I could respond, Kim said to April, "You're right—we don't understand."

Then Monica chimed in and said, "How could either of you possibly understand what happens in our lives?" I responded to the girls by saying, "Kim is right, and so are both of you. We don't understand what happens or has happened to either of you, because we aren't you. We haven't lived the same lives that you two have, and, even if we did, our lives would be different—no one experiences things the same way." Monica and April looked from Kim to me, waiting for one of us to say something. Finally, I said to both girls that sometimes people may not understand you, but you need to give people a chance. Help us to understand you by letting us know what's going on. Both girls nodded their heads in agreement. This session was truly powerful. Monica had shared a very traumatic experience with April, Kim, and me. Even though April was unwilling to share, it was an important moment in the group. After reflecting on this situation, I have come to realize that the girls were probably shocked by their own honesty and felt the need to retreat.

One can easily understand the anger carried around by these girls. Expressions of rage and escalation of negative behavior are often a call for help. They will continue until someone hears the hurt and begins to respond to the meaning of the behavior. These two group leaders are quickly learning that persistent and ongoing oppression and trauma can lead to expressions of anger that are then responded to by the systems (e.g., school, juvenile justice) as the problem, which misses the underlying message.

Fifth Session

When the girls first came in and took their seats, they were very quiet. I began the session by stating that I was so proud that they had shared last week. I also thanked them for being so open and honest and acknowledged that it must not have been easy for them to share such painful memories. The girls just kept staring at me. At that point, Monica and Samantha and April began chatting about their week, and they were unusually loud while they were talking. They were also using some very foul language, which usually Kim and I do not mind, but the way that they were speaking was disrespectful. They were calling other people derogatory names.

PRACTICE POINTS The members were using the painful n-word that had become part of their street culture. I believe that this use of the term in this meeting was significant and that they were actually raising another issue for their two white counselors that had to do with race and self-image. This is missed by the counselors, who probably have their own uncomfortable feelings in relation to the term and its racist connotations, particularly when used by Caucasians. Understanding that this is the next-to-last meeting, the counselors are tuned into the issues involved in ending the group. They reach for them as part of the ending process.

Kim asked them if they could settle down so that we could get to work. The girls ignored Kim's statement. At that point, I again asked them if they could finish their stories so that we could start talking as a group. The girls finished their stories and sat down. Kim and I began discussing some relapse prevention techniques with the girls. When the girls were asked for their feedback, no one spoke. They remained silent for about 1 minute. Kim and I also chose to remain silent. Finally, I asked the girls if they were acting the way they were because they realized that the next week would be our last session. Monica spoke up (as usual) and stated that she was sad that we would not be able to see one another anymore and that she was going to miss coming to the group. April then stated that she was worried that she wouldn't have anyone to talk to about her week and no one to tell when she had used the tools that we had taught her.

Kim and I were both stunned by these honest comments. Samantha then stated that she was going to miss the next week. At this point, I felt very angry and asked her why. She stated that she just couldn't be there. I chose to ignore this comment, and we continued on with the work. The session ended with a relaxation technique, and the girls were still not acting as they normally did. We reminded them before they left that we would have pizza and pop at the last meeting, and to bring anything in that they wanted to eat.

What happened during this session was very profound. The girls realized that we would no longer be meeting and were unable to function as they normally did. It was an important communication when April stated that she wouldn't have anyone to talk to, and I didn't grab that moment. It would have been very beneficial for me to discuss with April people in her life who she felt that she could talk to and, if she didn't have anyone, how we could help her develop new relationships with people whom she felt she could confide in and share her triumphs with. I was also, on reflection, very upset with myself for getting angry with Samantha. When I discussed the group with Kim after the girls left, it dawned on us that Samantha was saying that she wasn't going to come to the meeting because she knew that, if she missed it, she would have to repeat the whole program.

That communication from her was an opening to discuss how hard ending can be, and yet I missed it.

Sixth Session: Endings and Transitions

All three girls showed up to this session, and Kim and I immediately acknowledged that we were happy that they came and that we knew that it would be hard to say good-bye. We also discussed with the girls that they were free to contact us in the office if they ever needed any help. Monica said that she appreciated this, and April and Samantha smiled and nodded in agreement. We spent the rest of the session discussing whom the girls had in their lives as support and felt that they could talk to. Monica identified her mother as someone that she could count on and talk to if she had a problem. April identified her grandmother as a support, and, after some prodding, she also disclosed that she had a really good relationship with her counselor at school and that she could talk to her. Samantha also identified her mother as a support but stated that she wished that she could still come and see us every week.

I thanked Samantha for saying that and told her that I would miss her and the other girls as well. I continued by stating that, although we had only known the girls for 6 weeks, I felt that we had developed a great relationship and that I would think about them from time to time and wonder how they were doing. At this point, the girls were smiling, and I could tell that I had finally answered the question that they had been asking all along: Who was I, and would I care about them? I think I answered that question with those words. The rest of the group went smoothly; we spent the time discussing the girls' school and the different interests that they held, we ate pizza, and the girls filled out the postsurveys.

At the end of the group, Kim told the girls how much progress they had made and that the fact that they were so honest really helped all of us to get to know one another. I then stated that I thought it was wonderful that three girls who didn't know one another ended up being friends over a period of 6 weeks. We then gave each of the girls a hug and told them to call us if they ever needed anything. Samantha stated, "I wish that we could still come, but I'm glad that I got to know you guys for as long as I did." Monica chimed in, "I'm really going to miss you two white ladies." This got us all laughing, and April stated, "I didn't think that I would ever like two white ladies from the suburbs, but I gotta say I'm really gonna miss you guys." At this point, Kim and I both had tears in our eyes. I told the girls that I appreciated that they gave us a chance and hoped that they would continue to do that with other people in their lives. The girls nodded, and, with that, they were out the door.

PRACTICE SUMMARY

I sometimes wonder if new group leaders need a session on forgiveness, but with a focus on forgiving *themselves* for mistakes they make as new group leaders. The growth in understanding and skill, in dealing with very volatile and taboo issues—race, class, and sexual abuse—is a tribute to their courage and willingness to examine their own practice with honesty. They did very well in catching their mistakes and going back and correcting them. One of these co-leaders went on to work in an inner-city, school-based violence prevention project that I directed, so I am aware of her continued growth in her practice. An example of her work with a similar-aged group of girls is shared in the school counseling chapter. One can see she is now making more sophisticated mistakes.

Intracultural Issues: When the Group Leader Is the Same as Group Members

Earlier in the chapter, I introduced the idea of intracultural issues and their impact on group leadership. For example, in the illustration of the group for homosexual veterans with AIDS, the group leader, also gay, had to deal with his own feelings of loss of close friends to the illness in order to assist the group members in dealing with a member's death. In another painful example, an African American group leader in an inner-city school setting group for acting-out teens had to address indirect and then direct accusations that he was a "sell-out" and an "Oreo"—black on the outside and white on the inside—when group members raised these charges. What made it particularly painful for this group leader was his own struggle in trying to answer the question "Am I selling out?" In another example, a Latina leader in a group for Latina women had to address early accusations that the "white counselors" in the agency were biased against Hispanics. Dealing with the intracultural issues was particularly difficult because the group leader, at times, also perceived this agency racism. In later chapters, we will explore the importance of professionals not accepting such views and instead considering the agency or other setting as the "second client" needing a skillful intervention at least as much as the group members.

In the next example, an African American group leader of African American clients has to address the subtle and not-so-subtle comments on their experiences of what they perceive as racism on the part of their white welfare counselors. Her first response is to defend her colleagues even though she has similar concerns about racial attitudes in the agency.

African American Clients: Dealing with Issues of Authority and Racism

In the following example, an African American counselor leads a group for mothers on welfare, who are also African Americans, for the purpose of providing mutual aid on the problems of living on welfare. After some angry discussions about husbands who leave them all the bills and courts that garnish their wages if they work, they get to the authority issue in relation to their welfare counselors.

 PRACTICE POINTS Once again, the relationship to the group leader is raised indirectly by referring to another counselor. In addition, the taboo area of racism is broached as members describe a white counselor as racist. This is a classic dilemma for the group leader who, on the one hand, has experienced the prejudice and racism described by the clients but, on the other, feels a professional allegiance to the system of which she is part. After some initial defensiveness, she finally addresses the underlying issues.

> MRS. SMITH: I didn't know about Legal Aid until I got involved in the welfare rights group.
>
> MRS. MARTIN: Your counselor doesn't tell you anything. They always say they don't know. Well, what do they know? They're supposed to be trained and have an education.
>
> MRS. SMITH: They [counselors] are too young; they're not mature, and they are not exposed to life. What do they know about life and especially our problems?

> MRS. BROWN: How can I tell that child [the counselor] my real problems if I don't think she cares?
>
> MRS. SMITH: (To the group leader) Can't you get some older people to work instead of those young children?
>
> GROUP LEADER: Are you saying that because your counselor is young, she is not capable of being a good counselor? (Silence)
>
> GROUP LEADER: Sometimes, you know, it's hard to teach old dogs new tricks. We find that young people are not as set in their ways. Of course, there are exceptions to this rule. (Silence—a long one)
>
> GROUP LEADER: Are you trying to say something to me that you really have not stated?
>
> MRS. MARTIN: She [the counselor] is prejudiced. She doesn't like blacks.

PRACTICE POINTS

The group leader caught her initial defensiveness toward the anger directed at the other counselor and reached inside the silence for the unstated communication. Other group members countered Mrs. Martin's opinion of this counselor, offering examples of situations in which she had been helpful. Most of these were younger women. The group member has risked a powerful issue in sharing her feelings about the counselor's prejudice. The group leader was also African American, which may have been the reason for the member's honesty. The group leader remained defensive, however, and began to challenge Mrs. Martin, thus cutting off an important area for discussion.

> GROUP LEADER: Have you ever discussed this with your counselor?
>
> MRS. MARTIN: I sure did. I told her off good.
>
> GROUP LEADER: In the same manner in which you're speaking now?
>
> MRS. MARTIN: I sure didn't bite my tongue.
>
> GROUP LEADER: Then you were rude to her, yes? (Silence)
>
> GROUP LEADER: How would you feel if you were the counselor and she spoke to you in that manner? (Silence) Respect has nothing to do with age or color; it's a two-way street. (Silence)

PRACTICE POINTS

One of the members commented to Mrs. Martin that she thought she was wrong about the counselor, and this statement was followed by a quick change in the discussion. The group leader had not allowed this difficult area to be opened up and had not demonstrated an understanding of the client's perception. She felt required to identify with the other counselor, and perhaps even more so because she was African American and the other counselor was white. This is an example of an intracultural dilemma that can occur when counselors are dealing with someone who is the same as them (as opposed to intercultural). Professionals of color have told me that they feel a particular defensiveness in this area because they may privately agree that the other counselors in their own agency or other setting can be racist, or at least not ethnically sensitive in their practice. Before they can help their clients deal with intercultural issues, they must face their own.

In addition, in this example, the counselor did not reach for the implied question about her role and her authority. The discussion continued with complaints about the amount of money available, the difficulty of making ends meet, and so on. As each theme emerged, the group leader responded with a lecture or some advice, which was followed by silence. Each silence contained the message "You really don't understand."

As the group members sensed the group leader's honesty and directness, however, they began to take her on. For example, when they complained about making ends meet, the group leader asked them if they made out a list of what they needed at the end of the month before they went shopping. The response was "I need everything by the end of the month; the cupboard is bare. I don't need a list!" This was said with good nature, and the group members laughed in agreement. Their energy level was high, and as the group leader accepted their comments about her suggestions, laughing with them rather than getting angry, they warmed to her and took her on with even more gusto. Finally, after one piece of advice near the end of the meeting, there was a silence and the following exchange:

> **MRS. SMITH:** You see, Mrs. Powell, you just don't understand.
>
> **GROUP LEADER:** I was wondering when someone was going to say that. (The group members all broke up in laughter.)

Even though the group leader responded defensively at times and missed the indirect cues about her authority, the group members seemed to sense her honesty and her genuine concern for them. Her willingness to enter exchanges with them, to give and to take in the discussions, and to maintain her sense of humor helped overcome her early efforts at preaching and sermonizing. The group continued to meet, and as the leader become clearer about her function and demonstrated her capacity for empathy, the work improved. The important point is that group members can forgive a group leader's mistakes if they sense his or her genuine concern and honesty.

In my years of working with graduates of professional schools, one theme has remained constant. While many had experienced some discussion of intercultural practice, rarely had they had discussions of practice that was intracultural in nature. Many graduates of color described, when asked, how painful an area this could be and how helpful it would have been to have included it in the curriculum. This was true for others who also experienced minority status of one kind or another that would have a powerful impact on their practice.

Inter- and Intracultural Issues Between Group Members

Inter- and intracultural issues can emerge between members of the group as well as between the group leader and the members. For example, a group may polarize according to ethnicity, race, and, as in the next example, gender. This can lead to a negative impact on what was described in Chapter 8 as the members' alliance with the group-as-a-whole.

The following illustration takes place in a housing complex for the elderly sponsored by a community mental health agency. Most of the participants are of the same ethnicity (Jewish), but they divide along two dimensions. The first is gender, where the men bring a different perspective on the complex issues involved in living together. The second is length of time in the residence. A conflict emerges between the longer-term residents and new residents on the issue of making friends with neighbors.

Housing Complex Group for Elderly Persons

When elderly people leave their own homes to move into a residential complex, they are making a difficult transition stage in the life cycle. Familiar housing, neighbors, friends, and relatives may all be gone, leaving the person feeling lonely and lost. Recognizing the stress associated with this stage of life, the following group was organized specifically to deal with the issue of "Getting Along with Your Neighbor." In this example, the new group members are also new to the complex. The relationship to the group may well parallel their relationship to their new community.

> **CLIENT DESCRIPTION AND TIME FRAME:** This group was set up as a Growth and Education/ Support (short-term: 6 weeks) group for clients who ranged in age from 70 to 81 years old. Six were women and three were men; the group was primarily Jewish, with one Christian woman. All members were white. The dates covered in the record are from March 27 to April 24.

Description of the Problem

The group, called "Getting Along with Your Neighbor," was designed for residents of an elderly housing complex, to talk about their issues and concerns related to living in a community setting. The early culture of the group was a reflection of the culture of the housing community, and this has created some obstacles to mutual aid and productive work. Lines of division are made between the new (3 months to 1 year) and long-term (5–11 years) residents, between men and women, and between those who have developed support systems and those who have not. Other aspects of the culture that hinder mutual aid are judgment, gossip, and false assumptions. The taboo areas of loneliness, loss, and despair are fears they all have in common at this stage in their life cycle. Yet, unless the group norms shift, they will have difficulty offering support to each other in a meaningful way.

How the Problem Came to the Attention of the Group Leader(s)

The members of the group were having difficulty listening to each other without disagreeing, negating, or judging the others' comments. The lines were revealed almost immediately when one of the male members (Lou), a newcomer to the housing complex, said in the first session, "What I see is a big division between the men and the women. Most of us are lonely, and we need to get the men and the women together here." Some of the responses he got back were "Speak for yourself!" "Who needs men?" "He's new here," and "If you don't have any friends here, it's your own fault; there are plenty of opportunities to meet people."

PRACTICE POINTS The longer-term residents were defensive of their relative stability and were threatened by the more obvious vulnerability of the newcomers. This dynamic was repeated, with variations on a theme, for the first several group sessions. Once again we see the dynamic where process and content are integrated. In a group entitled "Getting Along with Your Neighbor," the members act out exactly how they don't get along. The group leader opens with a clear statement of purpose.

March 27 (First Session)

After welcoming everyone, I asked if anyone had been in a group before, and most of them raised their hands. I said that the name of this group is "Getting Along with Your Neighbor," and the purpose of being together is to talk about the benefits and difficulties of living in a community setting and the quality of relationships with others. I said that the group was their group, that the purpose was certainly broad enough so that the specific focus of discussion could be up to them. I explained that there were two main rules of the group, the first being confidentiality—that whatever is said in the group stays in the group; in other words, you can say you are in this group, but don't mention specific people or what someone else said. The other rule is, although this is a group about getting along with your neighbor, please do not mention specific people that are not in this group. This way, we avoid gossip and make it safe for people to share here. All agreed to these ground rules.

I tried to open the discussion by asking what I thought was a fairly tame question to break the ice. I asked the members to go around and say briefly how long they had lived in these apartments and where they had come from. After everyone had stated this, Lou said, "I'm here on behalf of the men's group, and we feel that the men and women are divided here. Most of us are lonely, and we need to get the women and men together. It's not natural to drift apart." Marie said, "Speak for yourself—I'm not lonely." Bea said, "Who needs men?" Anne said, "How long have you lived here?" I could see the group splitting on this issue.

PRACTICE POINTS   Noting that the group process is not going exactly as she had imagined it, the counselor tries to get the process under control. An alternative would be to point out that the group actually consisted of subgroups: long-term and short-term residents and men and women: "Each group may be experiencing living together differently."

I tried to introduce a way they could communicate that would allow for diversity of opinions. I suggested that they only try to speak for themselves and not for others. I added that each person is entitled to their opinions and feelings, and we need to respect that in this group. Although they were not afraid to speak up, there was no affective empathy for each other in their communication. I missed a lot of their initial hints of issues to "reach for" because I felt overwhelmed, and I stayed general. Murray said that he had been here a year and still hadn't met many people, and that the people here keep to themselves and barely say hello. Eva said she had many friends: "You just have to put yourself out there; it goes both ways." Mini said, "I agree with Murray. I've had a difficult time because of cliques." Bea said, "This is a wonderful place. You can't complain." I said, "What are some of the ways to meet people or feel more involved in activities?"

April 3 (Second Session)

Murray said again that he didn't find this a friendly place and that he would say hello and some people would walk right by. Ruth said, "Sometimes they can't hear you. I don't take it personally; I say hello to everyone anyway." I said, "It sounds like there are lots of different ways to interpret another's behavior." Eva said, "Not everyone is going to be your friend. It's got to be mutual." I asked, "What kind of behavior is supportive?" Bea said, "I like my friends to call me up and ask how I'm doing today." Mini said, "I don't have that kind of relationship with anyone here. I would feel like I was intruding to call up every day." Morris said, "I think there's a difference between friends and acquaintances."

Lou said, "The women, many of them, just sit around and play cards, and I think a man in their life, to call up and say 'How are you?' would make them feel good." Bea said, "Who cares if they play cards all day? If that's what they want to do, they're entitled." Marie said, "I had enough cooking and doing laundry, thank you." Lou said, "They are addicted to cards, some of them." I said, "Lou, you are going to have to speak for yourself only. I think that's why you get jumped on, because of the way you're saying it."

I felt stuck on how to handle the male/female conflict, so I just let them talk. Murray said, "What do you think if a man comes up to you and says hello?" Mini said, "I'd say hello back." Lou said, "If I'm the only one in an elevator with a woman, she looks at me like I'm going to molest her or something." Marie said, "Don't be ridiculous!" Lou said, "I'm serious." Eva said, "Some of the men here do just want to get their slippers under your bed." Murray said, "I'm just looking for friendship, but it seems the ladies don't really want to talk to the men." Mini said, "You have to understand, we were brought up not to be aggressive with men. I envy your [the group leader's] generation, which is much more outgoing. Women don't go to men first, and if they do, people talk."

PRACTICE POINTS

The discussion is raising an important issue about relationships between men and women at this stage of the life cycle and the difficulty in developing cross-gender intimacy without it leading to sexual relationship. Mini raises the very different culture these elderly men and women experienced in their lifetime and the obstacles presented to reaching out. This would be a good issue for discussion. The group leader does pick up the concern about gossip and raises it directly.

I said, "So how does gossip or fear of gossip affect your behavior?" Murray said, "I invited this one lady to my apartment for a cup of tea, and she said she doesn't go to men's apartments." Eva said, "You have people who meet here and become a couple. People talk at first, but so what?" Ruth said, "I don't let it bother me." Bea said, "If you want to be human and you want to talk to somebody, you've got to stick to your convictions regardless of what people are going to say."

PRACTICE POINTS

In the next session, as the relationships between counselor and group members and between some group members develop, the themes in groups for the elderly described earlier in the chapter begin to emerge. Bea becomes the "emotional leader," talking about losses of family members and physical ability. The leader's intervention is an example of sessional contracting.

April 10 (Third Session)

I asked if anyone had anything on their mind that they've been thinking about between sessions that they wanted to share with the group. Bea said she had lost her sister-in-law this week and wanted to thank the people who were supportive to her, that it really made a difference. I said, "Last week we talked about being supportive versus being intrusive. I hear you saying that you appreciated people reaching out to you." She said, "You know, I've been thinking about this adjustment that the new people are saying. But your whole life is an adjustment, from the moment you are born 'til the moment you go. When I first came here, I was walking with a cane. I had big plans for when I retired; I was going to travel and volunteer. But as you see, I'm now in a wheelchair. But you can't dwell in the past. I have a lot of friends here; you just have to put yourself out there." Her sharing changed the mood of the group; the members were really listening.

Lou got up out of his chair and went to shake Bea's hand. Lou said, "You are an inspiration, Bea. I know, because my wife—God rest her soul—she died last year. She was in a wheelchair, and she was so ashamed that she wouldn't even go out of the house. So I congratulate you for being out there and participating in things." Lou sat back down and his eyes teared up. I said, "Lou, thank you for being so open with us."

PRACTICE POINTS We can now see that Lou has been dealing not only with a new living situation but also with the loss of his wife. Lou's "first offerings" are about the difficulty in making new connections, while his "second offering", put more clearly in this session, is about the losses in his life. This is a profound loss that most members of the group, men and women, have also experienced. The leader at this point could have made that connection by noting that area of common ground. This would be an example of being with the individual (Lou) and the group at the same time. In the next session, the leader recognizes her difficulty in being with Lou because of his often negative impact on the group. She decided to change that.

April 17 (Fourth Session)

I realized that I was uncomfortable when Lou spoke because he tended to make the group members defensive. I decided to model nonjudgmental, patient listening as a way to help further the group. Lou said, "We have the settled residents and the new residents; I think we can all agree on that. The settled residents are more contented—they have had sufficient time to make lifetime friends. In other words, they are established here. Now we have the new residents. I'm here 4 months, and I'm lonely. Settled people know the ropes; I, on the other hand, lack that. There are a lot of people in my position, and I think the staff should do something further than the twice-a-year orientations. Maybe make a list of newcomers so we can contact them over the phone."

I said, "Let's keep whatever specific planning you might organize for later. I like what you are saying, though, because I think it would be useful to get a discussion going that helps us understand each other better." Bea said, "We all came in new like you. This place is not a country club; they don't have to provide you with friends; that's up to the individual. When I came here 5 years ago, I went downstairs every day and talked to people. You can't expect the staff to provide for your social activities, your loneliness, and your moods. It's an apartment building." I said, "Is that what you are saying, Lou?" Lou said, "Well, you see, this lady, God bless her, is not the shy type. Now there are many people that are, and don't have the nerve that this lady has." Ruth said, "Anyone who is lonely, it's their own fault. You have to reach out." I said, "What was it like when you first came?" Ruth said, "I was shy; I didn't want to push myself on people. But I made the effort." Mini said, "You were working when you first came here, that's the difference."

PRACTICE POINTS The key to getting past the conflicts in the group and in the building is for members to make an emotional connection to each other. The "all-in-the-same-boat" phenomenon, described in Chapter 3 on mutual aid processes, is a way to facilitate this. With the leader's help, the members begin to address the differences in social contact in this stage of the life cycle.

I attempted to help them break out of the debate nature of their interactions. I said, "Instead of putting blame or having a debate, let's see if we can just hear the experience of each person. They are just different perspectives. Given that the group is about getting along with your neighbor, hopefully that means having a better understanding of each other and being able to support each other in some of the difficulties." Marie said, "In every stage of life we are so different. We don't have the pep, we don't have the ambition to say, 'Come over for dinner, and I'll cook and bake.'" I said, "So what's it like for you now?" Marie said, "You just have to be content to sometimes be alone. Sometimes you're much better off alone. You don't have to dress up, don't have to get everything ready to serve, and do the dishes and everything. I really have to push myself to do things now."

Mini said, "I was told I was going to have a hard time adjusting here because I was working until I was 77 and my job ended, a sister died of cancer, and my daughter moved to England. The curtain went down, just like that, and I'm still adjusting. But I think this is my problem and not the problem of the housing. Here and there I make acquaintances, but it's going to take awhile. But it's OK." Lou said, "We forget; we say we'll never forget our problems, but we do. What I'm trying to bring out is that a newer person is faced with conditions the settled person had faced many years ago, and that it's a faded memory. I think about others; it's the way I was brought up, to look out for my fellow man. The way I see it is that the staff's purpose is to serve the residents, and maybe we can do something to help out the new residents."

PRACTICE POINTS As the group begins to develop a culture for work, additional areas of difficulty emerge related to language and ethnicity.

April 24 (Fifth Session)

I wanted to support them to extend their capacity for empathy to those outside the group. Murray said, "Then you have the Russians who you can't communicate with unless you speak Yiddish." Ruth said, "It's even worse with the Chinese, because we can't speak at all." I said, "We've talked about the difficulties in being a newcomer here. Can you imagine what it must be like to be uprooted from your country at this age, to a totally new culture?" Marie said, "It must be so difficult." Murray said, "There's only eight or nine in an English class. You'd think they'd make more of an effort to learn the language." Ruth said, "Learning a new language is very difficult at this age." Mini said, "It's frustrating because I can speak a little Yiddish, but the conversation only goes so far and we are stuck."

I said, "We communicate in many different ways, and, although we don't always speak the same language, we can show respect for one another just in our body language." Toward the end of the session, I asked the members their ages, initially just out of curiosity. Lou was talking about a 96-year-old man he knew in the building: "He showed me some pictures, and after one-year, from 95 to 96, you can barely recognize him. But his mind is very clear, that's what impresses me." I asked if anyone would be willing to share their age here. Mini said, "Sure, I'll tell you. I'm 79." They each proceeded to give their age proudly. Bea said, "Ruth, you're 70, what a baby!" Marie said, "Anne, I didn't know you were 80.

That's remarkable." I said, "So is it both inspiring but also difficult to live in housing with people mostly 70 and above?" Marie said, "No, I love 'em."

PRACTICE POINTS Mini's comment in the next excerpt is interesting because she points out the unique issues of living in a building where everyone is old. The taboo issue associated with living together at this age—the issue described as "moving on"—brings concerns to the surface about advanced illness and death.

I attempted to reach for their feelings about aging. I said, "You see people aging here." There were several nodding, confirming statements all at once. Bea said, "That's the part . . . ," and Marie finished, ". . . that's most difficult." Ruth said, "Yes. For me it's seeing the people move on, unfortunately, and their health." Mini said, "Susan, you are really confronted with your own mortality in a big rush. If you lived downtown, you'd see an occasional old person. But when everybody is in various stages of active and not active, it hits you, as it has to if you are thinking at all. This is what you have to learn to live with, the moment." Bea said, "After living in a place like this, it's true." Mini said, "You see very few kids around." Ruth said, "That's before the Chinese moved in!" Lou said, "When we were young, we had different problems; we had a family, most of us. And when you go to an advanced stage, it seems your perception changes. People think of looking in the obituary. When you're young, you don't even know it exists. Then you get a call that so-and-so is in a nursing home." Marie said, "Or you get a call and they're gone." Lou ended with, "I think we're fortunate to have the community agency. It provides us with good housing. So all in all, I think we are very fortunate to be here."

Where the Problem Stands Now

There has been a gradual shift in the way the members of the group interact with one another. They have begun to develop a more sophisticated level of group operation. At this point, there is much more of a sense of group cohesion; the divisions I mentioned in the problem statement do not seem to carry the same weight as they did early on. The long-term residents do less idealizing of the housing and are able to offer support from their experience. The newer residents are gaining some strength; they are seeing themselves in the process of an adjustment. Both have increased their level of self-disclosure, and the procedural norms have loosened up for more spontaneous interaction.

The group culture now supports members to give more empathetic listening. They have increased their ability to experience a common ground while still maintaining individuality, though the sense of interdependence is still somewhat suspect. The issues of loneliness and loss are still potent, of course, but they have developed an increased capacity to share this with each other.

PRACTICE POINTS In this example, the process of relating in the group modeled the content related to the group's purpose. The group became a microcosm of the housing community, with members having a chance to work on their connections. With the pain from so many losses a constant companion for many people in this stage of life, it is important to provide the help they need to continue to invest in new relationships, which, as described earlier in this chapter, are an important source of protective factors and help maintain a balance with threats to stability.

Chapter Summary

Diversity in a group can come in many forms, and each can have a unique impact on the culture of the group, group process, and the interventions of the group leader. In addition to understanding the culture of the population of group members, it is important for the group leader to understand his or her own cultural background as well as any biases or prejudices that can affect practice when working with group members who are different from themselves.

In addition to variations introduced by race and ethnicity, this chapter discussed and illustrates the application of these concepts to other populations such as gays and lesbians, the differently abled, immigrants, and the elderly. In each case, the impact of oppression and bias may be present and may help us understand elements of the culture. Culture and diversity can also provide a source of strength, contributing to resilience and the ability to overcome adversity. This chapter illustrated variations on this theme including the impact of ethnicity, race, age, physical ability, and sexual orientation.

In addition to understanding diverse cultures, the unique issues involved when counselors are different from the members (intercultural) and when counselors are the same as the members (intracultural) were described. Because of general society taboos, issues associated with differences between group leaders and members, as well as between members, may not be openly discussed without interventions by the group leader. These issues, when left beneath the surface, can have a powerful negative impact on group process. When addressed, they can often provide the energy for powerful growth and change.

Related Online Content and Activities

For learning tools such as glossary terms, InfoTrac® College Edition keywords, links to related websites, and chapter practice quizzes, visit this book's website at **www.cengage.com/counseling/shulman**.

CHAPTER 12

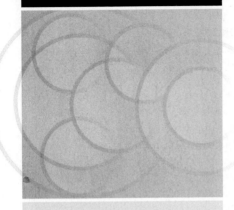

Models of Group Counseling

The counseling profession has a number of models and theoretical frameworks to draw upon for individual, family, and group practice. Although this book presents an approach to group practice that emphasizes mutual aid, the underlying assumptions about human behavior in general and groups in particular are congruent with other models. For example, all of the practice models and theories shared in this chapter start from a strengths perspective in thinking about individual clients and groups. All of the models believe that individuals have the capacity to change how they think, change their emotions, and change how they act. They also believe that changes in any of these elements, thoughts, feelings, or actions impact the others.

For example, some of the young women survivors of sexual abuse in the group described in Chapter 9 had perceived of themselves as "damaged goods" as a result of their childhood abuse experiences. This internalized view, along with the attached emotions, led to self-destructive behaviors such as the use of drugs and relationships with men who were abusive. As their understanding of their experiences changed, and they no longer accepted the guilt for their abuse (e.g., "I must have been provocative toward my father") and instead understood what happened to them was not their fault, their feelings about themselves also changed. As they were able to take more adaptive steps in their lives, end abusive relationships, stop self-medicating with drugs, and even assert themselves by confronting specific abusers and by acting together to participate in a Take Back the Night march, their strength increased, as did their capacity for change. Constructs and strategies from cognitive-behavioral therapy, solution-focused practice, and feminist practice can all be identified in this example.

In addition to practicing a specific group model, perhaps following the directions of the model's manual, a counselor can include specific techniques in an integrated group practice framework. For example, in a recovery group for substance abusers, the leader could use a solution-focused intervention by asking all the members to share with each other when in their lives they had been able to maintain their recovery for a longer period of time and what was going on at that time that helped them to do so. The all-in-the-same-boat phenomenon associated with a mutual aid model could enhance this sort of reflection since each member would be able to note similarities as well as differences.

In addition, core concepts from the mutual aid model can be used to understand group practice using other frameworks. For example, a crisis intervention group (an example later in this chapter) can be analyzed using the phases of work—preliminary, beginning, middle, and ending/transitions—to identify the dynamics and skills associated with each phase. Group leaders can draw upon a range of models as they create their own practice framework. In my view, the emphasis should be on finding what works for group members rather than on maintaining ideological purity.

A growing body of federally funded research has been helpful in identifying which models appear to offer advantages in dealing with specific populations and particular problems. The general rubric of *evidence-based practice (EBP)* has been used to describe frameworks that have been exposed to some level of rigorous testing and whose findings offer some support for their use in practice. The next section defines the criteria generally used to apply the EBP designation to a model. The following sections then summarize three of the identified EBP models that have already made major contributions to our understanding of practice. This is followed by a section describing other models that, while not yet noted as EBP, nevertheless also actively contribute to our understanding of group practice. The specific models included here were chosen because I believe that the concept of mutual aid could fit easily in their group versions and that their fundamental values are consistent with those espoused in this book. Other models could also have been included that meet these criteria, but space considerations limit the number shared. Many of the models are also relevant, and in fact may have been originally developed, for work with individuals and families and have been adapted here to the group context.

Evidence-Based Practice (EBP)

With so many models of practice, every professional must evaluate their frameworks and strategies in order to modify practices in the best interest of the client. The term *evidence-based practice (EBP)* describes a practice that has been determined to have some success, with some clients at certain times and with some outcomes.

Barker (2003) defines EBP as follows: "The use of the best available scientific knowledge derived from randomized controlled outcome studies, and meta-analyses of existing outcome studies, as one basis for guiding professional interventions and effective therapies, combined with professional ethical standards, clinical judgment, and practice wisdom" (p. 149). The elements of this definition that help define a model as an EBP include the following:

- "The best available scientific knowledge derived from randomized controlled outcome studies" (Randomized controlled outcome studies involve random assignment to treatment or no-treatment [or modified treatment] groups with efforts to control for other variables that may impact the outcomes.)

- "Meta-analyses of existing outcome studies"
- "Combined with professional ethical standards, clinical judgment, and practice wisdom"

McNeece and Thyer (2004, p. 10) suggest a hierarchy of scientific methodologies that should be considered, with some offering more credible support for EBP validation than others. In rough order from high to low, they are as follows:

Systematic reviews/meta-analyses

Randomized controlled trials

Quasi-experimental studies

Case control and cohort studies

Preexperimental group studies

Surveys

Qualitative studies

In addition, professional ethics, clinical judgments, and practice wisdom are integrated into the most effective EBP models. It would be hard, for example, to imagine an accepted EBP model that violated some of the basic ethical premises of the helping professions—for example, informed consent, as outlined in earlier chapters and described in detail in Chapter 13. In another example, some early models of treatment for addictive behavior involved extreme forms of confrontation designed to break down barriers and force acceptance of a problem. Addressing this issue, Miller and Rollnick (2006) point out that some therapy groups, particularly those organized around a Synanon therapeutic community model, have employed what is called "attack therapy," "the hot seat," or the "emotional haircut." After illustrating this with a particularly harsh and attacking example that has the therapist saying, "Now, Buster, I'm going to tell you what to do. And I'll show you. You either do it or you'll get the hell off Synanon property," the therapist in the example continues with a personally attacking and insulting verbal assault. Miller and Rollnick, referring to this illustration, comment, "Approaches such as these would be regarded as ludicrous and unprofessional treatment for the vast majority of psychological or medical problems from which people suffer. Imagine these same words being used as therapy for someone suffering from depression, anxiety, marital problems, sexual dysfunction, schizophrenia, cancer, hypertension, heart disease, or diabetes" (p. 6). This would be an example of an approach that violates ethical standards, clinical judgment, and practice wisdom. Most professionals in this field would agree that denial of the existence of a problem is a reality and that the client needs to face and accept a problem before it can be dealt with. Miller and Rollnick point out that confrontation is a goal, a purpose, and an aim. They continue, "The question, then, is this: What are the most effective ways for helping people to examine and accept reality, particularly uncomfortable reality?" (p. 13).

Whereas facilitative confrontation is an important element in any helping relationship, the emphasis is on the word *facilitative*. As described earlier in this book, confrontation that is integrated with genuine empathy and comes from caring is a crucial skill in a helping relationship. This concept emerges from both empirical research and practice wisdom.

As professionals consider claims that a particular approach is an evidence-based practice, it is important that they consider these crucial criteria: randomization, replication, professional ethics, effective assessment, and concepts that fit our established practice wisdom. Although our assessments and practice wisdom need to be challenged at times, our ethical standards are crucial to professional practice. The first three models described later have achieved the designation of being evidence based.

A resource for identifying EBP in the substance abuse and mental health fields is the National Registry of Evidence-Based Programs and Practices (NREPP), developed by the federal government's Department of Health and Human Services Substance Abuse and Mental Health Services Administration (SAMHSA). This registry (www.nrepp.samhsa.gov) is described as follows: "NREPP is a searchable database of interventions for the prevention and treatment of mental and substance abuse disorders. SAMHSA has developed this resource to help people, agencies, and organizations implement programs and practices in their communities" (NREPP, 2009, p. 1).

One note of caution has to be raised on the implementation of manualized practices associated with EBP. For both research and practice purposes, it is common to develop a manual that provides a structure for the practitioner that guides the implementation of the particular EDP model. In multisite research, projects manuals are used to ensure "dosage integrity," which means that the delivery of the model will be the same across sites. (The term *dosage* is borrowed from pharmaceutical research and refers to the way in which a particular drug is administered.) However, if the model and the manual are strictly observed in practice, it may, in some situations, prevent the use of innovative interventions or responses to unexpected events in the group.

In one example, I observed parenting groups that were part of a national 16-site federally funded project designed to use groups to prevent the intergenerational transmission of substance abuse. Group leaders were instructed to deliver parenting information at fixed times in a group session and for a required amount of presentation time. The leaders' presentations were videotaped and the tapes analyzed to see if dosage integrity was maintained when compared to the other 15 sites. The rigidity of this manualized approach led the group leaders to ignore parenting issues emerging from the group members as well as clear signals of reluctance to participate on the part of some mandated parents. This group would have benefited if the manual could have been adapted to the population's particular needs.

Motivational Interviewing (MI)

Examples of EBP-designated practices are found in major replications of a similar model funded by national organizations such as the National Institutes of Health. One example would be the use of *motivational interviewing (MI)* techniques to address addictive behavior (Miller & Rollnick, 1991).

Miller and Rollnick focus on the issue of motivation. "We suggest, then, that motivation should not be thought of as a personality problem, or as a trait that a person carries through the counselor's doorway. Rather, motivation is a *state* of readiness or eagerness to change, which may fluctuate from one time or situation to another. This state is one that can be influenced" (p. 14).

They build their framework on a stages-of-change model (Prochaska & DiClemente, 1982), described in more detail earlier in the text. In brief review, the six stages are the following:

- Precontemplation
- Contemplation
- Determination

- Action
- Maintenance
- Relapse

Key to the model is that the counselor uses interventions that are appropriate to the stage of change that is presented by the client. A counselor would not expect group members, for example, to begin to discuss actions to deal with the particular problem they are facing if they were still in a precontemplation or even contemplation stage. In the example of the court-mandated DWI group presented later in Chapter 14, the group leader did not attack the members' angry assertions in the first session that they were not alcoholics and should not be forced to attend the group. Instead, she worked with the resistance by having the men detail those things they did not want in the group such as being called alcoholics or made to feel guilty. It was a number of sessions into the group when they began to examine the "triggers" that had led to drinking so that they were able to move into open contemplation of their problems and, for some, determination to do something that preceded the action stage.

In a group I led for persons with AIDS in recovery from substance abuse, also presented in Chapter 14, most members were in the maintenance stage, using the mutual aid group and self-help groups such as AA to help them avoid relapse. One member was clearly in a precontemplation stage, refusing to accept both his drug use problem and his increasing issues with AIDS. Although he was able to do some work during the group, he eventually dropped out and moved to another city. Relapse did occur for one other member; as described in this model, his ability to learn from the relapse and renew his determination, followed by his move into the action stage, was a key to his success.

If the treatment approach involves the kind of confrontation described earlier in the Synanon example—when the client is in the precontemplation or even the contemplation stage—greater resistance is likely to be generated. Mandated clients could be forced to attend such a group, but they could not be forced to change. At best, in a mandatory situation, the group member will go through the motions and participate in what I have called the illusion of work.

Miller and Rollnick (1991) assert:

From time to time the balance tips, and for a span of time the person's statements reflect a good deal of what might be judged to be "motivation." At this "determination" stage, a client may say things like these:

I've *got* to do something about this problem!

This is serious! Something has to change.

What can I do? How can I change? (p. 17)

The MI model suggests the therapist's tasks at each stage of the change process:

Precontemplation: Raise doubt—increase the client's perception of risks and problems with current behavior.
Contemplation: Tip the balance—evoke reasons to change, risks of not changing, strengthen the client's self-efficacy for change of current behavior.
Determination: Help the client to determine the best course of action to take in seeking change.
Action: Help the client to take steps toward change.

Maintenance: Help the client to identify and use strategies to prevent relapse.
Relapse: Help the client to review the process of contemplation, determination, and action, without becoming stuck or demoralized because of relapse. (p. 18)

The elements of this model that closely parallel the major assumptions and strategies of the interactional mutual aid model central to this book include starting where the client is, working *with* the client and not *on* the client, recognizing the client's control over the outcome, developing a positive relationship through the use of empathy and other skills, and acknowledging the importance of facilitative confrontation. Although emphases may differ, the similarities are evident. A brief summary of the model's motivational strategies, which the authors set forth conveniently (for mnemonic purposes) using the letters *A* through *H*, is as follows:

- Giving ADVICE
- Removing BARRIERS
- Providing CHOICE
- Decreasing DESIRABILITY
- Practicing EMPATHY
- Providing FEEDBACK
- Clarifying GOALS
- Active HELPING (p. 20)

In the 2007 review of motivational interviewing research (NREPP, 2009), the National Registry describes the core elements of the model as follows:

Motivational Interviewing (MI) is a goal-directed, client-centered counseling style for eliciting behavioral change by helping clients to explore and resolve ambivalence. The operational assumption in MI is that ambivalent attitudes or lack of resolve is the primary obstacle to behavioral change, so that the examination and resolution of ambivalence becomes its key goal. MI has been applied to a wide range of problem behaviors related to alcohol and substance abuse as well as health promotion, medical treatment adherence, and mental health issues. Although many variations in technique exist, the MI counseling style generally includes the following elements:
- Establishing rapport with the client and listening reflectively.
- Asking open-ended questions to explore the client's own motivations for change.
- Affirming the client's change-related statements and efforts.
- Eliciting recognition of the gap between current behavior and desired life goals.
- Asking permission before providing information or advice.
- Responding to resistance without direct confrontation. (Resistance is used as a feedback signal to the therapist to adjust the approach.)
- Encouraging the client's self-efficacy for change.
- Developing an action plan to which the client is willing to commit.

While most of the development and research of MI has applied to individual treatment and has focused on treating addictive behavior, efforts have been made to translate the model into a group treatment modality. Van Horn (2003), describing a pilot-tested motivational interviewing group for dually diagnosed inpatients, points out that

> [m]otivational interviewing is a brief treatment approach designed to produce rapid, internally motivated changes in addictive behaviors. Motivational interviewing shows promise for engaging clients with dual psychiatric and psychoactive substance use diagnosis in treatment. While initially developed as an individual treatment approach, key motivations enhancement principles may be applied to structured group interventions to facilitate its introduction to inpatient dual-diagnosis treatment. (p. 1)

Researchers have proposed adaptations of the core MI model to group practice in the substance abuse field suggesting the development of a "core motivational group" as part of a treatment program (Ingersoll, Wagner, & Gharib, 2007). This framework uses topics such as the stages of change, decisional balance exploring the pros and cons of changing and staying the same, supporting self-efficacy by exploring strengths, and planning for change, in the group modality with a combination of presentation and group discussion and group support.

In a study of the impact of the use of a group-based motivational enhancement program prior to standard treatment, the authors report that the 73 clients who attended the motivation group, compared to the 94 who did not, had significantly more positive outcomes (Lincourt, Kuettel, & Bombardier, 2002). When controlling for diagnosis, employment, and age, those in the motivational group had a higher rate of attendance to the overall program as well as treatment completion.

Finally, a randomized-controlled study was conducted with 161 alcohol-dependent inpatients who received three individual counseling sessions on their ward in addition to detoxification treatment and 161 inpatients who received 2 weeks of inpatient treatment and four outpatient group sessions in addition to detoxification. Both interventions followed the principles and strategies of motivational interviewing (John, Veltrup, Driessen, Wetterling, & Dilling, 2003). The researchers found that group treatment resulted in a higher rate of participation in self-help groups at 6 months after treatment, but this difference disappeared after 12 months. There was no difference in the abstinence rate between the two groups.

Although the adaptation of MI approaches in the group context is still early in its development and reporting mixed results, it offers a promising model for strengthening the initial engagement of clients and their willingness to participate in and complete treatment.

Solution-Focused Practice (SFP)

Another model of practice with elements that fit nicely in the interactional framework is called *solution-focused practice (SFP)* or *solution-focused brief therapy* in group. Corey (2008) points to the underlying positive orientation as a key concept:

> Solution-focused brief therapy is grounded on the optimistic assumption that people are resilient, resourceful, and competent and have the ability to construct solutions that can change their lives. . . . Clients are believed to be competent regardless of the shape they are in when entering therapy, and the role of the counselor is to help clients recognize the resources they already

possess. Solution-focused therapists engage in conversations with their clients about what is going well, future possibilities and what will likely lead to a sense of accomplishment. (p. 424)

Several of its underlying assumptions and intervention techniques can be useful, particularly in the beginning phase of work. The practitioner needs to discern when they might be suitable or not for particular clients. This section provides a brief introduction to the model and identifies core techniques.

Major Assumptions on the Nature of the Helping Relationship

The solution-focused model is built on the strengths perspective. As a form of "existential" practice, it focuses on the client's current issues and assumes that, with the counselor's help, the client can identify and use inherent strengths that might be overlooked in a pathology-oriented practice. Put simply, the counselor thinks about what is *right* with the client rather than what is *wrong*. The counselor also believes that the source and methods of change will come from the client. This model emerged from an integration of the strengths perspective with interest in short-term treatment (deShazer, 1988; deShazer & Berg, 1992).

Some of the specific assumptions in the model include the following:

- Intervention should focus on the present and what clients bring with them to the process.
- Achieving behavioral changes takes place in and affects the present, rather than resolving problems of the past.
- Although it focuses on the present, the model recognizes that longer-term treatment may require examination and resolving of past issues (e.g., survivors of sexual abuse).
- When engaging the client, counselors might acknowledge the person's discomfort, but they do not engage in a prolonged discussion of etiology and pathology.
- Individuals have within themselves the resources and abilities to solve their own problems.
- Clients are often caught in feelings of powerlessness regarding their problems.
- Clients need to be helped to imagine what their future would look like without the problem—that is, if they were "unstuck."
- When working with mandated clients, the involuntary nature of the relationship must be acknowledged and used as the starting point for the work.

Prior to the engagement with the client and the first group meeting, the counselor will make minimal use of history and agency records, preferring to let the client tell the story. This can help the counselor avoid stereotyping the client based on the judgments of previous counselors. Assume, for example, that a new counselor tells her colleagues that she is going to have Fred Jones in her group and colleagues respond negatively: "Oh, no, not Fred Jones!" Mr. Jones may be the person I referred to early in the book as the "agency client." Many of the counselors have worked with him and found him hard to reach. (This is the client often assigned to new workers and students.) The counselor's perception that this will be a difficult client helps create conditions that can lead to a self-fulfilling prophecy.

As has been illustrated in several examples in previous chapters, with mandated clients, the group leader typically asks the members to share their views about the mandating agency's expectations and requirements. The group leader recognizes and acknowledges that, although the agency or court can demand certain changes, clients serve as the final "authority" with regard to what they want or need to change in their lives. When the group leader asks what the members want and the response is "Get the damn court (or anyone) off my back!" the counselor can respond, "OK, let's start with what all of you have to do to get the court off of your back." Essentially, the client is invited to be the "expert" who informs the counselor about her or his situation.

Role of the Solution-Focused Group Leader

Corey (2008) describes the solution-focused group counselor's role as follows:

> Solution-focused group counselors adopt a "not knowing" position as a route to putting group members into the position of being the experts about their own lives. In this approach, the therapist-as-expert is replaced by the client-as-expert, especially when it comes to what he or she wants in life. Although clients are viewed as experts on their own lives, they are often stuck in patterns that are not working for them. These practitioners disavow the role of expert, preferring a more collaborative or consultative stance, and they see their job as creating opportunity for clients to see themselves as experts in their lives. (p. 427)

One concern I would have with the "not knowing" position is that if rigidly or incorrectly implemented, it can stop the group leader from sharing data (information, values, beliefs, etc.) that might be helpful to the group members. The core concept of the solution-focused approach that the client is an expert in his or her own life is central to the model I have presented in this book, and the idea that the key to change rests with the client is also consistent. I would rather conceive of the group leader and clients as both experts but about different things. Clients are the experts about their lives, their troubles, possible solutions, and so on; the group leader is expert in leading groups. The group leader's role includes teaching all members about how to help each other, and at times, that may include the need to confront as well as support.

Defining Techniques

Several specific techniques have been associated with the SFP model. All of them share a common focus on the client's strength and capacity for coping with adversity. These techniques are as follows:

- **Asking about presession changes during the recruitment interview or first group session:** The group leader recognizes that change may have occurred even before the first session. The fact that a client has made an appointment to find out about the group, voluntarily or not, may begin a change process. The counselor will be curious and inquire about how the client made these changes and who was responsible for them.

- **Asking about between-session changes:** The group leader recognizes that the members have a life between sessions. Many factors will have influenced the client's life, and the counselor will want to explore these at the beginning of the session. For example, the counselor may ask group members,

"What, if anything, is better this week, compared with last week?" or "What issues are on your mind this week?" This is an element of the skill in the middle phase I called sessional contracting.

- **Asking about exceptions:** This technique asks the member to begin to examine when the problem did not occur in the past and what the conditions were that created these exceptions. For example, after a member in a substance abuse group discloses a relapse, the group leader could ask, "You've relapsed and started drinking again at least three times over the past 5 years, but you've also been able to maintain your recovery for longer and longer periods. What was going on during the time you maintained your recovery, and how were you able to do that?" A variation on this question would be to ask about times when the problem was not that serious or severe, was less frequent, or lasted a shorter time. The goal is to search for and reinforce those factors that made a difference. This is a subtle but important shift from focusing on the problem to identifying potential solutions. In the group context, other members can identify their own exceptions and, if possible, the leader can point to similarities as well as differences. Also, member support for each other can help in maintaining hope and a strengths perspective in dealing with the problem.

- **Asking the "miracle question":** Although there are different forms of the "miracle question," the most common is this: "Imagine you were to wake up tomorrow and a miracle had happened." The miracle would be that the client's life had changed for the better and the "problem" had been resolved. Questions such as "How would you first know that things were different?" or "What would others notice that would indicate that the problem was gone?" are designed to help the client conceptualize the desired change. A variation includes "Imagine this isn't so much of a problem" or "This group session has helped you in just the way you thought it would" or "It is 3 months in the future, we have been working together and you have been attending the group, and problems have been resolved. How would you know this? What would be different?" The one caveat that the counselor has to include when asking the question is that the client cannot answer that the problem itself did not exist. For example, a grieving widow cannot wake up the next day and find that her husband had not died.

- **Asking scaling questions:** This technique asks group members at the first meeting to identify the degree of the problem using a scale on which zero represents the worst end of a continuum and some other number represents the ideal. The group leader can then ask clients what number represents where they are in respect to this problem at a certain point in the work. In this way, group members may be able to identify incremental changes rather than see a problem as "solved" or "not solved."

- **Asking coping questions:** Another technique that emphasizes the clients' strengths and helps clients see themselves in new ways is to ask "coping" questions. For example, after a group member has shared a serious problem, after acknowledging the problem, the counselor might ask, "How have you managed to cope?" Another question might be "Given how bad things are, how come they are not worse? How have you kept things from getting worse?" Once again, in a group context, others in similar situations can share their experiences in coping if the group leader invites members to contribute them to the discussion.

Cognitive-Behavioral Therapy (CBT)

A third model considered to be an evidence-based practice borrows from *cognitive-behavioral psychology and therapy*. According to Corey (2008):

> Cognitive behavioral approaches are becoming increasingly popular in group work in part due to their emphasis on teaching clients self-management skills and how to restructure their thoughts. Clients can learn to use these techniques to control their lives, deal effectively with present and future problems and function well without ongoing therapy. (p. 338)

In CBT, the therapist uses strategies and techniques designed to help clients correct their negative, distorted views about themselves, the world, and the future, as well as the underlying maladaptive beliefs that gave rise to these cognitions (Beck, Rush, Shaw, & Emery, 1979; Elkin, Parloff, Hadley, & Autry, 1985).

Earlier in this book, I pointed out the powerful interaction between how we feel and how we act. Essentially, cognitive-behavioral approaches, which build on social learning theories, suggest that how one thinks also interacts with one's behavior. When feelings and cognitive distortions combine, they can result in maladaptive behaviors, which in turn strengthen the distortions, which then continue to affect the behavior. In cognitive-behavioral treatment models, the therapist would help the client identify and modify cognitive distortions and would reinforce behaviors that were more adaptive for the client.

Concepts drawn from a widely recognized and researched cognitive therapy model based on the work of Beck, who explored the causes and treatment of depression (Beck et al., 1979), can be usefully incorporated into the mutual aid model of practice. Oei and Shuttlewood (1996) summarize the three dimensions of Beck's theory.

First, life experiences lead people to form assumptions about themselves and the world ("schemata" or "underlying predispositions") that are then used to interpret new experiences and to govern and evaluate behavior. "Some assumptions reached on the basis of past negative experience may become rigid, extreme, and resistant to change and, hence, are termed dysfunctional or counterproductive" (p. 93).

Second, Beck posed the existence of "automatic thoughts," short pieces of "internal dialogue" that are associated with negative emotions and can lead to self-statements such as "I am a failure." According to Beck, a pattern of frequent and "highly negative automatic thoughts" can develop into a vicious cycle that leads to depression, which then leads to more depressive cognitions.

Third, automatic thoughts are seen as containing "errors of logic," which Beck termed "cognitive distortions." These could include overgeneralizing, disqualifying the positive, catastrophizing, minimization, and personalization.

Beck's treatment approach "disrupts the vicious cycle of depression by teaching the patients to question negative automatic thoughts and then to challenge the assumptions (schemata) on which they are based" (Oei & Shuttlewood, 1996, p. 94).

Cognitive-Behavioral and Supportive-Expressive Groups for Women Diagnosed with Breast Cancer

In a recent review of the literature on the effectiveness of cognitive-behavioral and supportive-expressive group therapy for women diagnosed with breast cancer, Boutin (2007) reviewed 20 studies that examined the extent to which CBT, supportive-expressive group therapy (SEGT), or a combination of these two treatments impact women with breast cancer. The 20 studies differed in methodology, with most (80%) using randomized assignment to the treatment or control groups. Studies also differed on the stage of the cancer and the ages of the women.

Outcomes varied for different studies and different designs and included less mood disturbance, no survival rate difference, less depression, higher self-esteem, increased vigor and "fighting spirit," less affect suppression, decreased anxiety, and less pain and suffering. Addressing the findings across studies, Boutin states:

> Despite evidence for success across all of the treatments, the pattern of results from the CBT, SEGT, and combination of CBT and SEGT studies are imbalanced. More repeated positive outcomes from studies implementing an experimental design were found for the SEGT treatments than for CBT as well as for the combination of CBT and SEGT treatments. Furthermore, studies with less experimental control were identified that support the outcomes of the more rigorous SEGT studies, but no supportive evidence was identified that support the outcomes of the more rigorous CBT or combination of CBT and SEGT studies. A contributing factor for the imbalance in results is the corresponding imbalance in the number of studies published for each treatment. (p. 279)

Boutin identifies limitations in both the review and individual studies. The differences in populations, length of time in treatment, and so forth, and the fact that treatment modalities were not directly compared with each other with the exception of one study, limits the ability to make inferences. Boutin does suggest that group treatment of using different modalities, particularly supportive-expressive group therapy, appears to have a positive impact on a number of important variables. An example of a CBT group that incorporates supportive-expressive group therapy within a mutual aid framework follows.

CBT Group for Chronic Mental Patients

In an example of how a group leader can incorporate constructs from the cognitive-behavioral model into the interactional framework, Albert (1994) writes about a mutual aid support group for chronic mental patients using a CBT approach. He describes a patient in a day treatment center—which had so many groups that patients often felt "grouped out"—who surprised staff by suggesting another group:

> She said, "We need to talk just about being mental patients, what it means, what it feels like." One patient after another seconded the motion. They wanted to address the mental patient identity. How were they thought of in their families and neighborhoods? How should they think of themselves? Was the mental patient stigma justified? Where did it come from? What were its effects? Although their "patienthood" was at the heart of what the patients had in common, it seemed to have remained an oppressive presence, at once too obvious and too painful to mention. (p. 109)

In one example from the group, patients were dealing with the ideation of permanent thinking—that when they are depressed, for example, treatment can seem "interminable and futile." This sense of failure and permanency, in turn, affects their ability to continue to cope.

> Sharon said, "I had the leaves raked into piles. Then the wind blew them all around the yard again. I thought, 'What's the use? They'll never get done.

There will always be leaves.' Then I went back to bed. My body started feeling heavy. I couldn't get out of bed." I (the counselor) pointed out that Sharon had used the word "always" when speaking about her hospitalization, too. ["I'll always go back to the hospital."] I asked, "Is it true that there will always be leaves? Is the job never done?" Sharon said, "That's one way of looking at it."

I asked the group for other ways. Members suggested that Sharon think about other tasks she has completed. [Disputation] Nick said, "Maybe you would have to redo the raking once or twice; maybe even three times—but not forever. [Disputation] I mean, you do what you can, then it snows and you're done." [Laughter] I repeated, "You do what you can." (Albert, 1994, p. 110)

The cognitive-behavioral approach is a good example of how most therapeutic frameworks, as long as they are based on core assumptions and beliefs about group member strengths, provide powerful ideas that can be integrated into other practice models. In addition, the emphasis by the cognitive-behavioral theoreticians on a practitioner-researcher model, in which the counselor continuously evaluates his or her own practice, is also healthy for the field because it accelerates the movement toward development of a more *empirically based practice*.

Feminist Practice

The models and theories discussed in the remainder of this chapter are those that may not yet qualify as evidence-based practice but may have elements that have proven to be consistently helpful, have achieved some research support, or may be driven by shared practice wisdom and experience. They may be in the early research stage, but they contain organized assumptions about behavior, valued outcomes, and intervention strategies that can be operationalized in a manner that can lead to consistent research findings.

Feminist practice consists of a number of models and frameworks that attempt to address the unique issues facing women in our society. These include issues of social and political oppression and the impact of having been generally placed in a subordinate position in respect to their gender. Efforts have also been made to develop a unique psychology of women in terms of how they relate and connect to others. Both of these approaches have direct impact on the structure and content of group work practice with women and will be explored and illustrated in this section. First, I begin with a brief introduction to a typology of feminist practice.

Feminist Practice Typology

Feminist approaches to practice have diverged into several identifiable streams. Saulnier (1996, 2000) has attempted to identify these various viewpoints. Her typology includes the following models: liberal feminism, radical feminism, socialist feminism, lesbian feminism, cultural and ecofeminism, womanism, African American women's feminism, postmodern feminism, and global feminism. Although some may disagree with the specific categorization of the models and the associated descriptions, analysis, and critiques, Saulnier's contribution highlights this important area of theory development and identifies implications for social policy and practice.

Sands and Nuccio (1992) specifically address the emergence of postmodern feminist theory and its impact on practice. The authors describe how the feminist literature has identified three general categories of philosophical and political feminist orientations: liberal, socialist, and radical feminism. Liberal feminism emphasizes the attainment of political rights, opportunities, and equality within the existing political system. Socialist feminism attributes women's oppression to the interaction among sexism, racism, and class divisions, which are produced by patriarchal capitalism. Radical feminism finds patriarchy an omnipresent influence that needs to be dismantled (p. 490).

Sands and Nuccio then trace the emergence of postmodern feminism from its postmodern philosophical and French feminist theoretical roots. Although they acknowledge differences between the roots and the emergent thinking of this model, they point to a shared political agenda with American feminism:

> Regardless of whether a feminist has a liberal, socialist, radical or other perspective, she has a desire to change the social and political order so that women will no longer be oppressed. Thus, organizing and taking political action to redress injustices are significant dimensions of postmodern feminism. (p. 492)

While the focus of this brief background is on the social justice and sociopolitical implications of the feminist approach, many of these concepts are translated into direct practice interventions, as will be illustrated later. First, I want to explore some of the work in developing a women-centered psychology that has implications for group practice.

The New Psychology of Women

A theoretical model that helps us understand some of the unique dimensions of practice with women is the relational model. This model has emerged from the work done at the Stone Center in Wellesley, Massachusetts, which is dedicated to studying the unique issues in the development of women and methods for working effectively with them. The center has built on the early work of Jean Baker Miller, whose book *Toward a New Psychology of Women* (Miller 1987; Miller & Stiver, 1991) laid the groundwork for the relational model. Much of the evolving work in this area can be found in publications and a series of working papers and books from the Stone Center. This framework is often classified under the general rubric of self-in-relation theory.

The framework was described in detail in Chapter 8 when I suggested it could serve as one of the four models presented to help us understand the dynamics of the group-as-a-whole. I will briefly review some of the core elements that directly relate to group work practice. The reader is urged to return to the discussion in Chapter 8 for a more detailed presentation.

In one example of a group work elaboration of this model, Fedele (1994, p. 7) draws on three central constructs repeatedly found in relational theory:

- Paradox (an apparent contradiction that contains a truth)
- Connection ("a joining in relationship between people who experience each other's presence in a full way and who accommodate both the correspondence and contrasts between them")
- Resonance ("a resounding; an echoing; the capacity to respond that, in its most sophisticated form, is empathy")

Referring to therapy, Fedele (1994) identifies several paradoxes: "Vulnerability leads to growth; pain can be experienced in safety; talking about disconnection leads to connection; and conflict between people can be best tolerated in their connection"

(p. 8). In describing the second major construct of relational theory, the idea of "connection," Fedele says:

> The primary task of the leader and the group members is to facilitate a feeling of connection. In a relational model of group work, the leader is careful to understand each interaction, each dynamic in the group as a means for maintaining connection or as a strategy to remain out of connection. As in interpersonal therapy groups, the leader encourages the members to be aware of their availability in the here-and-now relationship of the group by understanding and empathizing with their experiences of the past. But it is the yearning for connection, rather than an innate need for separation or individuation, that fuels their development both in the here-and-now and in the past. (p. 11)

Finally, the third major concept, resonance, asserts that the "power of experiencing pain within a healing connection stems from the ability of an individual to resonate with another" (p. 14). Fedele suggests that resonance manifests itself in group work in two ways:

> The first is the ability of one member to simply resonate with another's experience in the group and experience some vicarious relief because of that resonance. The member need not discuss the issue in the group, but the experience moves her that much closer to knowing and sharing her own truth without necessarily responding or articulating it. Another way resonance manifests itself in a group involves the ability of members to resonate with each other's issues and thereby recall or reconnect with their own issues. This is an important element of group process in all groups but is dramatically obvious in groups with women who have trauma histories. Often, when one woman talks about painful material, other women dissociate. It is a very powerful aspect of group work that, if acknowledged, can help women move into connection. (p 14)

These three elements all have their parallels in the mutual aid model in which ambivalence about closeness (paradox), the power of connecting with other members (connection), and mutual support through empathy (resonance) are described as elements in the mutual aid process.

Following the early publications addressing the relational model, Stone Center researchers focused on an inherent and acknowledged bias in their original work. Jordan (1997), referring to the early work, said that

> it represented largely white, middle-class, well-educated heterosexual experience. While we struggled not to reproduce the errors that occur when one subgroup speaks as if *its* reality is *the* reality, we inevitably were bound by our own blindspots and biases. We became more and more aware of the dangers of speaking about or for "all women." We were indeed speaking about "some women" or about partial aspects of many women's experience. Our appreciation of diversity needed to be broadened and deepened. (p. 1)

Jordan points out that the work in these later publications continued to elaborate and explore the relational theory with an emphasis on topics such as sexuality, shame, anger, and depression, as well as the complexity related to women's diverse life experiences.

> While all women suffer in a patriarchal society where our experience is not presented in the dominant discourse, women in various cultural/ethnic groups suffer additional marginalization based on race, sexual orientation, socioeconomic

standing, able-bodiedness, and age. Women who are marginalized also develop strengths that may differ from those of white, privileged heterosexual women. (p. 1)

Feminist Group Practice

Butler and Wintram (1991), writing about the development of feminist group work at that time, caution against crossing the line in writing about women as problem-bearers as opposed to problem-solvers.

> Effective therapy in groups should encourage women to value and develop inner strengths, regardless of societal norms. The institutional and social barriers that have impeded women are so wide-ranging that their erosion must occur on numerous fronts. Any feminist approach must harness the growing unrest among women with the aim of recognizing the dynamics of oppression whilst avoiding pathologizing them as vulnerable, weak and dependent. (p. 44)

The authors use their practice experiences working with inner-city women's groups in England to develop their model of practice designed to address the problems but also to develop solutions. "Our personal and professional experiences have shown us that women brought together can offer each other support, validation and strength, and a growing sense of personal awareness, in a way that is difficult to achieve otherwise" (p. 1). Their experiences revealed common themes:

> Fear, isolation and loneliness lay at the root of the experiences of many of the women with whom we were involved over the years. These three factors intertwine, forming their own perfect prism. The *fear* results from the threat of, or the actual occurrence of, physical, sexual and psychological violence. *Isolation* is caused by material constraints, such as lack of transport, money and child-care facilities, which in all restrict mobility. There is no real contact with other people. Each woman convinces herself that she is the only one to know what she is feeling and experiencing. The *loneliness* that arises from such circumstances needs little elaboration, especially when a woman is told often enough that she is a failure, receiving little if any positive reinforcement for the endless domestic labour and low-paid work she may perform. Feelings of unreality, of going or being mad, are all common amongst people divorced from any point of reference. Solitude, in such circumstances, breeds powerlessness. (p. 2)

The description of the factors impacting these women echoes the key *indicators of oppression* in the psychology of Fanon (Bulhan, 1985). Fanon's model, as described by Bulhan, was drawn from the experience of slavery. The oppression model was elaborated in Chapter 1 as an underlying framework for understanding maladaptive ways of coping with oppression as the "oppressor without" becomes the "oppressor within." The discussion of resilience and the strengths perspective, in the same chapter, focused on oppressed populations as potential problem solvers as described by Butler and Wintram.

Bulhan (1985) identifies several key indicators for objectively assessing oppression. He suggests that "all situations of oppression violate one's space, time, energy, mobility, bonding, and identity" (p. 124). He illustrates these indicators using the example of the slave:

> The male slave was allowed no physical space which he could call his own. The female slave had even less claim to space than the male slave. Even her body

was someone else's property. Commonly ignored is how this expropriation of one's body entailed even more dire consequences for female slaves. The waking hours of the slave were also expropriated for life without his or her consent. The slave labored in the field and in the kitchen for the gain and comfort of the master. The slave's mobility was curbed and he or she was never permitted to venture beyond a designated perimeter without a "pass."

The slave's bonding with others, even the natural relation between mother and child, was violated and eroded. The same violation of space, time, energy, mobility, bonding and identity prevailed under apartheid, which in effect, is modern-day slavery. (p. 124)

The slave model is an extreme example of the violation of space, time, energy, mobility, bonding, and identity as indicators of oppression. Although the slavery experience of African Americans in North America must be considered a unique example of oppression, the indicators may be used to assess degrees of oppression for other populations as well. In this way, a universal psychological model can help us understand the common elements that exist in any oppressive relationship.

Battered Women's Group

PRACTICE POINTS Consider the six indicators cited by Bulhan as you read a discussion among a group of women who have experienced and are experiencing abuse from their partners. Note how the description of fear, isolation, and loneliness described by Butler and Wintram is echoed in this work.

> Candy said one thing that she didn't like was that her husband had to be number one all the time. He felt he should come first, even before the children. She said, "The man's got to be number one. Just like the president. He's a man and he's number one. You don't see any female presidents, do you?" I said, "Are you saying that a man had the right to abuse his partner?" She said no and then turned to the women to say, "But, who's the one who always gives in, in the family? The woman does." All the women nodded to this remark. Linda said, "To keep peace in the family." Candy said, "In the long run, we're the ones who are wrong for not leaving the abusive situations." She said she finally came to the realization that her man was never going to be of any help to her. In the long run, she felt that her children would help her out if she gave them a good life now. She feels very strongly about her responsibilities to her children.

PRACTICE POINTS The comment about not seeing a female president was made a number of years ago when that seemed out of the question. The recent strong run for the Democratic nomination by a woman, Hillary Clinton, may be changing that view in spite of her loss. Candy's powerful decision to leave her husband represents the "problem-solver" element in her behavior.

> Another woman, Tina, said that when she called the police for help, they thought it was a big joke. She said when she had to fill out a report at the police station, the officer laughed about the incident. The women in the group talked about their own experiences with the police, which were not very good. One woman had to wait 35 minutes for the police to respond to her call after her husband had thrown a brick through her bedroom window. I said, "Dealing with the police must have been a humiliating situation for all of you. Here you are in need of help, and they laugh at you. It's just not right."

Linda talked about a woman in California who had been stabbed several times and the police didn't do anything about the incident. I brought up the recent case in Connecticut where an abused woman sued the police force and won millions of dollars. I said, "Because of this case, Connecticut police are now responding more quickly to abuse cases." I said, "I know this doesn't help you out now with your situations, but things are changing a little at a time." I thought this story would provide the women with some reassurance and let them know that some public officials do not think abuse is a laughing matter.

PRACTICE POINTS

The group leader's intervention is designed to address the feeling of powerlessness experienced by these women. The strength of their anger, finally fully expressed because of their ability to join with other women who can validate their feelings and, for some, freedom from the immediate fear of harm, emerges in the next comments. The devaluing of the work in the home, also identified by Butler and Wintram is expressed.

Joyce said that she wanted to kill her husband. This desire had been expressed by an abused woman in a previous group session. Other women in the group said it wouldn't be worth it for her. "All he does is yell at me all the time. He makes me go down to where he works every day at lunchtime. The kids and I have to sit and watch him eat. He never buys us anything to eat." I said, "What would you do? Eat before you would go to see him?" She said, "Yes. Plus, he wants to know where I am every minute of the day. He implies that I sit around the house all day long doing nothing." Marie said her ex-husband used to say that to her all the time. She said, "But now I'm collecting back pay from my divorce settlement for all the work I never did around the house."

PRACTICE POINTS

The trust and mutual support in the group allows Joyce to share her "secret" of sexual abuse experienced as a child. Her disclosure of the abuse to her current husband only results in further emotional abuse from him.

Then Joyce said she was going to tell us something that she had only told two other people in her life. Joyce said that she had been molested from the ages of five to seven by her next-door neighbor, Pat. She said that Pat was friendly with her parents. Her mother would say, "Bring a glass of lemonade over to Pat." The first time she did this, he molested her. After that incident, when her mother told her to bring something over to Pat, Joyce would try to get out of it. But her mother insisted that she go over. Pat had told Joyce not to tell anyone what went on. At this point in the session, Joyce began to cry. I said that I understood this was a difficult situation for her to talk about. Candy said, "Joyce, it wasn't your fault." Joyce said she had kept this incident to herself for approximately 25 years. Finally, when she told her husband, he said, "You probably deserved it." Joyce said she felt like killing him for saying that. Candy said, "See, you can't depend on nobody else but yourself. You're better off just not talking to anybody because when you get down to it you can't really rely on anyone but yourself."

I said that I thought there were people that Joyce could talk to, including professional people. I said it was unfortunate for Joyce that when she finally decided to talk about her experience, her husband didn't give her the support she needed. I said that we were listening to Joyce and realized what a terrible experience she had suffered as a child. After Joyce talked a little more about the situation and calmed down, I asked if anyone also had experienced or seen abuse in their families when they were growing up. Candy said she saw her father beat her mother. She said she used to ask her mother why she put up with it. She said now she sees that it's easier to say you want to get out of a relationship than it is to actually do it.

PRACTICE POINTS

The support of the group leads the members to begin to examine the "decision balance," a concept from motivational interviewing presented earlier in this chapter, between the problems of leaving an abusive situation versus the advantages of leaving. The group leader resists the urge to take a position on the matter since she respects the fact that this is an issue only the women can decide. In this situation, the group leader is truly an outsider.

Candy said, "I want to know whether we're better off leaving or staying in our abusive situations." I said, "Why don't we list on the blackboard the benefits of leaving and staying and see what we come up with." Candy said that leaving was better in the long run. By staying, the children will see their father abusing their mother. "What kind of example is that going to set for the children?" She felt her children would be happier by their leaving. Joyce said her children were happy to leave their father. She said, "They're tired of listening to him yell all the time." She said her son was more upset about leaving the dog behind than he was about leaving his father. Linda said another good reason for leaving is self-love. She said, "It comes to a point where you know he's going to kill you if you stay around." Linda said her boyfriend told her that he'd be happy to go to jail over killing her. Other good reasons for leaving that the women mentioned included: leaving an uncomfortable lifestyle, getting away from the pressure involved in an abusive relationship, and not having to take physical or mental abuse.

PRACTICE POINTS

In her next comment, the leader demonstrates how far she has come from her early efforts to preach to the women, reaching for the reasons a woman might find to stay in the relationship. By not allowing herself to act on the natural instinct of wanting to convince the women to leave abusive relationships, she creates the culture where they can honestly face their ambivalence and get the help they need from each other.

At this point, no one had mentioned reasons for staying in an abusive relationship, so I prompted the women to comment. The women said that money, belongings (many women leave their possessions behind when they seek shelter), and the convenience of the relationship were reasons for staying. Linda said, "Sometimes it's easier to stay because at least you know what's going to happen to you. If you leave, you don't have any idea what's in store for you. It's very hard."

Since group time had run out, I finished up the session by saying that it looked like the reasons for leaving an abusive situation outnumbered the reasons for staying. Candy said, "Yes, It's easy to see that leaving is the best thing to do." I said, "Even though we can see from the list that leaving is better than staying, that doesn't mean it's easy to follow through on a decision to leave. There are many women who decide to go back to their partners after they've left." I told the women that I thought they were very strong for having made the decision to leave, and I wished them luck with their new way of life. I thanked them for participating in the group session and said their discussion seemed to help everyone in the group.

Feminist Perspectives on Work with Other Populations

In another example of an application of feminist theory to practice, Holmes and Lundy (1990) present what they term a "feminist perspective" on work with men who batter. They provide specific prescriptions for intervention that are based on feminist theoretical and ideological assumptions. Other examples that draw on feminist perspectives include Berman-Rossi and Cohen (1989), who focus on work with homeless, mentally ill women; and Breton (1988), who provides an example of a "sistering" approach in a drop-in shelter for homeless women. O'Brien (1995) identifies the self-empowerment of a group of African American women, who were long-term public housing residents and activists, as a contributor to their resilience and effective mothering.

In an effort to merge a feminist perspective with a cognitive-behavioral approach, Srebnik and Saltzberg (1994) describe how internalized cultural messages negatively affect a woman's body image. The authors then propose interventions to influence thought patterns and dysfunctional behaviors.

In another example, Collins (1994) uses feminist theory to challenge the concept of codependency in substance abuse practice. The author refutes the idea that women need to view their relational strengths as pathology. Instead, she argues that they can get well by naming and discussing the injustices in their relational context.

In a more recent work in this area, Wood and Roche (2001) draw on feminist and social constructionist positions, anthropology, and narrative ideas to describe and illustrate a framework for practice with groups of women who are being battered and raped by husbands and boyfriends. They emphasize the role of resistance and protest in developing self-representation and proclaiming it in definitional ceremonies. The example that follows illustrates the power of resistance, protest, and definitional ceremonies.

Take Back the Night March

Most of the literature associated with this model emphasizes the impact of oppression and the importance of refusing to accept the internalized image of oneself as powerless in its face. In a group which integrated clinical practice with social action, the group first introduced in Chapter 9, the leaders approached the ending phase of work with a group of survivors of sexual abuse. After many months of difficult and powerful work on the impact of abuse on their lives, the counselor suggests that they consider attending a local march against sexual violence directed toward women.

> Then group members asked me to review information about the local Take Back the Night march with them. We had told them about the march against sexual violence against women a few weeks before and, after some exploration of their fears about participating in a public demonstration, they decided to march as a group. I supported the group's readiness to act independently and support one another in new experiences. I shared with them how good I felt that they wanted to march together and gave them the information they needed.
>
> At the next session, we supported the group's growing independence and shared our feelings with them. As the group processed how the march had felt for them, Jane and I shared how powerful it had felt for us to see them there, marching, chanting, and singing. We also shared that it was hard for us to see them and know that the group was ending. The group was special for us, and it would be hard to let it go.

Following their experience with the march, the group members decided to contribute samples of their poetry and art to an exhibit that dealt with issues of violence toward women. They also decided to contribute proceeds from the sale of their art to a fund devoted to support groups for survivors like themselves. This represents an example of a group combining the personal and the political, and deciding which part of their work was more "therapeutic" would be difficult. The cake they shared in their last session had even been decorated with the phrase "Survivors—Striving and Thriving!"

Finally, in an example of research in this area, Westbury and Tutty (1999) conducted a small, quasi-experimental study that compared women who were sexually abused as children and who were receiving individual and group treatment that included feminist techniques with women on a waiting list who were receiving only individual counseling. They found that the treatment group had significantly improved depression and anxiety scores, when compared with the waiting list group, as well as a near-significant improvement in self-image.

Religion and Spirituality

The helping professions have been taking an increased interest in the area of religion and spirituality in their practice. Formerly most evident in pastoral counseling, religion and spirituality have moved toward inclusion in many mainstream practice models.

Van Hook (2008) lists four reasons for incorporating spirituality into practice:

> First, those counseling models which stress the meaning of systems in the lives of individuals and families including spirituality and religion require counselors to understand the paradigms that shape how clients view their world. (p. 37)

> Second, there is a growing recognition by health professionals that spirituality and religion play important roles in the lives of people from a wide variety of cultural backgrounds. (p. 38)

> Third, a growing body of literature points out the positive role that spirituality and more specifically religion can play in promoting both mental and physical health. (p. 38)

> A fourth reason for including spirituality in the counseling process is that spirituality has been identified as promoting resiliency (the process by which people manage not only to endure hardships but also to create and sustain lives that have meaning and contribute to those around them). (p. 40)

Moody (2005), in his introduction to an edited collection of essays on the application of religion and spirituality to the aging population, points out that the precursor of early practice had roots in religious movements. Only recently have the helping professions begun to seriously explore the impact of religion and spirituality on our clients' lives and has the topic gained greater acceptance in the academic world. Spirituality and religion had been marginalized as outside our scientific model. Now, aided by the increased focus on work with the elderly in which religion and spirituality have been found to play an important role, this area has taken on new importance. It would be difficult to find professional training programs that do not include a course (or courses) on the topic.

Definitions

Moberg (2005) points out the difficulty of defining *spirituality*. He cites Aldridge (2002, pp. 25–54), who summarized nine definitions of spirituality that emphasize *meaning and unity* as the essence of spirituality, eight that interpret it as a dimension of persons, that *transcends* self or any experience at hand, three that focus upon it as *a motivating force or belief in a power* apart from a person's own existing, three that link it with *breath and its activities,* and four emerging from postmodern interpretations as something *non-observable and meta empirical.* There is no universally accepted definition, but we clearly are moving toward a universal consensus that there is a "something" about people that we can call "the human spirit" and therefore a reality that we can label as *spirituality.* (p. 13)

Moberg (2005) suggests that all of the definitions of spirituality, and even the scales developed to empirically measure it, only touch on aspects of the concept. He also suggests that for most people, although not all, spirituality and religion are so closely related that the terms may be easily linked. He argues that most of the empirical work has been on the topic of religion because the term *spirituality* is more elusive and difficult to "observe" and has only recently become a topic of research.

Van Hook (2008) points out that

> [t]he incorporation of spirituality into the healing process does not represent a specific treatment technique, but instead is recognition that spirituality can play a vital role in the healing process and that it is important to find appropriate ways to support this particular aspect of healing. Spirituality as part of the therapeutic reprocess opens the door to an important reality of human existence and taps the strengths and issues that are present within the individual. (p. 31)

Drescher (2006), in a chapter that addresses spirituality in the face of terrorist disasters, offers the following distinguishing definitions of religion and spirituality:

> [W]e will define religion as "a system of beliefs, values, rituals, and practices shared in common by a social community as a means of experiencing and connecting with the sacred or divine." And we will define spirituality quite broadly as "an individual's understanding of, experience with, and connection to that which transcends the self." The object of the understanding, experience, and connection may be God, nature, a universal energy, or something else unique to a particular individual. A person's spirituality may be realized in a religious context, or it may be entirely separate and distinct from religion of any sort. In most cases, however, religion can be understood as a spiritual experience, with spirituality a more broad, generic way of describing the experience. (p. 337)

Although some may question the use of a concept that is "meta-empirical" or difficult to define, there is no question that spirituality and religion can have a profound impact on our clients and therefore must be considered as part of our practice. It may be less a "model" of practice and more a recognition of the importance of these concepts in the lives of those with whom we work. Whereas Moberg (2005) points to the growing body of research findings that relate religion and spirituality to mental and even physical health, he also suggests caution when moving from the research findings to interventions. In particular, ethical issues may emerge that need to be considered.

He issues the following caveat:

> But spirituality deals so much with personal choice and other transcendental issues of the existential being itself that we may never know all of its components. There very likely are significant differences between individuals who

adopt spiritual or religious behaviors out of a desire to obtain the typical accompaniments of faith and those who do so out of an intrinsic personal faith without regard to "rewards," the latter receiving its fruits, but the former not.

Eventually, some prescribed therapies may prove harmful, while others that are proscribed may be recognized as aspects of positive spirituality. (p. 32)

Another concern about the potential negative impact of religion and spirituality is voiced by Van Hook (2008), who describes examples of the "shadow side" of this powerful resource and stresses the importance of assessment in determining who may or may not benefit.

An individual who contracts HIV through a homosexual relationship could find it difficult to seek help from a religion community that condemns such relationships. A person whose depression makes her or him feel alienated from God could feel burdened by additional guilt. People with perfectionists concepts of what is expected of them by the spiritual tradition can feel cut-off when he or she has failed to meet these standards. (p. 41)

Group Interventions: The Spiritual/Religious Autobiography

There may not be a spirituality/religious "model" of practice in the same sense as those models that were described earlier in this chapter; there are, however, interventions involved that foster respect for these ideas and for the structuring of new rituals and activities to address them. Encouraging members of a group, for whom religion or spirituality is important, to write a spiritual autobiography may provide one example. Schein et al. (2006) describe the exercise in a text on catastrophic disasters as follows:

The spiritual autobiography is an exercise that provides opportunity for personal reflection and sharing among group members. It is designed to enhance the third primary goal of group sessions by increasing the sense of social support among members. Because trauma frequently isolates survivors and leaves them thinking that no one else has experienced what they have or could possibly understand their experience, sharing spiritual history in the context of various life events reveals to members frequently how alike they are. (p. 357)

This concept was described earlier in this book as the all-in-the-same-boat phenomenon—one of the mutual aid processes. In the exercise described by Schein et al. (2006), a chart is used that has a time line along the bottom, from left to right. Symbols are used to describe either positive or negative events, such as a heart that represents relationship events (marriage, divorce, birth, and death), an upward-pointing arrow that represents positive events, and a downward-pointing arrow that represents negative events. The symbols are placed in the decade in which the events occurred. The left axis represents the importance, intensity, or value of spirituality or religion in a person's life at the time of the event, with a range from low to high. The group members each end up with their own personal autobiography in chart form. Connecting the symbols with a line provides a graphic view of the rise and fall of these influences in relation to these events (p. 358). Members then use the charts to share their autobiographies with one another.

In another group example of how religion and spirituality may emerge in a counseling session, a member, referring to her teenaged son's problems with the law, said, "It's in God's hands now." The group leader replied, "But maybe God wants to work his will through you." In another, a father accused of using excessive force in punishing his son responded by opening a Bible and citing a passage suggesting that if you spared the rod, you spoiled the child. The counselor, experienced in working with this population, opened her own Bible and read a passage that called for restraint. In both examples, the counselor integrated into her practice interventions specifically related to the clients' sense of spirituality and religious beliefs.

This mode of practice is still in an early stage, but as it develops, the challenges will be to ensure that it is client centered and not counselor centered, that it is respectful of boundaries and ethical issues, that it does not proselytize and evangelize rather than work within the client's existing religiosity, and that it remain faithful to the role of the counseling profession. It will be interesting to note how practice in this area differs from or is similar to a related profession, pastoral counseling. We will return to this discussion in the following section, in which we briefly examine practice with clients in response to traumatic events.

Practice in Response to Trauma and Extreme Events

During a training session with child welfare counselors in Hong Kong, one member of the group pointed out to me that the two Chinese characters for the term crisis mean "danger" and "opportunity." Most theories about crisis and response to disaster use a similar concept. The "danger," of course, is the potential for physical and emotional impact after experiencing any form of trauma. The "opportunity" refers to the unfreezing that occurs during or after a traumatic event, which leaves a client open and vulnerable to either a positive or negative change.

When we experience disasters such as the terrorist attacks on September 11, 2001, or Hurricane Katrina in 2005—to which outside response was slow and disorganized—the entire community may experience some level of trauma and, ultimately, posttraumatic stress. One does not have to be in the direct path of the disaster to experience the emotional impact, although those directly affected clearly are the most vulnerable.

In a coincidence, when I was originally writing this section, I received the following e-mail from a staff member at an antiviolence project I was directing in an urban, inner-city middle school:

> I was at the school today, and things are just so sad and bizarre! Last week a classroom witnessed an attempted carjacking in front of the school. Apparently two groups of men with shotguns came at the car from different directions, and the owner of the home/car released his pit bulls into the front yard, which caused the men to leave. The teacher of the classroom instructed all the kids to get down under their desks, which they did. She then instructed one youth to crawl out of the classroom to go get the principal while she stayed with the class. Jane, our site coordinator, and the other two full-time staff in the resource center, debriefed the classroom, but they were not instructed to do this until later, when the classroom was back to work (a bit of a delayed response).

This note provides an example of a small-scale traumatic event, although not insignificant for the students and staff in this classroom. Witnessing drive-by shootings, gang fights, robberies, rapes, and other physical attacks can take a toll on any group of children or adults. Although the term *extreme* event is most often used to describe a disaster, including the unchecked spread of a disease, a terrorist attack, or a devastating storm, I suggest that there are less obvious, persistent, and slow-moving extreme events in many communities that come to our attention only when they make the headlines. These more frequent, lower-profile events may affect as many or more children and adults than the widely publicized disasters. Violence, or the threat of violence, exists in many urban and suburban schools, and in higher education, but only when there are deaths and serious injuries involved does our attention focus on the event. The incident in 2007 at Virginia Tech provides one recent example of this category of high-profile tragedy.

An interesting example of a school-based program to address persistent trauma in Israel has been reported by Baum (2005). This program was designed to help Israeli children who were regularly exposed to ongoing trauma and stress from attacks on civilian populations. The author describes a national school intervention program designed to train teachers to deal with the persistent and long-term stress related to bombings and other forms of physical attack. The goal was to train teachers to work with class groups on an ongoing basis to help "build resistance" and "resilience." Initial and tentative analysis of the data supported a positive impact on teachers' attitudes and their confidence to implement the program. If the program is supported by ongoing research, and the teacher training results in positive outcomes for the Israeli children, this preventive approach could be useful for Palestinian and Iraqi children, and for any children who live in a persistent threatening environment—even in the inner cities of the United States. Of course, for all of these children the real issue is how to resolve the conflicts and restore a sense of peace and security.

In the next section, I will briefly introduce an evolving model of group practice that incorporates elements from crisis theory, disaster theory, and crisis intervention.

Crisis Theory and Crisis Intervention

Mitchel and Everly (2006) describe three main characteristics that are evident in any crisis:

1. The relative balance between a person's thinking and emotions is disrupted.
2. One's usual coping methods fail to work in the face of the critical incident.
3. Evidence of mild to severe impairment occurs in the individual or group involved in the crisis. (p. 428)

Mirabito and Rosenthal (2006) explore the issue of practice at the micro, mezzo, and macro level in the wake of the September 11 attacks on the World Trade Center. As faculty members at a university located in Lower Manhattan, they describe the experiences of counselors on a number of levels. Drawing upon the literature, they begin by setting out the underlying knowledge base for the intervention approach by exploring crisis theory. They refer to a model developed by Ell (1996) that includes the following:

- During a crisis, individuals frequently experience a state of acute emotional disequilibrium, which is marked by physical symptoms, cognitive impairment, and social disorganization.
- The state of acute situational distress that accompanies a crisis upsets an individual's usual steady state. It is important to emphasize that this state of disequilibrium is not a pathological condition. Moreover, crisis can happen to anyone at any time of life.

- During the state of disequilibrium that accompanies a crisis, individuals will naturally strive to return to a state of homeostasis or balance by mobilizing personal, familial, social and environmental supports.
- While struggling to return to the previous state of homeostasis, individuals experience a time-limited state of psychological, emotional, and, possibly, physical vulnerability that can be extremely difficult and distressing.
- During the heightened state of vulnerability that accompanies a crisis, individuals are often more receptive to and better able to utilize professional intervention.
- After the resolution of a crisis, individuals return to a state of functioning that may be either the same as, better or worse than the original state of equilibrium prior to the crisis. (p. 44)

When considering the stresses that result from a crisis, Mitchel and Everly (2006) identify four major categories: general stress, cumulative stress, critical incident stress, and posttraumatic stress disorder (PTSD). The authors suggest that general and critical incident stresses are normal reactions that people can usually overcome. The cumulative and posttraumatic stress, on the other hand, can produce significant life disruptions if not treated. They describe the goals of crisis intervention as follows:

1. To stabilize and control the situation
2. To mitigate the impact of the traumatic event
3. To mobilize the resources needed to manage the experience
4. To *normalize* (depathologize) the experience
5. To restore the person to an acceptable level of adaptive function (p. 430)

Crisis Intervention Stress Management

Mitchel and Everly (2006) identify four major crisis intervention stress management (CISM) group interventions in response to a terrorist event: "The two large-group interventions are called demobilization and crisis management briefings and are used to provide information and guidance. The two small-group interventions, called defusing and CISD, are useful in assisting a small group to discuss or process a shared traumatic experience" (p. 436).

The authors describe the demobilization intervention as a brief, large-group information session that focuses on personnel (e.g., the first responders) following their work-related exposure. The session provides information on possible symptoms, tries to normalize the experience, provides information on receiving additional help, and starts the process toward recovery.

A crisis management briefing is a large-group information session for people exposed to a distressing traumatic event. Accurate and practical information is supplied on the details of the event and on what is being done by the appropriate authorities to deal with the event (e.g., law enforcement, health, and fire services). This briefing may involve mental health personnel as well as community leaders.

Defusing is a small-group process to be used within hours after a homogenous group has endured the same traumatic event. It is a shortened version of critical incident stress debriefing (CISD) that is sometimes described as "storytelling" time. The goal is to normalize reactions and provide information about possible symptoms and resources. (The authors point out that early intervention is an area of contention in the field, with some studies arguing that the possibility of "retraumatizing" exists during a defusing session, and that not discussing the incident may be helpful to some in delaying a longer-term negative impact. Other studies provide support for this process.)

Finally, CISD is described by the authors as follows:

> [It is a] specific, seven-phase group crisis intervention process provided by a specially trained team. CISD is designed for a homogenous group, to mitigate the impact of a traumatic event on group members. It is typically provided several days after the crisis and lasts between two and three hours. The extended time allows a more detailed discussion of the event than the defusing. (p. 437)

In addition to the goals of the immediate defusing group (normalizing and providing information on potential physical and psychological impact), this session can serve as a screening tool to determine if any members of the group need additional individual attention or a referral for therapy or counseling.

The authors provide a description of the seven phases and a detailed discussion of the goals and interventions for each (pp. 456–459). Although their depth of detail is beyond the scope of this chapter, the seven phases described are the following:

- Introduction
- Fact phase
- Thought phase
- Reaction phase
- Symptoms
- Teaching
- Reentry

Trauma Groups

Attention to small-group process principles can strengthen groups that address trauma-focused issues. Davies, Burlingame, and Layne (2006) offer this view:

> Trauma treatment is complex and often requires interdisciplinary teamwork to address its multifaceted nature. Few circumstances are more complex than the aftermath of large-scale catastrophic events that result in hundreds, if not thousands, of individuals in need of care. In such cases, a variety of trauma treatment models may be employed, some of which target victims' initial reactions; others focus on the intermediate and long-term sequelae. (p. 385)

The authors cite research literature to support the notion that group treatment is as effective as individual or other forms of treatment to deal with trauma stress. They also point out that the result of a meta-analysis of relevant studies suggests that it is not the particular model of group treatment (e.g., cognitive-behavioral) that accounts for positive outcomes. Different models have been proven effective, ranging from those that emphasize didactic presentation to those that emphasize "process."

Many of the elements that have been shown to matter across practice models include those identified earlier in this book—for example, a positive relationship with the group leader; experiencing the commonality of the reaction to the event (I referred to this earlier in Chapter 3 as the all-in-the-same-boat phenomenon); emotional support from others in the group, information (data) that helps place the trauma in perspective, and so forth.

Different models identify specific exercises that can be implemented in the group to assist trauma survivors to develop effective coping skills. One illustration of these skills, forgiveness exercises, is described in a later section.

Groups for Children Dealing with the Trauma of 9/11

We have become increasingly aware of the unique impact of traumatic events on children, either an immediate event such as 9/11 or a more persistent chronic trauma such as community violence. According to Pfefferbaum (2005):

> A host of stressors, both natural and human-caused, have the potential to evoke symptoms. Naturally occurring stressors include, for example, tornadoes, earthquakes, and medical illnesses. Human-caused events include accidents, domestic and community violence, murder, terrorism, and war. Some of these are singular events; other involve chronic or repeated exposure. Trauma exposure appears to be common in children. (p. 19)

The author points out that most data are retrospective self-report and that a number of factors have not been well examined. Referring to the need for additional research, she suggests one example.

> Of great interest, particularly with the advent of major terrorist events in this country, are indirect forms of exposure and the PTSD spectrum. The impact of exposure has been measured primarily in relation to PTSD symptoms or reactions, potentially obscuring important differences between normal reactions and those that have clinical significance. . . . The child's subjective response is central to our understanding of the post-trauma process and the course of recovery, the relationship between the biology and psychology of the disease, the relative importance of specific symptoms, and treatment planning. Finally, the child's emotional response to a traumatic event or experience does not depend on exposure alone. A host of individual, family, and social factors influence the relationship and must be considered in the context of exposure in both clinical practice and research. (p. 24)

Cohen (2005) echoes the call for additional research on the impact of trauma on different categories of children and the effects of specific treatment responses:

> More research is needed to identify effective treatments for traumatized children, including those exposed to a variety of different traumatic events, those with comorbid psychiatric conditions, including substance abuse disorders, and those with serious functional impairments in a variety of domains. Research is also needed regarding the critical components and dosage of TF-CBT [trauma-focused–cognitive-behavioral treatment], the efficacy of alternative promising treatment models including those provided in the acute aftermath of mass disasters, and the efficacy of psychopharmacological agents used alone or in combination with psychosocial treatments. (pp. 117–118)

Malekoff (2008) describes a group example of an effort to treat the long-term impact of trauma for those children who were directly or indirectly influenced by the events of 9/11.

> The terrorist attacks of September 11, 2001 (9/11), demonstrate in the most horrific terms that violence, grief, and trauma know no bounds and have become a fact of life in communities across the United States. The aftermath of 9/11 involves a complex healing and recovery process for those were directly

affected, one that addresses the basic assumptions about self and community. September 11, 2001 has also had direct and rippling effects on the millions who saw it on television, know about it, and grieve with those who were there. Children and adolescents are particularly vulnerable to the consequents of this devastating life experience. (p. 32)

The impact of repeatedly watching the collapse of the towers on television, no less being involved through the loss of a family member, neighbor, or even living in Lower Manhattan, can have a profound emotional and cognitive impact that lingers long after the event itself. Malakoff describes some consequences as follows:

The troubling impact of the neurobiological and psychosocial consequences for trauma and violence include post-traumatic stress disorders and responses such as impaired cognitive, behavior, and psychosocial development, dysfunctional thinking and processing, altered attention and concentration, anxiety, depression, dissociation, aggression, violence, suspicion, mistrust, sense of foreshortened future, isolation, and changes in peer and family relationships. (p. 32)

Malekoff points out that a key question is how to regenerate a sense of interdependence and community. He suggests mutual aid support groups using verbal and nonverbal activities that can help children "calm down" and "soothe themselves in fun ways" can help prepare them for addressing more anxiety-raising memories. He then describes a number of strategies used to help children who had lost fathers in the 9/11 attack deal with difficult emotions and memories while still finding ways to remember the positive feelings toward those they lost. Some of these include the following:

- **Creating a Board Game to Remember Dad.** Used with a group of pre-teens who created a board game in which squares described emotions and cards dictated activities such as acting out particular events related to the person who died. Even the game pieces where designed by the children representing something memorable about their Dads (e.g., a football to remember watching games on Sunday with his Dad).
- **Cognitive-Behavioral Strategies in Group Work to Empower Young People to Cope with Intrusive Thoughts.** Activities that assist the child in taking control by regulating difficult feelings, soothing and calming oneself (e.g., drawing a stop sign on the back of a school book and dividing it into slices representing safe places or ideas or activities (e.g., call a friend, play a video game) or that engage their imagination, such as a park, a family vacation home, etc.).
- **Helping Young People to Make Waves: Giving Voice Through Group Work.** These can include involving them in community affairs where they can have some positive impact. Another example was a counselor preparing to present a paper at a national conference of bereavement counselors and asking members of her group what she should say helped. Their list was as follows:
  - Grown-ups need to know that kids have a voice.
  - Grown-ups need to listen.
  - Groups are important to feel better and not to feel alone.
  - Grown-ups need to be patient and to know that grieving takes a long time.

- It is okay to laugh. Laughing doesn't mean you forgot about your lost loved one, or aren't still hurting.
- It is okay to have fun. After all, "that is what our dads would want." (pp. 38–41)

Malekoff parallels group work principles and empowerment principles when working with children and youth in the aftermath of disaster (pp. 44–46). These include the following:

- Provide protection, support and safety.
- Create groups for survivors that reestablish connections and build a sense of community.
- Offer opportunities for action that represents triumph over the demoralization of helplessness and despair.
- Understand that traumatic grief is a two-sided coin that includes both welcome remembrances and unwelcome reminders.

Forgiveness Exercises

One group approach developed for work with victims of terrorist attacks is termed *forgiveness exercises*. Drescher (2006) writes:

> Exercises centered on forgiveness can be potentially important in working with victims of terrorist disasters. Because of the attributions of evil and malevolence attached to intentionally perpetrated traumatic events such as terrorist disasters, survivors and family members of victims frequently struggle with feelings of hatred, rage, and vengeance that are difficult to get rid of and may interfere with functioning. Forgiveness exercises strongly support the second primary goal of the group: cognitive processing of the meanings associated with the traumatic events. Group members may feel "stuck" with these feelings and unable to move forward. (p. 360)

The author suggests that "forgiveness interventions can focus on forgiving oneself, others (possibly even the perpetrators of terror), and even God" (p. 361). Drescher suggests that clear definitions of forgiveness are crucial:

> Members must understand that forgiveness does not mean condoning an act of terror or forgetting the victims. Moreover, there is no requirement that *reconciliation* with the perpetrator be part of the process. The primary purpose of forgiveness intervention is to allow the survivors to loosen the hold that the event and the related emotions have on them and begin to move forward. The goal is to help people get "unstuck." (p. 361)

The author proposes that steps in the process include the following:

- Clarify responsibility to deal with distortions or factual errors and self-blame or survivor guilt.
- Create an environment in which beliefs that are theological in nature (e.g., "This is God's punishment of me") be gently challenged without challenging the theological foundation.
- Help group members to move toward the decision to forgive, emphasizing that this is always a personal choice.

- Finally, reinforce the decision to forgive through, for example, retelling the story in a new context or reassuring members that the reemergence of old feelings is a normal part of the healing process.

Drescher (2006) appropriately mentions the controversy associated with the forgiveness approach, particularly with respect to female survivors of malevolent male-perpetrated trauma, such as incest, in which a significant differential in powers exists.

Some alternative models suggest that maintenance of a healthy level of compassion and anger is a more positive goal. In a clinician's manual for trauma-centered group psychotherapy for women, Lubin and Johnson (2008) address the issue of forgiveness of the perpetrator and the potential challenges involved. In response to a group member's question "Am I supposed to forgive my perpetrator?" they suggest the following:

> Some behaviors are not forgivable. You do not have to forgive the perpetrator. This is up to you. What we are talking about here is your capacity and readiness to forgive yourself. Many traumatized individuals blame the trauma on themselves and some of their self-destructive behavior may be an attempt to punish themselves. If you can remind yourself and accept that you were shortchanged, maybe you can forgive yourself. (p. 59)

The concept of forgiveness can also be understood as an element of spirituality and religion. Van Hook (2008) points out that forgiveness of self and others can be a powerful therapeutic tool. An appreciation for diversity and culture leads her to caution as follows:

> While forgiveness is supported by many religious traditions, the meaning of forgiveness varies depending on the tradition. As a result, counselors need to seek understanding of the meaning of forgiveness within the client's tradition. . . .
> In Judaism only the injured can grant forgiveness. Within Eastern religious traditions, harmful actions are viewed within a concept of worldwide suffering. (pp. 56–57)

Forgiveness has also emerged on a societal or national level through the use of "truth and reconciliation" processes, in which the perpetrators of acts of violence against whole populations accept their guilt and national reconciliation is the goal. The effort in South Africa to move past the atrocities committed by the white power structure during apartheid is one example.

Impact of Trauma on the Professional

When considering the impact of a disaster, it is important to understand how it can affect the helping professional who may have been exposed to the disaster or worked with survivors. Mirabito and Rosenthal (2006) provide this view on those who assisted survivors of September 11:

> Many of the professionals who volunteered to assist in the aftermath of September 11 did so in the dual capacity of professional helpers and individuals who were themselves affected in many different ways. Struck with their own grief, mourning, and shock, they struggled to make sense out of the extremely disturbing events. Moreover, they attempted to recover from the effects of the disaster as quickly as possible in order to begin to help others. (p. 55)

This is an important issue because helping professionals can experience a delayed impact following direct exposure to an immediate traumatic event, vicarious traumatization, and secondary trauma symptoms that result from working with the survivors. *Vicarious traumatization* refers to the changes in the helping professional when repeatedly exposed to the impact of trauma on clients.

In addition to the secondary trauma symptoms experienced by professionals dealing with mass disasters such as the 9/11 attack, there is evidence of compassion fatigue, sometimes referred to as *burnout*, experienced when exposed to long-term work in trauma-related areas. Professionals who deal with child abuse or sexual abuse groups, for example, may evidence personal and professional changes as they experience the emotions of the trauma victims in individual or group treatment.

A Single-Session Vicarious Traumatization Model for Trauma Workers

Clemans (2004) describes an example of a single-session psychoeducational group model for trauma workers to assist them in understanding and recognizing vicarious trauma in their own work experiences. The 2-hour sessions were organized using a mutual aid model with presentations, exercises, and discussions. These sessions were provided to agency-based trauma workers in settings dealing with rape crisis/sexual assault, domestic violence and child welfare/child protection. The groups were called "VT Seed Groups," and the purposes were "to provide workers with an overview of VT; to assess its occurrence among workers; and, through the process of mutual aid, to generate effective strategies to respond to VT" (p. 61)".

Each group was divided into four separate sections, each one attempting to answer a specific question:

1. Getting Started (Why are we here and what can I expect?)
2. Providing a Context (What is VT?)
3. Recognizing and Responding to VT (How can I help myself and, in turn, my clients?)
4. Ending and Transition (How did we do?)

The group leaders made use of a "stem sheet exercise," a writing exercise in which each participant shared their personal feelings about their trauma-specific work. Participants were asked to write in response to prompts such as "A specific way I am personally affected by my work with victims of domestic violence is . . ." or "One specific way I cope (either negatively or positively) with the stress of my work is . . ." (p. 64). Participants were then asked to introduce themselves and to share selected responses from their sheets. For example:

> B (participant reading her sheet): My name is B. I work in a domestic violence shelter. One specific way I cope with the stress of my work is by sleeping a lot.
> R (participant reading from her sheet): My name is R. A specific way I am affected by my work with rape victims is that I have become so overprotective of my 13-year-old daughter. (p. 64)

Responses were used to frame both the process and content elements of the group session.

The authors describe elements of mutual aid that emerged from the discussion such as the all-in-the-same-boat phenomenon, the normalization of their responses, and the ability to discuss taboo subjects such as the use of sleep or alcohol to deal with stress (citing Shulman, 2006). This opening was followed by presenting a brief definition and history of VT, three characteristics, and three specific effects, followed by case vignettes and discussion. Each vignette was read aloud by a member and introduced a theme: vulnerability and fear, difficulty in trusting, and a changed worldview. Strategies for coping were then discussed, including awareness (paying attention to feelings), balance (maintaining a healthy connection between work and home and outside activities), and connection (creation of positive connections with others). The ending phase of the session asked the participants to write a letter to themselves about the "lessons learned" and to make a commitment to address and transform VT. An evaluation of the group followed.

Impact of Traumatic Events on Practice

The impact of these events, either individually or cumulatively, can affect not only the person of the professional but also that counselor's direct practice. In my research on practice and supervision in child welfare (Shulman, 1993), I found that traumatic events (e.g., the death of a child in care or the physical attack on a professional) had a profound emotional impact on the worker as well as workers in the same unit or even the same geographic area. This impact directly affected practice for a time following the event unless group support was offered and the issue was addressed, often through the intervention of a supervisor.

For example, in one of my studies in British Columbia, Canada, when a high-profile death on a caseload was reported in a region of the province, the number of children served in that region sent into care increased, and the willingness of workers to recommend that children be returned to their biological parents decreased (Shulman, 1993). There were also significantly longer periods of time in alternative care arrangements. In contrast, in those district offices in a region where the supervisor or another administrator had created some form of mutual aid support groups, so that participants had an opportunity to deal with their own feelings and concerns and how they impacted practice, burnout, staff turnover, and less appropriate decisions around placement of children decreased. When traumatic events, such as the death of a child in care, received wide publicity and often unfair implied blame was placed on the workers, if the response of provincial and local administrators was experienced by the professionals as "Who is at fault?" rather than "How are you (the staff) doing?' the negative impact on the professionals and their practice was heightened. The inference I have made from my work with students, professionals in the field, and my research is that more effort needs to be made to care for the caretakers if we expect them to care for their clients.

Chapter Summary

A number of evidence-based practices (EBP) were described and illustrated. The three presented were motivational interviewing (MI), solution-focused practice (SFP) and cognitive-behavioral therapy (CBT). Three met the requirements for designation as EBP theories in that they use of the best available scientific knowledge derived from randomized controlled outcome studies and meta-analyses of existing outcome studies, as one basis for guiding professional interventions and effective therapies, combined with professional ethical standards, clinical judgment, and practice wisdom. It was suggested that some degree of flexibility was important so that implementing a manualized model did not prevent the group leader from responding in creative ways to the productions of the group and unexpected events.

A number of other models were also summarized, including feminist practice, spirituality and religion, and trauma and extreme event intervention. The feminist model includes issues of social and political oppression and the impact of having been generally placed in a subordinate position in respect to their gender. Efforts have also been made to develop a unique psychology of women in terms of how they relate and connect to others, with more recent efforts focusing on understanding diversity within a feminist model. Models of practice that integrate spirituality and religion were shared and illustrated with the argument that our practice has to be respectful and make use of these powerful factors that can influence the helping process. Finally, models developed to deal with traumatic and extreme events (e.g., 9/11) as well as the ongoing persistent trauma evident in many communities were discussed and illustrated. Crisis theory, crisis intervention, trauma groups, forgiveness approaches, and the impact on professionals of dealing with ongoing and immediate trauma (e.g., compassion fatigue) were discussed. A single-session vicarious traumatization group model was shared as a source of support for workers who had dealt with trauma victims.

Related Online Content and Activities

For learning tools such as glossary terms, InfoTrac® College Edition keywords, links to related websites, and chapter practice quizzes, visit this book's website at **www.cengage.com/counseling/shulman.**

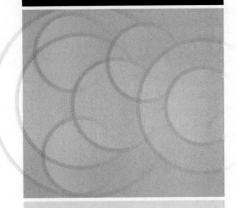

The Impact of Values, Ethics, and Legislation

I n this chapter, we explore several factors that can affect group counseling practice. These include professional values and ethics, social change, legislation, and the courts. We have discussed many of these issues in previous chapters. For example, informed consent, issues related to confidentiality, and boundaries on the role of the group leader were all presented in Chapter 3 on group formation and Chapter 4 on beginnings. The impact of court cases and the "duty to warn" is another example. In this chapter, we examine these issues and others in greater detail and bring them to the forefront.

Values and Ethics in Group Counseling Practice

In addition to knowledge and clarity about the professional role, specific values and ethics also guide the group leader's practice. In preparing to meet clients in a screening interview or a first group session, a counselor needs to consider these areas, which will affect the process and content of practice in significant ways.

In an introductory article to a two-part series exploring ethical problems and dilemmas for group psychotherapist, Barbender (2006) points out:

> In the training of group psychotherapist, considerable attention is devoted to the mastery of theory and technique that will enable the therapist to be effective in helping members to meet their individual and group goals. Cultivating the ethical group psychotherapist—training the therapist to be knowledgeable about ethical principles and be able to use them in everyday decision-making in the course of conducting psychotherapy groups—is a task that historically has been embraced with far less assiduousness. . . . Yet, intensive attention to this dimension of training of the group therapist is warranted. When exposed, ethical and legal errors made by group psychotherapists endanger the public's trust in psychotherapy in general and group psychotherapy specifically. Further, effective group work requires ethical practice. (pp. 395–396)

Barbender notes that when group members observe that the group leader's decision making is not informed by ethical considerations, a crisis in trust and diminished group commitment are likely.

Although preparing for every eventuality is impossible, familiarity with basic expectations of professional practice will alert a counselor to potentially serious situations and possible missteps, thus encouraging consultation with colleagues or a supervisor. The expectations may be spelled out, ranging from formal statements by agencies and other organizations to informal agreements concerning acceptable behavior on the group leader's part. In the next section, we examine how laws and the legal system more sharply define ethical issues such as informed consent, confidentiality, and the duty to protect. While many of the ethical and legal issues can apply to counseling in any client modality (e.g., individual, family, group), I shall play special attention to those that are unique to group work practice.

Gumpert and Black (2006), referring to this unique nature of practice with groups, point out that it is

> a complex, multi-leveled practice modality that requires assessment and intervention of interactions among group members, each group member and the worker, each member and the group as a whole, and the group and the worker. At minimum, the group practitioner must have a broad perspective and knowledge and skills to intervene in relation to many levels within the group process. Given the complexity of group practice, it is logical that ethical issues and dilemmas unique to group process might arise. (p. 62)

Definitions of Values and Ethics

For our purposes in this section, *values* are defined as "the customs, beliefs, standards of conduct, and principles considered desirable by a culture, a group of people, or an individual" (Barker, 2003, p. 453). *Ethics* is defined as "a system of moral principles and perceptions about right versus wrong and the resulting philosophy of conduct that is practiced by an individual, group, profession, or culture" (p. 147).

Loewenberg and Dolgoff (1996) define professional ethics as "a codification of the special obligations that arises out of a person's voluntary choice to become a professional, such as a social worker. Professional ethics clarify the ethical aspects of professional practice" (p. 6).

Dolgoff, Loewenberg, and Harrington (2005) highlight the difference between ethics and values and point to those professional practitioners who often "fail to distinguish between such terms as *values, ethics* and *morality* (or *virtues*). They use them rather loosely as if they all have the same meaning. Values, however, are not the same as virtues, though the two terms are often used interchangeably. Neither are values the same as ethics" (p. 16).

The authors argue that values imply a priority or preference and that the helping profession's values are generally drawn from the values of the larger society. They suggest that most professionals agree that client participation, self-determination, and confidentiality are among basic values. The authors point out that disagreements are likely when it comes to implementing these generalized professional values. For example, the value "enhancing the dignity of life" may be used by one counselor to support a client's request for an abortion or assisted suicide, while her colleague may call on the same generalized value to support her professional decision to try to persuade the client to go through a full-term pregnancy.

Code of Ethics

Most professional associations have developed specific codes of ethics to offer guidance to their practitioners. (Appendix D provides Internet links to a number of these). The drafters of professional codes recognized the difficulties involved when professionals attempt to make specific decisions based on general principles. To respond to this complexity, they also introduced the notion of peer review and peer standards for judging ethical behavior.

In itself, a code does not represent a set of rules that will prescribe all the behaviors of counselors in all of the complexities of professional life. Rather, a *code of ethics* offers general principles to guide conduct, as well as the judicious appraisal of conduct, in situations that have ethical implications. It provides the basis for making judgments about ethical actions before and after they occur. Frequently, the particular situation determines the ethical principles that apply and the manner of their application. In such cases, not only the particular ethical principles but also the entire code and its spirit are taken into consideration. One must judge specific applications of ethical principles in context. Ethical behavior in a given situation must satisfy not only the judgment of the individual counselor but also the judgment of an unbiased jury of professional peers.

Ethical Dilemmas and Ethical Decision Making

Of course, if all situations were clear and unambiguous, and if ethical codes were explicit enough to provide specific guidelines for all occasions (and all professionals could agree on these), ethical practice would simply involve a learning process and the strict implementation of agreed-on standards of practice. In reality, however, it does not work that way. The interplay among values, ethics, and practice is rarely simple and clear-cut. Counselors often face an ethical dilemma in which several possible solutions are equally desirable or undesirable.

Some ethical issues are reasonably clear-cut and provide unambiguous guidelines that are universally agreed on. Take, for example, the injunction against a counselor engaging in sexual activity with a client. Given the power differential between the helper and the client, as well as the serious potential for long-range damage to the client, such activity is universally condemned. In some places, legislation has defined such unprofessional acts a crime, with violators subject to criminal penalties. But what do professional codes of ethics say about nonprofessional relationships between counselors and clients after treatment has ended?

Even in these questions of boundary issues between counselors and clients, some areas of ambiguity exist. Consider the recent (2005) revision of the American Counseling Association's code of ethics (ACA, 2005):

> The standards related to boundary issues between counselors and clients and counselors and former clients seem to reflect a paradigm shift that is taking place in the counseling profession. Previously, there was an emphasis on the need to avoid any type of nonprofessional relationship with clients with no recognition that not all types of "dual relationships" may be harmful. The 2005 *Code* contains a new standard, A.5.d., which speaks, albeit with cautions, to potentially beneficial interactions between counselors and clients that go beyond the traditional professional counseling relationship. (p. 6)

The *Code* urges members to consult Standard A.5.d. to learn more about potentially beneficial relationships and factors that should be considered. Another change related to boundary issues is in Standard A.5.b., which changes the prohibition on having sexual or romantic relationships with former clients from 2 to 5 years while expanding the language to include such relationships with romantic partners or family members of former clients.

It is clear that many ethical dilemmas are not clear-cut and require careful thought and even consultation before action. Loewenberg and Dolgoff (1996) identify several factors that can contribute to such moments of serious uncertainty:

- Competing values (self-determination and the need to protect a client)
- Multiple-client systems (working with a children's group as well as one for the parents)
- Counselor difficulty in maintaining objectivity (the impact of the group leader's life experience)
- Ambiguity in the case (lack of clarity on the degree of danger to the client)

The authors believe by simply recognizing the factors contributing to the dilemma, the counselor begins the processes of managing the problem rather than having the problem manage the counselor.

Rather than naively operating under the assumption that practice is "value-free," counselors must recognize that the very act of intervening in a situation is based on value assumptions. In an increasingly complex and changing society, with value systems constantly in flux, every counselor must be knowledgeable about current ethical dilemmas and must develop a methodology to analyze value and ethics conflicts when they emerge. Many agencies and health settings have ethics committees in place to assist in this process.

For example, the counselor should have a forum either in supervision or in staff groups to raise a case that creates an ethical dilemma for consultation. An atmosphere should exist in which a counselor can feel free to share honestly his or her own personal value conflicts in such a situation and thereby sort through the conflicting pressures.

Perhaps the setting should set up a committee to examine the specific criteria used to make decisions about the degree of danger required before a counselor must implement the mandated reporter role. Would a checklist based on these criteria help reduce the amount of ambiguity in such cases? The agency or host setting would not provide a simple answer to a complex problem but would implement a process for recognizing and dealing with the complexity itself. In addition, the setting would take responsibility for actively assisting counselors to deal with these issues. In those situations where the counselor may be in private practice, it would be important to establish a network of colleagues for such consultation. Most professional associations provide some form of ethical consultation to their members whether working in an organization or in private practice.

Ethics Audit and Risk Management Strategy

Given the complexity involved in trying to respond appropriately when ethical dilemmas emerge, Reamer (2000) proposes an ethics audit and a risk management strategy (p. 355). Pointing out that agencies routinely conduct financial audits, he suggests that an ethical audit might determine

(1) The extent of counselors' familiarity with known ethics-related risks in practice settings, based on empirical trend data summarizing actual ethics complaints and lawsuits filed against counselors and summarizing ethics committee and court findings and dispositions; and

(2) Current agency procedures and protocols for handling ethical issues, dilemmas, and decisions. (p. 356)

Reamer further suggests that each topic, such as confidentiality procedures, can be assessed and assigned one of four risk categories:

(1) No risk—current practices are acceptable and do not require modification;

(2) Minimal risk—current practices are reasonably adequate; minor modifications would be useful;

(3) Moderate risk—current practices are problematic; modifications are necessary to minimize risks; and

(4) High risk—current practices are seriously flawed; significant modifications are necessary to minimize risks. (p. 356)

He identifies the areas to be addressed in an audit to include client rights, confidentiality and privacy, informed consent, service delivery, boundary issues and conflicts of interest, documentation, defamation of character, supervision, training, consultation, referral, fraud, termination of services, and practitioner impairment (pp. 357–359).

Guidelines for Practice in Group Work

Although many of the ethical guidelines for practice with individuals or families also apply to group work, seeing more than one client at a time presents unique ethical issues. For example, consider this variation on the confidentiality issue, introduced by the presence of other clients in group work, as raised in the *Ethical Guidelines for Group Counselors*:

- Members are made aware of the difficulties in enforcing and ensuring confidentiality in a group setting.
- The counselor provides examples of how confidentiality can non-maliciously be broken to increase members' awareness and helps to lessen the likelihood that this breach of confidence will occur.
- Group counselors inform group members about potential consequences of intentionally breaching confidentiality. (American Association for Counseling and Development, 1989)

Although a group leader can make clear his or her position on confidentiality, the leader must also acknowledge that a "rule" of confidentiality cannot be imposed on group members. The group itself must discuss the issue and develop appropriate ground rules.

In a recent confidential survey of group leaders who were U.S. and Canadian members of the Association for the Advancement of Social Work with Groups (AASWG), participants were asked to rank 17 ethical issues according to the frequency in which they were confronted in their practice (Gumpert & Black, 2006). The 17 issues were identified in two focus group discussions prior to the survey. Of the 350 mailed surveys, 90 (return rate of 27% usable surveys) ranked the following 10 ethical issues as most relevant (in order of importance):

- Communication among group members
- Conflict between the best interest of group and best interest of individual members
- Conflict between group norms and values and those of society
- Unanticipated termination of a group member
- Conflict between agency policy and best interest of group/member
- Breaches of confidentiality by group members
- Conflict between member independence and interdependence among group members
- Undemocratic group decision making
- Professional incompetence of worker
- Problems between co-workers that interfere with group process

Researchers in the field of group psychotherapy have raised complex issues associated with disclosures in multiperson practice (Roback, Purdon, Ochoa, & Bloch, 1992). The authors conducted a multidisciplinary survey of 100 members of the American Group Psychotherapy Association. Thirty-six of the respondents were counselors. The survey described six hypothetical group therapy incidents that posed threats to the confidentiality of the group:

(1) A group member has disclosed outside the group highly sensitive material about another group member, (2) a group member has disclosed current involvement in nonviolent criminal activity, (3) a moderately depressed outpatient group member has threatened physical harm to his ex-wife, (4) a moderately depressed inpatient group member has threatened physical harm to his ex-wife, (5) an adolescent group member has disclosed physical abuse that occurred for several years but is currently not present, and (6) an 8-year-old group member has disclosed an intention to run away from home, with no evidence of physical or sexual abuse. (p. 172)

Each of these examples takes on special significance because the disclosures took place in the group context. For example, in those states and circumstances in which confidential patient-therapist communications are protected, is the protection voided because of the presence of third parties, the other group members?

Respondents in the study answered four questions regarding each incident. These concerned the most appropriate context for dealing with the disclosure (group, individual, or both), with whom it should be discussed (therapist, group, or disclosing individual), who has primary decision-making responsibility for managing the situation, and what action the group leader should take.

Several of the study's findings provide insights into how group leaders would handle the ethical and practice issues associated with the six scenarios. For example, 80% of the group leaders indicated that they would not contact authorities in response to a disclosure of involvement in nonviolent criminal activities; however, 53% would encourage the group member to do so. Open-ended responses indicated that the nature of the crime and the potential threat to others would modify their response. Arson, for example, is much more serious than shoplifting.

Almost all therapists (94%) reported that they would contact the authorities if confronted with an outpatient's threat to harm others, and 92% would do so in response to an inpatient's threat. An interesting related finding was that gender affected the context within which such threats would be handled, with male group leaders more likely to deal with them within the group.

The same gender difference was found in the scenario in which a teenager disclosed prior physical abuse. Overall, 89% of the group leaders indicated that they would contact the authorities if confronted with such a disclosure. Approximately 50% of respondents would engage in each of the following four alternatives in response to a report of abuse that was no longer occurring:

(a) Discuss and assess the legitimacy of the allegation with the group member; (b) discuss with the member in group his or her feelings about the abuse and abide by what, if anything, he or she wants to do; (c) explain to the group the therapist's responsibility to report this information to the proper agency and proceed to do so; and (d) discuss with the group members their feelings about the abuse and honor their chosen strategy for resolving the situation. (Roback et al., 1992, p. 178)

Clearly, numerous unique issues and complicated dilemmas face even experienced and well-trained group leaders. To bring home the reality of the impact of these dilemmas, an example follows of work with a sexual abuse survivors group and the issue of the group leader as a mandated reporter.

Survivors of Sexual Abuse Group and the Mandated Reporter

Although the ethical issues and the guidelines for practice in situations in which someone is at risk are clearer, and the group leader's responsibility as a mandated reporter removes much of the ambiguity, the process can still be painful for all concerned. Consider the following example from a group of eight women who were survivors of childhood sexual abuse. It was a long-term open group, and, although the group had been meeting for 2 years, this was the group co-leader's first year. The student, a representative from the state child welfare agency, and a therapist from a local social service agency co-led the group.

The co-leaders had clearly indicated the limits on confidentiality during the contracting in the first session. Once that is clear, the co-leaders can assume that if a member shares information that requires reporting, they know the leaders are mandated to do so. Group members under these circumstances will often share the information with a conscious or unconscious desire that the leaders take the next step that they themselves find hard to take.

Confidentiality is a particularly salient issue, because, while the group was voluntary for these women, the fact of my being an employee of the child welfare agency was concerning for them until they got to know me and became comfortable with me.

The week prior to this meeting was very emotional, as one of the women had talked about concerns about how her son behaved when he returned from a recent visit with his father. The description of his behavior and the things that he said pointed to the father having digitally penetrated the boy's anus after they had showered together. I reminded the group of my role as a mandated reporter, and stated that I would be filing a report alleging sexual abuse of the young boy by his father. I told the mother that I thought that it was clear to me that the fact that she brought it up in group was her way of trying to get help. I praised her courage and her concern for her son.

Eileen, the mother of the young boy, did express some concern that her ex-husband, whom she was still emotionally attached to, was going to be mad at her. Mary, a young woman who was in the process of filing charges against her stepfather for her past sexual abuse as a child, expressed feeling empowered by what she saw as my immediate response to protect the child, because her mother had never believed her when she told her of the sexual abuse. After a short discussion, the group ended.

Although the leader's response was direct, honest, and required, and I believe she was correct in interpreting Eileen's raising the concern as a call for help, Eileen's reaction the following week is not uncommon. After returning to the home situation, the client now raises doubts about the event, second thoughts about having disclosed it, and anger at the group leader. The lack of defensiveness on the part of the group leader and the responses of other group members are crucial at this point.

At the start of the next group meeting, there was a long silence of about 2 minutes. Several members were glancing at Eileen, and she was moving about in her seat in an agitated manner.

GROUP LEADER: Eileen, you appear to be upset. Is something going on for you?

EILEEN: This is very hard for me. I'm really pissed at you, and I'm having a hard time confronting you. I spoke with Alice [her individual therapist] about what you did last week, and she told me that I should tell you how I feel.

GROUP LEADER: You sound very angry. I would very much like to hear what you have to say. (There is about 30 seconds of silence.)

EILEEN: Well, I thought what we said in group was supposed to be confidential! You took what I said in group when I was upset last week and then used it against me. How the hell am I supposed to ever trust you again?

GROUP LEADER: You feel I betrayed your trust by filing a report against Bobby, and you feel that it is not safe in the group because it is not really confidential.

EILEEN: Damned straight! How can I trust you anymore? Bobby is blaming me. I know my own son. I know when he's exaggerating and when he's not.

MARY: (Angrily) Right! I'm sure that's the same excuse that our mothers used when we were abused.

GROUP LEADER: Eileen, I wonder what it means to you that I reported Bobby. Do you think that it means that I don't trust you to protect your son or that I think that you are a bad mother? (Eileen starts to cry. As she sobs, others squirm about in their chairs.)

EILEEN: (Looking up) Yes, it means that I am no better than my mother!

PRACTICE SUMMARY In the group leader's analysis of this incident, she describes how, even though she knew that she was doing the right thing and that she had no choice, it was painful for her to hear the client's anger. The group leader's skill was evident in not falling into the trap of explaining and justifying her action but instead exploring the source of the member's distress. Because the counselor had clearly described her role as a mandated reporter and had stated under what circumstances she would have to disclose confidential information (see Chapter 4 for a full discussion of contracting), she could be reasonably certain that the member knew she would take action. Many nonoffending parents, who were themselves sexually abused and not protected by the other parent, report later that they wanted their counselors to intervene to protect their children because they were unable to do so themselves.

Social Changes and Their Impact on Ethical Practice

In a rapidly changing society that experiences regular advances in technology, new and evolving ethical issues emerge all the time. Dolgoff et al. (2005) identify areas that include "family and domestic violence, including elder abuse; managed care and mental health; technology in information systems and direct practice; genetics; and end-of-life decisions, as well as dilemmas related to evidenced-based practice and research in practice settings" (p. 192). In this section, we illustrate two examples of how these changes force counselors to renew and reevaluate generally accepted views on ethical practice.

Managed Care

New ethical dilemmas have arisen from trends in health care. The significant cost of health care in the United States has led to a growth in managed care as one major strategy to control health and mental health costs; this is done by monitoring what type of health care a patient will receive from a health care practitioner or from a health maintenance organization (HMO). The goal is to reduce costs by placing controls on health practitioners and by fostering competition among HMOs. Managed care plans attempt to reduce these costs by controlling the type of interventions health practitioners use, limiting access to service, and prescribing the type and length of service to be provided. In Canada, the cutbacks in resources available to the universal provincial health programs have resulted in some of the same efforts to reduce costs and manage care.

Loewenberg and Dolgoff (1996) address some of the ethical dilemmas that face counselors in this rapidly changing system. (Although the authors are not specifically referring to group counseling, the example is easily extrapolated to that form of treatment.) For example, most codes of ethics require that the counselor should not participate in, condone, or be associated with dishonesty, fraud, deceit, or misrepresentation. Loewenberg and Dolgoff describe a case situation in which a client's symptoms could be defined either as psychiatric or associated with alcoholism and drugs, but the counselor suspects the psychiatric assessment is not indicated. The dilemma is created by the third-party payer's rules, which would allow for more sessions if the diagnosis were psychiatric and fewer than needed if the diagnosis were substance abuse related. Should the counselor select the less likely diagnosis to assure that the client gets the necessary number of sessions?

In another example provided by these authors, most codes of ethics state that the counselor should be alert to and resist the influences and pressures that interfere with the exercise of professional discretion and impartial judgment required for the performance of professional functions. The authors then describe a scenario of a depressed college student who has been threatening suicide. The dilemma emerges when the claims reviewer for the third-party payer rejects hospitalization, citing recent research. The code of ethics holds the counselor responsible for ethical practice, but the legal system would hold the counselor responsible in the event that the student did commit suicide. (Even more striking is the case of the student at Virginia Tech who murdered fellow students before committing suicide in April 2007. Although the details of that case are different, ethical issues were raised with respect to treatment and/or lack of treatment and communications between professionals.)

To complicate the scenario suggested by these authors, let us add a third-party payer or an HMO that takes the position that the counselor (or doctor) cannot inform the client that a recommended service is not being provided; thus, a "gag rule" is in effect. This would eliminate the option of empowering the client to fight for his or her own rights in the situation. Fortunately, abuse of this practice has led to legislation in several states to bar such rules. However, if the counselor is a private practitioner who depends on referrals from this third-party payer and whose participation in the panel of approved clinicians is coming up for review, the ethical issues are further heightened.

The helping professions are starting to face some of the crucial debates associated with the emergence of managed care and increased control over practice. In a point-counterpoint debate, Gordon and Klein (in Gambrill & Pruger, 1997) argue whether counselors should even participate in for-profit managed care programs. Gordon argues that we should do so for several reasons, including the opportunity to influence the care provided. He draws on his own experience to support the ability to work ethically within a for-profit structure. Klein rejects this argument and suggests that working in a managed care program would lead to damaging effects on the client-counselor relationship, raise ethical issues because of competing economic pressures, and result in counselors justifying inadequate care with simplistic clinical reasoning (pp. 52–62).

Watt and Kallmann (1998) specifically address the issues involved in managing professional obligations within the constraints of managed care. They describe legal and ethical conflicts, such as confidentiality versus the requirement to report services to an employer. They also present legal-clinical conflicts. For example, under managed care, specific needed services may be limited to clients who have a specific diagnosis that may negatively label them and not be appropriate; this puts the counselor in the position of either denying the service or practicing a professional lie. The authors further point out that a decision in the legal-ethical area may impact issues in the legal-clinical areas, and vice versa.

The 2005 revision of the American Counseling Association's *Code of Ethics* provides additional clarity to counselors about ways to address potential conflicts between ethical guidelines and legal requirements:

Standard H.1.b. notes that in such situations, counselors "make known their commitment to the *ACA Code of Ethics* and take steps to resolve the conflict. If the conflict cannot be resolved by such means, counselors may adhere to the requirements of law, regulations, or other governing legal authority." (p. 8)

Clearly, the debate concerning these ethical issues and others has begun. It mandates that all helping professions and every professional counselor attend to issues of social policy, legislation, and court decisions that will influence the core of their practice and profession. With recent proposals for major changes in the health care system designed to broadly increase the number of Americans covered, we can expect that a closer look at the economics of health care will make sure these issues stay front and center for the professions.

End-of-Life Decisions

Although greater attention has been paid to a counselor's involvement in end-of-life decisions during recent decades, particularly because of the growth in practice in palliative care settings, it still remains a complicated area for ethical decision making. A highly publicized case generated a storm of emotionally charged activity, when the parents of a young woman, Terri Schiavo, who had been medically comatose for years requested withdrawal of life support. It was quickly (and publicly) connected to the "right to life" issue of the antiabortion movement and seized on by politicians as a cause. The low point in the debate may have been when a senior U.S. senator, who was also a medical practitioner, viewed a video of the patient and declared that he thought she was conscious of her surroundings—without ever physically examining her.

Passage of state legislation, such as an assisted suicide bill in 1997 in Oregon (the Death with Dignity Act), can initiate conflict as well. In response to the Death with Dignity Act, federal officials challenged the legitimacy of the act and threatened possible license revocation of doctors who participated. One can see that, with regard to such emotionally and politically charged issues, counselors may face serious ethical decisions in their work with patients individually and in groups at the end of their lives.

In a recent (2005) addition to the *ACA Code of Ethics*, the authors tried to provide guidance to counselors working with the terminally ill. While the ACA stressed it did not endorse a specific way of approaching this sensitive issue, it directed counselors to take measures that enable clients

1. to obtain high quality end-of-life care . . . ;
2. to exercise the highest degree of self determination possible;
3. to be given every opportunity to engage in informed decision making regarding their end-of-life care; and
4. to receive complete and adequate assessment regarding their ability to make competent, rational decisions on their own behalf from a mental health professional who is experienced in end-of-life care practice. (A.9.a., p. 5)

In addition, the document points out that counselors addressing end-of-life issues are also ethically responsible for seeking supervision and consultation from a wide range of professionals. The ACA offers its members access to an ethical consultation service when facing such dilemmas.

Dolgoff et al. (2005) point to an effort to address this issue by the National Association of Social Workers (NASW) Delegate Assembly in 1993 that approved a policy statement on "Client Self-Determination in End-of-Life Decisions." They list the central ideas contained in the statement as follows:

- The social work profession strives to enhance the quality of life; to encourage the exploration of life options; and to advocate for access to options, including providing all information to make appropriate choices.
- Counselors have an important role in helping individuals identify the end-of-life options available to them.
- Competent individuals should have the opportunity to make their own choices but only after being informed of all options and consequences. Choices should be made without coercion.
- Counselors should not promote any particular means to end one's life but should be open to a full discussion of the issues and care options.
- Counselors should be free to participate or not participate in assisted-suicide matters or other discussions concerning end-of-life decisions depending on their own beliefs, attitudes, and value systems. If a counselor is unable to help with the decisions about assisted suicide or other end-of-life choice, he or she has a professional obligation to refer patients and their families to competent professionals who are available to address end-of-life issues.
- It is inappropriate for counselors to deliver, supply, or personally participate in the commission of an act of assisted suicide when acting in their professional role.
- If legally permissible, it is not inappropriate for a counselor to be present during an assisted suicide if the client requests the counselor's presence.
- The involvement of counselors in assisted-suicide cases should not depend on race or ethnicity, religion, age, gender, economic factors, sexual orientation, or disability. (p. 209)

The authors assert that even the issuing of such a detailed policy statement did not remove ambiguity and ethical issues from the discussion. Some counselors claim that the statement suggests it is ethical to be involved, but others disagree. Dolgoff et al. (2005) claim that

> [t]he policy statement raises many questions, among which are the following: whose quality of life is supported by assisted suicide? Whose life harmed? What is competence in such a situation? How does one judge competency? Is coercion entirely absent when people are considering suicide? What should one do if the option chosen creates issues for other family members, significant others, friends, or other professionals? What should one do if there are conflicts among those involved—some wanting to maintain life at all costs, other supporting the person's decision? What does it mean to be present but not participate? Is this just another form of approval of the act? (p. 210)

It is clear that the passage of a policy statement with regard to such an emotional issue has not solved the potential dilemmas faced by practitioners in this area. It may, in fact, require the actions of the legislators and courts to help resolve the issue. We turn to this discussion in the next section.

The Impact of Legislation and the Courts

When exploring the impact of laws and the courts on practice, we need to discuss the growing body of case law (decisions of the courts) emerging from important legal decisions that involve helping professionals. Both the legislation and the case law are more sharply defining the rights, duties, and obligations for agencies, host settings (e.g., hospitals), and counselors. These two forces have helped clarify practice guidelines and reduce professional vulnerability. The principles of practice emerging from most of these changes reveal that many of the regulations and directives codify sound practice concepts.

In this section, we examine several examples of the growing influence of the law on practice issues. Specifically, we discuss three topics:

- confidentiality,
- informed consent, and
- the counselor's duty to protect a third party.

Confidentiality and Privileged Communications

I addressed the issue of confidentiality earlier in the book in the context of discussion of first sessions (contracting) and dealing with specific examples where the group leader had a mandated responsibility to report certain actions as revealed in the group. I return to this question with an expansion of the discussion in this area. *Confidentiality* is the right of a client not to have private information shared with third parties. To see the influence of legislation on practice, let us examine how confidentiality and the client's right to privacy can be protected or limited. (It is important for any counselor to check with both federal and state legislation that specifically addresses this right for their professional discipline in that state. The same is true for other obligations such as the duty to warn, described later in this chapter.)

In some states, acts regulating practice were passed and licensing boards were established to administer its provisions. The legislation was generally designed to protect communications between counselors and clients. These communications are held to be privileged, so that the counselor cannot disclose them without the client's permission, even in the course of legal proceedings. Counselor-client privileged communications are thus in a similar category to the privileges associated with doctor-patient or lawyer-client communications, although the exceptions differ. The client's or patient's right to privileged communications strengthens the confidential nature of the professional relationship. When the client's right to privacy is protected, the client will tend to share private information more freely.

Different states may have different statutory exceptions to privileged communications and may include the following circumstances:

- A child custody and/or adoption suit
- When the client introduces her or his mental health as an issue in a court
- When it is necessary to commit a client to a hospital in the event of danger to the client or someone else
- When a counselor is conducting a court-ordered evaluation
- In a malpractice action brought by the client against the counselor

- After the death of the client
- In the case of a child abuse investigation or certain other state investigations

Exceptions are also found in other state regulations. For example, professionals are required to report suspicions of child and elder abuse or neglect, as illustrated in the example presented earlier in this chapter. Although there are still gray areas in which professional judgment will come into play, regulations such as these provide helpful guidelines to counselors and clients. For example, limits of confidentiality may be spelled out in the first interview with a client or during the first group session.

In any case, counselors must be aware of the rights and obligations that flow from their own state's legislation and case law. Consider the example of a counselor who is approached by a police investigator requesting information about the counselor's client. The protections of confidentiality and, in some instances, privileged communications mean the counselor cannot be forced to disclose any information unless a clear exception exists or the client expressly consents. A counselor needs to be prepared to respond, for example, by stating, "I am not saying Mr. X is or is not my client; however, if he were my client, my communications with him would be confidential and protected, and I would not be able to share them with you."

Until a 1996 U.S. Supreme Court decision clarified the matter (*Jaffee v. Redmond*, 1996), the federal court system had held different views on whether communications between a counselor and a client were *privileged communications*. Although communications with psychotherapists were privileged in all 50 states and the District of Columbia, the inclusion of social workers and clinical counselors remained in question. Alexander (1997) points out that, in its 1996 decision, the Supreme Court recognized the "absoluteness of counselors' right to privileged communications; counselors can no longer be compelled to disclose confidential information in civil lawsuits filed in federal court" (p. 388). For example, if a licensed counselor is treating a child protective services counselor to assist in overcoming grief related to the death of a child on a caseload, the counselor cannot be compelled to testify in federal court.

Alexander also points out that the absoluteness of privileged immunity does not carry over to nonfederal cases in state court systems. He describes one difficult situation in which a criminal defendant may request access to a sexual assault victim's records. Based on *Jaffee v. Redmond*, the privilege is absolute in a case that occurs on federal property and is tried in a federal court. In most states, however, if the defense meets certain standards, such as demonstrating the relevance of the information to the defense, the trial judge will review the records and decide whether any information should be disclosed. Alexander emphasizes the importance of keeping these distinctions clear.

As also pointed out by Alexander (1997), this absoluteness of privileged communications in federal cases can raise significant moral dilemmas for the counselor (p. 390). The Court of Appeals and the Supreme Court in *Jaffee v. Redmond* recognized that the privilege is qualified and may not apply if "in the interest of justice, the evidentiary need for the disclosure of the contents of a patient's counseling sessions outweighs that patient's privacy interest." The Supreme Court itself, in a significant footnote to the Jaffee case, stated the following:

> Although it would be premature to speculate about most future developments in the federal psychotherapist privilege, we do not doubt that there are situations in which the privilege must give way, for example, if a serious threat of harm to the patient or to others can be averted only by means of a disclosure by the therapist.

Implications of the Federal Health Insurance Patient Protection Act (HIPPA)

More recently, the passage of the federal Health Insurance Patient Protection Act (HIPPA) in 2002 has further clarified and set limits on the ability of a counselor or other health professional to share confidential information and to whom such information can be shared. The reader has likely experienced these changes when visiting a doctor's office since the passage of this act. Patients now receive a description of their rights under HIPPA and must sign a release form that specifies what information can be released and to whom.

One immediate implication for students in professional programs is that case information presented in class or in papers needs to have all identifying information removed. That is, any information that would allow someone to know the identity of the person needs to be changed or eliminated. This includes obvious things like names and birth dates but may also include other information that is so unique to the person that it will allow for identification (e.g., diagnosis, race/ethnicity, or gender). If diagnosis, race/ethnicity, or gender is directly related to the case presentation, students can include it if they are confident it will not allow for identification. In most professional programs where student work with clients may be shared, the potential identifiers are usually cited by the school or the program itself.

Recent evidence of the difficulty in clarification of the conditions under which mental health information can be shared was evident in the tragic Virginia Tech campus shootings. Mental health staff apparently believed that HIPPA prevented them from sharing information about the student shooter that might have resulted in his receiving treatment or at least closer attention, which some believe could have prevented the tragedy. These events argue strongly for the need to train mental health professionals—and health professionals in general—on the meaning of the regulations and the conditions under which confidentiality is waived.

Confidentiality and Group Counseling: Unique Dilemmas

Lasky and Riva (2006), citing the work of Welfel (1998), outlined some of the unique confidentiality issues in group practice:

> In addition to disclosing personal information to a therapist, the group client discloses information to other group members with no guarantee that those others will keep that information private. The very effectiveness of the treatment is based on the interdependence and interaction among group members that entails the mutual disclosing of personal material. The group therapist has comparatively less control over how sessions progress, in terms of the nature and depth of material disclosed, or what happens between sessions, especially around issues of confidentiality. (p. 459)

The implications of the presence of these other members, who in most states are "third parties" (which invalidates the principle of privileged communications between counselor and patient), are profound. Group members may not be aware, unless clearly informed in giving consent to receive the service, that other group members could be required to testify in civil or criminal proceedings. The authors point out that even in those few states that do protect the privilege in group sessions for the group leader and the members, many therapists are not aware of this privilege, and other group members may not be as well. Even if aware, there are no consequences if other group members decide to waive this privilege and provide the information. Certainly, this is one of the most important distinctions between group and individual work. It heightens the need for a clear understanding of the principle of informed consent.

Informed Consent

The ethical and at times legal requirement of *informed consent* has been defined as follows:

> The requirement that the client provide informed consent to services offers another example of how legislation and the resulting codes of ethical practice influence a group leader's obligations. Informed consent is the client's granting of permission to the counselor and agency or other professional person to use specific intervention procedures, including diagnosis, treatment, follow-up, and research. This permission must be based on full disclosure of the facts needed to make the decision intelligently. Informed consent must be based on knowledge of the risks and alternatives. (Barker, 2003, p. 114)

Generally, true informed consent contains the following five elements:

- The counselor makes full disclosure of the nature and purposes of the service, including associated potential benefits and risks. The availability of alternatives must be explored.
- The client demonstrates an understanding of the information offered in the disclosure.
- The client must be competent to provide informed consent.
- The client's consent must be voluntary, with no coercion.
- The decision must be explicit and involve either consent to or refusal of services.

Although the guidelines for informed consent seem clear, one study (Lidz, 1984) identified several practical problems observed in an analysis of how informed consent actually works. For example, the study pointed out that the person responsible for obtaining informed consent was not always clearly identified. Informed consent was, in some cases, a "floating" responsibility. In addition, clients reported that family members often pressured them to act in a specific manner. Was consent under these circumstances really voluntary? Counselors were not always trained to educate clients. A counselor's perception of the client's intelligence and ability appeared to influence the disclosure process.

Informed consent was often obtained after the caregiver had made an assessment and decision in favor of a specific intervention. Were other alternatives really considered? Lidz (1984) also observed that a client's understanding appeared to occur over time rather than immediately. True informed consent might require revisiting the consent issue periodically as the client's understanding grows. The author argues that it is important to review the informed consent procedures in every setting and to actively promote strategies to ensure that informed consent is real rather than illusionary.

Given the discussion in the previous section, on the near-impossibility of guaranteeing confidentiality in the group context, informed consent takes on a special importance. Falon (2006) states that "[w]hile both ethically and legally it is clear that group therapists have an obligation to obtain informed consent from patients prior to beginning treatment, the therapist is given a great deal of latitude in deciding what, how and when this takes place" (p. 432). Falon points out the existence of some controversy in the group psychotherapy field about the nature of the informed consent and particularly how detailed it should be. The author, citing Jensen, McNamara, and Gustafson (1991), suggests that

> [i]n designing the consent process, the clinician must judge beforehand the kind of information that the patient would need in order to decide whether or not to enter this particular treatment. Here the clinician can be guided by the "reasonable person" doctrine used within the judicial system, which suggests that the information to be disclosed about the treatment is that which a reasonable person in the same situation would want and need to know in order to make a decision and give consent. "Reasonable person" in this context will vary as a function of the patient's attributes as age, diagnosis and ego strengths, the type of clinical setting (e.g., prison, outpatient), the acuity of the situation, the goals of those who have a vested interest in the treatment (e.g., patient, parents, insurance companies), and system constraints. (pp. 440–441)

A detailed discussion of the models of informed consent, including written outlines and so forth, would be beyond the scope of this book. However, in the group context, questions from the client's perspective that can be addressed in a conversation between the prospective group member and the group leader could include the following:

- How does group treatment work, and how does it compare to alternative treatments?
- Are there possible risks involved?
- What kinds of records are kept, and who has access to them?
- Will you be able to guarantee confidentiality on your part and on the part of other group members?
- Will I get better from group, or could I get worse?

While this conversation is important as a part of informed consent, it can never completely prepare either the group leader or the members for any eventuality. As Falon notes:

> The unplanned revelations of intimate details of the lives of group members mirror the often unanticipated events and actions that occur in life; their spontaneity is what enables the group to become a microcosm of the world outside. In these here-and-now interchanges members have opportunities to rediscover what has been hidden and rework what has been feared. But these very same processes are also risky events. (p. 447)

It is clear that informed consent is required prior to the commencement of any group activity. It is also clear that the multilevel complexity of the group, often beyond the group leader's control, makes it impossible to anticipate all circumstances, so the group leader simply needs to do the best he or she can.

The Duty to Warn

Another court decision has had a powerful impact on practice by defining the duties and obligations of a counselor in respect to her or his *duty to warn* (in some states, the "duty to protect") a third party if information shared by a client indicates that the third party may be in danger. An important California decision, *Tarasoff v. Regents of the University of California* (1976), severely limited privileged communications under certain circumstances involving duty to warn.

In this case, a client of a therapist at the Berkeley University Clinic indicated murderous fantasies about his former girlfriend, Tatiana (Tanya) Tarasoff. The therapist became concerned and notified campus police, requesting that they have the client committed. After a brief confinement, the police, believing the client was rational, released him. No further steps were taken, on the orders of the therapist's superior. Neither Tarasoff nor her immediate family was notified. The family sued after the client followed through on his threats to kill Tarasoff. The court held that the therapist had been negligent in not notifying Tarasoff directly or taking other steps to prevent the attack. The court said the following: "When a doctor or a psychotherapist, in the exercise of his professional skill and knowledge, determines, or should determine, that a warning is essential to avert danger arising from the medical or psychological condition of his patient, he incurs a legal obligation to give that warning."

This is another example in which the evolving rules for professional behavior provide structure and clarity for the professional. In this case, if a client communicates a threat toward a specific person and either has the intent and ability to implement a violent act or has a history of such acts, the counselor is required to take appropriate actions. These may include warning the victim, calling the police, asking the client to accept voluntary hospitalization, or attempting to arrange an involuntary hospitalization. Although helpful guidelines have emerged from legislation and court decisions, the counselor's judgment is still required.

Given the importance of understanding evolving legal requirements as they affect the obligations of the counselor, practitioners need to stay up-to-date with the law, federal and state, and its application to new sets of circumstances. Membership in a professional association, such as the American Counselor Association or the National Association of Social Workers, can provide a means for keeping abreast.

After reviewing the previous sections from the perspective of a student or any practicing counselor, it would not be surprising if, rather than feeling more prepared to meet a client, the reader might be having second thoughts about engaging in practice at all. Ethical issues, rules of professional conduct, and the still-evolving case law highlight the increasing clarity as well as the growing complexity of guidelines that affect practice. Understand that developing competency in practice takes time. When you introduce the complexity of group practice, as discussed earlier in this chapter, the issues increase in number.

The purpose of highlighting these issues is not to discourage you but to sensitize you to be more alert to the signs of ethical dilemmas or legal questions. This awareness should encourage all counselors to make use of supervisors, colleagues, agency procedural manuals, and other resources whenever such issues emerge. Thus, in a case-by-case manner, as the counselor raises her or his concerns about client disclosure in an interview or group meeting, the counselor will gradually learn when such a disclosure triggers the duty to warn or give an otherwise mandated report. This is an important part of the learning process, which in the long run will significantly strengthen a group leader's competency and practice effectiveness.

Chapter Summary

This chapter focused on some of the many value, ethical, and legal factors that can profoundly affect group as well as any modality of practice. Codes of ethics, legislation, and court decisions may help define the group leader's responsibilities. In spite of these guidelines, counselors may still face ethical dilemmas in serving clients—for example, in responding to social changes or managed care requirements. Group practice, itself, introduces a number of additional complications. For example, the leader may have difficulty guaranteeing confidentiality because of the presence of other group members. They may agree to a group norm of confidentiality, but they are not bound by professional ethical responsibility to respect it.

Helpful guidelines concerning how to be consistent with professional values when faced with dilemmas may come from many sources, including professional literature and professional organizations. With the constant evolving of new law and judicial case law that define specific ways in which counselors must act, agency and host settings are advised to make sure that all staff, not just counselors, are provided access to these requirements as soon as they are available. Given that the rules are evolving and at times still pose a dilemma or lack of clarity for professionals, agencies should develop some system for providing an ethical review body before which practitioners can share their potential dilemmas and receive collegial advice. Risk assessment management practices, when implemented by agency administrators, are also helpful. Examples of complex issues emerging from managed care requirements and end-of-life decisions were shared.

Finally, a more detailed discussion of confidentiality, privileged communications, the impact of HIPPA, informed consent, and the duty to warn alerts the reader of current and evolving issues in each of these areas. In each case the unique variations on the themes introduced by the presence of other group members need to be explored.

Related Online Content and Activities

For learning tools such as glossary terms, InfoTrac® College Edition keywords, links to related websites, and chapter practice quizzes, visit this book's website at **www.cengage.com/counseling/shulman.**

PART II

THE VARIANT ELEMENTS IN GROUP PRACTICE

Part 1 provided the foundation for understanding and implementing a mutual aid model of practice. In Part 2, I will describe how these core or constant elements vary according to the nature of the population served (e.g., children, adults), the problems dealt with (e.g., substance abuse, marriage and family issues), the purpose of the group (e.g., counseling, psychoeducational, informational), setting (e.g., school, community mental health agency), as well as counseling specialty (e.g., school, rehabilitation, career, substance abuse counseling).

While it was not possible to illustrate all of the variations in this book, the chapters selected are those that address issues for a large majority of counselors in the field. Also, each chapter was not meant to be a definitive discussion of the specialty or a complete review of the associated literature. It was meant, however, to illustrate how a group work model (the constant elements of group practice) can be elaborated differently (the variant elements of practice).

Each chapter begins with a section titled "What Do Counselors Do in . . ." the particular setting. I have chosen to use the U.S. Department of Labor's *Occupational Outlook Handbook* to describe the work of counselors in each chapter. Although other descriptions may be more inclusive or, for some areas, practice may be more limited than that described in the *Handbook*, it was used to provide some uniformity for all the chapters in this section.

The reader may have a special interest in certain chapters more than others; for example, school counselors would be particularly interested in Chapter 15. But other chapters may also contain useful information. The reader is urged to use the subject and case example indexes to find topics of particular interest. For instance, all illustrations dealing with children and some dealing with substance abuse can be easily identified in any chapter they appear.

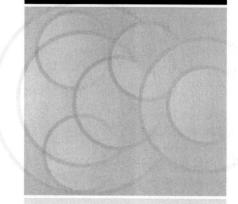

CHAPTER 14

Group Counseling in Substance Abuse Settings

This is the first chapter in which the general principles of group counseling outlined in Part 1 are adapted to address the unique issues and concerns of this particular population. This chapter and the next five in Part 2 are not meant to stand on their own as complete descriptions of the areas of practice but rather as extensions of Part 1. They are illustrations of how group practice adapts to purpose, setting, population, and problem.

While group work for behavior disorders and addictions covers a broad area of practice (e.g., gambling, eating, smoking, alcohol, and drugs), our focus in this chapter will be on group practice with the client population associated with substance abuse of alcohol and other drugs. I have chosen this population to begin to illustrate variant elements of practice because of the pervasive nature of the problem. Counselors in any of the other areas of practice—schools, community mental health settings, marriage and family settings, and others—will experience at some point substance abuse as an element emerging in their work. From prevention activities for youth in schools, addressed in Chapter 15, to recovery programs for the elderly or others addicted to prescription drugs, substance abuse can be a major source of client problems.

To begin, I will develop a framework for practice with this population, describe the role of self-help groups and the importance of an integrated approach, and provide a brief review of relevant research. I will then explore practice with active substance abusers who are at different stages of the change process. This section will include examples of groups for men as well as women and illustrations of court-mandated groups and a voluntary group for female trauma survivors. Next, I will examine the impact of dual diagnosis on the group process. This is illustrated with detailed excerpts from a group for women with mental illness who are also substance abusers and the author's work with persons with AIDS in early recovery from substance abuse. Because substance abuse powerfully affects those who are close to the abuser, I will also examine group work with significant others such as the abuser's partner or children.

What Do Counselors Do in Substance Abuse Settings?

In this chapter and the next five setting-, population-, and problem-specific chapters, I will use the U.S. Department of Labor's (2008–2009) *Occupational Outlook Handbook* to initially describe the work of counselors. The following is the Department of Labor's description of the role of counselors in the substance abuse and behavioral disorders area:

> Substance abuse and behavioral disorder counselors help people who have problems with alcohol, drugs, gambling, and eating disorders. They counsel individuals who are addicted to drugs, helping them to identify behaviors and problems related to their addiction. They also conduct programs aimed at preventing addictions from occurring in the first place. These counselors hold sessions designed for individuals, families, or groups. (**www.bls.gov/oco/home.htm**)

Group counseling for addictions in general (e.g., gambling, smoking, substance abuse) is a very broad area of practice and can take place in a wide range of institutional and community settings. It can include work starting with prevention at one end of the continuum to working with group members who struggle to maintain sobriety at the other. Issues of resistance and denial are often central to the practice with mandatory groups, such as those for driving while intoxicated (DWI) members common in every state. Because substance abuse can affect the entire family (and community), group counseling also needs to be available to family members to provide them support so that they, in turn, can support change for the substance abuser rather than serving as an *enabler*—that is, behaving in ways that enable continuation of the problem.

Jacobs, Mason, and Harvill (2006) stress the mutual aid element of groups for this population, noting:

> The value of addictions groups cannot be overstated. Addicts need to hear from other addicts, especially those who are struggling and those who are doing better than they are. Much support and help can be given each other because members feel a strong bond with those who are living what they are living. Also, other addicts can call each other on their "stuff." (p. 407)

Many of these variant elements will be discussed and illustrated in this chapter.

Substance Abuse and Substance Abuse Treatment

More than two decades ago, Googins (1984) identified a syndrome that he termed "Avoidance of the Alcoholic Client." He argued that while "problem drinkers" comprised 12% of the population (21% of men and 5% of women), counselors and their organizations tended to avoid offering service to this population or even recognizing the problem in their clients when it was masked by other issues.

In attempting to understand the widespread reluctance of counselors to deal with this specific social problem, Googins identifies a number of "myths" surrounding alcoholism. For example, informational myths leave many people unable to appreciate the fact that alcohol is a drug with properties and characteristics common to all drugs. Googins also identified "attitudinal myths" that lead to a moralizing approach that labels alcoholics as "morally inferior." Other attitudes, according to Googins, lead to labeling alcoholics as "undesirable, untreatable, and unmotivated" (p. 163).

Since the publication of this article, attitudes and practices have changed at least in part due to the expansion of services for this population and in particular, for the dually diagnosed clients who face both addiction and mental illness. Self-help organizations have also proved to be helpful in achieving and maintaining recovery. The federal government, through expanded support through National Institutes of Health (NIH) research in the areas of alcohol and other drugs (AOD) and mental health treatment, has influenced researchers to examine efficacy in work with these populations. In particular, group treatments have received a great deal of attention.

Self-Help Organizations

Among organizations that have labored long and hard to fill the treatment gap in the substance abuse field have been self-help groups such as Alcoholics Anonymous (AA), Narcotics Anonymous (NA), and a number of groups focusing on family members and friends of addicted persons, such as Alanon. While these groups differ in some ways, common themes include a focus on achieving and maintaining sobriety and helping others to do so, the use of structure to help bind anxiety, and the use of traditions and slogans to support recovery efforts. AA, for example, describes its purpose as follows:

> ALCOHOLICS ANONYMOUS® is a fellowship of men and women who share their experience, strength and hope with each other that they may solve their common problem and help others to recover from alcoholism.

> - The only requirement for membership is a desire to stop drinking. There are no dues or fees for A.A. membership; we are self-supporting through our own contributions.
> - A.A. is not allied with any sect, denomination, politics, organization or institution; does not wish to engage in any controversy; neither endorses nor opposes any causes.
> - Our primary purpose is to stay sober and help other alcoholics to achieve sobriety. (*A Brief Guide to Alcoholics Anonymous*, p. 1)

Many of these self-help groups adhere to *12-step models* that identify the route to achieve and maintain sobriety. My co-leader in a group for persons with AIDS in early recovery, described later in this chapter, and members of this group would often refer to these steps as guidelines for behavior when faced with difficult choices in their relationships with others. For example, steps 8 and 9 provide a means for members to deal with their guilt over their past behaviors by having "made a list of all persons we had harmed, and become willing to make amends to them all," and "made direct amends to such people whenever possible, except when to do so would injure them or others." These principles were invoked one night when men in my group for persons with AIDS in early substance abuse recovery talked about their guilt over having had unprotected sex with women after finding out that they were infected with AIDS.

AA follows an *abstinence model*, which suggests that this problem is a disease. One of the many AA sayings that guide members in their recovery is "For an alcoholic, one drink is too many and a thousand are not enough." Although disputes persist in the substance abuse field about the *disease model*, a focus on abstinence, the emphasis on spirituality, and other issues in 12-step programs, this structured recovery program and philosophy has worked for many and was reported as being crucial by three of our AIDS/recovery group members who attended AA and NA meetings while also attending our group. In addition, when the recovery of any member of our group appeared to be threatened, group members and my co-leader drew upon their 12-step experience to help protect the member's recovery.

There are other approaches to dealing with addiction, some of which are critical of the 12-step model. For example, the Rational Recovery movement (Trimpey, 1996) rejects the disease model of addiction and many of the central structures and approaches employed in 12-step programs. Advocates object to what they call the "jargon" of "relapse," "triggers," "enabler," "alcoholic," "addict," and other recovery group movement concepts.

Their central theme is that addictions can be conquered through use of "thinking" skills that radically reframe the problem of "addiction" by defining it as a "beast" that exists within the person. Trimpay (1996) and the Rational Recovery movement describe an "*addictive voice*" (AV), which is "your body talking to you, in thoughts and feelings, telling you to drink or use drugs. It is the sole cause of your substance addiction" (p. 36). Central to recovery is the use of an "addictive voice recognition technique" (AVRT) to recognize those thoughts and feelings that constitute the addictive voice as it constantly attempts to take control of the individual. This movement suggests that those thoughts and feelings that support abstinence are the real "you" speaking in a struggle with the enemy, the beast expressed by the addictive voice that encourages continued use.

It is beyond the scope of this book to describe in detail these approaches or others that offer aid in fighting addictions or to enter into the debate as to their relative efficacy. The real question may be which approach is most appropriate to a specific person at a particular time in his or her life and at a particular stage in their recovery. The two self-help approaches described here do agree on the importance of abstinence from substance abuse as central to dealing with addictions. Even this concept, however, has been challenged by proposals for *harm reduction* models that advocate attempting to help addicted persons moderate the negative impact of substances on their lives, rather than calling for abstinence. This debate exists within the professional treatment community as well. For example, an analysis of data from a national survey of outpatient substance abuse treatment units indicated a general rejection of the disease model by social work–trained managers, when compared with non–social work managers. Social work managers were also more likely to support continued treatment in the face of relapse and efforts at harm reduction activities when AIDS was involved (Burke & Clapp, 1997). I will avoid this debate as well.

Integrated Approach to Group Treatment

The focus in this book is on developing an integrated approach involving groups, led by professionals, with a strong mutual aid component. Concepts and strategies employed by other models will be used when they are judged to increase the effectiveness of the practice.

Matano and Yalom (1991) address the issue of integrating approaches in their efforts to synthesize an "interactional" approach to group therapy and the methods employed by traditional chemical dependency groups. While their interest is in a group therapy model in which the interpersonal interactions of the group members are used to develop insights and influence changes in interpersonal behaviors—a model somewhat different from the mutual aid support group described in this text—their principles for successful integration of approaches are relevant to this discussion. The authors suggest that

> an interactional approach can be effectively applied to alcoholics if the following guidelines are observed: (1) recovery is always accorded priority, (2) the patient accepts identification as an alcoholic, (3) anxiety is carefully modulated, (4) the proper distinction is made between what the alcoholic is and is not responsible for, (5) the therapist is thoroughly familiar with Alcoholics Anonymous language, steps, and traditions. It is important that therapists not permit misperceptions of AA to be used as therapy resistance and that they be able to harness the wisdom of AA for psychotherapeutic ends. (p. 269)

Research on the Use of Group Methods

Many group treatment programs for individuals with substance abuse-related problems are commonly based on (a) theories of self-efficacy, such as for women in substance abuse recovery (Washington & Moxley, 2003); (b) cognitive-behavioral therapies and medication, such as for the treatment of depression among gay men who are HIV-positive (Lee et al., 1999); (c) harm reduction models that espouse attempting to assist addicted persons to moderate the negative effects of substance abuse on their lives, rather than to abstain from substance use (Tatarsky, 2002); (d) self-help-based programs, such as AA (Davis & Jansen, 1998) and NA; (e) family-based support models, such as ALANON (Shulman, 1999); (f) therapeutic communities that use behavior modification approaches to treat addiction (Shavelson, 2001); and (g) group therapy models (Flores, 1997; McVinney, 1997). Many of the existing programs use psychoeducational support group models that focus on providing information to reduce intravenous (IV) drug risk-related behaviors (Levy, Tendler, VanDevanter, & Cleary, 1990).

Some models and program descriptions of group practice for at-risk drug users identify issues of oppression (Millan & Elia, 1997), gender (Benson, Quackenbush, & Haas, 1996), and race (Washington & Moxley, 2003) as important elements to consider in designing group practice. Other authors have focused on the problems of engaging substance-abusing clients, presenting models (Plasse, 2000). While suggesting the benefits of the group approach in the engagement process, research findings are either missing or limited by the design of the studies.

Studies involving group therapy for persons in recovery from substance abuse (who also have AIDS) show that group treatments generally have been supportive, with direct associations found between research interventions and positive outcomes for group members (e.g., Carroll et al., 2000; Felix-Ortiz, Salazar, Gonzalez, Sorenson, & Plock, 2000; Velasquez, Maurer, Crouch, & DiClemente, 2001; Washington & Moxley, 2003). Washington and Moxley used a quasi-experimental design with pre- and posttest measurements to study 93 individuals who composed two group therapy modalities, and they found significant posttest positive results.

Support for the influence of program factors on retention came from the National Institute on Drug Abuse (NIDA) Collaborative Cocaine Treatment Study, which found that retention in residential drug treatment was predicted by the program factor alliance to therapy (Barber et al., 2001). Among other findings, for example, alliance to supportive-expressive group therapy yielded higher levels of retention and engagement than individual-level drug treatment and cognitive therapy (Barber et al., 2001).

Retention and engagement in drug treatment also are influenced by factors outside the program that could help explain the mixed program effect findings. These factors include "level of burden," defined as the severity and number of problems faced by a client, including HIV/AIDS status, substance abuse history, impaired cognitive functioning, long-term health problems, and psychological problems (Brown, Huba, & Melchior, 1995). The combination of individual factors within the context of the program, specifically readiness for treatment and client motivation, were also found to increase treatment engagement in various residential substance abuse settings (Hiller, Knight, Leukefeld, & Simpson, 2002).

As this literature review suggests, both program and individual factors can influence retention and engagement in group-based treatment programs for AOD abusers, and the findings are often complex. This is consistent with the core interactional model presented in this text in that the group treatment itself can account for only a part of the outcome. The treatment modality can contribute to positive outcomes but only in interaction with group member–associated variables such as readiness, degree of personal readiness, and social stress and motivation.

Substance Abuse and Culture

Issues of diversity must also be taken into account, since attitudes towards the use of substances and issues of addiction and treatment may vary widely depending upon factors such as ethnicity, country of origin, immigration stage (e.g., recent immigrant vs. second generation), and community factors. In a publication for the NIH Center for Substance Abuse Prevention, Philleo and Brisbane (1995) point out:

> With the new wave of immigrants and the growing assertion of cultural identity of second- and third-generation immigrant groups, a new communication edict of cultural dialogue is part of the professional mandate. Therefore, the ability to interact with people who are culturally different from the professional is a prerequisite to providing culturally competent services to these groups. (p. ix)

This publication examines in detail five major cultural groups (American Indians, Hispanics/Latinos, African Americans, Asian Americans, and Pacific Islanders) as well as gay and lesbian persons, focusing on sexual diversity in a cultural context. While it is beyond the scope of this book to explore this area in detail, the reader is encouraged to review the material for each group listed that addresses the historical context, extent of the problem, cultural considerations, culture-specific interventions, and prevention.

In another example, in an article dealing with the use of foreign language interpreters, Amodeo, Grigg-Saito, and Robb (1997) identify difficulties non-English-speaking clients may experience in substance abuse interviews. Among these, they cite "worry about reports to referral agents . . . fear that the human service leader, interpreter, or both, will be disapproving or angry with them . . . shame and embarrassment about having to discuss with strangers an issue that is generally not discussed openly in their culture" (p. 81). The authors describe the difficulties that may be experienced by interpreters which, in turn, may affect their translation (e.g., annoyance or embarrassment at the client's behavior, leading to the impulse to reprimand the client). They describe strategies to increase the effectiveness of the clinician-interpreter-client relationship. They also stress the importance of increasing knowledge and skill in cross-cultural work and the value of attracting bilingual, bicultural leaders to the field. Some of these issues were discussed in Chapter 12 dealing with the general issue of the impact of diversity.

Because of the pervasive nature of the problem area and the range of prevention and treatment approaches, the balance of this chapter illustrates the core practice concepts with groups for

- active substance abusers,
- support groups for protection of recovery,
- dual-diagnosis clients, and
- the substance abuser's significant others.

Groups for substance abuse prevention will be described in Chapter 15, which addresses school counseling.

Group Counseling with Active Substance Abusers

This section will focus on group practice with active substance abusers. It is subdivided into groups for males and groups for females to illustrate the impact of gender on the abuse and the group process. Although the group members may be at different stages in accepting and addressing their substance abuse, they all have in common the unique issues raised when trying to address substance abuse while actively using.

Group Counseling with Male Active Substance Abusers

In this section we will examine work with two distinct groups. The first consists of clients who are actively abusing and could be defined as being in the *precontemplation* or *contemplation stage* of change (Prochaska & DiClemente, 1982) described earlier in this book. These clients have not yet accepted the idea that they have a problem or are just starting to think about the nature of their substance abuse. The second group consists of persons who have accepted their addictive behavior and are attempting to deal with it. Both examples are of court-mandated members who have been convicted of driving while intoxicated (DWI).

Court-Mandated Group for Male Drunk Drivers: The Precontemplation Stage

In the first meeting, we see a fairly typical start to a court-mandated group for persons convicted of DWI. Resistance and denial is in the air as the young female leader begins the session. Instead of confronting the resistance head-on and initiating the inevitable battle of wills (a not uncommon approach in some models of substance abuse treatment), she recognizes the resistance as a symptom of the precontemplation stage of acceptance most of the men are in. In groups such as this one, group leaders often feel a threat to their authority (and agenda) when complaints emerge. In this case, you also have a woman group leader dealing with a group of angry men, so gender issues can play out in the process.

Purpose: To introduce clients to support services; to encourage clients to explore their own use of substances and the role that alcohol and/or drugs play in their lives; to avoid re-arrest.

Gender of Members: Male

Age Range: 27–55 years

Cultural, Racial, or Ethnic Identification of Members: Two Irish males, one Native American Indian male, seven European American males

Excerpt from Process Recording

First Session

After going over the contract, I passed out a sheet that stated the purpose of the group and the topics to be covered. While some group members appeared to be reading the topics, others folded the sheet in half without a glance. I asked the group how they felt about the topics and if they had any questions. After a moment of silence one group member angrily stated, "You know, I shouldn't even be here. I was set up." (Nervous laughter from other group members.) He proceeded to tell his arrest story, while other group members appeared attentive. When he finished, I said, "It must be hard for you to be here when you don't even feel that the arrest was justified. I wonder if other people are feeling the same way."

PRACTICE POINTS

Instead of ignoring the resistance or confronting the men, she chooses to explore the resistance using empathy to begin to connect to their underlying feelings. The leader recognizes that the first member who challenged the need to attend the group was her "ally," not her "enemy." He raises feelings that are most likely experienced by all of the men. He, as well as other group members, are in the precontemplation stage. Instead of getting into a "battle of wills" designed to prove they need the group, she uses an exercise to help the group begin to explore what powers their negative reaction and thus is able to capture their energy in pursuit of the group's purpose.

Another member spoke up, saying, "Well, what I don't understand is why we're going to talk about things like alcoholism and AIDS in a class for drunk drivers" (referring to the handout). "Yeah, we made one mistake, and now we're all alcoholics." Other group members joined in, expressing similar dissatisfaction with the topics. I replied, "You're raising some important points. It sounds like one of the things you're especially concerned about is being labeled. I wonder if we can come up with a list of some other things that you don't want to have happen in this group."

As I wrote on the board "Don't Want" and under it put "to be labeled," I asked members for further suggestions. Another member said "to feel guilty. I don't want to feel guilty for what I did." As I wrote, "to feel guilty" on the board, I asked him if he could say more about this. He responded, "I mean, I know it was wrong, and I don't want to have people keep telling me it's wrong." Another member added, "Yeah, I feel like a criminal!" "Well, we are criminals, what do you expect?" another member commented. I asked, "Is it hard to see yourself in that way?" "Yeah, well, I guess we are criminals, but there are worse things we could have done."

It is striking that the group leader's use of the listing of "don't wants" actually allows the men to express the important issues to be dealt with in the group. They include feeling guilty, feeling like "criminals," concern about being branded as "alcoholics," and so forth. Each of these represents powerful themes to be explored in the group. The group members are creating their own version of the agenda, which actually, in many ways, mirrors the agenda of the leader and the agency. The example demonstrates the expression introduced in Part 1 of this book: "Resistance is part of the work."

Court-Mandated Group for Male Drunk Drivers: The Contemplation Stage

In the excerpts that follow, we see the beginning phase and the transition to the middle phase in a similar group to the one just described in which a number of the men have begun to face the fact they have a problem, confronting the profound negative impact on their lives of their abuse of alcohol. They have moved into the contemplation stage in preparation for a transition to the action stage. One man, the "deviant member" Phil, holds out and refuses to engage. While the leader misses his early signals and sees him as the "enemy" to the group, internal leaders emerge to help both the man and the leader understand the behavior as a signal of the intense pain and guilt associated with a traumatic event.

Purpose: To address substance abuse problems leading to DUI charges

Gender of Members: Male

Age Range: 18–45 years

Cultural, Racial, or Ethnic Identification of Members: Caucasian, African American, and Hispanic

The leader understands Phil's role as a gatekeeper, as described in Chapter 7, but does not understand why Phil chooses to play this role. This is an example of the mistake of being with the group but not being with the individual. Once again we see that the deviant member is someone in the group who faces the same issues as the other members but who feels them more strongly. This recognition allows the whole group to move into a deeper level of work.

Second Session

The group was struggling with their denial, Tom was starting to open up, but Phil was attempting to sabotage the movement of the group. It does appear that Phil is the gatekeeper, for every time the issue of drinking and driving is brought up he tries to prevent the process from occurring. I encouraged Tom to speak about his drinking and driving. Tom started talking about how he had three arrests in one year for drunk driving. I asked Tom if he could share with the group how he feels about this happening. He started to speak, but Phil jumped in and said that no one wanted to hear about this story. I tell Phil that Tom has the floor and ask him not to interrupt. I am starting to get upset that Phil is constantly interrupting, but I am hoping someone else will take a risk and say something.

Note that this is the moment that Phil needs the leader's help the most. Unclear about the "two-client" idea, the leader sides with group members who are angry with Phil and question his behavior.

Tom continues, saying he knows he needs help because he must have a problem, otherwise why all the arrests. Phil jumps in, but this time Pete speaks up and says that he has had enough of Phil and wants him to stop being rude. Inside I am excited that Pete, after having made overtures before as the internal leader, has stepped up to question Phil's behavior. I had asked myself how I might handle this challenge to my leadership (as a first-time leader) and my authority, but I realized the group had moved forward in the mutual aid process and that the group's work was going well. This was a good opportunity to point out to Phil, and to the group, that he was diverting the group's attention away from the emotional issue of drunk driving. I asked the group if they think this is a sign that they are beginning to be a more cohesive group, and they replied yes, except for Phil.

As the group culture develops, the leader begins to understand how easy it is for the members to create the illusion of work. When he confronts them about triggers, thoughts, feelings or events that lead to their drinking, the first reaction is a classic "flight" from pain through the use of humor and a "fight" reaction through a personal attack as described in Chapter 8 when I introduced Bion's emotionality theory. The group leader understands this and comments on the difficulty the men are having with a painful subject. He still, however, has not tuned in to Phil.

Third Session

While I think the group is starting to make progress, the illusion of work is holding the group members back. I make a demand for work by saying we are to discuss triggers that can cause them to drink. Jim speaks up and asks what I mean by triggers. Pete answers that was the Lone Ranger's horse. Tom jumps in and says that is what you use to shoot a gun with. I am not sure if the humor is a defensive tool to change the subject. I reply that this subject may have hit a sensitive spot, so I ask the group for feedback. Phil says that Jim asks the dumbest questions and wonders how Jim ever got his license. This is not the first time that Jim has been attacked when sensitive emotional issues are being brought to the surface. I am feeling some countertransference issues rising in me, about Jim being a scapegoat, and I tell the group that they must be feeling pretty powerful when they attack Jim. I ask why they feel it is necessary to do this. (In retrospect, I see that I have taken Jim's side and have forgotten the group as a whole. I am surprised I did not lose the group at this point.)

Pete, the internal leader, makes a leap of consciousness and apologizes to Jim for acting the way he did. Tom, Sam, and Phil all say the same. Pete continues and says that he had never considered anyone's feelings before and asks me why. I open it up to the group. The one member who has been noticeably quiet, Bob, speaks for the first time since the beginning of the first session. He says it has to do with the topic of the day—triggers. Bob says that everyone has triggers that can set them off, but he sees triggers as coming from his past. He lived in an alcoholic and abusive home. I was taken aback by Bob's speaking up and what he had to say. I asked him if there was more he would like to say. He said he grew up never being allowed to say much, nor have an opinion, without suffering a negative consequence. It has taken him this long to overcome his fear enough to talk in the group, but after hearing the apologies to Jim, he feels safe in the group. I said he was very brave to speak up and describe his feelings.

In this fourth session, we see the emergence of a strong internal leader who understands that Phil, the group's deviant member, may be reluctant to talk because he is thinking about his own triggers. As is often the case, it is a group member who understands and empathizes with another member and helps the group take the next step in its development. In this excerpt we also see why Phil has been resistant from the first meeting and has played the role of trying to block addressing more intense issues and feelings. Returning to our discussion in earlier chapters of informal roles adopted by members and the concept of the group as a dynamic system, we can see Phil's behavior in the first three sessions as functional for the group not quite ready to risk in areas of intense emotion. As the group culture changes and it becomes safer to share, Phil no longer has to play this role. In addition, once again we see that the member who takes on this functional role is the one who has tried and so far failed to live with the strongest guilt over his past behavior.

Fourth Session

I told the group that the last session showed the group is moving, and they should feel good about the work they have accomplished. I had a feeling that there was more work to be done with the issue of triggers, so I brought this out to the group. Pete said he had done some thinking over the week and wanted to know if the group could help him. All responded with a yes, except Phil. Tom asked Phil why he wouldn't, and Phil said he just didn't want to talk today. Bob said he thought Phil was struggling with his own triggers, and asked Phil if the group could get back to Phil's not wanting to talk after helping Pete. Phil, in a very quiet, subdued voice, said OK.

Pete said he wanted to revisit triggers because he feels that is where his major stumbling block is. Discussion was fruitful, and the group was beginning to take on a life of its own, dealing with intimacy and interpersonal relationships. Bob, Pete, and Sam were willing to look at these issues, while Phil and Tom were resisting any further intimate movements.

The group went back to Phil not wanting to talk, with Sam showing empathy and caring by saying that maybe Phil has some painful memories that have been triggered. The group as a whole struggled around how to help Phil. It seemed that the group had finally found a common ground to focus on—triggers. Other members took turns expressing how they have been affected by their triggers, how alcohol had taken over their lives, and the consequences. Bob talked about how he had lost his job; Sam said he had lost his job and his wife had divorced him; Pete said he had to go through bankruptcy; Jim finished by saying he had to spend eight months in jail for his drunk driving and this has affected how his children see him now. This was done with a lot of expressed emotions, with all members sitting in their chairs, but all leaning towards one another, as a way to begin to connect to the pains they had experienced due to alcohol.

As the group moves into a deeper and more emotional mode of work, we see the group leader practicing the skill of containment identified in Chapter 4 on the middle phase of group practice. The members have moved past the authority theme, as described by Bennis and Sheppard and discussed in Chapter 8, and are now into the intimacy theme.

They now turned to Phil, who looked like he had seen a ghost, and they asked if he was ready to share his triggers. Phil said that at first he had thought this group was foolish and felt that he had everything under control. We all sat with Phil's emotions. He started to cry, saying that he had for the first time since coming to group realized he was not alone in this fight over alcoholism. He said he felt this was a place for him to finally talk about his haunting nightmare. We all waited patiently, and I was overcome with the power of this group. Phil said that his trigger for all his years of drinking was he had never been able to forgive himself for driving the car and getting into an accident that had killed his wife. The group all sat in silence and cried for Phil and for their own losses.

Where the Problem Stands Now

I believe we have created a new phase of work whereby the group is able to open up and express their painful feelings. I am surprised at how much progress they have made in moving to the middle phase of group work. The difficulty of denial, defensiveness, challenging me to be in control, members wanting to take control, and the different roles each member has played has been fascinating. There has been a slow change in the manner in which the members have interacted with one another, each playing a dramatic role in moving the group to its current place.

The culture of the group has grown to the point where they can begin to use empathic listening skills. This was not present in the beginning phase. I knew the group had the opportunity to experience the finding of a common ground, but I was not sure how we were going to get there. In retrospect, the problem statement does not have the same meaning as in the beginning. I now see their denial and resistance as a tool they use to cope, with alcohol being the method they use to hide their fears and feelings. The group had begun to deal with some of their most sensitive issues and losses in a more honest and trustful way than they had initially presented. The members carry within them a history of pain and denial, and their allowing this to surface has been a thrill to observe. I know there is much more work to be done, but to have experienced Phil's growth to the point of allowing others access to his feelings will stay with me forever. Just as the members are taking risks, I hope that I too can do the same in my role, challenging each of them to work more on their issues.

PRACTICE SUMMARY While the leader admires the growth of Phil and the group, he should also acknowledge his own substantial growth. From a leader who at first identified with either the individual or the group, he has developed the ability to be with both "clients" at exactly the same time. This will be a crucial step in his professional growth as he moves from the contemplation stage to the action stage in his practice.

Group Counseling with Female Active Substance Abusers

Gender should be taken into account in considering the different meanings of group processes for men and women. For example, Hardesty and Greif (1994) described the common themes in groups for female IV drug users who were HIV-positive. Drawing upon their work with a mandatory women's group in a methadone maintenance clinic, they point out that substance abuse spanned a number of generations. Members discussed with the group their long histories of physical abuse and neglect at the hands of family members, friends, and strangers, which left an indelible impression of worthlessness that the women carry into their current relationships with their parents, friends, lovers, and children. Because of their belief in their own worthlessness, they fiercely guard secrets of shame and inadequacy (p. 290).

The authors describe the unique advantages of a women's group in creating a safe environment for disclosure of family-of-origin issues. The women in the following group clearly expressed their struggle with feelings of low self-worth that resulted in a vicious cycle of behaviors that maintained and often intensified their internalized negative self-concepts. A link for women between PTSD and substance abuse has been documented (Navajits, Weiss, & Shaw, 1997). Various studies have found frequent histories of childhood physical and/or sexual assault among women with current substance abuse, ranging from 32% to 66%. Moreover, if a woman experienced both physical and sexual abuse as a child, her likelihood of using illicit drugs was almost twice as high (44%) as if she had an earlier type of abuse alone (23%).

Women with substance abuse have also been found to have high rates of repeated trauma. In both studies of women in an inner-city neighborhood and a diverse outpatient sample of cocaine-addicted subjects, the average number of lifetime traumas among women was five. Moreover, the likelihood of PTSD diagnosis was increased in women exposed to a greater number of traumas and more violent traumas (p. 276).

Navajits et al. point out a number of differences between men and women documented in the studies, suggesting that PTSD in men is more often associated with victimization or witnessing of violence, in particular war experiences, while for women it is associated with physical and sexual abuse and trauma. "Female substance abusers have also been found to have significantly higher rates of repeated trauma and family perpetrators than male substance abusers." The authors describe women with PTSD and substance abuse diagnosis as also having more co-morbid disorders (mood, anxiety, and medical problems) as well as concurrent life problems (homelessness, loss of custody of children, etc.). They cite other studies that describe the women's "intense stigmatization, blame for failure in maternal roles, frequent sex-for-drugs exchanges, and the downward spiral of The Life, in which crack is used to manage the symptoms of trauma, retraumatization occurs in the context of crack use, and the cycle repeats" (p. 278).

These research findings come alive in the process recordings in this section involving groups for women and in the next section's example of an AIDS/early recovery group. In each instance, we can see the internalized oppressor at work in the lives of these women as well as the sources of strength for change.

Maintaining Sobriety for Women Trauma Survivors

Group Purpose: Learn new coping skills to help in maintaining sobriety. Members support each other in the use of the newly learned coping skills.

Members: 25- to 47-year-old white females, primarily low-income single mothers. Most are of European descent. All are substance abusers who have had at least three failed attempts at remaining abstinent from drugs and/or alcohol. All are also survivors of childhood trauma.

Dates: February 1 to April 19

Description of the Problem

The original time frame of this group was 8 weeks; after 4 weeks the group was extended to ongoing. The group faces the task of learning coping skills to deal with intense and overwhelming feelings that do not involve the use of alcohol or drugs. The task is complicated by the fact that all the women are trauma survivors and have used alcohol or drugs to numb their feelings since they were very young, beginning between the ages of 9 and 12 years old. It is my opinion that the group is having difficulty getting through the beginning stage and creating a group culture that allows the members to share openly. Since all the women are trauma survivors, I anticipated that it will be more difficult for them to trust each other and become a cohesive group. I pushed the group to move into the work phase of the group too soon, which resulted in the members engaging in flight or fight.

How the Problem Came to the Attention of the Group Leader(s)

During the initial interviews, the women all seemed to be excited about learning new coping skills and expressed a strong desire to stay abstinent. When the group actually began meeting it seemed difficult for the women to connect with each other. No one was willing to talk openly about their feelings or what led up to episodes of drinking. Linda is a good example of how the group is feeling; she sits, staring at her lap, saying very little. Every time I pushed them into what seemed to be work, it became obvious that the women moved into fight or flight; Linda did not show up the week after revealing personal information. It appeared that eight weeks was too short a time, so the group was extended and the women still could not connect. No matter how hard I reached, the group did not seem to be able to talk about feelings.

Summary of the Work with Process Excerpts

First Session

I noticed that the women entered the room silently. Each one seemed to be very guarded and apprehensive. The women took their seats; each one was looking down and very sad. I opened the group by talking about the common bond that each member of the group shared. I was hoping to lessen some of the shame associated with failed attempts at sobriety.

PRACTICE POINTS It is important that the group leader make an opening statement that defines the group's purpose clearly and identifies the areas of common ground between members as well as the fact that there may be differences. By explicitly defining the trauma experiences, the leader sends the message that it will be OK to discuss these sensitive and taboo subjects in the group. Even if group members do not respond immediately, not surprising in an early session, the stating of the words sends the message the group leader will be ready when the members feel safe enough to disclose.

I stated the purpose of the group. "As all of you know, this is the women's coping skills group. Everyone in this group has had difficulty remaining clean and sober; each of you has also had some type of trauma in your life. The trauma may be different for each of you. Some of you may have experienced childhood trauma, or possibly an abusive relationship as an adult, or you may have been raped. What you all have in common is that you all have intense and overwhelming feelings that lead you to drink or drug. Each one of you has expressed a desire to stop using substances and has tried on more than one occasion. When you stop drinking or drugging, the feelings flood in and then you have no ways to deal with them other than to return to numbing those feelings with alcohol or drugs. In this group we are going to talk about other ways that you can deal with the feelings and hopefully increase your ability to tolerate the feeling of being overwhelmed."

PRACTICE POINTS Although the leader is direct about the purpose of the group and even acknowledges the underlying pain, she will fail to reach for the signals from one member that she was feeling the pain in the moment. The leader comments that she was not sure that the group members were ready; yet in my view, it was the leader who was not ready.

As I spoke, I noticed that all but one of the women raised their heads and began to glance around at the other women. However, after a brief glance, each would return to looking at the table. Only two of the women looked up at me. One woman continued to stare at her lap. She appeared to be on the verge of tears. I knew that this would be a good time to address the pain that Linda was expressing and the entire group was probably feeling, but I chose not to because I feared it was too soon. I am not sure what would have happened if I had talked about the pain. It is possible the group could have responded by identifying with it or they could have fled from it as in Bion's fight-or-flight theory.

I asked the group if they would like to introduce themselves to each other at this point, telling them that they could say as much or as little as they felt comfortable with. Carol started. She seemed a little hesitant but told the group that she had relapsed (drank) two days before. Each woman took a turn; all had drunk in the previous week except Dot, who said she had not drunk in about a month.

When it was Linda's turn, she continued to look down and only said, "I'm Linda; I drank yesterday." I wanted to say, "You really seem to be in a lot of pain, Linda," but I did not. I let the group move on. I was not sure how to handle Linda's pain, so I ignored it. As the next woman was speaking, I noticed that Linda had tears in her eyes. After the introductions we went on to play the Ungame. In this game, the players draw cards and answer the question on each card. I continued to pay close attention to Linda. She answered all of her questions with as few words as possible, and I never saw her look up. I did not comment on Linda's answers or her obvious discomfort. I was afraid of making her more uncomfortable and afraid that she might not return to the group. Looking back, I could have acknowledged her pain by talking about the pain and frustration anyone feels when they try repeatedly to do something and fail and how much more painful it is when that something is trying to stop drinking.

PRACTICE POINTS

A comment is needed here about the use of a game in the first session or sessions of a group. It is common for leaders to try to structure an exercise, often calling it a "warm-up"; however, the exercise is often a way for the leader to deal with his or her own anxiety about getting started or, in this case, dealing with strong emotions. The leader's initial opening statement was excellent, and it evoked in members, one in particular, a response to the purpose of the group. In this instance, the game actually takes away from the power of the work and sends a mixed message to the group members.

Third Session

Carol opened the group by talking about her recent relapse. Dot, who is still sober, tried to encourage Carol by telling her about a women's AA meeting where she feels she gets a lot of help. Cindy began to cry at that point and talked about drinking over the weekend. I asked the group if they could identify an event or feeling that led to drinking. Three of the women said that they thought it was hanging out with friends who drink. I acknowledged that friends are certainly a powerful influence and asked if they could remember exactly what it was they hoped to get from drinking. Carol responded by saying, "Yeah! It makes it easier to talk and I feel more at ease when I've had a few."

At this point I am not sure where to go, so I remain silent. After a few moments of silence, Linda tentatively began to speak. She said she was embarrassed to admit it, especially now that she had kept quiet for so long, but she had relapsed. Linda then began to speak about her ex-boyfriend to whom she is still attached. He is a cross-dresser, and she does not feel that she can live with this, so they recently split up. Now every time she talks to him, she ends up drinking. Linda started crying when she began to speak. I wanted to give the group a chance to respond and identify with Linda's pain, so all I did was get up and get a box of tissues.

Once again we see how the skill of containment can allow the group members to become active with each other instead of waiting for the leader to respond. The leader commented that all she did was "get a box of tissues," as if that were not important. It was, since it said to Linda (and the group) that she understood the feelings and wanted to do something to help. It was actually a physical gesture of support.

Dot, who had become the leader, spoke up and said, "I know how you feel. When my boyfriend left and I lost my kids, I drank every time I saw him and it seemed like I was always seeing him since he lived in the same area that I did. Now I still see him but I call my sponsor instead of drinking." I asked, "When you see your ex-boyfriend or talk with him what is the feeling you are left with?" The group was silent for a few moments, and then Dot said, "Lonely." I was watching Linda, and she nodded in agreement. Cindy said that she usually drinks because she is feeling lonely. Carol denied that she ever felt lonely.

In retrospect, the leader could have taken some time at the end of this meeting to discuss the impact on all of the members, especially Linda, of sharing such painful material. Such a discussion might have made it easier for Linda to return for the next session. Members often feel embarrassed by sharing strong feelings and crying which is why some reflection at the end of the previous meeting might be helpful.

Fourth Session

Linda did not come to group today. Carol opened the meeting by telling the group she relapsed again. Dot told her about meetings again. I ask if anyone in the group can tell us what they go through before picking up a drink. Celia, who has not spoken before, offers that she drinks because she thinks it's going to make her feel better. I ask if anyone else drinks to feel better. Most of the group seems to identify. They seem ashamed to answer. No one openly said yes. However, there is a lot of muttering that sounds like agreement. I respond by asking how they respond to overwhelming feelings. Dot was the first to answer. She said, "I used to. I would feel overwhelmed with loneliness or sadness so I would drink to feel better. Now I go to a meeting or call my sponsor." Dot continued talking about how she stays sober; no one else responded. I think I pushed too soon, or maybe I should not have pushed at all.

The group leader made the not-uncommon mistake of failing to share her thoughts and feelings with the group. If she wonders if it is "too soon" to push, why not ask the group members? If she was concerned about Linda's absence, why not raise it with the group? Over and over, in workshop after workshop, when I ask the presenter what she or he felt or was concerned about, it becomes obvious that sharing it honestly with the group members is the best intervention.

Fifth Session

I opened the group meeting by telling the members that the group will not end after 8 weeks, it will go on for as long as we can keep it going. Carol asks if the present members can keep coming. I told her that they can. There was almost an audible sigh of relief. I asked how they felt about the group continuing. I was still hoping that someone would begin to talk about how hard it is to learn new coping skills and how hard it is to use them. Carol was the first to answer. She said that she was really glad to hear that the group would not end because she knows she needs more time. Carol seems to be the spokesperson for the entire group. Linda surprised me when she spoke; she said she was relieved to hear that the group will not end because she really wants to stop drinking and nothing has helped before so she is hoping that this group will make a difference. Others in the group agreed.

Now that I know that the group is not limited to eight sessions, maybe I can let the group work at its own pace. It is possible that my having an agenda every meeting has kept the group from doing the work that they need to do in the way that they need to do it. I think they are only giving the appearance of work when they are really in the beginning stages of the group.

PRACTICE POINTS The practice problem often comes down to trusting our own feelings and instincts. This group leader keeps writing about reactions she did not share in the group, yet each was right on target. As another example, in the previous session, she could say, "I wonder if my having an agenda every meeting actually makes it harder for all of you from doing the work you feel you need. Can we reflect on how we have been working and how we can strengthen our sessions?"

Sixth Session

Carol opens the meeting once again by telling the group that she relapsed over the weekend. This time when Dot responded to Carol, she did not sound as patient. She confronted Carol with the fact that she hangs out with people who drink. She said, "How can you expect to stay sober when all the people you hang out with are drunks? You never go to meetings so you can meet sober people. Then you drink and wonder why." I think Dot is the gatekeeper; every time anyone in the group gets too close to feelings, Dot starts talking about AA. When she does, the group seems to stop feeling.

PRACTICE POINTS While Dot may be a gatekeeper, she also represents what I have called earlier the "demand for work." If the group alliance has developed to the point where they all know that others care for them and they care for others, then confrontation by a group member can be facilitative. At some point, Carol has to ask herself why she places herself into vulnerable situations and start to take some responsibility for not doing so and then being surprised at her relapse.

While Dot is talking, I look around to see how the rest of the group is taking this confrontation of Carol. Linda has tears in her eyes. This time I want to draw Linda in and acknowledge her pain. I say, "I wonder if some of you are feeling like it's hard to make new friends, especially while you're sober?" Linda remains quiet and withdrawn, but I feel like I am beginning to reach her. Now she is openly crying. The group is silent, so I try to reach out to her. I say, "This seems like a very painful topic. Would anyone like to talk about their pain?"

She continued to cry and said very quietly, "I can't make friends, no one ever likes me. That's why Jack was so important to me. He liked me. I just can't stand his cross-dressing, but he's still my friend. That makes it really hard." The group remained silent. It seems like the group is having a hard time sitting with Linda's feelings. I want to bring the feeling of not being good enough to the group, so I say, "I'm wondering if others in this group feel like Linda?" It is almost like the group as a whole has been holding its breath and now begins to breathe again. Cindy, while hanging her head, mumbles, "Yeah." I can feel the pain in the room and want to keep it on the table, so I say, "It must hurt a lot to think no one really likes you." Linda nods. Dot gets the box of tissues. Cindy and Celia are crying now. Carol seems to be avoiding feeling anything; she stares up at the ceiling.

PRACTICE POINTS The intervention described in earlier examples, asking members to discuss how hard it is to talk about something, is appropriate at this moment. Once again, as members discuss how hard it is to talk about "it" (the process), they actually start to talk about "it" (the content).

I do not want to lose this moment, so I say, "I know how hard it is to talk about this; maybe we could spend some time talking about just how hard it is to talk." The group seems more comfortable with this. Cindy, still crying, says that she has always had a hard time talking about some things. Dot, who always seems to be full of helpful advice but never really joins the group, began talking about AA and how it has helped her to learn to talk. I can really see how Dot is the one who stops the group from feeling. Every time the group gets too close to talking about how they feel, Dot diverts the feelings by talking about AA. I may send Dot into fight or flight, but I decide to take a chance and bring this to her attention.

I say, "Dot, I know AA has been very helpful to you and that you have learned a lot about staying sober, but I'm wondering how you feel about talking about difficult things." Dot just sort of looked at me for a moment as if she did not understand what I had just said. Then she responded by telling me that even though she has learned to talk about a lot of things, it's still hard to feel it.

PRACTICE POINTS The leader is finally dealing with Dot's role in the group but could be a bit more direct. For example, she could say, "I notice, Dot, whenever we get very close to someone's pain, you raise AA as a solution. I know it's been helpful for you, but is it also tough for you to deal with other people's pain as well as your own?"

Eighth Session

The group is now working a little better together and seems to be gaining some degree of trust. I am hoping to draw Linda into the group more. Linda is still more withdrawn than the rest of the group and appears sad all of the time. I am not sure how to draw her out. She is difficult to engage and resists connecting with the group. This can be seen in her remaining separate from the group before and after the group session when the other women come and go together. Sometimes I feel like the group is leaving Linda behind. I am not sure that she is the scapegoat; however, she does serve a function in the group. She is like the part of each member that they all want to get rid of.

I am going to take a chance and ask the group how they feel about Linda's separateness from the group. I need to be very careful that Linda does not get attacked, or at least not more so than she can handle. Carol responds by saying that she has noticed that Linda is quiet most of the time and it makes her nervous. She is afraid that Linda is judging her. I reach for the pain. I ask Carol what she thinks the feeling is. Carol thinks for a moment and then says, "Fear." I am still reaching, so I ask whose fear. Carol replies, "Both of our pain." This is more what I am looking for, so I stick with it. I ask Linda how it feels to hear Carol talking about her. Linda finally looked up and said that she is really afraid of how she feels and what the group thinks of her because she cannot seem to stop drinking. Other members of the group pick up on what Linda has said. I think the group is coming together.

Where the Problem Stands Now

The group is beginning to come together. Linda's looking up at the other members of the group was a good sign. It seemed that when the group thought they would only be together for 8 weeks, they felt it was too risky to share painful information. After the members found out that they could continue longer, some members began to take some chances and talk about their pain. I was also able to give up my agenda to some extent and let the group set its own pace. The group reflected this when Linda talked about how much she wants to get sober. Each week there is a little progress. They begin to talk about their fear. This is real progress.

 PRACTICE SUMMARY
In reviewing the group's progress over time, it is important to note what was mentioned in the opening statement but does not emerge in the conversation: that they are all survivors of some form of trauma. The leader is aware this is not a trauma recovery group, although members may need a different intensive group focusing on the trauma. However, it is a group where it is appropriate to make the connection between feelings associated with trauma and how they impact the abuse of substances and threats to recovery. This apparent evasion of this sensitive, very painful area needs to be brought to the members' attention. The same intervention used earlier—asking the members what makes it hard to talk about this area of pain—may help the group members take the next step.

Support Groups for Protecting Recovery

Facing painful feelings is not the only threat to recovery. Most clients fight the recovery battle while still remaining in a community or family situation that may encourage relapse. In the next excerpt, one woman describes the drug dealer she had to deal with on her way to the meeting. The focus of the group is assertiveness, which is exactly the quality she will need.

Women's Recovery Group: Fending Off the Dealers

Purpose: Assertiveness group for women in recovery with 10 members
Gender: All female and all Caucasian
Age Range: 18–42

PRACTICE POINTS
Note how the theme of having to bypass drug dealers is raised using humor as a form of flight.

Susan talked about the frustration she was having in getting into a holding. I asked what a holding is. The group members explained that a holding is an unstructured, safe, and sober place they can stay before going to a halfway house. Diane then talked about the long waiting lists to get into halfway houses. I asked the group for suggestions on how to deal with these wait lists. Linda spoke about calling every day to show her interest in the houses. She also said that she stays clean by living in a shelter and coming to day treatment.

Robin responded by saying that she would never stay in a shelter because of the "lice, dirt, and rows and rows of cots." I asked Robin if she had been to a shelter like that. She said she had not but could just imagine it. Karen and Julie spoke about their positive experiences with specific shelters. Linda also said that the shelter she is at is clean but that the neighborhood has a lot of drug activity. I responded by saying, "That must be very difficult for you." Linda then shared a story about being approached by a dealer while she was on her way to day treatment this morning. She described how she got very nervous and gave him a comical and lengthy explanation of where she was going. The group (including myself) laughed at her story.

PRACTICE POINTS

In the previous excerpt, the leader laughed along with the group, but in the next excerpt, recognizing it is a form of flight, she asks for the feelings under the humor.

I then asked, "How did you feel after you said that?" Linda said that she was tempted and is nervous about how easy it would be to go back "to the streets." Linda also spoke about feeling in control and proud of herself about her decision. Wendy and Tricia said that they would not be able to live so close to the drugs because they would use. Chris said that she thought she'd be able to do it because even if she lives where there aren't any drugs, she knows where to get them. The entire group agreed. There was a brief silence. I asked if anyone wanted to share their plans about dealing with the easy access to drugs. Chris spoke about her living situation with a boyfriend who uses and how this situation may be impossible to continue if she wants to stay clean.

PRACTICE SUMMARY

Maintaining recovery requires energetic and active work on the part of the client at all times. In many day treatment programs, recognition that the weekend poses a particular threat to recovery has led to a focus on recovery-maintenance issues on Fridays. In the next example, the group leader deals with a number of common problems associated with such a group. First, it is one of five during the day. Second, it meets only once per week, and because of the open-ended nature of the group (and the program), keeping the contract clear can become a problem. These problems often lead to an illusion of work, as the co-leader of this group discovers.

Group Counseling with Clients with a Dual Diagnosis

As illustrated in the previous sections, substance abuse often accompanies another diagnosis such as posttraumatic stress, mental illness, or, as in one of the groups in this section, AIDS. It is important for the group leader to recognize that the group should not get stuck in focusing on the independent impact of each diagnosis on the life of the members. *There is a joint effect that needs to be explored: the specific impact of the substance abuse on the second diagnosis, and vice versa.*

In the first example in this section, a group of women discuss the impact of mental illness and substance abuse on their lives. A theme that often emerges in groups such as this one is the difficulty when they attend support groups for the alcoholism, such AA, in sharing issues related to their mental illness. This is echoed in the second example, in which members of a group I co-led explained at an early meeting how they could not discuss their having the "virus" at an AA meeting and that they could not discuss their substance abuse at support groups they attended for persons with AIDS. In this group, the feelings of shame at first led the members to avoid discussing the painful interaction between AIDS and their prolonged, polysubstance abuse. It is only in response to recontracting and a demand for work that they finally begin to address the concerns related to self-image and stigmatization.

A Dual-Diagnosis Group for Women: Mental Illness, Substance Abuse, and the Double Stigma

Purpose: A support group for women dealing with the double stigma

Gender of Members: Female

Cultural, Racial, or Ethnic Identification of Members: Caucasian and African American.

Age Range: 21–35

Excerpts from Process Recording
March 4 (Eighth Group Meeting)

Present: Leader, Barbara, Gloria, Rita, Pam, Nancy, and Theresa

Note how the leader reaches out to the group to respond to Theresa thus universalizing the issue.

After reading the opening, Gloria took an opportunity to read, "Accepting Differences."

THERESA: I want to comment on the last sentence that says we would leave our fear, secrecy, and isolation. I have felt isolated over the last few weeks, and several issues of abuse have come up for me over the last 2 weeks. I feel like I'm struggling. I really want to stay home.

LEADER: I wonder how other people are feeling about their ability to share their secrets in this group.

THERESA: I notice that I am very tired and that I have been holding onto things for a long time. I feel like I am very ashamed, and I am finally now getting angry.

NANCY: Being tired is a symptom of anger. I notice that when I am feeling ashamed, I am often angry.

BARBARA: I notice that when I am angry lately and very irritated at the people at the House [a residence], and I'm muttering under my breath, "You're an asshole." I don't know quite what to do with my anger because I can't really tell people in the AA community about it because most of my anger is about my mental illness. The other night when I was on a commitment [a trip to an AA meeting at which members from another group share their stories] with some other people with me in the car, the men started saying that people who are on psychotropic medications are not allowing themselves to go through their experience of being an alcoholic. They are taking medications, using the soft approach. I couldn't believe that they mentioned this right in the car when I was there, knowing that I take medication. I felt as though they were isolating me, and I find myself more and more angry that I have to take the medication, that I have to take it on time, that I have to check it with the pharmacist, and see my doctor. It is so much easier to be a drunk. All I have to do is stop drinking and show up to a meeting.

GLORIA: I feel very ashamed of my alcoholism, and I don't really tell anybody my story in AA, either. I can't imagine standing up and telling people that I have a mental illness and alcoholism.

NANCY: I feel as though some of the meetings would be accepting.

BARBARA: I'm just not sure where those are, and I am not willing to take the risk of being put down.

PRACTICE POINTS As the members begin to discuss their feelings of shame and the anger it provokes, the leader makes sure they return to the anger and a discussion of how they handle it. Stigmatism is a social problem; however, internalizing the negative self-image makes it the individual's problem.

LEADER: What do you do about your anger?

BARBARA: I don't do anything about it. I sometimes can call my sponsor, but he tells me to stop whining.

NANCY: I ignore it. I swallow it, pretend it's not there. I don't really know what to do with it.

THERESA: I swallow it. I used to self-medicate. Self-medication was easy for me. I would use any substance to make me not feel anger.

RITA: I ignore it.

LEADER: I tend to think that anger is a source of energy and that if you leave it inside after a while, it will just get more and more strong and want to get out. Some of us have rage attacks; others will feel the need to self-medicate. I even believe that the anger can turn into physical complications.

THERESA: I agree, but I don't have anywhere to go with it. It doesn't feel safe. I have a lot of anger about the abuse that I went through as a kid, but it doesn't feel right to yell and scream at my parents. But I do feel angry about what happened.

BARBARA: I still feel very angry at the mental illness. For a long time I was angry at life and my drinking habit. But I've noticed now that it has switched. I am very comfortable not drinking, but I am very much in denial about my mental illness.

RITA: I've accepted it.

NANCY: I still don't feel very comfortable with mine, although over the years I have grown to accept the mental illness. I remember once that I had a therapist who helped me a lot with my mental illness, but she wanted me to become a productive member of society, and I felt like she was pushing too hard and wasn't listening to me. It encouraged me to be mad at it.

PRACTICE POINTS An important theme has emerged, and the group leader tries to generalize it by bringing other members into the discussion

LEADER: I wonder if other people in the group feel angry at their mental illness. What do you think, Pam?

PAM: I sometimes feel angry at it because I really want to work. I want to contribute and have my own apartment, and I feel like my mental illness stops me from really being out there and working.

BARBARA: I want to work also. I don't know what I want to do, but I guess I could flip a few hamburgers or something.

RITA: I guess I just want to redefine work. I am volunteering now, but I can only volunteer about 6 hours a week and then I am very tired.

THERESA: I don't feel like I am working, either, and I can't imagine being in the work force for a long time. I am so anxious.

The group leader is attempting to reframe the issue for the members so that they understand that contributing at any level is an important step for them. One of the key advantages of mutual aid support groups is that they provide a medium or a safe place where members can discover strengths and the capacity to help others while helping themselves.

> LEADER: I wonder if there is a way to redefine "contribution." What is it like to be a leader or a participant right here in the group? What is it like to be a contributor? Rather than seeing ourselves as having to produce things, maybe being active contributors right here or in other parts of your treatment is enough work.
>
> BARBARA: I find work pretty easy because I am a manic, and I can just keep doing and doing and doing. (The group members laugh.)
>
> LEADER: When we feel like we are not contributors, isn't that what brings up our fear and isolation and secrecy that we talked about earlier and started the group with? Is that how we get the stigma that may be attached to the mental illness in the community and our alcoholism? (The group members nod.)
>
> GLORIA: I feel as though I have a lot of shame. I notice that I'm angry that I can't really work as much as I would like to. I started a new job, and I'm not able to manage it because it is too much.
>
> NANCY: It's so much like the therapist who tried to get me to be an active participant as a leader. I just couldn't imagine being able to do it. It would be really nice to redefine contribution.
>
> LEADER: It's 10:00, and we need to close the meeting. Who would like to read the closing?

The members have just begun to explore how their mental illness and substance abuse have in the past and even currently interact to increase their feelings of shame and their feelings that they "can't contribute." The leader tries to use the group itself as an example of contributing, but the members do not pick this up. Near the end the issue of stigma reemerges and will need to be explored at further meetings. As a doubly oppressed group, bearing the stigma of their mental illness and their substance abuse, the women will have to face their internalized negative self-image and, in Fanon's terms, the internalized oppressor, before they can take steps to change their lives. This meeting has just been the start of this process. Another issue, emerging in a comment about early abuse, may have to also be explored when members feel safe. The member's comment about not knowing what to do with anger at her parents over her childhood abuse may be a first offering of the need to explore in more detail the source of the anger and how to cope with it besides self-medication.

Group Work with Persons with AIDS Who Are in Early Substance Abuse Recovery

In the following example of a group I co-led, we see the dynamics of first sessions, discussed in Chapter 4, emerging as the members must begin to deal with the purpose of the group, the authority theme (relation to the leaders), and structural issues such as confidentiality.

Agency: AIDS Action Committee

Setting: Independent living for persons with AIDS (alcohol- and drug-free housing) with common rooms and 24-hour staff

Co-leaders: Full-time, African American substance abuse counselor working for AIDS Action; the author, a white social work professor

Group Purpose: A mutual aid support group for persons with AIDS who are also in early recovery from substance abuse. The focus is on the interaction between recovery and living with AIDS. Survivor issues emerged as central to the struggle for each of the members.

Timing: Eight initial sessions, 90 minutes each, with an agreement to consider renewal at the last session

Members: Jake (late 30s, African American man), Gerry (early 30s, African American man); Tania (early 40s, white transgendered woman); Theresa (late 20s, white woman); Kerry (late 20s, white gay man)

Each of the members has met individually with my co-leader prior to the first meeting. My co-leader is a substance abuse counselor and brings a background in 12-step groups to the session. We have agreed that we would be exploring how to integrate the mutual aid approach central to my work with the structured recovery (12-step) approach designed to help the members maintain their recovery. As the "outsider," I felt it was important that I cede the initial lead role to my co-leader. We had met prior to the session to work out our understanding of the group and how we would share the leadership role. Tania, Kerry, and Jake are residents in the housing unit, a "clean and sober" residence for persons with AIDS. Both Tania and Kerry had relapsed recently and acted out. They were required to attend some form of recovery group and reluctantly decided on this one since it was conveniently held in the house. The early themes include their anger and suspicion as well as the difficulty of dealing with the holidays. The authority theme is also central as Tania takes on the role of testing the leaders.

PRACTICE POINTS Note the initial theme has to do with the environment—staff in the housing unit—but also the authority theme and the crucial issue of confidentiality. While the members who live in the house complain about their lack of complete freedom, this housing unit is one of its kind in the city, and apartments are much sought after. My co-leader begins with the rules rather than a statement of purpose, and the members respond with some anger.

First Meeting

John (my co-leader) began the meeting by welcoming everyone and saying he thought it would be helpful to go over the rules for the sessions. He gave each member a list of 10 rules and asked them to read them and comment. The members responded positively, with Tania saying that she liked the one about confidentiality. She went on in a hyper manner, saying that she could deal with a lot, but she couldn't deal with anybody ratting on her—that if someone rats on her, she is out of here.

Jake picked up on Tania's theme with anger in his voice. He described an incident over the weekend, where a still active (drug-using) girlfriend visited him. When things got "out of hand," he told her to leave his room. He then imitated his girlfriend going to the staff office in the lobby and telling them that he had hit her. The police were called and he refused to answer his door. The others were listening intently as he, with a lot of anger, said that the incident was written down in his book and that he didn't understand what this was all about. If this was independent living, this was his apartment, and he could do what he wanted in his apartment.

Kerry and Tania, who also had apartments in the house, added their anger toward staff. I said that they seemed to be saying that they were living in independent housing, but that they didn't really feel they were independent. Members nodded and agreed.

PRACTICE POINTS

Tania's comment about "ratting" was interpreted by me as an indirect raising of the issue of the leaders and confidentiality. I responded directly and took this opportunity to address the issue. With some group members already placed on "probation" by house staff and all of the members having been involved in some form of illegal activity—even if only the use of drugs—confidentiality needed to be clarified. The rules governing this issue had been negotiated with the housing staff in presession meetings. Essentially, they were as follows:

- We would report any illegal activity such as selling drugs.
- We would report if we felt they were in danger of harming themselves or someone else.
- We would not report relapses since we understood they were part of recovery.

John returned to the contracting and asked if each one would initial or sign the contract. After they signed, I asked Tania whether she was concerned, not just about being "ratted" on by members of the group, but also about what John and I would share with staff. She said she was, and then she went on at some length about how she didn't have to be here and could leave if she wanted to.

John suggested that I explain the confidentiality rules that we would be following. I told them we had met with the house staff, and we had agreed that we would keep discussion in the group confidential, with the exception of any information they shared that indicated to us that they were personally at risk or that someone else was being put at risk. I also explained that any activities in the house that were illegal, like selling dope, would also have to be shared. Other than that, there would be no disclosures to staff. I went on to say that, since this is an early recovery group, in which there was always the possibility of relapse, staff and we had agreed that relapse incidents would not be reported. The group members nodded in agreement when I made this comment.

PRACTICE POINTS

Tania then raised a crucial issue. How could they trust that we meant what we said? All of the members of the group had been involved in recent years in a drug culture where trust was not common. They had been exploited and had exploited others so Tania's doubts were understandable. By my acknowledging that trust in us would have to be earned, I actually began to develop the working relationship.

I went on to tell them that the staff had also agreed that the only information they would share with us about resident activity at the house would be information that they felt indicated that a resident might be in danger of harming him- or herself or harming someone else. Other than that, we would meet with the staff in about 4 or 5 weeks to discuss how the group was going. Tania, with great agitation, said, "Well, that sounds good, but we'll have to see." She said that she had too many people in the past give her assurances and then not come through. I laughed and said, "Maybe we should sign the contract as well." The group members laughed and agreed that would be a good idea. I told Tania that I thought she was right not to trust us, since she had just met us, and that trust would be something we'd have to earn over time. She nodded her head in agreement.

PRACTICE POINTS

My co-leader returned to the issue of group purpose. However, he did not sharply focus on the issue of the interaction between AIDS and recovery. He was also introducing a structure that he felt comfortable with as an addictions counselor that involved presentation of information. It would take a while before we could fully integrate his AA recovery framework with my mutual aid support group framework. I decided I would have to come back later in the session to clarify specific purpose. When he mentions "family issues" as one of the things we could discuss, it triggers the feedback and problem-swapping stage of the group as members start to share their current concerns and issues. If I had initiated this group and had been responsible for the initial contracting, I would have invited problem swapping directly by giving examples of some of the issues they faced related to AIDS, recovery, housing, life in the residence, and family issues as we approached the holidays. As it was, I did not have to do this because the members began the discussion. Note that Tania's comment about not having a family is actually a first offering of a major theme of hurt that will be elaborated later—the violent response on the part of family members to her open change from a man to a woman.

John said that having clarified the rules, we should talk about the group. He told them that he saw this as their group, and that what we did in the group would be decided by the members. He said that he had some ideas about things that we could talk about, including, for example, issues around the medications they were taking. He suggested he could bring a medical person in to answer their questions. Personal and family issues would also be relevant. Tania interrupted, as she did often throughout the evening, and said, "Family issues—forget it." Thanksgiving was coming up, and, as far as she was concerned, she had no family.

Jake jumped in and said he wanted to tell a story about what had happened over the weekend. He had gone home to visit his family in another town in the state. He said, "I couldn't stay. They started to make me crazy right away. Everyone there was drinking and drugging, and I knew, if I stayed, they would pull me in, and I can't let them pull me in. I have to fight that. I know I can't control this. If I take one drink or use drugs once, I'm going to be back to going into the bar at 8:00 in the morning and staying right through until 2 A.M. drinking myself to death."

PRACTICE POINTS

As the members describe their family situations, I concentrate on empathizing with the underlying feelings. For example, I do this in response to Jake's comment, which I acknowledge as his having to give up his family. Also note that members may be at different stages of change. Kerry, the youngest member, sounds like he is in the precontemplation stage, while Jake is clearly in the action stage. It's important that we not challenge Kerry's statement that he can handle drinking. First sessions are not the time for confrontations, and my co-leader's comment starts to create more safety.

I said that it sounded like, in addition to giving up the drinking and drugging, he also had to give up his family. He agreed. Kerry said that he had been in a bar in the last week and had had two drinks. He said, "I can handle that. Just because I have two drinks doesn't mean

I am going back to where I was a year ago. I know you people (looking at the leaders) are going to say I am in denial, but it's not true. I know I can handle this." John said that we had to understand that recovery was different for each person and that we had to make room in the group for people to feel safe and not defensive as they described their own ways of handling recovery. I nodded in agreement. The rest of the group did as well.

PRACTICE POINTS

It's clear that most of the conversation, right from the initial chatter, is directed toward the authority theme: "Who are these leaders, and what kind of people will they be?" Kerry's comment allows John, who was in recovery himself, to acknowledge the individual ways in which members might handle their recovery without being judged by us or each other. I believe it also allows members to start to disclose difficult feelings and behaviors. At least three of the members—Theresa, Kerry, and Tania—had supported their drug habit through prostitution.

Theresa jumped in at that point and said that she was not living at this house. She was living in a single-room occupancy building two blocks away. She said that most of the people in that building were active users and, for her, it was a fight every day to make sure that she didn't get pulled in. She said that she knew that she didn't want to go back to all the drinking and drugging she had been doing. She told us that she had gotten out of the penitentiary after a 5-year sentence and that in the penitentiary she had dried out and learned not to use. She said that she didn't want to go back to when she hated herself and she would spend her time on street corners sucking old men's dicks in order to get enough money for a shot of crack.

Tania agreed and said that, when she thought of some of the things she did for the 10-year period that she was drinking and drugging all the time, she couldn't believe she had actually let herself do those things. Theresa said, "I still have to deal with the housing, even though I am not in this residence; but I know the real question is how we deal with ourselves. For me, religion has been the answer." And then she quickly said, "I know, John, you said that this isn't a religious group, but I can't help it. For me, religion is the answer." I told Theresa that I thought she'd misunderstood John. John wasn't saying that religion and spirituality couldn't be a part of what they talked about if that was what was important to them. He just wanted to make it clear that the group was not organized as a religious group. John agreed that that's what he had meant.

PRACTICE POINTS

Given their past experiences with counselors, advisors, family members, sponsors, and others, it was important for them to understand how John and I would respond to them. Also, they may hear our early comments differently than how we meant them. When John said to Theresa, in the intake session, that this wasn't a religious group, he was actually contrasting this to the AA groups that refer to a "higher power." This is an important process of testing that will continue for a number of sessions. Theresa continued:

Theresa said she had a boyfriend now. She went back to visit her family just last weekend, and she was really surprised that her father had actually invited the boyfriend into the house. She went on to say that her boyfriend was black and that her parents had a hard time accepting that. She said that her mother, in particular, was racist and couldn't believe she was going with a black boyfriend. Theresa said that this guy had been special to her and that it would have hurt a lot if her family had not accepted him.

She pointed out that he did not have AIDS and was not actively using and that he was very helpful to her. But she knew that she had to take responsibility for herself and that was why she made sure that they had safe sex. Her boyfriend, however, had had a lot of losses in life, including the death of his wife, and he felt afraid of having more losses.

PRACTICE POINTS At this point in the first session we see what will be an ongoing pattern as Tania plays the role of gatekeeper whenever we get close to painful issues. Theresa can be viewed as "leading" the group into real talk, while Tania can be understood as saying, "Wait a minute; this is very hard for me as well, and I don't know if I'm ready to get serious." Both members are important because they express the natural ambivalence about addressing issues that they have avoided through self-medication (substance abuse) for a good part of their lives.

Tania, still speaking with the same level of tension, said that the holidays were going to be impossible. Tania told us she was a part-time stand-up comic and did routines. She almost delivered her comments in the group as if it were a stand-up routine. I knew I was going to have to point that out at some point, but this first session was not the right time.

Tania went on about all the parties that were going on and how difficult it was for her now to party. She said, "I don't know how to party without first drinking and drugging. As I looked at the people at this party I attended last week, through clean and sober eyes, I said 'My God, was this me? Was this the way I lived my life?' I left the party when they started passing around the cocaine, because, if I had stayed, I might have given in." (Tania was only 1 month into her recovery and still obviously very shaky about it.) She commented, "I know you all know what I'm talking about, since you're in recovery as well, although I don't know about them" (pointing toward us).

PRACTICE POINTS The early discussion may have created safety to raise yet another issue in the authority theme—about whether my co-leader and I had "walked the walk" (been addicted) and "talked the talk" (been in recovery groups). Tania raises it indirectly, but we hear her real message because we have tuned in to this being an issue.

I decided to use this as an opportunity to address the authority theme. I pointed out that Tania had mentioned a couple of times her concern about confidentiality, and also she had raised the question indirectly about whether we were in recovery. I said that I would have to speak for myself. "I'm not in recovery, so I am an outsider." I went on to say that I thought the issue of trust in me and John was a major one for them today, and they were worried about what we might share and for three of them, whether or not what we might share could affect their ability to continue in the housing. They agreed that they wanted to hold onto their apartments, which were the best of this type available to them in the city. Theresa indicated that she was hoping to get into one of the apartments.

I told them that I was a counselor and that I taught group practice at the University. I told them I had asked John and AIDS Action if it would be possible for me to co-lead this group because I thought it was important, as a teacher that I continued to work directly with people. Tania exploded and said, "I thought you were a narc." I laughed and said, "A narc? You mean I look like a narcotics detective?" She continued, "I thought you were just going to sit there, take notes, and, right after this session, you were going to march me off to the police station and that I'd be arrested." I laughed again and said, "Look (holding my sweater up), no wire and no badge." They all laughed. I said, "I'm not a narc, but it's going to take a while for you to really believe and trust that we will keep what you raise here confidential, except for those conditions I mentioned earlier. I'm hoping we can earn your trust." All their heads were nodding in agreement.

At this point, I wanted to bring them back to the purpose of the group. I also wanted to reinforce the AIDS issue, which appeared to be in the background as they focused on recovery issues. I attempted to partialize the issues they had raised to begin forming an agenda for our work together.

I said, "Let's talk a little bit more about what the group is about." I pointed out there were groups for people in recovery, and there were groups for people who had the virus. I said, "The unique thing about this group is that you have the virus and also are in early recovery. I don't want to lose sight of the fact that we need to also look at how having the virus affects your ability to deal with your recovery. That's a powerful issue, and we should make sure we don't ignore it." There was a silence in the room at that point, and Theresa said, "You bet it affects our recovery." I said, "This should be a place we can talk about that."

At this point, my effort was to partialize and list the concerns they had raised thus far. This was designed to help the members see what kind of issues, experiences, feelings, and so forth, the group could address. Also, I try to provide some structure for the group's discussion. The work themes raised by the members included the following:

- Relationship to the immediate environment (the house and the staff)
- Losses including their drinking and drugging, family members, and friends
- Loss of a feeling of independence
- Concern about the approaching holidays and the threat to their recovery efforts.

I continued, "Thus far, I've heard you raise a number of issues. You have some concerns about what goes on in the house and your relationship with staff. If that's an area we discuss, we can talk about what you can do and the way you deal with staff around these issues that have caused you a great deal of concern.

"You have also pointed out that you've had a lot of losses. Not only have you lost the drinking and the drugging, which had been important to you, but you're also facing the loss of family members and friends who are associated with the drinking and drugging. These are powerful changes. You feel you've lost your independence. That's another issue we can discuss. My guess is, with Thanksgiving coming up in just a few weeks, how you deal with the holiday must also be a big concern."

Tania picks up the theme of the threat the holidays pose to their recovery efforts. We also see Theresa making the first effort to reach out and provide a support by offering to be available to Tania. This is the beginning of the mutual aid process.

Tania jumped in and said, "I'm scared stiff. From now until Christmas, it's going to be nonstop beer ads, drinking ads, parties—I'm not sure I know how I'm going to get through." Theresa said, "I know what you mean. That's a tough time, but, if you want, I'd be glad to help. I'll give you my telephone number and, if at any point, you feel you're really up against it and you just need someone to talk with about it, you can give me a call." Tania nodded her head, smiled, and said, "Thank you." Theresa went on to say, "However, if you're active and you're using when you give me the call, I will have to call someone else from AA in order to have someone to help me deal with the issue. I'd like to help you, Tania, but I don't want to get pulled in with your struggle. Mine is tough enough." Tania shook her head and then nodded in agreement.

PRACTICE POINTS

By this chapter in the book, it must be clear that the role of the group leader is complicated since one has to keep track of content, process, the group-as-a-whole, the clock, and each individual member. (Once again, I encourage the new group leader not to be discouraged since this integration comes with time, and the idea of going back to catch a mistake provides a practice buffer.) I had noticed a pattern with Kerry appearing to want to speak a number of times but missing his chance. I reached for his contribution.

I pointed out that a little earlier in the discussion I thought Kerry had wanted to get in but hadn't had a chance, and I wondered if there was something he wanted to say. Kerry was thoughtful for a moment and then said that he agreed with a lot of what was being said here, that the holiday times were pretty hard for him as well. He said he had boyfriends, but having the virus made it difficult for him. He described a trip he had just taken and some of the difficulties he ran into with his partner. (Kerry looks gaunt and, along with Tania, shows the most physical evidence of having AIDS.) Kerry went back to the issue of his being able to have a drink or two and not feeling he was out of control. Jake said that, for him, one or two drinks would be the end of it.

PRACTICE POINTS

My co-leader, John, intervened once again, suggesting that different people approach recovery in different ways. He was working on creating a culture in the group where support would be provided and each member would recognize their own recovery efforts might or might not work for everyone else.

"When I first began doing these groups, I would tell you, Tania, that just going to these parties is asking for trouble and that you should try to find clean and sober parties." Tania said, "I wish I could. I wouldn't know what to do at one of those." John continued, "Everyone has a different way of dealing with their recovery, and we have to make this a safe place for them to talk about it." Everyone agreed. John then pointed out that it was close to the end of the session and suggested that it might be useful to just go around the room and have each person comment on what they thought. He reminded them of the first step in the 12 steps, taking responsibility, and asked them to address that in a personal manner. Each member responded in turn.

PRACTICE POINTS

With John pointing out the session was coming to a close, he asked for each member to comment on the session thus far. We were both were aware that Kerry (and Tania) were attending reluctantly in order to keep their apartments. Although neither of us raised it at this time, we took Kerry's following comment about the timing of the group as a potential signal of his ambivalence about attending. On the other hand, a free dinner was important for him due to the fact that he was unable to work with his advanced symptoms of AIDS.

Kerry raised the question of the timing of the group. He attended a free dinner from six to seven, and thought we should end the group earlier. John pointed out that we ended at six. If Kerry had to leave a little bit earlier, that was his choice. Tania pointed out that, if Kerry really wanted to come, he could be a little late for dinner. She said, "If you're worried about that, we can cook you something upstairs." Kerry laughed and said, "OK," although both John and I felt there was some hesitancy on his part about attending the group.

PRACTICE POINTS As some members begin to articulate their need for interpersonal support, I suggest that this group might be able to provide it. Although it will take a while, it is my hope to begin even in this first session the process of creating the group alliance in addition to the therapeutic alliance, both so important in the emerging research cited earlier. Tania uses the "door-knob" comment to repeat her issue of trust and confidentiality. My co-leader John uses her comment to make clear the rules of the group on the issue of threats and intimidation.

Jake said he thought this meeting was a good start and he had found it helpful to talk to other people like himself. Theresa said she knew her way to salvation was through God but that she also needed other people to help her. I commented that maybe this group could make up a bit for the lost friends and family. They nodded their heads. Tania said, "As long as no one rats on me, this will be OK, but I want to let you know, if someone rats, you're going to hear from me, and I can be a mean bitch."

John picked up on that right away and said, "We can only tell you that we're not going to be sharing information, except under certain circumstances. But I also think, Tania, we ought to make it clear that this group should not be a place where there are any threats or intimidation." Tania said that she was sorry and that she hadn't meant it to be threatening.

When it was my turn, I said that I had appreciated their allowing me to join them in the group, and I looked forward to continuing to meet with them each week. John suggested that we end the group with the serenity prayer.

PRACTICE SUMMARY While in the first session we had clearly stated the purpose of the group as focusing on the interaction between AIDS and recovery, a pattern developed over the next few sessions of avoiding the AIDS element of the work. My co-leader and I identified this unstated norm of the group and agreed to confront it and make a demand for work on this taboo subject at the fifth meeting. I would describe this as recontracting. In reality, even if this had been said clearly in the first session, it does not mean that members heard it, understood it, and agreed with it.

PRACTICE POINTS My co-leader was ill for the fifth meeting, so I had to lead the group by myself for the first time. I felt some trepidation related to my ability to help the members keep recovery in the forefront as they explored the painful issues associated with the virus. This session is also useful as an illustration of a middle phase meeting, so it is shared in detail from my notes. The middle phase structure is also used to divide the session into its elements. The meeting actually begins in the common area in the lobby with what I have called earlier the "premeeting chatter."

December 9 (Session 5)

Preliminary Stage: Sessional Tuning-in
Kerry, Jake, and Tania were in the lobby when I arrived. Tania was angry because John (my co-leader) was not going to be there that evening. She said she had business with him.

I pointed out that I had passed along her concerns and that he would be there next week. She angrily said, "I don't think I'm coming to the meeting." She was in a bathrobe and looked terrible. She said she wasn't feeling well but said she would come just for the beginning. I spoke to Kerry, who was sulking as well, saying he could only come for the first half hour. I discussed his holidays with him for a few minutes and, at one point, he complained about the group as being just "bitching sessions." And then he said, "Some people" (and he secretively pointed toward Tania) "talk too much." I told him I understood what he was raising and that I would be dealing with it today. Jake was talking to another resident during this time. He joined us when we went upstairs.

PRACTICE POINTS While the early session had been dealing with the authority theme as well as a number of important work themes, the group was now ready to address the intimacy theme and to make the transition to the middle stage of the group in which the more difficult issues will emerge. It was clear to me that I needed to make a *facilitative confrontation* or what I also call a *demand for work*. The demand was for them to work for real on the issues they had agreed would be discussed in the group.

Theresa arrived. Tania said, "Maybe we should fill the people who weren't here in on what happened last week." Then she turned to me and said, "But I'm doing your job, aren't I?" I told her I could take all the help I could get. So she filled in both Jake and Theresa about the discussion they had around the house and some of their issues about the group.

PRACTICE POINTS At this point, I believed it was necessary to recontract and to make a demand for work that would reinforce our expectations for the group. I believed my co-leader and I had built enough of a fund of positive feeling, that element of the working relationship that signaled caring, that we could draw on the fund—somewhat like a bank account—and confront the members. I also wanted to make clear the importance of mutual aid. All of the members had been in recovery groups where intermember conversation and response was not encouraged. If one wanted help, one could turn to a "sponsor" outside the meeting. The idea of helping each other and letting go of your own concerns in order to invest in someone else was one they needed to understand. In many ways, the process of the group, mutual aid, was directly related to the content of the group, learning to find help and support from others in their lives and not depending on self-medicating.

Beginning Stage: Sessional Contracting and Recontracting

I said I wanted to raise a question right at the beginning. I had spoken to John, and we felt it was important to find out whether or not there was a real commitment to the group, in spite of the fact that some people had been asked to come or felt they were made to come at the risk of losing their housing. Tania said, "I suppose it helps to sit around and bitch each week. I guess that makes me feel a little bit better."

I told her that was not the purpose of the group and that I wanted to restate the purpose and to see whether we had some agreement on it. I pointed out, once again, that it was a group for people who were dealing with both the virus and early recovery, and how those two conditions affected each other. Tania said she didn't think that was the group's purpose. Theresa said, yes, that was exactly what she understood it to be, a place where she could deal with the impact of having the virus.

I went on to tell them that, unless this group could become a place where they could be helpful to each other, where they could make connections and be supportive to each other, it would not succeed. I told them that the purpose of the group was to help each of them figure out how to deal with some of the difficult issues in their lives, not just to complain about them. I said I knew it was hard to set aside some of your own concerns and invest yourself in someone else's issues, but that's what the group was about.

I thought all of them had had problems in their lives in trying to get close and make connections to people, and that this group was a place for them to learn to do that. I went on to say that the group would not be valuable unless they could learn to really care for each other, and that since most of them had experiences where either they were exploited by people or they exploited people, and where their only connection in recent years that was serious was the one they had with drugs and booze, this was what the struggle was all about.

PRACTICE POINTS I had also decided that I had built up enough of a working relationship with group members that I could confront Tania with her pattern of interruptive behavior. I understood it was important to do this in an empathic manner so that it was clear that it was coming from caring about Tania and the group.

Theresa enthusiastically said that that's why she wants the group; that's what she needs help with. She said she wanted to talk about her boyfriend and the impact of her HIV on their relationship. As she was talking, Tania interrupted her and started to complete her sentences. I stopped the group and pointed this out. I said, "Tania, you know, you haven't let Theresa finish a sentence." I said, "I could be wrong, but I think you get very anxious about these discussions and that talking is a way of dealing with it." She said, "Oh, did I?" and made as if to zipper her mouth and put her hand over it. I told her I would help her because I thought she had a lot to give, but I thought other peopled needed the chance to get involved as well. Tania accepted this and, for the rest of the evening, actively tried to catch herself when she was jumping in, cutting people off, or not leaving room for others to comment.

Middle Stage: Elaboration, Empathy, Confrontation, and Sharing Leader's Feelings

Theresa started to talk about her concerns. She said she was 18 months clean and sober, and so she was in the middle of the second year, which was a "feelings year." She went on to describe that this was the period when she and, she thought, everyone in recovery, started to face all those feelings they had been running from. She said it was a complex and difficult time and that it was hard to sort things out. She went on to say that her boyfriend had trouble sharing his feelings with her. When she wanted to talk to her boyfriend about issues like her AIDS, he pulled back and told her it was too painful. As a result, she backs off. She knows he's experienced a lot of losses, including the death of his wife from illness fairly recently, and she realizes he is still early in recovery, but she had things she wants to talk to him about. She has a closeness she wanted to achieve. She has some commitments she wants from him, and she is afraid that he can't make commitments at this point. He's holding back. I asked the others in the group if they had any advice for Theresa on this issue.

PRACTICE POINTS Theresa's response to my demand for work and her emotion-filled comments struck a cord with Kerry. For the first time he spoke with strong emotions. He also directed his comments, for the first time, as a means of offering support to another member.

Kerry, who usually sits quietly at the meetings and who had indicated earlier that he was going to leave as soon as he could, jumped right in. Kerry said he thought that her boyfriend was having trouble dealing with his losses and it wasn't easy. He described a very close relationship with his partner, Billy, that had ended 2 years ago, when his partner died of AIDS on Christmas Day. He said he still didn't think he'd come to grips with all the feelings that he had and the loss that he'd experienced. I said that must make each Christmas even more difficult for him, and he agreed. He went on to talk about how he had been raised by an extremely physically abusive mother and that his grandmother was the only person who had provided him with any support and love. He said he didn't think he had gotten over her dying, either. He told Theresa that she had to realize that the grieving process takes a long time and that it might not be that easy for her boyfriend to even discuss it with her, because he knew it wasn't easy for him to discuss his loss with other people.

As Kerry talked, I saw a sensitive and caring side of him that he keeps covered up with his abrasive, angry front, his consistently telling us he doesn't need anybody and, if they don't care about him, "the hell with them." This was the first time I felt that Kerry had really connected with the group. As discussed earlier in the chapters on the middle phase of group practice, when a member raises a general problem, a specific incident is often involved. Before I could ask Theresa if something had happened since last week, she took us right to the event.

Theresa acknowledged his comments and thanked Kerry for sharing that with her, as did the other members of the group. Tania came in at that point and reinforced what Kerry had been saying. Jake was shaking his head as if he understood that difficulty as well.

Theresa then took us to the issue that she was facing at the moment. She related an incident that had led to a major fight with her boyfriend. They were in a car together, and she was in the backseat. There was another woman in the front seat whom she experienced as coming on to her boyfriend. The woman was asking her boyfriend when they could get together and saying how much she'd like to "bump and grind" with him on the dance floor. Every time Theresa described this woman's comments, she did an imitation of her, making it sound flirtatious and seductive. Theresa went on with a great deal of anger, saying that her boyfriend didn't even acknowledge that she was in the backseat and that she was his woman. Therefore, this woman, a friend of his, was going on right in front of her, which she felt was disrespecting her. She thought her boyfriend was disrespecting her by not stopping the woman and not being aware of her feelings.

A common theme in groups dealing with relationships is that the other person should be able to "divine" our feelings if that person really cared. Now that we had the specific incident in front of the group, I asked Theresa if she had raised this with him.

I asked if she had talked to her boyfriend about this, and she said she had, but he had just told her that she was "insecure." Tania intervened at this point, asking if the other woman was a black woman. Theresa said she was. Tania said, "I thought so." She said, "My first husband was a black man, and I can tell you all those black women just hated the fact that he was going out with me. As far as they were concerned, I was his 'trophy,' and I was invading their turf and taking away their man from them." She said, "It didn't matter what I did or what I said or how I tried to be nice or how I tried to connect up with his family—they never accepted me as a white woman taking a black man."

As Tania was speaking, with much feeling, I noticed Jake, who was sitting next to her, rolling his eyes and looking up to the sky. Jake is usually very quiet, so I reached for him and asked what he was thinking. I said I realized that he wasn't able to speak for all black men, but he was the only black man in the room at this time (one member had relapsed and was in detox for the week). He went on to agree that there was a big issue when a black man dated a white woman and that people in the black community, in the black family—the black girlfriends—did resent it. He said he had found that when he had been dating white women, every time he did, there was a similar reaction from his family and others.

Theresa said, "Look, I don't know how to deal with this. I try to use a prayer I know from the 12-step program, that maybe I can pray he can change. But I don't think he's going to change because, even though he is in a 12-step program, I don't think he's really committed to it. I think he can talk the talk, but he doesn't walk the walk. He's got all the words, but he doesn't practice any of it. I'm not sure he's going to change at all."

Theresa continued, "I realize for both of us this is our first 'recovery relationship,' and I know I have to be patient because he's not where I am in recovery, but still it's hard to sit in the car and have him disrespect me in that way." She said that she was absolutely furious at this woman and that maybe she ought to go have a talk with the lady. She had a great deal of anger as she described the fact that she was just recently released from the penitentiary, and there she had learned how to fight (pointing to her two missing lower front teeth). She said, "I can ask this lady nicely first, but, if I don't get anywhere, then it's my boot up her ass."

PRACTICE POINTS At this point, I realized that some intervention was needed designed to help Theresa protect her recovery because a physical attack on the woman could easily end up with her returning to prison. I also wanted to stress that it would not solve the problem with the boyfriend.

I asked Theresa if that would solve the problem, since it might get rid of this woman, but if she doesn't resolve the issue with her boyfriend, wouldn't there just be another one? She agreed and seemed a bit deflated. I said that it seemed to me she had to talk to her boyfriend. Also, her anger was so strong that if she did take physical action against this other woman, she might be risking her own recovery and even her own freedom—and the last thing she wanted to do was to end up back in prison on an assault charge. She nodded her head and said, "I know it would mean I'd be losing control of my recovery and giving it to someone else, but I don't know if I could talk to him or if he'll listen to me without just putting me off."

PRACTICE POINTS By identifying Tania's pattern of interrupting because of her anxiety, and then actively helping her monitor the process during the meeting, I believed I was helping her begin to take control over her feelings. As she did so, she was able to invest herself in the thoughts, feelings, and concerns of the other group members. In the remainder of this report, we see her focusing in on Theresa's struggle and providing significant emotional and cognitive support. As she is helping Theresa, she is also helping herself and the other members of the group.

Tania came back in and spoke with great feeling about what an important and wonderful person Theresa was, and that she deserved respect and that, if she respected herself, which Tania thought she did, then she should stand up for herself and not let this guy get away with this. She had to tell him directly that she wanted him to make a commitment to her, to recognize her as his woman. Also, if there were these kinds of issues, she had to deal with them out in the open and couldn't let them just fester where she would get angrier and angrier. She said, "If you continue to get this angry, you're just going to hurt yourself, you're going to get sick and eventually you're going to threaten your recovery." Theresa agreed that this was going to be a problem for her.

PRACTICE POINTS

At this point in the session, I was getting the feeling that we were coming close to an important issue. Theresa had seemed to me and others in the group, to be a strong young woman. I was wondering why she didn't confront. I had noticed we had also veered away from the AIDS issue. I decided to confront her and credited her when she accepted her part in the problem.

I intervened and asked Theresa why she let him back off when she asked him to talk about the losses and these other issues and he said they were too painful. She said, "Well, he told me it was hard to talk about." I said to Theresa, "Well, you could have asked him what made it hard. So why do you back off when he resists conversations with you?" There was a long silence, and then Theresa's face softened and she said, "I guess I really don't want to hear." Everyone in the room nodded their head in agreement. I said, "Good for you, Theresa. Now you're taking some responsibility for your part. What are you afraid you're going to hear?" She went on and said, "I'm afraid I'm going to be rejected."

PRACTICE POINTS

Theresa's comment on her fear of rejection resonates with Jake, who takes us to the heart of their struggle over AIDS and the stigma that they all carry.

Jake jumped in at that point, with a lot of emotion, and said, "That's the problem when you've got the virus. People reject you." He went on and talked about his own family and how he'd gotten in trouble with the law over a fight, he was in court and nobody knew him in that court, and he was about to get released without having to do jail time because of the fight. He said, "My own mother was in the court, and she hurt me deeply—she really pained me—when she stood up and told the judge that I was HIV. Well, that changed everything. These people got real angry at me, and they didn't want a guy getting into fights that was HIV-positive, who had the AIDS bug, and they said, 'Go to jail.'" He said, "I couldn't believe the rejection I felt from my mother, and I tried to explain it to her later, and she didn't understand that I didn't want her telling people I was HIV, not in those circumstances." He then turned to Theresa and said, "So, I can understand why you're afraid of that rejection." He said, "I think we're all afraid of what people will do once they know we've got the virus."

PRACTICE POINTS

In addition to helping a member, Tania, control her interruptions, I also wanted to help her to participate in the work of the group. I reached for her acknowledging her nonverbal communications.

Tania had been very quiet, although I could tell she wanted to speak. At one point, I stopped and said, "I think Tania wants to get in here, and she's been well behaved this session, so we have to give her a chance." She smiled and jumped in, telling Theresa how much she admired her and how much strength she had, and that she hoped that she could handle her recovery in the way that Theresa was handling it. She told Theresa that she just deserved a lot more.

Theresa now starts to zero in on the core of her current struggle—the impact of her AIDS on how others view her. She begins with an indirect cue associated with a question. Later in the session, when she returns to this theme, I am able to understand it more clearly and to reach for the underlying feelings.

Theresa asked Tania whether she thought she was an attractive person. There was a silence, and Tania said, "I think you're a beautiful young woman, and you could have any man you want." Theresa went on at some length about how men come on to her and, if she wanted to, she could "bump and grind" with them as well. But she didn't want that. She wanted one relationship. She wanted a serious relationship. She said she was getting older now, and she wanted a commitment from someone and this was just not enough, and that was what the issue was all about.

I noticed that Kerry looked at his watch and was preparing to leave for his dinner. I wanted to make sure we acknowledged his contribution to the group.

At this point, Kerry had to leave to go to his dinner, and I said just before he left, "Kerry, I want to raise the question of commitment." I said, "I think you worked really hard today, and I think you gave an important gift to Theresa and to the whole group when you shared some of your own pain over the loss of Billy." I added, "I think you could get and also give a lot of help in the group, but you really have to commit to it, so I have to ask you: Is this something that you want to keep on coming to?" He hesitated, and then he said he would. He said he thought this was a helpful session but that he had to go.

I felt it was important to credit Kerry before he left, and although he said, somewhat hesitantly, that he would commit to the group, I felt his ambivalence and wondered if he would. I also realized we were approaching the end of the session, and as described earlier in the middle phase model, we needed to do some work on the ending and transition stage of this session.

We returned to Theresa, and I said, "Is the question really, Theresa, that you're afraid that he might not stay with you—that if you actually confront him on this issue of the other woman, he might leave you?" She agreed that it was her concern. At this point, I wondered if it might help Theresa to figure out what she might say to her boyfriend. Theresa said that would be helpful because she didn't know when and how to say it. Then she laughed and said, "Maybe I should say it in bed." Tania said, "Oh, no. Don't say if before sex and don't say it after sex." And I added, "And don't say it during sex." Everyone laughed at this point, and Tania did a hilarious imitation of having a conversation with Theresa's boyfriend, while pumping up and down on the couch as if she were in bed having sex with him. After the laughter, Tania returned to Theresa in a more quiet tone.

As noted in the chapters on the middle phase when members are facing a difficult task, some "rehearsal" in the ending and transition stage of a meeting can help. It can provide some support for the individual, but it can also reveal underlying ambivalence as well as issues not yet discussed.

Tania said, "You have to find a quiet time, not a time when you're in the middle of a fight, and you have to just put out your feelings." I asked Tania if she could show Theresa how she could do that. She started to speak as if she were talking to Theresa's boyfriend. I role-played the boyfriend, and said, "Oh, but Theresa, you're just insecure, aren't you?" Tania did a very good job of not letting me put her off and, instead, putting the issue right where it was—whether or not I was prepared to make a commitment or if I was too insecure.

Theresa said, "I know I have to talk to him, but you know, he's told me that he's not sure he wants to be tied down, that he likes to have his freedom." Jake nodded his head and said, "Yeah, that's the problem, they want their freedom and they don't want to make a commitment, and you're afraid, if you push him, he'll leave you because you got the virus." Theresa said she realized she had to sit down and talk to him because it couldn't keep up the same way. She would just get too angry and do something crazy and screw up her recovery. She said when she had a fight with him on Thanksgiving, he did call his sponsor and came back much more gently. She felt she had gotten through to him, but she had to find another way to get through to him and talk to him. Otherwise, this thing was just going to continue and it was going to tear her up inside.

As Theresa explores confronting this problem with her boyfriend, my concerns about the impact of such a discussion on her recovery emerge. Almost as if my co-leader's voice is reminding me about keeping recovery first in the work, I explore the availability of support. We are now into the ending and transition stage of this session. This brings from Tania a heartfelt offer to help as well as a poignant statement of what she was getting from the discussion. When Theresa returns to her question of her looks, I am ready this time and reach for the underlying core theme of the session—the impact of their AIDS.

Ending and Transition Stage: Where Do You Go from Here?

I said, if she did confront him, it was going to be very rough for her, especially with the holiday times, and I wondered whom she'd have for support, especially if he said he didn't want to continue the relationship. She said she had her sponsor, and Tania said, "You also have me. You can call me anytime you want." Tania said, "I didn't realize when I started this group there were people who have lived lives just like me, who had feelings just like me, who had struggles just like me. You—you're a woman—you've really helped me see that I'm just not the only one going through this. I'd do anything I could to help you."

Once again, Theresa asked Tania how she looked. She said, "You're a woman. I know, as a woman, you will be honest with me and just tell me what you think. Do you think I look OK?" Tania seemed confused and said, "Well, sure, you look wonderful." I said, "I wonder if Theresa is really asking, 'Am I pretty enough? Am I attractive enough? If my boyfriend leaves me, can I find someone else who could love me even though I have AIDS?'" She said, "That's it," and came close to tears. She said, "I'm so afraid, if I lose him, I won't find anyone else." She said, "I know I could have guys, and I could have sex, and I like the sex. I sure missed it during the time I was in prison, but can another guy love me?"

The group members tried to reassure her that she was a wonderful person. Tania said, "It's not what you look like on the outside; it's what you're like on the inside." And she said, "And you honey—you've really got it where it counts."

This had been a pivotal session with the members accepting my invitation to work embodied in the recontracting at the beginning of the session. I wanted them to reflect on the work.

I asked then, as we were coming to an end, what they thought about the evening. I pointed out it was already six o'clock, and some had been saying they thought 1 hour was too long for a group, yet we had gone an hour and a half, and the time had flown by. Theresa said everybody was really very helpful. Tania said, "You know, I didn't want to come, but, you know, it's turned out really to be OK." Jake said he really enjoyed tonight, and he liked my leading the group. He said, "You let us talk. You're not as serious about the rules."

PRACTICE SUMMARY

I had mixed feelings about this comment because I was uncomfortable about their comparison of this session, without my co-leader, with the previous ones in which he tried to be more structured. I knew I would have to meet with him to discuss what had happened and the implications for our future sessions. Jake had been bringing in copies of AA meeting handouts with phrases, sayings, things to do, and so on, and had handed them out at the end of each session. When I asked him why he did that, he told me that it appeared that I didn't know how to run a recovery meeting and he was trying to help. (Jake's only experiences in groups had been AA meetings, which are not structured as mutual aid sessions.) I told him I would take all of the help I could get. This was the first meeting that Jake did not distribute a handout, so I thought he might have thought I was improving. As Tania begins to talk about a problem she was having with my co-leader, I felt uncomfortable and suggested she hold off until next week when he would be present.

Tania got angry again, remembering her argument with my co-leader she had mentioned before the session. I said, "Look, we can discuss this next week. I think you ought to talk directly about this when John is present. We can talk about what kind of group really is the best group for us." I told them I knew that John had a real commitment to them and to their success in their recovery, and coping with AIDS, and I'm sure he'd be open to any discussion to help make the group work more effectively for them. I pointed out that they were all extremely helpful this evening, even though, for some of them, they didn't want to be there. I credited Tania for her ability to contain herself, even though many times she felt like just jumping in and speaking. I told her I thought she had been very helpful and supportive in her comments, and then I also credited Theresa for taking a big risk and sharing her problem with us. The meeting ended.

I was chatting with one of the staff members downstairs when Tania came down to sit down in the lobby area, and she said to me, "This was a really good meeting," and held up her hand for me to give her a high-five slap, which I did. I left the session feeling we had experienced an important turning point in the group's development.

Group Counseling with the Substance Abuser's Significant Others

Substance abuse takes its toll on everyone connected with the abuser. The impact of an addicted family member can emerge even years later to profoundly affect the ability of the survivor to create and maintain intimate relationships. The physical abuse often associated with the use of alcohol and drugs will also have profound consequences for those who have been abused as well as those who have only watched the abuse take place. It is not uncommon to find that someone struggling with a substance abuse or other addiction problem (e.g. gambling) have friends, colleagues, employers, and family members who act in ways which help to maintain the problem.

These people are often termed to be *codependent*. They have, in some ways, their own dependency on maintaining and not challenging the abuser and the problem. In many situations, helping the other person address his or her own needs and fears can be the most important step in helping the abuser face and deal with the problems. A partner who threatens to leave—and means it, an employer who indicates coming in high will result in the loss of a job, friends and children who confront the substance abuser rather than making excuses for that person are often the key people in helping the abuser move from precontemplation, to contemplation, and eventually to action. The group examples that follow illustrate groups for the significant others.

In the following section, we examine work with three common categories of significant others. The first is a group for adult daughters of alcoholics who struggle to revisit the pain of their traumatic childhoods and its impact on their current relationships. The second is a group for women who are currently living with abusers and experiencing physical abuse related to the substance use. The third example involves children living in homes where substances are or have been abused. In this example, we see clearly the struggle of a beginning leader as she tries to reach past the acting-out behavior that represents a flight-fight reaction and attempts to create a culture where the girls can feel safe enough to discuss the "family secret."

Adult Daughters of Alcoholics: Lowering the Walls of Denial

Children growing up in a family with an alcoholic parent are used to maintaining the *family secret*. They have observed widespread denial of a problem as a mechanism for avoiding pain and responsibility. When joining a group specifically for adult children of alcoholics, they take a first step toward public recognition of the problem and acknowledgment of the need to deal with it. In the record of service that follows, the leader attempts to help such a group begin to challenge the group culture that supports the notion that all of the pain and problems were in the past, the feelings have been resolved, and any current problems are usually the fault of significant others.

Group Purpose: A group for adult daughters of alcoholics. The purpose is for members to share with each other the experiences of growing up in an alcoholic home and, through the use of mutual aid, to help each other look at their behavior today and understand how it has been affected by past experiences.

Age Range of Members: Approximately ages 26–54. These are white, middle-class and working-class women.

Dates Covered in Record: From October 9 to November 20

Description of the Problem

The group is resistant to the discussion of painful past experiences having to do with growing up in alcoholic homes. They have difficulty sharing current or past problems without externalizing them by focusing on the faults and character defects of others. They refer to personal "issues," such as low self-esteem, as having been problems in the past, but not anymore. The problem facing the group and the leader lies in creating a culture for work and mutual aid in which the members trust each other enough to reach out and open up.

How the Problem Came to the Attention of the Group Leader(s)

On October 23, the third session, the group began discussing ACOA (*Adult Children of Alcoholics*) issues that were listed on a sheet I had handed out. One of the members stated with some anger that she "never lies"—a characteristic suggested as common to many ACOAs.

Most everyone agreed that they, too, never lie, but said that their husbands or other alcoholics they know lie all the time. Another member (Jane) pointed out that she agreed that adult children lie often—she said that she used to do it all the time, but that when she joined Alanon and began the 12-step program, she was forced to get honest. After this, the group continued discussing different degrees of lying, and individuals slowly admitted to exceptional situations in which they had lied. They generally denied having any behaviors possibly perceived as "bad." It seemed like it was too painful for them to examine and admit to any of their own maladaptive behaviors because it might mean looking back at a painful past where they learned these behaviors in order to cope.

PRACTICE POINTS

It is not unusual for a group leader to be contacted by a group member between group meetings. The leader understands that this is not really a withdrawal from the group but rather a request that the leader challenge the illusion of work. She responds by explaining the stage of group development and encouraging the member to give the group another try.

On October 26, a few days after the third session, Jane called to talk about the group and to tell me that she didn't think she was going to return. She felt that people were not talking about what they were in the group for. She felt everyone had been focusing on the problems of living with their alcoholic husbands instead of looking at their childhoods and being raised by alcoholic parents. She felt that people were not being honest about their feelings. I explained that the group was still new and that the members were testing each other out. I encouraged her to give it another trial period because I was pretty sure she had a lot to give and also a lot to receive if she would allow it in. She agreed to return for a few weeks.

Summary of Work

Third Session (October 23)

Paula stated that she had a problem with some of the statements on the worksheet. Ginnette quickly said she had seen this list before in something she's read. I asked Paula if she could talk a little bit about what she was having problems with on the sheet. She said she didn't like the statement about ACOAs lying when it is just as easy as telling the truth. She said she never lied, adding, "I'm so honest I can't stand it." Kate quickly agreed, saying that it's the alcoholic who lies all the time because he's always making excuses for himself. There were nods of agreement as other members joined in the talk of not being "liars." There was a brief silence.

Then Jane said she could see what the worksheet was talking about because she used to lie all the time, until she was 30 years old (24 years ago). She continued to say that it definitely had to do with growing up with an alcoholic parent. She said there was a lot of shame—she would never have friends over because they might find out how things were for her—she would lie about how things were. (Another brief silence.)

I asked Jane what happened then to make her change. She talked about being unhappy in a marriage with an alcoholic until she sought help through counseling and Alanon. She said the steps in Alanon (the 12 steps) made her look at her lies and why she was telling them. The other members got into a discussion of the 12 steps. Kate and Jane talked about how the steps are hard because they make you admit that you've done something wrong. Paula nodded and mentioned the step about making amends—said that because of it she has gotten good at apologizing. The others all nodded and smiled in agreement as Paula continued to tell a couple of stories to illustrate how she always "swallows her pride" and apologizes. She said that people always tell her that she's too honest.

Note that the leader has used the feedback from the member to prepare to confront the illusion of work and challenge the group by pointing out the defensive pattern in respect to lying. She then specifically points out how the group members avoid keeping the focus on themselves and their own behaviors by shifting discussion to the behavior of their husbands.

I commented that everyone seemed to get defensive about the idea of lying. I said I wondered what "lying" means to everybody—that maybe it means different things for different people. Diane looked at me and said that she used to have to lie for self-protection. I asked if she could say something more about that. She said that while growing up, her father used to get crazy and violent about things, so if she'd done something she thought he wouldn't like, she would lie to protect herself and her siblings. Kate and Ginnette agreed about self-protection lies. Others began sharing experiences of being a child and having to protect oneself—quick examples and lots of identification with each other. The focus evolved again to their alcoholic husbands and reasons why their husbands lied.

I commented that it seemed difficult keeping the focus on themselves and their behavior. Then Diane admitted that now she finds herself telling "little white lies" when she is trying to get herself or others out of a situation. People agreed about telling these kinds of lies and talked about feeling guilty after having told them. Paula and Kate shared stories about enabling by lying to cover for their husbands when they were drunk. Jane, who had been frowning, stated disbelief that Paula is in Susan's group (a family group offered at the same agency) and gets away with behavior like that. She chuckled rather smugly and said that she herself never would have gotten away with that ten years ago. I had been feeling annoyed with everyone's goody-goodiness and their unwillingness to "'fess up." Then I felt angry at Jane for acting so smug and righteous. I did not share my feelings, but in looking back, I see where it might have been helpful if I had been more open about them.

The leader in this excerpt did make a demand for work by exploring the issue of lying and not letting group members off the hook. It's interesting that the leader gets "annoyed" and "angry" when it should not be surprising that at only the third session members are acting out the very denial that has led them to attend the group. Even the term goody-goodiness has a disparaging element that suggests that the leader is really angry because the members are not responding the way she would want. The members have shared some very painful memories, and the leader might have helped them lower their defenses more easily with more empathic support that creates the relationship needed to confront from caring. For example, when she pointed out the difficulty of keeping focus on themselves and their own behaviors, she might have commented on or elicited the feelings that make it hard to do so.

Fourth Session (October 30)

The theme of this session seems to still be trust. The members are still trying to get to know me and each other. Throughout the session, they talk about what it means to look or feel normal, and they worry about making mistakes. They seem to be wondering how they can express themselves here and feel safe.

Paula brought up the phrase about "guessing at what normal is." She seemed angry and stated that she thinks she's normal. She said it makes her mad when "they" are made to sound like they all have the same problems. Kate said that she's just the opposite—that she likes reading it because it lets her know that she's not the only one who experiences these things, but that she also knows that they may not all apply to her. Jane agreed about how it makes her feel that she's not alone. Then she talked about this book being written about the experiences of many adult children and their issues—everything doesn't necessarily apply to everyone. Kate said that she does guess at what is normal, in a way—said she watches how other people do things and then tries to do what they do.

Ginnette said that she worries about it because she is afraid of repeating her parents' mistakes since she doesn't know any other way. Paula shared some of her worries that because of her husband's drinking she did terrible things to her sons while raising them. Kate and Diane both identified with these fears about raising their children. Kate and Paula began talking about their husbands—how they had met them, when they came to realize they were alcoholics, and how they haven't been able to leave them. The members also talked about how their kids' fathers are not very available but how, in the long run, it's probably better than being around and drunk.

I let my feelings of annoyance at the women's denial of their own faults hinder my ability to make interventions. I was unable to share my feelings openly in a way that could have been useful to the group, so I stayed silent.

PRACTICE POINTS Through analysis of her work over time, the group leader starts to see how her annoyance and anger are hindering her ability to provide support for the members as they enter these painful areas. She demonstrates greater empathy for the difficulty involved in the next section.

Fifth Session (November 6)

Then people got quiet, looking around at each other and at me expectantly. Paula commented that our "starter" isn't here. (Diane usually gives the group a cue to start with.) I said I wondered what someone else would say if they were to start the group. People seemed puzzled and asked what I meant. I asked what they would like to say—how they would like to start us off. Jane said she had an idea. She said she'd been thinking about last week's group, and she'd like to relate people's troubles in their lives now to troubles when they were growing up. Kate said that she didn't have anything bad happen as a child. I reached for elaboration from Jane. Jane said that since this is an ACOA group, she would like to hear people talk about experiences as children and how those experiences affect us now. She said that she realized this week that there was a similar pattern between her mother's behavior while drinking and her ex-husband's. (Silence.)

PRACTICE POINTS As the group members begin to explore more difficult material, their discomfort grows. At this point, the silence is signaling the need to address the process in the group and the difficulty in discussing these issues. An alternative intervention at this point might be to reach inside of the silence and explore what it means as a way of helping members move forward. The group leader does stay with the issue by trying to generalize the content.

I asked if anyone could see similarities between her husband's and parents' drinking. Ginnette began talking about how her father's drinking had affected her self-esteem, although it is better now. Said she wasn't sure why—"It's not like I was physically abused or anything—my parents never hit me . . . they told me I was stupid all the time." I recognized that emotional abuse can be just as painful and longer lasting than physical abuse. Diane talked about how she also used to have low self-esteem because of things at home, but that it's higher now. I asked what kinds of things happened at home.

Diane talked about her father's violent behavior while drunk and his complete emotional absence when sober. Diane told stories very animatedly and said that she knows it's weird, but that she used to feel excitement around these awful events. She said humor was the way to deal with the emotional and physical abuse. Ginnette said that she just felt shame and wanted to be invisible to everyone. Diane said she didn't—she felt like the commotion her family caused was a form of attention and any she could get was OK. She said it's sort of like, "Look at me! Look at me!" (Silence.)

<table>
<tr><td>**PRACTICE POINTS**</td><td>The conversation is moving to a deeper level; however, it is still painful for most of the members to recall their family experiences. If we consider that keeping the family secret was so central to their childhood, it is little wonder that taking down the veil of secrecy and talking about these experiences has to be hard. Diane describes a maladaptive way of coping, excitement and humor, while Ginnette discloses the deep feelings of shame.</td></tr>
</table>

I asked if anyone else remembered what it felt like when the alcoholic was drinking or when either parent was being abusive. Paula spoke up by saying she didn't really remember her childhood, but she began unfolding some of her childhood story anyway. Said she used to idolize her mother, and she hardly knew her father because he was more like a boarder than anything. She told about her mother going out to get drunk then returning, sick and crying, wanting to tell all her troubles to young Paula. Paula said she hated it, but she'd listen because she loved her mother. She talked about her father and how he didn't speak to anyone in the house—he would just stay out drinking until he came stumbling home and went to his room, where he lived off canned food.

<table>
<tr><td>**PRACTICE POINTS**</td><td>As we have seen so often in the examples in this book, the leader's capacity to share her feelings helps the group members deepen their work. In the next excerpt, the leader also demonstrates being able to "see" the group and monitor its emotional development, while simultaneously tracking the involvement of individual members. The leader notes that Jane "looks" as if she is ready to say something and reaches out to Jane to help her into the conversation.</td></tr>
</table>

I said that this is really painful to hear. It must have been a lot of pain for a child to carry—never having a father who would recognize her and wanting so much to have his attention; having to take care of her mother's physical and emotional needs. Paula responded that she'd never really thought of it as sad or painful—that's just the way it was. I had noticed that Jane looked like she'd wanted to say something, so I commented on that. Jane said she could relate to what Paula had said about not talking or questioning anything at home. She said at her house it was like having an arm cut off and no one saying anything.

I failed to acknowledge the intense pain in her powerful statement. It could have been an opportunity to say more about what it felt like rather than explaining what her situation looked like. Jane went on to talk about never having known her father and never being able to ask her mother any questions about him. She described her mother's reaction when she read about his death in the newspaper—all the anger and hurt came out. I said that it sounds like she has had to carry her mother's anger and shame for a long time.

Near the end of the session, Diane brought up that she had been planning to call her mother tonight and break 3 months of silence. But she said now she feels too angry. Said she feels a lot of anger at the mothers who weren't drunk but who sat there and watched the kids suffer. We were almost at the end of the session, so I wanted to validate Diane's anger and to acknowledge the heavy sharing of feelings that had gone on. I summed up the things that were shared. I said that I appreciated that people could be so honest tonight and bring up such painful memories. I said that there had been a lot of talk about childhood abuse and neglect. I said there had also been some minimizing of the neglect, and I just wanted to point out that it is abusive to a child when her needs—emotional and physical—aren't met. I said to Diane that she had shared experiences of having been hurt so I wasn't surprised that she was feeling angry. The members continued talking until I told them we had to clear the room for the next group.

PRACTICE POINTS Note the movement of the group into a discussion of how their growing-up experiences are affecting them now. Ginnette, in an internal leadership role, takes the group to a core issue of intimacy and affection.

Sixth Session (November 13)

Ginnette said that she wanted to discuss intimacy and affection—that it had been on her mind. She said it's difficult to show affection toward anyone except her kids and that she has a hard time receiving it. Paula said she could relate to that. She cried as she told about the absence of intimacy and affection in her marriage—said there's nothing left between her and her husband. She said she's really been thinking about it and almost didn't come tonight because she had been depressed. She talked about an argument with her husband over the weekend. She talked about how his inability to show affection toward her has been a disappointment from the beginning. (Silence.) People tried to comfort Paula by assuring her that he is acting this way because she is making positive changes without him.

PRACTICE POINTS This is a very difficult issue and the leader responds by reinforcing Ginnette's entry into a taboo subject.

I brought them back to Ginnette's demand for work. I asked how others felt about intimacy in their lives. There was much discussion about lack of affection and intimacy growing up and now with spouses. Members talked about what it means to love someone and to say and show it. Throughout the bulk of the session, I kept trying to help them get from general answers/talk to specific memories and feelings. I asked what it means to say or think that you love someone. They asked what I meant. I tried to clarify by asking how it feels to love. Paula said, "Well, I always thought it meant sex." People discussed their frequent confusion between sex and love. Kate related the inability to achieve intimacy after growing up without it. I reached back to her comment and put it out to the group. If you grew up "in the gutter" and never experienced intimacy, could you experience it now? Jane said yes, and Paula asked for a definition of intimacy.

PRACTICE POINTS In a beautiful example of synthesizing content and process, the leader asks the group members to relate their conversation about intimacy in their lives to the intimacy in the group.

The group is a microcosm of their world of relationships, and if they can face their fears of intimacy with each other, they increase their chances of taking risks with significant others in their lives.

After a lengthy conversation about the definition of intimacy, I realized there was a lot of indirect communication. I pointed it out to the group and related it specifically to what was happening in the group. I said that I was hearing several words mentioned around intimacy—vulnerability, trust, no judgment. Kate mentioned fear that people wouldn't understand. I said I wanted to make an observation. I was wondering if people have been talking all this time about not getting intimacy and not having their needs met because they're really afraid that they won't have them met here and they won't be able to trust each other, or that they will make themselves vulnerable and be judged. Kate immediately said she was glad I had brought that up because something had happened 2 weeks ago that had made her very uncomfortable. She said she was so worried about coming last week that she convinced herself that she was sick. She told the group that she had felt judged by a few people about something she had shared about herself. The members all talked about it, and Kate was given positive feedback about her courage to bring it up.

Current Status of the Problem

The group has begun to deal with some sensitive issues in a much more open, honest way. They continue to externalize problems to focus on safer issues, like their husbands. However, they are beginning to examine the role their own behavior plays in perpetuating the difficulties in their lives. For example, in the most recent session, I pointed out the connection between the way they communicate in the group and their frustration with never having their needs met "out there." They were able to start talking about it. They focused first on the lack of communication they get from their husbands, but with direction they looked at the patterns of communicating in their families of origin. Finally, they were able to start looking at their own communication skills and how that affects relationships.

At this point in the group—after eight sessions—the members seem to have developed some trust and are ready to do more work. With this population of women ACOAs, it will always be a challenge to keep up a culture for work because of their eagerness to agree and to avoid conflict. As the group leader, I am feeling more comfortable with my role. I feel more willing to take risks to challenge them to work.

The illustration points out how crucial it is for the leader to play an active role in pointing out what appears to be happening in the group. If the leader had shared her feelings earlier, the group process and development would have been speeded up. The other striking observation is how often the second client, the group, responded with silence at crucial moments in the conversation. Reaching inside the silences and exploring them might have been another way for the leader to move the group more quickly into its work. The leader's astuteness about how the group process related to the content of their work helped her develop more effective strategies.

In the example that follows, group members are currently living with the addicted partner and in most cases are experiencing physical or emotional abuse. The example also introduces the variation on the theme introduced by the open-ended nature of the group. We clearly see the impact of members' being at different stages in the group process (beginning, middle, and end/transition) and the importance of the group leader's sensitivity to the associated issues. A second issue is the fact that group members are at different stages in dealing with their problems: denial, passive acceptance, and, for some, the "taking action" stage that means ending the abusive relationship. It is important for the group leaders to acknowledge and respect the struggle for each member and to create a safe place for all of the women. Finally, a third element nicely illustrated in this group is the issue of co-leadership with one's supervisor. Once again, we see a sensitive handling of this dynamic by the student and a wonderful openness by the supervisor to the student's ideas and suggestions.

A Women's Open-Ended Codependent Group: Dealing with Substance and Physical Abuse

Group Purpose: Support and education group for women who are "codependent"

Age Range of Members: From 20 to 63 years

Gender, Ethnic, or Racial Information: All Caucasian: Italian, Portuguese, Greek, Irish, French Canadian, and Polish. Most members are Catholic.

Dates Covered in Record: From October 6 to November 17

The group is ongoing (has been meeting approximately 6 years) and open-ended. Some members have been in the group since it began. The leader of the group is my supervisor. She asked if I would like to co-lead the group as part of my fieldwork. This is the first time my supervisor has ever co-led a group.

Description of the Problem

The women in the group almost constantly focus on their partners' behaviors and feelings instead of on their own. Sometimes they discuss their reactions to their partners' behaviors. When feedback is given from one member to another, it is usually advice on how the person can "fix" her partner. The members are resistant in exploring who they are as individuals, what their individual goals are (separate from their partners'), and awareness of their own feelings. The contract aims to move the focus of the work off of the partners and onto group members.

How the Problem Came to the Attention of the Group Leader(s)

In my first meeting, members talked about how supported they felt by other women in the group, and they described the group as special time for themselves. Yet after a few meetings, I realized that little time was spent on their feelings. Whenever either leader tried to shift the focus away from partners and onto exploration of members' feelings, the subject was quickly changed. Members became quiet, and it seemed, full of shame. They either defended their partners or blamed themselves. They seemed secure in talking about their husbands' addictions. But it was clear to me that they had deep issues of insecurity and low self-esteem. They said things like, "But I'm always nagging him," or "I don't want to take up too much time talking tonight." I felt it was important to try to help them get at their root feelings of worthlessness.

PRACTICE POINTS Note that the leader, a student and new to the group, remains strategically silent during the first meeting. In part, that is to get to know the group, but it is also a natural reaction to joining a group in progress led by her supervisor. She shows courage in the second meeting by not only intervening but doing so by addressing the uncomfortable process taking place in the group.

Summary of the Work with Process Excerpts

In my first session with the group, I did not say much and basically observed. But at the second meeting, I knew if I did not speak up, I would be going along with a norm that implied "the student is an observer." The group got started, and as usual, each woman took her turn to speak. By the time the third woman got into her story, I felt ready to make an intervention.

Laura spoke at length about her husband, who is a compulsive gambler. She was highly agitated as she talked about how he gambles away his paycheck each week. She shared with the group how he had "pushed her onto the floor" during an argument over the weekend. This was the first time there had ever been any aggressive physical contact between them. She expressed concern about this incident. She said she had made a contract with herself that if he ever got physical with her, "that would be it, he would be out." She said she knew the statistics, that if it happened once, it was bound to happen again.

Suddenly, Celia (the scapegoat) could not contain herself any longer. Before my supervisor had a chance to respond, Celia jumped in. She said, "Well, is he out? Did you keep your contract, or is he still living with you?" Laura responded with her voice trailing off. "No, he's not out. He's still living at home." She seemed ashamed to have to admit it.

PRACTICE POINTS The student leader is demonstrating how to be with both members in a confrontation and crediting "real talk" at the same time. I believe she does not look at her supervisor, at least in part, because she is concerned at how her co-leader was reacting to her intervention. Taking it a next step, she could also comment that it was probably hard for all of them, even Celia, to confront their abusive partners.

I knew it was my time to jump in as well. I said, "Celia, it was great that you could challenge Laura on such a hard subject, as I'm sure it was really hard for you, Laura, to talk about such an upsetting incident with the group." I was validating Celia's confrontation of Laura. There was a real shift in the room. Celia beamed a large smile, while other members glanced around at one another and at my supervisor. I did not look at my supervisor because I was focused on what I was doing. Laura looked tentatively at me and then continued her discussion with Celia. Laura said, "I know I should have kicked his ass out right then and there, but I didn't. Instead I got up and pushed him back." Celia responded to Laura, "I know it's hard to keep to your bottom line. Believe me; I've broken mine many times . . . like when . . . ."

The discussion continued, and I felt great! For the rest of the session, members were more actively engaged with each other. There seemed to be a great relief that they could now talk to one another instead of just to the leader. At the end of the session, I made a process observation to the group. I commented on what a great job they were doing in addressing each other's problems.

PRACTICE POINTS This was a difficult step for the leader because her supervisor had co-led the group for a long time, and the student was stepping in to impact the culture. In retrospect, it might have been wise for the student to discuss this with her supervisor and develop a strategy for this intervention so that it did not come as a surprise. As it was, the supervisor took it well as she recognized an important change taking place in the group. The leader had done an excellent job through her intervention of being with both members and the group at the same time. With the taboo against discussing physical violence overcome, the discussion deepens.

In the next meeting, the members engaged in significantly more interaction. The taboo of physical violence had been broken the week before, and now Mary, the most timid member of the group, spoke up. She talked about an emotional/physical abuse situation that had taken place during the middle of the night, while she was in bed with her husband. Mary said, "He had been drinking all day and into the night. I just kept my distance from him most of the day and that night, too. A couple of times he snapped at me, and I just ignored it. Then, of course, it was time for bed and I got in. I knew he was still very drunk." Mary is quite light-skinned, and I could see the fear creep over her in the form of deep, red blotches on her neck.

She said he passed out and she eventually fell asleep. Then, at around 3:30 A.M., he woke up and started calling her names. She said she was half asleep and said some things she probably shouldn't have. Then the next thing she knew, he had backed her up against the bedroom wall and he had his fist placed ever so gently under her chin. She kept saying over and over, "He never hit me; he just held his fist under my chin." She made a fist and mimicked for the group what it was like.

My supervisor led a discussion around what constitutes physical abuse and tried to broaden Mary's and the group's definition of abuse. Other members jumped into the discussion, and they all intellectualized on the true meaning of physical abuse and domestic violence.

PRACTICE POINTS The intellectual discussion constituted a form of flight since the description of such an incident had to set off the anxiety, fear, and shame for all of the members. Once again, the student leader reaches for the underlying feelings. At some point, when the pattern persists, the group leaders will need to address with the members how fight and flight are maladaptive means for the members to deal with such a powerful issue. We also see the strength in the supervisor's response to the student and her self-reflection on how easy it can be to participate in the illusion of work.

There was a pause, and I caught Mary's eye. "Were you scared?" I asked gently. A hush fell over the room. Mary's eyes welled up with tears, and her face flushed bright red. "Yes," she said, "I was scared." Mary went on to describe her situation as "not even having a marriage." She was strong in her conviction that because he really didn't hit her, it wasn't physical abuse. But she commented several times that she "could no longer go on living this way." Celia challenged Mary on her bottom line and expressed concern for Mary's safety.

After the meeting, my supervisor told me it was excellent that I could get at Mary's feelings. She said she had been alone with the group for so long that sometimes she gets caught up with them. She encouraged me to continue the "feelings work" with the group.

At the next meeting, Betsy, also a timid woman had described living for 20 years with an abusive alcoholic husband. He was also sex addicted and had openly cheated on Betsy throughout their marriage. They have two sons together, a 17-year-old and a 2-year-old. A year ago (she's been in the group since it began), Betsy had found the courage to ask for a separation from him because she had found him in their bed with another woman. He begged her for forgiveness, and eventually she took him back. Then one night, he came home violently drunk, and he raped her.

Betsy is now filing for divorce. She has a restraining order on her husband, although he has visitation rights to the children. Somehow, Betsy got caught up in the oppression of the legal system and agreed to supervise her husband's visits with their young son. She says there were all kinds of pressure from different lawyers and the Department of Social Services, and she felt she had no other choice. Part of me believes she truly felt this way, and another part of me believes that at an unconscious level, she's not quite ready to let go of him.

PRACTICE POINTS This is a good example of the importance of "trusting your gut" because I believe the group leader is on target in her sense of Betsy's ambivalence. By exploring this with Betsy and the group, the member can get a better hold on what is making it so hard for her to take a next step.

Betsy talked about seeing her husband during one of the supervised visits. She said, "It's really bothering me that I have to see him at those visits with Matt. He keeps on talking about it, you know, that night. I'm not listening to him—I'm not! I know what he did to me that night! He keeps on trying to tell me it didn't happen, but I know what happened! Then I did something stupid. I'm so stupid. It just slipped out at the end of the day, and it was stupid."

My supervisor said, "What, Betsy, what did you do that you feel was stupid? Even though we all know you're not stupid, you're smart." Betsy looked hesitant, and then in a whisper she said, "I told him I loved him. I said, 'I love you, Tim.'" She lowered her head, and there was a long pause.

PRACTICE POINTS At moments such as this one, a not uncommon mistake would be to identify so strongly with the group member and have such strong anger at the perpetrator that the group leader tries to convince the member not to feel the way she feels. This would cut off Betsy and send a signal to the other members that these feelings should not exist and should not be shared. The leaders and others in the group will have to help Betsy make decisions that protect herself and her son in spite of these feelings. A first step is recognition of how hard this can be.

I said, "Betsy, it's only natural to feel that way. You did live with him for 20 years and have two boys with him. Of course you still love him. But that doesn't mean you can still live with him." She looked at me. Then I added, "I'll bet you're feeling very lonely these days." Betsy began to cry, "I am lonely. It's lonely in that big house with just me and Matt. And I'm starting to have more nightmares about that night."

The other members were silent and afraid. All this expression of buried feelings was new behavior for the group. Betsy is also living the other members' worst fears. She is leaving her husband this time and feeling the pain of what it means to let go and say good-bye. Even though it's an unhealthy relationship, it is indeed the only "love" she's ever known.

PRACTICE POINTS In Chapter 10, I discussed the issues raised when a group is open-ended. In a group such as this one where trust needs to be developed over time, it is particularly important to ask the group, if possible, to discuss the addition of a new member. Some tuning in to the feelings of the group members and the potential concerns of the new member would be helpful. Also, the members and the leaders could jointly discuss a strategy for bringing the new member into the ongoing group. This is not done and the result is a difficult first session.

Saying Good-bye to an Old Member and Hello to a New One

The group is open-ended, so when a long-term member terminates, a new member is added to the group. In this particular session, it was Faith's last meeting and Donna's first meeting.

Faith spoke at length about how supportive the group has been for her and how much she will miss all the members. She said she would like to continue phone contact with a few people she had gotten close to. She reported many changes in herself and realized that she had reached the goals she had set for herself when she started the group, especially getting her driver's license. She acknowledged that her husband would never stop drinking and that she had come to terms with that fact. She also knew she was not ready to leave him.

The group focus was clearly on Faith and her leaving. Donna sat quietly and listened. She seemed nervous and self-conscious and for good reason. Finally, my supervisor turned the attention to Donna. She introduced her and then asked all members to introduce themselves and tell Donna something about their situations. There was a long silence. I knew it was time to speak up: "It must be hard for people to reveal personal things to someone they don't know. Maybe you could just share something you feel comfortable about with Donna?"

PRACTICE POINTS

Although the supervisor had responded well to the student's interventions designed to change the culture of the group, eventually this will be a problem. It will become clear that the student does not agree with her co-leader, and her interventions, which impact the work, will be noted by the members. As discussed in an earlier chapter on co-leadership, the earlier a frank discussion with the supervisor takes place, the better it will be in the long run. I realize this is easy to say but hard to do when the co-leader will evaluate you on your performance. The issue in the next session of how to handle a termination and a new member would have been a good one to discuss.

> I think a termination should be done separately, without a new member present. I had so many mixed feelings with trying to say good-bye to Faith and hello to Donna. I'm sure the members also had lots of confusing feelings. Separation is a big issue for the women in the group. They need time to really feel the loss of a respected member. I would recommend a couple of sessions after the member left to discuss what it is like without her before a new member begins. This process would be beneficial for new, terminating, and current members.

PRACTICE POINTS

One might agree or disagree with the student leader on the wisdom of having a new member join at the same meeting one leaves. There may be advantages for the new member to hear the termination discussion and gain a sense of the group's intimacy. This only happens, however, if the group and the leader give consideration to the process and develop a strategy to make time to say hello and good-bye at the same session.

Where the Problem Stands Now

The women in the group are still focused on their partners' behaviors and feelings, though not quite as much. They have made progress in allowing themselves to experience more of their own feelings. This seems only natural as they take small steps in their emotional movement away from their partners. The members have truly shifted from one-on-one therapy with the leader, to dynamic group work. There is considerably more interaction amongst members. This interaction is no longer in the form of one-on-one advice giving on how to "fix" partners. Instead, it takes the form of open-ended questioning of other members. There also seems to be more genuine caring for other members.

The group is avoiding their deepest fear of abandonment and the loneliness that accompanies it. Although one member is beginning to openly work on it, the other women seem to communicate a "that's not me" attitude. They are dancing around the physical abuse issue, and I also believe that their feelings of worthlessness result from childhood sexual abuse. Perhaps this isn't the right forum for those issues to be worked on, but at some point, they need to be faced.

PRACTICE SUMMARY An important next step would be to have a frank discussion with her supervisor on those aspects of the group she found helpful and her ideas, some of them already demonstrated, of how the group could improve. The group will continue after she leaves. It would be important for the student to see as part of her ending with the agency and the supervisor that she needs some honest and respectful discussion of the experience they have had together.

Chapter Summary

This chapter began with a theoretical base for practice with this population. Substance abuse groups with members at different stages of the change process using stages of change model were described and illustrated. One group was generally described as the members in a precontemplation stage and the other in contemplation stages. The impact of gender was discussed with illustrations of working with active male abusers as well as female and some of the unique issues that affect each. The impact of dual diagnosis—substance abuse and mental illness or substance abuse and AIDS—was also illustrated as the unique problems as the two issues interacted with each were explored. This topic was described with detailed excerpts from a group for women with mental illness who are also substance abusers and the author's work with a group of persons with AIDS in early recovery from substance abuse. Because substance abuse was described as powerfully affecting those who are close to the abuser, group work with significant others such as the abuser's current partner or the adult child of a substance abuser was also illustrated. The strong shame and denial associated with these issues and the ongoing difficulty in addressing them and dealing with the profound impact on their lives were discussed.

Related Online Content and Activities

For learning tools such as glossary terms, InfoTrac® College Edition keywords, links to related websites, and chapter practice quizzes, visit this book's website at **www.cengage.com/counseling/shulman.**

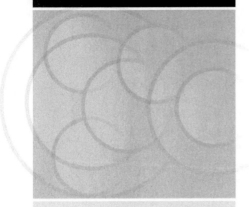

Group Counseling in the Schools

My focus in this chapter is to describe and illustrate group counseling in school settings with examples from elementary, middle, and high school. School counselors are active in a number of areas, and their work is influenced by their students' age and stage of the educational life cycle. Although discussing all the types of group work in school settings was not possible, I have chosen several with some emphasis on dealing with students with behavior problems. This population increasingly demands the attention of school counselors and can be the most challenging to work with in the group context. It is also the population for which group work may offer significant benefits.

In addition to discussing group counseling, the chapter also looks at the professional impact that the school counselor can have on system issues that emerge from practice. A focus on multicultural and social justice advocacy, as well as advocacy in general, is presented in terms of how the group leader helps the group deal with its environment—the school itself. This model could be applied to counselors in any of the six setting-specific chapters in Part 2, but I have chosen to elaborate on it here because of the crucial nature of the school environment and its daily impact on students.

Additional illustrations include prevention groups, groups to aid students in making the transition from elementary to middle school, and work with parents, as listed here:

Elementary School

- Ten-year-old girls in a first group meeting with an acting-out member
- Inner-city elementary school children: the impact of violence
- A group for sixth graders in transition to middle school
- Working with mothers of underachieving sixth grade boys

Middle School

- Adolescent boys group dealing with disruptive classroom behavior
- Peacemaking Circle group in the classroom—from acting out to krumping
- Informal lunchtime meeting with 9- to 12-year-old girls
- Alternative public day school: parents with children with emotional and behavioral disorders

High School

- Students suspended from school for violence, weapons possession, or drugs
- Educational substance abuse prevention: is it a class or a group?
- High school students in a diversion program

What Do Counselors Do in School Settings?

The U.S. Department of Labor's (2008–2009) *Occupational Outlook Handbook* describes the work of counselors in this area as follows:

> School counselors assist students of all levels, from elementary school to postsecondary education. They advocate for students and work with other individuals and organizations to promote the academic, career, personal, and social development of children and youth. School counselors help students evaluate their abilities, interests, talents, and personalities to develop realistic academic and career goals. Counselors use interviews, counseling sessions, interest and aptitude assessment tests, and other methods to evaluate and advise students. They also operate career information centers and career education programs. Often, counselors work with students who have academic and social development problems or other special needs.
>
> *Elementary school counselors* observe children during classroom and play activities and confer with their teachers and parents to evaluate the children's strengths, problems, or special needs. In conjunction with teachers and administrators, they make sure that the curriculum addresses both the academic and the developmental needs of students. Elementary school counselors do less vocational and academic counseling than high school counselors.
>
> *High school counselors* advise students regarding college majors, admission requirements, entrance exams, financial aid, trade or technical schools, and apprenticeship programs. They help students develop job search skills, such as resume writing and interviewing techniques. College career planning and placement counselors assist alumni or students with career development and job-hunting techniques.

School counselors at all levels help students to understand and deal with social, behavioral, and personal problems. These counselors emphasize preventive and developmental work to provide students with the life skills needed to deal with problems before they worsen and to enhance students' personal, social, and academic growth. Counselors provide special services, including alcohol and drug prevention programs and conflict resolution classes. They also try to identify cases of domestic abuse and other family problems that can affect a student's development.

Counselors interact with students individually, in small groups, or as an entire class. They consult and collaborate with parents, teachers, school administrators, school psychologists, medical professionals, and social leaders to develop and implement strategies to help students succeed. (www.bls.gov/oco/home.htm)

Group Work in Schools

Groups are the medium of choice for working with a range of students. The elements of mutual aid described in Chapter 2 can be particularly helpful to children, adolescents, and teens for whom peer influence is a powerful force for learning, healing, and changing maladaptive behaviors. Groups in schools deal with prevention, education, and treatment when needed. While individual and family counseling is also important, many counselor interventions are in a group format.

Corey and Corey (2006) point out:

> Counseling groups in schools consist of a wide array of topics and formats. These groups are the mainstay of psychological services offered by schools. . . . Such groups are generally brief, structured, problem focused, homogenous in membership, and have a cognitive behavioral orientation. Most of the research that has been conducted on groups for children and adolescents has also been done in the schools. This research tends to be clustered in the areas of social competence problems, adjustment to parent divorce, behavior problems, and learning disabilities. (p. 297)

These authors correctly point out that treatment of children with severe problems is generally not within the scope of counseling services offered in the school setting and is normally provided by outside agencies. However, the reality in many schools, particularly but not exclusively in urban areas, is that the number of students exhibiting serious maladaptive behaviors has grown. When students enter their schools, they may bring with them problems associated with poverty, family and school violence, racism, homophobia, substance abuse, and other challenges that can profoundly affect the ability to cope with school structure and their ability to learn. When widespread, the impact of these maladaptive behaviors on the overall culture of the school—on teachers, administrators, and other students—is serious.

An alternative model of bringing community services into the school for school-day or after-school programs, sometimes referred to as "extended school day" programs, has become more widely implemented in school districts in some states.[1] In addition to providing direct services, school counselors may take on the role of liaison to the

---

1. Some of the examples presented in this chapter were from group practice in an urban public school funded by the New York State Education Department's "Extended School Day" program, which allowed violence prevention services to be delivered during the regular school day. I have directed this project, offered in collaboration with a local agency, over the past 7 years, and it continues at the time of this writing.

agencies and coordinator of these programs. In addition, school counselors may work in special programs within a larger school or, as in an example described later in this chapter, in special schools set up for the purpose of dealing with suspended students or students with behavioral problems that cannot be dealt with in a regular school program.

Four General Types of Groups

DeLucia-Waack (2006) draws upon the definitions of the Association for Specialists in Group Work (2000) in delineating four types of groups based on their goals and interactional processes (p. 10):

- Task/work
- Psychoeducational/guidance
- Counseling
- Therapy

She suggests that distinguishing between these types of groups is important to "aid in the selection of the appropriate type of group for different populations (e.g., age groups) with different goals (e.g., combating depression, learning social skills, preventing eating disorders):

> This delineation is important because any type of group work previously and sometimes still today, is viewed as group therapy. Many people view group therapy or therapy in general, negatively, and so the understanding that groups can be preventive; focus on learning new skills, cognitive styles, and behaviors; or address developmental issues is useful in defining and promoting group work. It is very helpful in the schools and working with children and adolescents to provide all interested parties (staff, parents, children, and adolescents) with a description of what psychoeducational groups do, focusing on the preventive nature and the skill building emphasis.

DeLucia-Waack continues by distinguishing psychoeducational groups from the other three types as follows:

> By definition, counseling groups "address personal and interpersonal problems of living and promote personal and interpersonal growth and development" (ASGW, 2000, p. 331), whereas therapy groups "address personal and interpersonal problems of living, remediate perceptual and cognitive distortions or repetitive patterns of dysfunctional behavior, and promote personal and interpersonal growth and development" (ASGW, 2000, p. 331). Examples of counseling and therapy groups include general interpersonal groups; training groups for students learning to be counselors or therapists; and groups directed at amelioration of specific problems such as depression, eating disorders, or sexual abuse. By nature, counseling and therapy groups seem more appropriate for persons with severe interpersonal difficulties and for adults.
>
> In contract, psychoeducational groups/guidance groups use "group-based educational and developmental strategies" (ASGW, 2000, p. 330), particularly role playing, problem solving, decision making and communication skills training. Psychoeducational/guidance groups teach specific skills and coping strategies in an effort to prevent problems; such skills and strategies might include anger management, social skills, self-esteem, assertiveness, and making friends. (pp. 10–11)

Although defining different group types is helpful, particularly in communicating the range of purposes of groups to the parties concerned, many of the elements of each of the groups can be found, more or less, in the others. The lines are not always so clearly drawn so that the group counselor needs to be aware of emerging purposes that were not originally conceived of when the group was first formed. For example, in one anger management group for teenagers in trouble in school and with the juvenile justice system described in Chapter 11, as the relationship with the leaders and other members developed, it soon became clear that the angry outbursts and physical attacks on others were maladaptive means for addressing posttraumatic stress resulting from physical abuse and incest in their families. Rather than simply referring the youngsters to a "therapy" or "counseling" group, a step that was eventually taken, the group leaders incorporated concepts and skills that could be drawn from other group models into their psychoeducational group. As pointed out earlier in the discussion of this example, it was important not to turn this group into a long-term therapy group but to stay focused on how their anger over their physical and sexual abuse, their posttraumatic stress, and their general cognitions of themselves as "damaged goods" affected their coping abilities at school and in the community.

The argument here is that while identifying a general group type can be helpful, recognizing how easily a group can cross a boundary and incorporate elements, activities, and leader skills from other group types can increase the skill of the leader and the success of the group.

Race, Class, and the Emerging Adolescent

Levinksy and McAleer (2005) describe their group practice with young adolescents of color in an urban school setting.

> Children in our inner cities face many obstacles in their efforts to experience success in school. Their families, oppressed by chronic environmental stressors such as poverty, racism, limited or nonexistent medical care, hunger and malnutrition, violence, substance abuse, inadequate housing, and limited access to employment or educational resources, are struggling to survive. Their neighborhoods are often crowded, noisy, disintegrating, and dangerous. Their schools, old and poorly funded, reveal overcrowded classrooms, facilities in disrepair, and limited support services. (p. 203)

While these environmental and family issues sorely test the urban middle school student, as well as school staff, behavioral problems can be particularly difficult in any middle school—urban, suburban, or rural. Akos and Ellis (2008) describe middle school as follows:

> Conceptually, the emergence of middle schools is an attempt to attend to the unique growth and development of the emerging adolescent. The middle school format configures grades, classes, and learning opportunities to help facilitate development. Middle school counselors play a key role in the process. . . . [M]iddle school counselors advocate and systematically promote academic, career, and personal and social development. Although all three outcomes are important and interrelated, puberty often amplifies the personal and social developmental tasks in middle schools. (p. 26)

The authors point out that identity development is important in this stage of the life cycle for all students.

With so much at stake, it is important to consider racial and ethnic identity development of middle school student. For students of color, unlike their White counterparts, race and ethnicity are often central themes to identify and create differential challenges and opportunities.... When students of color become cognitively aware of racism and inequality in their environment, racial identity development adds an important layer to the development of the self. (p. 26)

In a recent article advocating an advocacy role for school counselors, Bemak and Chung (2008) cite the Education Trust (2006) to point out that

[r]acial/cultural disparities in academic performances have been clearly established by numerous researchers. Fifty-nine percent of African American, 56% of Latina/Latino, and 52% of Native American eighth-grade students in the United States are below a fourth-grade reading level in comparison with only 25% of their White counterparts. . . . Related research findings further indicate that low-income students are 6 times more likely to drop out of high school compared with youth from higher income families. (p. 373)

Social Justice, the Advocacy Role, and Idiosyncratic Credits

Bemak and Chung (2008) cite these and other statistics to support the notion of a crisis in education related to race and class and the need for school counselors to adopt a more assertive advocacy approach that incorporates a social justice element in counselor interventions. In addressing the barriers that might make it difficult for school counselors to implement this role, they refer to a "Nice Counselor Syndrome (NCS)" and describe it as follows:

Counselors exhibiting NCS are often noted to be comfortable assuming the roles of mediator and problem solver when working with students, parents, and other school personnel. However, the value these counselors place on being viewed as nice people by others overshadows their willingness to implement multicultural/social justice advocacy and organizational change services that predictably result in interpersonal disagreements and conflicts with other school personnel, especially those interested in maintaining the existing educational status quo (D'Andrea & Daniels, 1999). (p. 374)

The Nice Counselor Syndrome is something of an unfair stereotype, but the concern about school counselors not engaging in social justice advocacy within their schools may be accurate for some counselors, but for different reasons. One reason is clarity of role and the answer to the question "Who is the client?" The position I have presented in this book is that every counselor in every setting always has two clients; for school counselors, the school is the second client. This assumption leads to the position that to do one's job, the counselor must pay attention to issues of social justice as well as any other organizational problems that interfere with effective teaching and learning for all students. In this view of the role, counselors need to incorporate elements of skillful advocacy to do their job and to be effective.

I stress the term *skillful* because some arguments for advocacy seem to see the system—in this case, teachers, administrators, and even school boards—as the "other side" or the "enemy" and perceive advocacy as always confrontational. The two-client construct suggests that school counselors need to be at least as tuned in to the issues facing other staff as they are those facing students if they wish to be effective.

A passion for social justice and change has to be harnessed to a clear sense of the counselor's role and skill in being able to implement it.

In addition to lack of clarity about this core role, a second major reason that counselors may not consistently implement this role may have to do with minimal training in those skills required to be an effective advocate for organizational change. Although professional education is more consistently addressing this area of content, courses needs to go beyond understanding organizational theory and the dynamics of change and focus on the strategies and skills needed to actually implement change. Student counseling interns in placements need an opportunity to put their newly acquired understanding of organizational behavior and change into practice. Intern supervisors need to incorporate this area of skill development into learning contracts even if the impact involves one small area of change. Interns who experience some success in this role will later tend to be counselors who are more likely to understand and implement their social change responsibilities within the school and the community. If the student supervisor does not feel empowered to have professional impact and communicates a cynical "you can't fight city hall" attitude, this can result in disempowering the intern and, in turn, the students in the school groups.

An important first step is to recognize the need to establish a positive working relationship with others in the school. As with student clients, a good working relationship is the medium through which professional impact can occur. An interesting exercise for interns (and counselors) is to write a brief statement on how they think they are viewed by teachers, staff, and administrators at their placement school. What would these important constituencies say about them? How would they describe the intern? Based on this first part of the exercise, how would they like to see this viewpoint changed? Finally, what steps could be taken to influence this system's view of them as student counselors? In one example, interns thought that teachers and administrators did not see them as connected to the school's day-to-day life because their class and practicum schedules caused them to be absent on key days and to miss school faculty meetings. They wanted this perception changed so that they would be seen as "team players" sharing in the responsibilities of the other staff. Their strategies to change this perception included the following:

- They would start to help out in lunchroom coverage even though this was not part of their regular assignment.
- They would take their own lunch, when possible, in the teacher's staff room.
- They would ask for release from one class for one week so they could be at the school for at least one faculty meeting.
- They would offer to help on a committee planning a faculty/staff holiday party.

These are small steps, but they started the student counselor thinking about the importance of building a working relationship not just with students but with others in the school as well. They would also be developing what Hollander (1958) referred to as "idiosyncrasy credit"—that is, the process by which a member of a group builds credits by first conforming to the norms of the group, which then allows for idiosyncratic behavior. Put another way, a student intern or new counselor would not question policies, attitudes, or norms of behavior in the first week of work in the school. The exercise described here helps the student counselor develop these "credits," which then allows for deviation from the norms once the relationship is established.

A third reason for not assuming a social justice advocacy role may be related to the element of risk that can be involved. A student intern or a new counselor on probation, or even one with experience and tenure, may worry that raising concerns about school structure, rules, and the administration's approach to children, if not handled well, may result in negative consequences. In some settings, there may be validity to this concern. This concern may be related to the belief that advocacy involves "speaking loudly" when at times the counselor may be most effective by "speaking softly." For some, the advocacy role is only associated with confrontation and conflict. As in work with clients, a facilitative confrontation raising an issue in a supportive rather than attacking manner may be most effective. This is an effort to be not a "nice counselor" but rather a professional with an astute understanding of the nature of the organizational change process and the skills required to have a positive impact.

Bemak and Chung (2008, pp. 375–376) address many of the personal obstacles that may lead to counselor inaction, including the following:

- Personal fear
- Being labeled a troublemaker
- Apathy as a coping strategy
- Anxiety leading to guilt
- Anger that may lead to ineffective responses to injustices
- A false sense of powerlessness
- Personal discomfort

After detailing a number of professional obstacles to attempting change, including working in a culture of fear, concern for job security, and turf battles, the authors suggest strategies for attempting organizational change (pp. 378–379). These include aligning the changes with the school's mission, using data to drive change, not internalizing victimization, not taking things personally, allowing time for change while still taking calculated risks, developing political and personal partners (what I would call allying), being political astute and knowledgeable, and having a level of courage.

Although the authors address organizational change in respect to multicultural/ social justice, their analysis of the issues and many of their suggestions for intervention strategies can apply to any educational change issues and all student populations. Just as not all clients are ready for change at certain stages in their lives, the same can be true for the school as an organization. Environmental issues—including the impact of the district administration, the school board, and the local, state, and national political structures—can create obstacles for change or facilitate it. The school counselor who can respect and understand the meaning of resistance to change and "deviant behavior" from colleagues and administrators has an increased chance of overcoming it. All too often professionals react from a sense of the "should," how they expect others to respond, rather than the "is," the reality of human nature and interaction.

A crucial principle that underlies this approach is that there is always a next step. It may not always be the step one wants to take or allow change as fast as one wishes, but it is a step.

Group Work in the Elementary School

Each stage of developmental change with elementary school children involves some transitions and some challenges. Developmental psychologists have tended to focus on the issues of the crucial early stages of childhood, such as establishing basic trust versus mistrust, achieving autonomy versus shame/doubt, initiative versus guilt, and then usually focusing on the identify crisis of adolescence (Erikson, 1950). Less attention has been paid to one of the more difficult stages, the preteen group. These are students who have not yet left childhood but are not yet fully into their adolescence. Irrizary and Appel (2005) describe a group of 10- to 13-year-old girls who are struggling with the typical developmental tasks and stresses of this transitional stage: "By virtue of being preadolescent they were at the cognitive stage where they could begin to grasp, very likely for the first time, their marginal position: passing from childhood with some sense of loss at being compelled to give up this stage, into the unknown stage that was looming, that of early adolescence, and to feel oneself as not belonging fully to either" (p. 166).

DeLucia-Waack (2006) suggests that unlike with adults, child and adolescent groups need more structure, and the long periods of verbal interactions, common in adult groups, may be unsustainable with adolescents. The new group leader discovers just this in the next section's example.

Ten to Eleven-Year-Old Girls with an Acting-Out Group Member

With some groups, the intensity of the issues or the particular strengths of the members will cause an internal leader to emerge and to raise the work in spite of the lack of clear contracting by the group leader. An *internal leader* is a member of the group who assumes a leadership role in a situational or ongoing basis. The term *internal* distinguishes this leader from the counselor, who is an *external leader* with authority derived from the school and his or her professional function.

PRACTICE POINTS

In the following example, the group leader is unclear in her contracting with a group of 10- to 11-year-old girls in a school setting, and two internal leaders, Harriet and Vera, emerge to give direction to the group. The leader misses some of their early signals of issues for discussion. Fortunately, instead of reacting to these two members as competing for her leadership role or seeing their behavior as "deviant" (which is often the case with an insecure group leader), this counselor relinquishes control of the group's direction to the members. The contracting begins as the members use a book device introduced by the leader to start the feedback process.

This example also raises the issue of when, where, and how the subject of sex can be discussed in a school group. It's important for the school administration to be involved in clarifying the group leader's role and the appropriate boundaries. Some school districts and states require that such discussions be conducted by a staff member with specific training and certification in sex education. A school district may also require permissions from parents for their children to be involved in these conversations. A meeting with parents to discuss the purpose and limitations of such discussions is not uncommon. What the school counselor does not want is to have to explain to the principal the nature of the discussion after a concerned call from a distressed parent.

One way this can be resolved is to leave sex education to the certified counselor but leaving open permission for a general discussion of peer pressure—not just to get involved in sexual acts but also to use drugs, participate in bullying, settle conflicts with fights outside school, and to join formal or informal gangs. With the surge in school-age pregnancies as well as sexually transmitted diseases (STDs), young men and women need some place in addition to home to discuss how to resist peer pressure in order to make personal and responsible decisions. Some of these issues emerge in the group example that follows. Note how they are raised indirectly in the early part of the first session by pretending to take off clothing and asking about dressing up like "hookers." The leader misses the first offerings but gets back to them later. Note also how the group members, led by Harriet and Vera, also address the authority theme.

Purpose: Discussion group (with special attention to school and family problems)
Gender of Members: Female; age range: 10–11 years
Cultural, Racial, or Ethnic Identification of Members: Caucasian

---

First Session

The girls came in and sat in chairs in a circle, squirming around, flinging their legs over the chair arms. During the following conversation, the girls took off their shoes and sweatshirts. Vera and Harriet pretended to remove their shirts with their sweatshirts.

HARRIET: Is this group going to be boring?
LEADER: Do you think it'll be boring?
HARRIET: No.
VERA: Can we have parties?
LEADER: Well, what would we do at a party here?
VERA: Food, talking, dancing, and music.
LEADER: Yes, yes, yes, yes. Well, yes, I guess we can have parties here.
VERA: Today?
LEADER: No, not today.
HARRIET: Can we dress up like hookers?
LEADER: Is that fun?
(SEVERAL): Yes!
LEADER: Who does that?
VERA, HARRIET: Me!
LEADER: Oh, two me's! Let me tell you about the group. (Harriet mimics.) Harriet, stop. (Harriet continues.) Harriet, that's enough. OK? It's so you'll have a place that's special, just for you guys. This is your group, with me—our group. We're going to think about fun things that we can do together, and we'll do them. And it's also a place where you can bring things to talk about like things that happen at school or at home, at the Community House, at church, with friends . . . because this might be a time in your life when lots of things are changing, or maybe about to change, and it can help to talk about it. I'd like this to be a place where you can say things and know that no one's going to tell them to anyone outside the group. Now let me show you this; this is our book, for this group. (I open to a page with three headings: "Things we want to do," "Things we want to talk about," and "Things we want for snack." I put the book on the floor in the center of the circle and bring out Magic Markers.)

The leader has given a general statement of contract but has not included any "handles for work" that would make operational the concept of "things changing in your life." She also is unintentionally misleading in her statement about confidentiality, because she cannot guarantee things will not be shared outside the group. Although one can understand her reluctance to make clear the limits of confidentiality, it is important that she states that under certain conditions she may need to share what they say outside the group. The internal leaders return to the confidentiality issue, but the leader does not immediately respond.

> **VERA AND HARRIET:** We can't talk with Olive (absent today). She tells, she blabs, she says she won't, but she does. (All nod.)
>
> **LEADER:** I hope we can work together to help Olive. (To Fran, who seems quiet) What does your sweatshirt say?
>
> **VERA:** (To leader) What color is your shirt? (Points, then pokes finger up into leader's face) (Laughter) That's the oldest trick in the book!
>
> **LEADER:** Well, it didn't feel good to me.
>
> **VERA:** Oh, I'm sorry.
>
> **LEADER:** OK. (Reorienting around book)

The next comments raise issues about relationships with parents. Vera sends an early signal of the degree of stress between Harriet and her mother. This is a first offering that will be escalated by Harriet as the meeting continues.

> **VERA:** (To leader) My mom likes you, and she told Jean (the leader's supervisor).
>
> **LEADER:** That's nice. I liked meeting your moms. I've seen everyone's mother but Harriet's; she's coming next week.
>
> **VERA:** Harriet doesn't want you to meet her mother.
>
> **LEADER:** (To Harriet) Why not?
>
> **HARRIET:** She asks dumb questions—don't tell her I said that!
>
> **LEADER:** I won't. Like what?
>
> **HARRIET:** Like she asked my teacher, "Are you a good teacher?"
>
> **LEADER:** And the teacher could only give one answer, huh? She had to say yes. She couldn't very well say, "No, I'm a lousy teacher." (Laughter)
> (Vera seems ready to write in the book. I encourage others to take a turn, but they seem content to let Vera do it. Under "Snack" she writes Oreos, pretzels, Pepsi, pizza. . . . Then she moves to "What to talk about.")
>
> **VERA:** What we want to talk about . . . hmm. (Laughter) (Mouthing words to leader) Sex!
>
> **LEADER:** (Whispering to Vera) What about sex—boys or bodies?
>
> **VERA:** Both.
>
> **LEADER:** How do you want to write it? (Vera considers this for a moment and writes "sex.")
>
> **LEADER:** That's the simplest, isn't it? (Vera later adds "boys and bodies"—laughter, long and loud—particularly from Harriet.)
>
> **HARRIET:** (Laughing) Sex, we want to talk about sex!
>
> **LEADER:** Harriet, Harriet, you need to be quieter.
>
> **HARRIET:** (More laughter) Sex!
>
> **LEADER:** Do you want us to leave that on the paper, or does it make you too uncomfortable? (More laughter)

(Vera moves on to "Things we want to do": cooking, drama, art, ... I add some possibilities, some contributions from others, but most are from Vera.)

The leader, having passed the first test with her "boys or bodies?" comment, encourages members to open up with other, perhaps more painful, issues. Interestingly, the leader's own ambivalence is noted in her suggestion to modify the issue "family problems" to "families." It is further evidenced when the leader seems to try to slow the girls down when they want to start the discussion. The leader has a plan for the session and a structure she wishes to follow related to how they should complete their sections of the book. However, the group members have their own ideas about how to begin the work. Again, a member asserts her own (and the members') control over the process. Note the nonverbal signals sent by Harriet as she slaps herself for saying or doing something bad. It will be later in the session, when Harriet escalates her communication, that the group leader will pick up the underlying message.

VERA: We can talk about family problems, too.

LEADER: Yes, you could just write "families."

VERA: OK, family problems.

LEADER: Yes, put down "families."

FRAN: Can we talk now?

LEADER: Let me show you the next pages. This is our group book, and these pages are about each of you. (The page is divided into quarters. Each girl chooses a quarter. Vera describes the game as "4-square." Then each chooses a Magic Marker. Leader asks each to write her name and nickname if she has one. Two volunteer preferred other names).

FRAN: Don't laugh, but my baby cousin calls me _____ instead of my real name because she can't say it. (No one laughs. They write their schools, ages—all are 10 or 11—birth dates, grade in school.)

VERA: (To Fran) You were held back in school, right?

FRAN: Yes. But I was the youngest in my class before.

LEADER: So you were young for your old grade, and now you're with kids more your age.

(The girls then write names and ages and relationships of siblings, amid a discussion of "I hate . . ." and "We fight . . . ." As we write and talk, Harriet several times slaps herself for saying or doing something "bad.")

LEADER: (To Harriet) Harriet, you don't have to hit yourself.

HARRIET: Yes, I do.

(One girl suggests writing down names of best friends, which precipitates a discussion of the changing nature of friendships and alliances in the peer group. The group then moves on to boyfriends.)

VERA: I'm a two-timer!

HARRIET: I'm a two-timer, too!

LEADER: I think at this age you're allowed to be a two-timer.

(Several girls ask, "Are the boys going to see this?")

LEADER: No.

(Several girls say, "Don't let them! They might tell. . . . Are the mothers going to see?")

LEADER: No, this book is just for the group. The rest of the time it'll be locked up in my office.

HARRIET: My mother better not see it—she'd kill me!

LEADER: Why? Are you not allowed to have boyfriends?

HARRIET: No, I'm not allowed to have boyfriends.

VERA: (Circling two boys' names) These two boys are my babes.

LEADER: Are boys babes, or is that only for girls? (Lots of laughter) No, really—I don't know how you use the word.

(Vera stands up, does some gestures, and says boys look at girls' behinds. This is followed by lots of laughter.)

<table>
<tr><td>

PRACTICE POINTS

</td><td>

Note in the next section of dialogue how the group members, through Fran, continue to assert themselves since they do not want to follow the leader's prescription for structuring the group. Thus far, they have raised issues related to understanding sex, relationships with boys, family problems, and difficulty in school. These can all be part of the purpose of the group; however, the group leader will only hear them if she is actively listening for feedback on the group members' concerns. The counselor shows more skill as she puts her book aside and starts to respond more to the productions of the group members.

</td></tr>
</table>

HARRIET: (To Vera) Don't do that. What's next?

FRAN: Let's talk.

LEADER: Well, I thought we could think of a name for the group and make a cover for our book.

FRAN: No, let's talk.

LEADER: OK, what would you like to talk about? (Putting book aside)

FRAN: I want to talk about what Harriet wants to talk about.

VERA: Sex.

LEADER: (To Vera) Do you really want to talk about that already?

VERA: Yes. (General agreement)

LEADER: OK. What shall we say about sex?

HARRIET: Well, I don't get what my period is all about.

VERA: I know it all already; my Dad tells me everything. He told me about the birds and bees.

LEADER: (To Fran) Harriet doesn't get her period, and Vera's dad tells her everything.

VERA: I don't get my period, either.

FRAN: Me, neither.

VERA: Neither does Olive, but she'll lie.

HARRIET: Yeah, she'll tell the kids in school, "This girl Harriet gets her period." But I don't!

VERA: We can't talk when she's here; let's talk now.

LEADER: I didn't get my period 'til late. I was 11, and I thought everyone else got it before me. But that's how it was.

VERA: I don't want a period; you get cramps.

LEADER: Oh, not always. I didn't used to, not when I started. That didn't happen 'til later; it sometimes did. But it's different for different people. Do you know someone who gets cramps?

VERA: Yes, my stepmother. We were going to go to the beach, but she couldn't.

The discussion about a stepmother triggers a painful theme for Harriet. Also, as the session is coming to an end, the "doorknob" communication phenomenon is noted, with a member raising a most difficult issue as the session closes. She sends an indirect signal to the leader by kicking over a chair and then talks directly, and with force, about the family problems they were alluding to earlier in the session. The leader does not reach for the meaning of the behavior and instead brings out the snack. Harriet will escalate the responses until the leader gets the message and responds. Harriet also illustrates how she acts out her anger, and the hurt underneath, when she pours out the apple juice and throws a paper cup at the leader. The leader also misses, at first, the signal of the nervous laughter by the group in response to Harriet's emotion charged presentation.

(Harriet kicks over a folding chair; leader brings out a snack.)

VERA: (Holding up cup of juice) To a good group!
ALL: To a good group!
HARRIET: My stepmother hates me.

(Leader looks pained—girls laugh; Harriet spits out juice.)

HARRIET: One time she said to me, "I wanna rip the f—in' balls out of your head."

(Leader shows reaction of puzzlement/annoyance at the statement. Girls laugh.)

HARRIET: Then my stepmother, "I know you don't have any balls, but I wanna rip the f—in' hair out of your head." Excuse my language. And once when I was in the bathroom, I heard her say to my father, "When is she gonna get the f–k out of here?"

The leader is somewhat stunned by the intensity of the emotions and the pain that Harriet must be feeling. She responds with a comment that is somewhat behind Harriet's description since it is obvious from the statement that her stepmother does not want her there. She then tries to reach for Harriet's hurt feelings.

LEADER: Sounds like she doesn't want you there at your father's.
HARRIET: My dad hates me. What did I do to make him hate me?
LEADER: Maybe you didn't do anything. Maybe his life just went another way, but it hurts.

(Meanwhile there is nervous laughter from others.)

The leader is tuning in to Harriet's pain but misses the signal from the second client—the group—whose members are feeling anxious about the themes raised by Harriet. The laughter is a form of flight because the age of the members and the stage of group development make it difficult to address such powerful feelings. Vera also appears to be indirectly raising issues as she returns to the inappropriate sexual content of conversations with her father.

LEADER: Vera, it's hard enough for Harriet to say, without you laughing.

(Harriet is also laughing, hard, almost crying, pounding her empty cup into the floor, and then she throws it at the leader. She picks up the jug of apple juice, looks at each person, and begins to pour it onto the floor. All come forward to intervene, and Harriet puts the juice down. The leader gently takes Harriet by shoulders.)

LEADER: Harriet, you can't do that. If you're mad, you can tell us you're mad.

(As the leader goes back to her place in the circle, Fran, next to Harriet, also holds Harriet's shoulders kindly. Harriet lets her.)

LEADER: See, Harriet, Fran's also trying to help you calm down.

VERA: (Helping dry the rug and addressing the comment to the group leader) Look at what we put you through. . . .

LEADER: No, it's not that; we just can't do something like that.

HARRIET: I'm sorry. I spilled the juice on purpose.

LEADER: Yes, OK.

VERA: Harriet said "f" three times. . . . My father lets me swear, only not gross words, like c-nt . . . yuck.

LEADER: That's a slang word. Does your mother let you?

VERA: No. Can I say something dirty?

LEADER: (To Fran and Harriet) Is it OK or . . . ? (Nods, affirmation) OK.

(Vera tells about her father's collection of hats, including one with a raised middle finger, one with bird droppings painted on, and one with "boob inspector" and two plastic "boobs" on it. Harriet laughs and laughs and gleefully repeats.)

LEADER: If I saw someone wearing that on the street, I'd feel uncomfortable.

HARRIET: Not me, I'd laugh and laugh. (As she does)

VERA: My father was going to wear it when he took me to the dentist.

LEADER: What did you say?

VERA: I said, "Don't, you'll embarrass me."

LEADER: (To Fran, who has been listening intently, but not saying much) Do you have something you wanted to say?

FRAN: I'm not sure . . . .

LEADER: We'll have more chances next time. It's almost time to go now.

FRAN: (Starts to get giggly and jumpy) Sex! Can we write "sex" on the walls?

LEADER: No, we can't write anything on the walls; only in our minds but not really on the wall.

HARRIET: (Accusingly, to leader) Now you put it in my mind!

(The leader laughs, accepting the joke. Discussion continues about how they want to stay longer and "Can we keep talking?")

LEADER: You can keep talking downstairs, but I need to work.

(Someone asks, as we're all cleaning up, whether we'll meet all year.)

LEADER: Yes, from now until April, though we'll take a break around Christmas, because my school has a vacation.

FRAN: (Worriedly) Are you a teacher?

LEADER: No, I'm a student. I'm going to school to learn to be a counselor, and 2 days a week I'm here, working. On Fridays, from 3 to 4, I'm here with you for our group. We might want to start thinking about some rules, like one at a time talking. . . . I was thinking that next time we might go out for a walk. Is that OK?

HARRIET: Just around the block, then we should come back and talk.

(We finish planning where we'll walk next week, if the weather is good.)

It's clear that even with the uncertain contracting, the lack of leader clarity about her role, and the unresolved issue of confidentiality, the group members were anxious to have a female adult they could talk to about the themes of sex, family problems, friends, and school. It's interesting to note the leader's continued ambivalence, evident in her suggestion that they go on a walk at the next session. The internal leader, Harriet, is willing to compromise but insists that the walk be a short one.

PRACTICE SUMMARY

On reflection, this first meeting has raised some powerful issues and hinted at others—such as the sexually charged family life of one student and powerful feelings of rejection—which may be why these young girls are anxious to talk. The group leader has to be at least open to the idea that there may be some initial indirect offerings of themes related to physical and even sexual abuse behind some of the acting-out behavior. With good supervision and ongoing support, the leader should be able to begin to respond in more depth to the issues raised by the members. The devices, such as the book or other activities, can still be helpful as long as they are tools for the members rather than being tools for the leader.

Inner-City Elementary School Children: The Impact of Violence in the Family

In the next illustration, we get a good feel for some of the external community and family factors that are affecting the students' emotional and rational development and their performance in school. Students living often chaotic and at times dangerous lives cannot be expected to come to school, close the door, and leave all of those issues behind.

PRACTICE POINTS

The group leader makes a start in helping the members share these incidents and begin to get some emotional support. Note the counselor's willingness to examine her own feelings and fears as well as charting her next steps needed to address these powerful issues.

Purpose: Discussion group (with special attention to violent school behavior)

Gender of Members: Female

Cultural, Racial, or Ethnic Identification of Members: Two are African American, and the third is African American and Hispanic.

Meeting 2

I asked if anyone had something they wanted to talk about today. Both Shaquandra's and Asia's hands shot up. I told them to decide who goes first. They pointed at each other and said, "You go first." Maria said nothing. It went back and forth for a few minutes with "You," "No, you," "No, you," when finally Shaquandra said, "Oh, I will." She launched into a long, detailed account of how her stepfather tried to kill her mother. He was hiding in the room and she tried to get a gun but she could not get it because he pushed her down. She was talking very rapidly and staring blankly. She made no direct eye contact with anyone.

Finally, she paused, taking a deep breath. I said, "Wow, that's a lot of information all at once—sounds scary." She said, "Yeah." I asked her how that felt to her. She said, "It feels bad. I'm scared of him, but he's going to jail." Asia quickly chimed in, "Yeah, it feels bad."

Then she launched into a similar story about an uncle who tried to kill her mother, but Asia hit him. "He's going to jail too, but I'm scared if he gets out he'll try to kill my mother again." I asked how it felt to hit him. She said it felt good. I said, "Wow, you girls have a lot to deal with. It must be hard for you. Did you know that sometimes when kids have a lot going on at home, they sometimes have unhappy times at school?"

Group Leader's Written Summary

The major thing I would want to do if I had a chance would be to encourage a fuller development of statements the girls made. Due to my inexperience, and it's having been only the second group meeting, I was feeling my way and did not explore as much as I would now. At the time, there was nothing coming from the group that could explain my last intervention statement. I think it meant I was scared, so I threw in a safe (for me) training manual statement! The Student Support Program at the school prepared a manual with suggested wording of statements for working with the kids. Statements such as "Did you know that when kids are unhappy at home, they often have problems at school?" is a vintage example that I took verbatim. In retrospect, I would still want to tie the school behavior together with the home problems at some point, but I would not feel so compelled to run away from the violence issues. I have a much better comfort level with tougher issues now.

PRACTICE SUMMARY

The group leader's own summary is a good example of how reflection on one's practice is crucial for developing increased skill. In particular, her recognition of how she felt—scared—caused her to respond in a more ritualistic manner. She realizes she was "running away" from the unexpected statements about violence, which helps her develop an ability to address them.

A Group for Sixth-Grade Girls in Transition to Middle School

In the following example, the group leader recognizes that finishing sixth grade and moving on to middle school can be both exciting—the graduation quality—as well as frightening as the group members move from the familiar experiences in the grade school to starting fresh in a new setting. They also move from being the "seniors" to the "freshmen" with a loss of status and accompanying fears. The students' stage of the life cycle, moving through adolescence, can compound the issue as self-consciousness about one's body and the growing importance of peer acceptance can reach their peak.

PRACTICE POINTS

The example demonstrates how a group can ease the concerns associated with the transition. It also illustrates the task of helping the group members negotiate their environment. The two aspects of the environment that these girls must deal with are the school they are leaving and the middle school they will be attending. The counselor picks up this theme at the start of the meeting.

The girls began talking about going to a new school next year. Jean expressed her fear of leaving her current school, and I asked her why she felt this way. She said that she was happy at here and that she really does not want to leave. She also added that she did not know what her new middle school was like, and she had heard that they had some very strict teachers. I replied by saying that it seems as though Jean was worried about much more than just the strict teachers at her new school, and from what she said I got the feeling that she is telling us that it is scary to be leaving this school, a school that you have been at for many years and where you know the people, and now you have to go to a completely new school with many new people and many unknown things before you.

Jean agreed that she was quite scared of leaving and having to meet new teachers and new kids. I asked the others in the group how they felt about having to go to a new school next year. All the others shared Jean's feelings and expressed their fears about leaving. Mary said that she was worried about the first day at the new school and what it would be like. I asked them if any of them remembered their first day at elementary school and what it felt like. Vera and Soula, who had come to this elementary school 2 years ago, said they had been frightened but after the first few days began to feel less frightened, especially when some kids began to talk to them.

Betty said that she thinks that it is harder to make friends in Grade 7 than in Grades 4 or 5. I asked her why, and she said that she thinks kids are friendlier when they are younger and that older kids do not always want to be friends with you. I asked Betty whether she had ever experienced this herself. She said that she had moved to a new street this year and tried to become friends with a group of girls on her street, but they did not want her as a friend. I said that she must have been hurt when this happened, and Betty replied that she felt lousy, but she was able to make friends with some other girls on the street. A few other girls related their attempts to make friends on a new street or in the hospital, with some of their attempts being successful and others unsuccessful. They were able to understand how Betty had felt.

PRACTICE POINTS By asking the girls to think about their first day at the elementary school, the counselor was hoping to help them generalize from that experience to the new one that they faced. It was important that the leader neither underplayed the realities of their concerns nor allowed the group members to overplay them. Simply having them expressed this way was helpful, as it let the girls know that others felt the same way. This is an example of the mutual aid process I describe as the all-in-the-same-boat phenomenon. In this case, it was possible for the leader to try to arrange a visit to the new school. The counselor felt that fear of the unknown was part of the problem, and by helping the group members meet some of the junior high school staff and students, these fears might be lessened.

I said that from what they are saying, making friends can be easy at times, but sometimes it is not all that easy, and it is never a very happy thing when you try to become friends with people and they turn you down. I said that it is possible that it is harder to make friends as you get older, but I reminded them that in going to a new school they will probably be going with some of their old friends so it is a little easier than going in without any friends at all. Dmitra asked whether they would be in the same class with their friends. I said that I really did not know but would think that some would be together, whereas others would not. Taxia and some others said that they did not want to be separated from their friends. I said that I could understand their feelings of wanting to be together and that this would make it less frightening for them, but the decisions for this are really not in our control but are made by the principal and the teachers at the new school. I continued by saying that I realize that they are all worried about the unknowns of a new school and about being separated from their friends. These are real worries, and I can feel for them.

I told them that I had an idea that might help reduce some of their worries, and I wanted to share it with them for a few minutes. I asked them if it were possible for us to arrange a visit to visit their new school, to see the school, meet some of the teachers and students, would they would be interested. All of the girls were extremely excited and expressed their enthusiasm about the idea. I told them that I was glad that they wanted to go, and I would try very hard to see if it could be arranged, but I could not assure them that we would definitely go. The girls were able to accept this and told me that they hoped it would be possible. I then said that we would talk more about this next week, once I knew if it was at all possible, but perhaps now we could continue our discussion where we had left off before I introduced the idea.

Lola began to speak and said that she wants to make some new friends next year, but she is worried about what the kids at the new school will think of her. I encouraged her to elaborate on this point. She was concerned with what kids might think about her looks, the way she dresses, and just her in general. I asked her how she thinks others feel about her now. She said that she thinks others like her, but sometimes she is really not sure. At this point others in the group responded to what Lola said and began to express positive, warm feelings toward Lola and told her that they liked her. Lola seemed to feel better when she heard this. I credited Lola and the others for being able to express and share feelings that are often difficult to express. I then asked whether others were worried about what other kids at the new school will think about them. The girls continued this discussion for some time.

PRACTICE SUMMARY In this example, the leader was able to arrange a visit to the middle school, and the girls received a positive and accepting welcoming from the new school's counselor. They were able to share their concerns and their hopes that they might be able to even be in the same class. No promises were made, but they were assured that their preferences would be considered. The middle school counselor also showed them the location of her office and invited them to stop by to say hello when they arrived in the fall. She explained that she could try to help them with any problems they had and that she thought their teachers would also be willing to help them make their adjustment. The girls returned to their elementary school excited about attending their new school in the fall.

Working with Mothers of Underachieving Sixth-Grade Boys

In addition to working with students, counselors can also be helpful reaching out to parents to help them help their children. Recruiting parents into groups such as this one can be complicated depending on the parents' education, social class, race, and ethnicity. Parents may be intimidated at the idea of coming to their child's school. They may experience the call to attend a group as a sign of blaming them for the children's underachieving, which is a not uncommon attitude held and expressed by frustrated teachers and administrators. Also, if their own school experiences were negative—for example, if they are persons of color and they have experienced what they perceived as white teachers and staff relating to them in a stereotypical and racist manner—their reluctance to come in may be related to unfinished business from their own childhood.

Many of these barriers to participation were discussed earlier in the group formation discussion (Chapter 4). Other issues that need to be considered for parent groups include the time the group meeting is held to respect working schedules and the availability of child care at the school. It's important to understand that if the counselor does not get an immediate positive response, or if parents say yes but then do not show up, it may not be because they don't care about their children's education. Second and third efforts, with attention to the parents' previous experiences, may make the difference, as will the provision of structural supports that facilitate attendance. One of the best ways to help the children is by providing nonjudgmental support for the parents.

The following example is a group for mothers of sixth-grade boys who were underachieving in school. The purpose was to discuss how they could more effectively help their youngsters with their schoolwork. In the first meeting, the members began with a general discussion of their feelings when faced with their children's resistance to homework, their own memories of failure at school, their identification with their children's feelings, and their recognition that they sometimes push their children because of their own need for success.

At a later meeting reported here, the group leader recognized the need to focus on specific methods and techniques for helping their children with their work.

> I said that I thought it would be useful if they described what actually happens at home concerning the issue of homework—how they handle getting the kids started on and completing assignments, and then discuss the pros and cons of the various ways of handling this. I told them that they had come up with some good ideas during the past meetings and that if they could apply these with their own children, they might begin to resolve some of the difficulties they had been describing. I said that it seems to me that they already have found some alternate ways of dealing with their children related to schoolwork and homework, and it is just a matter of seeing where they can be applied in their own particular situations.
>
> I asked that each describe as fully as possible what goes on in their home concerning getting the children started on the homework and also to describe the means they may use to get them to complete it.

The members needed help to get into the details of their experiences. It is in analysis of the specific details of their efforts at home that the leader and the group can provide help. The intervention illustrates the skill described earlier as moving from the general to the specific. When specific examples were discussed, the leader and other members of the group were able to provide specific suggestions and ideas, particularly on how to empathize with the children's struggle with school while at the same time requiring that they make the effort. In retrospect, the leader is modeling for the group members the importance of providing support (the early discussions) with demand (the request for specificity).

Group Work in the Middle School

One of the major factors affecting student performance and behavior in general in middle schools is related to the powerful impact of puberty. Both the physical and emotional changes in this stage of the life cycle are profound. The coercive impact of the peer group may also affect behavior. However, it is this same peer group that can become a resource for more effective and adaptive coping with school-related issues if the group leader is skillful in introducing the concept of mutual aid.

Levinsky and McAleer (2006) address the developmental tasks and issues facing seventh grade adolescent girls in a group they led:

> Adolescents face a daunting set of developmental tasks and challenges as they transition, during their second decade of life, from childhood through early, middle, and late adolescence, to young adulthood. Our group members, ages twelve to fourteen years and in the seventh grade, are in their early adolescence. In addition to managing the many implications of the rapidly changing size and shape of their bodies, these young teenaged girls must also begin to psychologically and socially mature as they consider multiple, competing priorities and choices, refine their capacity for critical thinking, and self-reflection, and reassess and redefine their relationships with adults and peers. A barrage of new challenges, demands and expectations accompany this life stage, consuming much time, energy, thought and feeling. (p. 204)

Although the authors refer to challenges facing adolescent girls in their groups, many of the stressors and developmental tasks also apply to adolescent boys, as will be evident in the first group example in the next section.

DeLucia-Waack (2006) addresses the question of how child and adolescent groups differ from adult groups:

> Goals for child and adolescent groups tend to be much more preventative and skill based. Regardless of the type of group, much of the focus is on teaching and practicing social and interpersonal skills. Common topics in many psycho-educational groups are the identification and expression of feelings, friendship skills, communication skills, conflict-resolution skills, brainstorming, problem solving and decision making. Even in groups for children and adolescents who have been identified as being at risk or having some kind of difficulty, the focus is going to be on teaching new, more adaptive skills, cognitive strategies, and coping skills. (p. 14)

Adolescent Boys' Group Dealing with Disruptive Classroom Behavior

In this example, we see how a group leader returns to a follow-up session with a group of 12- to 14-year-old boys ready to apologize for his passivity in the first meeting and then attempts to recontract on group purpose and his leader's role. However, he makes the mistake of thinking of his job as teaching and preaching, which causes him to miss the indirect communications from the boys.

Purpose of the Group: To help members learn more appropriate ways to act in class

Gender and Age Range of Members: Male, 12–14

Cultural, Racial, or Ethnic Identification of Members: Three of the members are Caucasian, while the other three are African American.

I started the second session of by apologizing for not talking much during our first session. The group responded by nodding. Mike then said, "Were you judging us?" I said that I wasn't. I explained that because my supervisor was there I wanted to watch and see how to conduct the group. I also explained that this wasn't the best approach on my part because it is not mine and not my supervisor's group but it is their group and that they can help each other. At that point Mike spoke up and said, "Well, Mr. R., if it's our group, then we can do whatever we want, right?" I asked Mike what he had in mind. Mike said that because we discussed the possibility of watching a movie, he wanted to watch *The Dave Chappelle Show* in class. I looked around the class to observe the others' reactions to this statement.

Mike had stated that you guys (the leaders) probably don't know what we're talking about. Some other members in the group agreed. I then asked Mike if he were assuming that my supervisor and I were unaware of the content of this show. He had answered that we probably don't watch the show and that we should watch the part where Dave Chappelle does the video about R Kelly. I responded that that would be inappropriate for class. I then told the group that I did watch *The Dave Chappelle Show*.

PRACTICE POINTS Once again we can see how the group leader responds to what he perceives as a negative offering by the group members. It would be interesting if he had said, "What is it about that show that you find interesting, and why are you suggesting the R Kelly video? What would I get out of it"? Instead, he responds from a critical attitude and begins "preaching" rather than listening. This is the not uncommon response of starting to respond to a question or comment before we know the meaning behind it. I referred to this as the sessional contracting issue in the chapter on the work phase, suggesting that group leaders should always begin tentatively actively listening and assuming early comments and behaviors are first offerings of themes of concern that may be related to the group's purpose.

I also explained that there is a time and a place for that behavior, and in group it is not appropriate. I then asked the rest of the group if they knew why this behavior was inappropriate. Tom had answered it was because they sometimes swear on the show. The rest of the group laughed at this comment. I responded, "Judging by your laughter and smiles, it seems like a lot of you feel that this is acceptable or even cool behavior." Sam answered yes, and it's a relief to be able to laugh after class. I then stated to Sam that because class is hectic, he feels that he deserves to be able to laugh and be silly. Sam nodded yes. "Well, it is cool, isn't it, Mr. R" answered a few in the group. "That's a good question. Our purpose in having this group is to not only identify appropriate behavior but act on it as well. You've identified that this swearing on TV is cool, but does everyone here think it's appropriate for school?" They began discussing it among themselves.

PRACTICE SUMMARY If role were clear and the group leader had internalized the idea that group members were often reaching out for the very help he wishes to provide, but doing it in a way that is not direct, he might have responded to Sam's comment about it "being a relief to be able to laugh after class." This could have led to a discussion of what goes on in class rather than a discussion of the appropriateness of swearing.

The central point here, and in previous examples, is that something should happen in the group that is different from what happens in the classroom and the home. Group leaders fall into the trap of teaching and preaching when group members have heard these comments from adults before. Why should they have a different impact when spoken by a counselor in the group? One of the main differences in a counseling group should be that we are curious about the meaning of the behavior and comments, the questions behind the questions, the emotions that often drive the behavior, and so forth. A second major difference is that we recognize that much of the help provided, certainly at this stage of the life cycle, will come from the peer group members, not the leader.

Peacemaking Circle Group in the Classroom: From Acting Out to "Krumping"

One widely used model for intervention is the use of "peacemaking circles" in the classroom. In this model, all students and the teacher are involved in periodic discussion of classroom conflicts led by the counselor. The theory is that learning to talk about conflicts and to resolve them in a peaceful manner can make the class a better place for the teacher, the students, and the learning process. Specific structures are involved in the model such as the use of a "talking stick" that is passed to members when it is their turn to speak. This device provides structure to the group and stops students from all talking at once, interrupting each other, and not treating each person's contribution with respect.

This approach sounds useful and may work in some classrooms with some students, but the reality is that the principal often decides which classes will hold circles, and the classes he or she usually picks are ones that are currently chaotic. They may have young and inexperienced teachers who are having trouble setting limits and controlling behavior. In the school in the next example, the principal selected the special education classes, which contained all of the students who were not functioning well in their regular classes. Simply put, the students were not ready for this kind of structure, as is detailed in the description of one of the group leaders attempting to lead the circles.

Purpose of the Group: To help members learn more appropriate ways to act in class

Gender and Age Range of Members: Male and female, 12–14

Cultural, Racial, or Ethnic Identification of Members: Caucasian, African American, and Hispanic; teacher: Caucasian

The group leader soon understands that rather than fighting to impose a structure, which generates resistance and defiance, it is better to modify the structure to allow these students to use the circles in their own way and at their own pace. The krumping referred to in the subtitle is a form of dance—described in more detail later—which is also a creative means of expressing frustration and anger. What follows is one of the leader's descriptions of the early efforts at using a circles approach.

Report on the Peacemaking Circles

Peacemaking circles at this school always involve multiple instances of acting out behavior. When working with a student individually, issues can be addressed and discussed, with some indication of the student understanding the consequences of their actions. For example, during a one-on-one discussion during lunch, 13-year-old Tiana acknowledged how her disruptive behavior—entering a classroom loudly, swearing at the teacher and classmates, threatening to beat up a student, scribbling on desks and chairs with her pen—affects those around her. She can reflect on how idle and invalidated gossip can sometimes cause her to seek revenge in violent ways. She can even start to make connections between school and the real world, considering ways her impulsivity may impact her ability to maintain a job. I let her know her insights are valued and that she can bring much to her classroom's peacemaking circle. However, when escorting her back to class, her negative behaviors intensify, culminating in a loud and offensive entry into her classroom.

These behaviors are what we, as circle facilitators, experience during a circle, times 10. The biggest challenge for students in circles and in the school at large appears to be controlling impulses and behaving appropriately when surrounded by their peers. There is an ambience of one-upmanship, of saving face, of defending friends and self-appointed "sisters" and "cousins" from the demeaning comments and gestures of other students. The preferred method of appeasement is typically violent and belittling; fighting on and off school grounds, phone harassment, blatant insults written in bathroom stalls, and rude insults about each other and family members. This is the climate of the school, reinforced by a punitive disciplinary system of suspensions and occasional insensitive remarks by teachers and other staff. "If you don't take off that hoodie, you're out for five" (i.e., suspended for 5 days), or, as one teacher announced loudly to another in front of a line of students in the hallway, "All these kids need phone calls home to their parents, but the phone numbers are all wrong. Go figure."

PRACTICE POINTS

It's hard not to empathize with the feelings of frustration and impotence of the group leader writing this description. One can also understand how teachers and administrators may feel the same. Note how the leader refers to individual members of the group and suggest how hard it is work with individual problems. This represents the common mistake of not stepping back and seeing the group-as-a-whole as having a culture (norms, taboos, roles, etc.) that blocks work rather than facilitating it. As long as the leaders avoid addressing the behaviors as group as well as individual issues, they will not be able to keep up with all of the acting out. Later in this example, when structural changes are made, there is a noticeable shift in group culture. The group leader's description continues:

To address one student's behavior in a circle is to ignore another's. We could ask Jesse why he chooses not to participate with the rest of us in circle, or even try to engage him as he jumps from desktop to desktop across the room, but it might be at the expense of Keisha and Jacob. Both of them have remained seated and demonstrate interest in participating but are on the verge of beginning an argument laced with insults and need support to calm down. As Tiana, Brijon, and Scott intermittently leave the room, without permission, there is an occasional reprieve and the opportunity to focus on the issue between Keisha and Jacob. When Jesse begins to throw things into the circle, the dilemma for facilitators is whether or not to ask him to stop, join the circle, seek a motive behind his behavior, or ignore him. Ideally, the solution may be to encourage Keisha and Jacob to address Jesse's behavior, embracing the opportunity to model how asking someone patiently and diplomatically to stop doing something is often more effective that saying, "Knock it off before I beat the s–t out of you."

These moments of direct instruction can help students take responsibility for their classroom and their circle experience, but also contribute to the disjointed nature of these circles. Staying focused on one topic for any extended period of time is often difficult because of frequent interruptions and the exacerbation of behaviors by the students themselves.

PRACTICE POINTS

In the following comments, one can note the increasing understanding on the part of the group leader that behavior always has meaning but that the way it is communicated by the students can make it hard to understand. Although this understanding is a necessary precondition to attempting to change the group culture, it is not a sufficient condition. A change in strategy and a modification of the structure of the circles was needed.

In terms of finding the underlying messages behind behaviors, students can be very forthright and often share the complex stories that incite their confrontational and sometimes violent reactions. "We were on a three-way on my sister's cell phone with me and Shakayla and Mia and we was at my aunt's house and Shakayla called Shannon a bitch and she my cousin and I gotta watch out for her so I told her to hang up the phone and she better watch her back and then someone kept calling back on my sister's cell phone and my aunt got pissed and said she gonna call the cops and I know it was Shakayla because LaNiece say she had my name in her mouth this morning when she was on the bus and . . . ."

The stories are difficult to follow and can often be reduced to a case of "he said, she said," incorporating issues of their lives both in and out of school and expanding to include students only minimally involved. Many students are eager to fight and seek such an opportunity. In the circles, we have addressed some of the issues, validating their anger and their desire to protect their name or that of someone they care about. Still, even after clarifying misunderstandings and dispelling rumors with the help of their peers, the urge to confront remains. What students are really trying to say through their behaviors goes much deeper, but there is not enough trust and support in the circles to break through their reticence. The students are private about the impact poverty, sexual abuse, drive-by shootings, incarcerated family members, and other realities have on their lives. There are a few exceptions that reveal just how potent bringing these issues to the surface can be for the group.

For example, one student's sharing of her struggle in foster care and her very real fear of being placed in juvenile detention elicited genuine support from her peers. The immediacy of her plight seemed to affect the students directly, as her placement in juvenile detention would mean her removal from the school. In contrast, however, a circle several months later in which students shared stories of drugs, violence, and police involvement in their lives elicited only nervous laughter and apathy. "My father beat someone up, and he shot at our house with a gun." "We ran away from the cops when they went after my brother for the drugs he had stuffed in his sock." "This guy I know came to my house naked and shot in the head, and I had to calm him down so I could pour peroxide on his head." The influence these life events have on their behaviors is obvious, but how to address them amid disruptions, apathy, and an inconsistently supportive school environment is not so obvious.

PRACTICE POINTS A significant but limited change in behavior in the circles was noticed when the structure was modified in a number of ways. First, the group leaders stopped coming in with "topics" for discussion and instead opened up the beginning of the sessions as a time for sessional contracting. They also began to address some of the initial acting-out behavior as communications. Instead of engaging in a battle of wills over control, they began to verbalize these first offerings. For example, "Jesse seems upset and angry right now, and he is having trouble sitting with us. Jesse, can you tell us what happened? Does anyone in the group know why he is upset?" These comments, at times, would elicit a story from Jesse or whoever was upset, which eventually brought that member into the circle. Other times, members of the group would take turns trying to guess why he or another student was upset: "He had a fight in the hall"; "Mr. Smith (a teacher) was hollering at him in the hall"; "His cousin got shot on Saturday."

The rules were also changed so that if someone felt uncomfortable about what was happening in the circle, they could say so or simply stand up and move elsewhere in the room. There would not be a battle over getting them to stay put or come back. The talking stick was abandoned, and the group leaders recognized that for these kids, at this age, it was sometimes hard to talk one at a time. The group leader would acknowledge this and then by taking the role of "traffic director" rather than "rule enforcer" intervention was more easily accepted by the children.

A striking change took place when at one meeting one of the most troubled boys came into the room and started "krumping." The term was a new one for this author, and perhaps for some readers. *Wikipedia* defines *krumping* as follows:

> Krumping is an urban African American street dance form that developed on the streets of South Central Los Angeles, around 2001–2002. It is characterized by free, expressive, and highly energetic moves and is a major part of the hip hop dance culture, alongside other techniques, such as: breakdance, locking, popping and freestyling. . . . According to a major krump proponent, Tight Eyez, the word Krump stands for Kingdom Radically Uplifted Mighty Praise, and this acronymic formation can be seen on his videos. It began as a way to release anger, aggression and frustration in a positive, non-violent way and is now used to also praise God. Violent gangster activity was very common in South Central Los Angeles; Krumping was developed in resistance to such street violence. (*Wikipedia* entry, July 2008)

PRACTICE POINTS

The group members enjoyed the introduction of krumping into their meetings and provided praise to members for their skills. The group leaders also enjoyed it if not for the artistic presentation at least for the order it brought to the meetings. On further reflection, they began to see how addressing krumping was also an opportunity to address the origins of the dance and its meaning. The *Wikipedia* description continues:

> Krumping is a more aggressive dance form than clowning and is intended as an expression of anger or a release of pent-up emotion from the struggles of life through violent, exaggerated, and dramatic moves. Variation, individuality, and movement are the foundations of the Krump or bobble-bounce. "Dising" or jokes are often involved, as well as "sick" movements, such as snaking, grapples, pushing and grimey. Krumping also includes a little fight moves and gymnastics moves, as well as moments of heightened aggression called "buck" moves.

PRACTICE SUMMARY

For the co-leaders of this group, both young white women from the suburbs, this experience also reinforced the importance of understanding culture in its many forms: dance, song, music, and art and the way in which these mediums of exchange can be used to communicate if the counselors are willing to watch and listen.

Informal Lunchtime Meetings with 9- to 12-Year-Old Girls

In addition to regularly scheduled in-school and after-school groups, as well as classroom groups, counselors often work with informal existing peer groups or groups that they organize. One example is a lunchtime group in which students have a chance to discuss with each other and the leader events in their lives that impact their school behavior and performance. One example follows.

Purpose of the Group: To discuss life events that impact their school behavior
Gender and Age Range of Members: Female, 9–12

Cultural, Racial, or Ethnic Identification of Members: 8 African American female students ranging in age from 9 to 12 years old. Six of the girls were in fifth grade, and two were in sixth.

My co-leader and I, both Caucasian females, had decided to merge our two separate lunch-time groups. My group had originally come together for the purpose of attending a field trip. My co-leader's group had originally started after the girls were identified by my co-leader or their teachers as needing help with making and keeping friends. We decided to keep them together for a social skills/leadership group. This was our sixth meeting.

Before the meeting, we decided to have the girls from our two groups introduce themselves and then participate in a ball toss activity that focused on active listening and cooperation. I figured that by the time we were done with the ball toss activity, the group would be out of time (we only had 30 minutes over lunch). We had figured we would keep it light because of time.

PRACTICE POINTS

While program and warm-up exercises can be useful for many groups, especially those in schools with children, it is not uncommon for group leaders to use exercises because the leaders are the ones concerned and uncomfortable in early sessions, not the members. In this case, the co-leaders have structured the first session in a manner that guaranteed they would not have time for any substantive discussion. Once again, we note how the sense of urgency on the part of a group member, and the group's beginning trust in these two leaders who have been developing their working relationship with the girls, cause the leaders to abandon the planned program. What emerges from one member is the not uncommon story of violence in the neighborhood. Children exposed to family members and friends involved in what is often gang-related violence may maladaptively act out their feelings at home and in school. By providing a different way of dealing with these feelings, we see the beginning of the development of a mutual support system.

The group members picked up their lunch and proceeded to the room we used for the meeting. After introductions, one of the members asked if she could speak to me privately. We went into the hallway, and she explained that her cousin had been shot a few days earlier and she was very sad. I asked her if she thought it would help to talk to the group about it, and she agreed. Jennifer told the group what had happened to her cousin. While she was speaking, the other group members listened quietly. When she finished talking, tears began to stream down her face. As I looked at the group, all of the other members were crying as well. I asked the members who else had experienced a loss in her family or the loss of a friend. Every member raised her hand. For the next 40 minutes, the girls shared stories of loss and/or violence in their lives.

PRACTICE POINTS

In the next segment, one leader points out the all-in-the-same-boat connection between the girls. After some time for the expression of emotion, the second co-leader starts to help the members connect their expression of feelings to the purpose of the group. She points out how sadness can be expressed in ways that are hurtful rather than helpful. It is not uncommon for children to act out their feelings escalating their behavior until someone listens and understands.

My co-leader pointed out that the girls were not alone when it came to losing or almost losing a loved one. The girls seemed to take some comfort as they saw all of the other hands raised as well. At this point I began to discuss emotions—how we feel—and how when we were upset our emotions like sadness can come out in other ways. The girls were paying attention, so I continued. I explained that sometimes when we were sad it was expressed with anger—anger at classmates, teachers, and family members. The group members nodded in agreement. We then discussed what we could do with these feelings and who could be helpful when they were shared.

PRACTICE SUMMARY At the end of the session, one of the girls stayed behind and told the leader she was very upset by the discussion. When asked why she indicated that she had a fight with Jennifer early in the term, and although Jennifer had tried to make friends with her, she had ignored her. After listening to Jennifer and understanding how hurt she felt, she wanted help in how to go back to her and make amends for ignoring her. By providing a vehicle for addressing these painful feelings and pointing out the common ground, the group leaders also help the girls strengthen their support system in the school and community. This discussion helps the girls understand the "feeling-doing" connection and become more self-reflective about their behavior. It also teaches the girls how to more adaptively call for help.

Alternative Public Day School: Parents of Children with Emotional and Behavioral Difficulties

PRACTICE POINTS In this example, we see the not uncommon phenomenon of clients, in this case parents of children with emotional and behavioral difficulties, using a first session to externalize by angrily raising issues of dissatisfaction with the setting (e.g., the school, hospital) or professionals. Some of these will be legitimate concerns that should become part of the group's agenda. This behavior may also represent a form of avoidance of painful, personal issues.

> In an article on the nature of the stressful event when parents need to be reoriented to the reality of their child's disability, Roskam, Zech, Nills, and Nader-Grossbois (2008) suggest:

> An emotional event, such as learning of the necessity for school reorientation for their child, provides information that is disruptive to the parents' previous cognitions about and behavior toward their child. Because their cognitions or behavior may no longer be appropriate, parents have to engage in an adjustment process. This process may have either positive or negative outcomes. When the adjustment process has a negative outcome, parental development is seen to regress to a less-advanced stage. This means that the parents' cognitions become rigid, and maladjusted child-rearing behavior occurs. The regression may affect the child's autonomy because of parents' overprotective or inappropriate involvement. (p. 133)

PRACTICE POINTS In the following example, the group leaders do not begin with an opening statement but instead ask the group members how they wish to use the group. The group members new to the school accept the leaders' offer to provide feedback on the group's contract by externalizing until one member, at the end of the meeting (doorknob therapy), angrily brings home the pain they must all feel. The two student group leaders are too overwhelmed at this, their first group meeting, to be able to identify these themes as a way of helping the group reach a consensus on purpose. Their anxiety over this session also leads them to miss the cues about "helping professionals" that may actually refer to them. However, the student author's openness to listening and her astute postmeeting analysis bode well for her development and the group's potential for success.

Agency Type: Alternative public day school, Meeting #1

Purpose: Parent support group for parents of children with emotional, behavioral, and learning difficulties

Gender and Age Range of Members: Male and female; ages: 38–55

Cultural and Racial Identification: White, middle-class American

After introductions in which each member stated his or her name, I said that we needed to discuss how the group wanted to use the 1½ hours each week. I asked them if they would like to choose the issues and topics for discussion or if they would prefer that Dave (co-leader) and I prepare an agenda. Linda, a new parent who was sitting to my left, turned her body toward the group and said in an agitated voice, "I don't know about the rest of you, but I've had enough of psychiatrists, doctors, and teachers telling me what to do and that it's my fault that my kid is screwed up!" Several other parents joined in: "Boy, I sure know what you mean!" Karen, another new mother, said, "Can you believe that Kirk's teacher in public school last year, told me, in front of Kirk, that he's a bad kid who's going to end up in jail if I don't get him help? Like he hasn't been to shrink after shrink since he was eight!" I looked to Dave to respond, but he remained silent.

PRACTICE POINTS

One can understand this opening salvo in two ways: first, a legitimate theme for discussion in the group; second, an indirect offering of the authority theme with the group member expressing concern about what kind of professionals the group leaders will be. A clearer statement of group purpose at the start and clarification of their roles would have addressed this second issue. Also, a group leader comment such as "And are you wondering if we will be the same—giving unhelpful advice and seeming to blame you and criticize your parenting?" would get at this potential underlying issue.

Sharon, a parent whose child has been at the school for 4 years, turned to Karen and calmly and empathetically began telling stories about ways she and her family had been treated in the past by schools and professionals, but that this school was different. She said that the teachers and staff really cared about her son. Carol, another returning parent, agreed with Sharon and emphasized how much her son loved his teachers and counselors. Both Linda and Karen began to agree with Sharon and Carol. They said that they had noticed that, in the first month at this school, their children did seem happier. For half an hour the parents exchanged humorous accounts about their children while Dave and I remained silent.

PRACTICE POINTS

As the first meeting approaches the end, an example of a "doorknob" end-of-the-session comment is observed. Although humor can be an important way of coping with difficult and painful issues, it can also be a form of flight; a way of avoiding a difficult discussion. One way the group leaders could have intervened earlier during the humorous storytelling would have been to acknowledge the positive nature of the humor but also saying, "I know it can't always be something you can laugh about. There have to be painful moments and issues as well." As it is, a new member takes the lead and addresses the underlying issue directly. He also does so in a way that demonstrates how he uses "fight" and his anger to cope, while his wife sits silently beside him grieving. Thus we see in the first session the use of fight and flight as a way of avoiding the underlying issues.

Finally, I said, "We have about 15 minutes left, and I want to make sure that, before we end, we are clear about the way we will use this time as a group. It sounds like you all would like to bring in your own issues and topics to discuss. Does anyone have any comments or questions about this decision?" Jack, a new parent who had been silent throughout the meeting, began speaking to the group in an angry voice, while next to him, his wife, Joan, began crying. "What I don't understand is how all of you can laugh when you know you have a sick kid. It's not funny. Your kids are not normal members of society!"

PRACTICE POINTS In addition to raising the underlying pain and sadness, Jack was also showing the group how he and his wife Joan handled their feelings. He expresses the anger and she the pain. Although this is not a married couples' group, the specific ways that couples handle the impact of having a troubled child and how that affects their parenting and their relationship would be appropriate for discussion. This can easily be an issue for all of the parents who may, more or less, have a similar "division of labor" between husband and wife. How can they help each other deal with this ongoing stress and with the not uncommon grieving for the loss of the "normal" child they thought they would have? With this interpretation, we see another example of how the process can be integrated with the content as the leader identifies what is happening (the process) and helps deepen the discussion on the content.

The room went dead silent as each member avoided eye contact with anyone. After a minute of silence, I said, "I think people have different ways of dealing with pain. Some use anger, tears, laughter. Each of these emotions has been expressed here tonight. Does anyone have a response to Jack?" Sharon said, "I get angry and sad all the time, but sometimes I need to laugh. If I didn't have humor in my life, I wouldn't be able to get through the day." The other parents nodded in agreement. Jack was looking around the room, but not at the group. Joan was staring at the floor. Both remained silent. After a brief silence, Dave (the co-leader) said, "Looks like we're out of time. Thanks for coming, and we'll see you next week."

Summary of My Thoughts

These parents were ready to participate in the group. Because this was the first meeting of the group, my role as leader was to provide structure and create a safe environment in which they could begin to develop as a group. This analysis has made me aware that not listening to my own anxieties, thoughts, and feelings prevented me from tuning in to the needs of the group and of the individuals in the group. There were times throughout the session when I wanted to remain silent but did not. At other times, I wanted to speak. Instead, I was quiet.

I realize that if I had had a theoretical framework to work from when I began this group, I would not have felt overwhelmed. I would have been more responsive to the group process and my role in this process. Finally, I would have communicated with my co-leader prior to the group meeting.

Hindsight suggests that an opening statement encompassing the range of themes that emerged directly and indirectly may have facilitated a less confrontational start to this meeting. The moment of silence after the angry comment was an important form of group communication. Rather than commenting that each member had found their own way of coping, which was an important statement acknowledging that they all experienced the pain under the anger, the leader might have first simply said, "Everyone is quiet right now. I think you have all had a reaction to Jack's expression of his anger and Joan's crying. Can anyone say what it was?" This comment, addressing the process taking place in the group, would both help to establish a norm of honest communication as well as open up a central and painful issue for every parent—namely, "Our children are not normal and don't now and perhaps never will fit into our society." Given the effort to analyze her own feelings and practice in this first session, this group leader is well on the way to understanding these parents and helping them create a culture for work rather than an illusion of work. Jack is an important internal leader in this sense.

Group Work in the High School

Although many of the student-to-student and student-to-teacher conflict issues discussed in the previous session emerge at the higher grade levels, there are also differences. High dropout rates may mean that the many troubled and acting-out students are no longer in school. Conflicts between students in the classroom, in the halls, and outside school still occur, and many of the groups described in the previous session are still appropriate. A major difference is the stage of the educational cycle and of the life cycle these students are experiencing. While the initial turmoil of adolescence may be receding, students are preparing to move into a new stage of identity development. This transition can be difficult. For most students, their formal and required education experience is ending, and they need to consider moving on to early young adult roles involving work or further education and, for some, assuming a parent role.

This section begins with an example of work with students suspended from school for violence, substance abuse, or weapons possession. This project offers group counseling as well as ongoing educational support in a setting away from the suspending school.

The VISA Center: A 2-Week (10-Day) Intensive Intervention for Suspended Students

The VISA (Vision, Integrity, Service, and Accountability) Center was designed to offer suspended public school children in Buffalo, New York, an opportunity to explore alternatives to violence-related behaviors within a structured, supportive environment. I founded and directed the center, located at the University at Buffalo. Assignment to the VISA Center was offered as an alternative to the school district's regular formal suspension program, which consisted of 1 to 2 hours of daily home instruction provided by a teacher during after-school hours. In reality, by the time home instruction was arranged, students were often returning to school with no significant intervention or support. Resuspension was often the result. The 2-week program served 30 students at a time, in three groups of 10, with a combination of academics in four subject areas (three full-time teachers) designed to help the students not fall behind in the school work and psychoeducational groups as well as mutual aid support groups provided by full-time social workers and counselors. A summary of the research associated with this project can be found in Appendix A. For a full report on the project, go to www.socialwork.buffalo.edu/research/projectdocs/VISA_Center_Report.pdf.

One component of this program was a mutual aid group experience, based on my group counseling model (Gitterman & Shulman, 2005; Shulman, 2008). These groups were designed to promote discussion, peer support, learning, and behavior modification among students who described their problems and difficulties in school and their relationships with adults and peers at school, at home, and in their communities. For example, students would describe conflict situations with either teachers or other students and their inability to avoid physical fights without losing face. For most of the students, these discussions also revealed the extent of community violence as well as family violence they had witnessed, similar to the discussion in the earlier lunchtime group for girls, and how these incidents affected their interactions at school.

Problem behavior in their schools that had led to their suspensions and in the VISA program itself was seen as an important signal of underlying but unstated student issues that needed to be addressed by staff. The program's philosophy was that such behavior always represented a maladaptive form of communication. At times, students were seen as acting out the very behavior that had led to their suspensions from their regular school. Staff would attempt to respond by first setting limits and then exploring the message behind the behavior. It was not unusual to find that the specific behavior was connected to traumatic experiences at home or in the community. At times, the students' behavior was discussed in the mutual aid support groups with other students engaged in the effort. An attempt was made to help the student find a more adaptive way of handling issues and feelings that were influencing behavior.

In the example that follows, we see how the culture in the neighborhood and in the school can create pressures for students to respond to violent incidents, even ones that they are not personally involved in. For example, Tania was recently suspended and was attending her first group session:

> **COUNSELOR:** Tania, can you tell everyone why you were suspended?
>
> **TANIA:** It was not my fault! (Tania was an A student at her high school and had not been in trouble before.) My friend Latisha had gotten into a fight with another girl on Monday and gave it to her good.
>
> **COUNSELOR:** Were you involved in that?
>
> **TANIA:** No. But on Tuesday, the other girl's mother and two aunts came into the lunchroom and started beating on Latisha. I couldn't just stand by and let my friend get beat up. I jumped in with some other girls, and it was a real mess.
>
> **COUNSELOR:** Wow! Her mother and her aunts were just able to come into school like that and attack her. You must have felt like you had to defend your friend even if it got you in big trouble. Can any of you (the other group members) understand that?
>
> **JOHN:** If you don't jump in, then you lose face. Everyone knows it's your friend and you are just standing by not doing anything. What kind of friend are you if you don't stick up for your friend?
>
> **SERENA:** If you don't stick up for them, who is going to stick up for you if you get jumped?
>
> **COUNSELOR:** I think I understand the bind you were in, Tania, it was a tough choice. I wonder how you are feeling now.
>
> **TANIA:** I hate this. I'm an A student! I was going to try to go to college, and now I have this on my record.

The program recognized that it was crucial to provide feedback to the appropriate school staff in order to help staff be supportive when the student returned to the school. With intensive student contact at the VISA center, staff were often able to provide a different perspective on a student's behavior as well as a report on their use of the program. This group leader provides some reassurance responding to the student's concern and then asks the group to explore alternatives if she runs into the same problem. As the group members help Tania, they are also helping themselves.

COUNSELOR: You know, we write a report back to your principal when you return to school, and I can try to help him understand the bind that you were in and that this was really a one-time problem. I can also let him know that you used this program, assuming you do, to deal with this incident and that you are learning from it. Given your strong academic work and your good record, I can point out you have a good chance to graduate and go on to college but that you are worried about the impact of this incident. Perhaps that will help in terms of your record at the school. The problem is this could happen again, and if you respond in exactly the same way, then the school may not be so supportive. Does anyone have an idea of how Tania can handle this differently if it happens again?

SAM: I had the same problem a while back when three guys from the neighborhood came into the school and jumped my friend because of a beef they had with him. I didn't jump in to the fight, but I got the security guard at the door to come and help. He and a teacher broke up the fight and got the cops to deal with these guys. I'm glad I didn't jump in because one of the guys had a knife, and he would have pulled it if I did. I spoke to my friend later, and he understood that we both would have been in big trouble if I jumped in.

COUNSELOR: It seems to me there needs to be better security at the doors so you guys don't have be worried that someone is going to come into school and jump you. Tania, did what Sam say make any sense to you? Can you still be a good friend and not get yourself into a mess that you obviously are upset about?

TANIA: My jumping in didn't really help since there were three of them and they were adults. We both took a licking. I guess it would have been smarter to get some help the way Sam did. Sam, if you are so smart, why are you here now?

SAM: I was smart that time but not so smart when I brought some weed into school. They found it in my locker when they had a locker search.

COUNSELOR: What did you learn from that, Sam?

SAM: I learned to smoke outside of school! (Group members laugh).

COUNSELOR: Let's leave a discussion about drugs and alcohol for tomorrow. In the meantime I want to congratulate you, Tania, for your hard work, and I think the rest of the group was really helpful. What you all need are friends like this to help you when you get back to school and have to deal with the same stuff.

The combination of support and understanding for Tania's dilemma while at the same time opening up discussion of alternative ways of dealing with conflicts helped Tania consider how she might handle things differently. It was important for the counselor to also offer help with the school staff so that this one incident did not become an obstacle to Tania's future education. A report on every student was sent back to the referring school at the end of the 2 weeks in an effort to increase understanding of the student's life situation and, when appropriate, crediting his or her efforts to work on the problem that led to the suspension.

In other group sessions, students revealed traumatic situations in their homes and neighborhoods, including drive-by shootings, physical and sexual abuse in the family, family members incarcerated, rampant drug use by friends and family members, and pressures to join a gang for self-protection. In one example, when a young man was referred to an after-school job training program in construction, an area he hoped to work in, he indicated he could not go. He pointed out that attending the training center meant crossing through another gang's territory. When this was revealed by a number of students, we contacted the head of the training center and had him visit the program and speak with the students about how the center could bring some parts of the program to their neighborhood and how they could arrange some van transportation to take them safely to the center.

Perhaps the most poignant comment was by a young man who indicated he "didn't need school." He continued, "What's the point? By 21 I'm going to be dead or in jail." This triggered a group discussion about a persistent sense of hopelessness and helplessness and the need to find someone who believed enough in them to help them make it through a scary and dangerous stage of life. As pointed out in the earlier discussion of resilience, it can be one caring adult who can provide a buffer to help the student negotiate this stage of the life cycle and find a way to get through it.

Group Work and Substance Abuse Prevention

Another common high school group focuses on prevention and education dealing with substance abuse, dating, and relationships. With increased freedom and for some students income from part-time jobs, the potential for the use of abusive substances and unhealthy interpersonal relationships is high. Concern about the use and abuse of prescription drugs that can be found in the family medicine cabinet is also growing. If students are not experiencing the problems directly, they can observe them in friends and family members and are often at a loss for what to do. Educational support groups offer help in these areas, as do diversion groups for students already in trouble over substance abuse.

Group work is a modality of choice when considering substance abuse prevention approaches. The many ways in which mutual aid can occur in the group—for example, sharing of data, the all-in-the-same-boat phenomenon, and the opening of taboo areas—lend themselves to the learning process. As children and youth come to grips with the impact of substance abuse on their own lives and the lives of friends and significant others, as they attempt to cope with the pressures of growing up that may encourage conformity to unhealthy substance abuse norms, and as they experiment and learn to use substances in a controlled and limited manner, having an opportunity to meet with other youth experiencing similar struggles and having an adult who does not judge or lecture them may make all the difference in their successful negotiation of this vulnerable stage of life.

Educational Substance Abuse Group: Is It a Class or a Group?

This first example, which involves a teen group in a school, raises the not uncommon issue of confusion on the part of the school and the leader about group purpose. The school authorities have had bad experiences in the past when students have resisted substance abuse educational groups. Instead of considering that the source of resistance may be the way in which the group was conducted, the school staff suggests offering a "class." The leader's confusion is evident as she struggles to lead a "class" when she really believes it should be a "therapeutic group." In its strict sense, the term *therapy* implies something is wrong and needs to be fixed or cured. The term *psychoeducational group* would probably fit better. The alternative of offering the teens groups that can help them deal with the impact of substances on themselves and others, a group that can include educational content as well as mutual support and problem solving, was not part of the initial conceptualization. However, since this is what the group members really need, this purpose becomes evident as the group takes its members and the leaders where they need to go.

This example also illustrates the professional impact role of the school counselor as she recognizes the structural problem in how the group is conceived and begins to work with her own supervisor to bring about a change. This would be an illustration of the advocacy role described earlier in this chapter.

Group Purpose: Group members are 15 to 17 years old; one white female and six males (five white and one Puerto Rican); dates covered in record: September 19 to October 24

Description of the Problem

My assessment of the group problem involves its hidden agenda. In the past, the school has had difficulty creating an effective therapeutic group regarding substance abuse issues. Considering the tremendous need for a group of this type, as an alternative, the school has integrated a substance abuse class within its health science curriculum. Every Tuesday morning, during the students' health science period, I "teach" a substance abuse "class."

First Session

It was the second day of my placement and my first experience teaching a class. I had short notice to prepare a lesson plan and to prepare for my first session. I did not know what to expect. After briefly meeting the students the previous day and hearing an abundance of "horror stories" from the staff, my greatest fear was that the students would misbehave. As I explained to the students what this class was all about, I kept in mind the school's request to approach it as a class, not a group.

"Hi, guys, thanks for settling down so we can get started. As Mrs. Haft explained, I will be working with you every Tuesday at this time. This class will be focused on learning about substance abuse. I want everyone to know that any questions and/or comments you may have are welcome." The students remained silent. I was relieved that they were being well behaved, but I was hoping for some sort of interaction or feedback.

 PRACTICE POINTS The silence may have represented a number of concerns and feelings on the part of the group members: "What does a class like this deal with?"; "What about confidentiality?"; "I'm not sure I want to be the first to speak." If the opening statement was followed by the leader sharing some examples and then moving into problem swapping, that approach would have helped the members begin. Note how Jason responds with humor while raising a serious issue.

"Does anyone have any questions so far?" I questioned. A student asked what we would be learning about. I proceeded to briefly state that we would be covering everything from cigarettes to alcohol to cocaine, and that we would begin with substance abuse in general. Jason laughed as he asked, "Do we get to experiment with some stuff in class?"

The other students laughed and watched for my response. As I smiled and shook my head, I responded, "I don't think so, Jason, but we can definitely discuss any experiences anyone has with drugs or alcohol." Jason replied, "Cool. Rock on," as he nodded his head. I smiled and nodded my head as well.

Now looking back, I realize that would have been the perfect opportunity for me to mention the importance of confidentiality and respect within the class. We moved from the purpose and agenda of the class to the day's lesson. I provided the students with some information on substance abuse in general, gave them some time to complete a worksheet, and then we went over it together. Overall, the students were well behaved, fairly attentive, and somewhat enthusiastic. The atmosphere was that of a "class," something I enjoyed, but something to which I would have to get accustomed.

PRACTICE POINTS The students' growing confidence allows her to be flexible in response to the issues raised by the members. Driving under the influence (DUI) is a serious issue for students this age. Their own driving, feeling under pressure to get into a car with a friend who is driving and is drunk or stoned on drugs, and even parents and family members who have been convicted of driving under the influence are all real issues for students and should be discussed in this group. If the leader identifies some of these issues, the discussion will deepen.

Second Session

I entered the second "class" with a sense of confidence. I had adequate time to prepare a lesson, a good idea of what would occur, and had begun to develop a relationship with four of the seven students whom I had seen individually. "How's everybody doing?" I questioned as I entered the classroom. A few students responded as they settled into their seats. "What are you going to teach us about today?" questioned Derik. "I thought we would start with alcohol," I responded. "Are we going to talk about drunk driving and stuff?" asked Michael. "I hadn't planned on covering drunk driving until next week, but if that is something you want to discuss today, we can. Anytime anyone has something they want to discuss, please feel free to bring it up," I responded. I wanted to emphasize that we could talk about what they wanted, and that we did not have to abide strictly by the lesson plan.

PRACTICE POINTS Although the leader attributes skipping the confidentiality discussion to the school's perception of this group as a "class," the real reason is more likely that group leaders do not like to emphasize authority issues early in the relationship. They fear that bringing up the subject will cut off discussion, and this aspect of their role is often experienced as uncomfortable. In reality, raising it clears the air and actually encourages more discussion as participants understand the boundaries.

In the next excerpt, the student group leader begins to renegotiate the contract with her supervisor. Her honest sharing of her dilemma helps the supervisor respond positively. It also would have been helpful if she could have been as direct with her group members, thus helping them address group purpose and the working agreement.

Third Session

After spending a great deal of time thinking about the last class, I expressed my opinion to my supervisor regarding the "class" versus "group" dilemma. I explained that I understood where the school was coming from but that I had a strong feeling that the students would be willing to participate in and benefit from an integration of educational material into a group regarding substance abuse. My supervisor was very supportive as well as pleased to openly bring a therapeutic aspect into the students' substance abuse course. After all, a therapeutic substance abuse course had been the school's original desired goal.

PRACTICE POINTS

The leader's comments underline how important supportive supervision can be for a student and a relatively new counselor. In the next excerpt, the group leader drops the "agenda" and begins to respond to the productions of the group. We see a clear example of the sessional contracting skills described in the Part 1 discussion of the middle phase of group practice.

I entered the third session with my eyes and ears wide open for an opportunity to begin the shift. I felt prepared, supported, excited, and somewhat anxious. "OK, is everybody settled?" I questioned, as an attempt to get all of the students in their seats. "Last week we went over various facts about alcohol and issues related to it. We also completed some worksheets and had an opportunity to discuss questions some of you had in regard to alcohol. I thought today we could all talk about some reasons why you think people drink and abuse alcohol." As I looked around the classroom, I noticed heads nodding in agreement, but no one said a word. For a moment, I began to have doubts about making the "shift."

I contemplated recontracting but felt it was too soon, and I needed to observe a desire among the students to express personal experiences before I recontracted. However, I thought this was an appropriate time to mention the importance of confidentiality—not only to protect the rights of the students, but to increase the comfort level for sharing within the entire "group." "I just want to let all of you know that anything anyone shares in this class is confidential and is left in this classroom among the group. Does anyone have a comment, concern, or question about any of this?" All of the students felt good about the idea, especially the confidentiality.

PRACTICE POINTS

The student leader's first instinct to recontract was a good one. If she was concerned that it might be too early in the group, she could have shared that as well. Her handling of the group during the first sessions has started to build a sound working relationship that she could draw upon if she were direct with the members. As is often the case, the discussion of confidentiality is incomplete and unintentionally misleading. There are some things that, if shared in the group, the group leader is mandated to report. She would have been more accurate to limit confidentiality by explaining exceptions to that rule. She provides one exception in response to a question; however, there are others as well. For example, she would have been mandated to report illegal activity, such as drug dealing, and to report if a member were in danger from others (e.g., experiencing sexual or physical abuse) or could be a danger to others or a danger to themselves.

"Also, guys, it is important to remember to have respect for someone when they are talking. How does that sound to everyone?" I looked around the room for a response. All of the students nodded in agreement, and some commented "cool" and "sounds good." Paul (a student whom I see individually) questioned, "No matter what we say, you won't tell our parents?" "No, not unless you express harming yourself or someone else . . . and that is for your protection." "Rock on," commented Jason. I glanced over at Jason and, as I smiled, commented, "Jason, maybe you can start out and tell us a reason why you think people drink and/or abuse alcohol?" "To get drunk and forget about sh-t, you know," responded Jason. Jason's response was the true beginning of the shift. As the class/group continued, I got a strong sense the "group" atmosphere was truly developing among the students. Each student added something to the discussion. However, I noticed that the students whom I see individually expressed much more personal experiences than the others. I think their comfort level and counseling relationship with me may have something to do with it. As the period was about to end, I reminded the students about the confidentiality and thanked everyone for sharing.

PRACTICE POINTS The leader begins to note an interesting and not uncommon pattern in the group. Members she sees individually tend to respond in a different way than members who have just met her in the group. It is very possible that members have noted this difference as well. It is often helpful to simply acknowledge that two subgroups exist and that she has had time to develop a stronger positive relationship with some members than others. She can also indicate she hopes that she can do the same with members who are new to her. Just acknowledging this dual relationship with some group members can go a long way to removing any negative impact.

In the next session, the leader makes a significant shift by recontracting with the members. Although she may feel that the members are now ready, in reality, she is the one who is now ready. Her clarity about purpose sends that message to the group members.

Fourth Session

I entered the classroom with enthusiasm and a bit of anxiety. Shortly after entering the classroom, when the students were settled, I stated, "OK, are we all ready to move into the lounge to watch the movie?" The students responded positively, and we all moved into the lounge. After everyone was seated, I stated, "Each of you know that today we're going to watch *When a Man Loves a Woman*. This is kind of a 'tear-jerker' and may hit on some areas that are tough for some of you, but that is what the discussion with the group afterward is for. If anyone feels they need to leave, feel free and you can go to Mrs. Crawford's room." As I looked around, the students nodded their heads in agreement.

"Some of you may have noticed that we've been doing a lot more talking in this class lately and sort of developed into a group. I think it is important to learn about substance abuse, but the feelings involved and the effects of it are just as important as the factual information, if not more. It seems that substance abuse in some way affects just about everybody's life." (As I spoke, I noticed the students were listening intently.) "I think it is important to have a place where these effects and feelings can be shared and expressed as well as comforted and supported. How do you guys feel about having this class be a group where that can happen?"

"It sounds pretty good. I like that anything we say doesn't leave the room," responded Nicole (a student whom I do not see individually). I nodded my head empathetically and in agreement as she spoke. "Yes, the confidentiality is extremely important in a group like this . . . it helps to really develop trust, respect, and comfort, which make sharing a little bit easier," I responded. Derik commented, "I would still like to have you teach us some stuff, but I think it's pretty cool to talk about a lot of stuff, you know." "Does that sound OK to everyone? That we can learn some facts and then have a discussion as well?" I questioned and then looked around the room for a response. I observed several nods and "yeahs."

The shift seemed to be unanimously desired among the group. "Rock on, let's get the movie going," shouted Jason. The students laughed and then focused on the television. I started the video.

As the movie ended and the discussion developed, I felt the atmosphere of a group strengthen among the students. Some students appeared to be apprehensive at first, but as others shared, more students opened up. As the group ended, I went over the recontracting and the content of that day's group. I also checked in with the students that everyone was "OK" with the group. It seems as if all the students were comfortable with the shift and had already begun to form a bond.

PRACTICE SUMMARY These high school students were receptive to the offer of the group; and once the group leader was clear about the contract and the structure, they responded eagerly. All too often educational groups such as this take on a "teaching" and "preaching" approach that students have heard from adults, including their parents, and they simply tune out. Straight talk and an opportunity to connect the content to their life experiences and their own struggles or those of friends or family members will be experienced differently. However, as the next example demonstrates, it isn't always that easy.

High School Students in a Diversion Program

PRACTICE POINTS In the following excerpt from a middle-phase group meeting with older teen members, participants admit having used drugs prior to coming to school. The group leader must also face the challenge from one member for her to disclose her own drug use. While substance abuse is included in the contract in this group, it is only one issue among others. The leader is attuned enough to recognize that the members' disclosure of drug use prior to the meeting is a first offering, a way of both testing the leader and raising the issue. All of the members of the group have been assigned to a diversion program in a special school as an alternative to sentencing to a detention center. While the group members are older than those in earlier examples of work with teens, their behavior seems more adolescent. This is not unusual for older teens "stuck" in the stage of the life cycle that coincided with the beginning of their serious substance abuse.

Agency Type: Clinicians on the mental health agency staff lead or co-lead a number of school-based groups from the elementary to high school level.

Group Purpose: The group is made up of the students enrolled in the Diversion and Mainstream class at the local high school. The purpose of the group is to provide a safe haven where members can discuss their concerns, questions, thoughts, and feelings. The group focuses on issues related to self-esteem, conflict resolution, peer and familial relations, and substance use/abuse.

Gender of Members: Male

Age Range: 17–18

Cultural, Racial, or Ethnic Identification of Members: One is African American, one is Hispanic, and the remaining five are white.

Meeting 13

After a brief check-in with members, Don, Matt, and Jake began discussing their drug use prior to the start of the school day. I questioned their ability to participate in group while under the influence of drugs. Jake reported that it was easier to come to school high than straight. Others laughed. Mike jumped in, responding, "You guys are stupid, man. How the hell can you come here high? That's f—ing stupid!" I asked Mike if he has had an experience with using before school. Mike shook his head. Members laughed at Mike and called him a "fat liar." Referring to the contract, I emphasized the issue of respect for one another. Bob (a usually silent member) disclosed his history of drinking before school and firmly stated his decision against drugging. I thanked Bob for sharing and asked if he could say more about his experience. Before Bob could answer, Matt turned to me and questioned my history of drug use. I remained silent as I looked at my co-leader.

PRACTICE SUMMARY

While not falling into the trap of a battle of wills over the drug use prior to the meeting, and demonstrating some level of attunement as the leader starts to explore the reasons for this behavior, she does not ask the members to elaborate on the joking yet very serious comment of needing to use drugs in order to come to school. The group must also deal with the issue of limits and the leader's expectations that members will not be high during meetings. This is acknowledged by the group leader, but the limit is not clearly set.

Finally, the authority theme test experienced by the leader in the request for her drug history is, in part, an accurate perception. However, the question may also be an attempt to get at the experience of others who may have used drugs but are not currently addicted. An honest response could take many forms. For example, "I don't feel comfortable answering that question, yet I am asking you to share your experiences." Or "I did experiment with drugs, as all of my friends did, but at one point I decided I had to take control of the drugs before they took control of me." Or "I think I faced many of the same pressures you experience around drugs. I also didn't think any adults could understand and that most of them were just preaching to me and were hypocritical, since they used alcohol." There is no correct response to this question, only honest responses that may differ for each of us. The important thing is to address the real meaning of the question without turning our response into a full disclosure of all of our own experiences, if we had them, with drugs and/or alcohol or a defensive response designed to increase our own comfort at the expense of our group members. This is definitely a moment not to respond with "We're here to talk about you, not me."

Chapter Summary

The focus of this chapter was on group counseling in the school setting from elementary to high school. Selected examples illustrated how the group counseling framework presented in Part 1 can be elaborated taking into account the different group purposes, level of education, age and stage of the life cycle of the students, and other factors that introduce the variant elements of practice. For example, the difficulties faced by older elementary school students facing the awkward transition stage to adolescence created unique challenges to be addressed. Illustrations of dealing with the impact of stressful family life on school behavior as well as the normative transition process from elementary school to middle school illustrated the importance of recognizing the impact of the life cycle.

Examples of work with middle and high school students focused on group purposes that included violence prevention for suspended students as well as substance abuse prevention. The importance of including both educational material as well as discussion of the impact of violence and substance abuse on the lives of members and those they cared about was stressed.

Special emphasis was placed on working with urban students and dealing with the impact of violence in the family, the community, and the school. A multicultural/social justice advocacy approach for the school counselor was also explored, with the argument advanced that the school was the counselor's "second client."

Examples of support groups for parents that avoided preaching or making parents feel more guilty or responsible for the children's difficulties were also presented.

Related Online Content and Activities

For learning tools such as glossary terms, InfoTrac® College Edition keywords, links to related websites, and chapter practice quizzes, visit this book's website at **www.cengage.com/counseling/shulman.**

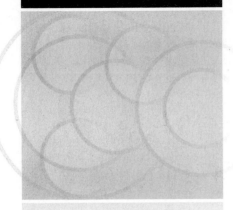

CHAPTER 16

Group Counseling in Marital and Family Settings

In this chapter, the term *family* includes a wide range of associations, many of which do not fit the traditional image of a two-parent family. The increasing number of single-parent families, as well as families headed by gay or lesbian partners, has broadened our understanding of the concept of family. The discussion in Chapter 11 of culturally competent practice also introduced the idea that even the word for *family* in some population groups refers to what the dominant culture would call the extended family. The illustrations in this chapter are mostly of more traditional couples, single-parent, and family groups; however, many of the core concepts could also be applied to other relationships as well.

What Do Counselors Do in Marital and Family Settings?

The U.S. Department of Labor's (2008–2009) *Occupational Outlook Handbook* describes the work of counselors in this area as follows:

> *Marriage and family therapists* apply family systems theory, principles and techniques to individuals, families, and couples to resolve emotional conflicts. In doing so, they modify people's perceptions and behaviors, enhance communication and understanding among family members, and help to prevent family and individual crises. Marriage and family therapists also may engage in psychotherapy of a non-medical nature, make appropriate referrals to psychiatric resources, perform research, and teach courses about human development and interpersonal relationships. (www.bls.gov/oco/home.htm)

Group counselors in the marital and family counseling field most often work with two kinds of couple or family groups: one that focuses on helping the couples or families function more effectively when dealing with the many normative developmental issues in a relationship or a family; or a second that focuses on a specific problem or issue such as a serious illness affecting a family member or when children are exhibiting severe behavioral problems in school. When the group brings more than one family together, the term *multiple family group therapy* (MFGT) is sometimes used to describe work. This form of group practice will be briefly described later in this chapter.

In either type of counseling group, the initial work may lead to the revelation of deeper, more long-term problems. In these situations, short-term couple or family support groups will often involve (1) helping the group members identify the real problems, (2) creating a positive working relationship with the group leader so that the family can begin to see helping professionals and counseling in a positive way, and (3) referring the couple or family members for more traditional forms of long-term family interventions.

The second type of group counseling involves providing couples or families with support that is directly connected to the specific services offered by the agency or host setting. For example, a hospital counselor in a medical setting might provide a group for a number of families dealing with their adjustment to a family member's common illness or medical condition. The all-in-the-same-boat phenomenon, described in Chapter 3 on mutual aid, or the ability of group members to share information about the illness with other families can be extremely helpful. Such a group in a hospital can provide an opportunity for medical staff to meet with members to answer questions about the illness and the treatments. This type of group counseling centers on a particular problem or life crisis that both guides and limits the nature of the work.

Clarity of the group's contract is essential since the focus has to be on the impact of the specific problem or illness. A major role for the group leader is "guarding the contract" so that the group does not go beyond its boundaries set by the contract or working agreement. For example, if members in a group for couples or families designed to provide support in dealing with a difficult child begin to discuss their longer-term marital issues, it would be important for the group leader to bring the discussion back to the group's purpose—for example, by saying, "It sounds like this problem has been stressful for your marriage. Can you let us know how it has affected your ability to work together as a couple in dealing with John (their child) and also how the stress with John affects you as a couple?" This is an example of guarding the contract where the group stays focused on the parenting issue and where the group leader might then makes a referral for the couple for couples counseling.

Examples discussed in this chapter illustrate work with

- multifamily group with Latino immigrants addressing 9/11 losses,
- married couples attempting to strengthen or save their marriage,
- single parents designed to help them cope with the unique problems they face, and
- preadoptive couples helping them explore the issues that they face as they make the decision to bring a child into their lives.

What Do We Know About Couples, Families, and Family Practice?

In Chapter 2, I explored a number of assumptions about individual psychology and behavior with a focus on an oppression psychology model, resilience, and a strengths perspective. In Chapter 8, I focused on the entity called the group-as-a-whole that had elements that could be described as more than the sum of its parts. In this chapter, we introduce two additional dynamic systems: the couple and the family. Each of these can have its own culture (e.g., norms of behavior, taboos, structure, roles) as well as its own unique dynamics. This adds a level of complexity in couple and multiple family groups. I suggested earlier that group leaders needed to be conscious of each individual member and the group itself. In this chapter, the group leader is faced with the challenge to also "see" the couple or family as a dynamic system within the dynamic system of the group. As I did for the individual in Chapter 2, I will present a summary of some theories of family dynamics and practice to lay the groundwork for considering the group illustrations.

In addition, many of the concepts and theories introduced in the earlier chapters can be applied to understanding family-related group work. For example, from the life span framework, the group leader would attempt to help family members identify the available baseline reserve capacity, both internal (within the family) and external, that could increase the family's ability to cope with the sources of stress. If, for example, the family crisis presented in a group involves an elderly parent or grandparent who can no longer cope independently because of physical deterioration, then the work might involve identifying the developmental reserve capacity potentially available through interventions such as the services of a home care aide or housekeeper.

Other practice models introduced earlier and described in more detail in Chapter 12 may provide constructs that are useful in this work. For example, cognitive-behavioral practice interventions can help couples or family members identify automatic thinking processes that cause them to misinterpret the reality of their interactions. This can allow group members to break maladaptive cycles of blaming and conflict and to identify individual and family strengths and sources of support. Feminist practice frameworks can help members of the family identify gender-stereotypical behavior that may have led to the internalization of anger and frustration as well as interactional-related depression on the part of parents or children. Solution-focused approaches that help family members identify their strengths and what helped them successfully cope with issues in the past can also be used. For example, as couples or family members explore in the group how they are dealing with a particular crisis, they can be asked when in their history did they feel things were going well and they had been able to handle other critical problems. A second question, asking what was going on in their lives as couples or as a family that helped them to cope, is a solution-focused technique that helps focus on their strengths rather than pathology.

Resilience theory and research would offer suggestions to the group leader, the couple, or the family on interventions, such as the involvement of extended family members or elders, or other resources in the community (e.g., Big Brothers or Big Sisters) designed to buffer the impact of a trauma on the children or the parents. In this sense, the work is essentially restorative, designed to strengthen the family and to lead to more normal or positive growth and development. The next section explores some selected concepts from family therapy that can help a group leader understand couple and family dynamics as well as consider intervention strategies.

What Is Unique About Working with Couples or Families?

When working with couples or families in a group, the group leader should take several unique factors into account. First, families have a history that goes back many generations. Family members beyond the nuclear family, both dead and alive, often affect the present. That is, the nuclear family's relationship—or lack of relationship—to the extended family or the community may play a large part in its functioning. Next, different family members exert different amounts of influence and power in relation to one another. For example, children (or a partner) may feel intimidated about speaking up or even face serious threats of retribution, including physical violence, when couples or family members return to their lives between group counseling sessions. Cultural variations discussed in Chapter 11 may influence members' ability to speak or disagree with another member of a family. The very fact that the couple or family usually returns to the same home means that they have a powerful between-session influence on each other as opposed to members of a group, who may only see each other for a brief period each week.

Finally, another issue is related to the fact that the stereotypes, roles, and communication patterns—the couple or family structure—have developed and been reinforced on a daily basis, 24 hours a day, over a number of years. This can create strong resistances to the "unfreezing" process needed for change. The family has had years to develop a *family facade*—a false front it presents to outsiders—and each family member has also had time to create the external role that he or she presents to the other family members. One of the major advantages of seeing whole families in a group, as opposed to working with one member of a family at a time, is that it allows the leader to observe many of these factors in the couple or family interaction (e.g., who sits where, who speaks for the family).

Selected Concepts from Family Therapy Theory

Family therapy theory can help us better understand couple and family dynamics and choose effective interventions when we work with them in groups. There are many different views about how families function and what counselors should do to help. One text on the subject describes 17 different models (Horne & Passmore, 1991). I shall identify and briefly describe key concepts from a few of these models. I have chosen some of the early foundation approaches since I believe many of the more recent family group work models, described in the balance of this chapter, have their roots in a number of fundamental concepts briefly reviewed in the following sections.

Nathan Ackerman

One early contributor to family therapy theory, whose work has influenced many of the current theories, is Nathan Ackerman (1958). My discussion about working with couples or family groups will draw on his framework for viewing a family and his practice strategies for implementing family work. Although he was not referring to work with families in groups, many of his theories about family dynamics and his description of the role of the therapist can be easily applied. Ackerman viewed family work as a special method of treatment of emotional disorders based on dynamically oriented interviews with the whole family. He sees the *family* as a natural living unit including all those persons who share identity with the family and are influenced by it in a circular exchange of emotions. The family has a potential for mutual support that can be blocked by communication problems and anxieties of individual members. This leads to family disorders and the family's inability to carry out its tasks.

Although Ackerman does not specifically define the function of the helping person as mediation, many of his treatment skills can be explained as implementing this function in action. For example, he recognizes that treatment usually begins at a time of crisis, when the emotional equilibrium of the family has been upset. In the beginning stages of work, after contracting to help the family members work together to improve their communications and deal with the family problems troubling them, the counselor employs the skill of observation to identify the idiosyncratic language of the family. Using personal emotions stirred by the feelings of the family members toward each other and the counselor, he or she tests hunches about the family and its feelings by sharing them with family members. In this way, the counselor helps the family move past the facade presented in the first stage toward a more honest disclosure of their interpersonal conflicts.

For example, the counselor might help the family move beyond viewing the family problem as concerning a single child, who serves as the family scapegoat. The child in this case is called the *identified patient (IP)* or the client in a family system that is identified as having the problem. (This IP phenomenon was evident in Chapter 4 in my description of the first session of the married couples' group when Lou, the 69-year-old member, began by describing his wife and her depression as the couple's problem.) This process of moving past the facade has been described by other family theorists as *reframing the problem* to help the couple or family see it in a new way.

The counselor would identify unhelpful patterns and roles (e.g., scapegoat, victim, persecutor, etc.), pointing them out to the family members. Facilitative confrontation is used to break the vicious cycle of blame and punishment that usually characterizes disordered family relationships. The counselor challenges the illusion of work using the "here and now" of the family session (and the couple or family group session) to bring out the central issues. Because the family acts out its dysfunctional patterns in front of the therapist and the group, the process of the family session is directly synthesized with the content of the work. In Ackerman's model, the therapist controls interpersonal danger, selectively supports family members, and attempts at all times to present a model of positive interpersonal functioning.

Murray Bowen

Another early foundation theorist whose ideas are helpful in understanding and working with couples and families in groups is Murray Bowen (1961, 1978). Bowen also views the family as guided in its activities by an emotional system that may have developed over years. He stresses the importance of understanding and exploring the intergenerational contribution made to the development of this family emotional system. Key concepts in Bowen's model include the importance of each individual being able to differentiate between emotional and thinking systems so that control can be maintained over behavior. Bowen also stresses the impact of anxiety on the family system. Increased anxiety, resulting from a perceived threat, can lead to efforts toward "togetherness" in the family as a maladaptive means of coping. One example is the process of *triangulation*, in which one party attempts to gain the allegiance of a second party in the struggle with a third party as a means of coping with anxiety. Each parent might try to pull in the child for support against the other parent, for instance. This is a maladaptive way of coping with a problem and can result in significant negative consequences, as in the case of the child forced to choose between parents. In a family support group, the process of triangulation that is hard to see in one's own family may become clearer when witnessed in another family in the group.

David Freeman

Without needing to adopt a particular model whole, we can borrow concepts and techniques that can be integrated into effective couple and family group work at any level. Freeman's work has been useful in explicating Bowen's theoretical model and describing and illustrating the method for its implementation (Freeman, 1981). In particular, his use of time in organizing his discussion of family work (beginning family therapy, the family therapy process, and the terminating stage) makes it easy to fit useful concepts within the model presented in this book. Although Freeman is referring to individual family sessions, many of his concepts and strategies can be applied, for example, to individual, couple, or family member interviews designed to recruit group members.

Freeman describes four phases in the first interview that can be equally applied to couples or family groups: warming up, defining the problem, reframing the family's thinking about the problem, and obtaining the commitment to work as a family. The warming-up phase helps reduce the family's anxiety. Defining the problem involves a form of contracting, trying to understand how all family members perceive the problem. The reframing phase involves helping the family see the problem in new ways (e.g., as a family problem, not just as a result of the behaviors of the identified patient). Finally, the commitment-to-work phase lays the groundwork for future sessions.

The middle phase of practice is where Bowen's theory adds its special emphasis on intergenerational work. As individuals take more responsibility for their own actions, and the sessions are thereby marked by less blaming and reactive behavior, the relative calm allows for identification of subsystems within the inter- and extra-familial networks to which the family can direct its attention. It is at these points in particular that the multigenerational concepts are used to help families expand their boundaries. The counselor tries to help the family understand the impact of the family history and use the extended family as a source of support. In group work with families, you can add the multigenerational influence of other group members to the equation. For example, the grandparent in one family may be able to offer insights to the parents in another.

Carl Rogers (Person-Centered Approach)

Another foundation of family therapy theory, termed the person-centered approach, builds on the ideas developed from the early work of Carl Rogers (1961). In this approach, as described by Thayer (1982),

> [t]he therapist works on establishing a healthy psychological climate which the
> family members can use to establish realness in family relationships, express true

feelings, remain separate and yet identify with the family, develop effective two-way communication, start a healthy process for family development and problem-solving, and clarify societal effects on the family as well as clarify conflicts, seek solutions, explore values, make decisions, experiment with new behaviors, and develop a family model/direction unique to its needs and wants. (p. 19)

The followers of this approach focus on the core helping skills that have been demonstrated repeatedly to facilitate change. These components of a healthy psychological climate include the therapist's genuineness (being real as a person), the therapist's caring and prizing of family members (unconditional positive regard for family members), and the therapist's willingness to listen carefully to what family members have to say (hearing and understanding family members' needs, wants, conflicts, fears, joys, loves, goals, values, hates, disappointments, dreams, sorrows, and worlds or realities). These core conditions will be familiar to the reader from Part 1 of this book.

Many of the core ideas in family therapy cut across early theories. For example, multigenerational issues are important in most models, with Satir (1967) interested in "family fact chronology" and Keith and Whitaker (1982) referring to a "longitudinally integrated, intra-psychic family of three generations." The core issue of integration and differentiation—how to be part of a family and at the same time a separate individual—appears in most formulations, although the terms used may differ (e.g., Keith and Whitaker refer to unification and separation).

Most theorists refer to the problem of triangulation, discussed earlier. Where they tend to differ is in their views of how to avoid the trap, change the pattern, or make strategic use of being the third party in the situation. The importance of developing a safe atmosphere is also stressed, although theories differ sharply in their timing and methods of confrontation for upsetting the dysfunctional patterns.

Working with Multiple Family Groups

Group practice in this area involves working with more than one family at a time in a group for a range of purposes, including group therapy, a psychoeducational focus, or a specific crisis intervention. For example, in one group project focusing on working with mothers and children in an effort to break intergenerational transmission of substance abuse patterns, participants were brought together for an evening program starting with dinner with each other and the group leaders.[1] After dinner separate groups were conducted for the children and the parents, followed by a group where all of the family members were brought together. The groups had both psychoeducational and mutual aid support elements. Group leaders reported some of the most important interactions emerged during the dinner segment when family members could be observed interacting in an informal setting.

Multiple Family Group Therapy (MFGT)

Thorngren (2006) has written about an MFGT approach that she and colleagues use (Thorngren, Christensen, & Kleist, 1998; Thorngren & Kleist, 2002). She defines the model and points out the advantages:

---

1. The project was part of a federally funded 16-site study of a psychoeducational model titled Families Working Together, conducted at the School of Social Work Research Center of the University at Buffalo, State University of New York.

Multiple family group therapy (MFGT) is a planned, psychosocial approach to treatment that involves two or more families. This approach combines elements of education and group process to harness the strengths of individual families and their members to bring about greater problem-solving abilities and enhanced functioning for the group as a whole. (p. 339)

Thorngren describes the multiplicity of subsystems within such a group such as all of the parents or all of the children. She suggests a number of ways in which subsystems can be helpful to each other. For example, adolescents in the larger group can confront adolescents in a particular family, or parents in the group can point out the strengths of their children to overcritical parents. In most cases, it may be easier to accept confrontation and hear advice from others in a similar situation.

Multiple family group therapy brings together families who are often experiencing severe stress and feelings of isolation. As families engage in risk-taking and self-disclosure to share their stories, trust is built, and it becomes apparent that they are not alone in their struggles. Difficulties may be slightly different, but each family has dealt with critical blows to its intactness. Often, one family has just gone through a stage that another family is beginning. These similarities and differences enable families to connect and impart hope. Each family has particular strengths that become apparent to other members. Members can provide effective confrontation and feedback from a place of experience. Families can impart information about what has worked for them and what has not been successful. Not only is the content of the information beneficial, the processes of socializing and learning through interpersonal interaction are invaluable for all members. (p. 340)

Psychoeducational Multifamily Groups (PMGs)

In a variation of a model for bringing families together in a group, psychoeducational multifamily groups (PMGs) have been used to assist individuals with mental illness (schizophrenia) to improve their participation in community and family life. In one example, family members, support people, and practitioners met every other week for 6 months in a program focused on providing information about mental illness, developing coping skills, solving problems, creating social supports, and developing an alliance between consumers and their families with practitioners or other support professionals.

A review of the PMG model conducted by the federal government's Substance Abuse and Mental Health Services Administration of the National Institutes of Health examined six studies that compared the results of PMG with other forms of treatment on the following outcomes:

- Employment
- Psychiatric relapse
- Symptoms of schizophrenia
- Family stress (SAMHSA's National Registry of Evidence-Based Programs and Practices, 2009)[2]

Although methodologies, research rigor, as well as findings varied in the studies, general results included the following:

---

2. Available at www.nrepp.samhsa.gov/programfulldetails.asp?PROGRAM_ID=103.

- Two of three studies reviewed found better employment outcomes for patients who were involved in PMG when compared with patients who received other forms of treatment.

- Patients involved in PMG demonstrated lower relapse and/or hospitalization rates than patients involved in other treatments in three studies reviewed.

- PMG patients had fewer negative symptoms of schizophrenia than patients receiving other forms of treatment in one of two studies reviewed.

- Families involved in PMG reported significantly reduced family stress in a variety of areas including improvements in objective and subjective report of burden, dissatisfaction with the patient, and lower levels of friction between the patient and others.

Multifamily Group with Latino Immigrants Addressing 9/11 Losses

Family groups can also be formed around specific events that have affected all of the families in the group. For example, Ludwig, Imberti, Rodriquez, and Torrens (2006) describe a collaboration with the building services union local to develop a community-based MFG that addressed traumatic loss experienced by families of community members who were missing after 9/11. The project began 5 months after the event and included family members who had lost a member working in the Windows on the World restaurant on the top floor of the North Tower of the World Trade Center.

> The families were mostly Spanish-speaking Latino immigrants from North America, South America and the Caribbean. This group met bi-monthly over a three-year period for full-day meetings in the union hall. The purpose of the group was to create a supportive healing community around the losses the families shared and to normalize the struggles that the families were experiencing both internally, within the family, and externally, with other people and institutions. Families were invited to bring as many people as they felt were important to their family network including friends, several generations of extended family, and important community members. A guiding belief was that families would be strengthened by becoming more connected to community and family resources, including each other. (p. 46)

The group described here was organized as a psychosocial intervention as contrasted with a medical model that focuses on posttraumatic stress disorder (PTSD; PTSD-oriented group practices were discussed in Chapter 12). The authors suggest that both types of groups may be needed for family members; however, their approach focuses on the social bond between members as the source of healing. Group leaders prepared for this project by receiving training in the unique family impacts associated with "ambiguous loss" in which the bodies of the family members were never found and many questions remain unanswered.

The authors focus on three facets of the work that they suggest would apply to any multifamily group work: (1) the meeting structure and activity level in relation to the developmental stage of the group, (2) cultural awareness, and (3) the group process of the workers.

Evolving Group Structure and Style

Ludwig et al. describe the development of the group using the framework of time—beginning, middle, and ending—described in Part 1. In the first sessions in February 2002, most families were still "reeling" from the traumatic losses they had experienced.

Many of the families were ambivalent and worried about attending, including those that were undocumented immigrants. Some families were still in denial about the death of their loved ones, and some parents had not found a way to tell their children that the family member was dead. The group leaders decided on a very structured approach to the first sessions.

> Since this was a multi-family group, the group leaders ensured that there was little demand for families to spontaneously interact with other families they did not yet know. In this beginning phase an individual worker was assigned to every family that was expected to attend. Workers had telephone contact with the families prior to the group meetings and would meet the families at the door when they arrived. They oriented families to space, the plan for the day, ate lunch with them, and initiated a check-in. After lunch, three to four families were directed to meet together in predetermined groups to continue conversations. During these meetings, group members began to discover how much they had in common. (p. 50)

In the middle phase, near the first anniversary, the number of workers was reduced, and families began to take more control over the sessions. Workers reported more intimacy (family members greeting each warmly at the start of the meetings) as well as the emergence of conflict when one member described how she was making changes in her life. Structure became more flexible, with family groups now meeting in one large group at the start of the meeting. After the large-group activities, families would break into smaller talking groups. The large group would be reunited at the end of the meeting. Activities involving all family members, such as creating a family portrait and sharing it with the other families, were suggested by the workers. The workers also asked family members to draw projections of where they wanted to be in respect to their losses and their families in the future.

> In contrast to the beginning of the group when children produced pictures of burning falling towers we now saw a range of towers including intact towers encompassed by hearts. Children were interested in how others were seeing the towers and ran around to see what their friends had made. Adults compared notes as they drew pictures of themselves traveling freely between New York and their countries of origin or as they drew their families united in one physical space. (p. 50)

One family-focused theme that emerged repeatedly in the small and large discussion groups involved cross-generational conversations between children and parents. For example, would parents be dating again, and did that mean they had forgotten the missing parent? By addressing these issues in the multifamily group, family members could see that these questions were part of a normal developmental process.

The ending of the group involved an overnight retreat to a summer camp shortly after the third anniversary of September 11. The retreat included a "graduation ceremony" and an ending of the relationship to the workers symbolized by the parents leaving the camp on the buses without the group leaders. One adult family member described this process to the workers as follows: "As much as we love you, we are like your adult children and we know that we must leave home someday" (p. 52).

Cultural Competence

Although most workers in this example were Spanish speaking, they did not necessarily share the Hispanic culture, even though some were immigrants themselves. They used what the authors described as "cultural curiosity" to increase their sensitivity to the particular cultural aspects related to loss. While there were differences between families, three main connecting points observed by workers were the native Spanish language, collective values and belief systems, and culturally based rituals. Members of the group spoke in Spanish and indicated that this was important for them to be able to express themselves directly and not through interpreters. They also expressed difficulty when participating in groups where the majority of the members were white and English speaking. While the families came from different countries, they shared "numerous culturally related codes which included traditional beliefs, family values, and spiritual principles" (p. 54). Group meetings became "a place where families could share in culturally specific rituals such as the celebration of Los Tres Reyes Magos or the Three Kings Day with gifts for children and traditional foods prepared by the families. . . . There were also more solemn and private rituals in the group such as the acknowledgement of 9/11 anniversaries and Father's Day" (p. 55).

Workers' Process

The authors point out that although most workers did not share in the losses, they lived in New York City and had a close proximity to the 9/11 event. It was therefore important to pay attention to the parallel process in which the group leaders needed to work on their own emotional reactions to the event and their own healing if they were to help the families. This goal was facilitated by holding meetings of the group leaders before and after the family sessions. These meetings gave them an opportunity to participate in the planning of the group, discuss their experiences and observations, and attend to their own healing process. From Ludwig et al.'s description, there developed a professional family group that provided the support needed to the group leaders so that they could in turn provide it to the families.

Married Couples' Groups

Three examples follow from my married couples' group. This group was first presented in Chapter 4 to illustrate the beginning phase of group practice and contracting. The examples in this chapter help spotlight some of the unique dynamics of working with couples in a group. The first illustrates the need to address the sexual taboo early in the life of the group. It is also a good example of the process/content integration, for example, since the difficulty in talking about sex in the group mirrors the difficulty between partners. The second example illustrates the importance of sessional tuning-in and sessional contracting as one couple shares a powerful issue in the 19th session as the group is coming to an end. The third illustrates how a couple raises a content issue through an angry attack on the group leaders. A fourth and final example, from a different couples' group that I did not lead, illustrates the difficulty of changing the group and couple culture to allow for the expression of anger and painful issues that underlie the anger.

Dealing with the Sexual Taboo

In earlier chapters, we explored how the skill of helping a client discuss subjects in taboo areas was important to the work. The social nature of taboos magnifies their impact in the group setting. Many taboos have their early roots in the first primary groups, such as the family, and thus can represent a powerful obstacle to group work. Sometimes the counselor simply needs to call the group's attention to the obstacle, but in the case of some of the stronger taboo areas, such as sex, the group may need more help.

The couples' group I led and described earlier in this book consisted of five couples trying to deal with conflicts that threatened their marriage. We met once a week in the University Health Science Center. I had two co-leaders, one a nurse and the other a social worker, who also saw the individual couples on a regular basis. Sexual concerns between members were hinted at toward the end of an early group session. I pointed this out to the group, suggesting that we pick up on this at our next session. The group agreed enthusiastically. I did not expect it to be that easy; because of the strength of the taboo in this area, simply calling the group's attention to the subject probably would not be sufficient. This group also took place at a time when the taboos around sex were much stronger than they are today.

PRACTICE POINTS

At the start of the next session, the members immediately began to discuss an unrelated area. In effect, by addressing another issue and avoiding the taboo subject, their behavior was saying to the group leaders, "That sexual thing we said we were going to discuss is difficult to address." I called their attention to what was happening after a few minutes and suggested that because of the taboo, the subject might be hard to discuss. I asked the group members to explore the obstacle that made it hard for them to discuss sexual subjects. This is an example of a group leader exploring resistance rather than ignoring it or trying to work around it. As they discussed what made it hard to talk about sex, they were actually talking about sex:

I said, "At the end of last week, we agreed to get into the whole sexual area, and yet we seem to be avoiding it this week. I have a hunch that this is a hard area to discuss in the group. Am I right?" There was a look of relief on their faces, and Lou (a 69-year-old member) responded, "Yes, I noticed that as well. You know, this is not easy to talk about in public. We're not used to it." I wanted the group to explore what it was about this area that made it hard: "Maybe it would help if we spent some time on what it is about this area, in particular, that makes it tough to discuss. That might make everyone feel a bit more comfortable."

Fran (in her 30s) responded, "When I was a kid, I got a clear message that this wasn't to be spoken about with my parents. The only thing said to me was that I should watch out because boys had only one thing on their mind—the problem was, I wasn't sure what that thing was." Group members were nodding and smiling at this. Lou said, "How many of you had your parents talk to you about sex?"

The group exchanged stories of how the topic of sex was first raised with them. In all cases, it had been done indirectly, if at all, and with some embarrassment. Those with older children described their own determination to do things differently, but somehow, their actual efforts to talk to their children were still marked by discomfort.

At one point, Frank (in his 50s) described his concerns as a teenager: "You know, from the talk I heard from the other guys, I thought everyone in the neighborhood was getting sex except me. It made me feel something was really wrong with me—and I made sure not to let on that I was really concerned about this." The conversation continued, with the group members noting that they had been raised in different generations, and that while some things were different in terms of attitudes toward sex, other things, particularly the taboos, were the same. I could sense a general relaxing as the discussion proceeded and members discovered that there were many similarities in their experiences. I said, "It's easy to see how these experiences would make it difficult for you to talk freely in this group; however, if we can't get at this critical area, we will be blocked in our work."

By encouraging discussion of the taboo and the reasons for its power, I was helping the members enter this area. It was important that I not blame or criticize them for their difficulty in getting started, but at the same time I needed to make a demand to move past the taboo. Once again, the connection between the process in the group and the group content is easy to see. The difficulty in discussing sex in the group mirrored the difficulty in discussing the subject with each other as partners.

"I can imagine that this difficulty in talking about sex must carry over in your marriages as well. I believe that, if you can discuss some of the problems you are having here in the group, we might be able to help you talk more freely to each other—and that might be the beginning of a change." Rick (Fran's husband in his 30s) responded, "We can never talk to each other about this without ending up in a fight." I asked Rick if he could expand on this. "We have this problem of me wanting more sex than Fran—sometimes we can go for months without sex, and I'm not sure I can take this anymore." Fran responded, "A relationship is more than just sex, you know, and I just can't turn it on or off because you happen to feel like having sex."

The rest of the evening was spent on Fran and Rick's relationship. The group was supportive to both as the couple's early conversation centered on who was to blame: Fran for her "frigidity" or Rick for his "premature ejaculation." During the next few sessions, the group kept discussing the sexual area as members explored the intricate patterns of action and reaction they had developed that led them to blame each other rather than take responsibility for their own feelings about sex. Once the taboo had been breached and group members found that they were not punished, it lost some of its power, and the discussion became more personal.

Sessional Contracting in the 19th Session

This second example illustrates the importance of sessional tuning-in and sessional contracting in the group context. The session was the 19th. At the previous group session, Louise (in her 20s) was present without her husband John (also in his 20s). She had revealed that John had developed a drinking problem. Her first offering of this issue can be traced back to the first session of this group (see Chapter 4) where Louise talked about something that had changed in their relationship but she could not put her finger on it right then. Now, as we were entering the ending and transition stage of the group's life (only five sessions left), each couple was raising the most difficult issue in their relationship. There was general agreement to pursue this concern with John present the next week.

In my sessional tuning-in session with my co-leaders prior to the start of the session, I had learned that Fran and Rick had had a particularly difficult week and had threatened separation during their individual counseling session. Rick had questioned returning to the group. This couple previously had made substantial progress in the group and in a related behaviorally oriented sexual therapy group program. However, they had hit a critical point in the other group program and were regressing. Over the course of the sessions, I had observed that this couple had a characteristic pattern of presenting their concerns in the group: Fran would express her own concerns and fears indirectly as she responded to other couples in the group, and Rick would physically retreat.

Having accomplished the preparatory work, we developed a strategy to reach for Fran's indirect cues if they were evident, and we prepared to help the group discuss priorities for this session. The session began with some hints from the group about the ending process, a topic to which I had planned to respond directly. After I acknowledged the group's sadness, and my own, about ending and the members had briefly discussed their feelings, there was a silence that was broken by John:

JOHN: I know about your discussion about my drinking last week, since I met with Larry (the leader) and he filled me in. If you have any questions, let me have them.

At this point, there was some relaxation of tension, and group members offered supportive comments for John for his having raised this difficult concern. I noticed that Fran and Rick had turned their chairs so that they faced slightly apart from each other. Rick was staring into space with a bland expression. Group members can also communicate by physical posture, expression, and so forth, so I was prepared to see this physical signal and ready for Fran to continue her pattern of raising issues by talking about other couples. Fran turned to face John.

FRAN: I want you to know, John, that I think it's great that you have come here prepared to talk about this problem. It takes a lot of courage on your part. It would have been a lot easier if you simply stayed away or refused to discuss it. That would have been the coward's way out.

LEADER: Fran, I wonder if that's what you think Rick is doing right now in relation to you. His chair is turned away from you, and you seem to be upset with each other.

FRAN: (After a period of silence) I don't understand how you do this, how you read my mind this way. It must be a form of magic. (Pause) But you're right, we had a really bad fight this week, and we're not over it. Rick didn't want to come this week, and he won't talk to me about it. (Fran shows signs of becoming upset emotionally.)

LEADER: How do you see it, Rick?

PRACTICE SUMMARY

After Rick's confirmation of the seriousness of the situation, both he and Fran state they are concerned because this was supposed to be the week for John and Louise. I raised the issue with the whole group, and they decided to stay with Rick and Fran because of the degree of urgency in their situation. John and Louise felt they could wait another week. The session turned out to be an important turning point for the couple (Rick and Fran), as well as one that yielded important insights for the other couples into their own relationships.

There was no magic in picking up Fran's cues; tuning in and identifying the couple's pattern of raising issues in the group had helped. Also important was the recognition that comments from members early in the meeting may be indirect efforts to raise themes of concern.

Emergence of Anger at the Group Leaders and the Process/Content Integration

Another example from the same group was the issue raised by Lou, the member of the group who was in his 60s. He was the member in the first session of this group, described in Chapter 4, who challenged indirectly and then directly the authority of the group leaders.

In this illustration, the problem of identifying the issue was compounded, because the nature of the concern was not clear to the member and was presented indirectly as a part of an angry attack on the group leaders. In the previous session, a videotaped segment of a meeting when the partners of one of the couples had blown up at each other had been viewed by the group with the couple's consent. Lou was upset that this painful exchange had been replayed in the group. He began with an angry attack on helping professionals, denouncing "the way they played games with people's lives." He was extremely upset at the way leaders encouraged the expression of bitter feelings between couples, feeling that this tore them apart emotionally. He argued that this was not necessary. I reached for the specific meaning of his opening comments.

> **LEADER:** Lou, I think you're talking about us and last week's session—when we watched the tape. (I had missed this session due to an accident but had reviewed the videotape. The session had been led by my co-leaders.)
> **LOU:** Of course I am! I've never been more upset. It tore my guts watching what you people (referring to my co-leaders) put them through.

Lou went on to attack the helping professions in general as well as us in particular. My co-leaders responded by attempting to explain what they had done. We were generally made to feel defensive and incompetent. Group members will often make the leaders feel exactly the way they feel themselves. When they are unaware of or unable to express their own pain and the hurt under their anger, one way to deal with it is to project it onto the leaders or other members. Bion (1961) described this process as *"projective identification,"* in which the group member communicates his or her feelings by stimulating the same feelings in the leader. The difficulty for the leader is that there is always some element of truth in the attack, which is usually aimed at an area in which the leader feels vulnerable and less confident. In this situation, we stayed with the issue raised by Lou.

> **LEADER:** Lou, you're angry with us and also feeling that we really hurt Len and Sally last week. Obviously we missed how hard it hit you to see their pain. Why don't you ask them how they felt?
> **LOU:** Well, am I right? Wasn't that terrible for you to go through?
> **LEN:** It wasn't easy, and it hurt, but I think it helped to get it out in the open. It also helped to have all of you care about us and feel the pain with us.
> **LOU:** But there must be some way to do this without having to tear your guts out. (Lou seemed a bit taken aback by Len's comments, which were echoed by his wife, Sally.)
> **LEADER:** When you attacked us, Lou, I have to admit it hit me hard. A part of me doesn't want to get at the anger and pain that you all feel, and yet anther part of me feels it's the way back to a stronger relationship. I have to admit you shook me.
> **ROSE:** (Lou's wife) I think you have to understand this has been a hard week for us.
> **LEADER:** How come?
> **ROSE:** We just got word that Lesley, our granddaughter who lives in London, is splitting up with her husband.

Lou and Rose have spoken before in the group about their children and the pain it has caused them to see each of them experience difficulties in their own marriages. Lou has been particularly angry with helping professionals in the past who have helped neither him nor his family members. This was their first grandchild to experience marital problems, and it signified to Lou and Rose the continuation of the family's instability into another generation. Under much of the anger is their pain as well as their feelings of defensiveness and doubt, to which Rose responded by clarifying Lou's signal.

> **LEADER:** It must have hit you very hard, Lou, having the first grandchild experience marital problems.
>
> **LOU:** (Seemingly deflated, the anger gone, slumped in his chair, speaking with a tone of resignation and bitterness) After 45 years, you learn you have to live with these things. It's just another notch that you have to add to all to the other hurts.

The discussion continued with Lou and Rose describing their feelings of helplessness as they watched their family disintegrating and their desire to show the children that it did not have to be that way. The group members commiserated as Lou and Rose described their feelings of impotence to affect the lives of their children and their grandchildren.

PRACTICE SUMMARY

In the first illustration with Fran and in the second with Lou, the individual (and couple) was reaching out to the group indirectly through her or his opening comments. With Fran, the concern was presented in the guise of a response to a group member, while with Lou it appeared as an attack on the leaders. In both cases, the communication had two meanings. The first was the actual statement of fact, while the second was a disguised call for help. Unless leaders are tuned in, listen hard for potential offerings from group members, and are clear about their own function in the group, it is easy to miss the early, indirect productions of group members. Of course, the member will often present a concern more directly, thus making it easier for the group to hear. And sometimes an issue may emerge at a later point in the meeting.

In Rose and Lou's situation, the most powerful issue did not emerge until after the group had ended. They had requested a session with me a few months after the last session. At that session they disclosed that their son, who now lived in California, had been in therapy and had told them that his psychiatrist had indicated that all of his problems stemmed from his parenting—in effect, that Lou and Rose were the cause of his marital difficulties. Two years before, he had indicated that he did not want them to contact or visit him. This was actually the precipitating incident that had led to Rose's most recent episode of depression and her hospitalization. They asked to see me since they now felt strong enough to visit him in spite of his injunction and they wanted to discuss it with me. If one looks back to the first session of this group in Chapter 4 on contracting, at that session Lou mentions during his speech on incompetent therapists that there were other incidents having to do with his son that he didn't want to talk about at this first session. With hindsight, that was his first offering of a deeply painful concern only fully emerging after the group had ended. As with John and Louise, and Lou and Rose, each of the five couples had hinted in the first session of the group at the issue that would only emerge as the urgency of the group ending in the last five sessions forced it to the surface.

Legitimizing the Expression of Anger

In an example from a different married couples' group led by another group leader, an effort is made to help the group change its norms to develop a culture that is more conducive to work. The counselor notices the group members' reluctance to get involved when couples share very personal and angry feelings. She brings this to their attention.

By the sixth session (following Christmas vacation, during which the group had adjourned for 2 weeks), most of the group's work seemed to involve each couple presenting problems that had been decided on by both partners and within limits felt by both to be fairly comfortable. If there was intracouple disagreement and challenge, such conflict seemed to be on safe topics—for example, related to problems of the others in the group or, if pertaining to their own marriage, then almost always at the level of the more reluctant spouse. Don, at the fifth session, challenged Liz directly. Liz responded to his charge that she was "always covering up the truth" with a return challenge, asking him why he had married her—daring him to share with the group the real reason: her pregnancy.

When he tried to evade her by deliberately misinterpreting her question, she stuck with it and said she had always suspected that he had felt an obligation to marry and had never really loved her. The group seemed reluctant at first to step into this interchange—they seemed to be giving the couple a chance to "unsay" what had been said.

The group leader intervenes and points out the pattern she has observed. This is similar to my pointing out the pattern of avoiding talking about sex in the earlier excerpt with the couples' group. A common mistake would be for the group leader to jump in and start doing couples' counseling. This would be a sign of the leader's own anxiety and lack of clarity of role. By intervening as she does, she asks the group to move to a new level of intimacy and mutual aid.

I pointed out the difference between their reaction to this problem and others they had picked up on unhesitatingly, and I asked if they agreed that there was a difference. A few members did, and I asked why they thought they hadn't wanted to get involved. Most felt it was "extremely intimate," and that made the difference. I agreed that it was and that I felt it really took guts to bring up something intimate. I said that problems were not often brought up because they were so personal and because we were so used to keeping anything personal as private as possible.

The group talked about family and friends and "how far" one could go in these relationships and how this group was different from "out there." Something clicked for Reisa, because, without even checking it out with Jack, she told the group that she and Jack had been forced to marry because she had been pregnant, too. They talked about her family's reaction and how this had affected their marriage and their feelings about their first child.

Although group counseling is complex, and doing it with couples or families adds other processes for the group leader to monitor, by being clear about the leader's role in helping the individual, couple, or family, reaching out to the group, and helping the group members respond, finding the right intervention is much easier.

Single-Parent Groups

This section focuses on the practice issues involved in working with single parents in groups. Our understanding of the average family being composed of a working father, a mother at home, and two to three children has become a myth. According to the U.S. Census Bureau (2007):

- The percentage of households headed by single parents showed little variation from 1994 through 2006, at about 9%, up from 5% in 1970, according to the latest data on America's families and households released by the U.S. Census Bureau.

- According to *Families and Living Arrangements: 2006*, there were 12.9 million one-parent families in 2006—10.4 million single-mother families and 2.5 million single-father families.

- Just over two-thirds (67%) of the nation's 73.7 million children younger than 18 lived with two married parents in 2006. Also in 2006, there were an estimated 5.8 million stay-at-home parents: 5.6 million mothers and 159,000 fathers.

These single-parent families are the result of divorce, widowhood, separation, and unmarried parenthood. It is interesting and somewhat revealing to note that this report did not include the number of same-sex couples or gay or lesbian single parents in the analysis. With the emerging acceptance of gay marriage and other legalized forms of same-sex relationships in a growing number of states, this omission may be corrected one day.

Life Cycle Developmental Issues

The parents and children in a single-parent family must face all the normative developmental tasks for their age and stage of life; however, in addition, they must face the stresses generated by significant transitions in status. For example, one member of the group who is discussed later in this section was in his late 20s and had just become a parent. His ability to cope with the transition to the parent role was severely affected by his wife's decision to leave him and the new baby. Thus, he had to deal with the change in status from nonparent to parent, a difficult enough transition, while simultaneously coping with the change in status from married partner to single parent.[3]

The teenage children of another group participant were facing the normative transitional stresses associated with adolescence but now found themselves also having to cope with the inevitable stresses associated with the disruption of their family and the departure of their father. The impact of the change in status from child in a "normal" family to child in a "broken" family exacerbated the already difficult transitional issues associated with adolescence. Other associated status changes included a sharply decreased family income after the split. Thus, both the parent and the children were faced with changes in their economic status from well-off and secure, to indigent and insecure. As will be illustrated later, in the discussion of the difficulties single women, without work and credit experience of their own, encounter when they try to establish their own credit, the prejudicial responses of the community may mean resources needed to cope with this change (e.g., credit in their own name) are unavailable. Given the current economic crisis in the United States, including tightening of credit, unemployment and home foreclosures, these problems can easily become exacerbated.

Compounding all of these issues faced by single-parent families is the reality that the single parent often has to handle these problems alone. Another added problem is referred to as the "Noah's Ark syndrome," in which friends seem to operate under the general belief that people come "two by two." Old friends seem to slip away, and new friends seem to be hard to find.

---

3. Parts of this section are based on a chapter by this author on work with single parents published in Gitterman and Shulman (2005).

In addition is the difficulty of trying to balance personal needs against all of the responsibilities of raising a family. At the time when the single parent is most vulnerable and most needy, he or she must also deal with school meetings, dental appointments, homework, and all the rest. Finding time for oneself can be extremely difficult.

The ongoing relationship with the ex-spouse, whether or not he or she is still actively in the picture, can be a major problem in trying to work out a new relationship that could overcome the bitterness and hard feelings associated with the split, so that the children don't feel torn between parents. Often, the ongoing legacy of anger from the marriage and from the way in which the split was handled by overzealous lawyers can remain to haunt all members of the family even when the ex-spouse is no longer around.

Finally, dealing with the children can take its toll. For example, finding child care assistance, either during the evening for a night out or during the day to facilitate working, can be difficult and expensive. The makeshift arrangements that are often necessary in such situations can lead to heightened anxiety for the parent and an increased sense of guilt.

In addition to the concrete issues related to children, there are the problems of dealing with their emotional needs. These can cause even more difficulty for the single parent whose own emotions are still raw. Although reactions differ according to age and according to the specific situation, it is not uncommon for children to react to the split in the family by going through the phases of grieving similar to those associated with death and dying.

First, there is the shock, followed by depression and denial. Then comes anger and a lowered sense of self-esteem. Often, there is also a feeling of being responsible for the split in the marriage. These feelings are expressed in different ways, ranging from regression for toddlers to problems in school and with peer group for young teens. The children's anger at the parent thought to be at fault, their struggle with the loyalty problem when parents force them to take sides, and their feelings of sadness, depression, anger, and guilt can cut them off from friends and other close people, just at the time they need them the most. Often, one of the hardest times for the single parent is trying to help the child deal with these strains at precisely the same time they are feeling most vulnerable themselves.

Many of these issues facing single parents and their children emerge in the example that follows.

A Single-Parents' Group: Short-Term Interventions

This author was the group leader for a single-parents' group held in a small town in British Columbia, Canada. The service was offered as part of a university community psychiatry *outreach program*. The group had both service and training purposes and was thus attended by clients and local service providers. The group met for one evening (3 hours) and the following day for 7 hours. Participants included eight single mothers, three single fathers, and three community professionals who worked with single parents.

PRACTICE POINTS The session began with our contracting work. I hoped to set the stage by using the skills of clarifying purpose and clarifying my role. To help them understand the purpose, I had tuned in to possible themes of concern and included in my opening statement some handles for work by partializing the overall purpose into potential issues for discussion. This was followed by my reaching for feedback from the group members.

I explained the purpose of the group as an opportunity for single parents to discuss with each other some of the special problems they faced because they were alone. I said that my role was not as an expert with answers for them, but rather as someone who would try to help them to talk to and listen to each other and to provide help to each other from their own experiences. In addition, I would throw in any ideas I had which might be helpful. I then offered a few examples of possible concerns (these were similar to those described earlier in this section).

There was much head nodding in agreement as I spoke. I completed my opening by describing some of the phases that both parents and children go through after a separation, as outlined earlier. I invited the participants to share some of their own experiences, their concerns and problems, and suggested that we could use their issues as an agenda for our discussion. There was a brief silence, and then Irene asked how long it took to go through the phases. I asked her why she was asking, and she said it was 3 years since her separation, and she didn't think she had passed through all of them yet. The group members laughed, acknowledging their understanding of the comment.

PRACTICE POINTS

Although Irene had responded in a lighthearted manner, I wanted to be sure to communicate to the members that if they were prepared to discuss even these painful areas, I was ready as well. Because it was a short-term group, I also felt I had to get right to the issues that were residing beneath the humorous comment.

I said I thought there must have been a great deal of pain and sadness both at the time of the split and since then to cause it still to hurt after 3 years. I asked Irene if she could speak some more about this. Irene continued in a more serious tone by describing her ongoing depression. She described days in which she felt she was finally getting over things and picking herself up, followed by days when she felt right back to square one. Others in the group agreed and shared their own experiences when I encouraged them to respond to Irene's comments. I told them it might help just to know that they were in the same boat with their feelings.

PRACTICE POINTS

I then asked if the group members could be more specific about what made the breakup difficult. A number of areas were raised by members, which I kept track of in my written notes. They included dealing with money and finances, problems with the ex-spouse, problems with the kids, and the strain in their relationships with friends and family. A great deal of emotion was expressed in discussion of this last area, with anger directed toward others who "didn't understand" and who related to them in ways that hurt more than helped. Dick, a young man in his mid-20s, spoke with great agitation about his wife who had left him with their 6-month-old baby only 6 weeks before. The group seemed to focus on Dick, who expressed a particularly strong sense of urgency and was clearly still in a state of shock and crisis.

Dick had arrived early and had carried on a long and animated discussion with another member in the premeeting "chatter," listing all of the crises he had to get through in order to get to the session that evening. I had noted this and considered it a first offering and an indirect message to me, the leader, that he was in a difficult state and wanted help.

I pointed out to the group that it seemed like Dick was feeling this concern about friends and relatives rather strongly and, in fact, had had a great deal of difficulty even getting here tonight. I asked if they would like to focus on friends and relatives first, perhaps using Dick's example to get us started. All agreed that would be helpful.

In the opening session of this group, the members begin by externalizing the problems. That is, the first theme dealt with others who didn't understand. It was friends and family who created the problems. It was important to begin with the members' sense of urgency and to respect their need for defenses. However, since there were only an evening and a day for work with this group, I had to move rather quickly to confront the participants with the need to look at their part in the proceedings; it was also important that I take some time to acknowledge how it felt to them. During the course of the following discussion, I was struck by how the crisis for the single parent was simultaneously a crisis for friends and relatives. It appeared that the single parent was sending mixed messages to "significant others." On the one hand, I heard, "I'm hurt, lost, overwhelmed. Help me." The contrary message was "Don't get too close. I'm afraid of losing my independence."

After Dick described the details of his separation and his current living situation with his 6-month-old child, he went on to describe the problems. He emphasized the difficulty of living in a small town and, in his particular case, being in a personal service occupation that put him in daily contact with many town residents. He said, "Sure I feel lousy, depressed, and alone. But some days I feel I'm getting over things a bit, feeling a little bit up, and everywhere I go people constantly stop me to tell me how terrible things are. If I didn't feel lousy before I went out, I sure do by the time I get home."

Dick added a further complication in that the baby had a serious case of colic and was crying all the time. He told the group that everyone was always criticizing how he handled the baby, and even his mother was telling him he wasn't competent and should move back home with her. He continued by saying he was so depressed by this that he had taken to not talking to anyone anymore, avoiding his friends, and staying home alone at night, and he was going out of his mind. Others in the group shared similar versions of this experience. I said to Dick, "And that's the dilemma, isn't it? Just at the time you really need help the most, you feel you have to cut yourself off from it to maintain your sense of personal integrity and sanity. You would like some help because the going is rough, but you are not sure you want to have to depend on all of these people, and you are not sure you like the costs involved." Dick nodded, and the other group members agreed.

It became clear to the group members and me that Dick was actively sending two apparently conflicting messages to those in his support systems and not being really clear about either. It appeared that his ambivalence about the central issue of independence and dependence was the major dynamic in relating to friends and family. The crisis appeared to evoke unresolved conflicts. Dick was feeling that he wanted to give up and let someone else handle things for him. This frightened him and made it difficult for him to take any help at all. All of the group members expressed one variation or another on this same theme.

After providing recognition and support for these feelings, I tried to move the group members into an examination of what they could do about the feelings in terms of how they handled their conversations with friends and relatives. I encountered a good deal of resistance to this idea, with Dick balking each time I tried to get him to look at how he might have handled a conversation differently. He evaded this by jumping quickly to other comments or examples or by saying, "If you only knew my mother/friends, you would realize it is hopeless." When Rose, a member of the group in her early 50s with children close to Dick's age, confronted him from the perspective of his mother, he rejected her comments.

I interpreted this as the point at which Dick, and all of the group members, needed to make a second decision. Coming to the group was the first decision to face their problems.

Starting to take some personal responsibility for them was the second and more difficult decision. I wanted to integrate, at this moment, empathic support for their struggle with a clear demand for work. Because it was a short-term group, I believed I had to do this during the first of the three segments of work.

I pointed out what was happening. I said, "It seems to me that when I or a group member suggests that you [Dick] look at your part in the proceedings, you won't take in what we are saying. I only have a day and a half with this group, so I really can't pussy-foot around with you." I wondered if it was tough for Dick, and all of them, to take responsibility for their part in their problems. Dick smiled and admitted that it was hard. He already felt lousy enough. Others joined in on how easy it was to blame everyone else and how hard it was to accept any blame themselves. I agreed that it was tough, but I didn't think I would be of any help to them if I just sat here for a day and a half agreeing about how tough things were for them. The group members laughed, and a number said they didn't want that.

PRACTICE POINTS At this point, Doris, one of the three counselors participating in the group, surprised us all by saying that she had intended to listen and not talk during the session but that listening to Dick's problem made her want to share hers.

Doris said she had come to the group as an observer; however, she was pregnant, unmarried, and, therefore, about to become a single parent. She thought she was having the same problem in communicating with her mother as Dick was having with his. It was a classic example of a conflict between a mother who is hurt and embarrassed and a daughter who feels rejected at a critical moment in her life. At my suggestion, Rose offered to role-play the mother as Doris tried to find a new way to talk to her mother. The group was supportive, but at the same time, following my example, they confronted each other during the discussion in a healthy way.

Dick listened and participated in the work on Doris's problem and, as is often the case, was able to learn something about his own situation as he watched someone else struggling with the same concerns. When I asked him later if he had taken something from it, he said it had helped him a lot to see how he was holding back his real feelings from friends and his own mother. I pointed out to all of the group members what a shock their situation was to their friends and close relatives and how at first contact they could not respond in a way which met their needs. I said, "This does not mean they don't love you. It just means that they have feelings and aren't always able to express them. Your mixed messages also make it difficult."

PRACTICE POINTS At the core of the mutual aid concept described in Chapter 3 is the idea that listening to others with similar issues and concerns can help a member see more clearly their own issues and understand their own behavior. Cerrise, another counselor/observer in the group, joined the discussion at this point and described how she had felt when close friends had separated.

She said that she realized now that it had taken her a couple of months to get over being so angry at them for ending their marriage because she loved them both. She hadn't been able to reach out to support them. They, however, had not given up on her, and she had been able to work it out. Dick said that hearing that helped a lot. That was what was probably going on with some of his friends. Carrie, who was both an unmarried parent and a counselor in the community, described her own experiences with her mother when she split up. She shared how she had involved her mother in the process, had let her know her feelings, and that she wanted her mother's love and support but felt she had to handle the problems herself. Dick listened closely and said that this was probably what he had not been able to do. We did some role play on how Dick could handle the conversation with his mother and how he could articulate his real feelings. The group was supportive.

PRACTICE POINTS As the evening session was coming to an end, I wanted some sense of how the members had experienced the group thus far. As is often the case, the cause of the intensity of Dick's feelings emerges at the end of the session, the "doorknob therapy" syndrome, as Dick describes a friend in a similar single-parent situation who had committed suicide. My first concern was the issue of safety, and I wondered if Dick were indirectly signaling some of his own despair.

When I asked the group how they felt about this discussion thus far, Doris said it was helpful because I kept stressing the positive aspect, the reaching out and caring between people. Most of them had been so upset they could only see the negatives. The discussion turned to the question of how much they needed others to talk to about what they were going through. Near the end of the session, in typical "doorknob" fashion, Dick revealed that a close male friend of his, in a similar situation with a young child, had told him he was considering committing suicide. He went on to tell us, with tears in his eyes, that the friend had carried through with the threat and had just killed himself. I said, "It must have hit you very hard when that happened, and you must have wondered if you could have done something more to help." Dick agreed that was so, and the group members offered him support.

PRACTICE POINTS I felt that while Dick was referring to his friend, the parallels in their life situation caused me to wonder if he was having similar thoughts about suicide. One of the reasons for having community service providers present was to make sure that when I left at the end of the day and a half, resources would be available for individual work as needed.

After some time, I asked Dick if he was worried about his own situation, since he had many of the same feelings as his friend. He said he was worried but that he thought he would be strong enough to keep going with the goal in his life to make it for his child. I told him he had shown a lot of strength just coming to the group and working so hard on his problem. Carrie said that he was not alone and that he could call her if he needed someone to talk to as a friend or as a counselor. Rose pointed out that there was a single-parent social group at the church, and Dick said he had not realized that. Others in the group also offered support. I asked Dick how he felt now, and he said, "I feel a lot better. I realize now that I'm not so alone." Irene, who had opened the discussion by saying she had not yet gone through all the phases, summarized the evening's work when she said, "I guess we are all struggling to find ways of saying to friends and close relatives, Please love me now. I need you." The discussion ended, and we agreed to pick up again in the morning.

Relationship to the Children

A central theme that emerged when the group members discussed their problems with their children had to do with their guilt over their feelings of failure as parents.

They expressed feelings of responsibility for the marital split and therefore also felt responsible for their children's reactions. Thus, when indirect cues of the children's negative reactions emerged, they had difficulty in dealing with them. Also, the guilt made it hard for them to make appropriate demands on their children.

PRACTICE POINTS

For example, in the first part of the discussion that follows, one mother has difficulty in asking for an older child's help in baby-sitting a younger child. When the mother raises the general question, I intervene by moving from the general to the specific, in order to obtain details for our discussion. As in all mutual aid groups, as they help this member, they are also helping themselves.

There were some new members in the morning, so I took some time to review the contract. The discussion picked up again with Irene raising the problem of dealing with the children. She described how tough it was on her when she asked her 11-year-old boy to baby-sit his 5-year-old brother. I asked if she could describe a specific incident, and she told us about one that had occurred the previous day. Her older son was about to go out to play when she asked him to cover for her, because she needed to take care of some business. His face dropped but he did not say anything. I asked her if she could tell us how she felt when she saw his face drop. She said, "Miserable!" I asked her what she said to him, and she replied, "Nothing!" I pointed out how Irene had not leveled with her son and how she had avoided a frank discussion about her expectations on him and his feelings about having to carry some of the load. I asked if she had any ideas why it was so tough on her. She said he had not been getting along with his friends for a while after the split and, in fact, was moping around alone. Now that she saw him out and around, she hated to do anything that interfered.

John, a new member, revealed that he had been a son in a single-parent family and that he felt the same way her son felt. He resented having to be responsible at such a young age. He said he would have very much appreciated it if his mom had talked directly to him about it and had allowed him to get some of his feelings off his chest. I said, "I wonder if you parents really want to hear how your kids are feeling? I wonder if your kids' feelings are too close to your own." Gary said there was a lot of guilt in these situations. You feel responsible for your kid's problems because you've split up. He went on to say, "I'm also a little bit like a third-year medical student. Every time I see any sign of trouble with my kid, I'm sure it's going to be something really terrible."

PRACTICE POINTS

As Irene was describing her problem, I kept reaching for her feelings associated with their conversation. Group members often describe an incident without explaining their associated affect. In a sense, I was asking Irene to go back to the moment and try to remember and then share with us how it felt to her. By pointing out the gap between how she felt and what she said, I was trying to help all of the group members see how hard it is to be honest in expression of our feelings. We often expect the other person to "divine" our feelings, without accepting the responsibility of letting them know what those feelings are. In the group situation, I wanted to move further than just understanding, since I wanted to help the group members develop the skills needed to relate differently to those people who were important in their lives.

I suggested a quick role play, consciously trying not to make it a major production—for example, "Let's put two chairs in the middle of the circle." Role play in the group is difficult enough without the complications associated with formal structure. Irene resisted the suggestion. This resistance was important and was in many ways part of the work. Just as Rick's defensiveness in the opening session was a signal of underlying feelings, Irene's hesitation was also sending a signal. I tried to be empathic by exploring the reason for her hesitation, while simultaneously making a demand for work.

> I asked if a little role play might help here, and since John was a child in a family like this, maybe he could help by playing Irene's son. There was some hesitation by Irene, who said that was hard to do. When I asked about the hesitation, she said she was afraid she would make mistakes. Carrie pointed out they would be the same mistakes they all make, so she shouldn't worry about it. Irene responded by saying it was hard to role-play. I agreed and then told her that I never said this work would be easy. She agreed to give it a try. The role play revealed how hard it was for them to reach for the underlying feelings that they sensed were expressed indirectly by their children.
>
> I introduced the skill of looking for trouble when everything is going your way as an active way of reaching for the underlying feelings that were not easily expressed by their children. I illustrated how they could ask the child for negative feelings even when the child seemed to say everything was fine. There was a general recognition of how immobilized they often felt by their guilt. Irene tried again, and this time was direct in opening up the question of mutual responsibility and her son's feelings. John told her that as her son he would be relieved to have it out in the open and would feel good that she respected him and needed him in this way. He still would not like to stay home and baby-sit, but it would sure make it easier. Irene said, "I guess if I get this off my chest, it will be a lot easier for me as well."

PRACTICE POINTS As is often the case, when the group members saw how a first offering of a feeling-laden theme is handled by the leader and other members, they felt safer about moving into a deeper, more painful area. The difficulties arising from their guilt and their reluctance to make demands on their children were real problems but, still, only "*near problems*"; that is, each issue exposed just the surface of a much more difficult area of feeling. Maureen raised the issue directly in a way that touched each of the other members. Their first reaction was to avoid the feelings that were just under the surface of her question. Interestingly enough, this process in the group replicates the way in which they avoid the feelings under their children's questions. Once again, the group leader's task is to confront the members, but to do it gently and in recognition of the understandable reasons for the denial.

> Maureen jumped in and asked how you handle it when your kid says, "Why can't we be a normal family?" This hit the group like a bomb, and they all jumped in with their versions of how they would answer the child's question. Most of the responses were variations of defensive explanations, long analogies or examples, and so on, all designed to provide the "good parent's answer." I intervened and said, "You know, you have jumped in to answer Maureen's child's question, but I wonder if we really know what the question is?" I explain that it often takes some time for others really to tell us what they are feeling and that a quick response may not be getting at the real feelings, particularly when a question hits us in our gut and touches our feelings. I asked, "What would happen if you asked your child what he or she meant by the question?" There was a thoughtful silence in the room, and then Rose said, "Then we might really find out, and I'm not sure I want to hear."
>
> I asked if we could get back to Maureen's example, and Maureen said, "Could we go on to someone else's example? I've been in the spotlight too long, and people are probably

bored with my problem." I asked the group members if this was true. They vigorously shook their heads, indicating they were very interested. I said to Maureen, "Look, they are interested. Why is it you want to get off the spot? Is it very tough to be on the spot?" Maureen replied, "It's hitting too close to home." The group members laughed in acknowledgment. I credited her for being honest and asked what she meant by "hitting close to home." She said, "I want to feel like I'm a good mother." There was silence in the room, and Lenore finally said, "I know what you mean. I feel I failed in my marriage, and now I'm desperate about not wanting to feel I have failed as a mother."

PRACTICE POINTS

This was followed by a discussion of their sense of guilt, of how harsh they were on themselves, and how their feelings of failure in their marriages and their fears of failure as parents often translated into over concern and overprotection in relation to their children, with a resulting fear of revealing the underlying, painful feelings. We returned to Maureen's example. She role-played a number of ways she might reach for her daughter's real feelings and the meaning of the question "Why can't we be like a normal family?"

PRACTICE SUMMARY

Group counselors often believe they face a dilemma in having to deal with either their group's process or its content. The dilemma is experienced only because the counselor believes in the existence of what is really a false dichotomy. In this group, the process by which the members attempted to avoid the pain underlying questions raised by other group members was simply an illustration of the same problem they had with their children's questions. Thus, the process and the content are synthesized, not dichotomized, and as the group counselor deals with process, he or she is simultaneously dealing with content.

PRACTICE POINTS

I try to use this dynamic by asking the members to reflect briefly on the morning's discussion. The briefness is designed to ensure that the group does not lose its purpose and become lost in a discussion of its process.

Before we broke for lunch, I asked the group members to reflect on what had just happened in our group. I thought in some ways our group was an illustration of some of the problems they faced. I pointed out how Maureen had said she wanted to be off the spot because others were bored. Instead of just accepting that, I reached for other feelings that might be behind her discomfort. It turned out that she was feeling many things, and her concerns were very much the concerns of the whole group. I wondered what they thought about my observation. Irene said that she could see what I meant. They had feelings they needed to talk about and they would only get to them if I helped them. The same was probably true for their kids. I said, "Lecture's over—how about lunch?"

Other themes emerged in the afternoon session, including the problem facing one woman, Rose, who had found that her credit rating disappeared with her husband when he divorced her. Another theme emerged dealing with how to handle their children's feelings of being abandoned by the partner who moved out. This led to a discussion of the need to deal with their own feelings of rejection before they could deal with those of their children.

The final theme, saved for the ending of the afternoon session, dealt with issues of loneliness and the fear of risking. For most of the parents in this group, the change to single-parent status, for whatever the reason, had resulted in a state of loneliness. After having experienced years of being integrated, for better or worse, as part of a couple, they were suddenly facing the problem of being differentiated and alone. While many single parents enter into new relationships, the members of this group had not. Perhaps that is why they attended the group.

PRACTICE POINTS What became even more striking, as the following discussion reveals in a most dramatic fashion, is that the hurt they experienced in their separations has created a fear of risking in new relationships. They wanted closeness but were afraid to be vulnerable again to the pain of another separation. The crucial aspect to this work involved the group members' understanding the connections between the ways they felt and the way they acted. Also, they needed to see that changing their state of loneliness might be up to them.

The conversation about loneliness began when Rose told us she was afraid of being alone when her last child, now 15, grew up and moved out. All of her other children had left the home. Even though Rose wanted to deal with this question of loneliness, a part of her wanted to avoid it. It is interesting to note that the group members and the group leader backed off and, in a silent conspiracy, allowed the subject to change to the issue of finances. What follows is the start of that discussion.

Maureen said to Rose, "Maybe the problem is you've never been Rose. You've always been somebody's mother or somebody's wife." Louise said that it was almost another form of rejection, being alone. She continued, "My kids aren't moving out, but I find myself feeling the same way just putting them on the school bus in the mornings." I asked Rose if she could be specific about the loneliness, when she felt it and what was it like. She said the worst time was the emptiness in the house in the evenings.

PRACTICE POINTS After a few more comments by other group members, I noted that discussion had shifted to Rose's concern about the loss of her credit rating when her husband left her.

I intervened at the end of the credit discussion and said, "You know, it seems you have all decided to drop the issue Rose raised at the beginning—that is, how to handle the terrible loneliness of the empty house." They all laughed, recognizing they had silently agreed to drop the hot potato. Brett spoke for the first time and said that when we figured out that answer, to let her know, because she had the same problem. I commented that probably they all did, and that was why it was hard to help Rose.

Carrie wanted to know what Rose did about finding friends. I said I thought that was a good start in helping Rose. Rose described how she had been invited to a dance by a group of her friends, all couples, and then spent the whole night sitting there while no one asked her to dance. I said I could imagine how uncomfortable they might all have felt. Lenore said that when she goes to a dance and no one asks her, she asks them. Connie wondered if she couldn't find a female friend to go to dances with. A pattern started to emerge with Rose saying, "Yes, but . . ." to each suggestion. When I asked her if she had spoken to her friends about her discomfort directly, so they could better appreciate her feelings, it was obvious that she had not. Instead, she had been hurt and angry and had cut herself further off from her closest friends.

PRACTICE POINTS As her resistance stiffened, and with the group close to ending, I finally confronted her and said it appeared as though she was not willing to work at maintaining her close relationships.

She seemed to be saying that she wanted friends once again to divine her feelings, but she was not willing to take the risk and let them know what they were. At the same time she was complaining about being alone. The confrontation associated with my demand for work led her to the most painful of her feelings.

There was a long silence, and then with great feeling she said, "I don't want anyone to ever get close to me again." The group was somewhat stunned at the force of her feelings, since she had been speaking quietly and in control for most of the session. I asked her why she felt this so strongly. Rose went on to tell us that her husband had left her for her best friend. I said, "So you really had two losses. You must have felt betrayed and very bitter." She replied that she still felt that way, hurt and bitter. This initiated a powerful discussion by all group members of their feelings about intimacy. Their losses made them wonder if they should ever let themselves get close to anyone again. Irene said, "I think that's what I meant last night when I asked when you get over the last phase. I realize I have been depressed because I'm holding back. I'm not risking getting hurt again." The conversation dealt with their feelings about risking with friends of the same sex as well as with members of the opposite sex. Many of them described men who had attempted to date them whom they had liked but whom they had been afraid to get to know.

I tried to take us back to Rose by asking what she thought about this conversation. She shrugged her shoulders and said, "Well, maybe in a couple of years it will get better." I said, "And maybe in a couple of years, it will get a lot worse." I pointed out how all of them had been concerned that the kids come out of the situation whole, and yet their message to their kids appeared to be that when one gets hurt, it's better not to try again. Rose pointed out how much she has done about her life, even learning to drive a car so she could be a bit more independent. I agreed that she had shown a great deal of strength in tackling the strains of being alone, and that was why I felt she had the strength to even tackle this one, perhaps the hardest one for all of them. Irene said, "You're right, you know. We complain about being alone, but we are afraid to let ourselves be vulnerable again, afraid to get hurt." I said, "And that's the real dilemma, isn't it? It hurt so much to lose what you've had, you're afraid to risk. And then you find it also hurts to be alone. The important point, right now, is that you are aware of the question of loneliness and that what to do about it is really in your hands."

PRACTICE SUMMARY When we evaluated the group in the ending phase, the participants felt it was helpful to see other people with the same problems. They also appreciated my pushing them to be specific about their problems, even to the point of asking them to recount their actual conversations. They liked getting new ideas about what to say and do and didn't feel quite so helpless about some of their concerns. They also felt it was important that I didn't let them off the hook. Finally, they felt I was really listening to them and that I could understand what they were struggling with. I pointed out that these were probably some of the same qualities their children wanted from them.

I thanked them for their honesty and for teaching me a great deal more about the problems of being a single parent. There were exchanges of positive feeling at the end and some discussion about how they might continue to stay in touch. They also discussed other sources of support in the community. The counselors, who had been invited to attend the group in part to be available to the members for follow-up counseling, offered their telephone numbers and invited group members to contact them if they wanted to talk.

Preadoption Groups for Couples

The next two brief examples illustrate work with couples who are taking the adoption route to expanding their families. This would be an example of work designed to help the couple deal with issues related to adoption, the adoption process, the adoption agency, as well as any issues or concerns between them.

First Session of a Preadoption Group for Couples: Confidentiality and the Illusion of Work

PRACTICE POINTS

The issue illustrated in the first excerpt is dealing with the members' anxiety over whether they will be accepted as good adoptive parents. This can lead to an illusion of work in which the members say what they think the group leaders want to hear rather than using the group session to honestly explore real concerns. The group leaders take steps by acknowledging this difficulty in an effort to avoid the illusion of work. The couples' anxiety is signaled in both direct and indirect ways.

> Within a minute Mr. O'Hare followed her. I recognized that he was uncomfortable in the group and talked with him while his wife was cleaning up. I went with them to rejoin the group. I also recognized that Mr. and Mrs. Thomas, who were one of the last couples to arrive, seemed tense and flustered. Mrs. Thomas said her husband hadn't come home for supper and had met her at the door. I commented about whether he might be working late as we were entering. Mr. Thomas looked a little sheepish. Mr. Aronson arrived and apologized to the group. I opened by welcoming everyone and requesting that we all introduce ourselves and give the following information: whether you have children, if adopted or biological, age and sex; child desired—age, sex, anything else specific. Everyone responded quite comfortably to this, with the men speaking for both (as is usually the case).

PRACTICE POINTS

As the group leader shares the purpose of the meeting, she recognizes the degree of discomfort about honest sharing, which puts the issue on the table. She also emphasizes the issue of confidentiality of information shared previously in individual sessions. Her contracting includes a brief statement of the leaders' role.

> I explained the purpose of the meeting as being an opportunity for them to share thoughts and feelings about adoption. Discussion in a group might be helpful to them in sorting out what their attitudes are, what they're comfortable with, and whether adoption is for them. I wondered if they might be feeling uneasy about sharing their concerns with us. We recognize their feelings about this and it being part of our getting to know them. We're not looking for perfect people, but we want to get to know them and what they are suited for. They might find it helpful to discuss questions with others who may be having the same concerns.
>
> I continued that the information they shared from my previous visits with them is confidential, and what they share with the group of what they've told us is up to them. It's their group. Our role as co-leaders is to see that we stay on topics related to adoption and to clarify policy matters, but we hope that they'll be free in talking about what's on their minds. I asked the group's permission to take notes of tonight's meeting. The purpose of this recording was for us to use it in a group training session on how to work with groups. Confidentiality of the group members would be protected, and they would be identified only by initials. Staff members from other departments would be present at the training session. We hoped to improve how we work with groups.

The group leader's request for permission to take notes leads a member to get to the core issue for all of them: was this part of the assessment process?

> Mr. Aronson wondered if what they said was confidential or part of the assessment of them. I replied that the groups are part of the total study and process of getting to know them, but the recording as we would use it would not identify anyone. It will be about how we work in a group and not thoughts and feelings they were expressing. The group members laughed. I asked if they felt free to move ahead. They nodded and said yes.
>
> Mr. Thomas began by asking how long it takes to get a child and what the ratio of applicants to children is. Mrs. Thomas followed his question by asking when they would know if they were approved. I explained that we try to let people know what we are thinking all along. Adoption brings happiness to many, but it's not right for everyone. I also explained the contacts we would have with them following the group sessions.

The group members' response to this opening was to move immediately into questions of criteria and procedures involved in adopting. After some discussion, the focus shifted once again to a more general discussion rather than the specific concerns of the couples. In addition to dealing with the authority theme (the leader's role and authority in the decision-making process), the counselor must stress that the purpose of the group is to deal with the concerns and feelings of the preadoptive parents. Sometimes, group leaders have a different purpose and view the group as a medium for "educating" the parents. They then develop set agendas for a preadoptive parent "curriculum." For example, such a counselor might begin by discussing "how to tell your child he is adopted," even though all the couples are awaiting infants who will not need to be told for a number of years.

As one listens to such discussions with an ear for the themes important to these couples in their immediate situation, one can often hear subtle undercurrents. For example, when they discuss whether the child will love them as parents once the child knows about being adopted, they are often indirectly expressing their own concerns about how they will feel toward an adopted child—whether they will be able to love the child as if the child were their own.

Even though the counselor has been honest about the judging function, the group will still need help to enter taboo areas. They will need support to open up potentially difficult and dangerous subjects, yet these are precisely the concerns they need to share to discover that they are all in the same boat. Once the counselor is clear that the group is offered to the couples as clients in their own right, then attention can be directed to their concerns. One way to do this would be to raise examples—what we have called handles for work—and to emphasize the fact that simply sharing these concerns would not disqualify a couple from adoption. In fact, the honesty of the couple in facing these issues might make them even more desirable as adoptive parents.

Preadoption Group: Dealing with Friends and Relatives

In the next example, the counselor's empathetic responses open up an important discussion about how friends and relatives respond to the adoption. The supportive atmosphere established by the counselor has encouraged members to share problems rather than to attempt to convince the counselor that everything is going well.

MRS. THOMAS: We have a problem with a grandmother who is against the idea of adoption, but we feel that once a child is placed with us, she'll love the child the same as she does the others.

MRS. CHARLES: People can change their opinions also. When my husband's grandmother first heard of me being adopted, she regarded it as very hush-hush. Now that she knows that we are adopting a child, she thinks it's great—she's going to be a great-grandmother, and she is very thrilled about that.

MR. CHARLES: At work, many people are asking me how the adoption is proceeding.

COUNSELOR: What do you say?

MR. CHARLES: I say that we're going to more meetings. (Laughter)

MRS. KURTZ: It's a necessary thing in getting ready for adoptive parenthood.

COUNSELOR: Are many of you feeling that this is a hard way to get a baby?

MR. KURTZ: It's more difficult; it's easier to have your own.

MRS. KURTZ: For you men, maybe. (Laughter)

MRS. CHARLES: What I find so difficult is not knowing how long we'll have to wait. When a woman is pregnant, she knows it's 9 months, but this way, it's unknown just how long it will be.

MRS. GARVIN: I was taking a friend's baby for a walk, and someone said to me, "Don't you wish it was yours?"

COUNSELOR: How do you feel when people say things like that?

MRS. GARVIN: It bugs me.

MRS. THOMAS: They're giving you a dig, don't you think? People ask at work, "When are you having a family?" and "Are you pregnant?" It bothers and hurts me, too, but they don't seem to realize it.

MR. GARVIN: Even my brothers-in-law, who are really good fellows, they tease me about why we aren't having any children. I know that they're kidding, but on a down day, it can hurt.

MRS. THOMAS: Have you told anyone it hurts? I told a friend that it hurt me when he kept asking about us having children. He is a reference for us, and now he is the most interested and considerate person to talk to about our adoption. He's always asking me how things are going with the adoption, and he seems to really care.

MRS. KURTZ: I like the way you said that.

COUNSELOR: I think it's good that you were able to say that it does hurt.

MRS. THOMAS: It's a door closed if a couple are not able to have children born to them. You feel so alone and that you're the only person that this has ever happened to. My husband and I both love children so much, and we've always wanted to have children, and when we think of a life ahead of us with just the two of us, it seems so shallow. We have to adopt, and that's why we are nervous. We were nervous when Mrs. Smith came to our home because we want to be accepted—this is our only way.

Chapter Summary

In this chapter, the term *family* included a wide range of associations, many of which do not fit the traditional two-parent-family image. The increasing number of single-parent families, as well as families headed by gay or lesbian partners, has broadened our understanding of the concept of family. The unique aspects of working with couples or family members in groups were described including the fact that the group members bring a history, family culture, roles, and more to the first session and have significant intersession contact. A number of models suggested by family therapists were reviewed and their implications for working with family members in groups elaborated.

Some of the unique aspects of group work with couples and multifamily groups were also explored. Added to the complication of attending to each member of the group as well as the group-as-a-whole, the leader must observe the interaction of the couple or family system within the group.

Examples discussed in this chapter included work with

- multiple-family groups for family therapy, psychoeducational purposes, and community crises;
- married couples attempting to strengthen or save their marriage;
- single parents designed to help them cope with the unique problems they have; and
- preadoptive couples helping them explore the issues that they face as they make the decision to bring a child into their lives.

The argument was made that working with couples or families in a group introduced a number of variant elements, but the basic core principles of group practice would still guide the group leader.

Related Online Content and Activities

For learning tools such as glossary terms, InfoTrac® College Edition keywords, links to related websites, and chapter practice quizzes, visit this book's website at **www.cengage.com/counseling/shulman.**

CHAPTER 17

Group Counseling in Community Mental Health Settings

What Do Group Counselors Do in Community Mental Health Settings?

The U.S. Department of Labor's (2008–2009) *Occupational Outlook Handbook* describes the work of counselors in this area as follows:

> *Mental health counselors* work with individuals, families, and groups to address and treat mental and emotional disorders and to promote mental health. They are trained in a variety of therapeutic techniques used to address issues, including depression, addiction and substance abuse, suicidal impulses, stress, problems with self-esteem, and grief. They also help with job and career concerns, educational decisions, issues related to mental and emotional health, and family, parenting, marital, or other relationship problems. Mental health counselors often work closely with other mental health specialists, such as psychiatrists, psychologists, clinical social workers, psychiatric nurses, and school counselors.

The American Mental Health Counselors Association (www.amhca.org) describes mental health counseling as follows:

> Mental health counseling is a distinct profession with national standards for education, training and clinical practice.

The American Mental Health Counselors Association (AMHCA) is the professional membership organization that represents the mental health counseling profession. Clinical membership in AMHCA requires a master's degree in counseling or a closely related mental health field and adherence to AMHCA's National Standards for Clinical Practice.

Graduate education and clinical training prepare mental health counselors to provide a full range of services for individuals, couples, families, adolescents and children. The core areas of mental health programs approved by the Council for Accreditation of Counseling and Related Educational Programs (CACREP) include:

- Diagnosis and psychopathology
- Psychotherapy
- Psychological testing and assessment
- Professional orientation
- Research and program evaluation
- Group counseling
- Human growth and development
- Counseling theory
- Social and cultural foundations
- Lifestyle and career development
- Supervised practicum and internship

AMHCA points out that counselors practice in a number of settings providing a full range of services:

Mental health counselors practice in a variety of settings, including independent practice, community agencies, managed behavioral health care organizations, integrated delivery systems, hospitals, employee assistance programs and substance abuse treatment centers. Mental health counselors are highly skilled professionals who provide a full range of services including:

- Assessment and diagnosis
- Psychotherapy
- Treatment planning and utilization review
- Brief and solution-focused therapy
- Alcoholism and substance abuse treatment
- Psychoeducational and prevention programs
- Crisis management

With community mental health counselors working in many different roles, with a wide range of clients and client issues, within so many different settings, it is hard to define and illustrate their range of work in one chapter. For example, group practice can take place in counseling agencies, outpatient clinics, day treatment facilities, and community centers for the elderly. These settings may be government agencies (e.g., state or county) or not-for-profit private contract agencies dependent on government or community funding. Group counseling can also take place as part of a private practice of an individual counselor or a counseling group. While all settings and populations cannot be illustrated in this chapter, selected examples will include the following:

- An outpatient teen psychiatric group
- A group for depressed men and women with relationship problems
- A pain and stress management group for veterans in an outpatient clinic
- A fathers' group for men with children attending a clinic for behavior problems
- A group for visually impaired elderly when a member dies

Each of these groups will introduce themes of concern associated with the mental health problems as well as group dynamics and group leadership issues. Once again, I will share the work of novice and experienced group counselors so the reader can see how reflective practice leads to more skillful group leadership.

Group Counseling with Troubled Teenagers

Gladding (2003) points out that adolescence, which he defines as the age span from 13 to 19, is a difficult period in the life of many young people.

> Young adults during this time grow up physically and mature mentally, but they struggle with psychological and social issues related to their growth and development. . . . Adolescents are expected to behave as adults in their relationships with their peers and adults. They are given some adult privileges, such as obtaining a driver's license and registering to vote. However, most adolescents experience frustration and stress in being independent, on one hand, and yet dependent on their parents and school/community authorities on the other. Some of their turmoil may also be exacerbated by teens officially being denied some of the most tempting status symbols of adulthood such as sanctioned sex and the legal consumption of alcohol. (p. 275).

Adolescents in the examples that follow have to deal with an extraordinary number of developmental tasks and issues. Malekoff (1997) describes them as follows:

- Separating from family: includes testing and experimentation in relationships with adults and authority figures, in pursuit of emotional independence, increased autonomy, and more intimacy with peers;
- Forging a healthy sexual identity: includes body image, self-esteem, capacity for making safe and healthy choices, developing social roles;
- Preparing for the future: including skill development, career exploration, relationship development and planning;
- Developing a moral value system: includes forming and assessing values and ethical beliefs to guide socially responsible behaviors. (p. 24)

The members of the group described next have to deal with all of these issues and at the same time address the stigma associated with mental illness and mental illness treatment. This stigma can be difficult for anyone at any age, but when one considers how important peer acceptance is during this period of developing one's identity and how intensely teenagers feel the impact of inclusion or exclusion from the peer group, accepting a psychiatric diagnosis is understandably difficult.

Outpatient Teen Psychiatric Group

Purpose: To provide education and support to teenagers referred by their psychiatrist to an outpatient psychiatric setting

Gender/Age of Members: Mixed; age range: 14–18

Cultural, Racial, or Ethnic Identification of Members: Caucasian, African American, and Hispanic

PRACTICE POINTS

In earlier chapters, I have stressed the importance of working with the two clients, the individual and the group. In reality, it is not possible to deal with them as separate entities. The following example is a report of a group leader's efforts, over time, to help a group develop a "structure and culture for work." She does this by paying consistent attention to the individual–group connection. The time period covered is 6 weeks. Once again, the deviant member, Dave, plays an important role in expressing the feelings of the other group members.

Description of the Problem

The group members' struggle to share real feelings with each other is an ongoing process. Dave often expresses the widely held feelings of the group, communicating indirectly by being loud and overactive, and by doing so hiding the deep feelings behind his actions. On occasion he alienates group members. His anxiety and concerns are similar to what each member is feeling, so I hoped I could reach beyond his behavior to help Dave communicate and relate effectively to the group, and also help the group see past Dave's behavior to the commonality of their feelings.

How the Problem came to the Attention of the Group Leader(s)

At our first session, all of the group members were uptight. Dave's uncooperative behavior was the manifestation of all the members' anxiety. Both verbally and nonverbally, he brought up many of the concerns of the group. For instance, the day the group started, all members were sitting on cushions on the floor. However, Dave perched on a table and refused to sit on the floor. "I'm here just to listen—I won't be doing any talking. My psychiatrist made me come to this group." Thus, Dave started to articulate concerns felt by all members:

The concern of being involved with a psychiatrist—Am I nuts?

Is this a group for crazies?

I'm not going to share my feelings with anyone here, it's too risky.

Am I going to be accepted by other group members?

I am here involuntarily.

I felt that if I could reach beyond the behavior to bring out the common feelings of all the group members, Dave could become an important ally to me in the group.

PRACTICE POINTS Note that taking this attitude in the first session helps the leader avoid the not uncommon struggle to convince the members that they are here for a reason. Instead, she understands Dave's comment to represent the resistance and fears of the group and tries to generalize its meaning.

Summary of the Work

First Session

The first week of the group, when Dave made his comment "I'm just here to listen—I won't be doing any talking. My psychiatrist made me come to this group," I was in a dilemma as to which lead to take, he had given me so many. I turned to him, saying, "Yeah, it is tough, isn't it, when you come into a group like this and you don't know anyone." There was a slight pause. Dave said, "Yeah." I tried again and said, "I guess all of you were wondering and maybe feeling anxious about what the kids were going to be like in the group." Connie jumped in and said, "You know I figured you had to be whacko to be in this group." Wanda agreed, "I really thought this was a group for crazy kids, you know, but when I walked in— you all looked—well, normal." I said that it's hard to come to any group, but especially at a psychiatry clinic, and I could understand them being concerned. Several other members agreed, and Brian said it was easier now that he had met the others.

PRACTICE POINTS The group leader picks up nicely on the theme of being seen as "crazy" and by articulating it helps the members begin to feel more comfortable. She correctly read that part of Dave's message. A further discussion of the central theme—that is, the stigma associated with being involved with psychiatric treatment—will need to be further explored. A second issue also raised by Dave, being mandated to come by their psychiatrists, is left unexplored. The underlying authority theme, described in earlier chapters, emerges indirectly as once again, Dave, leads the way opening up the discussion of psychiatrists and social workers who just don't understand. Indirectly, the group members are asking if this group leader will understand. The mandated nature of the group and the authority theme will be acted out in the group until the leader addresses it.

Second Session

The concern with the authority theme was especially apparent in our first few weeks. Dave, as usual, had a greater sense of urgency and neatly brought it to the fore. He marched into the group session the second week and said, "Anyone mind if I lead the group today?" No objections. "Good, we won't allow psychiatrists in." I asked Dave what he meant. "My psychiatrist is about to drive me crazy. I just saw her for an hour." I asked what it was about his psychiatrist that made him feel that way. "Well, she lays trips on me." I asked if other people felt the same way. They all nodded. "I can't talk to my social worker," said Connie. "I can't talk to people who haven't done drugs or gotten drunk," said Gayle. "They don't treat us like we know what we're doing," said Chris.

PRACTICE POINTS The group leaders pick up on the indirect communications of the teens who are wondering what kind of helpers they will be. Even though the group members do not immediately respond, they have heard the counselors and know that this taboo subject can be open for discussion.

I said, "Are you afraid Tom [co-therapist] and I won't treat you as if you know what you're doing?" (Silence.) I added that it was important that they all understood that this was their group, and we were here to help them talk to each other, and listen, and maybe give suggestions, but not to dump on them. The group did not take me up right away on this.

PRACTICE POINTS In the next session, we see the teenage struggle described earlier between independence and dependence, particularly in relation to parents. The group leaders suggest a parents' night, which evokes immediate resistance from Dave who appears to have fully accepted the role of the internal leader. It's interesting to note that Dave, who at first resisted the idea of the group, now describes it as "our group." Once again, the process-content connection becomes obvious as the group leaders skillfully explore the process—their rejection of a parents' night—and the content—their relationship to parents. Note also that the leaders see their roles as helping the "group" negotiate the system, the clinic, and do so by representing their concerns about the policy of requiring parents' nights. The leaders also explore the feelings under the rejection of a parents' night.

Fourth Session

A few weeks later, Tom and I raised the idea of having a parents' night (a clinic policy) where the parents came and participated in the group. The group was immediately against this and, led by Dave, unanimously voted against our suggestion. "This is our group," Dave said. "If we don't want to have a parents' night, we won't have it." I said I'd clear it with the head of the clinic that we would not plan a parents' night, as the group didn't feel they wanted it. I did so over the next week.

Later, I explored what it was about having parents come that the group didn't like. "I wouldn't say a word," said Gayle, "I can't talk to my parents." Chris said, "I always fight with my parents, and we'd get into a big battle." "My parents wouldn't come," said Tracy. "Sounds like most of you have real difficulties talking to your parents," I said. "No kidding" was the generally fervent reply. I asked Gayle to tell us a bit of what goes on at home for her. Gayle started talking and led us into an excellent discussion of problems with parents. Several of the members made suggestions to Gayle about how she could do things differently.

PRACTICE POINTS In the fifth session the group members begin to address the intimacy theme—the relationship between members. The group leader has built up a fund of positive relationship and can now draw upon it by gently confronting Dave on his pattern of behavior. It is also interesting that Dave acts out by singing nursery rhymes, which can be seen as immature and childish behavior. The critical issue to adolescence of acceptance in the peer group emerges. While the focus is on Dave, all of the members struggle with this question, especially having been identified as needing psychiatric intervention. Note how the leader inquires as to the meaning of Dave's behavior.

Fifth Session

Dave was seeking attention, singing nursery rhymes into the microphone and being flippant. The group members were trying to ignore him. I confronted him on his behavior. "Dave, it seems you act out just to bug the group, but I'm sure something's going on." Gayle said, "Dave talks too much. He always seems to be doing something. I bet he's not showing his real self." Chris suggested, "Maybe he's insecure." I said, "Dave, I'm sure it bothers you that people are getting angry with you. Is it something to do with being accepted in here? It seems you set yourself up to get put down." No reply. Gayle said, "You want us to know you and like you; you won't admit it, but it's true." Gayle had hit it beautifully, whereas I had missed the right words.

Dave looked at her, and quietly said, "I guess you're right. I guess I feel uptight when I come in here." I then added I was sure each person was feeling what Dave was feeling; he just showed it differently. Gayle said, "Sure, I wonder what you guys think when I talk." I said that perhaps the group could help each other in that regard. I said I thought it was important for them to recognize that they were all wondering about each other, and that they were all tense, and each of them understood how hard it was to really express how they were feeling.

<hr>

PRACTICE POINTS

As the group reaches the halfway point, the leaders skillfully ask the members to reflect on how things have been going as well as to give them feedback on their roles. They also start the process of thinking about the endings, which will only be five sessions away. This gives the members and the leaders the time needed to make sure the ending is experienced as a process and not a rude shock, as described in Part 1.

Through the weeks, I had been encouraging the group to give feedback to Tom and me. At the fifth session, I said, "OK, we're halfway through our sessions now, and we'd really like some feedback on the group, what we've done, where we're going." I said sometimes I felt frustrated at the flight behavior and sometimes their rambunctious moods. The group started to talk about the help they gave each other and how they felt. A constructive mutual exchange occurred. I said I thought they should know that after the group ended, Tom and I would no longer be at the clinic. They asked what would be happening. We explained. I said it would be hard for us to leave and hard for the group to end because I felt really good about the work we had all done together. There was a silence. Then the group began to deal carefully with the ending.

<hr>

PRACTICE POINTS

By pointing out the impending endings, the leaders have begun the process of dealing with termination and transition so that they have time to address the various common phases: denial, anger, sadness, trying it on for size, and so on. As the group is approaching the ending, the doorknob therapy phenomenon described earlier will result in the members starting to address the more difficult issues. With the help of the group leader, playing the role of mediating between the individual (Dave) and the group, the growing ability to provide mutual aid to each other becomes apparent.

Sixth Session

Dave was flippant and inappropriate more than usual. He obviously had something on his mind. I confronted Dave: "You're really high today, Dave, bouncing all over the room. What's going on?" The group picked up my use of the word *high*, and a discussion ensued on whether Dave was stoned or not. I asked the group to get back to the question. I said maybe it would help for all of us to talk about what was going on for Dave, even if it was hard. The group settled down and waited. I said we knew by now that when Dave had something on his mind he got really hyped and so communicated his uptightness by being noisy, and that we hoped he could feel he could talk to us.

Chris picked that up and encouraged Dave to talk: "Is something going on, Dave?" Connie said, "What's going on?" (Pause) Dave looked down. Then he said, "I moved yesterday." I encouraged him to continue. "I moved from Franklin House into a foster home." I commented that was a big move. "Well," Dave said, "I was in Franklin House for 8 months. I really liked it there." I tuned in to his feelings of loss, "It hurts, doesn't it, when you have to leave someplace familiar? You've had a lot of moves." Chris asked what it was like to move into a foster home. The group began to reach out supportively to Dave.

PRACTICE POINTS The group has learned to read Dave's behavior and to reach for the message behind it. This thoughtful and caring addressing of his anxiety is not lost on the other members. It creates a new level of trust that allows other important but difficult issues to emerge. The group leader's persistence in pointing out what is happening in the group (the process) pays off as in the next excerpt group members are able to find a capacity for caring and mutual aid in responding to Carol instead of just ignoring her because of her difficult speech.

Ingrid, sitting quietly in the corner, was confronted by Chris about never speaking in the group. Ingrid felt put on the spot and was able to say so. I asked her what made it hard for her to talk in the group. She said there were too many people around. I guessed she wasn't used to talking in a group, probably not even in school. She said right. Tracy agreed, and said it was easier for her to talk to friends at school whom she saw every day. Chris said sometimes she felt her problems weren't very important and not worth talking about. There was a thoughtful silence.

PRACTICE POINTS In the powerful excerpt that follows, we see the group leader implementing the mediating role described repeatedly in this book by searching out the common ground between members. In this case, it is the fear of the members of being laughed at and not liked by other teens.

Then Carol, who has a speech difficulty that makes her almost incomprehensible, started talking. It was the first time she had spoken in the group. She said she felt uncomfortable talking in the group because she was afraid she'd get laughed at. There was a long silence. I said, "I guess Carol's really hit the nail on the head for all of us, eh?" There were nods. Chris said, "No one will laugh; we're here to help each other." I said, "The concerns you have, Carol, are the same as the feelings Ingrid has, but she expressed them by being quiet. Dave, on the other hand, is loud. You are each wondering how the others will react." Gayle asked, "What can we do to make it easier?" Carol said she felt worse because she felt the group couldn't understand her speech. Tom said that if she spoke really slowly that we could all pitch in and help. The group started shouting encouragement to each other. I said I guess they were all feeling the same inside, even if it showed in different ways, and if they knew that, maybe it would be easier to talk, to take the risk. They all laughed and agreed.

PRACTICE POINTS The following excerpt, in which the group leader points out that the members have stopped listening to Carol, requires a high level of trust in the members and skill. It would be so understandable if the leader let this drop because of not wanting to hurt Carol. However, Carol is already hurt and the leader's ignoring the group's response replicates the very behavior she faces all the time. Note the tremendous power of teens to care for and help each other—even, perhaps especially, teens who themselves are troubled.

Seventh Session

Carol, painfully, was talking. She was difficult to understand. Dave decided he wanted to talk about points of interest, rather than difficulties. The group started talking about their various weekends. I said to the group, "How come you changed so quickly from listening to Carol?" There was an uncomfortable silence. I said I had noticed that they became restless when Carol spoke, and it seemed as if they felt uncomfortable listening to her. Carol started crying and said it was the same as at school—no one understood her. Chris asked Carol how long she had her speech difficulty. Carol said since birth. The group started to reach out for her. Dave said he had a hard time understanding her, and the group agreed. Brian said, "Let's make sure that Carol has the opportunity to speak." Gayle said, "I guess it's hard to talk about difficult things for all of us, but with Carol, it's doubly difficult to talk about difficult things." I agreed, but said I thought they were doing a great job at this point. (Crediting the work)

PRACTICE SUMMARY

The power of the peer group to hurt, block the work, and create tremendous stress for teenagers is matched by the power of the group to heal. Of all age groups, mutual aid between teens and peers has the potential not only to help the individual, such as Carol, but also to help each member as they discover their ability to care for others and to transform these positive emotions into skills of living as they reach out to help. These skills will be important to them in all areas of their lives, as friends, partners, parents, children, and other roles. The mutual aid support group is a place to discover their inherent caring for others and a place to practice.

Group Counseling with Adult Clients with Relationship Problems

There are different approaches to organizing groups for adults (and others), including structured "topic-oriented" groups. According to Corey and Corey (2006):

> Topic-oriented groups have many advantages for adults. If topics reflect the life issues of the participants, they can be powerful catalysts. Several factors must be considered if you decide to structure your groups around topics, but perhaps the most important is to think about the common developmental life concerns characteristic of the group membership. The topics selected also reflect the main goals of the group. (pp. 364–365)

An alternative approach is to have the topics flow from the day-to-day experiences of the group members so that the focus of each session is guided by the sense of urgency of the members and the ability to find commonality in their experiences. In the example that follows, individual members bring their current life experiences to the group; as these are explored in some detail, the group leader is able to discern the "topic" and helps generalize it to the other members.

Chen and Ryback (2004) point out that most problems faced by adults are interpersonal in nature.

> All humans have an inner drive to search, in one way or another, for happiness. At times that search leads them to seek answers in counseling or therapy. People

use counseling or therapy for many different reasons. They may feel isolated or depressed. They may be having problems with their spouse, coworkers, or other significant others. They may have a taxing issue that holds them back from building the lives they desire. (p. 12)

For many adult clients, maladaptive patterns of relating to other adults, friends, family members, partners, and so forth, such as the unreasonable expectations that others should "devine" what they are thinking and feeling, are at the core of their problems. These modes of behavior can be formed early in their development and reinforced by dysfunctional family life. Many adults lack the skills of living that are very similar to the professional skills described in Part 1. The capacity to tune in, emphasize, confront, understand "deviant behavior," be honest in expression of one's feelings and concerns—all of these and others make for healthy interactions with persons we care about or even those we work alongside. If our early family models (e.g., parents) did not practice these skills in their family roles, it is not surprising that for many adults they need to be learned or relearned.

A first issue in groups such as this is to help the participants move past the tendency to externalize and blame others for their problems and the associated feelings. The group leader needs to empathize with the expressed perceptions and feelings, because they are real to the members, but it is also important not to get stuck in a spiral of depression and hopelessness. An important transition from blaming others to taking responsibility for one's own behavior is crucial for success in improving interpersonal relationships. A guiding principle is that although you can't change someone else's behavior, you are in control of your own.

The group itself can become a medium for learning about how one relates to others and for practicing the skills needed in the outside-the-group world. As illustrated in the next example, by looking at the process in the group, the leader can help members make the connection to the relationship problems that initially brought them to the group. In effect, the group member acts out the problem in the group almost as if to say, "Do you want to see how I get messed up in my relationships? Watch!"

It is important to distinguish this attention to process as different from a preoccupation with process. By that I refer to models described in Part 1 in which the discussion of group process and member interaction appears to be the sole purpose of the group. These are sometimes referred to as T groups or encounter or process groups. While much can be learned by members by considering how they act in such a group without an external purpose—a task—the process often becomes artificial. In this case, the task is to learn how to improve relationships outside the group in the members' real worlds; however, reflection on the internal process can help members to accomplish this goal.

A Group for Depressed Men and Women with Relationship Problems

Purpose: This group was offered in a community-based family agency to provide education and support to adults who are experiencing problems in their relationships to friends, partners, and family members and an associated state of depression.

Members: The five women and two men in the group, between the ages of 20 and 35, were separated, divorced, or widowed. All of them had experienced heavy depression and difficulties in their interpersonal relationships.

Cultural, Racial, or Ethnic Identification of Members: Caucasian and African American

In the session that follows, one member raises a conflict with a separated husband for discussion. Note in particular as the leader encourages elaboration, what was actually said and how the presenter felt, the other group members will get an idea of how this member related to her separated husband and how she was partly responsible for the results. This is an example of the middle stage skill of elaboration and the particular version of the skill I called "moving from the general to the specific." Instead of having a general conversation of her relationship with her separated husband, the group leader pushes for the details of the conversation.

At the same time, by calling attention to how she related to group members in the here and now of the group, this behavior could be related to her general relationship issues. The emerging issue is the not uncommon communication problem in which we are indirect at best in our communications and expect significant others in our life to divine how we feel without telling them. We are then upset when they have not figured it out. A not uncommon expression is "He/she should have known I would be upset."

The session began with a young woman, Sheila, asking for help. The first response from group members was to offer consolation. The leader asked for elaboration while offering empathic support.

> Sheila suddenly broke in and in a choked voice said, "I am feeling so down tonight." Bob quickly responded, "You, too?" Sheila continued that she had called Don in Montreal; he had been busy and had not wanted to talk to her. I said, "You sound very hurt." Tears filled her eyes, and Sheila said, "Yes, I am. I blew up and acted like a baby, and now I have to apologize when he comes down on Saturday." Roberta and Bob rushed in to support Sheila saying they would be hurt, too, if they called someone and he was too busy to listen. Libby nodded but said nothing. I asked Sheila why she had called and why she blew up. She softly and sadly replied that she had called Don because she was lonely. Evelyn questioned if she had told Don this. Sheila hadn't. Bob asked why. Sheila smiled and said, "That wasn't the only reason I telephoned. I sometimes call to check up and see if he is really working." Roberta said, "You can't dwell on the fact that he had an affair, and Joan is going to have his baby."
>
> Sheila began to talk about Don and Joan and the baby. I suggested, after listening a few minutes, that it seemed to me that Sheila's relationship with Don right now was important, rather than again talking about what had happened in the past. I asked the others in the group, "What do you think?"

The leader refused to allow Sheila to discuss ground that had already been covered in group. Instead, she made a demand for work by focusing Sheila on the here-and-now details of her discussion with Don. A major step in such work involves asking the group members to take some responsibility for their part in their problems. Our defenses often cause us to explain our problems by projecting the blame onto others in our lives or justifying the present difficulty by describing past reasons. In this case, the leader focused the group member and the group on the immediate situation in the belief that this was the only way to help. The member's responses elaborated on the specifics of the concern.

> Sheila did not wait for a response and replied directly to me, "I feel so tense. I don't know what to talk to Don about. I don't want it to be like it was before we separated." I said, "You sound scared to death." Sheila became very sad and nodded. Evelyn added, "I have felt the same way with Jacques. I was his shadow. When he left and moved in with a girlfriend, I thought I could not exist on my own. I have learned to do so. Sheila, you talk as if you had no life of your own." Libby continued, "Do you always do what Don wants?"

Sheila then revealed the reason she was angry on the telephone with Don. She had earlier thought of going on a trip to England on her own and had wanted Don to say no. He had not, and when financially she had been unable to make the trip, she had called Don expecting him to be very happy that she was staying. He was busy and had not said much. Sheila had then accused him of not caring and hung up crying.

PRACTICE POINTS As the details emerged, so did a fuller picture of the problem. The leader recognized a common problem in intimate relationships—that is, one partner feels that the other should divine what she is feeling and wants to hear and then is hurt when it is not forthcoming. This is a specific example of the general problem of the difficulty of risking oneself by sharing real thoughts, feelings, and needs directly with those who are important to us. As a group member began to provide feedback to Sheila on her part in the proceedings, she cut him off, and the leader moved quickly to point this out. The process-content connection is clear as Sheila recognizes that she is acting in the group the way she acts with Don.

Bob started to say that Sheila had put Don on the spot, when Sheila interrupted and continued talking. I stopped her and said to the group, "Did you notice what just happened?" Everyone except Sheila and Bob smiled but said nothing. I said to Sheila, "Bob was trying to say something to you when you cut him off." She cut in to say anxiously, "Did I? I'm sorry, Bob." Bob quietly said, "My God, I didn't even notice. It has happened to me so often I guess I just expected to be cut off." She picked this up and said Don and Bob were alike and that Don let her get away with talking too much and cutting him off. Roberta commented, "Don seems hard to get close to," and there followed a few more comments on how Don seemed unapproachable.

PRACTICE POINTS The leader then challenged Sheila's view of the event and asked her to take some responsibility for creating part of the problem. Because the leader had already built a positive working relationship with the group members, Sheila was able to accept the confrontation and to examine her own actions. As the group members worked on the details of this specific example, it is easy to see how they were also working on their own variations on the theme. Note that the group leader has built up a supportive relationship with Sheila, a form of a "bank account" that the leader can now draw upon by directly confronting Sheila with her pattern of behavior with Don and the group members.

I then went back to Sheila's telephone call and asked Sheila why she had called Don at work when he was likely to be busy, rather than calling him at home. She stumbled around and didn't answer the question. I kept pressing her with the same question and then asked the group if they had any ideas on this. Bob said, "I don't know what you are getting at." I said, "Let me check this out with all of you. My feeling is that Sheila called Don when she knew he would be likely to be busy and set it up so that he would probably be annoyed with her. Once again, she gets very hurt." Evelyn added, "You did that with Don around the trip. Had he told you not to go to England, you would have been angry. If he told you to go, you would have said he did not care. I did the same thing with Jacques, and I never knew what I wanted. I was the little girl who asked her father's permission for everything."

Sheila said, "I guess I set things up so that I am the sad little girl and everyone feels sorry for me, just like I am trying to do tonight. How do I stop?" Bob said, "How do we stop hating ourselves—that is what it comes down to." Sheila continued thoughtfully, "You know I took the job at the airline so that Don and I could travel, and he really doesn't like traveling. I also bought him a bicycle to go cycling, but then found out he hates it." I said, "It sounds like you assume things about Don but somehow never check them out with him. How come?" There was a short silence, and I continued, "Is it because when, as Bob said, we hate ourselves, we are too scared to say what we feel or want?"

PRACTICE POINTS The leader has picked up on the member's comment about self-hatred and how the way we feel about ourselves affects how we act, which in turn impacts how we feel. It can be a vicious cycle needing to be broken. Self-reflection and recognizing the pattern is a first step.

Sheila talked about how horrible and stupid she feels she is, and the group members gave her much support. They also reminded her of the one area where she feels she has accomplished something—teaching piano. She brightened and talked of her love of music and how she enjoyed teaching.

Roberta then remarked on how much everyone needs to be told they do some things well. She recounted an incident at work where she had been praised and how pleased she was. The others in the group, except Libby, agreed. She said it depended on whether or not you believed it. Sheila agreed and stated it was hard for her to accept praise. Evelyn went back to Sheila's relationship with Don, saying Sheila had given indications that she knew the marriage was breaking up, although she had said Don's decision to separate was a complete surprise. Sheila said she partly knew but did not want to admit it to herself. She had been withholding sexually, although they had had good sexual relations prior to marriage. I asked if she often gets angry at Don, and Sheila replied angrily, "I get furious at him, but I end up being bitchy, which I don't like. I am also scared he will leave." As the end of the group session was approaching, the members began making some suggestions around dealing with Don on the weekend. She should be a little more independent, say what she is feeling and not always what she thinks she should say.

PRACTICE SUMMARY As the group members work on a specific problem, leaders should share their own thoughts and ideas that may help place the problem in a new perspective. To do this, they must draw upon their own life experience, the information they have gathered by working with people, either individually or in groups, who have had similar concerns, and the professional literature. For example, in the previous example, group members were learning something about taking responsibility for one's own actions, the difficulties involved in interpersonal communications, and specific interactional skills that might promote more effective interpersonal relationships.

These agenda items were set in the context of their own experiences as they explored their often mixed feelings about themselves and others. Group leaders frequently provide data (information, values, observations, etc.) that may be unavailable to group members and may provide help with the problem or issue of the moment. In working with a couples' group, for example, the leader could draw upon communications theory, "fair fighting in marriage" ideas, developmental life theory, game model theory, gestalt, and other orientations. As leaders deepen their own life experiences, as they use group leadership experiences to learn more about the complexities of life, and as they review the literature, they can enrich their contributions to the group members' struggles.

Groups for Management of Chronic Pain and Posttraumatic Stress

With a growing interest in noninvasive procedures and efforts to limit the use of pain medication, chronic pain management clinics and groups for this purpose have grown in use. The members of the next group were Vietnam veterans. However, with the significant increase in severely injured veterans surviving bombing and other forms of attack in the current wars in Iraq and Afghanistan, we have seen a rise in the number of returning soldiers with injuries that will lead to chronic pain as well as what we now understand as posttraumatic stress. We have also seen that for many in the military, admitting they need some form of counseling can be a problem. The norm of being able to handle everything by yourself and not taking help, especially emotional or counseling help, is just now being seriously recognized and challenged by the military.

Veterans' Outpatient Clinic

PRACTICE POINTS In this example, we see the use of group work as part of a larger pain management program. The group is structured as a psychoeducational group with information presented by experts in their respective areas. The student group leader uses this written exercise to focus on the apparent resistance of one member, George, who is sending nonverbal negative signals from the first group meeting.

Ages: 31–58

Dates Covered: October 3 to December 12

Group Purpose: This group consists of nine Caucasian men, all veterans, all suffering from chronic pain. The source of each man's pain differs, but they have come together to learn techniques for trying to decrease their constant, chronic pain.

Description of the Problem

At our first meeting, George sat as close to the door as he could and wore dark sunglasses and a baseball cap with the visor tilted down over his eyes. His arms were tightly clasped around his chest. The major problem that I could see immediately was George's nonverbal message that being in the group was difficult for him.

How the Problem Came to the Attention of the Group Leader(s)

Sitting as close as he did suggested to me that George was ready to race out of the room at any time. His dark sunglasses and cap, being worn in a room in an outpatient clinic, told me that he wanted to be invisible or perhaps that he wanted to observe this new group situation without being seen. By clutching his chest tightly with his arms, George was keeping himself safe and defended from this potentially dangerous group meeting.

Summary of the Work
First Session

I was quite nervous anticipating this first meeting. I was new to this setting and had only minimal contact with veterans. The members were all referred to the group by their primary doctors. The group's description was "pain management—coping with chronic pain." As we went through the introductions, it was clear that group members joined in order to be "free from pain." I told the group what I had in mind for our meetings. I gave them an overview of the "guest speakers" whom I had arranged to come to speak. Some of the people scheduled were a pharmacist and a nutritionist; other professionals, more experienced people than I, would be a part of some of our meetings. The scheduled "experts" would have concrete suggestions for these men in their struggle to deal with their pain. My role, as group leader, would be that of a discussion leader rather than an expert. When each veteran introduced himself in terms of his injuries, number of surgeries, and list of daily medications, I sensed a kind of contest was in play: Who hurt more? Who took more codeine?

PRACTICE POINTS
The initial contracting did suggest that the group would focus on pain relief. However, post-traumatic stress issues and how they relate to pain was also part of the group's purpose. The leader does not make this part clear, although from the record of the fifth session (of eight), it appears that group discussions did go beyond simple steps for pain relief. George, who sent signals of resistance in the first session, challenges this believing he was misled into a "therapy group." The novice group leader responds at first with defensive feelings.

Fifth Session

GEORGE: I was told this was gonna be a pain relief group—it seems to be more of a therapy group. This really pisses me off. I don't like opening up in this kind of setting, and my pain is just as bad as ever. (I felt angry at George. What did he want, anyway—a miracle? He made me feel that I had failed the group. I bet he makes people feel inadequate frequently. He has a powerful effect on me and the group. He's so angry. What exactly does he mean by "relief"? Can he give me concrete suggestions on what would be helpful to him?)

FRANK: No way this was supposed to be a "pain relief" group. I didn't expect any major pain relief.

LEADER: Frank, I hear you saying you didn't expect pain relief. But it sounds like George did expect relief from his pain. (I tried to validate both members' statements. "I'm sorry that this group hasn't filled your expectations, George." I then restated the goals for the group.)

PRACTICE POINTS
While the leader hides her initial anger at George's complaint, she fails to explore the reason behind the anger. What is it about "talking" about pain, not only in the group but with others in our lives, that gives George—and perhaps all of the members—such difficulty? She picks up on the pain relief rather than the talking. The leader does acknowledge George's anger but in relation to Ken. In reality, his anger toward the group was actually also hurtful to her. Her reflection on her being "punitive" is on target, but the reason is not. He made her angry and defensive. Thinking back to the earlier group theorists described in Part 1, for example Bion (1961), we see that the idea of projective identification may fit very nicely here. She is feeling what George is feeling and acting out.

LEADER: George, I know it's difficult for some of us to open up. I think you've shared quite a bit with this group.

KEN: What works for me is accepting what I can't change and being grateful for what's good in my life.

GEORGE: You a minister or something?

LEADER: George, you sound angry today. What makes you so angry? I think the remark you just made to Ken was hurtful. Ken, do you agree with me?

KEN: Not really—he has done it before. I'll get over it.

LEADER: I think I needed to restate the boundaries (maybe at the onset of each meeting, actually) so that members treat each other with respect in order to keep the group feeling safe. George needs these boundaries to feel more in control, and I must keep setting limits for him and also modeling respectful behavior myself. In hindsight, I wouldn't have been so punitive toward George and thus given the group the opportunity to speak to George's rudeness. I think I intervene too much.

GEORGE: To tell you the truth, I'd rather be alone than at this meeting getting picked on.

PRACTICE POINTS

Whereas the group leader sees George's comments as rude and needing control, another interpretation, one that integrates process and content, could understand his behavior as his demonstrating to the leader and the group how he handles his physical, and probably emotional, pain: by lashing out in anger. The leader is concerned about intervening too much when the real issue is what is the appropriate role for the leader and how to intervene in a manner that helps George connect with the group.

An alternative intervention by the leader might be "I suspect when the pain gets to be too much, for George and perhaps for all of you, it can lead to anger and perhaps acting angry with friends and family members as well. I wonder, George, when Ken talked about accepting what he can't change and focusing on what's good in life, did you feel he didn't really understand how hard that is for you to do that? Am I close?"

Instead, it is clear in her next comment that the leader is still feeling defensive and holding back her anger at George's remarks that she is taking personally. By sitting on her feelings instead of trying to express them more directly, she cuts herself off from her capacity for empathy and ends up suggesting that George take his problems to the individual therapist. Perhaps if she could have expressed some of her frustration at trying to help and just getting anger in return, she might have broken the cycle while demonstrating how to express hurt and angry feelings in an appropriate manner. If we reflect back on the discussion of Bion's (1961) theory of projective identification, that our clients may project their feelings on us in order to make us experience what they feel, then George has clearly gotten through to this group leader.

I felt quite insulted. Here I thought I was trying to help this guy, and all I get is angry barbs that I felt were directed toward me personally and professionally. "You sound really depressed today, George; more so than I've ever seen you. What would you think about discussing this with Cheryl?" (his individual therapist). I thought that by mentioning Cheryl, I might get him grounded. George responds to my suggestion, "Yeah, I'll ask her."

PRACTICE POINTS

As we approach the ending of the group, we see the adjustment that George has made and his beginning acceptance of the need for help. The leader starts the important evaluation discussion. Note, it is now "our man George" as the leader has also come to a new understanding of George's behavior.

Last Meeting

LEADER: Should we wait for the others?

GEORGE: Hell, no. They might not show up. They don't feel like us guys do about this group. I haven't missed once.

Our man, George, who started out with sunglasses on, a hat covering his eyes and great resistance, now is comfortable expressing his identification with the group. He had perfect attendance. "Before we have our farewell party, I'd like to hear from each of you about how these meetings were for you. And if you have any criticisms or suggestions for me."

George was the first to respond. "The first day, I really didn't want to be here—but Cheryl coaxed me to give it a try. I don't do well with groups—but I gotta tell you, it's been OK. I learned some stuff. My pain is not different, but I think I'm more relaxed. I'm sleeping much better." This is a certain sign that group helped. "George, it sounds like there were parts of being in the group that were helpful for you. I think you've been an important member of this group. You've shared your symptoms, coping skills, gripes—you've opened up a lot to this group. And yes I do remember you felt quite uncomfortable the first day and sat nearest the door. Remember?"

GEORGE: Yeah, I thought I'd have to make a quick exit, but I never did.

<table>
<tr><td>**PRACTICE POINTS**</td><td>George's comments indicate that we can't always judge how much a member is getting from a group. The open expression of negative feelings and anger may be just what the group member needed. It was also clearly related to his pain although not discussed in that way. It is not clear from the record why the leader asks the next question of Ken; however, it does evoke a powerful doorknob therapy response and opens up an important area of trauma for all of the members. It also, in hindsight, explains George's initial concern about the group being a "therapy" group.</td></tr>
</table>

LEADER: Ken, other than your brother, do you have any other family? (God, did I step on a minefield, unknowingly.)

KEN: No, he and I were orphaned when I was 6 months old and he was 19 months old. We lived in an orphanage until I was seven and he was eight. Then we were adopted by some people—they were terrible drunks, and I still don't understand why they took us in—Dave and me. We were better off in the orphanage. My adoptive parents beat us a lot, and the day I turned 17, I enlisted and never saw them again.

GEORGE: Hey, guy, me too! My father was a bastard, a mean drunk. Man, did I hate the guy. I never shed a tear when he kicked the bucket. I could never feel relaxed in my own house or my bedroom, 'cause I never knew when he was gonna make me take the trash out in the pouring rain or some idiot thing like that. He made me full of shame. I never had any friends because I was so ashamed of my father and his boozing.

(Here we were, in the last minutes of the group meetings, and the common theme of being adult children of alcoholics is just being brought to the surface.) I said, "Oh, George and Ken—it sounds like your early years were painful and full of shame."

FRANK: (Another member) We're still in pain. My father and mother were the drinking Bobbsey Twins. We six kids had to do all the stuff at home—even clean up their puke. I hated them both. They ruined me and my sisters. I'll never forgive them their drinking. They were bums and never should have had kids. I've tried to be a good husband and father and breadwinner all through my pain.

It's important to note that the group was not set up to deal with these other issues, and it would be important for the leader to "guard" the contract. However, she does make a nice connection between their painful personal experiences and the current experiences of pain. It might still be helpful to make referral possibilities available to the men to address these other issues that still haunt them. The positive experience in the group may help them seriously consider other sources of help for these issues that may still contribute to their stress and their ability to manage pain.

These men have many common experiences, including a painful childhood. This information will be helpful to me in preparing for subsequent groups—what are the common threads? I responded, "Yes, Frank, I can see that you've worked hard and your wife and daughters are very devoted to you. Wow, you men have been through your own personal wars and then you enlisted in the service and went to Vietnam, and now your legacy is chronic pain. Speaking for myself, I have a lot of feelings about you men. Firstly, respect for what you've endured lifelong. I also feel sadness. But more importantly, faith and hope that you are all willing to work on the pain management and stress relievers.

"There's very little we can do about your alcoholic parents and the scars they left on you. But one major technique for releasing those memories and maybe in the process, a little of your pain, is to talk about it. This hour today has been a very emotional time for me and I suspect for all of you. Forums such as this, after you've built up trust among each other, can be very healthy and kind of cleansing." Because we were terminating today, I praised them sincerely for their hard work and left them with some final suggestions. This may possibly be the first positive termination they've ever experienced.

Where the Problem Stands Now

This group became cohesive. They discovered they had much in common and shared willingly with one another. The member who progressed the most was George. He was talking in the last session about getting together with Ken to show him his collection of model airplanes (Ken was a bomber pilot). George was not hiding behind sunglasses or a hat with a visor. He still suffers with his pain daily, but I feel he will carry his feelings of success in this group with him for a long time. He trusted enough to share painful memories and discovered others had similar experiences. He is sleeping better, which certainly will improve the quality of his life overall.

After the final meeting of this group with the revelations that took place, I can certainly see how oppressed George has been his whole life. What looked to me initially like deviant behavior in the first meeting now looks like a maladaptive effort to protect himself. George has spent his life fighting. He became quite used to risking alienation due to his external persona. After this group experience, I predict that he will need his old defenses less, as he begins to trust more.

The disclosure of the alcoholic and abusive parents in the last meeting came as a surprise to the group leader. While the leader is correct that nothing can be done about this history, two areas of discussion might have been helpful in this last session. First, how did these childhood experiences affect how they handle or don't handle their anger over their pain? Second, they may want to consider sharing this information, if they have not already done so, with their individual therapists. Other groups that focus on helping adult children of alcoholics—groups that may be offered by professional associations as well as self-help groups offered in the community—may also be of use.

Groups for Parents and Caretakers

As we have seen in earlier chapters, some of the most important help we can give children is the help we provide for their parents and caretakers. While helping professionals may work with the children a limited number of times a week, the parents and caretakers are with them all the time. They provide the most important influence, and their ability to take care of themselves strengthens them in being able to care for the children. In the following example, clinic has provided a group for fathers whose children are attending a special clinic for behavior problems.

Fathers of Children Attending a Clinic for Behavior Problems

PRACTICE POINTS

In this example, the leader had noted a pattern of withdrawal by group members. He had observed indirect cues (e.g., facial expressions) of feelings toward Mr. Abrams, who had not shared his problems as the others had done. In addition, Mr. Wilson, who had spoken often, had hinted that he feared he might have been speaking too much. At the start of this session, a number of indirect cues led the leader to believe members were questioning the way the group operated. These signals indicated to the worker an issue in the intimacy theme—the way in which members related to each other. The two central members in the discussion are Mr. Wilson, who talks often, and Mr. Abrams, who does not freely share his problems and often seems defensive. By asking the group members to reflect on the intimacy theme and surfacing concerns and feelings about members' participation, they remove the block and the work deepens.

After a dispirited opening marked by a rambling discussion, the leader challenged the illusion of work by asking the group members to reflect on the way they worked as a group, explaining that he felt the discussion tended to be "impersonal" at times and that he thought they had reactions to each other's ways of participating. The group leader recognizes that conflict between members is often avoided in a group by members and the leader. When this happens, it goes beneath the surface and can lead to the illusion of work that is lacking in serious content and feeling. The leader takes the step of reaching for the underlying feelings.

> Mr. Wilson quickly challenged the view that the group should be personal. When I asked him to say a little bit more about this, he explained that he felt he could come here and talk about these things very objectively, but then he was pretty sure that he would never see these men during the week. He was supported very strongly in his feelings about the "impersonal" nature of the group by Mr. Lewis, Mr. Abrams, and Mr. Russel, with Mr. Moran playing a quiet, listening role. Mr. Moran still seemed to be a little bit confused about where this discussion would lead but said that he would prefer to sort of listen until he got the "hang of things."

PRACTICE POINTS

This is a piece of work many group leaders would like to avoid. Even after creating safety for members to confront them, the authority theme, group leaders have great hesitation about encouraging, even allowing, members to confront each other. It is not unusual to jump in at a point such as the one that follows and try to smooth out the interaction by defending members and calling for apologies or a minimizing of confrontation. It takes a while for leaders to have enough experience to understand that the emotions in the intimacy theme, the relationship between members, can provide the energy to make the work real and not an illusion.

I encouraged each of the three men, in addition to Mr. Wilson, to talk about how they saw this. All said that there was not much investment of feeling in the group, although each of them said that they certainly liked everyone who came and really looked forward to the sessions. At this point I wondered whether in addition to the feelings of liking and friendship, there might also be some feelings of dislike or perhaps some people whom they liked more than others. Mr. Russel was the first to comment on this, bringing out a great deal of his feeling, while looking at Mr. Abrams, about people who just rambled on about subjects and on the other hand persons who could really talk about themselves but also give a lot of opportunity for other people to identify with them. He said that his preference was for the latter person in the group, and he could recognize that there were times when he wished the former would keep quiet.

Mr. Wilson (the member who spoke often) responded to this by saying that certainly there were differences in how much one participated or what one thought of somebody's participation but that he didn't see this as really being based on competition of any sort. He pointed out that for him there were various ways of participating, that it wasn't always a matter of talking or not talking about one's own problem but that one could sit back and listen and get perspective from the way in which other people spoke about their problems. He said that at the beginning, particularly, this allowed him to get help without exposing problem areas that he felt he could not share with the group. Gradually, he said, as he felt more at ease in the group and really could see where it was helpful to him he began to share some of these problems as well. He pointed out that of course his feeling of liking was for a person who could help by talking or commenting on problems that he brought up and that he felt this was rather selfish of him, but that after all this was why he was coming to the clinic.

PRACTICE POINTS With the discussion of group process and the intimacy theme out in the open, the group leader moves to generalize the issue by inquiring if other members felt the same way. This exercise is intended to modify the culture of the group in respect to both how they work together but also to deepen the level of content.

After Mr. Wilson had spoken, the leader asked if what he had said was true for the others as well—they weren't always motivated to talk about their own problems, and there were times when they could gain by listening to others. All the members agreed verbally. Mr. Wilson continued on the question of the impersonality of the group, using as an example that he was not missed when he did not attend a session. He also raised his concern about "talking too much" and was surprised when one member contradicted him.

Mr. Wilson said that he was fairly confident that he wasn't really missed and that the group proceeded anyhow, even though when he was there he did a great deal of talking and that perhaps it was even better when he stayed away. To this, Mr. Russel, with a great deal of feeling, looked right at Mr. Wilson and said in a fairly strong and loud voice, "I miss you when you're not here, and I can tell when you're not here. It makes for a difference in what we talk about. It's not that I don't get anything when you're not here, because I do, but we talk about different things sometimes when you're not here." I pointed out that they were able to recognize that it was with a great deal of feeling that they came to the group and that these feelings were not related specifically to the content and that they had really an investment in each other as well as in the clinic. Mr. Wilson reacted in a very surprised way to Mr. Russell's statement that he really had missed him and could see in looking back over his own participation in the group that he had similar feelings about people being present or not being present.

Mr. Abrams, too, felt that there were differences in how he felt about other men in the group and that while he didn't want to talk specifically about which ones they were, he knew that this was so. He said that in spite of the difference, most of his feeling was in a positive direction and he did like most or all of the men in the group. Mr. Moran entered the discussion at this time, trying hard to make a point. When I recognized him, he said that he could now get an idea of what I had been driving at when I focused the discussion as I did on how people felt about each other in the group.

Mr. Moran continued by discussing his role in the group. He explained that he was quiet in the beginning because he had wanted to make sure that they might have some of the same feelings before he ventured his own opinion. He explained that, at this point, he felt they were enough like him that he was willing to jump in more quickly and risk his ideas.

There was further discussion, at the leader's request, of the topic of competition in the group that had been mentioned by Mr. Moran. Mr. Wilson once again raised his concerns about "talking too much," and the members reassured him that they were interested in what he had to say.

<table>
<tr><td>

PRACTICE POINTS

</td><td>

As the members of this group began to express some of the feelings they had toward their own participation and the participation of others, their honesty helped Mr. Abrams, a usually defensive member, to bring his problems to their attention for the first time. When all of these negative and positive feelings remained under the surface, they served to block the ability of the group members to develop a real sense of trust. In the new culture of honesty about their mutual participation, the group members acknowledge their reactions to Mr. Abrams but now reach out to him in support. Note once again the striking process and content integration. Mr. Abrams has not shared his feelings in the group, and that is the problem he appears to be having with his children as well.

</td></tr>
</table>

Mr. Abrams said that now that we had discussed what had happened in the group, he had something else he wanted to bring up. In a very sharp contrast, he said that as long as we were talking about feelings, he wanted the group's opinion about something that he was struggling with. He said that in his contacts with the clinic, he had been "accused" of withholding a great deal of his feeling, particularly in regard to his children. He wasn't quite sure about this and what effect it had on the children, but he was just wondering if any of the others had ever felt the same way. When I asked what it was tonight that enabled him to ask the group this, Mr. Abrams replied that he sort of felt that all of the men would really understand and would be able to help him to look at this.

Mr. Russel, Mr. Lewis, and Mr. Wilson all reacted visibly to this, each looking up, Mr. Russel smiling, Mr. Lewis nodding his head, and Mr. Wilson leaning back in his chair and looking directly at Mr. Abrams. Mr. Russel responded first. With a broad grin and in a very pleased and warm tone, he welcomed Mr. Abrams to the group. When Mr. Abrams wondered what he meant by this, Mr. Russel went on to explain that it seemed that Mr. Abrams no longer had to hide the fact that he really had some problems of his own. Mr. Russel said that it seemed to him that any time Mr. Abrams had talked before this, he talked in a very general way and that it was really hard to feel that he had any real problems, but now it seemed that he was bringing them out into the open more. Mr. Lewis confirmed this, saying that if nothing else tonight, he could really tell that Mr. Abrams was concerned about his feelings with his children as well as "what the book says one should do."

Although previously unspoken, the group's feeling that Mr. Abrams was remaining outside their work was evident in their reactions to his comments. His lack of emotional and personal involvement had been an obstacle to the group's movement. By pointing out the need to discuss the way the members worked with each other and by holding the group to this discussion, the leader played a key role in helping the members talk about their relationships. This freed Mr. Abrams and the other group members to risk discussing ideas in more intimate ways. As the next excerpt reveals, the connections between Mr. Abrams's feelings and those of the group became evident.

Mr. Wilson looked up, paused, and then asked Mr. Abrams if he could say more about what he meant, to which Mr. Abrams replied that what he thought he was asking about had to do with the difficulty or the ease with which one really showed how one felt. He said that tonight the group seemed able to do it, and this is what encouraged him to bring his concern and the question that had been raised by his counselor. At this point, he wanted to understand how this might influence his son and his daughter as well as his own participation in his family life. With this, Mr. Wilson nodded and said this is really what he thought Mr. Abrams was driving at and that he had a notion that this was something that was not only Mr. Abrams's problem, but that as far as he was concerned, this seemed to be the way that most men in the group felt. He asked whether this was not so. He said that for him, this had been and still continues to be somewhat of a concern and that he could feel what Mr. Abrams was driving at.

As Mr. Wilson stopped talking, he looked up and all of the others in the group very thoughtfully looked at him, looked at each other, at me, and finally at Mr. Lewis. I remarked that if this was so, it gave us something else that could be of some help because as we had discussed that evening, the group was one place where they could really show how they felt and look at some of these feelings in order to understand better what motivated them. Mr. Moran summarized this by saying that he thought that if the group could continue with this topic of discussion, he would have a much better understanding of what role feelings played in the behavior of his children, how these were influenced, what they represented to him, and consequently, that would give him a much better understanding of how he behaves, as well as what makes his children tick.

The session ended soon after this conversation; the leader acknowledged that the group had worked hard and set an agenda to continue with Mr. Abrams's concern. This excerpt demonstrated the group's need to deal with the intimacy theme as well as the connection between the process of the group and the content of the work, a connection that Mr. Moran pointed out in his last comments.

Groups in an Elder Community Setting

Mental health group counseling can also take place in a setting other than a community-based mental health agency. For example, the mission of an elder care center may focus on providing a place for socialization, food, activity (cards, singing, dancing, etc.) and education to elders who might otherwise be isolated at home. With greater geographic mobility of family members, it's possible for an elder who has lost friends and partners to need a structure that encourages and supports getting out of the house for some form of social activity.

Orr (2005) points out that

> [f]or the 95 percent of the population over the age of sixty-five in this country who live independently or semi-independently in the community, a community-based facility such as a local senior center can serve as a primary resource. Attending a senior center is synonymous with group involvement, whether the older person actively participates in various group activities or programs or merely attends the center for a hot meal in a congregate setting. Both formally and informally, older people are involved in mutual aid in a senior center. Many may not even perceive their involvement as such, nor may the professionals who plan and implement the service think of it as mutual aid, but it is. The informal groups that naturally form around an activity or topic of mutual interest (these can range from a crafts program to a lobbying effort) informally serve as mutual aid for the members of the group. (p. 471)

Discussion in earlier chapters of the factors that facilitate resiliency and protect against vulnerabilities in this age range emphasized the importance of social contact. This contact provides a buffer against the impact of the physical, emotional, mental, and personal losses often associated with this age.

Orr, discussing her group for visually impaired elderly who have recently lost their vision, describes the potential losses associated with this stage of the life cycle.

> The stresses and strains characteristic of the older person are represented by the loss of income and financial security, loss of the work role and sense of productivity, loss of spouse and/or significant others, loss of other meaningful interpersonal relationships such as friends and neighbors, loss of close geographic proximity to children, loss of health through physical illness or impairment, loss of physical functioning, such as that experienced by those with severe arthritis or heart disease, or less commonly thought of, visual impairment, loss of opportunities for self expression—and the list goes on. (p. 473)

In the example that follows, we can see how the availability of social support through a community-based setting can help provide the resources needed for elderly clients who may have to live for 20 or 30 more years coping with the many losses just described. In this example, Orr illustrates how such a group can help with the immediate trauma of the death of a member.

A Group for the Visually Impaired Elderly: The Death of a Member

Group Purpose: The group described in the following example meets once a week at an elder center for 1 hour serving as the members' primary and at times sole source of support (Orr, 2005).

Group Membership: The group consists of 12 visually impaired or blind elderly people, 4 of whom are also hearing impaired. They range in age from 61 to 92. Ten members, male and female, are widowed and live alone.

PRACTICE POINTS The session described is one that follows their being informed by the van driver of the death of a member, Maddie, who was 75 and died of a massive heart attack the day before.

Losses are very central in the life of people of this age. They have lost their former lives and, in this case, their eyesight, family members and friends, and others. With so many living alone, they need a source of support to cope with the losses and to build up their "reserve" during this often painful time of life. The group conversation began without a formal opening.

TESSIE: I just can't believe Maddie died. I've been calling her house every day to speak to her husband, and no answer. I knew something was wrong (said softly and with despair). (Brief silence.)

ROSE: Are you crying, Tessie?

TESSIE: I don't know whether I'm crying or not (said with frustration).

GOLDIE: Don't cry, Tessie; you'll only get all upset.

TESSIE: How can I not cry? Now it's Maddie; every week it's someone else (begins to cry openly). Rose leans over, reaches out to find Tessie, and puts her arm around her.

ROSE: But we are upset, Goldie, why shouldn't she cry? Why shouldn't we? I cried this morning when I found out in the van. We're all upset.

HANNAH: (Who is severely hearing impaired) Who's crying?

GOLDIE: (Whispers to the worker) We shouldn't tell Hannah; she lives in the nursing home; she gets upset when people die there. She doesn't have to know.

PRACTICE POINTS

One can see Goldie as, in part, trying to avoid the painful feelings associated with the death and trying to protect a member as well. Depending on the nursing home, Hannah may be in a place where the death of residents is not addressed because staff believes it can be too upsetting for residents. Someone dies, the door to all the rooms are closed, the body is removed, and the next thing the residents know, a new person occupies the room. In reality, that is the part that is most upsetting: a death of a resident going unnoticed rather than an appropriate intervention with the remaining residents. At this point the leader intervenes to support Hannah's right to know and to receive support.

LEADER: (To Goldie) How do you think Hannah will feel when she finds out?

GOLDIE: (After a long pause) She'll be upset.

LEADER: I think Rose is right, that we're all upset. Hannah is part of the group.

GOLDIE: (Loudly to Hannah) Maddie died yesterday.

HANNAH: I knew something was wrong. I could feel it. Oh, my . . . that's terrible about Maddie.

PRACTICE POINTS

The ambivalence about discussing the death of a member, a reminder to all of their other losses and their own inevitable death, emerges as one member suggests standing for a moment of silence, donating money to the center in her memory, and then another states:

RUTH: And then we can stop talking about it. Tessie's upset and Josephine's upset and I'm getting upset, too. Talking about it won't help. We can go on to something else. We had something on the agenda.

The leader understands the part of each member that wants to avoid facing the reality of this loss and as they do so facing all of the other losses in their lives. She understands, however, that each member is going home for the weekend, and the impact of this death when no one is around to provide support will be even greater. She makes what I have called an empathic demand for work and makes it in her own artistic way:

> **LEADER:** What are we going to do with all that we're feeling, though, if we don't talk about it here, in the group? I'm thinking that it's Friday, and we've done a lot of talking over the past few months about how difficult the weekends alone are for so many of you, especially when something upsetting has happened. Are we going to take all that sadness and pain and emptiness home with us for the weekend? (see Orr, 2005, pp. 480–483).

The leader consciously uses the word *we* because the loss of a member has an impact on her as well. The resulting discussion deals with the difficulty of having no one to speak with at home, their own recent losses, and a powerful discussion of the recognition of their own mortality. At the leader's suggestion, the group also talks about what Maddie meant to them, not only the impact of her death. The leader also shares her own feelings and initiates a discussion of the difficulty she feels in not being able to say good-bye and come to closure. During this discussion, the leader walks over to Tessie and puts her arms around her. After further discussion and association to their own losses, the leader ends the meeting by saying:

> **LEADER:** We've lost someone very special. Maddie touched each of our lives in a very special way. I think we've all touched each other's lives today. We've shared an awful lot of what we we're feeling. (p. 489)

Chapter Summary

This chapter has examined many forms of mental health group work that take place in the community. The range of ages included teenagers to elders and many of the stages in between. Settings included outpatient clinics, day treatment centers for teens, community centers for the elderly, and traditional mental health counseling agencies. Populations and issues addressed included teens with a psychiatric diagnosis, young adult clients with relationship problems, veterans with pain management and stress issues, parents who have children attending a clinic for behavior problems, and a group for the blind elderly.

With each population group, the importance of understanding issues related to their life cycle stage of development and how these affect the members' lives and participation in the group itself was stressed. A strengths perspective suggested that the mutual aid potential in the group could be a key element helping each population cope with the stresses that added to their vulnerabilities, while also strengthening the protective factors that allowed for resilience in the face of life's negative events.

The importance of addressing the issue of stigma associated with mental health problems and treatment, particularly with teenagers, was stressed. Strategies were suggested for engaging even reluctant group members. In examples of work with adults with relationship problems, the requirement that the group leader make a demand for work that asks members to take responsibility for their part in the problems was highlighted. Group examples in an elder community setting stressed the importance of helping members build new social networks as well as dealing with the losses associated with the death of a member.

Related Online Content and Activities

For learning tools such as glossary terms, InfoTrac® College Edition keywords, links to related websites, and chapter practice quizzes, visit this book's website at **www.cengage.com/counseling/shulman.**

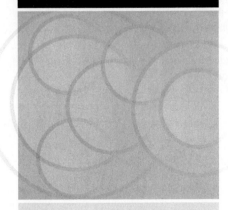

CHAPTER 18

Group Counseling in Job and Career Settings

What Do Counselors Do in Job and Career Settings?

The U.S. Department of Labor's (2008–2009) *Occupational Outlook Handbook* describes the work of counselors in this area as follows:

> Vocational counselors, also called employment or career counselors, provide mainly career counseling outside the school setting. Their chief focus is helping individuals with career decisions. Vocational counselors explore and evaluate the client's education, training, work history, interests, skills, and personality traits. They may arrange for aptitude and achievement tests to help the client make career decisions. They also work with individuals to develop their job-search skills and assist clients in locating and applying for jobs. In addition, career counselors provide support to people experiencing job loss, job stress, or other career transition issues.

While group programs can be set up to provide education and skills training (e.g., how to write a résumé or prepare for an interview), there are often serious physical, emotional, and social barriers to employment that job counseling groups need to address. One model of counseling entitled the Self-Determined Career Development Model (SDCDM) was developed by Wehmeyer and colleagues (2003), with a particular focus on working with persons with disabilities to assist them in obtaining their desired careers and jobs. This model is used in individual counseling, but it can also provide a structure for discussion in group counseling. This is a problem-solving model that is implemented in three phases. In each phase, the individual identifies the problem, potential solutions to the problem, barriers to solving the problem, and the consequences of each solution. The three phases address three questions:

- What are my career or job goals?
- What is my plan?
- What have I achieved?

For example, in work during the first phase, each group member would identify their desired career or job, what knowledge they have about this job or career, what must change for them to get this job/career, and what they would have to do to make this happen. A similar approach answering questions in phases 2 and 3 would result in group members participating in a systematic problem-solving process, ending in a plan for proceeding. An important element in this model is identifying barriers to achieving the client's goals and steps to overcome them.

These barriers can be addressed in a supportive manner if job and career counseling groups include an element of mutual aid. For example, take the first illustration in this chapter of a group for single-parent women on public assistance seeking employment. One core issue that emerges as a barrier is their guilt about not being home for their children. In another example, men who have been unemployed for a period of time have to deal with a sense of hopelessness that emerges in a member's angry comment stating that role-playing interviews in the group is a waste of time when there are no jobs or job interviews available. These comments take on a special emphasis in the current economy, at the time this is written, with long-term unemployment rising. Ex-offenders on parole must face the discrimination against them when prospective employers ask what they have been doing the past few years or notice their prison tattoos (referred to as "toos" by the ex-offenders). Some older teenagers in the child welfare system making a transition to independence must also deal with their internalized perception of themselves as "losers" in order to develop the confidence needed to enter the workforce. In a final example, a defensive male group member who has lost three straight jobs because of his temper and his angry fights with supervisors has to be helped to lower his defenses and take some responsibility for his own part in his employment problems.

In reality, job and career counseling groups do not always operate according to the plan, the structure, or the model. Personal as well as group issues will emerge and must be integrated into the work. The common element of the illustrations in this chapter is a focus on how mutual aid can assist participants in identifying barriers to their success and addressing them. Because there are significant differences in terms of the life cycle and other issues between adults seeking work compared to older teenagers, the chapter is divided by age. The first part of the chapter focuses on work with adults and the second with teenagers. The chapter presents the following examples:

- A job counseling group for women on public assistance
- A first session for ex-offenders mandated to attend a job training group
- Dealing with despair and long-term unemployment
- Employment groups including persons with special needs
- Losing a job: the gatekeeper role
- Getting angry on the job and then getting fired: the defensive member
- Older teens in a transition to independence group: the scapegoat phenomenon
- A worksite training program for teenagers: addressing sexual harassment

Group Counseling for Adult Clients Seeking Work

The examples in this section all involve unemployed adults seeking employment. Some are attending sessions voluntarily, some reluctantly, and some are mandated. All share similar concerns about being able to obtain and keep a job. In the first two examples, resistance and mandated attendance need to be addressed. In the example that follows, I will provide a more detailed analysis of a first session, reaching back to the discussion in Part 1 and applying it to the issue of resistance. No matter what the model of career counseling being implemented, it will not have the desired effect unless members of the group are engaged and begin to "own" the group even if mandated to attend. I believed it was worth a more detailed discussion than will be found in some of the other examples in this chapter.

Engaging Group Members in First Sessions in the Face of Resistance

Group members attending job counseling groups may be voluntary, semivoluntary, or mandated by some authority. For example, persons on welfare may need to make an effort to obtain employment as part of the conditions for receiving support. Parolees may be required to attend job training as a requirement for remaining on parole and not being remanded to prison. Even voluntary and semivoluntary (attendance was suggested but not required) participants may bring resistance to the group and the idea of returning to the workforce to the first session. The following two groups illustrate the dynamics and skills of engaging even somewhat reluctant group members.

A Job Counseling Group for Women on Public Assistance

This example is of a first session of a group for women who had been receiving welfare for a number of years. Some were attending voluntarily as they began to feel the so-called empty nest syndrome. Their children were growing up and preparing to leave home. Other group members were semivoluntary, with their financial assistance caseworkers suggesting that they attend. Although attendance was not mandatory, there was a suggestion that their lack of effort to find a job would be viewed negatively and could affect their eligibility for financial aid. A third group of clients consisted of women who expressed strong feelings of ambivalence about returning to the workforce.

All of the women in each of the three subgroups had children at home of various ages, but all of the children were old enough to be somewhat independent. Each of the women also faced significant barriers to moving into the workforce. These included their children, their lifestyles, their feelings and anxieties about working, their lack of work experience, and others.

Group Purpose: The members were non-job-ready, and the purpose of the group was to help them to deal with barriers to employment.

Group Members: Although there were areas of common ground between these group members, there were also significant differences. A number of them were women living in environments with few supports, either financial or emotional. There were single mothers, widows, and others strongly motivated (often desperate) to get back into the workforce. At times, these clients would appear to be lacking in motivation, hesitant about leaving their roles as caregivers, and apprehensive about the changes and challenges facing them. The lack of financial and emotional support and reasonable child care was also important.

PRACTICE POINTS

The sessions were scheduled in the morning at a time when most of the clients' children would be at school. Twelve group members arrived (15 had been invited) to a room with chairs set in a circle. The group leader warmly welcomed each group member by introducing herself, asking their names, and offering some coffee. When she felt most of those who were going to arrive had done so, she began the meeting by introducing herself, and asking if each of them could tell the others their names and briefly describe their children. She followed this with a brief statement of purpose and her role as group leader and included a description of some of the barriers they may have faced. This was important because it sent a message that they were able to talk about these issues and that the group leaders were not just going to "sell" the idea of returning to work or be "cheerleaders" without recognition of the significant obstacles. She also acknowledges the semi- or involuntary nature of attendance for some of the members.

> I began by saying that all of the members of the group had a number of things in common: "You all have children who are starting to be more grown up and independent, and as a result, you may be thinking about what you would like to do with your lives when the children are gone. I know from my past work with moms like yourselves that there are many obstacles in your way when you even think about looking for a job. Some of you may have mixed feelings about being away from home when your kids are still around. Others may be worried about whether or not you would be able to handle a job—some of you have not worked for years, and some never really worked at full-time work, even though you all have shown your ability to handle a big job, just by raising your kids and keeping a home. Some of you may still feel lacking in confidence, afraid of interviews, worried about the competition from younger women with more experience, or just doubting your skills. For some of you who are ready to work, the competition for jobs must seem overwhelming. I also realize that some of you are not too eager to look for work right now; in fact, you may not be so pleased about having to come to this group."

PRACTICE POINTS

In her next comments, she clarifies her role as not the expert giving them all of the answers but rather the person who can help them help each other. For members who may already lack confidence in themselves, the group leader is crediting them with her perception of their abilities to own the group and to help each other.

Because we realize that there are a lot of factors to consider before someone switches from being a full-time homemaker to a full- or even part-time employee, we set up the group so that you can talk to each other about these concerns, perhaps even be able to help each other think them through. It might help a lot just to know that other people feel the same way as you—a kind of everyone-is-in-the-same-boat feeling. My job as group leader would be to help you to help each other. We will try to help you talk to each other, listen to each other, support each other, provide ideas from your experiences, and let you know some of what we have learned that may be helpful to you. The important thing is that it must be your group if it's going to be helpful. This is pretty much what the group is all about and how we will try to help. I wonder if I can get your reactions to the group and some of the problems I raised. Did any of them seem familiar to you? Does the group sound like it might be helpful? Can you share your reactions with each other for a while, and perhaps we can see if you also think the group might be useful? Who would like to start?

PRACTICE POINTS

Although the dynamics and skills of first group sessions were discussed in Part 1, it is worth revisiting them in the context of this area of practice. These opening comments by the group leader are important in setting the stage for work. They provide a structure that can free the members to begin their work. Without this structure, there can be no freedom. At the same time, the structure provided by the group leader should not be so prescriptive that it blocks the members from making a start. If the group leader immediately began to implement any structure or models, such as the one described earlier, with a group containing some women who didn't want to be there and others who were very ambivalent about work, then an illusion of work would occur.

By openly acknowledging the resistance of some group members, the group leader has given them permission to talk about their feelings if they wish. While group discussion during the meetings will address many of the questions suggested in the SDCDM model described earlier, the first step and the priority in the first session is on connecting the members' sense of need to the purpose of the group. The group leader wants the members to make what I have called the "first decision" to even engage in the group.

The purpose of the problem swapping, in which the members exchange with each other some of their concerns, is twofold. First, it provides the feedback necessary to develop the client's side of the working contract. These are the issues and concerns that will be the starting point for the group's work. It is quite possible that in the initial stage, group members will share near problems, usually more superficial ones, which do not bear directly on some of the more difficult and hard-to-talk-about issues. This is their way of testing, of trying to determine how safe it is to use the group. The group leader must respect and understand their defenses as being an appropriate way to begin a new experience. The second function of the problem-swapping exercise is to encourage intermember interaction. For most of their lives, clients have participated in groups where the discussion has essentially been between the group member and the leader, the person in authority. This is a long-standing habit. They now need to learn new ways of relating in a group, and the problem-swapping exercise is a good way to start.

Silence is not unusual in the first group session when the leader has completed the opening statement. This silence can represent a number of communications, a different one for each group member. Some may be thinking of what they are willing to share with the group at that time. Others may be shy and afraid to be the first one to speak. Still others are expressing their wariness of being put on the spot if they raise a concern, not knowing how other group members or the leader will react. These are the moments that inexperienced group leaders dread. The silence, they feel, is the beginning of a recurring nightmare they have had about their first group session. They are worried that after making their opening statement and inviting feedback, nobody will speak. It is not unusual for group leaders to take over the group at this point and to offer subjects for discussion or, in some cases, present prepared films or presentations or involve group members in exercises. This, of course, leads to a self-fulfilling prophecy, where the message conveyed to the members by the leader is that although their participation is being asked for, there is not a willingness to wait for it.

PRACTICE POINTS

In the example of the welfare mothers' group, after waiting a few seconds, the leader used the skill of reaching inside the silence to articulate what the members might be feeling.

> There was a brief silence when I finished my statement. I smiled and said I realized it wasn't easy to be the first one to speak in the group so that I would give them a moment. After another brief pause, Joan raised her hand, and I invited her to begin. She said she had been thinking about going back to work, but whenever she mentioned it at home, the kids seemed to get upset over the idea. I asked her to tell us more about that. What did the kids say? She said her 10-year-old looked shocked when she said she was coming to this group session to consider getting a job. He had asked her who was going to cook their dinner in the afternoon if she went to work? I asked if she could remember how she felt when he said that. She said she felt lousy, like she was abandoning him. I wondered if she felt he was really asking, "Who is going to be home for me after school?" and if that hadn't hit home hard at her own mixed feelings. She agreed that it did, since she already felt guilty enough at being just a single parent. I said it must have felt even worse for her, because he had lost his dad, and now it seemed like he was losing his mom.

PRACTICE POINTS

The way in which the group leader responded to Joan, the first member to speak, set an important tone for the group. She invited Joan to elaborate on her first comments, and as she did so, the group leader concentrated on trying to get in touch with Joan's feelings. She did this first when she reached for the real concern raised by the child who suddenly worried about who was going to care for him, and second by acknowledging the feelings of guilt a single parent might experience about abandoning her child. As the group leader responds in a caring and supportive manner, the other members watch closely, getting some hints about the group leader and how she might respond to them if they were to speak up in the group. The group leader resisted the temptation to provide answers, solutions, or other arguments in favor of working. Inexperienced group leaders, under organizational pressure to have successful sessions that result in clients pursuing and obtaining jobs, might respond in a manner that cuts off consideration of these concerns. This leader's containment is important, because she is trying to set a tone for mutual aid in which the help is coming from other group members as well as the leader, and she is trying to demonstrate her understanding of the group members' feelings. She also understands that success in terms of group members actually moving into the workforce may depend on surfacing and addressing these concerns and others.

> I said that Joan had gotten us started with one of the tougher problems facing moms in their particular situation, but it probably was one most of them experienced. I asked if others in the group might want to comment on what Joan just said or add another issue for our discussion. We wouldn't solve all of the problems before the coffee break (some of them smiled),

but perhaps we could get some idea of what they were. Louise said she had to deal with the same feelings the first time she went to work. The kids started to act up and were a real handful for a few weeks. She also had second thoughts about it, but then she finally sat down with them and had it out. They admitted they missed her being home, and she admitted to them that she missed being home. But then she went on to explain why she felt she needed to work and that this did not mean she didn't love them anymore. She also said she was going to continue, so they just better work out how they were going to live with it. She felt clearing the air had helped a lot and that things had been going much better since then. In fact, the kids were being very helpful in picking up some of the chores around the house. Theresa said she felt it was the best thing that ever happened to her kids. They began to get more independent around the house, and the better she felt about herself, the better she seemed to get along with the kids.

PRACTICE POINTS

The tuning-in exercise discussed in a previous chapter, as well as the group leader's experience in individual job and career counseling, was most helpful in shaping her responses. After acknowledging the client's feelings about the problem, the group leader asked other group members to respond. In the role suggested earlier in this book, the group leader concentrated on helping the individual, Joan, raise the concern with her second client, the group. In turn, she tried to help the group members respond to Joan. Two of the members were quick to take the group leader up on her invitation. By crediting Joan with having raised an important and difficult problem, the group leader was encouraging a culture in the group in which raising problems and concerns would be viewed positively. This message was also noticed by the other group members who may have been more hesitant to risk.

Returning to the example, the initial conversation about the guilt arising from leaving the kids was followed by the raising of some of the other concerns included in the group leader's opening statement. As the members shared these, the group leader acknowledged them and recorded them in her notes. She had previously explained she would use her notes to keep track of what they discussed. After 5 minutes of this, Lorraine finally raised the taboo subject of the leader's authority. As is often the case, she raised it indirectly by referring to other employment counselors who had not been helpful:

Lorraine said it was all good and well to talk about these things, but in the end, the fact was there were no jobs for them to get. She continued by saying her caseworker at the welfare place had been pushing her to consider taking work for a while, but that the caseworker was just a kid, wasn't married herself, and couldn't appreciate how tough it would be on her. She said she felt her caseworker was actually telling her she was just lazy and if she would simply get off of her ass, she would be fine. She resented it and had simply stopped listening. At the end of her speech, which seemed to have a lot of anger in it, she turned and stared at me. I told her that perhaps her caseworker really thought she needed some encouragement. She laughed with a sarcastic tone and folded her arms.

Elaine said there were lots of problems that made it hard for her, including transportation. She didn't have a car, the bus schedule from her area was lousy, and she didn't think her caseworker, who had a car, understood that kind of problem. Others started to discuss how they would handle the transportation issue and I just sat and listened.

PRACTICE POINTS

Lorraine had made a first offering of her feelings related to the authority theme. As is often the case, even with experienced leaders who are tuned in and ready to deal with the issue, our own feelings cause us to pass up the invitation. The leader in this example tried to protect the welfare caseworker but, in reality, was protecting herself. She sensed the anger in

Lorraine's comments; however, her message back to the group was "I'm not so sure I want to discuss this with her." Fortunately, her ability to catch her mistake in the same session, which I earlier defined as skillful practice, helped her reopen the issue. Even if she missed it in the first session, as long as she demonstrated genuine concern and feelings for her group members, they would have given her the benefit of some time to deal with the authority theme. By addressing it openly, she speeds up the process of group development.

> I interrupted the conversation and said that I thought Lorraine had raised an important issue earlier that I had ducked because it made me feel uncomfortable. She had talked about her welfare caseworker who hadn't really understood her. Instead of listening, I had jumped in and defended the caseworker. I'm sure they have all had experiences with people giving them advice without appreciating what they faced and they were probably wondering if I would be just like those other counselors. I didn't want to be like that because the only way I could be helpful to them was if I did try to understand.
>
> Someone asked me if I had children. I told them I did not, and, in fact, I had never experienced being out of work. I said that I had been continuously employed since I graduated from school. I was really an outsider in this group compared to all of them. Lorraine said, "Well, don't worry too much about it—the way things are going with the economy and all of the job cuts, you may get your chance to experience it." The group members and I laughed at this, responding to Lorraine's more friendly tone of voice.

PRACTICE POINTS

With a 2-hour session, it is possible to move past the contracting work with beginning efforts to focus on an example of the work. It is not unusual for group members to use the early sessions to start with "near" problems. These are issues related to the work of the group, but they are not core issues. This may be done because the group members must test the reaction of a group leader and the other members. Group members often feel it would be unwise to rush right in until they know how their feelings and thoughts are going to be treated, whether they will be met with support or confrontation, and whether it is OK to share the real feelings and concerns. Not only must the members in this group be concerned about the leader, but they must also be concerned about the other members. With these concerns in the background, it is not unusual for group members to come close to a concern while watching to see how the other group members and the leader react. Timing is important in a first session, and it would therefore be a mistake for a group leader to attack defenses at a point when the group member is too vulnerable.

PRACTICE POINTS

Returning to the example, a clear contract and some work in the beginning of the session helped create the safe conditions within the group so that members felt free to begin to risk themselves. After the discussion of the authority theme, the group members returned to one of the core issues facing women with families considering a return to work. What is striking is the way in which the group members themselves directed the emergence of this theme.

> The members accepted my suggestion that we return to some of the concerns listed in the problem swapping. Fran, who had not spoken yet, commented that while she agreed with some of the comments about how it could be helpful to the kids to gain some independence, she also felt she could understand Joan's feelings about leaving them to go to work; she had some of these as well. I invited her to tell the group more about how she felt. She said that in her mind she could understand how it would be really good for her to get out of the house, and that the kids probably could do with some independence. She paused, and I said, "But

there is a big gap, isn't there, between what your head tells you and what your heart feels." Fran, who seemed close to tears, said, "Sometimes I feel like I failed as a wife when my marriage split up, and now I'm afraid I might fail as a mother."

I said that I felt Fran had shared something with us that she felt very deeply about, and I wondered if some of the other group members didn't have some of the same feelings. Theresa, who had earlier responded to Joan's raising of the question with a report of how positive it had been for her kids when she had gone to work, spoke directly to Fran and told her that although she felt it had been a good decision to return to work, she sometimes forgot how hard it had been on her when she finally decided. She had felt the same way Fran did. She now realized that she had been too hard on herself, that she had taken on too much guilt about her marital split and had taken all the responsibility for all of the kids' problems. Now looking back, she realized that she had actually done a good job in raising the kids by herself, at least the best she was able to do. After all, her husband had taken off scot-free; he hadn't taken any of the responsibility, financial or otherwise, for the kids. She had stuck with them and she felt that in spite of the problems, the kids knew she really loved them. She didn't have to stay home every day to be there at 3:30, after school, to let them know she cared. It was time she had started to look after herself and she felt Fran probably needed to do the same. In the long run, she felt if Fran took care herself, she would be a lot better mother and would have more to give the kids.

I asked Fran and Joan, and any of the others who were feeling guilty about leaving the kids, if what Theresa had just said had been helpful. They nodded, and Joan, who originally raised the question, said it helped just to hear that other people felt the same way, and that Theresa had been able to do something about it even though she also had felt guilty. I told them I felt they all had worked hard today and had shown a lot of strength in just raising the issue and discussing it so they should be pleased about this first session and how they handled it.

PRACTICE POINTS Each group is different, since it reflects the strengths and experiences of its members. Louise, the member who took on the leader early in the session, brought a sense of urgency and a willingness to risk herself in the group that helped members not only tackle the issue of authority directly and constructively but also helped them move past their early defenses into their common concerns about working and about their children. This group moved directly into an emotionally charged issue in the first session. I do not believe the level of the work or the speed with which it began is at all unusual. I believe it reflected the urgency of the group members, the clarity of group purpose and the leader's role, the members' willingness to attack the issue of authority directly, and the worker's consistent efforts to articulate the feelings expressed by the group members, or even slightly ahead of them. Given these core conditions, the impetus of the group members carried them toward productive work.

Now that the session was nearly over and a consensus had been reached on a theme for additional work, the ending and transition phase of this session began as the group leader credited the work of the members, summarized the discussion, identified issues for future work, discussed her expectations of them, and provided an opportunity for evaluative comments. The leader wanted to encourage members to feel free to talk about the group and the leader.

Since our time was running out, I wondered if we could plan to discuss this issue, dealing with the kids, in more detail next week. I said, "For example, we could discuss how to talk to your kids about your plans to go back to work, what kinds of expectations of them would be fair, how you can help them to talk about how they feel about your going to work, and any other questions that you might think of during the week. We could also begin on some of the other barriers that you identified as making it hard for you to seek and find employment. Maybe each week, we could take one or more of these issues, and with all of you helping, just as you started to do today, and with me throwing in some of my ideas that might help, we could work toward the goal of helping you to overcome these barriers. I believe you can do it with the help of each other. I think you made a really good start today." The group members nodded in agreement.

I continued: "We only have a few minutes left. This was our first session, and I wonder how you feel it went. It's important to me that you feel free to feed your reactions into the group session as we go along." Joan said it was very helpful just to know others felt the same way. Theresa said that even though she was telling Joan and Fran that it would be all right and that they needed to look after themselves, she was probably still trying to convince herself. I said that this was the way group mutual aid worked, as I saw it. When you helped another group member with a problem, it helps you as well. Sara spoke for the first time and said she realized that she hadn't said anything during the group, but that she felt it was helpful just to listen. She hoped she could contribute more in the future. I said that each group member would begin in their own way and that I could tell from her expression, and the expressions of others who had not spoken a great deal, that they were still very much involved. A number of the more quiet members shook their heads in agreement.

PRACTICE POINTS In the next intervention, the group leader shows continued courage and skill as she returns to the authority theme and the resistance of members who were pressured to attend. By returning to the issue, she clearly sends a message that she is open to feedback and meant what she said earlier in the session.

I then asked how those people who felt they were pressured to come by their financial aid workers felt after this session. I thought they may have started the session angry at having to come. Louise said she was still mad at the pressure, but after listening to the discussion, she thought it might not be as bad as she had thought it would be. I asked why she felt that way, and she said that I at least tried to understand what they were going through, that I didn't just seem superior to them or have all of the answers. I told her that I thought I could only be helpful to them if I could understand, and that she and the others in the group had made a good start on my education. Louise laughed and said I might pass this course after all.

Cathy said that she had come to the group really wanting to get back to work. She felt she didn't have the same concerns as some of the other group members, although some had meaning for her. Her problem was that she wasn't sure she had the paid work experience she would need to get a job when there was so much competition out there. She wasn't sure if this group was going to deal with her problems. I said that I thought this was an important issue as well and wondered if we could agree to put it on our agenda for early discussion. How could they make the most out of what they had in order to sell themselves in a tough job market? The other members agreed this would be an important. I credited Cathy with raising her concern about the first meeting. By being direct, she had focused our attention on another problem. I hoped all of the other members would do the same, because it was important that we be honest with each other in the group if we were going to be successful.

PRACTICE POINTS It is important for the group leader to address the issue of confidentiality and in particular the limits to her being able to maintain it. Once again, Louise plays the internal leader role by being direct about a crucial issue for members who have been mandated to attend. The group leader should also be clear about her role as a mandated reporter in respect to safety issues with the children, which she skips, probably reluctant to raise another authority issue.

Since the evaluation seemed to be coming to an end, I pointed out that there were three rules I felt we should follow in the group. I explained that members were expected to come each week and that information they shared with each other should be treated as confidential. I also asked that if anyone wanted to drop out of the group at any time before the end of the eight scheduled sessions, they would agree to come back and discuss it with the group before quitting. All agreed that these seemed to be reasonable rules.

Louise asked if the confidentiality extended back to their financial aid workers. I explained that I would need to let their caseworkers know if they stopped attending because that was part of our agreement with their workers; however, what they said in the group would not be shared. I thought there might be times when they might want me to share information with their financial aid workers but that we would discuss that if it came up, and I would only share information with their permission. Louise said that seemed fair enough.

I told them we were all a little nervous since this was a first meeting, but I felt they had made a good start. The session ended at this point, but most of the members stayed around and chatted with me and with each other while they had another cup of coffee.

PRACTICE SUMMARY

In ending the group, it was important that the group leader credit negative as well as positive comments. There are many times during group sessions when members have negative reactions, and it is crucial that they feel the group leader really wants to hear them. As is often the case, the negative reaction in this group (Cathy wondering if the group would be for her) helped the leader further refine the contract to include an issue that Cathy and probably most of the other members needed to know was on the agenda. When the worker credits Cathy, she sends a message to the other group members that it is OK to say what you really think and feel, not what you think the leader wants to hear. Although this is a little scary for the new group leader, in the long run such honesty will help ensure the success of the group.

It is interesting to note that Louise, who challenged the group leader early in the session and might have been diagnosed as a deviant member, turned out to be a candidate for internal leader. If Louise had not raised the issue of confidentiality in relation to the financial aid caseworker, it would have been wise for the group leader to have raised it herself. Unless the rules of the game were clarified (part of the development of a working contract), the question might have stayed beneath the surface, blocking open expression in areas that the group needed to address. Once again, it is important to note that the leader has not completely shared the limitations around confidentiality. She would need to come back to the next meeting and point out that she was a mandated reporter if discussion indicated there were issues of potential or actual abuse of children by them or by others and under what conditions she would be required to share information from the group.

This first session also points out how the structured approach to career and job seeking described earlier, SDCDM, can provide important questions for group members to discuss; with the type of groups described in this chapter, it would need to be modified. The group leader needed to address first session group issues including authority and the reluctance of some members to attend before she could begin to use the structure to focus discussion.

First Session for Ex-Offenders Mandated to Attend a Job Training Group: The Meaning of Resistance

In the previous example of the first session with the welfare mothers' group, traces of resistance were evidenced and acknowledged. In that situation, honest recognition of the problem was all that was needed to help the group members overcome the barrier. In other groups, the resistance may be much stronger, with all of the group members having been forced to attend. In this next example, attendance was a condition of their parole. Resistance, often associated with anger, may be evidenced directly or indirectly at the start of the group session. It is not possible to begin without addressing the issue. This type of group can generate fear in the leader as he or she anticipates spending 2 hours with a group of resistant and angry clients.

To develop a strategy for dealing with this scenario, I need to begin by revisiting our earlier discussion in Part 1 of the nature of resistance. First, it is important to realize that resistance, in which clients seemingly dig in their heels and refuse to take help, is a part of the group counseling process. Rather than viewing it as a barrier, it should be viewed as an essential element. Group leaders may be concerned when they encounter resistance and immediately begin to wonder if they have done something wrong. In reality, resistance may be a sign that the group leader has done something right. If we understand that all change is difficult, and that each of us has built in defenses that allow us to avoid facing problems directly by denying responsibility for our own part in our problems, then resistance may be a sign that the work is hitting home.

I would be more concerned if I never sensed resistance on the part of my group members. It might mean I was participating in an illusion of work and avoiding sensitive and difficult issues. Underground, or passive resistance, is actually more difficult to deal with than when it is out in the open. Therefore, resistance in a first session may be a signal that the purpose of the group is actually very relevant to the members. If we also understand our clients may have ambivalent feelings about change, we can reach for the part of the client that wants to change, to take responsibility for his or her life, to overcome the barriers to employment, and so forth. For some clients, the part of them that wants to avoid change may be stronger. That is why we may not be able to reach some clients at particular stages in their lives. However, if we are ever to help them, we must believe in and reach for the positive side of their ambivalence, using a strengths perspective, and not be overwhelmed or fooled by the negatives. Resistance in a first session may be an unconscious indirect signal of how strongly group members sense they need help. The more they protest, the greater their need.

With this approach to resistance, the group leader does not have to fear it or interpret it as a signal of leader incompetence or lack of relevance of the group and its content. Instead, the tuning-in skill can be used before the first session to develop some understanding of the feelings of the client hidden beneath the resistance (e.g., poor self-image; fear of being harshly judged by others; a deep sense of hopelessness about their futures) and thus to become prepared to reach for and acknowledge these emotions.

A second major issue underlying resistance in a first session is the group members' fear of loss of control. This is associated with the members' view of the group leader as someone who is going to do something to them. They have often had so many experiences of "being done to" that they believe most all helping professionals have a hidden agenda up their sleeves and fear possible manipulation. Manipulation is defined here as the secret use of power to attempt to influence people. Obviously the group leader is present to try to influence the individual clients and the group toward a positive group experience. The only question is whether the group leader will act *with* the members and be open about his or her interventions, or whether he or she will act *on* the clients using indirect means.

Finally, we need to remember we are dealing with men who have been incarcerated and have experienced a frightening and at times brutal culture. It is not unusual for convicts in prison to refuse to attend group or individual counseling sessions out of fear that they may be seen as weak and vulnerable. Convicts, at times, need to invent practical and plausible reasons for speaking to a counselor because the very act of having a private interview with a member of the prison staff can lead to suspicion on the part of other convicts. Fear of being identified as a "rat" who squeals on other convicts is frightening because even if not true, the accusation can lead to a brutal outcome. Men recently released from prison on parole will bring some of these cultural issues with them to the first meeting.

PRACTICE POINTS

With these three ideas in mind, we turn to a first session with a group of ex-offenders on parole attending a mandatory job counseling group. This example illustrates a group leader dealing directly with the resistance and the issue of control, attempting to reach for the underlying feelings related to both. He makes his opening statement in the face of nonverbal signals of resistance and tries to connect to the men by sharing concerns he believes must be under the tough surface they present. He understands that he can't wait for the emergence of the authority theme, because this is central to their lives on parole where many important decisions are made by others, so he reaches for it directly.

Group Purpose: A mandatory job counseling group for parolees to provide assistance in their job searches

Group Members: Seven men and one women of mixed ages and races all recently released from prison, with a male Caucasian group leader

First Session

I began by welcoming the men to the group. I explained the purpose as follows: "We at the center realize how tough it is out there to get a job right now. We know that, as ex-offenders with a record, you may face a tougher time than most. We set this group up as a way of offering you some help in dealing with some of the barriers that may make it tougher for you. For example, some of our clients in your situation have wondered how to handle the questions that may come up in a job interview about the gap in their résumé and where you have spent the last few years. For some, the toos (tattoos) that they obtained while in prison because they needed them to survive are hard to cover up, and the concern is that employers and others only see the toos and don't really see them. Others have had problems holding down jobs, for a variety of reasons, such as difficulties with bosses who seem to push them around. For others the problem is trying to find work that will pay enough to help them support their families. It's hard to be in prison and know that your wife and kids are trying to make it on welfare, and it's important to get the kind of work that might help make it up to them."

"We hope the group can be a place where you men can help each other tackle these problems, or any others that you feel might make it harder for you to find employment. My job will be to help you help each other, and to pass along any ideas or suggestions that we have found to be helpful in the past. The important thing is that it will be your group." I asked what they thought of the idea of the group. Nobody spoke; they just kept staring at me looking defiant or simply smirking.

PRACTICE POINTS

The next intervention is an example of reaching inside silences and surfacing the underlying issues of being mandated and the worker's use of authority.

I said that I felt the silence probably meant that some, or all of them, were not to happy about being here today. I wanted them to know that at this moment, I wasn't too sure I liked the idea, either. I realized they were being forced to come as a condition of their parole and that they probably resented it. I wanted them to know that even though I would keep attendance and had to report them if they didn't show up, and even though their parole officers could pressure them to attend, I realized that no one could actually make them treat the group seriously or change. That was still in their hands. So, if we were going to make this group work effectively, it would really be up to them. I paused, and this time I felt it was a more thoughtful silence. I said, "How about it? Am I right about your being mad at having to come to the group?"

PRACTICE POINTS The group leader's surfacing the resistance directly and his honesty in sharing his own feelings about leading a resistant group helped break the ice. His recognition of the control the men held over their own involvement is also important. These are men who have just emerged from prison where control over their daily lives was in the hands of prison guards and other officials. When they ate, slept, and had recreation opportunities and what prison jobs they held were mostly determined by prison authorities. The only areas in their lives where they maintained absolute control, in prison and in the group, was their control over their thoughts and feelings. Frank, an internal leader, responds by addressing the authority theme. His honest admission of their experience at "conning" group leaders is extremely helpful.

Frank said that having to come to group was nothing new. They were forced to attend a group session once a week with some jerk psychologist who sat around for hours and didn't say anything. When he did talk, he wanted us to discuss our personal lives so he could change our personalities. Frank smiled, and said they all decided to play along with the guy and discuss their problems. Others in the group smiled in recognition of what he was saying. He continued by laughing and saying "We didn't tell him a thing about us that was real and he never realized he was being conned. He really thought he was changing our personalities. We all thanked him for helping us change in the end, and the jerk believed it all."

PRACTICE POINTS Once again we see the common phenomenon of group members raising the authority theme and their concerns about this group leader by talking about another professional. The group leader responds directly, and his admission that they could "con" him as well is crucial to their making what I have called the first decision.

I asked if they wondered if this group would be the same as that one. Did they think I was out to change their personalities? Frank laughed and said that I could try, since he had gotten pretty good at making up a life story if I wanted one. I said I didn't see the group in that way. I felt that all of them had real concerns about work, whether they could get a job, could they support their families, would they end up having to go back inside, and other things that could keep them up at night. I didn't think some of these things were going to be easy to talk about, especially since they had learned in the joint (prison) to keep things to themselves for self-protection. I really wanted to help them to help each other. I felt there was a lot they could get out of such a group that could be helpful to them. I wanted a chance to show that to them, but I realized it was really up to them if they wanted to give it a chance. They were experts at conning, and they could con me as well. I hoped they didn't do that, since I thought even though it was tough to admit, they really did need some help with these problems. I said, "How about it—will you give it a try?"

There was a short period of silence, and Lou asked how the group would work, how would they help each other. I said that to begin, I'd like to know if any of the problems I had listed earlier sounded like they fit their concerns.

PRACTICE SUMMARY

Frank, who another group leader might have experienced as the deviant member and an enemy, was clearly the ally as he raised the issue of conning so directly. If we believe these men did have some concerns about their lives, work, family, and so forth, then Frank's comments could be seen as an indirect call for real help instead of the con job they have experienced in the past. That's the part of the message to which the skilled leader responded.

The Emotional Impact of the Reality of the Job Market

Job training and employment programs have an underlying assumption that once the participants have completed the exercises, learned to write résumés, have developed interview skills, and finished other preparatory work, the jobs will be there for them. In reality, training programs such as these are often offered at a time when the job market may be shrinking, jobs are being sent overseas, and the general economy is not expanding. At the time this is being written, in late 2009, the United States is in the midst of one of the worst economies in decades, dubbed the Great Recession because in some ways it is highly comparable to the Great Depression of the 1930s. In such times, despair may be understandable and unavoidable, but also a major barrier to continuing to try to find work. The number of unemployed who move off the unemployment list because they are no longer seeking work can grow. In the example that follows, an internal leader raises these powerful feelings.

Dealing with Despair and Long-Term Unemployment

PRACTICE POINTS

When a job training group is highly structured with written and verbal exercises as well as information presentation, it is possible to miss the underlying feelings of participants that may have a powerful impact on their ability to make use of the information and skill training. In the next example, we see the group leader first reacting defensively to a negative comment by a member in the second group session but then catching himself in midsession to explore the meaning behind the words. It's not surprising because the group leader will also have feelings about the discouraging job situation when he tries to lead a group that tries to develop hope. This "deviant member" turns out to be an internal leader raising important issues that need to be integrated into the discussion.

Tim said he had something to say before we started the meeting. He went on to say that he had found last week's exercises and role plays a waste of time. He felt it had avoided the real issues they faced in trying to get jobs. I felt angry and floored by his comment. I said, "Well, I'm sorry you didn't find the group that helpful. I hope this week will be more useful. It might help if you got more involved in the discussion instead of just being critical." The group was subdued after my comments, and I had the sinking feeling that I was blowing it, but I had absolutely no way of figuring out how to stop myself and change directions. I just put my head down and plowed ahead with this week's scheduled presentation, sinking deeper as I went along.

PRACTICE POINTS

The next intervention, catching his mistake, is crucial. By apologizing, he models effective adult behavior in the face of criticism and opens the door for a real discussion. Catching a mistake in the same session is, in my view, very skillful practice indeed.

> About halfway through the session, I recovered enough to try to get back to Tim. I stopped the group and said, "I want to apologize to Tim. I told you folks that I wanted honest feedback on how the group was going, and the first time someone gave me feedback I didn't like hearing, I got defensive. Tim, will you give me another chance? What did you mean when you said we were not getting at the real issues last week? What are the real issues for you?" After some silence, Tim said it's all right to talk about job interviews and using the telephone for finding positions and résumé writing, but what if you have given up all hope? What good is it to keep trying if all you get is a lot of rejections? I was quiet for a moment as I began to feel his despair.
>
> I asked if others in the group shared some of Tim's feelings. I said, "I wonder how many of you were also going through the role play while you were wondering if it was worth all the effort?" After a brief silence, Tammy said she was feeling low as well, that it wasn't just Tim. I said that perhaps I was rushing into trying to discuss ways to find jobs, and I hadn't really taken enough time to let them talk about what was going on inside them. I thought that was important to talk about as well, and I thanked Tim for having the guts to slow me down. I said we should talk about what they are going through, and then we can see if some of these exercises can be helpful at all.

PRACTICE SUMMARY

By treating the deviant member as an ally, the leader gave permission for the group to begin a frank discussion of how they were experiencing the group but also their disappointing job search. Others in the group felt the freedom to express their dissatisfaction, and as a result, the group members began to take responsibility for making the group more effective. The issue led some group members to point out the need to be determined in the face of adversity and not to allow all of the rejections, as painful as they were, to stop them from making the effort. This also led to efforts to improve their job search skills, which were the essential purposes of the group.

The Impact of Group Member Differences in More Heterogeneous Groups

In each of the preceding groups, the members had most issues in common. That is not always the case, and at times groups may be organized in which there are significant differences between participants. These difference may enhance the group if the group leader can help the members identify the more general issues associated with the employment barriers. The barriers facing the welfare mothers in the first example in this chapter and those facing the ex-offenders are very different; however, the general problems of lack of confidence and internalized negative self-image that exacerbated the impact of those barriers create a common theme of concern. The specific stages of emotional stress facing a person who has recently exhausted his or her unemployment insurance, such as those in the previous example, may be quite different from those encountered by someone who has been out of work for 2 years and has apparently become resigned to it. However, both clients may face depression, the problem of how to use their time effectively, and the challenge to maintain a sense of hope. With the group leader's help, these variations in the concerns may not be insurmountable obstacles to the group's development.

Some differences in concerns may indeed make mutual aid extremely difficult. For example, the issues facing youth at risk who are recruited from the street by an outreach worker may be so different from those facing an unemployed adult with a family that bringing these two populations together for anything other than a general meeting may not be productive. Street youth who need to deal with sensitive and taboo issues such as the impact of their involvement in prostitution to survive will not be able to work effectively in a group with a mixed population. In addition, the age differential between the youth population and the adult population may be too much to overcome because they are facing significantly different developmental tasks. In the next example, a group for unemployed adults, many with special needs, the group leader addresses the differences in the group while attempting to identify the common ground.

In another example, the problems facing ESL (English as a second language) clients in obtaining a job will be replicated in the process of a mutual aid group. That is, they will have difficulty talking in a larger English-speaking group, which mirrors the problem they will face in the job market. The group process attempting to overcome this difficulty can be central to their work. However, this work may not be as useful to English-speaking members in a mixed group.

I am suggesting that there are no hard and fast rules in deciding on the range of acceptable variation in group composition for employment groups. Each program must develop its rules from its own experiences. However, in the first session of a heterogeneous group, the group leader should be sensitive to the importance of this issue and should be prepared to raise it for discussion, as is illustrated in the next example.

Employment Groups Including Persons with Special Needs

Employment counseling agencies, government and private sponsored, do not always have the luxury of forming groups with distinct populations. Funding issues and the availability of enough potential members of a particular population may mean some groups need to be offered to members with a variety of issues. It is important to address the heterogeneous nature of a group's population as well as to identify the common ground early in the first session. Consider this group leader's opening statement in the first session.

Group Purpose: To provide assistance in finding a job for members who have one form of special need or another

Group Members: Ten men and women, most but not all of whom have special needs such as a physical disability, language issues, minimal reading and/or writing ability, and so forth

After welcoming the members, I explained the purpose of the group: "We set up this group because we recognize that getting a job is not that easy, particularly if you face any special problems that can make it even more difficult. For example, some of you in this group have a physical disability that may make it more difficult for you to convince an employer that you can do the job. Others are relatively new immigrants who face having to find and hold a job using a second language. It can be frustrating trying to communicate that you can do the job in a language you did not grow up with. Finally, some of you have a hidden, less obvious barrier to cope with. For example, your in ability to read and write may stand in your way, or you may have a physical problem whose symptoms can come and go, such as epilepsy, that may prejudice employers against you. Even though the specific barriers are different for each of you, the common problem is how to find and keep a job in spite of them. We think you can help each other in tackling this issue and that we can help you with that. What do you think?"

An important aspect of this opening statement is the group leader's direct mentioning of the barriers. Members of the group have physical and health disabilities, literacy problems, and difficulties with the English language. Each of these difficulties can produce a level of shame in the participant and make it difficult not only to hear what is said but also to speak. For example, in our society, not being able to read and write is such an embarrassing problem that many people work almost full-time at ways to cover up this lack of ability. The group leader opens by stressing the common ground between members but also articulates the differences. This honest opening allows one of the members, Fran, to raise directly the issue of potential lack of common ground. The group leader credits her for raising the concern and then uses her comment to help group members begin to explore whether their commonalities can overcome their differences.

> After a pause, Fran said she didn't think they had as much in common as I did. I said I was glad Fran could say that right away, because I thought others in the group might have the same concern. Could she elaborate on why she felt that way? She said she didn't have the same problems they did because she wasn't physically handicapped, she could read and write, and she spoke English just fine. She was wondering what she was doing in this group. She asked if she might have been placed in this group by mistake.
>
> I asked her to specify some of the barriers she faced in finding work, and she said her problem was her kids. A lot of employers felt that single parents with kids would not be reliable workers, and so she felt they were prejudiced against her from the start. I commented that her major concern was how to convince employers that she could and would do the job. I wondered if we might take a minute to see if there was a connection between Fran's concern and what the others faced. It might help all of them to decide if they were in the right group as well.

Rather than being thrown by the comment, the group leader encourages Fran to discuss her issues and then tries to search out the common ground by inviting other participants to respond.

> Terry, who was a paraplegic in a wheelchair, felt that he also ran into bosses who had their mind made up before they even spoke to him. He was applying for jobs that did not require the use of his legs, yet they always asked questions in the interview that made him mad. I asked him what the questions were. He recalled a recent interview in which it was obvious the boss felt he might be accident-prone even though he had worked before and had an excellent accident-free record. I responded that most employees don't understand that physically challenged workers often have better work records in terms of sick leave and the like, than nondisabled workers. Many employers also do not understand the rules in hiring that are spelled out in the Americans with Disabilities Act (ADA) and end up asking subtle or not so subtle questions that they shouldn't ask. Terry said you bet we have good work records, because when we get a job we really want to hold onto it.

It's important that the group leader not try to convince the members of the common ground. It has to come from their stories and has to be discovered by them as they listen.

> I asked if others in the group could relate to this issue of convincing employers that you could do the job. I noted Fran and the whole group watching intently as other members shared their examples of prejudice against them. I was surprised when Lou, an epileptic, talked about his

experiences and about the fears bosses had about him having a seizure on the job. He had told me in the premeeting interview with me that he didn't feel comfortable talking about his epilepsy in the group. The conversation was marked by a lot of anger toward others, particularly bosses who judged him as unreliable and were unwilling to give him a chance.

The core skill described in Part 1 of searching out the common ground between members when all they can see is their differences is illustrated in the preceding interventions. Each member may still have to decide if the differences outweigh the similarities, but at least it can be an informed decision.

I summarized after a while and said we could do some work in this group on what some of the ways were to increase their chances of making their cases in interviews with potential employers. We could also discuss their rights in those situations where they feel they were not considered solely because of their disability or gender or the fact they had a family.

I told them that as I listened to them, they sounded to me like a very reliable group who needed better ways of getting their message across. I turned to Fran and asked her what she thought now about whether this was the right group for her. I asked if she could see any connections. She said, "You know, its funny, but I was complaining about bosses prejudging me and not giving me a chance, and yet in this group, I think I did the same thing. I was ready to assume that I was really very different from everyone else. After listening for a while, I can see we are all fighting for the same thing; we want people to have some faith in us and to believe we can do the job. Perhaps I should give it a try. I smiled and told her I really appreciated her honesty. I thought she could make an important contribution to the group and was glad she would give it a try. I went on to tell all of the group members that if they ever felt the group discussion was not relevant to them, they should speak up, just like Fran did, and we could check that out.

PRACTICE POINTS

In addition to helping the group members decide whether to make that first decision—whether to invest in the group or not—the group leader has started to help the group develop a culture for work that will allow for honest conversation as the work proceeds. Also, it was important for other members for Fran to own up to her own prejudgment of them and the reasons for it. In many ways, the process in the group takes the members directly into the content.

Taking Some Responsibility for Employment Problems

It is not uncommon for group members to externalize their problems. That is, they blame everyone else and everything else except taking some responsibility for their part in the problems. The next two examples illustrate this phenomenon and how the group leader can intervene.

Losing a Job: The Gatekeeper Role

In the previous examples, we saw how the "deviant member" is often the one who feels a sense of urgency about a particular issue more strongly than the others. In a sense, the behavior is an effort to move the group toward real work if we understand the message as "Wait a minute, group leader. There are some things we need to address before you go any further." The internal leader, such as Fran in the previous group, often serves this function in a healthier, more direct way. A group can be ambivalent about work in the same way an individual may be; an individual member can assume the function of expressing that ambivalence for the group. This is sometimes seen as the gatekeeper role in which a member guards the gates through which the group must pass before the work can deepen.

It appears as a pattern, for example, when the group approaches a difficult subject, and the gatekeeper diverts the discussion. Humor is often used to guard the gate in difficult areas. While humor can make an important contribution to the work of the group by helping develop a positive group atmosphere, it can also be used as a subtle distraction from difficult areas of discussion. When a pattern persists in which one member plays this role and is encouraged by the reactions of the other group members, then gatekeeping may be at work. In a dynamic system, the gatekeeper's behavior is a signal of not just the individual's denial but of the group-as-a-whole. In the next excerpt, the group leader tries to help the group enter a taboo area.

Group Purpose: Helping members look at the reasons for their job losses and how to deal with stressful issues in the future

Group Members: Ten Caucasian men, all in their early to mid-20s, with recent job losses related to poor job performance

Louis had been talking about how he had lost his last job because of an argument with his supervisor. Since all of the young adults in the group had a record of poor job performance, I felt this issue was an important one. As Louis spoke, it was obvious that he was feeling discouraged, wondering if he could ever find or hold a job. I felt he was getting close to taking some responsibility for his part in the firings, rather than always blaming the bosses. I wanted to encourage this, but Terry interrupted by telling a story about how he got fired on his last job. It was a hilarious description of how he screwed up on a large order, and no matter how he had tried to cover it up, he kept getting deeper in trouble. As usual, Terry was effective in his storytelling, with the whole group joining in the laughter. I had mixed feelings. I was laughing with the rest of the group, but I also realized that once again Terry had sidetracked us at a crucial moment.

It's important to acknowledge the humor as well as the issues under the surface. Once the pattern is observed, the leader has to find a nonoffensive way of reaching for the underlying feelings without making the gatekeeper feel badly. The leader also needs to generalize to the group-as-a-whole since all of the members feel some of the resistance to talk about real issues—not just Terry the gatekeeper.

I tried to point this out to the group: I said I thought Terry's story was very funny, and I genuinely appreciated his humor; however, Louis was just talking about some difficult feelings he was having, and Terry's story had taken us right off Louis and his problem. I said this happened quite a bit. When we approached some tough issues, Terry would tell another funny story, and the rest of the group encouraged him. I was beginning to wonder if they, especially Terry, found it difficult to talk about some of these things. I suggested that maybe they all found it easier to joke than to face their feelings.

After a brief silence, Frank turned to Louis and asked him to remind them of what he was telling them when Terry told the story. They got back to the issue of their personal responsibility for losing their jobs, and this time, they were all in the discussion.

The important point in this excerpt is that the group leader confronted the group and Terry, by pointing out a pattern of what he saw happening each week. Even as he confronted Terry and the group, he was still supportive because he could genuinely understand how hard it might be to face the issues. He did not blame Terry and, instead, raised it as a group issue. Once the issue of gatekeeping was brought out into the open, it was not necessary to discuss it at length, making the topic Terry's role rather than job conflicts and difficulties. Simply articulating the pattern that can block the work—the existence of an obstacle to effective mutual aid—may be all that is necessary to help a group achieve a greater degree of sophistication and effectiveness. If the problem persists, further discussion may be necessary, and Terry may have to share some of his feelings that are hidden by the humor. However, it is crucial that the contract of the group not be subverted so that the group purpose is lost in the process (e.g., becomes a therapy or an encounter group) and the task of addressing employment issues forgotten.

Getting Angry on the Job and Then Getting Fired: The Defensive Member

Although defensiveness on the part of a group member has already been discussed in connection with other roles and with the issue of resistance in the beginning phase of work, it deserves some special attention. One often notices group members who seem to be particularly defensive about any criticism or self-reflection. The more serious the issue, the more deeply the individual feels a challenge to the sense of the core self and the more rigid will be the defenses.

Defensiveness on the part of a group member is a signal to the leader that the work is real, as opposed to an illusion of work. The individual struggling to deal with change needs to be challenged and confronted by other group members or the leader, in order to begin the process of lowering defenses. That is why the skill grouping I call the demand for work is so crucial. It serves as one of the catalysts for change; however, the individual will need all the support, understanding, and help possible to translate the defensive moment into movement to a new level of acceptance. Leaders often underestimate the difficulty of what they and group members are asking people to do in the way of making changes in their lives. The difficulty of this process needs to be respected. It requires a delicate integration of support and demand to create the conditions in which the group member may feel free enough to let down the barriers.

In the example that follows, a continuation of the previous group example, a group member resists any suggestions that he had anything to do with his getting fired from three different jobs. The more he denied the problem, the harder the group members pushed him to take responsibility. The key point to note is that the group leader understands he has two "clients"—the group and the defensive member—and tries to be with both.

> I said, "I think we are at a standstill right now. Everyone seems to be trying to convince Ted that he needs to take some responsibility for his problems with his bosses, own up to his temper problem, but the more you push him, the more he denies he has a problem. You all seem about to give up on him, and he must feel backed into a corner." Ray said that Ted was just too stubborn to admit he could have made some mistakes. He just wanted to blame things on his bosses. I said to Ted that he seemed to be having a hard time taking in what the group members were saying and could he tell us why? He said they just didn't understand what it really was like. I asked if he could explain it to the group so they could understand. He said

all he really wanted was a little appreciation on the job, instead of always getting criticized for what he did wrong. He told us when he started on his jobs, he really wanted to make it, not to get fired. But it didn't take long for his bosses to get on his back. They never told him he did anything right, only put him down. That was why he got so angry at them, and when the first conflicts came along, he just blew up and let them have it.

I said it must be tough to feel you are putting out on the job and getting no strokes or positives at all. No wonder he got mad. I asked if he ever tried to let his supervisors know he wanted to do a good job and would appreciate hearing from them when he was doing things right as well as when he was doing them wrong. He said he had never tried that. It was like brown nosing, sucking up to the supervisor.

PRACTICE POINTS

We have here another example discussed in the previous chapter of expecting someone to "divine" how you are feeling and then being angry when they don't meet your expectations. The worker has made a reasonable suggestion, but the member interprets it as a form of supplication. It takes another member to address it in a way that Ted can hear it.

Gene said he didn't agree. If you asked a supervisor straight out to let you know how you were doing, he found that it often helped a lot. Some supervisors were just impossible, and you had to learn to live with them if you wanted to hold a job or else find another job. But others, he had found, had really appreciated being asked for feedback. I said, "So I guess the problem for Ted is how to deal with his supervisor in a way that lets Ted keep his self-respect and, at the same time, receive some positive as well as negatives comments." Ted said that he had been through it so often that he begins with a chip on his shoulder and assumes the worst. Then, he usually gets the worst. I asked if any other group members had found ways to deal with this problem.

PRACTICE SUMMARY

It is interesting to note that as soon as the group leader broke into the vicious cycle of confronting and denying, by pointing out what was happening, and by asking Ted why it was so hard to take in the advice, the process began to move forward. As Ted talked about what he feels under the denial, as he explores his resistance, he starts to move toward new insights. The key to the process is to integrate some understanding of the source of the denial while continuing to push. With Ted, some movement began. With other clients, at certain stages in their lives, or maybe at a particular group meeting, they will not be able to let down their defenses. The fear of the unknown when they let go of defenses may be stronger at that moment than the desire to change and grow. It is important for the group leader to point out that he or she senses the change is too difficult at the moment. If Ted had continued to deny, the leader could have said, "We can't seem to get anywhere on this today. Maybe we should let it drop and give Ted a chance to think about it." Often, the time in between can make a difference.

Job-Related Group Counseling with Youth

Job and career counseling with youth may focus more on issues of deciding on career or job preferences and preparing for employment. The structured approach of the Self-Determined Career Development Model may be more useful in group counseling with youth than with adults who already have career choices made and skills required for a job. We have seen how important life transitions from adolescence to teenage to young adult have inherent stresses that need to be addressed. Also, more immature patterns of coping with these stresses can be observed in many in this age group. In the next example, we see how older teenagers maladaptively deal with their negative internalized self-image by scapegoating the member having the most difficulty with the program.

In a second example, a summer program for high school students experiencing on-the-job training, the group counselor needs to help one female member address issues of self-confidence as well as subtle and overt sexual harassment on the job site.

Older Teens in a Transition to Independence Group: The Scapegoat Phenomenon

The following example is of an employment preparation group offered to older teenagers who are making two powerful transitions: the transition from being wards of the state child welfare system to independence, and the transition to young adulthood and employment. Both are powerful life-changing events, and they can easily interact with each other. All of the members have at some point been in the foster care or residential treatment system. These clients will not be continuing their education after high school, so they need to develop their own means of support perhaps for the first time in their lives. Young adults entering the workforce during difficult employment times usually have their family of origin to turn to for support. Some even return home to repopulate the recently "empty nest." For these teenagers there is no empty nest.

> **Group Purpose:** To help older teenagers prepare for employment as they make the transition from foster or residential care to independence
>
> **Group Membership:** Seven teenagers (age 17 and 18), male and female, who have been long-term state wards in the child welfare system

PRACTICE POINTS Many of these group members have experienced trauma in their family of origin and have not had much success in their lives. In recent years, they may have been considered "drawer kids" by their child welfare foster care workers. That is, after some intensive tracking and services in their early teens, their files were "put in the file drawer" with only superficial agency involvement. They now face moving into a young adult role but without all of the supports provided by family. As they struggle to gain the skills needed for competing in the work environment, they fall back into old patterns of using a scapegoat, Fred, on whom they project all of their own self-perceived deficiencies. After having worked with this group for a period of time and having developed a good working relationship with the members, the group leader decides it is time to confront this scapegoating pattern.

> Fred had frozen during the role play of the interview with the prospective employer. He mumbled his answers, lost his train of thought, and in general was a disaster. Before I could say anything, a few of the group members made sarcastic comments about him being a "retard" and a "real nerd." Some of the group members laughed, joining in on the teasing.

PRACTICE POINTS As discussed in Part 1 when I dealt with the issue of members' roles in the group, it is crucial for the group leader not to give in to the normal tendency to simply side with the scapegoat and try to protect him from the hurt. The two-client idea helps the group leader by reminding him that simply shutting down the scapegoat is not the answer since it does not address the reason the group uses Fred to deal with their own insecurities.

I restrained my first impulse to express anger at them and instead said, "Could we stop and take a look at what's going on here? Fred has been struggling for weeks in this group, and most of you guys have been unmerciful in making fun of him. I've been thinking about it a lot. Sure, Fred has trouble in the role plays and the exercises, but I think it's because he doesn't have a hell of a lot of confidence in himself. The fact is most of you don't have much confidence in yourselves, either. Are you so unsure of yourselves that you can't help Fred with his feelings? Is it so scary for you that it's easier to give Fred a hard time than to deal with what you are feeling?"

The group was silent for a few moments as the force of my comments and my tone of voice seemed to hit home. Louise said she has never given Fred a hard time and had felt uncomfortable at all of the kidding. She just didn't have the guts to say so. Terry said he didn't understand what I meant. I said, "All of you are in this group because in some ways you have been struggling with the same problems in trying to get a job that Fred has. Maybe Fred has less confidence in himself than most of you, but it's my sense that all of you are worried about making it, ending up with no job and no future. I think all of you are wondering who you are, where you are going with your life, and whether you are going to make it. It's a tough time for all of you, but I think you might be able to help yourselves more if you faced it. Maybe, if you could help Fred gain more confidence, you might just be able to help yourselves as well."

PRACTICE POINTS The leader's understanding of the scapegoating process lets him tune in to the fact that the members' negative comments toward Fred reflect their own internalized feelings toward themselves. In a dynamic way, the group is using Fred and the scapegoating process to show the leader exactly what they need to work on in their own lives. All behavior by individuals and the group is a form of communication. By confronting the pattern, making a demand for work, and at the same time expressing his understanding of their underlying feelings, the leader has avoided the trap of identifying with the scapegoat versus the group members. Instead, he demonstrates how to be with both clients, the individual and the group, at the same time. Note how he credits a member's helpful intervention trying to create a new norm for member behavior.

The group was quiet again, until Louise turned to Fred and said, "Fred, how come you seem so down on yourself? If one of these guys doesn't put you down, you end up doing it yourself." I said, "That is better, Louise; that may start to be helpful." Fred looked pained so I said: "I know this is hard to talk about, Fred. I'll try to help you through it." Fred said, "You can't have a hell of a lot of confidence if everyone you know—your parents, your foster parents, your teachers, your friends—all tell you you're just a jerk. I guess after a while, you just begin to believe it." The other kids were quiet as they sensed the deep feelings in Fred's voice. I said, "It must be awfully painful to begin to believe you're not worth much. It must be hard to like yourself. It must be hard to think you have a chance, to keep on trying to do something with your life, to get a job, to make it." Fred seemed close to tears. He said, "I'm not so sure it's worth it, to keep trying."

The silence in the group went on for almost 30 seconds as the meaning of his words, the sense that he may be talking about suicide, sunk in to the other members. Chris said, "Look, man, I've been one of the guys giving you a hard time, and I'm sorry. I guess I never realized just how much you were hurting. I had a friend once, in high school, he carried a lot of hurt around inside and never let us know. One day, he tried to kill himself and almost made it. He pulled through, but I felt awful guilty about it. I thought about all of the times I didn't hear him when he was asking for help. I also felt mad at him because he had so much to live for.

"I know I've given you a hard time, but you know nothing is so bad that you should give up. We're all afraid about what's going to happen in the future. I know I bullshit a lot about the good life, and becoming a ski bum, but that's because I'm scared I'm going to become just a plain bum. I'm scared, but I'm not going to give up. I've still got some fight in me." I said, "I think that helps, too, Chris. How about the rest of you? Do you have anything to say to Fred?"

PRACTICE SUMMARY The session continued with other members of the group offering support and encouragement to Fred. As they were speaking to Fred, one could imagine they were also speaking to the part of themselves that also felt hopeless and close to giving up. The group leader had been helpful in starting to bridge the gap between the individual and the group by confronting the group members, but also by doing it in a way that was supportive and caring. He understood his role and the importance of being with both clients—the individual and the group. He asked them to understand how Fred was feeling, but as he did it, he demonstrated his understanding and feelings for them. This was the beginning of a mutual aid process in which emotional support as well as constructive criticism was used by the group members to help Fred begin to assert himself and to master the skills he needed to develop.

Worksite Training Program for Teenagers: Addressing Sexual Harassment

In the following example, an employment counselor leads a group for older high school students who are employed in a summer on-site job training program in the construction field. The focus of the leader's report is her work with one individual member of the group to help her become more assertive with other, male group members. The group leader, also female, does not address early in the group that the member is the "only one"—that is, the only female in a male group. In the course of the work, the counselor discovers that the job site used by the agency has workers and supervisors who make sexual comments and express gender-biased attitudes that amount to harassment. Given the persistence of sexists attitudes in many areas of the workforce, helping this member deal with an all-male group and discriminatory work experiences is an important way of helping her prepare for the reality of the world of work. The group leader's work with the group's job site supervisors and her own agency illustrates clearly the importance of the two-client concept. In approaching this example, the group leader concentrates on work with the individual member and the group.

Type of Group: Work ethic oriented, educational group for older teens

Age Range of Members: 16–18

Gender, Ethnic, Sexual Orientation, and Racial Information: All group members were Caucasian, descending from several white ethnic backgrounds including Irish, German, and English. These group members lived in a rural, secluded community. This educational group consisted of three males and one female.

Dates Covered in Record: June 3 to August 10

Description of Problem

Brenda is unable to vocalize her own feelings or thoughts to the group as a whole or to the individual group members. When specifically asked a question, Brenda seems to disappear into herself, staring away blankly from the perceived threat of demand

and its source. I experience Brenda as depressed, lonely, and insecure; a small girl who recoils from attention regardless of the level of threat. I often encounter great difficulty engaging her in conversation or group participation.

PRACTICE POINTS In the early notations by this group leader, we can note a pattern of trying to use humor as a way of reaching group members. The group leader soon realizes her use of humor is her way of dealing with stress and not helpful to the group or the members.

How the Problem Came to the Attention of the Group Leader(s)

When filling out the required paperwork and discussing the upcoming experience in the workforce, Brenda would not make eye contact with any other group member or myself. The other group members quickly began to converse regarding a number of subjects, giving little regard to Brenda sitting to the left of them. When I questioned her directly about her hope for the summer experience, she lowered her head, appeared uncomfortable, and quickly began to fill out the paperwork. As the first session came to a close, her demeanor had not changed, and I found myself almost "performing" to get some reaction from Brenda. When no reaction was given, I quickly realized this particular member would be difficult to incorporate into the group process. This problem was further evident through the other group members' complete lack of acknowledgment of Brenda's presence, through lack of greetings, discussion, and eye contact during the entire hour.

PRACTICE POINTS An important step for this group leader is to tune in to her feelings and to recognize her own use of humor as a form of flight—as described in earlier chapters—when experiencing her own anxiety. In this case, the humor blocks rather than enhances the work.

Summary of the Work

I tried to break any awkward silence by utilizing humor to begin the discussion of the first week of work and develop a rapport, which did not work. This "intervention," the use of humor, becomes most evident when I am feeling insecure of my abilities. This is evidenced by the beginning week of the program, when I met Brenda first in the hallway. She promptly avoided eye contact by lowering her head. I nervously smiled and began a lengthy salutation by mentioning traffic, parking, and the impact the school's construction has on both previously mentioned topics. Brenda did not respond to any comment or question. I then asked her if she knew where the meeting room was in the school. Brenda nodded slightly and quickly turned to walk in the opposite direction. I commented on her fast walking, making joking references to her fast pace. My statements were met with dead silence, with no facial or bodily reactions.

PRACTICE POINTS As we have seen so often, the group member's behavior is a form of communication. The crucial skill is for the group leader to recognize this and to inquire as to what it means.

At this point we had discovered the other members of the group and moved to the meeting room. During the session, all members but Brenda made eye contact, spoke with other group members, and smiled or laughed at one point in the meeting. Brenda's head remained lowered, only to rise when I would turn slightly to gather paperwork or reach into the briefcase. When I was not looking directly at her, she would study me with her eyes, scanning my body while focusing on my speech as well. Several times during the session, I caught her staring at me intently with my peripheral vision. When I would look directly at her, she would appear as if she had never lifted her head or averted her eyes. Brenda's evaluation of me made me very uncomfortable, resulting in small jokes and nervous laughter on my part.

PRACTICE POINTS

It is not unusual for group leaders to also use humor to cover their own anxiety. By joking with Brenda rather than addressing her pattern of avoidance and apparent shyness, the group leader has to find out what is upsetting her through a forwarded e-mail from her own supervisor. It also becomes clear that the group leader is not receiving helpful supervision from her supervisors.

Approximately 3 weeks into the program, I received a forwarded e-mail from Brenda, sent to my supervisor, in which she discusses her purse being stolen by another member of the group, the lack of work by the other members of the group, and inappropriate comments concerning her ability to work due to her gender by the group members. This original e-mail was sent to the director of the program, as Brenda knew her outside the program. This e-mail was the first contact I had ever had with Brenda, even though the e-mail was not directly sent to me. I sent her an e-mail explaining my intentions to discuss these matters in group and with their on-site supervisor, since I believed these actions were not suitable for a healthy work atmosphere. I emphasized my gratefulness for her information but suggested she bring up this information when I am visiting the work site, and I would act promptly on the issue. I stated she should feel welcome to contact me through e-mail, if the subject was too uncomfortable to discuss in person.

PRACTICE POINTS

The response from the supervisor described next is not supportive of the group leader and in fact reveals the not uncommon lack of understanding of group process and the role of a group counselor.

After the information I received from Brenda was evaluated by my superiors and their on-site supervisor, it was made clear I was to "lecture" the group and "give them a slap on the wrist" because "boys will be boys." It should be mentioned the agency's stance on this subject was sent to Brenda via e-mail by the director, stating the same plan as above. However, the issue was stated in ambiguous terms and was unclear. When I arrived on the site, I found the group all in one room, painting with no ventilation and paint thinner uncapped. Only Brenda appeared uncomfortable, with her shirt pulled over her face, while squinting her eyes. The other members were giggling and joking until they saw me enter the room. I requested they enter the group room immediately and watched while they slowly prepared their area for work later in the day.

PRACTICE POINTS

The group leader is concerned about the safety issues involved but also about the dangerous use of solvents to get high. This kind of behavior on the work site needed to be addressed. The group leader makes clear that limits will be enforced and the boys could be expelled from the program.

As they entered the room, the boys all exchanged nervous glances as they had been previously warned on proper painting ventilation and the policy against the use of paint thinner. At this time, I reexplained the procedures and the causes for expulsion from the program. Brenda and the rest of the group remained still, as all appeared very nervous. Brenda appeared to be fearful of future statements I would make, as she was intensely concentrating on the conversation.

I then listed off the offenses I had witnessed that day and that have been reported to the agency, at which time I included Brenda's complaints without mention of her name.

The group members looked around at each other seemingly confused on how I knew all the behaviors for the past 3 weeks. I then explained how many of their offenses could be utilized for expulsion for each member and spent considerable time on the issues of sexual harassment, respect for co-workers, and what would happen in the "real world" if these behaviors occurred. I stated if they would like to work and earn a salary, then they were going to actively work in group meetings and avoid feeding me inaccurate information. I stated this was an opportunity for each of the members to learn from their mistakes, and I suggested they take advantage for this experience, while not abusing their privilege. Each member agreed and contracted to actively bring work related issues to group.

PRACTICE POINTS The group leader, following her supervisor's suggestions, has "laid down the law" to the group members. Of course, doing so avoids any discussion of what is going on for the group and each of the members. It also guarantees the group members will not be open with the group leader, fearing the results. She was correct in setting limits but needed to go further dealing with the meaning of the behaviors.

During this discussion and confrontation, Brenda at first seemed nervous but made eye contact with me the entire session. When I addressed the sexual harassment, paint thinner, and purse stealing, Brenda would glance at her fellow group members to seemingly gauge their reaction. Once I was finished with the session, I glanced over to see Brenda mouth "thank you," before lowering her head for the remainder of the session. This was the first contact directly made from Brenda toward me.

PRACTICE POINTS While the group leader has read the "riot act" to the male group members, she has still not talked directly to Brenda. This is where her supervision on the incident fell short. Brenda needs to be able to assert herself as the only female in the group and, as will become clear, stand up for herself in response to the sexist put-downs from group members and workers on the site.

I regret the use of authority regarding this session; however, I was still responsible for the agency's expectations to instill a work ethic into these youths. In retrospect, these issues could have been dealt with when they were smaller and less extreme if I had effectively utilized a group check-in, while steadily working toward a rapport.

After the previously mentioned group session, Brenda began writing me routinely. I wrote back every time, as e-mail was expected by the agency, and I hoped she would be comfortable enough to speak in person to the group after becoming comfortable with myself. As the e-mails continued, she would speak a few more words in the group, gradually increasing as the weeks progressed. In these letters she would thank me for "sticking up" for her and indirectly "vent" concerning the abuse she encountered at home and from her boyfriend. However, as she was 18 years old, there was nothing that could be reported as she was "willingly" staying with her parents, according to the director of the agency.

PRACTICE POINTS The mention of abuse at home deserved more discussion, in person and not by e-mail. Was the abuse emotional, physical, and/or sexual? Were there younger siblings living at home? If so, then a report might be required. Did Brenda want to discuss her situation at home and consider alternatives since she was 18? The e-mail correspondence starts to raise additional issues that while not directly related to work clearly can have an impact on Brenda's work experience. Mental health and behavioral counseling are not part of this counselor's role, but identifying these issues, understanding how they impact Brenda's work, and making referrals to appropriate resources should be addressed.

Through these e-mails, she explained she is uncomfortable speaking with anyone and tries to avoid eye contact, regardless of the environment. When I would ask her to explain when these behaviors began, she wrote of her early teenage years and later divulged an incident of date rape that resulted in pregnancy at the age of 14. It was vaguely explained when she informed her parents of the event, she was physically beaten and emotionally abused. Brenda eventually lost the fetus due a miscarriage, which she attributed to the physical abuse. Her behaviors then began to make sense, as she was reacting as an abused individual and was extremely meek in all situations. Her abuse was later confirmed by records within the agency, as well as by her previous social services caseworker.

At this time, I realized I had spent so much time with papers and generalized work ethic material, I was ignoring the group members and concentrating on Brenda solely due to the ease of replying to her e-mails when it was convenient. However, through her story I was aware of remaining ignorant to the issues at home for all the group members, and the factors that would contribute to the adverse behaviors at the work site. In essence, I was failing my group by focusing on the desired result, and I was not spending time on what issues were barriers to the members to succeed. If faced with this issue again, I would refrain from connecting so closely to one member and focus on the group as a whole.

PRACTICE POINTS As the group becomes more actively involved in discussion another issue emerged: the behavior of the worksite full-time staff. This time the group leader does intervene directly with the staff and their supervisor.

After the previous session when I confronted the group, they began to work on their issues related to work. Brenda began to participate, although speaking less than most of the other members. Brenda even developed a friend from the group. Also, the group would routinely discuss the regular construction staff in vague terms, never telling an entire story and seemingly avoiding the actual details. This subject remained unclear, even when I actively probed for details. I believed some negative events had taken place, but I was blocked from questioning staff by the on-site supervisor.

After the fifth session, I ran into the regular staff during their lunch break in a main hallway. I began to make small talk with the employees and noticed the members of my group were staying apart from the staff. Brenda exited the hall immediately and nervously began working in a nearby room, completing tasks that she had not mentioned were on her list. This strong reaction from the group caused me to question further into the staff's perception and treatment of the group members. I was nervous, so I used humor again by jokingly asking which one of the group members was the strongest. One of the older men stated, "The boys do just fine, for being small. You have to repeat yourself often, but all she's good for [gesturing toward Brenda] is washing windows and sweeping." This comment caused a roar of laugher from the other staff, with several other comments concerning women in maintenance. They continued by expressing a negative view of Brenda's worth.

PRACTICE POINTS This comment finally revealed the abusive situation that Brenda was working in. While one can understand how sexist attitudes have developed in largely male work groups in the construction field, and even their real fears of being replaced by women or minorities at a time when work opportunities are limited, this behavior is unacceptable, and it becomes part of the group leader's role to make this clear.

I explained to the group of men the contribution all of the group members had made to the completion of the summer's improvements. I continued by pointing out that their supervisor would not be too happy if the group members were pulled from the worksite. As I continued to explain, the students stopped working and moved into the doorway of the hallway. They stayed there until I completed my speech on the students' worth to the agency, the worksite, and to myself. As I began to explain the concept of sexual harassment, the on-site supervisor walked in. I asked the supervisor to speak in private with the group members to discuss the degrading comments made by the staff. The group members were all exchanging nervous smiles, and all spoke of their experiences with the staff to their onsite supervisor.

Brenda spoke of the offensive comments made by staff and made eye contact for a majority of the conversation. The on-site supervisor apologized for the treatment of my group members and promised to "thoroughly investigate the issues at hand."

PRACTICE POINTS It was important for the group leader to confront the negative work atmosphere and to make clear to the group members that this was not acceptable behavior. However, important issues were also raised that should be dealt with in terms of agency policy. For example, how does the agency choose work sites? Does the program include segments of discussion that clarify legal and ethical issues of worksite harassment and help participants develop strategies for dealing with it on the training site and potentially on a future job? Wouldn't it be important to work with the male members of the group on their responsibilities when on a worksite and sexist comments or activities emerge? All of these issues are related to work ethics and need to be incorporated into the work preparation program.

Where the Problem Stands Now

The group has since ended, but during the final stages of the program, Brenda appeared to blossom. Her friendship within the group was strengthening, as they were discovering mutual friends and making plans outside the group. The other group members began to treat one another as equals, a matter that was helped by the maintenance staff being strictly informed of inappropriate language. Brenda would speak up in group but still remained primarily a listener. After the confrontation with the regular staff, the group seemed to merge into one of mutual aid and support. Each member appeared to care about the difficulties experienced by the others. Brenda has since been working on making eye contact and conversing freely with other individuals.

When the program ended, I recommended a prolonged work experience for Brenda and was able to place her in a human services organization that works with individuals with varying levels of intensity. Since Brenda dropped out of school at her parents' suggestion, the supervisor of the agency has enrolled her into GED (General Education Degree) classes and is sending her to counseling for dealing with her issues related to her abuse.

PRACTICE SUMMARY A major theme of this chapter is that job and career counseling groups, for young people and adults, have to address the personal and social obstacles that they face. For counseling to be effective, the group leader has to find a way to connect attention to these issues while staying focused on the core purpose of the setting. It was appropriate to work with Brenda on her ability to assert herself in work situations but would have been inappropriate to use the group to deal with unresolved issues resulting from her sexual, physical, and emotional abuse. The referral to other agencies that serve young men and women like Brenda was the appropriate step. It's a mistake for job and career counseling groups to work from a predetermined framework without recognizing the need for a flexibility that responds to the job and career related needs of the participants.

Chapter Summary

Vocational counselors, also called employment or career counselors, provide their services mainly outside the school setting. Individual and group counseling models, such as the Self-Determined Career Development Model (SDCDM), offer a structured way of assisting clients in thinking about their career and job choices and the steps needed to achieve them.

Employment group counseling should also address the barriers that can block participants from achieving their job and career goals. These can be addressed in a supportive manner if job and career counseling groups include an element of mutual aid. Examples of barriers illustrated in this chapter included a group for single-parent women on public assistance seeking employment who experience guilt feelings about not being home for their children. In another example, men who have been unemployed for a period of time in a poor job market have to deal with a sense of hopelessness that emerges when they find themselves role-playing interviews when no jobs or job interviews are available. Another example was ex-offenders on parole who must face the discrimination against them when prospective employers ask what they have been doing the past few years or notice their prison tattoos. The importance of addressing initial resistance to participate in mandated groups was once more emphasized. The skills required to address the defensiveness of group members who have lost their jobs, in part because of their own behavior, were also described.

Older teenagers face their own set of issues as they make the transition associated with the young adult stage of the life cycle and attempt to enter the workforce. Examples in the chapter included working with youth who must also make the transition from being clients in a child welfare system to independence for which they feel unprepared. Groups in job training programs such as on-site work experiences need to incorporate discussion of the barriers facing participants including sexual harassment, lack of social skills, and negative experiences with discrimination. These issues can affect a young person's confidence and ability to acquire the job skills needed to function in the world of work. Illustrations of these struggles were provided, and the argument was made that for teens and adults, mutual aid can be an important element in any employment group experience.

Related Online Content and Activities

For learning tools such as glossary terms, InfoTrac® College Edition keywords, links to related websites, and chapter practice quizzes, visit this book's website at **www.cengage.com/counseling/shulman**.

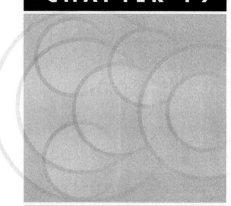

CHAPTER 19

Group Counseling in Medical and Rehabilitation Settings

What Do Counselors Do in Medical and Rehabilitation Settings?

Counselors dealing with medically related issues practice in a variety of work settings, including hospitals, outpatient clinics, rehabilitation, and long-term care settings. Although such settings are not specifically defined as a counseling specialty, with the exception of rehabilitation and gerontological counseling, group practice can play an important part in helping patients, caretakers, and family members cope with the impact of physical and emotional illness and disability within the medical setting or in outpatient services. Group counseling in a hospital, rehabilitation, or long-term care facility can serve many purposes, some related to medical issues (e.g., information on the illness or injury, treatment options, etc.) and others to the patient's interaction with the setting itself.

The examples used in this chapter to illustrate practice in this setting include the following:

- Group counseling with paraplegics in a rehabilitation center
- Caregiver support group in a hospice setting
- Patient empowerment through a newspaper in a VA hospital
- A living-with-cancer group

Stages of the Problem and Engagement with the Setting

In Part 1, I used the framework of time to describe the phases of the helping process: preliminary, beginning, work, and ending/transitions. The impact of time can also be helpful in thinking about the issues associated with the medical problem or the relationship to the setting. For example, there is the beginning stage when the patient is first diagnosed with the illness or assessed as having a physical or mental problem requiring long-term care. This often coincides with the beginning stage of engagement with the hospital, rehabilitation, or long-term care setting.

The ongoing or middle stage is illustrated by the example in this chapter of patients with a long-term experience with cancer who are undergoing chemotherapy over a number of months or years. Instead of dealing with the shock of the diagnosis, they and their significant others must now deal with the profound changes in their lives caused by the illness and its treatment.

If the medical problems require long-term hospitalization, such as in two examples in this chapter—a group for paraplegics in a rehabilitation setting or psychiatric patients in a Veterans Administration (VA) hospital—then the group counselor needs to consider the setting itself as the second client. Helping the group negotiate its environment, the "external system" as discussed in the presentation of Homans's (1950) social systems model in Chapter 8, can be central in empowering patients to deal with both their medical problems and their environment.

Finally, patients may be in an ending stage with their illness or rehabilitation procedure. This situation is illustrated in an excerpt from group work with caretakers for patients in the end-of-life stage of their illness residing in a hospice. Whatever the stage of the illness and treatment, or the stage of engagement with the setting, group practice can provide an important source of support for patients and their significant others.

Group Counseling for Hospital and Rehabilitation Inpatients

The examples that follow touch on all three stages of engagement with the medical problem as well as with the facility. Each example shows how the interaction with the external facility impacts the patient's ability to address the medical issues involved. The unique role of the counselor in monitoring each member of the group, the group process, and the group members' relationship to the environment are illustrated.

Group Counseling with Paraplegics in a Rehabilitation Center

In an example from a Canadian physical rehabilitation center for paraplegics who are still early in their rehabilitation treatment, a middle-stage issue emerges. A patients' council group was formed to allow the mostly young male patients to provide feedback to the center on medical and other services. At one meeting, they were informed by their counselor that the medical director was considering canceling the policy of allowing weekend passes to return to their homes. The reason for this change was that many of them were returning to the hospital with bed sores. The patient members of the council erupted in anger, and the following conversation took place:

LEADER: Dr. Mansfield met with me and told me that many patients are returning with bedsores. He is deeply concerned about this and feels that he may have to revoke the weekend pass policy.

LOUIS: (With great anger). He can't do that. If he takes away that privilege, we will wheel down to his office, and he'll have a sit-in on his hands.

JOHN: Who does he think he is, anyway? We fought hard for that privilege, and he can't take it away. (Others murmur in angry agreement.)

LEADER: I can understand why you are so angry. The pass is really important to you. It's important to see your families. But, tell me, I don't understand: Why are so many people coming back with bedsores? (A very long silence)

TERRY: (Speaking slowly and staring at the floor) Here at the center, the nurses turn us in our beds all the time. When we go home, our families do not.

WORKER: (Suddenly understanding) And you are too ashamed to ask them, isn't that it?

PRACTICE POINTS

In the discussion that followed, the group members talked poignantly about their feelings concerning their newfound dependency. Many felt they had lost their "manhood" and were ashamed to need help with going to the bathroom and turning in their beds. So, they simply did not ask for help. At this time, a number of years ago, routine provision of home care services was not provided through their government health care plans. As the men in the group discussed their family's reactions, it emerged that their wives or partners were also often too embarrassed to ask what kind of help they needed. It soon became clear to the worker that the problem of bedsores was an indirect communication of the need for an important new area of service: addressing the problem of dependency, patients' and family members' feelings about it, and how to handle it.

The group leader's next step was to ask for a meeting with the medical director, and, after sharing the discussion with the patients, the leader enlisted his support in calling a meeting with the various department heads to report on the session. At the meeting he said, "A most interesting issue was raised when I talked to the patients at the council meeting about the bedsores, and I wanted to share it with you to get your reactions and ideas." After the group leader recounted the discussion, the staff fell silent as the department heads thought about the implications of this feedback for their areas. The group leader suggested it might be helpful to explore this question of dependency as it was handled throughout the institution and to see if some special attention could be paid to the problem.

PRACTICE SUMMARY

Once again, as in Chapter 15 on school counseling, we can see the importance of the group leader taking the stance of involving his professional colleagues in a mutual discussion of an issue that was relevant to their work. From this discussion emerged a plan to raise the issue in the various departments and to develop new services to deal with the problem. One proposal was to hold groups for relatives of recently paralyzed patients that would specifically focus on their reactions to the accident and their questions about their ongoing relationships—particularly how to handle the feelings of dependency they were sure to encounter. Programs for patients were also proposed, and staff training implications were discussed. The group leader suggested that these discussions should involve the patient council so that their input could be considered.

Caregiver Support Group in a Hospice Setting

Group Purpose: To provide support to family and friends while their loved one is in the inpatient unit

Age Range of Members: Late 20s to early 80s

Gender, Ethnic, Sexual Orientation, and Racial Information: Because this was an open-ended group, the group composition was continually changing. In the two sessions described in this record of service, all members were Caucasian. In the first session there were four females and three males, and in the second session there were three females and one male.

Background

When I began my internship at Hospice Inpatient Unit, there were no groups running. With support from my supervisor, I constructed this caregiver support group for the family and friends of the patients in the unit. The patients on this unit can stay up to 2 weeks only, but the average stay is about 3–5 days. At this point the patient either passes or is discharged home or to a nursing home. Due to this unique environment, the most number of group sessions one person will attend is two. I have led two groups to this date, and both have had completely new members.

Description of the Problem

In a hospice inpatient unit, family members and friends often hold vigil with their dying loved ones. Although counselors are available at all times to assist these family members in their time of need, a sense of loneliness is very evident in these families. The ability to hear that others are experiencing similar feelings and thoughts as themselves, the all-in-the-same-boat phenomenon, is comforting to these families. Although this group offers multiple positive therapeutic interventions, problems are also associated with holding an open-ended group. Often members attend only a single session. Problems such as addressing taboo subjects, dealing with group roles such as monopolizer and scapegoat, and being able to work through all three stages of a group within a single session exist for the members and well as the group leaders.

How This Problem Came to the Attention of the Group Leader(s)

Dealing with the issues of death and dying is a strong taboo subject for most of our society. Avoidance of taboo subjects can lead to the illusion of work. An example of this would be a conversation held in the first session. The conversation was about the lack of government funding for cancer research. A 10-minute conversation about the anger these families held for the government was really just an avoidance mechanism from dealing with the sadness they were feeling about the death of their loved one.

The second occurred during a conversation within the group with a father who was losing his daughter to breast cancer. At the end of his revelation to the group of his feelings on this matter, he just stood up and left, which prompted the rest of the group to stand up and leave as well. The group had not ended.

I have discussed in earlier chapters the difficulty in dealing with taboo subjects such as death and dying. It seems a bit ironic that in a *hospice*—a setting devoted to helping patients and family members and friends deal with the end stage of life—the subject of death remains taboo. The group leader recognizes this in her analysis of her first session. In Chapter 9 on the ending phase of group practice, I referred to the stages of death and dying described by Kübler-Ross (1969) that suggested that anger, following denial, was one way to avoid dealing with painful endings. This group leader's first session appears to have been dominated by anger and an avoidance of the painful feelings underneath. In the anger we see the "fight" defense; and in members' leaving the session early, we see a clear example of "flight."

First Session

Before the first session, I practiced tuning in to this population with my co-leader. We spoke at length and brainstormed about what feelings and fears these individuals would bring to the group. We drew on prior experiences and knowledge of the population. I walked around the unit about 15 minutes prior to the start of the group session and informed families who had just arrived that a group was being offered, some information about the group, and the location. Seven people showed up, three on time, and four walked in about 10 minutes late.

My co-leader began the session by introducing herself and me. She reviewed the purpose and the ground rules of the group. The purpose she presented was to provide a safe and comfortable environment where people could share their fears and feelings and provide support to each other in a respectful and empathetic way. We then began introductions around the circle.

Mike and Shelly began. They were brother and sister whose mother had been admitted the day before the group started for pain issues that could not be treated in the home. About 2 weeks prior, their father had been admitted to the unit for similar reasons. They shared how it was difficult to care for both of their parents at the same time, especially when the daughter lived out of town and could only stay for a couple weeks at a time to assist her brother with their care.

The group leaders are conscious of the need to bring the new members into the group. Coming into a group in the middle of a session can feel like arriving in the middle of a movie after missing the first reel. The task is to bring the new members in without starting all over.

At this point the remaining four members entered the room. The members were seated, and my co-leader asked the first members who shared to give a brief overview of what they had just said for the newest members of the group. Shelly was honest and said she could not go through it again as she was very emotional from the first time. Mike agreed and gave a succinct review of what they had just revealed. The newest group members thanked him.

The next person to introduce himself is an elderly man named Pat. Pat was outwardly upset and started to talk but quickly stopped and asked if we could get back to him. The group all nodded yes. Next was an elderly married couple named Ben and Mary. Ben began to speak as if he was speaking for both of them. He told the group that their daughter was in the unit with breast cancer for end-of-life care. This was common hospice lingo that these families have unfortunately come to know very well, meaning their daughter would die very soon. Another group member said aloud that it "just wasn't right for a child to go before a parent." The rest of the group nodded in agreement. The couple was silent after this comment.

The next member, Diane, said that she would continue the introductions. Diane was an elderly woman. She told the group that she was on the unit because her boyfriend had been admitted 3 days prior and was here for end-of-life care as well. She spoke about how he had been her companion for many years since her husband had died, and she did not know what she was going to do when he was gone. She was visibly upset and asked if the she could stop there. My co-leader quickly thanked her for sharing and encouraged the next member to speak.

The next member to speak was Carol. Carol was a woman in middle age whose husband was admitted for end-of-life care as well for pancreatic cancer. She ended her introduction there.

<table>
<tr><td>

PRACTICE POINTS

</td><td>

As the introductions finish, one member of the group asks a question of the leader. Indirectly raising the authority theme, he wonders if a young person could understand what they were experiencing. Note that the group leader feels caught off guard but does not share that understandable response.

</td></tr>
</table>

There was a slight pause in the group after the last group member finished. One of the men, Mike, spoke up and started talking to no one in particular about Elizabeth Kübler-Ross's stages of grief. He asked when and if acceptance, the last stage in grief, ever comes. I decided to remain silent, as did my co-leader, in hopes that either the group would respond with support or that he would continue with his own feelings on the topic. It was then that Mike directly addressed me with his next statement. (I have not spoken at this point.) He asked if I was attending school. I told him yes and where I attend. He said, "OK, then, you're a student. Tell me, when will I accept my mother's death? Will I ever accept it?" I was caught off guard by this direct challenge by Mike. I was silent for a moment and then told him that that was a tough question that isn't easily answered.

<table>
<tr><td>

PRACTICE POINTS

</td><td>

Once again, the authority theme introduced in Chapter 4 on the beginning phase of practice is raised indirectly. The reader has seen this issue raised throughout the book in one example after another, which suggests its almost universal nature. The inexperienced leader is thrown at first but recovers well to respond to the question.

</td></tr>
</table>

My silence was not a therapeutic intervention; he had just completely caught me off guard. My response was one of a deer in headlights, my mind had gone blank. My co-leader then began to speak about the stages of grief and how they do not necessarily go in the order they are written down in the textbooks. She spoke some more on the topic, which allowed time to gather my thoughts again. When she finished speaking, I took advantage of a short silence and directed my response to Mike. I asked him for another chance at answering that question. He nodded his head in agreement. I told him that acceptance of someone's death means different things to different people. Some people may accept a loss quickly; others may take many years. Some people may never accept a loss but do go on living in the comfort of their memories. There is no set time limit; everyone handles their grief in different ways.

Mike nodded his head in agreement, as did the rest of the group. Diane, another group member, spoke about how she had lost her father many years ago and still has not come to accept it, but that she feels better every day that goes by. Mike then directly asked me if I had lost someone close to me and if I have accepted the loss. I shared that I had lost my grandmother many years ago and that I have similar feelings as James, but that doesn't mean that

that is the only or correct way to grieve. Mike nodded his head in agreement once again. I believe this encounter led our group from the beginning phase of the session to the middle phase where the real work began.

PRACTICE POINTS Even in a single session, the authority theme must be addressed and done so quickly. By raising it indirectly and then directly, Mike was helpful to the leaders and the group.

It was then that Pat spoke up again. He apologized for not being able to speak in the beginning; it was just that it was so hard for him to talk about his wife. Pat's wife was in the unit for a respite visit. These visits can be up to 5 days and allow the caregivers some time for themselves. Pat went on to explain how he and his wife had volunteered for hospice for the last 10 years, visiting people enrolled in hospice who live in their homes. He said his wife had always been a caring person who always put others first. Now that she is sick herself, she won't accept any help from anyone but her husband. He described how terribly hard it was for him to see her so angry and not wanting to see friends when her whole life she had been the socialite and always doing for others. I waited to see if the group would provide some emotional support for Pat, and it came immediately. Carol, who had been very quiet throughout the meeting, agreed with Pat that it is hard to see the people you have loved your whole life change into people you hardly know. She said she understands his pain. Pat was visibly comforted with her interpretation of his experience.

PRACTICE POINTS In addition to support, Pat might also have wanted some help in how to deal with his wife. The irony of her being available for others but not accepting help herself must be difficult for him to accept. In addition, it puts the burden on Pat. While a single session would not provide a "solution" to this issue, recognizing it and encouraging Pat to seek some individual and perhaps couple counseling would take the group's work to the next step. Mike then jumps in and starts to express the anger under the pain, which moves away from direct emotions. The group leader points this out and asks directly what they are really angry about.

Mike began to speak about how cancer is such a growing problem in this country. Everyone in the group agreed. He continued to speak about the government and the need for more funding on cancer research. He spoke about canceling the space explorations and putting that money into research. He continued this conversation for a period of time, and the other group members are encouraging this behavior by agreeing and adding short responses and ideas. I acknowledged that the group seemed very angry about this issue and posed the question of what were they really angry about? The response I had hoped for came from Mike himself. He said that he thought maybe it was a "Why me?"/"Why my loved one?" anger. Others in the group agreed. One person even acknowledged that they were mad at God, which brought on numerous responses of having the same feeling.

Ben began to talk about how those feelings are very difficult for his family, as taking a child before a parent seems so senseless. He talked about the wonderful things his daughter had already accomplished in her life and how far she could have gone. Mary would add small details as Ben continued his praise of his daughter. This was when Ben stood up and announced that they had to leave, and he took his wife's hand and led her out of the room. The group was slightly stunned, as were my co-leader and I. We were barely able to say good-bye as they exited the room. This is when Carol also got up to leave, saying she better get back to her husband as well. Diane then stood, which signaled to the rest of the group that the group was over. Talk about behaviors communicating group norms!

The rest of the group stood, and my co-leader said, "Well, I guess we are done here." I quickly passed out some handouts on other support groups that I had been planning on passing out at the conclusion of the group. We said good-bye and that was it. There was no closure for the group members or the group leaders. My co-leader and I spoke at length following the meeting, analyzing the skills and group responses. I believe that when Ben and Mary left, they were sending a signal to the group that the work was over for them, possibly because it was getting too hard and too painful. The rest of the group took the cue and left as well without having to face another ending.

PRACTICE SUMMARY

This single session was very powerful and touched on deep emotions. Those going through this experience will feel the need to control how and when those emotions are expressed. The group was helpful, but the members did send a signal that this was all they could handle at that time. The group leaders need to be respectful of their decision. Given this experience, it might be helpful in the future to directly point this out at the start of each meeting, reinforcing the importance of group members controlling how much they wished to share and to feel in the group. The group leaders could also indicate that if members felt it was too difficult for them, they could share this with the group and feel free to leave.

Second Session

I made the rounds on the unit, stopping at each room and inviting them to the meeting. Three women and one man all arrived promptly to the meeting. I introduced myself and then reviewed the purpose and ground rules of the group. I began this meeting in a similar fashion as the last one, and the go-around introductions spurred some sharing of feelings right off the bat, also as occurred in the previous session.

PRACTICE POINTS

One of the variations on the group leadership role that is introduced by a short-term (possibly one-session) group dealing with very emotional issues is that the group leader needs to take more control over the process. One member, Vicky, is unable to contain her anxiety and becomes a monopolizer. The group leader recognizes the need to help her contain (bind) her anxiety by stopping her. The other group members are waiting for the leader to take this step.

A woman named Vicky, who looked to be in her mid-50s, who was sitting directly next to me, offered to go first. She told the group her husband was in the unit for pain relief issues as well as respite. She describes their marriage as rocky but had recently improved greatly, which was making the idea of losing him now very difficult for her. He was also a very demanding patient, which made her caregiving job difficult. She continued about how her faith in God was what kept her moving, and how she was the black sheep of her family, and that she was worried about her daughter and multiple other stresses in her life.

Although her concerns were valid, due to the time restraint inherent with single-session groups, her monopolizing of the group could lead to the other members feeling unneeded or annoyed. They were also attempting to speak, but Vicky would continue to use their inputs as catalysts to her stories. After the third interruption, I thanked Vicky for her contributions and carefully suggested she allow others to complete their stories and then speak on them. She agreed, and the group seemed relieved I had said something. In doing this, I empowered the other members to speak.

It was important for the leader to intervene and provide some structure. However, one could see that the leader was "with" the group and may have momentarily been unable to be with the member Vicky at the same time. This crucial role for the leader, outlined in detail in Chapter 7, of working with the individual in the group, might have been accomplished by her also saying:

Sometimes, Vicky, when our own concerns and feelings are so strong, it is hard to hold them in and be able to listen to others. I think that is hard for you right now, but I think it could be helpful to you and others in the group if you could work on doing that and try listening more. I would be glad to help.

In another example of the integration of process and content, evident throughout this book, Vicky was actually acting out her problem by overwhelming the group members in a way that she probably did with her family, friends, and even her husband. Also, she had described her husband as "demanding" and is acting in the same way in the group. By providing some structure for Vicky, the group leader is modeling what Vicky may need to do with her husband.

> The next introduction was Abe and Lori. Lori spoke first, telling the group that Abe was her father and that her brother was in the unit for end-of-life care due to lung cancer. Lori told the group that she was not from the area but had moved here to help care for her brother while her sister-in-law went to work. Lori expressed frustrations with letting others care for her brother as she has been so used to it. I asked the group if this was something many of them felt when they entered the unit and relinquished their caregiving role to the nurses and doctors. Every person in the room agreed. I asked the group to think about the loss of that role as a gain of the original role, such as Lori would now be able to be her brother's *sister* and Vicki could now be her husband's *wife* instead of their caretakers. The group agreed that this might help with some of the feelings of helplessness in this environment.

In the next excerpt, we see the group leader once again caught off guard. However, her level of experience, as in the first meeting, helps her catch her mistake in the same session.

> It was now Emily's turn. Emily was a woman about the age of 30. She stated in her opening introduction that being in this group was difficult for her as she was facing her own mortality. This caught me off guard as the group is usually composed of family and friends of the dying, not those facing their own death. I paused for a moment and then directed a question to another member of the group that was completely off the topic of what this woman just brought to the table.
>
> As soon as I did that, I realized that I had just completely avoided that taboo subject and had set an example for the group that it was not safe to talk about *those things* in *my* group.

I had set a norm in the group, and if I did not address my response, the norm would remain. At a point later in the group, I took advantage of a moment when I could apologize to Emily for my veering away from the toughest issues and give her an opportunity to share some her feelings on what was happening in her life. She went on to explain how it is difficult for her because none of her friends and family want to talk about her illness, but that's all she really wants from them. She talked about how when people ask her how she is, she always answers with what they want to hear, which is "fine." I then validated her frustrations and again pointed out that I had done the same thing to her by avoiding the topic. She thanked me for acknowledging that.

 PRACTICE POINTS

A next step for the worker might be to point out that this may be a common problem for all of the members. They avoid discussing tough issues with the dying patient out of fear of hurting the other. This would be a good example to use to help Emily figure out how to open the conversation with her friends and family members and for others in the group to address their own avoidance. It is often harder for the caretakers to talk about the death than it is for the dying family member. Each tries to protect the other, which leads to an inability to have final and important conversations and to deal with unfinished business.

At about 10 minutes left in the group, my co-leader suggested we wrap some things up before we say good-bye. The members agreed. I said to the group, "I have to admit that for such a small group I think we accomplished a lot today. What do you think?" The group all agreed that this was helpful, and they appreciated everyone's support throughout the meeting. My co-leader did the same. The group filed out, and as they were leaving, I noticed two of the women, Vicki and Lori, were going to have a cigarette together. It is my hopes that the skills of mutual aid that were performed in the group would continue to work outside the group.

PRACTICE SUMMARY

These sessions illustrate both the problems of dealing with emotional issues in a short-term and open-ended group as well as the possibilities. One thing to note is the importance of moving past just sharing of feelings, which by itself is helpful. The concept of dealing with feelings in pursuit of purpose can be helpful if we think of each example and how the leaders can find the next steps available to the members. In the last powerful example as a group member talks about her family and friends' avoidance of her impending death, the leaders can ask if the other members find themselves doing the same thing with their loved ones. Does this suggest it would be helpful for them to open up the painful conversation as Emily would have liked in her situation? Each of the powerful emotions shared in the group can be connected to the group's purpose, which includes helping family and friends find ways of coping with the death of a loved one.

Group Counseling and the Impact of the Setting

In this section, we focus on the setting or milieu as community and the use of activity—in this case, production of a patient newspaper—as a medium for effective group work. For many long-term patients, their community is a residential center or a hospital ward. Although group treatment programs affect their lives, the day-to-day experiences of living and working with staff and other residents will have the most powerful effects. If a treatment group teaches about life empowerment but its members feel disempowered in the setting, the real message reinforces weakness rather than strength, pathology rather than resiliency.

In Chapter 8, I focused on the group as the second client. A number of early and more recent models of group dynamics were presented. The one most relevant here is Homans's (1950) social systems theory. In brief review, Homans proposed that a group was a *dynamic system* and described the "internal system" as consisting of the interactions, activities, and sentiments between members. Each of these "elements of behavior" interacted with each other so that, for example, if there were positive sentiments (feelings) between members, that would increase their tendency to interact and affect their activities. In a like manner, greater interaction could impact the sentiment in the group either positively or negatively. He also described the "external system" consisting of the interactions, activities, and sentiments between the group (as a whole) and the environment.

Finally, the internal and external systems, each consisting of the three elements of behavior, would interact with each other. In the example that follows, it is not possible to understand the internal system (what goes on in the group) without understanding it in the context of the external system (the nature of the relationship between the patients and the staff at the VA hospital). This would be true as well in the earlier example of the rehabilitation group. In the next example, we see how a skilled leader helps a group develop a new form of relationship with the staff system that profoundly affects the interaction, activities, and sentiments within both systems and between them.

Patient Empowerment Through a Newspaper in a VA Hospital

In this illustration, the group leader creatively (and courageously) uses the medium of a ward newsletter to help psychiatric patients in a VA hospital negotiate their hospital community more effectively. In Chapter 10, I discussed how activity, such as art, song, and writing (the poetry example), could be used as a medium for mutual aid. I suggested that healing did not come from words alone. This is an example of how the group leader helped veterans with diagnosed psychiatric conditions use the newspaper to change their image of themselves and the view of patients held by staff. Once again, we see the two-client idea providing direction for the group leader and serving as a powerful tool for empowerment for patients.

With the group leader's help, the newspaper became a vehicle for communication with staff as well as a means for members to discover their own strengths. It also becomes a medium through which the members can communicate their inner feelings about having to deal with the oppression and stigma associated with mental illness. The example takes us from the early, enthusiastic beginning phase, through the problems of the middle phase and the need to make the "*second decision*," and finally to the way in which the worker (a student) helps the group and the system build in the structures needed to continue after she has left.

Members: White male veterans who are patients in a VA psychiatric setting
Dates: September 30 to December 2

Description of the Problem

The task this group faces is one of negotiating the larger system in order to produce a patient newsletter. Some of the challenges faced by the group are resistance from the larger system (the hospital), resistance within the group (fear of making waves), members' fear of retribution from staff, feelings of disempowerment, and suspicion from inside and outside the group. The major problem centers on the feelings of disempowerment embodied by the group members. This is illustrated by their reluctance to express themselves honestly in the newsletter. A second, related problem is the hospital's low expectations of the patients and the ambivalence of the hospital toward change. The problem I face is to find a way to mediate between these two systems.

How the Problem Came to the Attention of the Group Leader(s)

In beginning the newsletter, I initially observed a great deal of enthusiasm, from both group members and staff, but this enthusiasm began to falter after the first few meetings. Many of the members failed to complete the assignments for which they had volunteered, and support from the outside system was not forthcoming, as had been promised. Staff members discussed the need to censor the newsletter before it was distributed, which heightened and reinforced group members' fear and reservations.

Summary of the Work

The first session was exciting. It was filled with hope and expectations on the part of the worker as well as the members. It was a large group, with 17 members in all. Most of the veterans had gotten to know me well enough to suspect that something different was happening—that this group would be different from other groups in the program.

PRACTICE POINTS The group leader's comment about the members feeling something would be different from other groups in the program is important. It is not unusual for patients in settings such as these to attend many groups during the day. A common complaint is that the groups lack substance and emotion. A cycle can develop where staff are not expecting much from the group members, and they have limited group leadership skills. This combination can create an illusion of work. The illusion of work leads the group members to go through the motions, reinforcing the staff's negative impression of the patients' interest and abilities. The group leader is trying to break this cycle. With so many of the groups dominated and highly structured by staff, she stresses the patients' ownership of the newspaper group.

In the beginning of the session, I explained to the group what I had in mind for the newsletter. "As some of you already know, I had an idea to start a newsletter. The newsletter would be created by all of you. You would write the articles, decide what went into it, how often it would be published, and things like that. In other words, it would be your newsletter. I also thought of it as a way to help everyone get connected with one another and to keep one another informed as to what happens here. We could send copies to your friends and families. I would also contribute my own ideas from time to time and be available to help you with any problems you might have. There will also be some other students and volunteers who have offered to help in any way if you have trouble with writing. I'd like to hear from you now. Do you have any thoughts about this?"

Many members expressed interest and said it was a good idea, though I sensed some doubt on their part. I had the vague sense that some were just humoring me. Instead of confronting it directly, I went on, hoping that in time they would become more invested. Had I confronted it then, it might have opened up the discussion and raised some of the concerns and doubts they were feeling.

The student's sense of patient ambivalence was on target; however, she fell into the group formation trap of hoping the problem would go away rather than addressing it directly. If she used the skill described earlier in Chapter 3 on group formation, described as "looking for trouble when everything is going your way," she would have helped the members explore their concerns. She will get another chance.

> We decided on a name for the newsletter, and people volunteered for jobs. There was much debate about what to call the newsletter. One member sarcastically offered the *Elite Newspaper of the East* as a possible title. He seemed very angry. I commented that I thought it was an interesting name. He did not respond, and I went on collecting other titles. I realized I had not picked up the message he was indirectly sending me. I had missed the opportunity to address some of the anger he was feeling, and I was not tuned in to what was urgent to him at that moment. I was unable to set aside my own agenda. Had I picked up on his anger, I would have been able to recognize that his feelings were representative of much of what the group was feeling. Fortunately for the group (and for me), this anger would surface again in later groups and help break through the illusion of work.

In her excitement about getting the paper going, the student has ignored the irony in the suggested title since these veterans felt anything but "elite." (The eventual selected name was the *War Memorial Gazette*). These veterans experience both the stigma of being branded as psychiatric patients and the sense of being treated by staff more as children rather than as adults with emotional problems. The initial first decision to become involved and the associated excitement start to fade as the group begins to deal with the realities of being vulnerable patients as well as their own personal vulnerabilities. We have an example of group members needing to make a "second decision" that involves continuing in spite of their concerns.

> In the second session, the members volunteered one another for jobs. In a somewhat derisive manner, an older man named George volunteered Dana, one of the younger members, to be the editor. Dana was generally very quiet and reserved and seldom participated in other groups. I responded that I thought it was a great idea and asked Dana if he would consider accepting the position. He seemed pleased at this and accepted. Everyone applauded. At this point, Harold, another older man, said that when he was in the army, he used to take a lot of pictures. I asked him if he wanted to be the photographer, and he agreed. The energy in the room seemed to increase, and everyone started volunteering for jobs. We decided to meet once a week as a group and to put the newsletter out once a month.
>
> During the month, some of the members were busy interviewing people and writing their stories. Others were not doing their jobs and were coming up with excuses for why they couldn't do them. I felt this was due to a lack of confidence, so I concentrated on expressing my belief in their abilities to do the job. I began to recognize that a general theme was emerging with regard to how disempowered the members were feeling.

The issues avoided in the early stages of this group reemerge in the form of group apathy and difficulty in following through on assignments. This time the student picks up on the nonverbal signals and opens up a discussion of a common complaint by patients in hospital and rehabilitation settings: that all they do all day is go to meaningless group meetings.

During the fifth session, I noticed that many of the members were having difficulty concentrating and seemed completely disinterested in the group. I reached for what was happening. "What is going on today? Everyone seems to be having trouble focusing on the topic. You all look bored and tired." Dan responded, "We all just went out for a long walk. We are tired." Richard added, "They keep us too busy around here, and all we do is go to groups. They never leave us alone." I asked if anyone else felt this way and, if so, whether they wanted to spend a few minutes talking about this. Many members responded by agreeing that there were too many groups and they were feeling overwhelmed.

I tried to validate their feelings by saying that sometimes there were a lot of groups to attend, and then I asked if they had ever spoken to the staff and voiced their concerns. Jim, the member who had been so angry in the first session, responded by saying that it did no good, that the staff didn't care what they wanted and treated them all like children. I knew I had to be careful here. My natural inclination was to side with the group members. I had often been angered by the patronizing manner in which these men were treated. It would have been easy for me to have jumped on the bandwagon and started criticizing the hospital, but I knew that would not have been useful. I responded instead by reaching for his feelings, saying, "It must feel pretty frustrating to be treated in this way. After all, you're not children—you're grown men."

As the group approaches the second and more difficult decision on whether to really engage with the newsletter idea, different members take on different roles. In many ways, these members articulate the ambivalent feelings of all group members. Jim articulates the anger and cynicism over the way they have been treated in the hospital. Roland articulates the fear of angering the staff members who have so much power over the patients. It is important to understand that to different degrees, there is some of Jim and some of Roland in all of the members.

This opened the door for a lengthy discussion about how it felt for the members to be psychiatric patients and to lose so much control over one's life. I tried to bring the conversation back into focus by suggesting that the newsletter might be a forum the men could use to voice some of their concerns. Roland, a member whom I have always thought of as very ingratiating to the staff, eager and cooperative, fearful of making trouble, and generally considered a "good" patient, said, "Oh, no, we couldn't do that—they would never let us print it. Besides, it's not really so bad around here. The staff is all nice, and they treat us well." Another member was made anxious by the interchange and completely changed the subject. Time was almost up, so I said that, if the group wanted to, we could continue talking about this the next time we met.

Once again we see a powerful and taboo issue emerging at the "doorknob" as the session is about to end. The key for the group leader is to step back and to understand the behavior of these two members, Jim and Roland, in a dynamic way and as representing the general ambivalence felt by all group members. It's as if the group-as-a-whole is speaking to the leader through these two members. Both are allies for the leader, bringing out both sides of the struggle. We see the important growth in the group leader's skill as she reaches past the surface humor expressed by staff in the next session and reaches for the staff concerns.

The next session involved a field trip we had planned, and the session after that, the recreational therapist joined the group. Apparently, the news had gotten out about our discussion. I told the staff I was encouraging the members to write about things that were meaningful to them and that, at times, this might involve an expression of criticism toward the hospital. They joked about how I was getting the patients all riled up. I sensed some suspicion beneath the humor, so I asked if they thought this was a bad thing. This brought the issue to the surface and opened up the opportunity for me to speak with the staff about some of the feelings the patients were having. Staff were also able to share some of their concerns about public sharing of problems since the hospital was part of the larger Veterans Administration system. I outlined some of the ways I could involve staff in reviewing the newspapers before they were released.

PRACTICE POINTS This was a crucial step in the process. The VA is a hierarchal system and one that is politically sensitive. As has been seen recently in respect to criticisms of conditions in VA hospitals for wounded soldiers returning from Afghanistan and Iraq, staff at this hospital had some legitimate concerns. The skill described in the chapter on group formation of "looking for trouble when everything is going your way" would have been helpful in the initial discussions with staff on the whole idea of starting a newspaper. By understanding this and working with the staff, the group leader was able to address these concerns. In the next group session, we see how the issues related to their illness and their medications interact with issues related to their environment.

During the next group session, we got back to the discussion and returned to the earlier topic. The members seemed distracted and uninterested. They were also having difficulties finishing the assignments for which they had volunteered. I asked them what was going on. Jimmy, a member who attended only occasionally, responded, "How do you expect us to do anything? I can't write; look at my hands." He held up his hands, which were shaking visibly. "They keep us so medicated around here, we can't even think straight." Jake agreed, "These doctors use us as guinea pigs. They try one medication after another on us. We are subjects in their experiments; they don't treat us like human beings." Roland began to get nervous. "Yes, but we need to take our medication because it helps us. I'm ready for my next shot. I get too agitated if I don't get my shot."

Jake responded, saying the medication didn't help him and that it had ruined his life. He spoke of how he was not able to have a relationship with women or to live a normal life. He said, "Any member in this room will tell you that the medicines make you impotent. How are you ever supposed to meet a girl or think about getting married?" Several of the men nodded their heads in agreement. I said that must be very difficult for them and asked if they had ever let the doctors know about the problems they had with the medications. Jake again responded, "They don't care. If you refuse to take the medications, they will just lock you up." He went on to tell of how he had been forcibly locked up in the hospital. Several other group members agreed, telling stories of how they had been locked in the seclusion room, beaten up by orderlies, or admitted to the hospital against their will. They said that when they told someone, the doctors responded by saying it was just a symptom of their paranoia. Jake said that he was learning not to fight, that he was not a young man anymore.

PRACTICE POINTS The growing positive relationship between the group leader and members allows them to surface powerful and up to now taboo subjects: the impact of the medicine on their sexual functioning and incidents of abusive behavior by staff. The disclosure of abusive behavior, as perceived by the patients, raises ethical issues for the group leader. At minimum, she should be raising this with her supervisor and discussing what appropriate steps should be taken. The issue of lack of communication around the impact of the medicine is an issue of a different order and opens up possibilities for improving communication.

> I empathized with the things that the group members had gone through and said it must be really difficult to always have someone questioning their reality. I then suggested that Jake might want to write about his experiences for the newsletter. I hoped to begin to help empower them and to show them a way to have their concerns heard. Jake expressed ambivalence about doing this. I said I could understand his reservations and that, if he wanted to, he could take some time and think about it, or he could write it anonymously. This all proved to be more than Roland could stand.

PRACTICE POINTS In this next part of the group meeting, we can see many of the ideas on group dynamics suggested in Chapter 8 emerging. Homans's (1950) social systems model is evident as the relationship with the external system, the hospital and staff, is strongly affecting the group's internal system. Bion's (1961) notion of the "work group" being subverted by the "fight-flight" group when the discussion gets too close to painful material is another explanation of Roland's outburst. At this moment, Roland is the group's fight-flight leader.

> Under his breath but loud enough for everyone to hear, he said, "Communist!" I was taken aback by this expression of anger from Roland. I was also not sure to whom he was talking. Jake responded angrily, "What did you call me?" Roland looked in his direction and said, louder this time, "A communist. You're nothing but a communist. The doctors are just trying to help us. You're always going around trying to stir things up." Jake was very angry at this; a veteran considers this to be the worst kind of insult. Jake responded to Roland, "I'm no communist, and don't you call me that. I have a right to say what I feel." I was afraid the situation might escalate into violence, because Jake was extremely angry.
>
> I interjected, "Roland, it seems as if you see the situation in one way, and Jake sees it from a different perspective. But I don't think it is useful for us to call one another names." I had intended to try to create a culture in which discussions of such matters were allowed and also one in which members respected and listened to one another. But, in rushing to Jake's defense, I was sending a message that I didn't believe he could take care of himself and that he needed my protection. This was not a useful message to send to someone who already feels oppressed and powerless. I might have done better if I had waited a little longer and allowed them to work things out themselves.
>
> Roland apologized to Jake and said he was just a little "off" because he had not gotten his shot yet. Jake accepted this apology, and the conversation returned to a discussion of an article someone was writing for the newsletter. The session ended with me encouraging the members to consider writing about their hospital experiences for the newsletter.

PRACTICE POINTS In retrospect, the problem with the intervention is not that the leader intervened, because setting clear limits and not allowing anger to escalate was the right thing to do. However, the leader could have gone a bit further by pointing out that Roland's comment came from his anxiety about confronting staff, and this was the same anxiety probably felt by all in the group, including Jake. After this pivotal event and the expression of emotions, the group leader continued to support the men who began, as will be evident later in this report, to take some initial risks and to make the important second decision to continue the newsletter. One also has to credit the staff at the hospital who also took a risk in allowing and eventually encouraging the publication of the newsletter.

Current Status of the Problem: Where It Stands Now

I can safely say that the newsletter has become firmly established as a part of the program. I've noticed more staff members becoming invested in its continuation. There has been discussion of who will take over the project after I am gone. The director of the program requested a copy of the newsletter to be sent with his semiannual report, and another staff member included it in a presentation she was giving about the program. I have witnessed some positive change, in that the system now relates to the veterans in a different manner. I notice some staff now saying "members" or "veterans" instead of "patients." Several staff members have expressed surprise with regard to the talent that the men are exhibiting. There is also less fear and suspicion about what kinds of things I am doing with the group. We are still working on the issue of censorship, as I continue to advocate for as little as possible to make sure the newsletter remains within the patients' control.

The group members are still working on how much they want to express themselves in the newsletter. Many of the members still feel very disempowered and alienated, but they have received a lot of positive reinforcement from the hospital community, which has led to a tremendous boost in self-confidence and self-esteem.

Some of the members of the newsletter group are working on submitting articles to a national journal that publishes works by disabled and hospitalized veterans. Others have expressed an interest in learning how to type so they can type the newsletter themselves. One member has decided to begin to study for his high school equivalency exam. This is truly an exciting process to watch.

PRACTICE SUMMARY

It seems appropriate to conclude this example with some excerpts from the newsletter published by these veterans, the *War Memorial Gazette*. Their first issue did not deal directly with some of their concerns and feelings about the hospital and the staff; however, they did appear to employ indirect communications. For example, the comedy section of the first issue contained the following three jokes about psychiatrists.

Jokes by Ed

1. What's the difference between a neurotic, a psychotic, and a psychiatrist? A neurotic builds castles in the clouds. A psychotic lives in them. A psychiatrist collects the rent for them.
2. How many psychiatrists does it take to change a lightbulb? One, but the lightbulb has to be willing to change.
3. This guy goes to the psychiatrist, and he talks to the psychiatrist, and the psychiatrist says, "You're crazy!" And the guy says, "I want a second opinion." And the psychiatrist says, "OK, I think you're ugly, too."

As the members' confidence grew, they began to be more direct, including writing columns about their concerns over the ward policies and procedures, balanced with positive interviews that highlighted the efforts of members of the staff. In their third issue, they included editorial and poetry pages, excerpts of which follow.

This newsletter is a project of the Community Support Program of this Veterans Administration Hospital. The opinions and views expressed do not necessarily reflect those of the staff or administration of the hospital.

Personal Philosophy: I'm a Vietnam combat vet. I've been in and out of the Veterans Hospital for many years for physical and mental problems. This doesn't mean I haven't got a good IQ or common sense.

On politics: It's about time we look at our representatives and the policies they put forward. Are they voting for money, people, and special interest groups or for the American people? Stop the political slander and get to the economic issues. We have a beautiful system of checks and balances between the Congress, Presidency, and Supreme Court. We also have the right of petition if we disagree with what's going on. If we don't examine and vote, we stand a chance of losing this system.

Poetry: By Tom

Feeling Blue

When I'm out under the trees
I watch the flowers dance in the breeze
I feel the pain and sorrow that surround me
All I want is the sun to shine, the rain to fall
And no one to be left standing small.

The veterans published the *War Memorial Gazette* for over 5 years (and may still be publishing it). It has matured as a paper and has earned the respect and support of the staff. When the patients held a 5-year celebration of the inception of the newsletter, they invited the student, now a professional, who had helped them organize it, to thank her for her initiative and her faith in their ability. These excerpts serve as a tribute to the resilience and courage of clients and to the profound impact of one student who refused to give up on them or the system, her second client. It sends an important and appropriate message to the helping professions, reminding us of the importance of the two-client concept.

Group Counseling for Medical Outpatients and Their Families

When a serious illness or accident results in hospitalization, it has a profound impact on the patient and also on family members and friends. Because family members may constitute an important part of the support system assisting the patient to deal with medical, emotional, and life change issues (e.g., inability to work or the need for ongoing medical treatments), support for the patient's significant others must be considered as part of the total treatment plan. A common misconception on the part of both health professionals and participants is that the focus of the group is only on the patient. In order for such a group to be effective, it must also address medical, emotional, and life change issues for the family and friends as well. This issue is explored in the context of a living-with-cancer group in the next example.

Denial, Gender, and Culture in a Living-with-Cancer Group

The following illustration explores the denial exhibited by people with cancer and their family members in a group designed to help them cope with this life-threatening disease. I will focus on the role of one defensive member, Al, who helps the group avoid the taboo subject of death. In addition, the members' different responses to the disease of cancer illustrate the impact of gender and ethnicity. The two men in the group, for example, respond by using increased work activity as part of a strong pattern of denial of their emotions about their wives' cancer. At one point, Al says, "You have to understand what it's like to be an engineer. Engineers are used to working with problems that can be resolved, and her cancer is a problem that I can't resolve."

Furthermore, as a Hispanic mother and daughter describe their reactions and those of their husband and father who has cancer, we see a contrast with the non-Hispanic members of the group that reflects the influence of culture, as described by Schaefer and Pozzaglia (1986):

> Unlike their uninhibited expression of grief and sadness, Hispanics try to control their anger. This, however, is not necessarily the case with white, middle-class families who are more comfortable in openly expressing their anger at the disease and their frustration with the hospital system. The Hispanic family's strong belief in God and His will is used to explain why the child is ill and minimizes their anger. (pp. 298–299)

Devore and Schlesinger (1996) suggest that the Hispanic father contemplates suicide rather than becoming a burden on his family; his reactions of shame to his diagnosis of cancer can be partly explained by machismo: "As macho, he is the head of the family, responsible for their protection and well-being, defender of their honor. His word is his contract" (p. 81).

Client Description and Time Frame: This is a weekly support and education group for people with cancer and their family members. It is a 6-week, time-limited, closed group. The setting is a large teaching hospital, and the group is offered free of charge through the social services department.

Age Range of Members: Members are between 30 and 78 years old. Ten group members are Caucasian American. Two members, a mother and daughter, are Latin American. There are 10 women and 2 men in the group; 5 are patients, and 7 are family members.

Dates Covered in the Record: February 1–March 8

Description of the Problem: The problem is the group's avoidance of painful issues that would lead to a discussion of the taboo subject of death. The taboo needs to be breached so that the group may begin to redefine its norms to include direct discussion of the reality of cancer. Though there is reality-based discussion of living with cancer, there is resistance to discussing the reality of dying from cancer. An additional problem is our collusion as co-leaders in the process of avoidance.

How the Problem Came to the Attention of the Group Leader(s)

As an observer of a previous 6-week cancer group, I was witness to and aware of the incredible courage and depth of hope displayed by two patients in the group. They and their struggle were an inspiration. As the group ended, I wondered if they had gotten what they needed from the group. I had a sense that they had never faced up to the harsh reality and finality of cancer as they had maybe hoped they would in the group. As a co-leader of this new group, I found myself again caught up in the inspirational comments shared among members. In an attempt to refocus the group on more painful issues, I felt a resistance and retreated from interventions, thus colluding with group members in their hopefulness.

The group leader's recognition of her resistance to discussing the "reality of the disease" may mirror the resistance of doctors and nurses and others in the health setting. There is a tendency to hold out hope even when the medical prognosis is clear. While hope may be important at the beginning stage of the illness and the beginning stage of the patient's and family's engagement with the health care system, as a transition takes place to ongoing treatment and especially in the end stage of the illness, reality-based information may be important for patient and family members in order to deal effectively with the possibility of death. This can partially account for the tendency of patients and family members to wait until the very end of life, often just 1 to 2 weeks before death, to take advantage of available hospice care that can increase a dying patient's comfort as well as significantly decrease pain.

Summary of the Work

February 1

Rosina and her mother, Maria, talked quite a bit about their father and husband, who had lost interest in everything since his diagnosis of cancer. They talked about what he had been like before cancer and how he had changed. People were trying to be very helpful and supportive in giving advice to them. I wondered to myself if the members responded this way because if you give advice and people accept it, then you have helped and possibly resolved a problem—the very thing you cannot do with cancer. I did not share this with the group.

Faith, the daughter of a nonlocal patient, said her mother described cancer as the great liberator, and she said that this part of the disease was contagious. Both she and her mother were becoming more assertive as well as expressive. She talked about friends who are there for her parents and how wonderful they are. I wondered (to myself) what about cancer was liberating.

Frances (a patient attending the group with her daughter and the widow of a cancer victim) began to talk about her husband after Rosina said her father would rather die of a heart attack than live feeling like a burden to her and her mother. Frances said her husband felt the same way. He had lung cancer (here, she pointed to Sara, who has lung cancer) and was given a year to live. He died in 7 months. She said she was working when he was first diagnosed, but one day she came home and found him trying to commit suicide. She said, "We held each other and cried, and I said, 'We're going to fight this thing on my shirttails' . . . and we did . . . one day at a time." Sara, always an inspiration, said, "You need to fight; you need to find something to make every day count," and she began to talk to Rosina and Maria about ways they could help their father and husband make every day count. I wondered (to myself) if the return to advice giving was the group's response to the pain of Frances's disclosure about her own husband's painful death.

As is evident throughout this book, the group leader's reactions, thoughts, and feelings are right on target but not always shared. In the examples in Part 1, I described this hesitancy to act and the group leader's fear of making a mistake. What this leader is also recognizing is that in addition to a fear of saying the "wrong" thing, when dealing with these painful subjects, the leader may be fearful of saying the "right" thing. Taboos in our society exist for a reason, and the group leader may be just as vulnerable to their impact as the members.

February 15

As in the two previous groups, Doris talked about her allergic reaction to the chemotherapy drugs. She focused on how much she had been "digging" for information, calling the manufacturer and even the inventor. She was discouraged to find out she was the only patient to have such a severe reaction to the drug, but she seemed to feel better by taking some action. Group members seemed to admire her initiative. I failed to recognize the underlying disappointment that there may be no satisfactory resolution and to note the pain masked by a hopeful discussion of drugs and experts.

I also missed the connection of an individual's themes to the purpose of the group. Al, Doris's husband, talked about what a hard week it had been for him. He had overslept that morning after working night and day for 3 weeks on a contract that was meant to be in the mail that day. The group (and I) ignored this comment. Instead, the group attempted to resolve the problem with more advice about drugs and experts. I was caught up in the hope of resolution. Faith asked Doris if the dosage of the drug might be diluted. Christine shared that her mother was participating in a drug study and gave Doris the name of the physician conducting it.

I thought about reaching for feelings, but I held back. Doris talked about having no pain and discomfort except for the rash on her legs. I wondered to myself what it was like for her to have no pain and discomfort and still be sick with colon cancer. I would have liked to support a group member's progress, but I remained silent. Faith read a poem from her mother. She began to cry as she read it. She reiterated her mother's description of cancer as a blessed, terrible happening. Faith said she had been crying daily for 10 weeks. She said that, in all that time, she thinks it never quite sunk in that her mother has cancer, and she said the word that she previously could not say. She said she was angry about it.

PRACTICE POINTS It is interesting to note that it appears to be easier for the group leader and the members to discuss the anger at the disease rather than the ongoing pain and sadness that usually exist under the anger. This replicates the behavior noted earlier in the hospice example. Faith is expressing that part of the feeling through her tears. The group leader is more comfortable reaching for the anger.

I said I wondered if anger was something they had all experienced. There were many nods. Maria asked Faith who she was angry at and why she was angry. Faith talked about how her mother had not taken care of herself, though she did not directly say she was angry at her mother. She said she did not know whether or not to blame God. Al said, "You can't blame the person with the disease, and you can't blame God. It's nobody's fault—it just happens." Christine asked Maria if she was angry. Maria said, "No, never." She had never been angry at God or her husband. She talked about how wonderful their life had been and said she thought God needed to give them some pain and that whatever happened they would accept. Rosina said, "You haven't always felt this way. In the beginning, you were really depressed and feeling badly when he was sick." Maria said, "That's true." Rosina said she even got sympathy pains. Maria said they don't talk that much about his cancer. They just hold hands and that's enough; they don't have to talk about cancer.

PRACTICE POINTS In the excerpt that follows, Al, one of the two men in the group, begins to describe how he tries to handle his feelings by denying they exist. He uses a coping mechanism, somewhat supported by the reality of his job, of working all the time, which is another form of flight from the underlying pain. His argument with the group members, a form of fight, allows both him and the other members to avoid discussing the pain itself. In reality, all of the family members must feel torn at times between the need to get on with their lives, to take care of themselves, and then their guilt over not being there for the person with cancer. This scenario will become more apparent in the meeting following this one.

> Al said he understood where she was coming from, but that you cannot sacrifice and change your life because of your husband's illness. He said, "I haven't. I go to work and do what I need to do, and, of course, I've given up some things." "Not many," Doris said. "No, not many," he said. "You just have to go on with your life; otherwise you'll just get depressed. You just can't let yourself get depressed."
>
> I said, "I understand what you're saying about needing to have a life of your own, but what do you do with the feelings? You may not want to get depressed, but the disease is depressing." Al responded somewhat angrily, saying, "I only allow myself 15 minutes of depression a year. Any more than 15 minutes is too long."
>
> I backed off in response to the angry tone in his response and remained silent. Al said he gets depressed around Christmas but always brings himself out of it. Grace (co-leader) said his feelings around Doris's disease were coming out somehow and that it sounded like he was avoiding them by being away so much. He denied this and talked about how crucial it is that he put in the evening and weekend hours at work. Christine said, "With all due respect, I don't know about your relationship, and I think I'm talking to you so much because I'm thinking of my parent [her mother has colon cancer like Doris], but I think Doris is asking you to spend more time with her and be there more."

PRACTICE POINTS

As discussed in Chapter 16 on marital and family counseling group sessions, we have a complex set of group dynamics. There is each individual, the group-as-a-whole, and the dynamics between couples. This is not a married couples' group designed to address issues in Doris and Al's marriage. However, it is important to address issues in relation to how they are coping with the illness. As long as the group leader keeps this focus in mind, she can avoid the problem of the group being subverted to another purpose. Al and Doris will have to go to another group, if they wish, to deal with what appears to be more ongoing marital concerns.

> All group members got involved in this discussion, speaking for Doris to Al. When other members said they did not want to attack him, he responded by saying this was nothing—he was used to handling this kind of argument at work all the time. He defended his need to be at work. Sara said, "But Doris needs you there, too." I missed an opportunity to ask if Al may have been speaking for the whole group and allowed the discussion to return to a struggle between the group and Al.

PRACTICE POINTS

Once again we see how the "deviant member" may be speaking for the group—a rejection of the often noted belief in a false dichotomy between the individual and the group. Although Al is a more extreme version, probably related to his way of dealing with all painful issues in his life, the desire to get on with a normal life and not have to cope with their partner's or family member's illness must be felt, in part, by all family members. Both group leaders identify with his wife, Doris, and the other group members, as the members attack

Al for his position. Even the co-leader's comment on his avoidance of pain is expressed in an accusatory tone rather than as a real understanding of what he is feeling. This is the moment when being with Al and Doris as individuals and as a couple, and being with the group is crucial since searching out the common ground—the similar feelings felt but denied by group members—is important to deepening the discussion.

February 22

I attempted to connect present group activity and previous content with the issue of avoidance. Al talked for a while about the pressures on him at work. He talked about having spent 35 years building his career. Sharon (Frances's daughter) said, "I'm sitting here listening to you, Al, and I'm not sure what went on last week (she and her mother had been absent because of poor weather), but I can say that I see a lot of myself in how you're dealing with this." She talked about when her father had gotten sick. She was in Washington, and her parents were in Pennsylvania. She talked about the sense of relief she felt every time she got on the plane to go back to DC. She did not want to and couldn't face her father's illness. She said that, when her mother called and said, "You'd better come," she even waited then to go to Pennsylvania. She said, "I know about career pressures. I work for an agency that regulates the same type of company you work for, and I know about those pressures. When my mother got sick, it was the same time that a promotion came up that I'd been working toward for years, and I passed it up because I needed to be with my mother."

Al said, "But there's a difference. You're at the beginning of your career—I'm in the last 10 years of it, when my entire pension and retirement are determined." Sharon said, "None of us know if we're even going to be here tomorrow."

PRACTICE POINTS

In the following exchange, with the presence of the other male in the group (Sid), an opportunity surfaces to point out issues that may be related to gender. Although they are joking, the underlying feelings are real. The group leaders pass up this opportunity although they are also aware of the gender issue.

At that point, Sylvia and Sid came in with their daughter, Laura (not a member of the group). Grace briefed them on what was going on, and everyone quickly introduced themselves. Sid asked what they had missed last week, because they had also been absent. Al laughed as he said, "They all ganged up on me." He had already been through this with the other people who'd been absent the previous week. Sid said he was sorry he'd missed it. Al said, "So you could join in?" Sid said, "Who knows, maybe I would have joined in with you against everyone else." (These two were the only men in the group.) Frances asked Sylvia (the patient) how she was doing. She said her treatment had been going well, though she had been sleeping a lot. Laura said that she always sleeps a lot and that she even falls asleep at movies.

Then Doris and Al got into a discussion with them about how he loves movies and she hates to go to them. I said I wondered, as I thought Sharon had been saying to Al, if there was a tendency to avoid thinking, feeling, and talking about cancer—even in the group right now. I wondered if people found that they tended to or felt like avoiding it all. Frances said, "You avoid it and then don't know that you're doing it." Al said, "I'm not avoiding it—it's just my way of coping. You just can't think about it all the time."

Al said, "This isn't the first time I've been through it." "But it's not the same," Doris said. "But I was 10 when my father died of cancer," said Al. "You were just a child—it's not the same." "My mother died of leukemia," said Al. "But you weren't in the house; your brother and sister took care of her." Al said, "That's true." Frances said, "It's different when you're living with the person than if you're away." I said it's different and it's the same. Al said, "No, it's definitely different when you're living with the person." Sylvia asked if anyone had seen the television show *20/20* that week. Group members said they had not. Sylvia said it had been about chemotherapy drugs.

PRACTICE POINTS

For the first time, Al begins to share some of his history that may be influencing his current struggle. Al having had a father die of cancer when he was age 10, and then his mother died of leukemia, and with the possibility that he still had many unresolved issues and feelings, it is not surprising that he feels not thinking about it is the only way to cope.

Frances asked Maria how her husband was doing. Maria and Rosina looked at each other, and Rosina said it had been a discouraging week for them. Her father was no longer responding to the chemotherapy. Maria talked some but mostly cried as Rosina talked about a new lump her father had found behind his ear. Frances said that was the last thing he needed, to find that lump. She said her husband had gotten a great big tumor on his neck and couldn't stand it, so she had to shave him. She spoke eloquently about her husband, her experience with him, and his death.

I overlooked Frances's own need to confront her own cancer, which she only talked about in terms of beating it. The group was engrossed. Al asked, "How do you do it?" Frances looked at him and said, "Sometimes you just hold each other and cry." She said again, "I told him to grab onto my shirttails, and we'll make it though this thing." After a while, her husband had said, "I'm not going to make it." She told the story of how he had died in the hospital, not at home. I wondered how everyone felt. I imagined that everyone was moved by Frances's story but that they also related it to themselves or their own loved one. I didn't raise this, so we missed the boat.

PRACTICE POINTS

In the next excerpt, the group is preparing to come to an end. Many of the dynamics discussed in Chapter 9 on endings are evident as the group members begin to face the fact that they will no longer have the support of the group. Endings in this group carry a particular poignancy since members are also struggling with their fear of a permanent ending with their loved ones.

March 1

Grace mentioned that this was the fifth group and that we had one more left. Doris said, "That's a bummer," and that was all that was said by her or anyone about the group ending. Al talked about what a tough couple of weeks it had been. He said it had been emotionally draining, and he attributed it mostly to work.

In the middle of the group, I said that Doris had said it was "a bummer" that the group was ending next week, and I wondered how others were feeling about it. After an attempt to confront the denial, I copped out and colluded with it, allowing their discussion of how they could keep the group going. Sid asked if it could be extended. Doris said that it was a bummer and that she always felt better after the group. Then everyone talked about ideas for how it could continue rather than talking about what it was like that it was ending. I wished I had said, "But this group as it exists now is ending next week."

This phase of work is called the "ending and transition" phase for a reason. As the group members discuss their feelings of loss in the group, they need to also evaluate the group's effectiveness and identify what they found helpful. The group leader needs to also address their attention to how and where they can continue to get what they need even after the group has ended. The implications of the "empty chairs" are also important because they raise concern about Rosina's father and Maria's husband dying.

Grace said that the tone of the group seemed different tonight and wondered if it had anything to do with the two unexplained empty chairs. Rosina and her mother, Maria, were unexplainably absent after having spoken of their father and husband's turn for the worse the previous week. Frances, often the "cheerleader" and major source of group inspiration, said they were occupying her mind. The conversation for the next 10 minutes revolved around the group's concern for the missing members and their loved one.

March 6 (Last Session)

I listened intently to information I wished had been shared by members earlier in the 6 weeks. I felt sad that I had not helped facilitate its earlier entrance to the group. At the end, Christine talked about what had gotten her to come to the group. She said she didn't know if people could tell what kind of person she was, but that she went on a cross-country bike trip alone and hiked and camped and was very independent.

She's also organized and likes to keep things in order and be healthy. She said that, a few weeks after hearing her mother's diagnosis, she had a terrible headache one night and realized she hadn't eaten in 3 days. She said she made some cream of wheat but couldn't eat it. She looked around her apartment. There were clothes in every room and dirty dishes in the sink. She said she didn't know who was living in her apartment. She saw the flyer the next day and said, "I've got to get into that group."

Christine said the group had been keeping her in touch with the disease but that she wasn't really facing that her mother could die from this. She said she talked to her boyfriend, and he got so upset and said to her, "I can't believe you're in this group and you're not dealing with death." She said it as if she were the only one in the group who was not. I looked at Grace and thought that Christine said what I had been thinking throughout the 6 weeks of group. We had 5 minutes left of our final group. Sadly, this group did not confront death.

Current Status of the Problem

This group ended, though the members have made a commitment to informally continue their meetings. Possibly they will begin to confront their own avoidance, particularly if members begin to become sick. I am looking forward to the start of another 6-week group on March 22. I hope to be more cognizant of the ways in which avoidance surfaces and to be more assertive in noting and helping the group confront its avoidance without letting the discussion drop. I am also more acutely aware of how attractive it is to collude with the hope of group members as a defense against not only their fear of death and dying but mine as well. I want to support their struggle to heal from the disease without cheating them of an opportunity to talk openly about the painful reality of cancer. Having taken a closer look at the issues of avoidance, I feel better prepared to facilitate that process.

The group leader in this illustration has used the experience to deepen her understanding of her clients and herself. Typical of new group leaders, she is overcritical of her work, focusing on what she did not do and not crediting herself enough for what she accomplished. A little guilt is helpful for professional growth; however, group leaders should not undervalue their work along the way.

In exploring the group leader's hesitancy about dealing with the subject of death, you may have noticed a piece missing—the support system for staff that is essential in such emotionally draining practice. Case-related stressors on staff can directly affect practice (Shulman, 1991). Davidson (1985) examined the impact of the special stresses that affect counselors who work with cancer patients and their families. He hypothesized that workers experience their work as stressful and lack adequate support to help them cope with the emotional impact of working with clients affected by a chronic and life-threatening illness. Pilsecker (1979) found that counselors, like other hospital staff, used strategies to deal with their painful emotions, including reduction of their direct involvement with patients. By recognizing, accepting, and trying to meet their own needs, group workers can better support their clients.

Chapter Summary

Rehabilitation and health counselors practice in a variety of work settings: private nonprofit agencies, hospital medical settings, educational programs, private for-profit business, state/federal agencies, private practice, unions, and others. In addition to working directly with patients, counselors also provide support for caretakers and family members.

Patients were viewed as being at different stages in relation to their illness as well as in relation to their engagement with the health or rehabilitation facility. An example of inpatient counseling included a short-term group in a hospice dealing with end-of-life care and the difficulty members had in discussing the taboo subject of death and dying.

The setting was also addressed as a community that the group members have to deal with on a day-in and day-out basis. An example of the creative use of a ward newsletter in a VA psychiatric hospital illustrated how group work can empower patients and impact the hospital system.

Finally, outpatient services were illustrated using a living-with-cancer group for patients and their significant others. The issue of addressing denial on the part of the members as well as the group leader was central to the discussion.

Related Online Content and Activities

For learning tools such as glossary terms, InfoTrac® College Edition keywords, links to related websites, and chapter practice quizzes, visit this book's website at **www.cengage.com/counseling/shulman.**

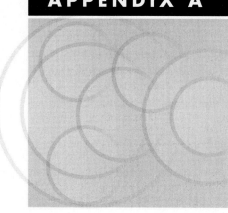

Research Methodology and Selected Findings

A number of my research studies have contributed to the ideas shared in this book and have been cited in the text. This appendix provides additional information on methods used, sample, limitations, and some selected significant outcomes. The reader is referred to the full studies for a more detailed discussion.

Starting with the basic interactional framework, in four studies instruments were developed to measure skill use by counselors and social workers in individual and group practice and to relate the use of these skills to the development of a positive working relationship and to effective outcomes for clients. The findings were then used to analyze the practice approach critically, to confirm some hypotheses, while also generating new assumptions for future research. In addition, in a number of these studies, the research incorporated analysis of the impact of supervision and management on practice and eventual client outcomes.

Study design, methodology, sample, and a number of findings from four of the studies cited in this book are shared in this appendix:

Child Welfare Practice and Supervision Study: an early study into the impact of child welfare worker practice skill on working relationship and client outcomes (Shulman, 1978)

Child Welfare Practice and Supervision Study 2: a later study replicating and modifying the early project by adding the impact of supervision and management on worker behavior, working relationship, and client outcomes (Shulman, 1993)

Category Observation System for Analyzing Counselor-Client Interaction in Individual and Group Practice: In this subdesign of an earlier study, I developed a Category Observation System for analysis of individual and group practice. Over 120 hours of videotaped individual and group sessions were analyzed by entering numbers that characterized the nature of the interaction as perceived by trained raters (Shulman, 1981).

The VISA Center for Students Suspended From School for Violence, Substance Abuse, or Possession of Weapons: a 2-year project with over 300 students treated in a 2-week intensive academic, psychoeducational, and social skills program (Shulman & Maguin, 2006)

Each successive study built on the preceding ones as well as on the knowledge base in related professions and disciplines. The reader is referred to my publications cited above, (Shulman, 1970, 1979a, 1979b, 1982, 1991, 2009) for more detailed descriptions of the methodology of each study and their findings. Although all findings reported in this text are tentative and should be considered in light of each study's limitations, some findings have been replicated in a number of my studies as well as the work of other researchers.

Child Welfare Practice and Supervision Study

This major study was conducted in a provincial government child welfare agency in British Columbia, Canada. Project staff reviewed family files that had been recently opened in 68 district offices. Of the 1,056 families identified as potential subjects, 348 (33%) agreed to participate. The final sample consisted of 305 families with 449 children served by 171 workers supervised by front-line supervisors in 68 district offices. Ten managers and 5 province-wide executive directors also participated.

Most of the data were gathered during the first 3 months of the project. In-home interviews were conducted with the parent(s). A mail survey of staff at all levels (workers, supervisors, managers, etc.) was carried out at the same time. Project staff also read client agency files every 3 months during the project. Much of the analysis is based on the data obtained during this time period. Follow-up data were obtained through surveys mailed to clients and staff at intervals over the subsequent 15-month period. Twenty-three questionnaires and interview guides were developed and tested for various forms of reliability and validity.

Description of Study Participants

The five executive directors in this early study had MSW degrees; however, only 60% of the regional managers, 44% of the district supervisors, and 20% of the child welfare workers held that degree. When MSWs, BSWs, and other professional degrees were included, 90% of the managers, 60% of the supervisors, and 68% of the child welfare workers held professional degrees.

Two-thirds of the families were headed by a single parent. One-third of the families also reported "some" or "severe" disability with respect to physical and emotional health, learning problems, or drug and alcohol problems. Fourteen percent reported some or severe alcohol or drug problems for themselves. Eight percent reported that their spouses had similar problems. Unemployment was present for one-third of the families. Forty-seven percent of the families were living on welfare or unemployment insurance benefits. Finally, in 10% of the families, at least one family member was a Native American (of Canadian origin).

Family problems included periodic and severe neglect of children, inability of parents to care for children (because of illness, addictions, etc.), and physical and sexual abuse. By the end of the study, 28% of the families had been listed on the child abuse registry. Forty-nine percent of the families had at least one child in care during the study period.

Study Limitations

The study is limited by the self-selection of the families involved from whom we requested informed consent. We compared the participating and nonparticipating groups on several demographic variables and found no significant differences between them. An additional limitation was added when British Columbia cut back funding and services to the province-wide child welfare program. In particular, these cutbacks led to the nonrenewal of over 600 family support workers across the province. Because the cutbacks were implemented differentially in regions, we could gather data on their impact over time. Thus, we could incorporate the impact of these cutbacks into the study design. The findings of this aspect of the study take on added meaning today, as practitioners face an increasingly conservative climate that encourages politicians to demonstrate their ability cut funding thus shredding the safety net developed over the years to protect our most vulnerable populations.

Findings on Skills Related to Silences

In addition to the findings reported in this text, the analysis of the use of skills related to silence deserves a more detailed presentation. The skill of reaching inside silences was one of the 5 skills used least often of the 27 skills studied (Shulman, 1978). However, another analysis showed it to be the one of the most significant. The 15 workers (of 155) who had the most positive overall skill scores were compared with those workers who had the most negative. The former were found to have more positive working relationships and were more helpful than the latter. The practice skill profiles of the workers were compared according to their scores on 27 specific skills. The skill of reaching inside silences was one of the three most important in which the positive skill group of workers differed from the negative skill group (p. 281). Additional findings related to the response to silences are shared in the studies described later.

Child Welfare Practice and Supervision Study 2

In the more recent study, reaching inside silences was one of the four skills included in a grouping termed the skills to help clients manage their feelings (Shulman, 1991). This grouping was related to the client's sense that the worker cared—one element of the working relationship. When the skill was examined by itself, workers were perceived by their clients to use it seldom. In fact, out of the eight skills examined, it was almost the least-used skill, only slightly ahead of the worker sharing his or her feelings (p. 61).

The particular impact of each of the four skills on the development of the working relationship (rapport, caring, and trust) as well as the member's perception of the worker's helpfulness was also examined (Shulman, 1993). The results, which replicated the general findings of the 1978 study, indicated that this skill—when used in the beginning phase of practice—showed the highest correlation with the client's perception of the worker's caring ($r = .56$) and trust in the worker (.68). It was fifth in importance in terms of the client's perception of worker helpfulness (.51). The findings of both studies support the notion that workers need to actively explore the hidden meaning of silences in interviews.

Category Observation System for Analyzing Counselor-Client Interaction in Individual and Group Practice

Another finding from a separate design of the 1978 study yielded additional evidence that this important skill may not be used as often in practice as it should. In this part of the study, the individual interviews and group sessions of 11 volunteer workers were videotaped and then analyzed by trained raters using a category observation system I developed. The system assigned a number to categories of behavior such as addressing silences, empathic responses, sharing worker's feelings, and so forth. It also analyzed whether in our judgment the worker was responding to the client's or group member's "production" or working on his or her own agenda. In an analysis of 32 individual interviews and 32 group sessions, raters scored the worker's or group leader's or the member's behavior by entering a number that described the interaction at least every 3 seconds. A total of 103,248 individual observations of sessions were scored and then analyzed by computer. In one analysis, I was able to determine which behaviors of the workers most often followed silences of 3 seconds or longer.

The findings were striking.

- Of all the entries scored, only 1,742 (4%) indicated that a silence of 3 seconds or more had taken place. Brief silences were rare in both the individual and group sessions.

- A 3-second silence was followed by another 3-second silence only 26% of the time. This meant that three out of four times there was a brief silence someone responded.

- Raters found that member comments followed 3-second silences only 38% of the time.

- Group leaders' active comments in response to silences occurred 36% of the time.

When these ratings were examined more closely, they revealed the following results:

- When workers actively intervened after a silence, they attempted to encourage elaboration 31% of the time.

- Their efforts to deal with the member's feelings or share their own feelings were noted in only 4% of their responses.

- The most common active action in response to silence was to direct the member or the group away from the member's presented theme of concern. This occurred 49% of the time.

Remember, however, that the subdesign involved only 11 workers in one agency, each of whom faced the unusual pressure of being videotaped as part of a research project. My attempt to generalize from these findings to other settings or workers is tentative; even so, my observations as a training consultant and the findings of the more recent study support these conclusions (Shulman, 1991).

Videotape analysis data indicated less attention to group member affect on the part of group leaders than the overall study suggested. Group leaders shared their own feelings or dealt with member feelings in only 2.3% of their interventions in the individual sessions and in 5.3% of their interventions in the group sessions. When total interactions in the session were analyzed, including times when the member was speaking and the group leader listening, the total interventions that dealt with the affect in the group sessions dropped to 1.4%. This figure is very close to Flanders's (1970) results from analyzing classroom teaching behaviors.

When examining the skill profile of the average worker in the larger study, I found that clients perceived their worker as acknowledging their feelings "fairly often" and as articulating their feelings without their having to share them between "seldom" and "fairly often" (Shulman, 1993). When the correlation between this skill and the development of the caring dimension of the working relationship was examined, it was the second-strongest associating skill when used in the beginning phase of practice ($r = .54$) and the strongest associating skill when used in the middle phase (.77). Similar patterns were found in relation to trust and worker helpfulness.

Related and Relevant Studies

Supporting Clients in Taboo Areas

In my early study, the skill of supporting clients in taboo areas was one of four skills that distinguished the most effective workers from the least effective, from their client's perspective (Shulman, 1978). In the more recent study, this skill was only the sixth-most used out of the eight skills examined (Shulman, 1991). Clients reported that their workers used this skill between "seldom" and "fairly often." This result is not unexpected, because workers face the same taboos that group members do. Group leaders need experience and supervision to find the courage to speak directly about many of these issues.

The introduction of time to the analysis of this skill yielded some interesting findings. Supporting clients in taboo areas, when used in the beginning phase of work (first sessions), was the third-strongest skill (out of eight) that correlated with the client's perception of the worker's caring ($r = .52$). The correlation for the use of the skill in the middle phase of work was slightly higher (.58). These findings were expected, because support of any kind, particularly in sensitive and painful areas of work, could contribute to the client's perception that the worker was concerned about him or her.

When the association between the beginning phase use of this skill and trust was examined, however, it was significant but smaller ($r = .37$). The correlation was higher when the skill was used in the middle phase (.57). A similar pattern was found when the skill use was correlated with client perception of the worker's helpfulness ($r = .39$ in the beginning phase and .50 in the middle phase). One inference from these findings might be that the use of this skill in the early phases of work, before a solid working relationship has been established, primarily contributes to the working relationship through the development of a client's sense of the worker's caring. This provides some justification for the argument that it is better for the group leader to risk and be ahead of the member than to be overly cautious and behind, such as in always only reflecting the client's stated feelings.

The use of the skill may have less of an impact on trust and helpfulness early in the work because of the lower levels of trust in the beginning phase of any relationship. In short, the member needs to feel somewhat safe with the group leader before the group leader's efforts to explore taboo areas have their largest impact on trust.

The VISA Center for Students Suspended from School for Violence, Substance Abuse, or Possession of Weapons

Chapter 15 on school counseling reported on my VISA project with students suspended from school for violence. Additional details on the methodology, sample, and findings are shared here.

Profile of Suspended Students

Of the total study sample of 886 students, 280 (32%) participated in VISA, and 606 (68%) did not.[1] The 886 students had a mean age of 15 years, were predominantly male (69%) and black (69%), and were overwhelmingly served by the free lunch program (80%). (On average, 58% of the school district's student population was African American.) The profile of the total suspended group of students (VISA and control) indicated that

- 18 (2%) were in 6th grade,
- 191 (22%) in 7th grade,
- 244 (27%) in 8th grade,
- 132 (15%) in 9th grade,
- 155 (17%) in 10th grade,
- 86 (10%) in 11th grade,
- 40 (5%) in 12th grade, and
- 20 (2%) did not specify their grade.

Almost 7 out of 10 suspended students were male, equal proportions were black, and 8 out of 10 were economically disadvantaged. Some portion of these figures may be explained by the fact that almost 6 out of 10 students in the school district were also black at that time. Our profile data do not tell us if being a poor, black male student leads to behavior that results in suspension or that race, gender, and class tend to be factors that cause school staff to respond differently to their behavior. The schools in our study showed a wide range of percentages of total school population suspended, and our work in these schools indicated very different criteria were used for in-school versus out-of-school suspensions.

Also, our work in the community and in the schools has suggested to us that community-based factors in some lower-income communities of color, such as gang and drug activity, may also be an external contributing factor. Certainly, students' verbal reports in the VISA support groups on the impact of traumatic events, such as drive-by shootings, seem to suggest that these events may constitute an additional risk factor or may also magnify the impact of preexisting risk factors.

It is important to point out that there were also thousands of male, black, economically disadvantaged students in the district schools who were not suspended or resuspended. In addition, 3 out of 10 suspended students were white, 3 out of 10 were female, and 2 out of 10 were not economically disadvantaged.

Impact on Survival Rate (Length of Time Between Resuspensions)

The reader is referred to the complete report on the project for a full discussion of the impact of participating in the VISA program (Shulman & Maguin, 2006). One outcome measure was survival rate—that is, if a student was resuspended, the length of time before the second suspension. The survival rate is seen as an important interim outcome measure. For example, in the field of substance abuse counseling, the phrase "relapse is a part of recovery" recognizes that change may not be a straight line and

---

1. Students may not have participated in the VISA program out of their choice or their parents', or because there were no spaces at the VISA Center for them at the time of suspension. A major limitation of the study is the lack of random assignment to the VISA and the non-VISA groups.

in fact is a process. The key to understanding relapse as potentially positive is whether the substance abuser has learned from the relapse and can change his or her behavior.

In a like manner, students who are able to manage their interactions in school for a longer period may be demonstrating increased skill in avoiding resuspension (relapse). The relatively low number of students who were resuspended in our study and the even lower percentage of students who were resuspended more than once may be an indication that learning has taken place for all students. In addition, a finding in the full report indicated that when controlling for age and ethnicity, participation in VISA was associated with a longer time before resuspension (trend level). This suggests that while resuspended students were not able to avoid resuspension, they were able to postpone it.

Exit Interview Findings and Other Outcomes

When the students in the VISA program were asked in an exit interview if they were helped by VISA, 55% indicated they were helped a lot and 39% helped a little. When asked what was the most useful thing learned in VISA, 75% of the respondents indicated social skills (e.g., conflict avoidance, anger management, thinking before acting), 4% identified academic skills, 11% learning about black history and racism, and the remaining 10% cited none or other.

Finally, analysis of outcome data indicated that VISA participation appeared to have a positive impact on some students; however, the impact was affected by demographic factors. For example, none of the white VISA participants were resuspended compared to 12% of the white students in the control group. When we controlled for ethnicity and suspension quarter marks (i.e., the grades received in the quarter prior to the suspension), VISA participants had a significantly lower resuspension risk of .85 compared to students in the comparison group. In another example of the interaction between VISA participation and other variables, VISA students with a GPA over 80 were about half as likely to be resuspended as students with a GPA under 60. Students with a GPA between 70 and 80 were only two-thirds as likely to be resuspended as those with GPAs below 60.

Longer-term analysis of the impact of this type of program was limited due to the suspension of funding in the third year. The program had been funded through the efforts of the deputy speaker of the New York State Assembly, a local state representative. Funding was lost after 9/11 when available funds were diverted to dealing with the impact of that attack on Lower Manhattan.

Summary

A more detailed discussion of methodology, sample, limitations, and selected findings from a number of my studies cited in the text are shared in this appendix, as are findings from related and relevant studies. The four studies include (1) an early study into the impact of child welfare worker practice skill on working relationship and client outcomes; (2) a later study replicating and modifying the early project adding the impact of supervision and management on worker behavior, working relationship, and client outcomes; (3) an analysis of 120 hours of videotaped individual and group sessions using a category observation system; and (4) the design and results of a 2-year project with 280 students treated in a 2-week intensive academic, psychoeducational, and social skills program for students suspended from school for violence.

Findings from the first three studies supported a number of constructs about the importance of the use of skills such as reaching inside silences, exploring taboo areas, and expressing empathy. They also raised questions about the low frequency of use of some of these skills. The impact of these skills at different times in the relationship were also explored with some, such as expressing empathy and exploring taboo areas, appearing to be more important in the middle phases of work. Some related studies by other researchers supported these findings.

The findings in the VISA project indicated that involvement in the program had some positive impact on some students in terms of lowering resuspension rates as well as lengthening the time between suspensions (or relapses). Variables such as race, income, school attended, and grade point average in the quarter before suspension all influenced the findings.

APPENDIX B

Resilience Theory and Research

Resilience theory and research were introduced in the text in relation to children and the elderly. This appendix expands somewhat on the definitions and research findings in this area of knowledge about human growth and behavior.

Developmental Psychology Theory and Research

A landmark study in developmental psychology involved 698 infants on the Hawaiian island of Kauai who, in 1955, became participants in a 30-year longitudinal study of "how some individuals triumph over physical disadvantages and deprived childhoods" (Werner, 1989, p. 106). Werner discussed the goals that she and her collaborators shared "to assess the long-term consequences of prenatal and perinatal stress and to document the effects of adverse early rearing conditions on children's physical, cognitive, and psychosocial development" (p. 106). She described their growing interest in resilience as follows:

> But as our study progressed we began to take a special interest in certain "high risk" children who, in spite of exposure to reproductive stress, discordant and impoverished home lives and uneducated, alcoholic, or mentally disturbed parents, went on to develop healthy personalities, stable careers, and strong interpersonal relations. We decided to try to identify the protective factors that contributed to the resilience of these children. (p. 106)

The researchers identified 201 "vulnerable" children (30% of the surviving children) as high risk if they encountered four or more risk factors by the age of 2 (severe perinatal stress, chronic poverty, uneducated parents, or troubled family environments marked by discord, divorce, parental alcoholism, or mental illness). Two-thirds of this group (129) developed serious learning or behavior problems by the age of 10 or had delinquency records, mental health problems, or pregnancies by the time they were 18.

It was the other third (72) of these high-risk children—those who "grew into competent young adults who loved well, worked well and played well"—that attracted the researchers' attention (Werner, 1989, p. 108). They identified several constitutional factors as sources of resilience (e.g., high activity level, low degree of excitability and distress, high degrees of sociability, ability to concentrate at school, problem-solving and reading skills, and effective use of their talents). They also identified the following environmental factors:

- Coming from families with four or fewer children
- Spaces of 2 or more years between themselves and their next siblings
- The opportunity to establish a close bond with at least one caretaker who provided positive attention during the first years of life

These resilient children were found to be "particularly adept at recruiting such surrogate parents when a biological parent was unavailable or incapacitated" (Werner, 1989, p. 108). These children were also able to use their network of neighbors, school friends and teachers, church groups, and so forth, to provide emotional support in order to succeed "against the odds" (p. 110).

The researchers concluded on a hopeful note:

As long as the balance between stressful life events and protective factors is favorable, successful adaptation is possible. When stressful events outweigh the protective factors, however, even the most resilient child can have problems. It may be possible to shift the balance from vulnerability to resilience through intervention, either by decreasing exposure to risk factors or stressful events or by increasing the number of protective factors and sources of support that are available. (p. 111)

Stressors, Risk, and Personal and Environmental Factors

Researchers and theorists have built on this basic set of ideas: Life stressors can lead to negative outcomes for people at high risk; however, personal and environmental factors can buffer the individual, thereby providing the resilience to overcome adversity. For example, Fonagy, Steele, Steele, and Higgitt (1994) examined attachment theory, which focuses on the impact of early infant-caregiver attachments in a child's development and the security of such attachments. They examined the intergenerational transmission of insecure attachments, focusing on factors that might disrupt a negative cycle—in other words, ways to help mothers who had themselves experienced insecure attachments avoid transmitting these to their own children.

Other researchers have applied the basic model to specific populations (as defined by race, ethnicity, etc.), economic status (poverty), or community variables (inner-city location, level of violence). For example, Daly et al. (1995) make use of an "Afri-centric paradigm" to describe an emphasis on collectivity that is expressed as shared concern and responsibility for others: "Scholarship using this perspective identifies positive aspects of African American life richly embedded in spirituality and a world-view that incorporates African traits and commitment to common causes" (p. 241).

As an example on the individual level, specifically referring to the resilience of successful African American men, the authors cite research findings (Gary & Leashore, 1982; Hacker, 1992) that suggest the following:

Much of their success can be attributed to individual and family resilience, the ability to "bounce back" after defeat or near defeat, and the mobilization of limited resources while simultaneously protecting the ego against a constant array of social and economic assaults. To varying degrees, success results from a strong value system that includes belief in self, industrious efforts, desire and motivation to achieve, religious beliefs, self-respect and respect for others, and responsibility toward one's family and community, and cooperation. (Daly et al., 1995, p. 242)

In another example, researchers examined age, race, and setting by focusing on risk and resilience for African American youths in school settings (Connell, Spencer, & Aber, 1994). They developed a theoretical model that they tested using data from two large samples in two cities: New York and Atlanta. Their findings confirm that family involvement is an important target for these interventions. This study's results also support efforts to develop intervention strategies that increase poor African American youths' beliefs in their own abilities to affect their academic outcomes and for improving their relationships with peers in the school context.

Parental Involvement

Perhaps the most intriguing and disturbing implication of this study for our understanding of risk and resilience is that disaffected behavior in low-income African American youth can lessen parental involvement, which in turn contributes to negative appraisals of self that exacerbate disaffected patterns of action and contribute to negative educational outcomes.

Christian and Barbarin (2001) also examined the importance of parental involvement on the adjustment of low-income African American children. They found that children of parents who attended church at least weekly had fewer behavior problems than did those who attended church less frequently. This supported the importance of religiosity as a sociocultural resource for African American families with children who are potentially at risk for behavioral and emotional maladjustments related to growing up in poor families and communities. In a second and related line of inquiry, the researchers hypothesized that parents who reported a positive racial identity, as well as those who tended to externalize by attributing the causes of negative African American life outcomes to outside forces, would have children with fewer behavioral problems. Although these two variables might relate to parental self-esteem, they did not directly affect the children's incidence of behavioral problems. In fact, parents who tended to internalize explanations of poor outcomes (e.g., not working hard enough, lack of persistence) had children with fewer behavioral problems. The authors concede that the limitations of the study do not allow wider generalizations; nonetheless, their findings were both unexpected and intriguing.

Community Violence

Richters and Martinez (1993) offer an example of resilience research that examines the impact of community violence on childhood development. They examined factors that contributed to resilience on the part of 72 children attending their first year of elementary school in a violent neighborhood of Washington, DC. Their findings indicate the following:

Despite the fact that these children were being raised in violent neighborhoods, had been exposed to relatively high levels of violence in the community, and were experiencing associated distress symptoms, community violence exposure levels were not predictive of adaptational failure or success. Instead, adaptational status was systematically related to characteristics of the children's homes. (p. 609)

The authors point out that only when the environmental adversities contaminated the safety and stability of the children's homes did their odds of adaptational failure increase.

In a study of the risk and protective factors associated with gang involvement among urban African American adolescents, researchers found that youths with current or past gang membership documented higher levels of risk involvement, lower levels of resilience, higher exposure to violence, and higher distress symptoms than did youths with no gang affiliations (Li et al., 2002). The findings persisted when controlled for age, gender, and risk involvement. The authors suggest that gang membership itself is associated with increased risk and ill effects on psychological well-being. They also found that strong family involvement and resiliency protects against gang involvement.

Poverty

Garmezy (1991) focused on the resilience and vulnerability of children in relation to the impact of poverty. He states, "The evidence is sturdy that many children and adults do overcome life's difficulties. Since good outcomes are frequently present in a large number of life histories, it is critical to identify those "protective" factors that seemingly enable individuals to circumvent life stressors" (p. 421). The author points to a core of variables that serve as resilience factors, including "warmth, cohesion, and the presence of some caring adults (such as a grandparent) in the absence of responsive parents or in the presence of marked marital discord" (p. 421). Similar findings in studies that examine the resiliency of children who are exposed to poverty and other traumas have identified emotional responsivity in the parent-child relationship as a buffering factor (Egeland et al., 1993).

In a review of the literature on resilience and poverty, Garmezy (1993) suggests that these findings provide new questions and avenues for research. What factors are involved in the seeming diminution over time of resilience in some hitherto adaptive children and adults? Prolonged and cumulated stress would appear to be a prime candidate for examination. Another factor worthy of consideration would be the absence of a support structure and its availability over time. Other candidates for effecting change may include critical modifications in the child's environment, such as the physical dissolution of the family (p. 130). Other examples of population-specific resilience studies include research on youths with high incidence of disabilities (Murray, 2003), homeless students (Reed-Victor, E., & Stronge, J. (2002), and adolescents who experience marital transitions (Rodgers & Rose, 2002).

Cognitive Hardiness and Coping Style

Researchers have also examined the concept of "cognitive hardiness" and coping style as buffering or moderating variables between life stress events and trauma and psychological and somatic distress (Beasley, Thompson, & Davidson, 2003). The study involved analysis of questionnaires completed by 187 students who had returned to the university as mature adults. In general, findings supported a direct effect on outcomes of life stress and psychological health. Cognitive hardiness, coping style, and negative life events also impacted outcomes. Several cases supported the concept that cognitive hardiness moderated the impact of emotional coping styles and adverse life events on psychological distress. The researchers used Kobasa and Pucetti's (1983) definition of cognitive hardiness as a personality variable—specifically, "the quality of hardy individuals who believe that they can control or influence events, have a commitment to activities and their interpersonal relationships and to self, in that they recognize their own distinct values, goals and priorities in life, and view change as a challenge rather than a threat. In the latter regard, they are predisposed to be cognitively flexible" (p. 841).

Summary

Resilience theory and research help inform our understanding about why some individuals appear to be able to deal with adversity, both personally and in their community, and others are not as able to cope. An early landmark study of resilience identified (1) coming from a family with four or fewer children, (2) spaces of 2 or more years between siblings, and (3) a close bond with at least one caretaker during the first years of life. The study indicated that the balance between vulnerability and resilience could be shifted in a positive manner either by decreasing stressful events or risk factors or by increasing protective factors.

This basic model of life stressors potentially leading to negative outcomes for people at high risk that can be buffered by personal and environmental factors is central to this theory of human development. Researchers have explored this model in relation to positive attachments, the impact of race and poverty, and community factors such as violence. Lack of parental involvement, community violence, and poverty have been found to increase risk factors; however, the individual's cognitive hardiness and coping style, as well as support system, can buffer this risk and allow the individual to overcome adversity.

Association for Specialists in Group Work (ASGW) Best Practice Guidelines

Approved by the ASGW Executive Board, March 29, 1998
Prepared by: Lynn Rapin and Linda Keel, ASGW Ethics Committee Co-chairs
Revised by: R. Valorie Thomas and Deborah A. Pender, ASGW Ethics Committee Co-chairs
Revisions Approved by the ASGW Executive Board, March 23, 2007

The Association for Specialists in Group Work (ASGW) is a division of the American Counseling Association whose members are interested in and specialize in group work. Group Workers are defined as mental health professionals who use a group modality as an intervention when working with diverse populations. We value the creation of community while recognizing diverse perspectives; service to our members, clients, and the profession; and value leadership as a process to facilitate the growth and development of individuals and groups within their social and cultural contexts.

Preamble

The Association for Specialists in Group Work recognizes the commitment of its members to the Code of Ethics (as revised in 2005) of its parent organization, the American Counseling Association, and nothing in this document shall be construed to supplant that code. These Best Practice Guidelines are intended to clarify the application of the ACA Code of Ethics to the field of group work by defining Group Workers' responsibility and scope of practice involving those activities, strategies and interventions that are consistent and current with effective and appropriate professional ethical and community standards. ASGW views ethical process as being integral to group work and views Group Workers as ethical agents. Group Workers, by their very nature in being responsible and responsive to their group members, necessarily embrace a certain potential for ethical vulnerability. It is incumbent upon Group Workers to give considerable attention to the intent and context of their actions because the attempts of Group Workers to influence human behavior through group work always have ethical implications. These Best Practice Guidelines address Group Workers' responsibilities in planning, performing and processing groups.

Section A: Best Practice in Planning

A.1. Professional Context and Regulatory Requirements

Group Workers actively know, understand and apply the ACA Code of Ethics (2005), the ASGW Professional Standards for the Training of Group Workers, these ASGW

Best Practice Guidelines, the ASGW diversity competencies, and the AMCD Multicultural Counseling Competencies and Standards, relevant state laws, accreditation requirements, relevant National Board for Certified Counselors Codes and Standards, their organization's standards, and insurance requirements impacting the practice of group work.

A.2. Scope of Practice and Conceptual Framework

Group Workers define the scope of practice related to the core and specialization competencies defined in the ASGW Training Standards. Group Workers are aware of personal strengths and weaknesses in leading groups. Group Workers develop and are able to articulate a general conceptual framework to guide practice and a rationale for use of techniques that are to be used. Group Workers limit their practice to those areas for which they meet the training criteria established by the ASGW Training Standards.

A.3. Assessment

a. Assessment of self. Group Workers actively assess their knowledge and skills related to the specific group(s) offered. Group Workers assess their values, beliefs and theoretical orientation and how these impact upon the group, particularly when working with a diverse and multicultural population.

b. Ecological assessment. Group Workers assess community needs, agency or organization resources, sponsoring organization mission, staff competency, attitudes regarding group work, professional training levels of potential group leaders regarding group work; client attitudes regarding group work, and multicultural and diversity considerations. Group Workers use this information as the basis for making decisions related to their group practice, or to the implementation of groups for which they have supervisory, evaluation, or oversight responsibilities.

A.4. Program Development and Evaluation

a. Group Workers identify the type(s) of group(s) to be offered and how they relate to community needs.

b. Group Workers concisely state in writing the purpose and goals of the group. Group Workers also identify the role of the group members in influencing or determining the group goals.

c. Group Workers set fees consistent with the organization's fee schedule, taking into consideration the financial status and locality of prospective group members.

d. Group Workers choose techniques and a leadership style appropriate to the type(s) of group(s) being offered.

e. Group Workers have an evaluation plan consistent with regulatory, organization and insurance requirements, where appropriate.

f. Group Workers take into consideration current professional guidelines when using technology, including but not limited to Internet communication.

A.5. Resources

Group Workers coordinate resources related to the kind of group(s) and group activities to be provided, such as: adequate funding; the appropriateness and availability of a trained co-leader; space and privacy requirements for the type(s) of group(s) being offered; marketing and recruiting; and appropriate collaboration with other community agencies and organizations.

A.6. Professional Disclosure Statement

Group Workers maintain awareness and sensitivity regarding cultural meaning of confidentiality and privacy. Group Workers respect differing views towards disclosure of information. They have a professional disclosure statement which includes information on confidentiality and exceptions to confidentiality, theoretical orientation, information on the nature, purpose(s) and goals of the group, the group services that can be provided, the role and responsibility of group members and leaders, Group Workers qualifications to conduct the specific group(s), specific licenses, certifications and professional affiliations, and address of licensing/credentialing body.

A.7. Group and Member Preparation

a. Group Workers screen prospective group members if appropriate to the type of group being offered. When selection of group members is appropriate, Group Workers identify group members whose needs and goals are compatible with the goals of the group.

b. Group Workers facilitate informed consent. They communicate information in ways that are both developmentally and culturally appropriate. Group Workers provide in oral and written form to prospective members (when appropriate to group type): the professional disclosure statement; group purpose and goals; group participation expectations including voluntary and involuntary membership; role expectations of members and leader(s); policies related to entering and exiting the group; policies governing substance use; policies and procedures governing mandated groups (where relevant); documentation requirements; disclosure of information to others; implications of out-of-group contact or involvement among members; procedures for consultation between group leader(s) and group member(s); fees and time parameters; and potential impacts of group participation.

c. Group Workers obtain the appropriate consent/assent forms for work with minors and other dependent group members.

d. Group Workers define confidentiality and its limits (for example, legal and ethical exceptions and expectations; waivers implicit with treatment plans, documentation and insurance usage). Group Workers have the responsibility to inform all group participants of the need for confidentiality, potential consequences of breaching confidentiality and that legal privilege does not apply to group discussions (unless provided by state statute).

A.8. Professional Development

Group Workers recognize that professional growth is a continuous, ongoing, developmental process throughout their career.

a. Group Workers remain current and increase knowledge and skill competencies through activities such as continuing education, professional supervision, and participation in personal and professional development activities.

b. Group Workers seek consultation and/or supervision regarding ethical concerns that interfere with effective functioning as a group leader. Supervisors have the responsibility to keep abreast of consultation, group theory, process, and adhere to related ethical guidelines.

c. Group Workers seek appropriate professional assistance for their own personal problems or conflicts that are likely to impair their professional judgement or work performance.

d. Group Workers seek consultation and supervision to ensure appropriate practice whenever working with a group for which all knowledge and skill competencies have not been achieved.

e. Group Workers keep abreast of group research and development.

A.9. Trends and Technological Changes

Group Workers are aware of and responsive to technological changes as they affect society and the profession. These include but are not limited to changes in mental health delivery systems; legislative and insurance industry reforms; shifting population demographics and client needs; and technological advances in Internet and other communication devices and delivery systems. Group Workers adhere to ethical guidelines related to the use of developing technologies.

Section B: Best Practice in Performing

B.1. Self Knowledge

Group Workers are aware of and monitor their strengths and weaknesses and the effects these have on group members. They explore their own cultural identities and how these affect their values and beliefs about group work.

B.2. Group Competencies

Group Workers have a basic knowledge of groups and the principles of group dynamics, and are able to perform the core group competencies, as described in the ASGW Professional Standards for the Training of Group Workers. They gain knowledge, personal awareness, sensitivity, and skills pertinent to working with a diverse client population. Additionally, Group Workers have adequate understanding and skill in any group specialty area chosen for practice (psychotherapy, counseling, task, psychoeducation, as described in the ASGW Training Standards).

B.3. Group Plan Adaptation

a. Group Workers apply and modify knowledge, skills and techniques appropriate to group type and stage, and to the unique needs of various cultural and ethnic groups.

b. Group Workers monitor the group's progress toward the group goals and plan.

c. Group Workers clearly define and maintain ethical, professional, and social relationship boundaries with group members as appropriate to their role in the organization and the type of group being offered.

B.4. Therapeutic Conditions and Dynamics

Group Workers understand and are able to implement appropriate models of group development, process observation and therapeutic conditions. Group Workers manage the flow of communication, addressing safety and pacing of disclosures as to protect group members from physical, emotional, or psychological trauma.

B.5. Meaning

Group Workers assist members in generating meaning from the group experience.

B.6. Collaboration

Group Workers assist members in developing individual goals and respect group members as co-equal partners in the group experience.

B.7. Evaluation

Group Workers include evaluation (both formal and informal) between sessions and at the conclusion of the group.

B.8. Diversity

Group Workers practice with broad sensitivity to client differences including but not limited to ethnic, gender, religious, sexual, psychological maturity, economic class, family history, physical characteristics or limitations, and geographic location. Group Workers continuously seek information regarding the cultural issues of the diverse population with whom they are working both by interaction with participants and from using outside resources.

B.9. Ethical Surveillance

Group Workers employ an appropriate ethical decision making model in responding to ethical challenges and issues and in determining courses of action and behavior for self and group members. In addition, Group Workers employ applicable standards as promulgated by ACA, ASGW, or other appropriate professional organizations.

Section C: Best Practice in Group Processing

C.1. Processing Schedule

Group Workers process the workings of the group with themselves, group members, supervisors or other colleagues, as appropriate. This may include assessing progress on group and member goals, leader behaviors and techniques, group dynamics and interventions; developing understanding and acceptance of meaning. Processing may occur both within sessions and before and after each session, at time of termination, and later follow-up, as appropriate.

C.2. Reflective Practice

Group Workers attend to opportunities to synthesize theory and practice and to incorporate learning outcomes into ongoing groups. Group Workers attend to session dynamics of members and their interactions and also attend to the relationship between session dynamics and leader values, cognition and affect.

C.3. Evaluation and Follow-Up

a. Group Workers evaluate process and outcomes. Results are used for ongoing program planning, improvement and revisions of current group and/or to contribute to professional research literature. Group Workers follow all applicable policies and standards in using group material for research and reports.

b. Group Workers conduct follow-up contact with group members, as appropriate, to assess outcomes or when requested by a group member(s).

C.4. Consultation and Training with Other Organizations

Group Workers provide consultation and training to organizations in and out of their setting, when appropriate. Group Workers seek out consultation as needed with competent professional persons knowledgeable about group work.

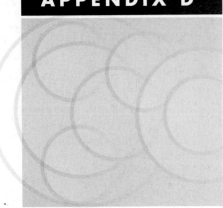

Links to Associations, Practice Guidelines, and Codes of Ethics

- Association for Specialists in Group Work: www.asgw.org
- Standards for Social Work Practice with Groups: Association for the Advancement of Social Work with Groups: http://www.aaswg.org/node/377
- Practice Guidelines for Group Psychotherapy: American Group Psychotherapy Association. www.agpa.org/guidelines/index.html
- Council for the Accreditation of Counseling and Related Educational Programs: http://www.cacrep.org/template/index.cfm
- American Counseling Association: www.counseling.org
- American School Counselor Association: www.schoolcounselor.org
- American Mental Health Counselors Association: www.amhca.org
- American Association for Marriage and Family Therapy: www.aamft.org
- National Association of Social Workers: http://www.socialworkers.org/
- National Rehabilitation Counseling Association: http://nrca-net.org
- National Employment Counseling Association: www.employmentcounseling.org
- American Psychological Association: www.apa.org
- National Board for Certified Counselors: www.nbcc.org
- The Association for Addiction Professionals: www.naadac.org

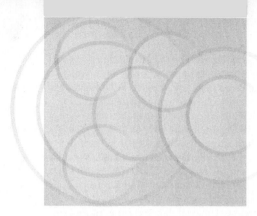

Glossary

12-step model A model of recovery in which the participants follow 12 clearly defined steps to achieve recovery from drug and alcohol abuse. Although this model is closely associated with the Alcoholics Anonymous movement, it has been used in other recovery programs as well.

abstinence model An approach to recovery suggesting that complete abstinence from the use of drugs or alcohol is required for achieving and maintaining recovery.

ACOA (Adult Children of Alcoholics) A recovery movement organization for people with alcoholic parents, designed to help them deal with the long-term emotional impact of growing up in a household with an alcoholic parent.

act out To communicate thoughts and feelings through behavior, often in a disruptive manner.

activity group A term usually applied to groups involved in a range of activities other than just conversation. "Program" is another term used to describe the activities implemented in such groups, such as the expressive arts (painting, dancing), games, folk singing, social parties, cooking, and so on.

addictive voice Defined by the Rational Recovery movement as an addictive voice (AV), which is your body talking to you in thoughts and feelings, telling you to drink or use drugs.

all-in-the-same-boat phenomenon A mutual aid process in which group members gain support from discovering that other group members have similar problems, concerns, feelings, and experiences.

ambivalence Mixed feelings about a problem, person, or issue. For example, a group member may wish to finally deal with an issue, but because of the painful feelings associated with it, the member may also wish to deny that the problem exists.

anger about the ending A stage in the ending/transition phase whereby group members appear to be angry at the group leader because of the ending of the relationship. This anger appears in direct or indirect forms.

authority theme Issues related to the relationship between the group members and the group leader.

barometric events In the Bennis and Shepard (1956) model of group development, these events mark the shift from one phase or subphase to the next—for example, when the leader is "overthrown."

baseline reserve capacity The individual's current "maximum performance potential" with existing internal and external resources.

basic assumption groups Bion's (1961) idea that group members appear to be acting as if their behavior were motivated by a shared basic assumption—other than the expressed group goal—about the purpose of the group.

beginning (or engagement) phase The engagement phase of work, during which the group leader contracts with the group members by clarifying the purpose of the group, by clarifying the role he or she will play, and by reaching for members' feedback on the content of the work. Authority issues are also dealt with in this phase.

bisexuals Individuals who can be attracted to either men or women or, as they say, to a person, not a gender.

burnout A common problem in stressful practice situations in which the group leader's emotional reactions lead to leaving the job or maladaptive behaviors such as overworking or closing off all emotional reactions.

caring One element of the construct "working relationship"; the group member's sense that the group leader is concerned about him or her and that the group leader wishes to help with those concerns the group member feels are important.

check-in An exercise used in some groups at the start of a session, in which each member briefly shares what has happened to him or her during the preceding week.

checking for underlying ambivalence Exploring group member ambivalence that may be hidden by an artificial agreement.

clarifying the group leader's purpose and role Establishing the purpose of the group, the various services offered by the agency or setting, and the specific ways in which the group leader can help.

cleavage A process in a group in which the members split into distinct racial subgroups in response to a changing racial ratio. It can occur with an increase of the minority or "out-group" members past the tipping point.

closed group A fixed-membership group in which the same people meet for a defined period of time. Members may drop out and new members may be added in the early sessions, but in general, the membership of the group remains constant.

code of ethics The explication of the values, rules, and principles of ethical conduct that apply to all professional counselors.

codependents Friends, colleagues, employers, and family members who act in ways that help maintain the addict's substance abuse or other addiction problems (i.e., gambling).

cognition The way in which group members think about themselves and their environment.

cognitive-behavioral psychology and therapy In cognitive-behavioral therapy, the therapist uses strategies and techniques designed to help group members correct their negative, distorted views about themselves, the world, and the future, as well as the underlying maladaptive beliefs that gave rise to these cognitions.

cohesion The property of the group that describes the mutual attraction members feel for one another.

common ground The overlap or commonality between the specific services of the setting and the felt needs of the group member.

computer-mediated counseling "Any type of counseling that uses a computer for delivery of services whether via e-mail, chat rooms, online support-groups or video conferencing" (Kennedy, 2008. p. 34).

confidentiality The right of a group member not to have private information shared with third parties.

consciousness-raising groups Groups designed to help women become more aware of gender stereotyping and oppression issues that have affected their lives.

consensual validation The third subphase of the interdependence phase of group development (Bennis & Shepard, 1956), in which the unconflicted members once again provide the leadership needed for the group to move to a new level of work characterized by honest communication among members.

containment The skill of refraining from responding immediately to a group member's comment or question.

contemplation stage The second stage in the addiction change model suggested by DiClemente (1991), in which the addicted person is considering his or her use of substances and exploring the possibility of the existence of an addiction problem. This stage precedes any efforts at change.

content The substance of the work, consisting of ideas, issues, problems, concerns, and so on, that are part of the working contract.

contracting A group leader–initiated effort, usually in the beginning phase of a group, to establish the purpose of the group, to explain the group leader's role, to gain some sense of the group members' issues (feedback), to help group members see their connections to one another, and to deal with issues of authority.

correlation A nondirectional measure of association between two variables, with the correlation coefficient r ranging from –1.0 to 1.0.

counterdependence-flight The second subphase of the dependency phase of group development, in which the internal leader (a group member) attempts to take over the group and group members are in flight, exhibiting behaviors indicating fear of the leader's authority (Bennis & Shepard, 1956).

counterdependent member A member of the group who, during the counterdependence-flight subphase of group development, acts as if she or he is not dependent on the group leader and attempts to take over the group (Bennis & Shepard, 1956).

countertransference The complex of feelings of a group leader toward a group member or members.

crisis A term used in two ways: "(1) an internal experience of emotional change and distress and (2) a social event in which a disastrous event disrupts some essential functions of existing social institutions" (Barker, 2003, p. 103).

crisis intervention "The therapeutic practice used in helping group members in crisis promote effective coping that can lead to positive growth and change by acknowledging the problem, recognizing its impact, and learning new or more effective behaviors for coping with similar predictable experiences" (Barker, 2003, p. 103).

culture "A commonly used concept that is difficult to define. It revolves around the fact that human groups differ in the way they structure their behavior, in their worldview, in the perspectives on the rhythms and patterns of life, and in their concept of the essential nature of the human condition" (Devore & Schlesinger, 1996, p. 43).

culture for work An explicit or implied set of values, taboos, rules of interaction, and other concepts that are shared by the group members and that positively affect the group's ability to work at its tasks.

data gathering One of the functions of group activities, designed to help members obtain more information central to their tasks.

dealing with issues of authority The group leader's efforts to clarify mutual expectations, confidentiality issues, and the authority theme.

defensive member The defensive member refuses to admit there is a problem, to accept responsibility for his or her part in a problem, or to take suggestions or help from the group after a problem has been raised. The "yes, but . . ." syndrome is not uncommon as the defensive member has all of the reasons why he or she cannot deal with a problem.

demand for work The group leader's confrontation of the group or group members to work effectively on their tasks and to invest that work with energy and affect.

denial of the ending A stage in the ending/transition phase whereby group members appear to ignore the imminent end of the sessions.

dependence-flight The first subphase of the dependency phase of group development, in which group members are in flight, exhibiting behaviors indicating dependence on the leaders (Bennis & Shepard, 1956).

dependence phase The first phase of the group development, which is marked by group members' preoccupation with authority issues (Bennis & Shepard, 1956).

dependent group One of Bion's (1961) basic assumption groups. The group appears to be meeting in order to be sustained by the leader rather than working on its purposes.

dependent member A member of a group who, during the dependence-flight subphase of group development, acts as if she or he is dependent on the group leader, wanting the leader to take control of the group (Bennis & Shepard, 1956).

detecting and challenging the obstacles to work Perceiving and then confronting directly the obstacles that impede the group's work.

developing a universal perspective A mutual aid process in the group in which members begin to perceive universal issues, particularly in relation to oppression, thus allowing them to view their own problems in a more social context and with less personal blame.

developmental reserve capacity Refers to an individual's resources that can be activated or increased.

deviant member A group member who acts significantly differently from other group members in the system but may actually be sending an indirect signal of feelings and concerns on behalf of the other group members.

deviational allowance One of the functions of group activities, designed to create a flow of affect among members that builds up a positive relationship, allowing members to deviate from the accepted norms and raise concerns that might otherwise be taboo.

dialectical process A mutual aid process in which group members confront each other's ideas in an effort to develop a synthesis for all group members.

discussing a taboo area A mutual aid process in which one member enters a taboo area of discussion, thereby freeing other members to enter as well.

disease model The belief that addiction is inherently a disease and should be treated as such.

disenchantment-flight The second subphase of the interdependence phase of group development, in which the counterpersonals take over from the overpersonals in reaction to the growing intimacy (Bennis & Shepard, 1956).

displaying understanding of the group member's feelings The skill of acknowledging to the group member, through words or nonverbal means, that the group leader has understood how the group member feels after the affect has been expressed by the member (e.g., the group leader's response to crying).

division of labor The development of group structure in which the tasks to be performed are distributed among members in a formal or informal manner.

"doorknob" communication A group member communication usually shared at the very end of a session (hand on the doorknob) or in the last sessions. Recognizing doorknob communications and addressing them is one of the sessional ending and transition skills.

duty to warn The legal obligation by counselors and other professionals to warn a third party when they, in exercising their professional skill and knowledge, determine that a warning is essential to avert danger arising from the medical or psychological condition of their group member.

dynamic interaction Interaction in which the parties involved affect each other reciprocally—that is, with the movements of one party affecting the other(s), moment by moment, in the interaction.

dynamic system A system in which the behavior of each participant in the system (e.g., all group members) affects and is affected by the behaviors of all other members of the system.

elaboration Helping the group member tell his or her story.

empathic demand for work A facilitative confrontation integrated with an empathic understanding.

empathy Helping the group member share the affective part of the message.

empirically based practice A research-based description of a counselor's valued outcomes and interventions, which are based on a set of underlying assumptions about human behavior and social organization and on a set of professional ethics and values.

enabler A person in the life of a substance abuser whose behavior, often including acceptance of the abuse, tends to preserve the status quo, thus enabling the abuser to maintain the addiction.

enchantment-flight The first subphase of the interdependence phase of group development, in which good feelings abound and efforts are directed toward healing wounds (Bennis & Shepard, 1956).

ending and transition phase The termination phase of work, in which the group leader prepares to end the relationship and to help the group members review their work together as well as to prepare for transitions to new experiences.

entry One of the functions of group activities, designed as a way to enter an area of difficult discussion.

ethics "A system of moral principles and perceptions about right versus wrong and the resulting philosophy of conduct that is practiced by an individual, group, profession, or culture" (Barker, 2003, p. 147).

evidence-based practice (EBP) "The use of the best available scientific knowledge derived from randomized controlled outcome studies, and meta-analyses of existing outcome studies, as one basis for guiding professional interventions and effective therapies, combined with professional ethical standards, clinical judgment, and practice wisdom" (Barker, 2003, p. 149).

exploring resistance Identifying and discussing, with the group member or the group, the meaning of the signals of a resistance.

external leader The group leader who derives his or her authority from external sources such as the sponsoring agency. This is in contrast to the internal leader, who is a member of the group and who derives his or her authority from other group members.

extreme event Most often used to describe a disaster, including the unchecked spread of a disease, a terrorist attack, or a devastating storm.

facilitative confrontation Drawing on the fund of positive work with the group or group member to use confrontation in a supportive manner.

family façade A false front presented by the family or the family member in the group in early contacts or group meetings. The facade demonstrates how the family collaborates in hiding its problems from the social environment.

family secret An explicit or unspoken agreement in which all family members agree not to deal directly with a sensitive and taboo concern. Family violence, alcoholism, and sexual abuse are examples of family secrets often hidden behind a family facade.

farewell-party syndrome The tendency on the group's part, in the ending/transition phase, to avoid the pain of ending by planning some form of celebration. Also, the tendency to express only positive reactions about the group experience, rather than being critical.

fear-of-groups syndrome The anxieties experienced by group leaders as they prepare to work with groups for the first time.

feeling-thinking-doing connection A process in which how we feel affects how we act and think, and how we act affects how we think and feel.

feminist practice "The integration of the values, skills, and knowledge of social work with a feminist orientation to help group members overcome the emotional and social problems that result from gender discrimination" (Barker, 2003, p. 161).

first decision The group member's commitment to engage with the leader and the group in a meaningful way and begin to develop a therapeutic and group alliance.

first offering An indirect communication from the group member or group offering the group leader a clue about the nature of the group member's concerns. Often followed by a second (more direct) and even third or fourth offering designed to increase the signal's clarity.

flight-fight The natural tendency on the part of any organism to respond to a threat by either running from it (flight) or attacking it (fight). In human relationships, flight-fight usually (but not always) characterizes a maladaptive response to emotional pain that can lead to the avoidance of real work.

In a group, conflict between members can be a form of fight, and forced humor an example of flight.

flight-fight group One of Bion's (1961) basic assumption groups. When the work group gets close to painful feelings, the members sometimes unite in an instantaneous, unconscious process to form the flight-fight group, acting from the basic assumption that the group goal is to avoid the pain associated with the work group processes through flight (an immediate change of subject from the painful area) or fight (an argument developing in the group that moves from the emotional level to an intellectual one).

focused listening Concentrating on a specific part of the group member's message.

function In counseling, the specific part the professional plays in the helping process.

gatekeeper A group member who may intervene to distract the group each time the discussion approaches a painful subject.

gay and lesbian Parallel and equal terms to refer to male and female homosexuality, respectively.

generalizing Using specific instances to help the group member identify general principles (e.g., the importance of being honest about one's feelings in different situations). This is one of the sessional ending and transition skills.

grounded theory An approach to theory building, first described by Glaser and Strauss (1967) in the field of sociology, in which formal and informal observations from the field are used to develop constructs of the theory. Formal research is conducted to test propositions and to generate new ones.

group Two or more people who meet, usually face-to-face, to pursue a commonly agreed-on purpose.

group-as-a-whole The entity that is formed that is more than the sum of the individual members that can be recognized by the way in which members act in respect to such elements as norms of behavior, stated and unstated rules, concern about discussing taboo subjects, and so forth.

group culture The norms, taboos, rules, and member roles that guide the generally accepted ways of acting within the group. In a group's early stage, the group members usually re-create a group culture representative of the larger community. This culture can be modified over time to become more conducive to effective work.

group method A collection of skills that are integrated into an overall understanding of how groups work and how group leaders help group members to do their work.

guarding the contract Efforts on the part of the group leader to prevent a member from subverting the contract by raising other unrelated issues.

handles for work Concerns and problems, suggested by the group leader in an opening or contracting statement, that offer possible areas of connection between the group member's needs and the agency's services.

harm reduction A treatment model that advocates attempting to help addicted persons moderate the negative impact of substances on their life rather than calling for abstinence.

helping the group member see life in new ways Skills designed to help group members modify their cognitions about themselves and their world (e.g., reframing a situation in a more positive way).

heterocentrism The phenomenon of viewing the world through the eyes of the dominant group.

heterosexual privilege The rights and advantages that heterosexuals have and take for granted every day.

holding to focus Asking the group member to stay focused on one theme as opposed to jumping from issue to issue. It is one of the demand-for-work skills.

homosexuality Sexual attraction between members of the same gender, often but not always accompanied by sexual behavior.

hospice A residential setting for people who are usually in the final stage of a terminal illness.

human communication A complex process in which messages are encoded by a sender, transmitted through some medium (e.g., words or facial expressions), and received by the receiver, who must then decode the message. The response of the receiver involves encoding a new message and transmitting it, which keeps the cycle going.

human contact One of the functions of group activities, designed to focus on meeting a basic human need for social interaction.

identified patient (IP) The group member in a family system who is identified as having the problem.

identifying process and content connections A skill set allowing the group leader to see how the group member uses the working relationship (process) as a medium for raising and working on issues central to the substantive issues under discussion (content).

identifying the next steps Helping the group member use the current discussion to develop ideas about future actions. This is one of the sessional ending and transition skills.

identifying the stage of the ending process The skill of naming for the group the stage of the ending process for the purpose of helping the group feel more in control of the endings. These stages are denial, indirect and direct expressions of anger, mourning, trying it on for size, and the farewell-party syndrome.

illusion of work A process in which the group leader and the group members engage in a conversation that is empty of real meaning and affect. It may be a form of passive resistance in which the group member tries to please the group leader by pretending to work.

impression management (IM) A term from social psychology describing how people, consciously or not, present themselves to others to control the impression they make.

indicators of oppression Bulhan (1985) identifies several key indicators for objectively assessing oppression. He suggests that "all situations of oppression violate one's space, time, energy, mobility, bonding, and identity" (p. 124).

individual counseling in the group A common pattern in which the group leader provides individual counseling to a group member within a group setting. This contrasts with an effort to mobilize mutual aid for the group member by involving the other members.

individual problem solving A mutual aid process through which group members help one member solve a particular problem, receiving help themselves while offering it to another.

informed consent "The group member's granting of permission to the counselor and agency or other professional person to use specific intervention procedures, including diagnosis, treatment, follow-up, and research. This permission must be based on full disclosure of the facts needed to make the decision intelligently. Informed consent must be based upon knowledge of the risks and alternatives" (Barker, 2003, p. 114)

interactional model A model of practice that emphasizes the interactional nature of the helping process. The group member and the group in this model are viewed as a self-realizing, energy-producing persons with certain tasks to perform, and the group leader as having a specific function to carry out. They engage each other as interdependent actors within an organic system that is best described as reciprocal, with each person affecting and being affected by the other moment to moment. The group leader–group member relationship is understood within the social context and is influenced by the impact of time.

intercultural A relationship between the group leader and the group members or between group members that is marked by difference in ethnicity, race, gender, sexual orientation, class, or another variable.

interdependence phase The second phase of group development, which has to do with questions of intimacy—that is, the group members' concerns about how close they wish to get to one another (Bennis & Shepard, 1956).

internal leader A member of the group who assumes a leadership role in a situational or ongoing basis. This role needs to be implicitly or explicitly confirmed by the other group members.

intimacy theme Concerns related to the interactions among the members of a group.

intracultural A relationship between the group leader and the group members or between group members that is marked by similarity in ethnicity, race, gender, sexual orientation, class, or another variable.

LGBT An acronym that stands for lesbian, gay, bisexual, and transgender people.

life span theory A theory that suggests that development throughout life is characterized by the joint occurrence of increases (gains), decreases (losses), and maintenance (stability) in adaptive capacity

listen first—talk later An approach used in work with information groups, in which the leader first listens to the group members' questions, issues, and concerns and then presents the required information.

looking for trouble when everything seems to be going your way The skill of exploring hidden ambivalence or a negative response when a group member immediately responds positively to a difficult suggestion or to participating in the group.

macabre humor Humor that can be funny but has a dark or sarcastic element.

mandated reporter A professional who is required by law to report if certain categories of group members (e.g., children and the elderly) are at risk (posing a threat to themselves or others or experiencing serious abuse or neglect).

mandatory group member A group member who is required to engage in services involuntarily, usually by an agency policy, a court (as in male batterers' groups), an employer (as in alcohol counseling), or a family member (as in support groups for spouses of addicts).

medical model The four-step process of organizing one's thinking about practice, commonly described as study, diagnosis, treatment, and evaluation. Also sometimes used to describe a "pathology" model for diagnosing group member problems.

microsociety A description of the small group as a special case of the larger individual-social interaction in society.

middle (or work) phase The phase of work in which the group members and the group leader focus on dealing with issues raised in the beginning phase or with new issues that have emerged since then.

middle stage The stage of a single group session that follows the completion of the sessional contracting work. It is the segment of the session in which the work of the group takes place as identified in the sessional contracting process. It precedes the ending and transition stage, which brings the session to a close.

mixed transactional model A way of seeing practice in terms of transactions, exchanges in which people give

to and take from each other through different mediums of exchange, including words, facial and body expressions, touch, shared experiences of various kinds, and other forms of communication (often used simultaneously).

model A concrete, symbolic representation of an abstract phenomenon.

monitoring the group The skill of observing the second client—the group—by watching for verbal and nonverbal clues as to their reactions while a member is speaking.

monitoring the individual The skill of observing individual group members, remaining alert to verbal and nonverbal clues signaled by each individual. This is an acquired skill. When this skill is integrated, a group leader can simultaneously monitor the group and each individual.

monopolizer A member of a group who talks a great deal and appears to dominate (monopolize) the conversation. The monopolizer is usually described as someone who does not listen well to others.

motivational interviewing (MI) A technique to address addictive behavior focusing on the issue of increasing group member motivation and drawing upon the stages-of-change model.

mourning period A stage in the ending process of a group, usually characterized by apathy and a general tone of sadness.

moving from the general to the specific Helping a group member share specific details about an issue first brought up on a more general level.

multiple family group therapy (MFGT) A planned, psychosocial approach to treatment that involves two or more families who share some common problems or area of concern.

mutual aid A process in which group members form an alliance to work on certain specific problems by providing help to each other.

mutual demand A mutual aid process in which group members offer each other help by making demands and setting expectations on personal behavior.

mutual support A mutual aid process in which group members provide emotional support to one another.

near problems Legitimate issues raised by group members, early in the relationship, to establish trust before raising more difficult and often threatening issues.

nonverbal forms of communication The transmission of a communication without the use of words—for example, the client's posture or facial expression, where the client sits, the client standing and leaving an interview or an affectionate touch between clients.

norms of behavior The rules of behavior generally accepted by a dominant group in society. These norms can be re-created within a group or other system. The existence of the norms is evident when the group members act as if the norms existed.

open-ended group A group in which new members can join at any point and ongoing members may leave at different times. For example, a ward group on a hospital may have new members join when admitted to the hospital and others leave when discharged.

opening statement The group leader's statement, during the first contact, that attempts to identify the purpose of the encounter, the group leader's role, and possible areas of connection with the felt needs of the group member.

oppression psychology A theory of the impact of societal oppression on vulnerable populations.

organismic model A metaphor suggesting a capacity for growth and emergent behavior—that is, a process in which a system transcends itself and creates something new that is more than just the sum of its parts.

outreach program A program that attempts to bring services directly to group members, usually in their own homes or neighborhoods.

pairing group One of Bion's (1961) basic assumption groups, in which the group, often through a conversation between two members, avoids the pain of the work by discussing some future great event.

parallel process The way in which the process on one level (e.g., supervisor–group leader) parallels the process on another level (e.g., group leader–group member).

partializing the group member's concerns Helping the group member deal with complex problems by breaking them down into their component parts and addressing the parts one at a time.

plasticity Defined as the individual's ability to be flexible in response to stress.

pointing out endings early The skill of reminding group members, far enough ahead of the last sessions to be helpful, that the working relationship is coming to a close. How early this is depends on the length of the working relationship, among other factors.

positive working relationship A professional relationship between the group member or members and the group leader that is the medium through which the leader influences the group members. A positive working relationship is characterized by good rapport and a sense on the part of the group members that they can trust the group leader and that the group leader cares for the group members.

practitioner-researcher A group leader who is continuously involved in evaluating his or her own practice and developing generalizations from the practice experience.

precontemplation stage One of the stages in the addiction change model suggested by DiClemente (1991). In this stage, the addicted person has not even begun to contemplate the idea that there may be an addiction problem.

preemptive intervention A common mistake in practice in which the group leader intervenes between the scapegoat and the group and preempts the opportunity for the group and the individual to deal with the problem.

preliminary or preparatory phase The phase of work prior to the group leader engaging with the group member. Usually used by the group leader to develop a preliminary empathy about the group member's issues and concerns.

privileged communication Group leader–group member communications are held to be privileged, so that the counselor cannot disclose them without the group member's permission, even in the course of legal proceedings. Specific exceptions to privilege are usually listed in the state legislation that establishes the privilege.

process The interaction that takes place between the group leader and the group members during a group session, or between a group member and another group member, which characterizes the way of working versus the content of the work.

professional impact The activities of group leaders designed to effect changes in (1) policies and services in their own setting and others, as well as broader social policies that affect group members, and (2) the work culture that influences interstaff relationships within a setting and with other institutions.

projective identification According to Bion (1961), a situation in which the group member communicates his or her feelings by stimulating the same feelings in the leader. The group member or the group projects those feelings onto the group leader.

protective factors Variables that may provide a buffer of protection against life events that affect at-risk children.

putting the group member's feelings into words The skill of articulating the group member's feelings, in response to tuning in or perceiving the group member's indirect communications, prior to the group member's direct expression of affect.

quasi-stationary social equilibrium A term used by Lewin (1951) to describe a stage in the change process at which a person is in balance with his or her social environment. This balance can be upset by external or internal forces, resulting in a state of disequilibrium that can lead to change and a new quasi-stationary equilibrium.

queer An insider term that is being reclaimed—as in, for example, queer art and queer theory.

questioning In the elaboration process, the group leader's requests for more information from the group member regarding the group member's problem, including who, what, where, when, and why.

quiet member A member of the group who remains noticeably silent over an extended period of time.

rapport One element of the construct "working relationship"; a general sense on the group member's or the group's part that they get along well with the group leader.

reaching for feelings The empathic skill of asking the group member to share the affective portion of the message.

reaching for the group member's feedback Inviting a group member to share his or her concerns related to the purpose of the contact and the agency service. This may be a simple question or a statement of specific illustrative examples of possible concerns (see *handles for work*).

reaching inside silences The skill of exploring the meaning of a silence by putting the group member's possible feelings into words (e.g., "Are you angry right now?").

recontracting The process in which the group leader reopens the issues of contracting by providing a clearer statement of purpose or exploring the group members' resistance or lack of connection to the service.

record of service (ROS) A written record that describes the group, identifies the central problem area, describes and illustrates the practice over time, assesses the status of the problem after a period of work, and then identifies next group leader interventions to continue the work.

reflective practice The counselor's ability to reflect on his or her personal and professional experiences as a means to improve.

reframing the problem The process, described by family theorists, as helping the family see a problem in a new way. One example of this would be helping the family move beyond viewing the family problem as concerning a single child (the identified patient) who may be serving as a family scapegoat.

rehearsal (1) The process in which the group member has an opportunity to practice a difficult next step in an informal role play, with the group leader usually playing the role of the other person. This is one of the sessional ending and transition skills. (2) A mutual aid process in which group members help one another by providing a forum in which members can try out ideas or skills. (3) One of the functions of group activities, designed to develop skills for specific life tasks.

relapse The period when an addicted person who is in recovery but goes back to using the addictive substance (i.e., heroin, alcohol).

resiliency "The human capacity (individual, group, and/ or community) to deal with crisis, stressors, and normal experiences in an emotionally and physically healthy way; an effective coping style" (Barker, 2003, p. 369).

resistance Behavior on the part of the group member that appears to resist the group leader's efforts to deal with the group member's problems. Resistance may be open (active) or indirect (passive). It is usually a sign of the group member's pain associated with the work.

resolution-catharsis The third subphase of the dependency phase in group development, in which group leadership is assumed by members who are unconflicted (independent) (Bennis & Shepard, 1956). This "overthrow" of the group leader leads to each member taking responsibility for the group: the group leader is no longer seen as "magical," and the power struggles are replaced by work on shared goals.

resolution stage The stage of work in which a session is brought to some form of closure or resolution, which may include recognizing the lack of closure and determining next steps.

role In the psychodynamic frame of reference, an "adaptational unit of personality in action" (Ackerman, 1958, p. 53).

scapegoat A member of the group attacked, verbally or physically, by other members who project onto the member their own negative feelings about themselves. The scapegoat role is often interactive in nature, with the scapegoat fulfilling a functional role in the group.

second decision The group member's decision to continue engaging with the group and the leader in the middle phase of work. This decision is made in the face of challenges such as dealing with painful issues and accepting personal responsibility for addressing issues.

sessional contracting skills The skills usually employed at the start of a group session to clarify the immediate work at hand. These include listening, exploring group member resistance, identifying process and content connections, and reaching inside silences.

sessional ending and transition skills The skills designed to bring a session to a close and to make the connections between a single session and future work or issues in the life of the group members. These include summarizing, generalizing, identifying the next steps, rehearsal, and identifying "doorknob" communications.

sessional tuning-in skills The skills designed to sensitize the group leader, prior to each session, to the potential themes that may emerge during the work. These include tuning in to the group members' potential sense of urgency, to the group leader's own feelings, to events in the life of the group or individual members, or events in the community.

sexual orientation Refers to the inclination of an individual toward sexual or affectional partners of the same sex, opposite sex, or both sexes.

sharing data Sharing facts, ideas, values, and beliefs that group leaders and group members have accumulated from their own experiences and can make available to the group.

sharing the group leader's feelings The skill of appropriately sharing with the group members the group leader's own affect. These feelings should be shared in pursuit of professional purposes as the group leader implements the professional function.

single-session group A one-session group in which all of the phases—preliminary, beginning, middle, and ending/transition—are contained.

skill factor A set of closely related group leader skills.

skills Specific behaviors on the part of the group leader that are used in the implementation of the social work function.

societal taboos Commonly shared injunctions in our society that directly or indirectly inhibit our ability to talk about certain areas (e.g., sexual abuse, death and dying). More generally, taboos are social prohibitions that result from conventions or traditions. Norms and taboos are closely related, because a group norm may be one that upholds the tradition of making certain subjects taboo.

solution-focused practice (SFP) This model is built on the strengths perspective. It focuses on the group member's current issues and assumes that, with the group leader's help, the group member can identify and use inherent strengths that might be overlooked in a pathology-oriented practice.

spirituality "Devotion to the immaterial part of humanity and nature rather than worldly things such as possessions; an orientation to people's religion, moral, or emotional nature" (Barker, 2003, p. 414).

"strength-in-numbers" phenomenon The mutual aid process in which group members are strengthened to take on difficult tasks (e.g., challenging the leader or setting policy) through the support of other group members.

strengths perspective The view of the group member that focuses on what's right rather than what's wrong.

structure for work The formal or informal rules, roles, communication patterns, rituals, and procedures developed by the group members to facilitate the work of the group.

summarizing Helping a group member identify the main themes of discussion during a session. This is one of the sessional ending and transition skills, to be employed at key moments, not necessarily in every session.

supporting group members in taboo areas Encouraging a group member or the group to discuss a sensitive or difficult area or concern (e.g., sex, loss).

systems or ecological approach A view of the group member that takes into account his or her dynamic interaction with the social context.

systems work The set of activities through which counselors attempt to influence the systems and systems representatives (e.g., doctors, administrators, teachers) that are important to their group members.

taboos See *societal taboos*.

theoretical generalizations Testable propositions that receive repeated support from research.

theory A framework consisting of facts, ideas, constructs, and/or models that helps explain a physical or social phenomenon.

therapeutic alliance The relationship developed between the group leader and group members characterized by elements such as rapport, trust, and caring.

third decision The decision group members make to deal with their most difficult issues as they approach the end of the working relationship.

tipping point The "saturation point" in the changing racial ratio of a group that leads majority group members to respond with anxiety and aggression toward the "out-group." Reaching the tipping point can generate such processes as cleavage and white flight.

transgender Several different types of sexual identities and sets of behaviors that involve taking on the attributes of the opposite sex.

triggers Feelings and memories that may cause individuals to relapse and begin to use alcohol or drugs to dull the pain.

trust An element of the construct "working relationship"—the group member's perception that she or he can risk sharing thoughts, feelings, mistakes, and failures with the group leader and/or members.

trying the ending on for size A stage in the ending/transition phase in which group members operate independently of the group leader or spend a great deal of time talking about new groups or new group leaders.

tuning-in The skill of getting in touch with potential feelings and concerns that the group member may bring to the helping encounter. For this to be done effectively, the group leader has to actually experience the feelings, or an approximation, by using his or her life experiences to recall similar emotions.

two-group construct A view of the group leader as always having two clients at any moment in time (e.g., the group member and the group; the group and the system).

unconflicted member A member of the group who is independent and untroubled by authority.

universal perspective The view developed by group members as they recognize that a source of their problems may be external to themselves and shared by others.

valued outcomes The hoped-for results of a group leader's interventions based on an underlying knowledge.

values "The customs, beliefs, standards of conduct, and principles considered desirable by a culture, a group of people, or an individual" (Barker, 2003, p. 453).

vulnerable group member A group member who is particularly exposed to the impact of oppression and stressful life events because of personal and/or social factors (e.g., lack of a strong social support system of family or friends; limited economic resources).

white flight The process of white members leaving a group when the racial composition ratio of the group changes, resulting in an increase in minority group members past the tipping point.

who owns the client A maladaptive struggle in which helping professionals appear to fight over "ownership" or responsibility for a group member.

work group The mental activity related to a group's task (Bion, 1961). When the work group is operating, one can see group members translating their thoughts and feelings into actions that are adaptive to reality.

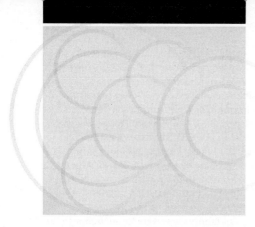

References

Ackerman, N. (1958). *Psychodynamics of family life* (3rd ed.). New York: Basic Books.

Akos, P., & Marcellus, E. (2008). Racial identity development in middle school: A case for school counselor individual and systemic intervention. *Journal of Counseling and Development, 86,* 26–33.

Albert, J. (1994). Rethinking difference: A cognitive therapy group for chronic mental patients. *Social Work with Groups, 17,* 105–122.

Alcoholics Anonymous World Services, Inc. (1972). *A brief guide to alcoholics anonymous.* New York: Author.

Aldridge, D. (2000). *Spirituality, healing and medicine: A return to silence.* London: Kinsgley.

Alexander, R., Jr. (1997). Social workers and privileged communication in the federal legal system. *Social Work, 42,* 387–391.

American Association for Counseling and Development. (1989). *Ethical guidelines for group counselors.* Alexandria, VA: Author.

American Counseling Association. (2005). *ACA code of ethics.* Alexandria, VA: Author.

Amodeo, M., Wilson, S., & Cox, D. (1996). Mounting a community-based alcohol and drug abuse prevention effort in a multicultural urban setting: Challenges and lessons learned. *Journal of Primary Prevention, 16,* 165–185.

Amodeo, M., Grigg-Saito, D., & Robb, N. (1997). Working with foreign language interpreters: Guidelines for substance abuse clinicians and human service practitioners. *Alcoholism Treatment Quarterly, Vol 15*(4), 1997. pp. 75–87.

Association for Specialists in Group Work. (2000). Professional standards for the training of group workers. *Journal for Specialists in Group Work, 25,* 327–342.

Atieno, J. E. (2008). Reflective practice in group co-leadership. *Journal for Specialists in Group Work, 33*(3), 236–252.

Barbender, V. (2006). The ethical group psychotherapist. *International Journal of Group Psychotherapy, 56*(4), 395–414.

Barber, J. P., Luborsky, L., Gallop, R., Crits-Christoph, P., Arlene, F., Weiss, R. D., Thase, M. E., Connolly, M. B., Gladis, M., Foltz, C., & Siqueland, L. (2001). Therapeutic alliance as a predictor of outcome and retention in the National Institute on Drug Abuse Collaborative Cocaine Treatment Study. *Journal of Consulting and Clinical Psychology, 69*(1), 119–124.

Barker, R. (2003). *The social work dictionary* (5th ed.). Silver Springs, MD: National Association of Social Workers.

Baum, N. L. (2005). Building resistance: A school-based intervention for children exposed to ongoing trauma and stress. In Y. Danieli, D. Brom, & J. Sills (Eds.), *The trauma of terrorism: Sharing knowledge and shared care—An international handbook* (pp. 487–498). New York: Haworth Press.

Beasley, M., Thompson, T., & Davidson, J. (2003). Resilience in response to life stress: The effects of coping style and cognitive hardiness. *Personality and Individual Differences, 34,* 77–95.

Beck, A., Rush, A., Shaw, B., & Emery, G. (1979). *Cognitive theory of depression.* New York: Guilford Press.

Bell, N. W., & Vogel, E. F. (1960). The emotionally disturbed child as the family scapegoat. In N. W. Bell & E. F. Vogel (Eds.), *A modern introduction to the family* (pp. 382–397). New York: Free Press.

Bemak, F., & Chung, R. C. (2008). New professional roles and advocacy strategies for school counselors: A multicultural/social justice perspective to move beyond the Nice Counselor Syndrome. *Journal of Counseling & Development, 86*(3), 372–381.

Bennis, W. G., & Shepard, H. A. (1956). A theory of group development. *Human Relations, 9,* 415–437.

Benson, J. D., Quackenbush, M., & Haas, D. K. (1996). HIV, women and alcohol recovery: Risks, reality and responses. *Journal of Chemical Dependency Treatment, 6*(1/2), 109–127.

Berlin, S. B. (1983). Cognitive-behavioral approaches. In A. Rosenblatt & D. Wald Fogel (Eds.), *Handbook of clinical social work* (pp. 1095–1119). San Francisco: Jossey-Bass.

Berlin, S. B., & Kravetz, D. (1981). Women as victims: A feminist social work perspective. *Social Work, 26,* 449.

Berman-Rossi, T., & Cohen, M. B. (1989). Group development and shared decision making working with homeless mentally ill women. In J. A. Lee (Ed.), *Group work with the poor and oppressed* (pp. 63–74). New York: Haworth Press.

Bion, W. R. (1961). *Experience in groups.* New York: Basic Books.

Boutin, D. L. (2007). Effectiveness of cognitive behavioral and supportive-expressive group therapy for women diagnosed with breast cancer: A review of the literature. *Journal for Specialists in Group Work, 32*(3), 267–284.

Bowen, M. (1961). The family as a unit of study and treatment. *American Journal of Orthopsychiatry, 31,* 40–60.

Bowen, M. (1978). *Family therapy in clinical practice.* New York: Aronson.

Braeger, G., & Holloway, S. (1978). *Changing human service organizations: Politics and practice.* New York: Free Press.

Breton, M. (1988). The need for mutual-aid groups in a drop-in for homeless women: The sistering case. In J. A. Lee (Ed.), *Group work with the poor and oppressed* (pp. 47–60). New York: Haworth Press.

Brown, S. (1985). *Treating the alcoholic: A developmental model of recovery.* New York: Wiley.

Brown, V. B., Huba, G. J., & Melchior, L. A. (1995). Level of burden: Women with more than one co-occurring disorder. *Journal of Psychoactive Drugs, 27*(4), 339–346.

Bulhan, H. A. (1985). *Franz Fanon and the psychology of oppression.* New York: Plenum Press.

Burke, A. C., & Clapp. J. (1997, November). Ideology and social work practice in substance abuse settings. *Social Work, 42*(6), 537–632.

Butler, K. (1997, March/April). The anatomy of resilience. *Networker,* pp. 22–31.

Butler, S., & Wintram, C. (1991). *Feminist group work.* London: Sage.

Carroll, J. F., McGovern, J. J., McGinley, J. J., Torres, J. C., Walker, J. R., Pagan, E. S., & Biafora, F. A. (2000). A program evaluation study of a nursing home operated as a modified therapeutic community for chemically dependent persons with AIDS: Project Samaritan. *Journal of Substance Abuse Treatment, 18*(4), 373–386.

Castex, G. M. (1994). Providing services to Hispanic/Latino populations: Profiles in diversity. *Social Work, 39,* 288–296.

Chen, M., & Rybak, C. J. (2004). *Group leadership skills: Interpersonal process in group counseling and therapy.* Belmont, CA: Wadsworth/Thomson.

Christian, M. D., & Barbarin, O. A. (2001). Cultural resources and psychological adjustment of African American children: Effects of spirituality and racial attribution. *Journal of Black Psychology, 27,* 43–63.

Chung, R. C.-Y., & Bemak, F. (2002). The relationship of culture and empathy in cross-cultural counseling. *Journal of Counseling and Development, 80,* 154–159.

Clay, C., & Shulman, L. (1993). *Teaching about practice and diversity: Content and process in the classroom and the field* [Videotape]. Produced and distributed by the Council on Social Work Education.

Clemans, S. E. (2004). Recognizing vicarious traumatization: A single session group model for trauma workers. *Social Work with Groups, 27*(3), pp. 55–74.

Cohen, Judith A. (2005). "Treating Traumatized Children: Current Status and Future Directions." In *Acute Reactions to Trauma and Psychotherapy: A Multidisciplinary and International Perspective,* 109–121. New York, NY US: Haworth Press, 2005.

Collins, B. G. (1994). Reconstructing codependency using self-in-relation theory: A feminist perspective. *Social Work, 38,* 470–476.

Connell, J. P., Spencer, M. B., & Aber, J. L. (1994, April). Educational risk and resilience in African American youth: Context, self, action, and outcomes in school. *Child Development, 65*(2), 493–506.

Corey, G. (2008). *Theory and practice of group counseling* (7th ed.). Belmont, CA: Thomson, Brooks/Cole.

Corey, M. S., & Corey, G. (2006). *Groups: Process and practice* (7th ed.). Belmont, CA: Thomson, Brooks/Cole.

Daly, A., Jennings, J., Beckett, J. O., & Leashore, B. R. (1995). Effective coping strategies of African Americans. *Social Work, 40,* 240–248.

Damianakis, T., Climans, R., & Marziali, E. (2008). Social workers' experiences of virtual psychotherapeutic support groups of family caregivers for Alzheimer's, Parkinson's, stroke, front temporal dementia and traumatic brain injury. *Social Work with Groups, 31,* 99–116.

D'Andrea, M., & Daniels, J. (1999). *Youth advocacy.* Alexandria, VA: American Counseling Association.

Davidson, K. W. (1985). Social work with cancer patients: Stresses and coping patterns. *Social Work in Health Care, 10,* 73–82.

Davies, D. R., Burlingame, G. M., & Layne, C. M. (2006). Integrating Small-Group Process Principles into Trauma-Focused Group Psychotherapy: What Should a Group Trauma Therapist Know? In *Psychological effects of catastrophic disasters: Group approaches to treatment.* Eds. Schein, L. A., Spitz, H. I., Burlingame, G. M., Muskin, P. R., & Vargo, S. pp. 385–423. New York, NY, US: Haworth Press.

Davis, D. R., & Jansen, G. G. (1998). Making meaning of Alcoholics Anonymous for social workers: Myths, metaphors, and realities. *Social Work, 43*(2), 169–182.

Davis, L. E. (1979). Racial composition of groups. *Social Work, 24,* 208–213.

Davis, L. E. (1981). Racial issues in the training of group workers. *Journal of Specialists in Group Work,* 155–160.

Davis, L. E. (1984). *Ethnicity in social group work practice.* New York: Haworth Press.

Davis, L. E. (1999). *Working with African American males: A guide to practice.* Newbury Park, CA: Sage.

Davis, L. E., & Proctor, E. K. (1989). *Race, gender, and class: Guidelines for practice with individuals, families, and groups.* Englewood Cliffs, NJ: Prentice Hall.

DeLucia-Waack, J. L. (2006). *Leading psychoeducational groups for children and adolescents.* Thousand Oaks, CA: Sage.

DeLucia-Waack, J. L., & J. Donigian (2004). *The practice of multicultural group work: Visions and perspectives from the field.* Belmont, CA: Thomson-Brooks/Cole.

deShazer, S. (1988). *Clues: Investigating solutions in brief therapy.* New York: Norton.

deShazer, S., & Berg, R. (1992). Doing therapy: A poststructural revision. *Journal of Marital and Family Therapy, 18,* 71–81.

Devore, W., & Schlesinger, E. G. (1996). *Ethnic-sensitive social work practice* (4th ed.). New York: Macmillan.

Diaz, T. P. (2002). Group work from an Asian Pacific Island perspective: making connections between group worker ethnicity and practice. *Social Work with Groups: A Journal of Community and Clinical Practice, 25*(3), 43–60.

DiClemente, C. C., Prochaska, J. O., Fairhurst, S. K., & Velicer, W. F. (1991). The process of smoking cessation: An analysis of precontemplation, contemplation, and preparation stages of change. *Journal of Consulting and Clinical Psychology, 59,* 191–204.

Doel, M., & Sawdon, C. (2001). *The essential groupworker: Teaching and learning creative group work.* Philadelphia: Kingsley.

Dolgoff, R., Loewenberg, F. M., & Harrington, D. (2005). *Ethical decisions for social work practice* (7th ed.). Belmont, CA: Brooks/Cole.

Douglas, T. (1995). *Scapegoats: Transferring blame.* New York: Routledge.

Drescher, J., D'Ercole, A., & Shoenberg, E., editors (2003). *Psychotherapy with gay men and lesbians: Contemporary dynamic approaches.* New York: Haworth Press.

Drescher, K. D. (2006). Spirituality in the face of terrorist disasters. In L. A. Schein, H. I. Spitz, G. M. Burlinghame, P. R. Muskin, & S. Vergo (Eds.), *Psychological effects of catastrophic disasters: Group approaches to treatment.* Binghamton, NY: Haworth Press.

Education Trust. (2006). *Key education facts and figures: Achievement, attainment and opportunity from elementary school through college.* Education Watch: The Nation. Retrieved March 20, 2008, from www2.edtrust.org/edtrusst/summaries2006/USA.pdf

Egeland, B. R., Carlson, E., & Sroufe, L. A. (1993). Resilience as process. *Development and Psychopathology, 5,* 517–528.

Elkin, I., Parloff, M. B., Hadley, S. W., & Autry, J. H. (1985). NIMH treatment of Depression Collaborative Research Program: Background and research plan. *Archives of General Psychiatry, 42,* 305–316.

Ell, K. (1996). Crisis theory and social work practice. In F. Turner (Ed.), *Social work treatment: Interlocking theoretical approaches* (4th ed., pp. 168–190). New York: Free Press.

Elze, D. (2006). Working with gay, lesbian, bisexual and transgender students. In C. Franklin, M. B. Harris, & P. Allen-Meares (Eds.), *The school services sourcebook: A guide for school-based professionals* (pp. 861–870). New York: Oxford University Press.

Erikson, E. H. (1950). *Childhood and society.* New York: Norton.

Falon, A. (2006). Informed consent in the practice of group psychotherapy. *International Journal of Group Psychotherapy, 56*(4), 431–454.

Fanon, F. (1968). *The wretched of the earth.* New York: Grove Press.

Fedele, N. (1994). *Relationships in groups: Connection, resonance, and paradox.* Wellesley, MA: Stone Center Working Papers.

Felix-Ortiz, M., Salazar, M. R., Gonzalez, J. R., Sorenson, J. L., & Plock, D. (2000). A qualitative evaluation of an assisted self-help group for drug-addicted clients in a structured outpatient treatment setting. *Community Mental Health Journal, 36*(4), 339–350.

Flanders, N. A. (1970). *Analyzing teaching behaviors.* Reading, MA: Addison-Wesley.

Flores, P. J. (1997). *Group psychotherapy with addicted populations: An integration of twelve-step and psychodynamic theory* (2nd ed.). Binghamton, NY: Haworth Press.

Fonagy, P., Steele, M., Steele, H., & Higgitt, A. (1994). The Emanuel Miller Memorial Lecture 1992: The theory and practice of resilience. *Journal of Child Psychology and Psychiatry and Allied Disciplines, 35,* 231–257.

Freeman, D. S. (1981). *Techniques of family therapy.* New York: Jason Aronson.

Galloway, V. A., & Brodsky, S. L. (2003). Caring less, doing more: The role of therapeutic detachment with volatile and unmotivated clients. *American Journal of Psychotherapy, 57,* 32–38.

Gambrill, E., & Pruger, R. (1997). *Controversial issues in social work ethics, values, and obligations.* Boston: Allyn and Bacon.

Garfield, G. P., & Irizary, C. R. (1971). Recording the "record of service": Describing social work practice. In W. Schwartz & S. Zalba (Eds.), *The practice of group work* (pp. 241–265). New York: Columbia University Press.

Garland, J. A., Jones, H. E., & Kolodny, R. L. (1965). A model for stages of development in social work groups. In S. Bernstein (Ed.), *Explorations in group work* (pp. 17–71). Boston: Boston University School of Social Work.

Garland, J. A., & Kolodny, R. L. (1965). Characteristics and resolution of scapegoating. In S. Bernstein (Ed.), *Explorations in group work.* Boston: Boston University School of Social Work. (Published later under the same title by Boston: Charles River Books, 1976; Hebron, CT: Practitioner's Press, 1984)

Garmezy, N. (1991). Resilience and vulnerability to adverse developmental outcomes associated with poverty. *American Behavioral Scientist, 34,* 416–430.

Garmezy, N. (1993). Children in poverty: Resilience despite risk. *Psychiatry, 56,* 127–136.

Garmezy, N., Masten, A. S., & Tellegen, A. (1984). The study of stress and competence in children: A building block for developmental psychopathology. *Child Development, 55,* 98–111.

Gary, L. E., & Leashore, B. R. (1982). High-risk status of black men. *Social Work, 27,* 54–58.

Gilligan, C., Lyons, N. P., & Hammer, T. J. (1990). *Making connections: The relational worlds of adolescent girls at Emma Willard School.* Cambridge, MA: Harvard University Press.

Gitterman, A., & Germain, C. B. (2008). *The life model of social work practice: Advances in theory and practice* (3rd ed.). New York: Columbia University Press.

Gitterman, A., & Shulman, L. (Eds.). (2005). *Mutual aid groups, vulnerable and resilient populations, and the life cycle* (3rd ed.). New York: Columbia University Press.

Gladding, S. T. (2003). *Group work: A counseling specialty* (4th ed.). Upper Saddle River, NJ: Merrill/Pearson Education.

Glaser, B., & Strauss, A. (1967). *Grounded theory.* Chicago: Aldine.

Goffman, E. (1959). *The presentation of self in everyday life.* New York: Doubleday.

Googins, B. (1984). Avoidance of the alcoholic client. *Social Work, 29*(2): 161–166.

Gordon, R., & Klein, P. M. (1997). Should social workers enroll as preferred providers with for-profit managed care groups? In E. Gambrill & R. Proger (Eds.), *Controversial issues in social work ethics, values, and obligations.* Boston: Allyn and Bacon, pp. 52–62.

Gumpert, J., & Black, P. N. (2006). Ethical issues in group work: What are they and how are they managed? *Social Work with Groups: A Journal of Community and Clinical Practice, 29*(4).

Guttmann, D. (2006). *Ethics in social work: A context of caring.* Binghamton, NY: Haworth Press.

Hacker, A. (1992). *Two nations: Black and white, separate, hostile, unequal.* New York: Scribner.

Hakansson, J., & Montgomery, H. (2002). The role of action in empathy from the perspective of the empathizer and the target. *Current Research in Social Psychology, 8,* 50–62.

Hakansson, J., & Montgomery, H. (2003). Empathy as an interpersonal phenomenon. *Journal of Social and Personal Relationships, 20,* 267–284.

Hardesty, L., & Greif, G. L. (1994, July–September). Common themes in a group for female IV drug users who are HIV-positive. *Journal of Psychoactive Drugs, 26*(3), 289–293.

Hare, P. A. (1962). *Handbook of small group research.* New York: Free Press.

Harvard Mental Health Letter. (2006, December). Cambridge, MA: Harvard University.

Haug, S. (2008, January). Group processes and process evaluations in a new treatment setting: Inpatient group psychotherapy followed by Internet-chat aftercare groups. *International Journal of Group Psychotherapy, 58*(1), 35–53.

Hiller, M. L., Knight, K., Leukefeld, C., & Simpson, D. D. (2002). Motivation as a predictor of therapeutic engagement in mandated residential substance abuse treatment. *Criminal Justice and Behavior, 29*(1), 56–75.

Hollander, E. P. (1958). Conformity, status, and idiosyncrasy credit. *Psychological Review, 65,* 117–127.

Holmes, M., & Lundy, C. (1990). Group work for abusive men: A profeminist response. *Canada's Mental Health, 38,* 12–17.

Homans, G. (1950). *The human group.* New York: Harcourt Brace Jovanovich.

Horne, A. M., & Passmore, J. L. (1991). *Family counseling and therapy* (2nd ed.). Itasca, IL: Peacock.

Ingersoll, K. S., Wagner, C. C., & Gharib, S. (2007). *Motivational groups for community substance abuse programs.* Richmond, VA: Mid-Atlantic Addiction Technology Transfer Center.

Irrizary, C., & Appel, Y. H. (2005). Preteens in double jeopardy: Supporting developmental growth through a natural friendship group. In A. Gitterman & L. Shulman (Eds.), *Mutual aid groups, vulnerable populations, and the life cycle* (3rd ed., pp. 119–149). New York: Columbia University Press.

Jacobs, E. E., Masson R. L., & Harvill, R. L. (2006). *Group counseling: Strategies and skills* (5th ed.). Belmont, CA: Brooks/Cole.

Jaffee v. Redmond, 116 S.Ct. 1923 (1996). [Lexis, U.U. 3879].

Jensen, J. A., McNamara, J. R., & Gustafson, K. E. (1991). Parents' and clinicians' attitudes toward the risks and benefits of child psychotherapy: A study of informed-consent content. *Professional Psychology: Research and Practice, Vol 22*(2), pp. 161–170.

John, U., Veltrup, C., Driessen, M., Wetterling, T., & Dilling, H. (2003). Motivational intervention: an individual counselling vs a group treatment approach for alcohol-dependent in-patients, *Alcohol, 38,* 263–269.

Jordan, J. V. (1991). Empathy, mutuality, and therapeutic change: Clinical implications of a relational model. In J. V. Jordan, A. G. Kaplan, J. B. Miller, I. P. Stiver, & J. L. Surrey (Eds.), *Women's growth in connections: Writings from the Stone Center.* New York: Guilford Press.

Jordan, J. V. (1993). *Challenges to connection.* Work in Progress, No. 60. Stone Center Working Paper Series, Wellesley, MA.

Jordan, J. V. (1997). *Women's growth in diversity: More writings from the Stone Center.* New York: Guilford Press.

Joyce, A. S., Piper, W. E., & Ogrodniczuk, J. S. (2007). Therapeutic alliance and cohesion variables as predictors of outcome in short-term group psychotherapy. *International Journal of Group Psychotherapy, 57*(3), 269–296.

Keith, D. V., & Whitaker, C. A. (1982). Experiential/symbolic family therapy. In A. M. Horne & M. M. Ohlsen (Eds.), *Family counseling and therapy.* Itasca, IL: Peacock.

Kendler, H. (2002). "Truth and reconciliation": Worker's fear of conflict in groups. *Social Work with Groups: A Journal of Community and Clinical Practice, 25*(3), 25–41.

Kennedy, A. (2008). Plugged in, turned on and wired up: How technology and the computer age are changing the counseling profession. *Counseling Today, 51*(2), 34–38.

Kobasa, S. C., & Pucetti, M. C. (1983). Personality and social resources in stress resistance. *Journal of Personality and Social Psychology, 45,* 839–850.

Kübler-Ross, E. (1969). *On death and dying.* New York: Macmillan.

Kuhn, T. H. (1962). *The structure of scientific revolution.* Chicago: University of Chicago Press.

Kurland, R., & Salmon, R. (2006). Purpose: A misunderstood and misused keystone of group work practice. In *Social Work with Groups: A Journal of Community and Clinical Practice, 29*(2/3).

Lasky, G. B., & Riva, M. T. (2006). Confidentiality and privileged communication in group psychotherapy. *International Journal of Group Psychotherapy, 56*(4), 455–476.

Learly, M. R. (1996). *Self presentation: Impression management and interpersonal behavior.* Boulder, CO: Westview Press.

Lee, M. R., Cohen, L., Hadley, S. W., & Goodwin, F. K. (1999). Cognitive-behavioral group therapy with medication for depressed gay men with AIDS or symptomatic HIV infection. *Psychiatric Services, 50*(7), 948–952.

Levinsky, L., & McAleer, K. (2005). Listen to us! Young adolescents in urban schools. In A. Gitterman & L. Shulman (Eds.), *Mutual aid groups, vulnerable and resilient populations, and the life cycle* (3rd ed., pp. 203–219). New York: Columbia University Press.

Levounis, P. (2003). Gay patient—gay therapist: A case report of Stephen. In J. Dreschler, A. d'Ercole, & E. Schoenberg (Eds.), *Psychotherapy with gay men and lesbians.* New York: Harrington Park Press.

Levy, R. S., Tendler, C., VanDevanter, N., & Cleary, P. D. (1990). A group intervention model for individuals testing positive for HIV antibody. *American Journal of Orthopsychiatry, 60*(3), 452–459.

Lewin, K. (1935). *Field theory in social science: Selected theoretical papers.* New York: McGraw-Hill.

Lewin, K. (1951). *A dynamic theory of personality: Selected theoretical papers.* New York: McGraw-Hill.

Li, X., Stanton, B., Pack, R., Harris, C., Cottrell, L., & Burns, J. (2002). Risk and protective factors associated with gang involvement among urban African American adolescents. *Youth and Society, 34,* 172–194.

Lidz, C. (1984). *Informed consent.* New York: Guilford Press.

Lincourt, P., Kuettel, T. J., & Bombardier, C. H. (2002). Motivational interviewing in a group setting with mandated clients: A pilot study. *Addictive Behaviors, 27*(3), 381–391.

Lindgren, A., Barber, J. P., & Sandahl, C. (2008). Alliance to the group-as-a-whole as a predictor of outcome in psychodynamic group therapy. *International Journal of Group Psychotherapy, 58*(2), 142–163.

Loewenberg, F., & Dolgoff, R. (1996). *Ethical decisions for social work practice* (5th ed.). Itasca, IL: Peacock.

Lu, Y. E., Organista, K. C., Manzo, S. J., Wong, L., & Phung, J. (2001). Exploring dimensions of culturally sensitive clinical styles with Latinos. *Journal of Ethnic and Cultural Diversity in Social Work, 10,* 45–66.

Lubin, H., & Johnson, D. R. (2008). *Trauma-centered group psychotherapy for women: A clinician's manual.* New York: Haworth Press.

Ludwig, K., Imberti, P., Rodriguez, R., & Torrens, A. (2006). Healing trauma and loss through a community-based multi-family group with Latino immigrants? *Social Work with Groups: A Journal of Community and Clinical Practice, 29*(4), 45–59.

Lum, D. (1996). *Social work practice and people of color: A process-stage approach* (3rd ed.). Pacific Grove, CA: Brooks/Cole.

Malekoff, A. (1997). *Group work with adolescents: Principles and practice.* New York: Guilford Press.

Malekoff, A. (2007). What could happen and what couldn't happen": A poetry club for kids. In *Social Work with Groups: A Journal of Community and Clinical Practice* (pp. 121–132). Binghamton, NY: Haworth Press.

Malekoff, A. (2008). Transforming trauma and empowering children and adolescents in the aftermath of disaster through group work. In *Social Work with Groups: A Journal of Community and Clinical Practice* (pp. 29–52). Binghamton, NY: Haworth Press.

Mangione, L., Forti, R., & Iacuzzi, C. M. (2007). Ethics and endings in group psychotherapy: Saying good-bye and saying it well. *International Journal of Group Psychotherapy, 57*(1), 25–40.

Masten, A. S. (2001). Ordinary magic: Resilience processes in development. *American Psychologist, 56,* 227–238.

Matano, R. A., & Yalom, I. D. (1991, July). Approaches to chemical dependency: Chemical dependency and interactive group therapy: A synthesis. *International Journal of Group Psychotherapy, 41*(3), 269–293.

McEachern, A. G., Oyaziwo, A., & Kenny, M. C. (2008). Emotional abuse in the classroom: Implications and interventions for counselors. *Journal of Counseling & Development, 86*(1), 3–10.

McNeece, C. A., & Thyer, B. A. (2004). Evidence-based practice and social work. *Journal of Evidence-Based Social Work, 1*(1), 7–26.

McVinney, L. D. (Ed.). (1997). *Chemical dependency treatment: Innovative group approaches.* New York: Haworth Press.

Millan, F., & Elia, N. (1997). The model of multiple oppression in group psychotherapy with HIV-infected injecting drug users. *Journal of Chemical Dependency 7*(1), 97–117.

Miller, J. B. (1987). *Toward a new psychology of women* (2nd ed.). Boston: Beacon Press.

Miller, J. B. (1988). *Connections, disconnections, and violations.* Wellesley, MA: Stone Center Working Papers.

Miller, J. B., & Stiver, I. P. (1991). *A relational framing of therapy.* Wellesley, MA: Stone Center Working Papers.

Miller, J. B., & Stiver, I. P. (1993). A relational approach to understanding women's lives and problems. *Psychiatric Annals, 23,* 424–431.

Miller, W. R., & Rollnick, S. (1991). *Motivational interviewing: Preparing people to change addictive behavior.* New York: Guilford Press.

Miller, S. (2005). What it's like being the 'holder of the space': A narrative on working with reflective practice in groups. *Reflective Practice, 6,* 367–377.

Mirabito, D., & Rosenthal, C. (2006). *Generalist social work practice in the wake of disaster: September 11th and beyond.* Belmont, CA: Thomson.

Mitchel, J. T., & Everly, G. S., Jr. (2006). Critical incident stress management in terrorists events and disasters. In L. A. Schein, H. I. Spitz, G. M. Burlingame, P. R. Muskin, & S. Vargo (Eds.), *Psychological effects of catastrophic disasters.* Binghamton, NY: Haworth Press.

Moberg, D. O. (2005). Research in spirituality, religion and aging. In H. R. Moody (Ed.), *Religion, spirituality, and aging: A social work perspective* (pp. 11–40). Binghamton, NY: Haworth Press.

Moody, H. R. (Ed.). (2005). *Religion, spirituality, and aging: A social work perspective.* Binghamton, NY: Haworth Press.

Murray, C. (2003). Risk factors, protective factors, vulnerability, and resilience: A framework for understanding and supporting the adult transitions of youth with high-incidence disabilities. *Remedial and Special Education, 24,* 16–26.

National Association of Social Workers. (1997). *National Association of Social Workers code of ethics.* Washington, DC: Author. Accessed November 4, 2009, at www .socialworkers.org/pubs/codenew/code.asp

National Registry of Evidenced-Based Programs and Practices. (2009). Retrieved November 5, 2009, from www.nrepp. samhsa.gov/programfulldetails.asp?PROGRAM_ID=103

Navajits, I. M., Weiss, R. D., & Shaw, S. R. (1997). The link between substance abuse and posttraumatic stress disorder in women: a research review. *American Journal of Addictions, 6*(4): 273–283.

O'Brien, P. (1995). From surviving to thriving: The complex experience of living in public housing. *Affilia, 10,* 155–178.

Oei, T. P. S., & Shuttlewood, G. J. (1996). Specific and nonspecific factors in psychotherapy: A case of cognitive therapy for depression. *Clinical Psychology Review, 16,* 83–103.

Orr, A. L. (2005). Dealing with the death of a group member: visually impaired elderly in the community. In A. Gitterman & L. Shulman (Eds.), *Mutual aid groups, vulnerable & resilient populations, and the life cycle* (3rd ed., pp. 471–492). New York: Columbia University Press.

Perlman, H. H. (1957). *Social casework: A problem-solving process.* Chicago: University of Chicago Press.

Pfefferbaum, B. (2005). Aspects of exposure in childhood trauma: the stressor criterion. In E. Cardena & K. Croyle (Eds.), *Acute reactions to trauma and psychotherapy: A multidisciplinary and international perspective.* Binghamton, NY: Haworth Press.

Philleo, J., & Brisbane, F. S. (Eds.). (1995). *Cultural competence for social workers: A guide for alcohol and other drug abuse prevention professionals working with racial/ ethnic communities* (DHHS Publication No. SMA 95-3075). Washington DC: U.S. Government Printing Office.

Pilsecker, C. (1979). Terminal cancer. *Social Work in Health Care, 4,* 237–264.

Plasse, B. R. (2000). Components of engagement: women in psychoeducational parenting skills group in substance abuse treatment. *Social Work with Groups 22*(4), 33–50.

Prochaska, J. O., & DiClemente, C. C. (1982). Transtheoretical therapy: Toward a more integrative model of change. *Psychotherapy: Theory, Research and Practice, 19,* 276–288.

Proctor, E. K., & Davis, L. E. (1994). The challenge of racial difference: Skills for clinical practice. *Social Work, 39,* 314–323.

Pudil, J. (2007, January). I'm gone when you're gone: How a group can survive when its leader takes a leave of absence. *Social Work with Groups, 29*(2/3), 217–233.

Rak, C. F., & Patterson, L. E. (1996). Promoting resilience in at-risk children. *Journal of Counseling and Development, 74,* 368–373.

Rapin, L., & Keel, L. (1998). *ASWG best practices guidelines.* Washington, DC: Association for Specialists in Group Work.

Reamer, F. G. (1990). *Ethical dilemmas in social services* (2nd ed.). New York: Columbia University Press.

Reamer, F. G. (1998). The evolution of social work ethics. *Social Work, 43,* 488.

Reamer, F. G. (2000). The social work ethics audit: A risk management strategy. *Social Work, 45,* 355–366.

Reed-Victor, E., & Stronge, J. (2002). Homeless students and resilience: Staff perspectives on individual and environmental factors. *Journal of Children and Poverty, 8,* 159–183.

Reid, W. J., & Shyne, A. W. (1969). *Brief and extended casework.* New York: Columbia University Press.

Reitzes, D., & Reitzes, D. (1986). Alinsky in the 1980's: Two contemporary Chicago community organizations. *Sociological Quarterly, 28,* 265–283.

Richters, J. E., & Martinez, P. E. (1993). Violent communities, family choices, and children's chances: An algorithm for improving the odds. *Development and Psychopathology, 5,* 609–627.

Roback, H. B., Purdon, S. E., Ochoa, E., & Bloch, F. (1992). Confidentiality dilemmas in group psychotherapy: Management strategies and utility of guidelines. *Small Group Research, 23,* 169–184.

Rodgers, K. B., & Rose, H. A. (2002). Risk and resilience factors among adolescents who experience marital transitions. *Journal of Marriage and Family, 64,* 1024–1037.

Rodriquez, R. L. (1998). Challenging demographic reductionism. *Small Group Research, 29,* 744–759.

Rogers, C. R. (1961). *On becoming a person.* Boston: Houghton Mifflin.

Rogers, C. R. (1969). *Freedom to learn.* Columbus, OH: Merrill.

Rogers, N. (1993). *The creative connection: Expressive arts as healing.* Palo Alto, CA: Science & Behavior Books.

Rosenberg, M. (1978). *Logic of survey analysis.* New York: Basic Books.

Roskam, I., Zech, E., Nils, F., & Nader-Grossbois, N. (2008). School reorientation for children with disabilities: A stressful life event challenging parental cognitive and behavioral adjustment. *Journal of Counseling & Development, 86,* 132–142.

Sands, R., & Nuccio, K. (1992). Post-modern feminist theory and social work. *Social Work, 37,* 489–494.

Satir, V. (1967). *Conjoint family therapy.* Palo Alto, CA: Science and Behavior Books.

Saulnier, C. F. (1996). *Feminist theories and social work: Approaches and applications.* New York: Haworth Press.

Saulnier, C. F. (2000). Incorporating feminist theory into social work practice: Group work examples. *Social Work with Groups, 23,* 5–29.

Schaefer, D. S., & Pozzaglia, D. (1994). Living with a nightmare: Hispanic parents of children with cancer. In A. Gitterman & L. Shulman (Eds.), *Mutual aid groups, vulnerable populations and the life cycle* (2nd ed.). New York: Columbia University Press.

Schein, L. A., Spitz, H. I., Burlingame, G. M., Muskin, P. R., & Vargo, S. (2006). *Psychological effects of catastrophic disasters.* Binghamton, NY: Haworth Press.

Schiller, L. Y. (1993). *Stages of group development in women's groups: A relational model.* Paper presented at the 15th Annual Symposium of the Association for the Advancement of Social Work with Groups, New York.

Schlenker, B. (2003). Self-presentation. In R. Learly & J. P. Tangney (Eds.), *Handbook of self and identity* (pp. 492–518). New York: Guilford Press.

Schopler, M. D., Galinsky, M. J., & Abell, M. D. (1997). Connecting group members through telephone and computer groups. *Health and Social Work, 22,* 91–100.

Schwartz, W. (1961). The social worker in the group. In *New perspectives on services to groups: Theory, organization, and practice* (pp. 7–34). New York: National Association of Social Workers.

Schwartz, W. (1969). Private troubles and public issues: One social work job or two? In *The social welfare forum* (pp. 22–43). New York: Columbia University Press.

Schwartz, W. (1971). On the use of groups in social work practice. In W. Schwartz & S. Zalba (Eds.), *The practice of group work* (pp. 3–24). New York: Columbia University Press.

Severin, H., Sedqay, J., & Kordy, H. (2008). Group processes and process evaluations in a new treatment setting: Inpatient group therapy followed by Internet-chat aftercare groups. *International Journal of Group Psychotherapy, 58*(1), 35–53.

Shavelson, L. (2001) *Hooked: Five addicts challenge our misguided rehab system.* New York: New Press.

Shulman, L. (1967). Scapegoats, group workers, and the pre-emptive intervention. *Social Work, 12,* 43.

Shulman, L. (1970). Client, staff, and the social agency. In *Social work practice* (pp. 21–40). New York: Columbia University Press.

Shulman, L. (1971). Programs in group work: Another look. In W. Schwartz & S. Zalba (Eds.), *The practice of group work* (pp. 221–240). New York: Columbia University Press.

Shulman, L. (1978). A study of practice skills. *Social Work, 23,* 281.

Shulman, L. (1979a). *The skills of helping.* Montreal: Instructional Communications Centre, McGill University.

Shulman, L. (1979b). *A study of the helping process.* Vancouver: University of British Columbia, School of Social Work.

Shulman, L. (1980). Social work practice with foster parents. *Canadian Journal of Social Work Education, 6,* 71.

Shulman, L. (1981). *Identifying, measuring, and teaching helping skills.* New York: Council on Social Work Education and the Canadian Association of Schools of Social Work.

Shulman, L. (1982). *The skills of helping individuals and groups.* Itasca, IL: Peacock.

Shulman, L. (1984). *The skills of supervision and staff management.* Itasca, IL: Peacock.

Shulman, L. (1991). *Interactional social work practice: Toward an empirical theory.* Itasca, IL: Peacock.

Shulman, L. (1993). *Interactional supervision.* Silver Springs, MD: National Association of Social Workers.

Shulman, L. (1999). *The skills of helping individuals, families, groups and communities* (4th ed.). Belmont, CA: Cengage Publishers.

Shulman, L. (2005). Healing the hurts: A short-term group for separated, widowed and divorced single parents. In A. Gitterman & L. Shulman (Eds.), *Mutual aid groups, vulnerable and resilient populations, and the life cycle* (3rd ed., pp. 448–470). New York: Columbia University Press.

Shulman, L. (2009). *The skills of helping individuals, families, groups and communities* (6th ed.). Belmont, CA: Cengage Publishers.

Shulman, L., & Buchan, W. (1982). *The impact of the family physician's communication, relationship, and technical skills on patient compliance, satisfaction, reassurance, comprehension, and improvement.* Vancouver: University of British Columbia.

Shulman, L., & Clay, C. (1994). *Teaching about practice and diversity: Content and process in the classroom and the field.* Alexandria, VA: Council on Social Work Education.

Shulman, L., & Maguin, E. (2006). *VISA report.* Buffalo, NY: University at Buffalo Social Research Center. Available: www.socialwork.buffalo.edu/research/visa.asp

Smalley, R. E. (1967). *Theory for social work practice.* New York: Columbia University Press.

Smith, A., & Siegel, R. (1985). Feminist therapy: Redefining power for the powerless. In L. B. Rosewater & L. E. Walker

(Eds.), *Handbook of feminist therapy: Women's issues in psychotherapy* (pp. 13–21). New York: Springer.

Srebnik, D. S., & Saltzberg, E. A. (1994). Feminist cognitive-behavioral therapy for negative body image. *Women and Therapy, 15,* 117–133.

Staudinger, U. M., Marsiske, M., & Baltes, P. B. (1993). Resilience and levels of reserve capacity in later adulthood: Perspectives from life-span theory. *Development and Psychopathology, 5,* 541–566.

Strean, H. (1979). *Clinical social work theory and practice.* New York: Free Press.

Taft, J. (1933). Living and feeling. *Child Study, 10,* 100–112.

Taft, J. (1949). Time as the medium of the helping process. *Jewish Social Service Quarterly, 26,* 230–243.

Tarasoff v. Regents of the University of California, 551 P.2d 334 (1976).

Tatarsky, A. (Ed.). (2002) *Harm reduction psychotherapy: A new treatment for drug and alcohol problems.* Northvale, NJ: Aronson.

Thayer, L. (1982). A person-centered approach to family therapy. In A. M. Horne & M. M. Ohlsen (Eds.), *Family counseling and therapy* (pp. 175–213). Itasca, IL: Peacock.

Thomas, R. V., & Pender, D. A. (2007). *ASGW best practices guidelines.* N.p.: Association for Specialists in Group Work.

Thorngren, J. M. (2006). Multiple family group therapy. In M. S. Corey & G. Corey (Eds.), *Groups: Process and practice* (7th ed., pp. 339–341). Belmont, CA: Thomson, Brooks/Cole.

Thorngren, J. M., Christensen, T. M., & Kleist, D. M. (1998). Multiple-family group treatment: The underexplored therapy. *The Family Journal: Counseling and Therapy for Couples and Families, 6,* 125–131.

Thorngren, J. M., & Kleist, D. M. (2002). Multiple family group therapy: An interpersonal/postmodern approach. *The Family Journal: Counseling and Therapy for Couples and Families, 10*(2), 167–176.

Toseland, R. W. (1995). *Group work with the elderly and family caregivers.* New York: Springer.

Toseland, R. W., & Rivas, R. F. (2005). *An introduction to group work practice.* Boston: Allyn and Bacon.

Toseland, R. W., & Rizzo, V. M. (2004). What's different about working with older people in groups? In R. Salmon & R. Graziano (Eds.), *Group work and aging: Issues in practice, research, and education* (pp. 5–23). New York: Haworth Press.

Trimble, D. (2005). Uncovering kindness and respect: Men who have practiced violence in intimate relationships. In A. Gitterman & L. Shulman (Eds.), *Mutual aid groups, vulnerable populations, and the life cycle* (3rd ed., pp. 352–372). New York: Columbia University Press.

Trimpey, J. (1996). An overview of AVRT and rational recovery. In *Rational Recovery* (pp. 29–44). New York: Simon and Schuster.

Truax, C. B. (1966). Therapist empathy, warmth, genuineness, and patient personality change in group psychotherapy: A comparison between interaction unit measures, time sample measures, and patient perception measures. *Journal of Clinical Psychology, 71,* 1–9.

U.S. Census Bureau News. (2007, March 27). Single-parent households showed little variation since 1994, Census Bureau reports. Retrieved November 5, 2009, www.census.gov/Press-Release/www/releases/archives/families_households/009842.html

U.S. Department of Labor, Bureau of Labor Statistics. (2008–2009). *Occupational outlook handbook.* Retrieved November 5, 2009, from www.bls.gov/oco/home.htm

Van Hook, M. P. (2008). Spirituality. In A. L. Strozier & J. Carpenter (Eds.), *Introduction to alternative and complementary therapies* (pp. 39–63). New York: Haworth Press.

Van Horn, D. (2002). A pilot test of motivational interviewing groups for dually diagnosed inpatients. *Journal of Substance Abuse Treatment, 20*(2), 191–195.

Vannicelli, M. (1992). *Removing the roadblocks: Group psychotherapy with substance abusers and family members.* New York: Guilford Press.

van Wormer, K., Wells, J., & Boes, M. (2000). *Social work with lesbians, gays, and bisexuals: A strengths perspective.* Needham Heights, MA: Allyn & Bacon.

Vastola, J., Nierenberg, A., & Graham, E. H. (1994). The lost and found group: Group work and bereaved children. In A. Gitterman & L. Shulman (Eds.), *Mutual aid groups, vulnerable populations, and the life cycle* (2nd ed., pp. 81–96). New York: Columbia University Press.

Velasquez, M. M., Maurer, G. G., Crouch, C., & DiClemente, C. C. (2001). *Group treatment for substance abuse: A stages-of-change therapy manual.* New York: Guilford Press.

Washington, O. G. M., & Moxley, D. P. (2003). Group interventions with low-income African American women recovering from chemical dependency. *Health and Social Work, 28*(2), 146–156.

Watson, D. L., & Tharp, R. G. (2007). *Self-directed behavior: Self-modification for personal adjustment* (9th ed.). Belmont, CA: Thomson Wadsworth.

Watt, J. W., & Kallmann, G. L. (1998). Managing professional obligations under managed care: A social work perspective. *Family and Community Health, 21,* 40–48.

Wehmeyer, M. L., Lattimore, J., Jorgensen, J. D., Palmer, S. B., Thompson, E., & Schumaker, K. (2003). The self-determined career development model: A pilot study. *Journal of Vocational Rehabilitation, 19*(2), 79–87.

Welfel, E. R. (1998). *Ethics in counseling and psychotherapy: Standards, research, and emerging issues.* Boston: Brooks/Cole.

Werner, E. E. (1989). Children of the garden. *Scientific American, 260,* 106–111.

Westbury, E., & Tutty, L. M. (1999). The efficacy of group treatment for survivors of childhood abuse. *Child Abuse and Neglect, 23,* 31–44.

Wood, G. G., & Roche, S. E. (2001). Representing selves, reconstructing lives: Feminist group work with women survivors of male violence. *Social Work with Groups, 23,* 5–23.

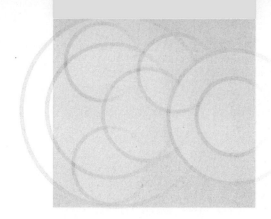

Name Index

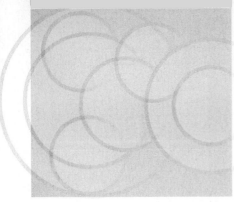

Subject Index

for management of chronic pain and
posttraumatic stress, 529–533
Vietnam veterans, 200–206
Vicarious traumatization, 367
trauma workers, victims of, group
for, 367–368
Videoconferencing, 280
Video support groups, 279
Vietnam veterans' groups, for
management of chronic pain and
posttraumatic stress, 529–533
Vietnam War, 204
Violence
in families, inner-city elementary
school group on, 458–459
impact of community violence,
609–610
mandated reporting of sexual
abuse, 376–378
in schools, 8–10
September eleventh terrorist
attacks, groups for children
following, 363–365
Take Back the Night marches
against, 252, 336, 355–356
traumatic, 359–360
witnessed by school students, 469, 474
Virginia Tech shootings, 360, 379,
384
VISA Center (Vision-Integrity-
Structure-Accountability), 8–10,
144, 473–476, 603–605
Visually impaired elderly, group for,
538–540
Vocational counselors, 542

War Memorial Gazette, 585, 589–590
Washington (D. C.), 609–610
Web-based video support groups, 279
Welfare. *See* Public assistance

White flight, 50
Whites
in group composition, 50
as leaders of African American
inner-city high school girls'
group, 316–325
Women (females; girls)
adult daughters of alcoholics,
430–437
adult female survivors of sexual
abuse, 247–255, 336,
376–378
African American inner-city high
school girls' group, 316–325
battered, groups for, 87–91,
352–354
with cancer, support group for,
215–220
codependent group, substance
abuse and physical abuse,
437–442
as co-leader of posttraumatic stress
disorder Vietnam veterans'
group, 201–206
consciousness-raising groups of, 28
diagnosed with breast cancer,
346–347
lunchtime meetings with nine to
twelve-year-old girls, 468–470
with mental illness and substance
abuse, group for, 411–413
new psychology of, 349–351
public assistance, job counseling
for, 544–552
in recovery from substance abuse,
groups for, 409–410
self-blame resulting from sexual
abuse of, 16–17
sexual harassment problems for,
566–571
sixth-grade girls in transition to
middle school group, 459–461

substance abusers, group for,
402–409
teenager survivors of sexual abuse,
176–180
ten to eleven year olds, 451–458
victims of others' substance abuse,
315–316
See also Feminist practice and
perspective; Gender
Work
culture for, 222–227
demands for, 132–139, 200–206
developing structure for, 227–230
illusions of, 138–139
Work groups, 223–225
Work phase of group counseling. *See*
Middle (work) phase of group
counseling
World Trade Center
multifamily group for Latino
immigrants working at,
492–494
See also September eleventh terrorist
attacks

Yom Hashoah (Holocaust
remembrance day), 263–264
Youth
African American inner-city high
school girls' group, 316–325
employment counseling for,
563–572
lesbians, gays, bisexuals, and
transgender students,
308–309
recovering addicts group,
228–230
troubled, group counseling with,
518–524
See also Adolescents; Teenagers